A Guide to Materials Bearing on Cultural Relations in New Mexico

compiled by

LYLE SAUNDERS
Research Associate
School of Inter-American Affairs

THE UNIVERSITY OF NEW MEXICO PRESS
ALBUQUERQUE
1944

INTRODUCTION

This *Guide* represents, even with its acknowledged shortcomings, the most consistent and important effort of our School since its establishment in 1941. After an unsuccessful attempt to secure financial support from the outside, we decided to embark with our own personnel and resources on an exploration of materials, both published and unpublished, bearing on cultural relations in New Mexico. The task has been difficult and is not yet completed. However, the information collected is worth placing at the disposal of students.

Professor Paul Walter, Jr., Head of the Department of Sociology at the University of New Mexico, conceived the idea of the *Guide*. Mr. Lyle Saunders, Research Associate of the School of Inter-American Affairs, brought it to realization with the assistance of many individuals and institutions.

The main motivation of the undertaking was purely academic. When our School was founded it was keenly felt that any discerning work we might be able to do in the field of cultural relations in the Southwest must be based on authoritative knowledge of the work that had been done before. Bibliographical research is tedious, but rewarding. It brings to the scholar the awareness of the field and a perspective for the evaluation of what has been accomplished in it. It points to original contributions not generally known, to duplications which should have been avoided, to areas which are waiting to be animated by study. A critical bibliography is the essential tool of the investigator—his directive, his brakes, and his spring board.

Within the Southwestern region, New Mexico has a personality of its own. It is a land of sand and sun, of desert and mountain and mesa, of bare rock and green valleys—all these natural elements merging into a symphony of distances, masses, and color. The people of New Mexico are the peoples of the Americas—Pueblo Indians and tribal Indians, descendants of the early Spanish settlers, sons and daughters of the Anglo pioneers who conquered the West. The kiva and hogan stand side by side with the squat adobe house of the Hispano and the brick or stone building of the Anglo. And inside the dwellings of New Mexico one finds the Indian pottery, the Hispano *santo,* and the efficient American gadgets fully reconciled.

Narrow patches of land barely providing subsistence to their tillers border ranch empires where thousands of cattle and sheep roam, and where produce is harvested by hundreds of hired hands. People live on lonely plateaus, on the slopes of mountains, in crowded valleys. Our resources are those of the forest, the mine, the grassy plain, and the irrigated strips which follow our humble rivers. Indian tongues and the Spanish tongue and the English tongue punctuate the landscape. A gamut of psychologies injects itself into rural and urban life. Though the dominant culture has imposed its tone, there are deep undertones of other cultures. These undertones affect our thinking and our attitudes. They make us conscious that here in New Mexico we have a synthesis of the Americas—the aboriginal population and the two main conquering ethnic groups. They make us conscious of the fact that if we are intelligent and flexible we have a destiny to fulfill in adding distinctive elements to our national life and in becoming the "meeting place" of the peoples of all the Hemisphere. For here in the Southwest has developed a new culture which is neither Indian, nor Spanish, nor Anglo, but a blend of all three. As is the case with the natural elements, the human elements have also merged into a symphony.

In spite of our relative youth in the pattern of the civilization of the United States, there has grown a great body of literature— scholarly, artistic, folk—which compares both in quantity and quality with that of any other region. This literature, which we have tried to list in our *Guide,* sheds much light on the processes of acculturation we have undergone and are still undergoing. New Mexico has a long history of culture accommodation under Spain, Mexico, and the United States. With the leading role assumed by our country in international affairs, and particularly so in the New World, it is obvious that the experience of New Mexico has significance both as a lesson of the past and guidance for the future. For New Mexico can and should be the testing ground for our ability as a people to get along with other peoples.

It was said at the beginning of this Introduction that search for knowledge was the moving spirit of our little enterprise. But soon we saw many utilitarian by-products, which it will be pertinent to enumerate:

1. The *Guide* would effect enormous savings of time, energy, and money on the part of scholars, writers, institutions, governmental and private agencies, and others interested in studying life in New Mexico or in carrying on practical programs, by providing them with ready references to what has been written or done in their particular fields. Especially benefited would be governmental agencies which now spend a good part of the monies allocated for particular projects on preliminary surveys and the compiling of background information. An experienced worker in federal agencies told us, when we consulted with him on the validity of our plan for preparing this *Guide,* that in

most projects about one-third of the appropriation was used "to get one's bearings." It is not excessive to claim that these preliminary steps would be facilitated and speeded by our *Guide,* thus saving resources that could and should be applied to the action program proper.

2. It would provide a fairly complete bibliographical background for two of our most important minority groups—the Indians and the Spanish-speaking citizens of our State.

3. It would facilitate in general terms the study of culture accommodation, which is to play an important role in the post-war period. Where the people of New Mexico have adjusted to each other smoothly and without friction, much can be learned; where they have failed to adjust can be found an object lesson in what to avoid in furthering accommodations.

4. The *Guide* would be a stimulus to the preservation of a great body of materials, many of which are now either lost or not readily accessible.

5. It would indicate gaps in our existing knowledge of life in this area and point the way to new studies whereby those gaps could be closed.

6. It would provide the necessary information through which projects and programs dealing with life in our region could be coordinated, preventing duplication of effort on the part of students and agencies and suggesting sound norms for cooperation.

7. It would help in the successful development of any research project bearing on New Mexico, by providing a handbook of organized reference in libraries which should prove a useful tool in the training of personnel for service in our area. Such a *vade mecum* to existing materials should become an instrumentality for the study of techniques of investigation so that the best might be followed, and mistakes of the less apt methods of approach avoided.

8. It would be a means whereby persons who have done good work on any phase of cultural relations in New Mexico could be located for further work where their abilities and knowledge could be effectively utilized.

9. The *Guide* may stimulate the compilation of similar ones for the literature relating to other states of the Southwestern region and in general to other areas where Indian and Spanish-speaking minorities exist, until we could have available a complete picture of the field. As a matter of fact, our School is already considering a plan for expanding our studies to cover the whole Southwest.

10. Serious students of inter-American relations know that certain conditions prevailing between Anglo-American and Spanish-American groups on this side of the border have proved to be a great impediment to the rapidly growing *entente cordiale* of all countries of the Americas. The facilitation of means of acquiring a clearer understanding of the problems involved in the contacts of different cultures helps break down prejudices and stereotyped attitudes. The *Guide* would furthermore serve the purpose of bringing to the attention of our friends in Latin America the fact that, though the situation is far from perfect, a great deal of thought and effort has been devoted to it by earnest students and governmental and private agencies. As practically all these studies of acculturation are sympathetic to the Indians and the Spanish-speaking people, they should somewhat neutralize the widespread impression in Latin America that our minorities have been neglected.

After work began in the preparation of the *Guide,* the University created in June, 1942, a Research Bureau in the Social Sciences to function through cooperative arrangements with other institutions, agencies, and individuals. Some of the tasks going on or planned for this Bureau insofar as studies on Latin America and cultural relations in the Southwest are concerned are: (1) to continue gathering data for periodic supplements to this *Guide*. The cooperation of the readers is eagerly requested to point to errors or omissions; (2) to expand our bibliographical research to include all the Southwest; (3) to compile and publish in *The New Mexico Quarterly Review* "A Guide to the Literature of the Southwest," listing all current publications which deal with any phase of life in this region. Eight issues have appeared, beginning with items published since January, 1942. A limited supply of reprints of these quarterly bibliographies is being made available to libraries and scholars; (4) to organize and complete a library of books, pamphlets, periodicals, reports, manuscripts, photostats, microfilms, pictorial material, etc., relating to the history of cultural relations in the Southwest, so that all entries in our bibliographies may be made available under one roof. There will eventually be a new wing in the University Library, properly decorated with Southwestern motifs, to house this collection as a separate unit; (5) to establish a service thereof of mimeographed digests and microfilms of rare or unpublished materials for agencies and bona fide students. Many have already made use of our bibliographical facilities; (6) to promote and support whatever research is necessary for the development of the action programs of our School, and to collaborate in significant undertakings of other entities; we have undertaken a statistical health study of several hundred New Mexican families and have planned studies on nutrition, one of them consisting of a model rural school for the scientific determination of the relationship of proper farming practices and sound food to educational achievement and adaptation to the environment; (7) to provide facilities and headquarters for scholars from other institutions doing research work in this region; (8) to assist in supervising the editorial work connected with the publication of our Inter-Americana series; (9) to prepare and publish special bibliographies on Latin America. Besides our general bibliography in the field of economics, politics, and sociology, we expect to issue soon special ones on the German element in Argentina, labor and social conditions in the banana industry of Costa Rica, and social and economic conditions in highland Bolivia. There are plans also for undertaking a compilation of bibliographical references to everything printed in Latin America (including even newspaper items) bearing on the Spanish-speaking minorities of the United States; (10) to organize a repository of information on Latin America, consisting chiefly of pamphlets, reprints, governmental reports or circulars, periodicals, booksellers' catalogs, syllabi, pictures, bibliographies, posters, and other printed or processed "perishable" material not likely to be found classified and cataloged in libraries; (11) to publish a quarterly review of authoritative articles on folklore, linguistics, and other aspects of the culture of our Spanish-speaking people; socio-economic studies of education, health, levels of living, land use, nutrition, youth problems, recreation, etc., among our Southwestern populations; occasional brief fiction which contributes to an understanding of Southwestern life; progress reports of significant projects or experiments concerned with improving conditions and relations among Southwesterners; news summaries of important events relating to the Southwest; reviews of pertinent books; and critical bibliographies of all published and unpublished materials bearing on the region. The need for such a periodical is indicated in the fact that although the Southwest has attracted and is attracting considerable attention, both general and scholarly, there exists at present no organ especially devoted to a uniform and consistent presentation of our basic problems. This periodical will not be the organ of any particular group nor will it expound any particular point of view, but rather be a vehicle for serious and unbiased study of the vital questions that affect all citizens of the Southwest. Naturally the inter-relationships of the different ethnic groups must be considered, but they will not be particularly emphasized, for we believe that the harmonious solution of certain social and economic problems will inevitably improve human relations without the necessity of making any distinct issue of them.

Our actual and potential performance may appear too ambitious, but the challenge for service is great. The University of New Mexico under the able leadership of President J. F. Zimmerman—a man of vision—is doing more than its resources and the physical endurance of the persons devoted to these activities permit. Until substantial support comes our way, we shall continue working the best we can and asking indulgence for deficiencies which might have been overcome had we had at our disposal means commensurate with the task.

J. ORTEGA
General Editor of the Series

PREFACE

This is not a complete bibliography of New Mexico. No bibliography is ever really complete, nor was it our purpose to include here everything ever written about New Mexico. This is merely an attempt to list, with as much thoroughness as possible, those published and manuscript materials having some relevance to problems of cultural relations between the three main ethnic groups within the state of New Mexico, and to indicate in some detail the specific contents of the various titles which bear most directly upon those problems.

In selecting items for inclusion here, we have defined cultural relations quite broadly and have assumed that even those titles which treat of only one particular phase of one particular culture (none of the cultures is, of course, unique or entirely distinct from the others) are pertinent to our subject. We have included also a number of items which, at first glance, might seem to have no bearing at all on cultural relations—studies of plant and animal life; of soils, irrigation, and erosion; of mineral resources, etc.—because we feel that it is impossible to understand any cultural group without knowing something of the physical environment in which they live, and because in New Mexico the physical environment has given direction to if not actually determined the cultural development of the Indian groups and, to a lesser extent, that of the Spanish-Americans and Anglos as well. Although a considerable amount of archaeological and historical material has been included because of its value as a background for the understanding of present day cultural relations, no attempt has been made to exhaustively cover these fields.

Although we have aimed at including only those items which deal wholly or in part with New Mexico, some few titles have been listed—studies of Navajos or Apaches or of Mexican immigrants into the United States, for example—which, while not dealing specifically with New Mexico, do treat of topics applicable to New Mexico and thus do contribute to an understanding of cultural relations in this state. Items about whose appropriateness we were doubtful have, in general, been included.

We have included references to a goodly amount of manuscript material, but this field has by no means been exhaustively covered. Lacking the resources both of time and money necessary for the extensive travel and correspondence needed to root out unpublished materials, we have been forced to depend upon the help of friends, colleagues, state and federal officials, and other interested persons in locating manuscripts for inclusion here. That this help has been considerable is attested by the number of manuscript items included; that all relevant unpublished materials have been listed, we do not for a moment believe.

It has not been possible in all cases to indicate the location of unpublished manuscripts. In general, however, those for which an author is listed are in possession of the author; unpublished studies and manuscript materials of federal agencies will be found on file in the Albuquerque office of the particular agency concerned or in the USDA library at Albuquerque. All New Mexico Writers' Project manuscripts are now on file at the New Mexico State Museum in Santa Fe.

Newspaper articles, college and university catalogs, and reports of the Bureau of the Census have not been included, either because, as in the case of the Census reports, they are so well known as not to require listing or because of the impossibility of adequately examining them in the time at our disposal.

The opening section, "Dictionary-Guide," represents an attempt to index with some thoroughness the contents of the available works which have the most relevance for a study of cultural relations in New Mexico and, at the same time, to summarize with extreme brevity the more important facts and opinions included in the works examined. The selection of topics for treatment in the "Dictionary-Guide" was not pre-determined, but rather grew out of the topics treated in the studies themselves, a fact which accounts for certain apparent duplications such as, for instance, that between the topics *Land Holdings* and *Land Ownership.* Although these headings, for all practical purposes, mean the same thing, we have included information under both because reference in the materials indexed was in some cases to one, in some cases to the other.

It was our original purpose to include in the "Dictionary-Guide" all the items which in any way deal with cultural relations in New Mexico and to let the degree to which any item was oriented specifically towards the field of cultural relations determine the intensity with which it would be treated. It was soon found, however, that the large number of titles with relevance to the field made such a plan impractical, so that we have been forced to limit the items included in this section to those which have a more or less direct connection with cultural relations in New Mexico and which would be of most value to anyone seeking information in that field. Some few items of lesser importance were included before the limitation was decided upon and have been left in; conversely, several other titles which should have been included were received after the "Dictionary-Guide" was already in print and have, therefore, been placed in one or another of the supplementary bibliographical lists.

Arrangement of material under the topics in the "Dictionary-Guide" is roughly alphabetical by place, although at times the nature of the material has forced a departure from this practice. Under *Cost of Living*, for example, (p. 15) information about Albuquerque, Atarque, Bosque, and Cuba Valley is given in that order. The information concerning Jemez, San Ildefonso, and Taos Pueblos, however, is lumped together, so that, to avoid needless repetition, all three have been placed under Jemez in the alphabetical order. The emphasis in the "Dictionary-Guide" has been on crowding the utmost material into the least possible space, so that the niceties of both grammar and style have been largely ignored. Commas, for example, are not generally used to mark elisions when the meaning is clear without them, and all words which could be omitted without sacrificing clarity have been left out.

One caution is necessary in connection with the "Dictionary-Guide." In it a number of statements have been made in the present tense with no qualifying date being given (e. g., of 1,062 families in twenty villages in upper Rio Grande area, 64 per cent have total incomes of $600 or less) (p. 41). Such statements must be understood as applying not to the date of publication of this *Guide* but rather to the date of the particular work from which the statement has been abstracted.

Certain items, particularly in the list of selected titles included in the "Dictionary-Guide," have been marked with one, two, or three asterisks to indicate their relative importance to the student of *present day* cultural relations. These ratings, which are of course highly subjective, are not to be construed as evaluations of the quality of the works rated, but are rather to be regarded as signposts indicating that the organization and orientation of the subjects treated are such that the work is thought to be of special value to a student of cultural relations.

Some few items in the list of selected titles, most of which will be found to be unpublished studies or others difficult to obtain, are marked with the symbol (D) to indicate that digests of their contents have been prepared and will be made available in mimeographed form to anyone who does not have access to the original studies or who prefers to examine a condensed version to determine the suitability of the material for his particular purpose. The extent of this service will of necessity be determined by the demand for it, since it will be very unprofitable to mimeograph digests for which there are few or no requests.

The great bulk of the *Guide* is made up of "Supplementary Bibliographies" grouped into eleven categories. These are not the only groupings which could have been made, but since these have the advantages of dividing the included materials into types (Fiction, Bibliographies), into historical periods (Pre-Spanish, Spanish-Colonial and Mexican, American Frontier), and into materials dealing with specific cultural groups (Apaches, Navajos, Pueblos, etc.), they have been adopted as being more useful to workers in all the social sciences than would have been the case had the groupings been made in the light of the particular interests of students of anthropology, economics, history, sociology, or any other of the more specialized fields in the social sciences. Items which did not seem to fit under any of the categories have been grouped together under the heading "General." Those titles which include materials coming under two or more of the categorical headings have been classified according to major emphasis or, where it was impossible to determine major emphasis, have been listed under "General."

Arrangement of the materials in the "Supplementary Bibliographies" is alphabetical by author under each category, with the works of each author being listed alphabetically according to title under his name. Items having no author listed, but which could be identified with some institution, are listed under the institution; otherwise they are arranged alphabetically under *Anonymous*. Numbering of items is consecutive throughout the "Supplementary Bibliographies" so that any item referred to in the "Dictionary-Guide" or in the subject or author indexes may be easily located. In order to make the *Guide* as up to date as possible, certain items were added while the manuscript was in press. To fit these into the alphabetical arrangement in each category, numbers ending in *a, b, c,* and *d* have been assigned them. Thus items numbered 1783a and 1783b, for instance, will be located after 1783 but before 1784.

A number of titles published or located after the first parts of the manuscript were printed have been included in an "Addenda" following the "Supplementary Bibliographies."

The necessary bibliographical information for each item is given in as brief a form as possible. For magazines in which the paging is continuous throughout a volume, we have given volume number, inclusive pages, and year in that order. If the paging is not continuous, the issue number is placed in parenthesis after the volume number (e.g., 13 (4): 91-102, 1927) or the specific date is given. For books and other non-periodical material, we have given the place of publication, name of the publishers (in abridged form), and date of publication. In some instances the complete bibliographical information has not been available to us. In such cases we have assumed that half a loaf is better than no bread and have listed the items with as much completeness as our information permitted.

It will be noted that no attempt has been made to achieve a uniform spelling of words occurring in titles listed. On the contrary, we have tried to preserve the spelling and punctuation of each title exactly as it appeared in the source from which we obtained it, with the result that frequently such spellings as Navahos, Navajos, Navahoes may occur on a single page. Accents on foreign words, with the single exception of the tilde, have been uniformly omitted in the interest of simplicity.

Naturally a work of the scope and nature of this one could not result from the efforts of a single person. Lack of space precludes the possibility of here listing all the persons from whom helpful suggestions and contributions have been received, but particular thanks are due to Mrs. Ethel A. Fleming of the Education-Information Division of the Soil Conservation Service and Dr. Edward W. Hardies, Assistant Agronomist of the United Pueblos Agency, who helped with the compiling of the materials from their respective agencies; to Mr. David French, Junior Administrative Technician of the Indian Service, who permitted us to use an extensive bibliography on Southwestern Indians which he had compiled; to the staffs of the libraries of the University of New Mexico, New Mexico State College, and the New Mexico State Museum at Santa Fe for much patient assistance; to the state and federal agency officials who gave such generous help; to Dr. Paul Walter, Jr., Head of the Department of Sociology at the University of New Mexico, for much advice and assistance in the early stages of the work; to Joaquin Ortega, Director of the School of Inter-American Affairs, whose interest and support made the whole work possible; and, of course, to the bibliographers whose works are listed in the section beginning on page 124 and from whom we have pilfered freely.

A special debt of gratitude is due Mr. Theo Crevenna, graduate student in sociology at the University of New Mexico, now in the United States Army, who performed far more than a fair share of the drudgery and whose ideas and suggestions have been of particular value.

To the authors whose names we have misspelled, whose titles we have misquoted, whose pages we have listed incorrectly, or, what is worse, whose works we have omitted, we apologize in advance. Most

of the work of compiling, typing, checking, and editing this *Guide*
was done between January and August, 1942, with only the services
of one full time and one part time person. After August, 1942, it was
entirely on a part time basis, with months intervening sometimes between successive stages of the work. This, together with the fact that
for most items we did not have access to the original material but were
compelled to obtain our listings from secondary sources, has led to a
number of inconsistencies in the form of entering items and may be
responsible for other errors of which we are not aware. We shall
appreciate having our attention called to any errors, either of omission
or commission, in the *Guide* and shall undertake to make the necessary
corrections in any subsequent editions or supplements which may be
issued.

LYLE SAUNDERS.

CONTENTS

LIST OF ABBREVIATIONS*

AA	American Anthropologist
A&A	Art and Archaeology
AAA	American Anthropological Association
AAAS	American Association for the Advancement of Science
AAES	Arizona Agricultural Experiment Station
AIA	Archaeological Institute of America
AMNH	American Museum of Natural History
BAE	Bureau of Agricultural Economics
DAM	Denver Art Museum
EAIA	Eastern Association on Indian Affairs
EP	El Palacio
FERA	Federal Emergency Relief Administration
FSA	Farm Security Administration
GPO	Government Printing Office
ICA	International Congress of Americanists
IECW	Indian Emergency Conservation Work
IW	Indians at Work
JAF	Journal of American Folklore
JAP	Journal of Applied Psychology
LMC	Lake Mohonk Conference of Friends of the Indian
MRGCD	Middle Rio Grande Conservancy District
NH	Natural History
NM	New Mexico Magazine
NMAES	New Mexico Agricultural Experiment Station
NMHR	New Mexico Historical Review
NMSC	New Mexico State College
NYA	National Youth Administration
SCS	Soil Conservation Service
SR	Southwest Review
SW	Southern Workman
UCP	University of California Press
UCPAAE	University of California Publications in American Archaeology and Ethnology
UNM	University of New Mexico
UOP	University of Oklahoma Press
UPA	United Pueblos Agency
USC	University of Southern California
USDA	United States Department of Agriculture
USDC	United States Department of Commerce
USDI	United States Department of the Interior
WPA	Works Progress Administration
YUPA	Yale University Publications in Anthropology

*We have tried to avoid as much as possible the use of abbreviations, the jargon into which bibliographers seem to fall so readily. In some cases, however, the considerable repetition of certain magazine titles or institutional names has made it advisable that they be abbreviated in order to save space.

DICTIONARY-GUIDE*

Indexing 263 Selected Titles

ABIQUIU Statistical description covering location, population, work, land, livestock, crops, and trade, (241).

ABSENTEE OWNERSHIP Not a problem in Clovis Project area, (220).

ACCEPTANCE A sub-configuration in the behavior patterns at Atarque, (103) ;—by Spanish-speaking New Mexicans of poverty and hardship, (24).

ACCOMMODATION Importance in social and cultural relations in rural Dona Ana County, (93).

ACCULTURATION Attempt to establish Anglo judicial system at Acoma, (155) ;—Anglo culture needs to adopt some of the Spanish-American non-utilitarian values, (260) ;—change in Anglo culture since frontier times, (80) ;—adoption of peyote by Mescalero Apaches influenced by contact with Anglos, (147) ;—complete description of acculturation at Atarque, (103) ;—among all groups at El Cerrito there is regret that changes have been wrought in the old way of life and agreement that people were better satisfied and life more complete under old conditions. El Cerrito has managed to keep the greater part of its culture intact after losing a large share of its economic base. Definitely submarginal in its capacity to support its population, it is highly integrated and socially unified, (108) ;—in Guadalupe, Sandoval, Alameda there is close relationship among family institutions, church, and *patron-peon* patterns. Any alteration in one brings equally significant changes in the other two, (248) ;—resistance and vitality of Spanish and Indian cultures in New Mexico, (99) ;—extent of among New Mexico Indians, (80) ;—at Isleta, (119) ;—Laguna Indians use Spanish names for all days of week except Wednesday. Spanish orgin of many Laguna holidays, (44) ;—aboriginal Navajo culture has survived to a remarkable extent. Navajos have integrated Anglo material traits into their existing culture pattern, (72) ;—divergencies in degree of among various Navajo groups, (72) ;—Navajo borrowed traits from Hopi, (100) ;—Navajo ritual connected with salt gathering modified by contact with other tribal groups, (71) ; —Navajos have kept old non-material culture traits while making

*Numbers in parentheses refer to titles in selected list beginning on p. 96.

ACCULTURATION (Continued)

great changes in economic and material life, (35) ;—acculturation one of main problems facing the Navajos, (83) ;—summary of Navajo acculturation, (104) ;—conclusions from a study of processes of acculturation in Pueblos: 1. processes of acculturation are common to other social situations; 2. process of acculturation is unique for every situation; 3. processes most characteristic of acculturation among the Pueblos start with warfare and end with accommodation, with exploitation, competition, conflict, and superordination appearing frequently; 4. adoption of material traits involves immediate shifts in non-material behavior of group; 5. rapid acculturation is related to the demoralization of leadership when the culture base is conservative; 6. personal disorganization of the Pueblo people has resulted from the discrediting and malfunctioning of the traditional personality type; 7. aims of intentional or directed acculturation are never achieved without compensating shifts in the affected culture; 8. in directed acculturation, incidental changes are more important than those sought, (90) ;—the way in which white culture has most changed Pueblo life has been in presenting Indians with new wants and new ways of satisfying them, (90) ;—one of the most subtle ways in which acculturation has affected Pueblos is through extension of dependence beyond the confines of the Pueblo, (90) ;—Pueblos were able to adopt European crops without much change in the social organization of agriculture, (90) ;—there is evidence of conflict in Pueblo attitudes towards European crops and European machinery, (90) ;—domesticated animals were acquired by Pueblos from Spaniards, but were never raised on a large scale, (90) ;— acceptance of material traits is governed not only by the utility of the trait offered, but also by the fear the subordinate group has of losing its culture, (90) ;—directed acculturation has not been very successful among the Pueblos. The unforseen or unplanned contacts, and unforseen effects of supposedly controlled contacts are the basis of most acculturation, (90) ;—the present threat to the Pueblos arises from the apparent impossibility of adjusting to an individualistic competitive economy in the same way they met earlier threats, (90) ;—Pueblo Indian dances are becoming less primitive, more self-consciously performed, (142) ;—the non-purposeful and incidental phases of acculturation are sweeping the foundations from under the traditional Pueblo life far faster than any of the agencies of acculturation can restore them, (90) ; —infiltration of kinship terms between Pueblo groups, (153) ;—

ACCULTURATION (Continued)

failure of Spanish to impose their cultural objectives on Pueblos, (6) ;—rural New Mexican is highly inaccessible physically and culturally to agencies of incorporation, (176) ;—since 1900 tempo of cultural change at San Ildefonso has increased. Money economy has been introduced: cooperation is giving way to competition: pottery is displacing agriculture: women are beginning to dominate Pueblo policies. People have adopted economically productive traits. Religious concepts and Catholic morality have been adapted to meet existing Pueblo attitudes and prejudices. Traditional division of labor between the sexes is disrupted: village is divided into two quarrelsome factions: traditional leadership patterns are no longer effective, (254) ;—at Sandia Pueblo, (49) ;—Anglo material objects adopted by Spanish-Americans with no regard for elements of beauty or adaptability, (25) ;—progressive adoption by Spanish colonists of Indian traits, (62) ;— degree of among Spanish-speaking New Mexicans, (80) ;—at Taos will be delayed by poverty, (174) ;—word borrowing as an index of degree of acculturation, (161) ;—work relief programs are proving influential in breaking down some of the compactness of rural communities, (108) .

ACOMA Attempt to establish Anglo judicial system, (155) ;—clan system, (156) ;—religion, traditions, mythology, history, (190) ;— history of land grant litigation, (15) ;—use of plants for medicine, (190) . *See also* ceremonials, religion.

ADAPTATION Apaches achieved good adaptation to environment, (31) ; —well adapted to survive in the New Mexico of the conquest, the New Mexican was not prepared to withstand the effects of a new culture, a new economy, and a new type of administration, (176) ; —Spanish-American New Mexicans have been remarkably successful in adapting to environment, (62) ;—Spanish colonials adapted to Indian methods and materials, (25) .

ADJUSTMENT Cundiyo adjusting well to outside world, (117) ;—the basis of Indian adjustment to environment in pre-Spanish times was a well developed agriculture and an excellent pottery industry. Indians are demonstrating their ability to adjust to American culture as individuals whenever the opportunity presents, (90) ;— Navajos have achieved a satisfactory adjustment to Anglo material culture, (102) ;—of Navajos to nomadic life, (79) ;—Pueblos find it difficult to adjust to Anglo competitive economy, (90) ;—difficulty of Spanish-American adjustment to Anglo economic ways in

ADJUSTMENT (Continued)

Cuba Valley, (146) ;—Spanish-Americans not well adjusted to the land, (63) ;—of Spanish-speaking New Mexicans to harsh living conditions, (24) ;—Spanish-speaking people's adjustment to poverty has resulted in an almost complete lack of incentive for group betterment and a consequent retarding of assimilation, (248).

ADOPTION   Of children by relatives frequent at Atarque, (103).

ADULT EDUCATION   At Capulin, (75) ;—at Des Moines, (75) ;—necessary at El Pueblo, (62) ;—at Folsom, (75) ;—among Navajos, (163) ; —proposals for program in Taos County, (174) ;—1,298 men given vocational training in New Mexico since 1939, (139).

AGAVE   Importance to Southwestern Indian culture, (30).

AGGRESSIVE TENDENCIES   Among Spanish-Americans in rural communities in Dona Ana County, (93).

AGRICULTURAL LABOR   Supply augmented by dispossessed farmers in Dona Ana County, (93) ;—survey of migratory labor in southern New Mexico, (208). *See also* farm labor, migratory labor, migratory workers, wage work.

AGRICULTURAL PRODUCTION   Principal crops in Middle Rio Grande Valley, alfalfa, corn, grain, fruits, and truck garden crops: total valuation of crops in 1927, $1,235,000, (65). *See also* agriculture, cash crops, crop failures, crops.

AGRICULTURE   Physical, biological, economic forces in the development of in New Mexico, (86) ;—types of farming, Alamosa River watershed, (198) ;—type introduced by Anglo contributed to decline in land and water resources and to growth of a landless and impoverished labor class, (239) ;—Anglos introduced no plants of importance into New Mexico, (28) ;—only recently practiced by Apaches, (31) ;—trend in Cuba Valley is towards more dry farming, less irrigation, from subsistence farming to farming as a supplement to wage work: farming resources of Cuba Valley consist of about seventy-five hundred acres, 2,149 irrigated. Evenly distributed this would provide four acres of semi-irrigated and ten acres of dry land for each consumption group, (225) ;—history of and type of farming in Curry County, (162) ;—Curry County, (134) ;—De Baca County, (134) ;—Dona Ana County, (93), (134) ; Dry Cimarron Valley, (141) ;—Eddy County, (134) ;—general pattern at El Cerrito little changed from that of original settlers, (108) ;—El Pueblo farm families are producing an average of 69 per cent of their food, (62) ;—farm practices improving at El Pueblo, (62) ;—Española Valley, (236) ;—crop yields in Estancia

AGRICULTURE (Continued)

Valley low and uncertain because of lack of water. Low prices and low yields make large scale operations necessary, (223) ;—Estancia Valley, (87), (141), (236), (238) ;—Hammond irrigation project, (196) ;—statistics on crops, yields, values for Harding County, (255) ;—brief history of in New Mexico, (86) ;—proposals regarding in Jemez River rehabilitation area, (125) ;—agriculture in Jemez-Tewa area is predominantly non-commercial, with nearly every land-holder devoting part of his acreage to cash crops, (223) ; —importance and methods in early Manzano, (88) ;—Mesilla Valley, (87), (223), (236) ;—change in agriculture in MRGCD due to urban growth and development of transportation, (217) ;—acreage decline in MRGCD since 1890's, (217) ;—types and characteristics of farming areas in MRGCD, (217) ;—cost of producing crops in MRGCD, (245) ;—Mora County, (134) ;—Mora River area, (200) ; Mora River Valley, (141) ;—contributed half subsistence of Navajos, (72) ;—Navajo methods, (72) ;—illustrative of Navajo acculturation, (72) ;—Navajo basic techniques and ritual aspects remain intact, (72) ;—development on Navajo reservation, (131) ; —status of among Navajos, (83) ;—possibilities for Navajos, (242) ; —among Navajos, (87), (163), (240) ;—limitations on in New Mexico, (142) ;—specific recommendations by New Mexico Land Use Advisory Council for meeting agricultural problems in the state, (133) ;—types of farming and crops, Ocate Creek area, (204) ; —Otero County, (134) ;—Pecos Valley, (87) ;—growing of cotton in Pueblos declined after coming of Spaniards, (95) ;—since coming of Spaniards use of native plants by Pueblo Indians declining, (28) ;—crop yields, Quay-Curry area, (199) ;—Rincon Valley, (87) ;—Rio Hondo watershed, (222) ;—history of in Rio Puerco watershed, (231) ;—Rio Puerco watershed, (203) ;—types practiced and historical development, Roswell region, (18) ;— dwindling in importance at San Ildefonso because of increasing importance of pottery, (254) ;—declining in importance in San Jose: only 2.5 per cent of San Jose families grow anything, (243) ;—San Juan Basin, (87) ;—San Juan Valley, (141) ;—trends in and statistics for in San Miguel County; (167) ;—in Santa Cruz area capable of improvement through use of fertilizer, better planting methods, better use of water, (227) ;—Santa Cruz area, (235) ;—most Spanish-Americans part-time farmers, (63) ;—most of land in Taos County unfit for cultivation: overuse and misuse have combined with erosion to further deplete the land resources of the county, (176) ;—Taos County, (134) ;—in Tewa Basin

AGRICULTURE (Continued)
predominantly non-commercial with a large part of the acreage in basic subsistence crops. Melons, peas, beans, onions are grown, but chili alone produced in surplus of diet quantities, (213);—Torrance County, (134);—Valencia County, (134);—Villanueva, (138);—Zuni reservation, (87). *See also* agricultural labor, agricultural production, cash crops, commercial agriculture, commercialization, crop failures, crops.

ALABADOS Description, (25).

ALAMEDA History, population, community and family organization, leadership patterns, occupations, (248). *See also* acculturation, assimilation, education, family organization, isolation, *patron-peon* system, poverty, religion, social change.

ALAMOSA RIVER WATERSHED Physical description, irrigation, present use of resources, types of farming, land ownership, tenure, and use, population, land values, tax delinquency, relief, (198). *See also* relief, water rights.

ALBUQUERQUE Cost of living, (187);—history, hospitality, military importance, (191);—housing survey, (89);—marriage customs in, (50);—life prior to coming of railroad, (50). *See also* expenditures, hospitality, housing, income, tenancy.

ALFALFA *See* cash crops.

ALLOTMENT ACT Effect on Indian lands in New Mexico, (81).

AMALGAMATION Of Spaniards and Indians in seventeenth century, (25);—of Spanish colonists and Indians, (63).

AMERICANIZATION Of Spanish-Americans delayed by racial differences, (184).

ANGLO OCCUPATION Three factors encouraged Anglo settlement in Rio Grande area: extension of railroads: the homestead policy of the government: and introduction of commercial cattle and sheep industry, (90).

ANGOSTURA Statistical description covering location, population, work, land, livestock, health, (241).

ANGOSTURA (Dona Ana County) Historical background, economic agencies, population characteristics, education, occupational characteristics, housing, sanitation, water supply, transportation and communication, economic services, institutions, recreation, mobility, family interrelationships, (93).

ANNUAL CYCLE In activity of Navajos, (72).

ANTAGONISM   Present between Anglos and Spanish-Americans in Dona Ana County, (93) ;—between Spanish-Americans and Anglos analyzed, (103).

ANTHONY-LA TUNA   As a community center in Dona Ana County, (93).

APACHES   Ceremonial life, (31) ;—cultural differences between Chiricahua and Mescalero, (31) ;—summary of Jicarilla culture, (148) ; —population, location, resources, (142) ;—recreation, (31) ;—social organization, (31). *See also* acculturation, adaptation, agriculture, beverages, economic life, food habits, Mescalero Apaches, peyote, mescal, narcotics.

APODACA   *See* Embudo.

ARCHITECTURE   Overuse of Indian and Spanish colonial design in New Mexico, (130).

ARENAL   Description of presentation of a *pastorela* at, (25).

ARROYO DEL AGUA   Land use, economic status, resources, and proposals for improvement, (123).

ARROYO HONDO   Feast of *La Percinguala* at, (164) ;—*penitentes,* (164).

ART   Pueblo art closely related to religion, (2) ;—Pueblo art contrasted and compared with that of Spanish colonial, (3). *See also* crafts and craftsmanship, painting, religious art.

ART, INDIAN   *See* painting.

ART, RELIGIOUS   *See* religious art.

ARTS AND CRAFTS   Indian Arts and Crafts Act of 1935 designed to assist in expansion of Indian handicraft market, (128) ;—urgency of commercial economy has hastened evolution of Indian craftsmanship, partly to its destruction, (128) ;—at Isleta, (119) ;—possibilities for production and marketing, Jemez River rehabilitation area, (125) ;—introduction of Anglo containers led to decline in Navajo pottery and basket production, (102) ;—importance in Navajo culture, (83) ;—Spanish colonial arts and crafts, (6) ;— part of curriculum at San Jose Training School, (194). *See also* crafts and craftsmanship, handicrafts.

ASSIMILATION   In acquiring New Mexico, the United States got sixty thousand impoverished and illiterate people alienated by language, faith, customs, and education, (166) ;—New Mexico will remain Spanish as long as it remains poor, (58) ;—era of stratified civilization in New Mexico ending: era of melting pot beginning, (179) ;—there is a differential in the rate and kind of social change between various economic and occupational groups, (248) ;— language and poverty are among the factors tending to retard

ASSIMILATION (Continued)

assimilative process at Alameda, Guadalupe, Sandoval, (248) ;—
Indian assimilation retarded by adoption of Wheeler-Howard Act,
(90) ;—Indians of Rio Grande Pueblos are more assimilated to
American economic ways than are Spanish-Americans of rural
areas, (90) ;—many Indians assimilated into Spanish-American
culture, (25) ;—where family, *patron-peon,* and church institutions
can withstand shifting forces they are most effective in retarding
changes and assimilation, (248) ;—Laguna migrants assimilated
completely into Isleta culture, (154) ;—language differences a
factor in retarding assimilation, (248) ;—leadership a factor in
retarding assimilation, (248) ;—Navajo attitude towards, (83) ;—
of Pueblos hampered by Indian Service policies, (90) ;—race
prejudice as a delaying factor, (54) ;—resistance to assimilation is
greater in villages with freest contacts with the alien culture and
with each other: it takes the form of hostility, unfavorable prejudice, and suspicion, (248) ;—impossible for Spanish-speaking New
Mexicans, (184) ;—retarded among Spanish-speaking people because of their adjustment to poverty, (248) .

ASSOCIATION   Between families at Bosque Farms and at Tortugas as
shown by extent of visiting, exchanging work, borrowing, (110) .

ATARQUE   Acceptance a sub-configuration in the behavior pattern,
(103) ;—cost of living, (103) ;—history, economic activities, social
organization, supernaturalism, population composition, birth and
death rates, health, marriage, (103) ;—behavior explained in terms
of four interrelated configurations, (103) ;—level of living by class
of family, (103) ;—migration, (103) . *See also* adoption, authority,
behavior, *comba* configuration, community conflict, community
organization, configurations, *costumbres* configuration, courtship,
custom, dances, diet, disease, division of labor, economic life,
education, ethnocentricism, expenditures, extra-community relations, *familia* configuration, family organization, family relationships, family size, fear, *fiestas,* food habits, health, *hermano mayor,*
housing, income, infant mortality, inheritance, inter-community
relations, isolation, *jefe politico,* land ownership, land problem,
mañana configuration, marriage, paternalism, *patron, patron-peon*
system, personality, political relations, property, relief, religion,
santos, siblings, supernaturalism, superstition, tradition.

ATTITUDE   Spanish-American attitude, backward, suspicious, and un-
acquisitive, the core of his problem, (62) .

AUTHORITY   A function of the family at Atarque, (103) .

AUTOMOBILES Bosque, (112);—Capulin, (75);—Des Moines, (75); —Folsom, (75);—few autos in Taos, Jemez, San Ildefonso: average age of those owned, five and one-half years, (90);—ownership and use among Navajos, (102);—37½ per cent of families in San Jose own auto or truck, (243);—Villanueva, (138).

AUTONOMY Ideal of autonomy for a minority group within a nation cannot be achieved as long as that group is submerged in the dominant group and dependent upon it, (90).

BAILES Typical Spanish-American *bailes* described, (142).

BALLADS Historical development and present place in New Mexican folk culture, (25).

BARRANCA Statistical description covering location, population, work, land, livestock, health, and crops, (241).

BASKETRY Development of among Indians, (27);—is being modified by demands of white buyers, (27);—description of construction, (27);—future of the craft, (27);—among Navajos, (72). *See also* income, marketing.

BEADS A medium of exchange among Indians in pre-Columbian time: about 1800 only a means of decoration, (27).

BEADWORK History of among Indians, (27);—greatest development at Zuni, (27);—exclusively women's work, (27). *See also* income, marketing.

BEANS Seventy-seven per cent of total crop of Estancia Valley is beans with 78 per cent of farmers producing beans as a principal crop, (223);—role in economy of Estancia Valley, (223);—importance to Estancia Valley, (42).

BEARGRASS Utilization by Southwestern Indians, (12).

BEHAVIOR Of Spanish-Americans at Atarque based on four fundamental configurations, (103);—of Spanish-Americans analyzed, (24). *See also* customs.

BEHAVIOR PATTERNS Analysis of at Atarque in terms of four basic configurations, (103).

BERINO Historical background, economic agencies, population characteristics, education, occupational status, housing, sanitation, water supply, transportation and communication, economic services, institutions, recreation, mobility, family interrelationships, (93).

BERNALILLO COUNTY Recommendations for increasing farm production, (134);—farm tenancy in, (140);—history, present conditions, and problems of land use, (134);—largest number of relief applications by migrants in New Mexico, (137).

BEVERAGES   Use of native plants in preparation of by Apaches, (31).

BILINGUALISM   Needs to be encouraged in New Mexico, (96);—essential in New Mexico culture, (161);—should be developed at UNM, (99);—will increase in New Mexico, (149);—an educational problem in the Southwest, (175);—makes for poor schools at El Cerrito, (108);—extent in New Mexico, (9);—in New Mexico legislature, (184);—affects education at Guadalupe, (248);—development of at San Jose Training School, (194);—use of Spanish language being discouraged at Sandoval, (248);—Spanish and Indian words in common use in New Mexico, (161);—renders education ineffective in Taos County, (176). *See also* language, Spanish language.

BIRTH RATE   At Atarque, (103);—of Pueblo Indians, (249).

BLOCK, JOHN   Organizer of Santa Cruz irrigation system, (229).

BLUEWATER   History of settlement by Mormons, (53).

BOSQUE   Extent of association between families as shown by visiting, exchanging work, borrowing, (110);—automobile ownership, (112);—culture conflict, (111);—economic conditions, (112);—expenditures, (112);—family size, 4.1: comparison with six other resettlement communities, (112);—food, (112);—housing, (112);—income, (112);—level of living, (112);—in-group dissolution, (111);—illustrative of process of integration, (110);—relief, (112);—participation in religion as shown by attendance, (110). *See also,* cost of living,, food consumption, health, informal relationships, integration, religion, self sufficiency.

BRADY   *See* Leyden.

BUREAU OF AGRICULTURAL ECONOMICS   Publications of, (20), (21), (108), (109), (110), (112), (113), (115), (162), (189), (196-204).

BURSUM BILL   Protests against, (22), (261).

CABEZON   Survey of history, resources, problems, (225).

CACTUS   Importance in culture of Southwestern Indians, (29).

CANCION POPULAR   Origin and development, (25).

CAÑON DE JEMEZ   Income, population, relief, (125).

CAÑONCITO   *See* Embudo.

CANYON DE SAN DIEGO GRANT   History and present status of lands, (219);—natural features, acreage, relation to irrigation projects, physical and climatic conditions, soils, forest value, use of timber, settlements, transportation facilities, (125).

CAPULIN   Population: home, car, and radio ownership: family size: income: housing: adult education: use of leisure time: number of books per home: magazine and newspaper subscriptions: hobbies: participation in social life: health: attitudes towards education, (75).

CARNUEL   Statistical description covering population, resources, livestock, business, cash income, relief, rural rehabilitation loans, community conditions, (238).

CARSON NATIONAL FOREST   *See* commercial grazing.

CASA SALAZAR   Survey of history, resources, problems, (225).

CASE STUDIES   Of Atarque families, (103);—of Navajo families on various economic levels and of Navajo individuals at various age levels, (83).

CASH CROPS   Not very important in MRGCD: principal one, alfalfa, in 1929 worth about 16 per cent of total value of all crops, (223); —importance of chili as, (213).

CASTE   An unfortunate result of the arrival of new peoples in Taos has been the development of caste lines and barriers, (176).

CATRON COUNTY   Recommendations on livestock, range improvement, land use, crop production, dairy, poultry, subsistence farming, (134);—classification of land use, (134);—water facilities program, (134);—discussion of conditions of farm tenancy, (140).

CATTLE INDUSTRY   Problem of overgrazing, (41). *See also* commercial grazing, commercial livestock, commercialization, livestock.

CEDAR CREST   Crops, farm size, income, land tenure, population, relief, (238).

CENSUS   Criticism of in regard to agriculture and farm tenancy in New Mexico, (140).

CEREMONIAL LIFE   Of Apaches, (31);—of Jicarilla Apaches, (148);— in Navajo groups south of Gallup men give one productive day out of four to ceremonial activity, (101);—interdependence of economic and ceremonial activity among Navajos, (101);—at Zuni, (13);—Zuni calendar of ceremonies, (158);—ceremonialism beginning to decay at Zuni, (158);—role of kinship in at Zuni, (158).

CEREMONIALS   Original purpose of religious ceremonies being lost sight of in isolated New Mexican villages, (164);—description of dance accompanying installation of local governmental officials at Acoma and Laguna, (155);—Indian dislike of Anglo spectators increasing, (142);—at Isleta, (119);—Isleta ceremonial calendar, (152);—Isleta birth and christening ceremonies, (152);—associated

CEREMONIALS (Continued)
with clan system at Isleta, Santa Ana, and Acoma, (156);—
description and interpretation of *Ahwanyu* at Nambe, (43);—
description of Navajo ceremonials, (142);—at Picuris, (159);—
Pueblo ceremonials often incorporate foreign ideas, (142);—at
Sandia Pueblo, (49). *See also* dances.

CHAMA DISTRICT   Forest Service policies in regard to dependency, livestock, grazing, recreation, wildlife, (59). *See also* livestock,
recreation.

CHAMBERINO   Historical background, economic agencies, population
characteristics, education, occupational status, housing, sanitation,
water supply, transportation and communication, economic services, institutions, recreation, mobility, family interrelationships,
(93).

CHAMISAL   *See* Rio Pueblo District.

CHAMITA   Statistical description covering location, population, work,
land, livestock, and health, (241).

CHAVES COUNTY   Crops, (134);—farm tenancy, (140);—housing, (77);
—land use, livestock, water resources, (134).

CHESTS   Place in culture of early Spanish-speaking people in New
Mexico, (6);—use of borrowed by Indians from Spaniards, (6).

CHILD LABOR   2.1 per cent of 439 working members of migratory families studied were under nine years of age: 21 per cent under
fourteen, (92);—9.2 per cent of ninety-eight children studied, aged
five-nine, worked: 71.6 per cent of the ten-fourteen age group
worked, (92).

CHILD TRAINING   Among Navajos, (72).

CHILDREN   Personality of Navajo children, (83);—Navajo attitude
towards, (83). *See also* discipline.

CHILI   In the Tewa Basin is the single cash crop, making possible
income with which to buy flour, beans, lard, sugar, coffee, and
clothing. It occupies a key position in the economy of the area
and around its production a culture complex has grown. Annual
production is about sixty thousand strings of which 50 per cent
is sold through three merchants. Chili is a source of income not
only as a crop marketed, but by means of the wage work made
possible through its harvesting, (213).

CHILILI GRANT   History, economic status of families on, (207);—
population relies on agriculture for livelihood, (207). *See also*
population, relief.

CHIMAYO Statistical description covering location, economic condition, population, work, crafts, trade, land, water, livestock, health, education, history, (241).

CHIRICAHUA APACHES *See* Apaches.

CHIZ COMMUNITY Population, land, water supply, (198).

CHUPADERO Vocational school at, (180).

CHUPADERO AND EN MEDIO Statistical description covering location, population, work, tillable land, livestock, health, (241).

CHURCH Analysis of role of in assimilation, (248);—a factor in retarding assimilation, (248). *See also* religion.

CIBOLA NATIONAL FOREST AREA Irrigated land, livestock, population, (124). *See also* irrigated land.

CIENEGA *See* Embudo.

CITIZENSHIP Status of Indians, (81);—guaranteed citizenship status by Treaty of Guadalupe-Hidalgo, by State Constitution of 1911, and by blanket act of Congress, 1934, Pueblo Indians are nevertheless deprived of a number of privileges of citizenship and are held in a twilight status under the control of the Office of Indian Affairs. Denial of rights of citizenship to Pueblos precludes possibility of their adjusting to American culture on a civic level and is prejudicial to their assimilation in other fields, (90).

CLANS At Isleta, Santa Ana, and Acoma, (156);—importance and function in social organization of the Navajo, (72);—role in social organization of Pueblos, (69);—at Santo Domingo and San Felipe, (157).

CLARO *See* Leyden.

CLIMATE Mesilla Valley, (52);—Navajo Reservation, (87) (150);—Navajo territory, (83);—in Rio Grande Basin, (144).

CLOTHING Inadequate in Jemez rehabilitation area, (125);—costumes of early *ricos* in Albuquerque, (50). *See also* costumes, cost of living, dress and ornament, expenditures.

CLOVIS AREA *See* land use.

CLOVIS PROJECT AREA Crops, land ownership and use, livestock, (220). *See also* farm investment, income, indebtedness, land value.

COCHINEAL History of use as a dye in New Mexico, (6).

COCHITI Land grant litigation, (15). *See also* drum-making, shell work, weaving.

COLFAX COUNTY Farm tenancy, (140);—irrigation, land use, (134).

COMBA CONFIGURATION Analysis of behavior at Atarque in terms of, (103).

COMMERCIAL AGRICULTURE   Tewa Basin area not suited to, (235). *See also* commercialization.

COMMERCIAL GRAZING   Four per cent of permit holders in Carson and Santa Fe National Forests have use of 42 per cent of grazing capacity, (239).

COMMERCIAL LIVESTOCK   Commercial operators dominant in Cuba Valley from earliest settlement, (224) ;—a factor in Anglo settlement of Rio Grande area, (90).

COMMERCIALIZATION   Trend in Mesilla Valley is towards more highly commercialized farms, resulting in concentrated ownership and loss of land by Spanish-Americans. Only 4 per cent of all farms in Mesilla Valley with about 1 per cent of total crop acreage are of non-commercial type, (223) ;—degree to which Pueblo Indians are dependent on commercial transactions is emphasized by fact that in Pueblos surveyed 84 per cent of living is purchased, 16 per cent home produced, (90) ;—pottery and painting became major economic dependence at San Ildefonso, displacing agriculture which had only a subsistence value. Standardization of techniques and adoption of mass production methods is inevitable result of producing for cash market. Craftwork has upset traditional organization of Pueblo by disrupting division of labor and placing women in dominant positions. Cooperative, non-assertive personality is being replaced by competitive type. Artists profane esoteric life of the community by reproducing and selling sacred designs, (90) ;—upper Rio Grande region cannot support commercial cattle and sheep industry for the benefit of a few large operators and at the same time subsistence enterprises for the 101,000 Indians and Spanish-Americans in the same area, (90).

COMMON LAW   Among Navajos, (72).

COMMUNITY   Strongest socio-political organization among Navajos, (83).

COMMUNITY CONFLICT   Between Fence Lake and Atarque, (103).

COMMUNITY CONSCIOUSNESS   Attempts to cultivate at El Pueblo by FSA, (63).

COMMUNITY DISORGANIZATION   Breakdown of old patterns of reciprocal behavior at San Ildefonso is a large factor in the present disorganization of the Pueblo, (241) ;—at Sandoval, (248). *See also* disintegration, disorganization.

COMMUNITY HOUSE   Construction and use at El Pueblo, (62). *See also* Tesuque.

COMMUNITY ORGANIZATION   At Alameda, (248) ;—extra-familial organization largely lacking at Atarque, (103) ;—Guadalupe, (248) ;—organization of Spanish-speaking communities has followed old Spanish *patron-peon* pattern, (248). *See also* integration.

COMMUNITY RELATIONSHIPS   In Dona Ana County, (93).

CONFIGURATIONS   As general principles for understanding behavior at Atarque, (103).

CONFLICT   Role in social organization of rural Dona Ana County, (93).

CONSERVATION   Navajo attitude towards, (221).

CONSTITUTION   As a factor in regionalism, (171).

CONSTITUTIONAL CONVENTION, 1910   Distribution of members between Anglos and Spanish-Americans, (171) ;—concern with rights and privileges of Spanish-Americans, (171).

CONTINENCE   Ceremonial aspects of at Zuni, (158).

COOPERATION   Role in social organization of rural Dona Ana County, (93) ;—operates most strongly within family group in Dona Ana County, (93) ;—practice of cooperation and mutual aid is still dominant trait at El Cerrito, (108) ;—cooperation at El Cerrito is on informal basis: borrowing of household goods is frequent, (109).

COOPERATIVE HEALTH PROGRAM   USDA sponsored program has 12,342 members in eighteen counties, (239).

COOPERATIVE MARKETING   Plan to market cooperatively with the help of SCS surplus crops of families of Santa Cruz area with two and one-half to eight acres of land, (235).

COOPERATIVE PRODUCTION   Plan to establish subsistence production level in Santa Cruz area by having families with two and one-half to eight acres of land work under supervision of SCS, (235).

COOPERATIVES   Progress during 1941 on El Pueblo farms, (84).

CORDOVA   Statistical description covering location, population, work, crafts, trade, manual labor, land, livestock, health, (241).

CORRIDOS   Description of, (25).

COST OF LIVING   Albuquerque, 1935, compared with fifty-eight other cities, (187) ;—Atarque, (103) ;—Bosque (family per year) : food, $584; housing, $125; clothing, $122; health, birth, deaths, $66; advancement, $43; automobile, $159; incidentals, $32, (112) ;—comparison of Bosque with six other resettlement communities, (112) ;—Cuba Valley, (146) ;—average annual value of family living at Jemez, San Ildefonso, Taos for families surveyed (9.5

COST OF LIVING (Continued)

per cent of total number in Pueblos) was $482.11 of which only $78.83 in value was produced at home, (90);—fuel consumption largest single item of home maintenance at Jemez, Taos, San Ildefonso, valued at $15-18 a year. Average cost of food per family varies from $175 to $258 (42-48 per cent of total expenditure). Clothing $75-85 per year. Cost of living at Jemez, Taos, San Ildefonso: food 45.5 per cent; housing 11 per cent; clothing 17 per cent; health, births, deaths, feasts, 13 per cent; education and recreation, 5.5 per cent; incidentals, 8 per cent, (90);—four-fifths of Pueblo wants are satisfied by purchase. Desire for American goods exceeds purchasing power, and is affecting traditional Pueblo personality, (90);—each family group in Jemez-Tewa area required roughly $250 annually for clothing, additional food, household and farm equipment, (223);—mining shacks at Madrid cost $100, rent about $60 per room per year, (188);—in MRGCD, (245);—at Tortugas: thirty-seven families studied averaged $347 a year living cost, 96 per cent purchased, (113);—expenditures per family per year at Tortugas: food $193; housing $55; clothing $50; health, births, deaths, $20; advancement $6; auto $10; incidental and other $13, (113). See also expenditures, level of living.

COSTUMBRES CONFIGURATION   Analysis of behavior at Atarque in terms of, (103).

COSTUME   Navajo costume modified by historical experience of the group, (102). See also clothing, dress and ornament.

COTTON   Introduced to Mesilla Valley in 1918, occupied 105,000 acres (76 per cent of total) in 1929. Cotton completed the process by which the commercially isolated and stable agricultural community of 1900 and 1910 was annexed to a commercial system of industrially organized production and a world market, (223); —effect of introduction of as a principal cash crop on economy of Mesilla Valley, (223);—relation to migratory labor problem, (92); —widely used in ancient Pueblos. Growing declined following coming of Spaniards, (95);—a recent development in southern New Mexico, (208);—principal crop in Roswell region in 1935, (18).

COUNTY ELECTIONS   A factor in regionalism, (171);—analysis of distribution of offices between Anglos and Spanish-Americans by county, 1920-1936, (171).

COURT OF PRIVATE LAND CLAIMS Activities, (219) ;—accomplishments, (195) ;—evaluation of efforts, (160).

COURTS A factor in regionalism, (171).

COURTSHIP Patterns of behavior associated with at Atarque, (103) ;— patterns of changing at Manzano, (88).

COYOTE AREA Education, lands, population, range, resources, water supply, (123) ;—Forest Service recommendations for resource management, (123). *See also* Arroyo del Agua, education, land, Mesa Poleo, range, timber, water supply, Youngsville.

CRAFTS AND CRAFTSMANSHIP Indian crafts an outcome of necessity, only incidentally a medium of self expression, (27) ;—ten crafts: basketry, beadwork, belt and cloth weaving, blanket weaving, drum-making, painting, pottery, turquoise work, silversmithing, and tanning, rather universal throughout Indian areas of New Mexico, (27) ;—at Chimayo, Cordova, Cundiyo, (241) ;—because of widespread Anglo acceptance of their work, San Ildefonso potters (most famous of those of any Pueblo) have lost much of their artistic creativeness while raising their purely technical skill to a high level of achievement. Stereotyped work, under small scale "mass production" methods, has become the rule, with most of the women engaged in commercial pottery making and many of the husbands assisting. Painting, too, as it came to be a source of income, lost its vigorous originality and tended to become stereotyped. The commercialization of old artistic techniques has had a profound effect on the community life of San Ildefonso and upon the people, (241) ;—greater income from relief wage labor may lead to a decline of Pueblo craft production, (241) ;—Spanish colonial arts and crafts, (6). *See also* arts and crafts, basketry, beadwork, drum-making, handicrafts, leather work, painting, pottery, shell and turquoise work, silversmithing, silver work, tanning and mocassin making, tinwork, weaving.

CREDIT *See* debt, farm credit.

CRIME Fairly prevalent in nineteenth century Manzano, (88) ;— Navajo attitude toward defined by common law, (72).

CROP FAILURES In the past fifteen years there have been three complete failures in Estancia Valley region, with bean yields in other years ranging from one hundred to one thousand pounds per acre, (238).

CROP FARMING On Navajo reservation, (163).

CROPS Abiquiu, (241) ;—Barranca, (241) ;—Cedar Crest, (238) ;— Chaves County, (134) ;—Clovis Project area, (220) ;—Cundiyo,

CROPS (Continued)

(117) ;—Curry County, (162) ;—Dona Ana County, (134) ;—staple crops at El Cerrito are corn, beans, alfalfa. Most families have orchards. Piñon nuts produce some income, (108) ;—El Pueblo, (63), (84) ;—main crops of Española Valley are corn, wheat, garden products, (236) ;—Estancia Valley, (87), (223), (236), (238) ;— Guadalupe, (248) ;—Hammond irrigation project, (196) —Hope irrigated area, (197) ;—at Jemez, Taos, San Ildefonso, cotton, beans, squash are neglected while wheat, alfalfa, chili, other vegetables and fruits are cultivated, (90) ;—Jemez Springs, (125) ;— Laguna Reservation, (87) ;—Lincoln County, (134) ;—Lower Vallecitos, (125) ;—Mesilla Valley, (52), (87), (223) ;—Middle Rio Grande Valley, (87), (223) ;—situation in relation to migratory casual workers, (92) ;—cotton, broomcorn, peas require migrant workers, (92), (137) ;—Navajo Reservation, (87) ;—Ocate Creek area, (204) ;—Pecos Valley, (87) ;—European crops adopted by Pueblos without much change in social organization of agriculture, (90) ;—yields per acre, Quay-Curry area, (199) ;—Rincon Valley, (87) ;—Rio Arriba County, (134) ;—Rio Moquino watershed, (201) ;—Rio Puerco watershed, (203) ;—Roosevelt County, (134) ;—San Juan basin, (87) ;—San Juan County, (134) ;—Sandia Park, (238) ;—Sandoval, (248) ;—Sandoval County, (134) ;—Santa Clara, (244) ;—Santa Cruz area, (202) ;—Santa Cruz Valley, (39) ; —Santa Fe County, (134) ;—entire Tewa Basin area depends upon subsistence crops with the people afraid to concentrate on more productive vegetable or fruit crops because of unstable markets, (241) ;—Torrance County, (134) ;—Zia, (64) ;—Zuni Reservation, (87). *See also* agricultural production, agriculture, Bernalillo County, cash crops, cotton, crop failures, commercial agriculture, commercialization.

CUANDOS Description of, (25).

CUARTELES AND PUEBLA Statistical description covering location, population, work, trade, land, livestock, and health, (241).

CUBA VALLEY Cost of living, (146) ;—economic conditions, (224) ;— not a homogeneous social unit, (224) ;—relation of economic and cultural factors to land use adjustment program, (224) ;—economic and cultural differences between Anglos and Spanish-Americans, (224) ;—history of settlement, (224) ;—land use, ethnic groups, social and physical conditions, income, level of living, expenditures, (146) ;—relief, rural rehabilitation, tenant herding, (225). *See also* adjustment, agriculture, commercial livestock, economic life,

CUBA VALLEY (Continued)
economic status, expenditures, income, integration, irrigation, land ownership, livestock, rehabilitation, tenant herding, wage work.

CULBERSON-STEPHENS BILL (S. 453, H. R. 115, 57th Congress, 1st Session) Analysis of and protest against provision prohibiting impounding of Rio Grande water in New Mexico, (14).

CULTURAL CHANGE Rather superficial among Navajos, (104).

CULTURAL DIFFERENCES Between Anglos and Spanish-Americans in Cuba Valley, (224);—between Fence Lake and Atarque, (103).

CULTURAL DIVERSITY Should be encouraged, (83).

CULTURAL EFFICIENCY Evaluation of efficiency of Navajo culture, (83).

CULTURAL EVOLUTION Of Southwestern Indians, (165).

CULTURAL INERTIA Causes of among Spanish-Americans in Dona Ana County, (93).

CULTURAL RESISTANCE Strong at El Pueblo, (62);—Navajos have retained their non-material culture pattern while adjusting to Anglo material culture, (102);—Santo Domingo people reject much of Anglo culture, (253);—of Spanish and Indian groups in New Mexico, (99);—reasons for among Spanish-Americans, (63).

CULTURAL STRATIFICATION Occurrence in New Mexico, (25).

CULTURE Of El Cerrito, (108);—brief description of Navajo culture covering handicrafts, housing, marriage, material possessions, personality, health, (82);—the typical Spanish-speaking community is a relatively self-sufficing rural village, somewhat communal in economic organization, and characterized by an extremely low standard of living, (247);—of New Mexico's Spanish-speaking people derives partly from 16th century Spain, partly from sedentary Indian cultures of the Pueblo groups. Only recently has industrial culture of United States made any considerable impression, (248);—of Taos inadequate to meet current problems, (176).

CULTURE CONFLICT At Bosque Farms, (111).

CULTURE CONTACT Manzano long a center for between Navajo, Apache, and Pueblo groups, (88).

CULTURE PATTERN Of El Cerrito, (108).

CUNDIYO Crafts, (241);—crops, (117);—economic problems, (117); —health, (117), (241);—housing, income, irrigation, land use, (117);—livestock, (241);—population, trade, (117), (241);— work, (241). See also adjustment, income, inheritance, tax delinquency, weaving.

CUNDIYO GRANT   History and present status of lands, (219).

CURRY COUNTY   Agricultural economics, (97), (162);—agricultural history, (162);—climate, crop yields, (162);—erosion, (134);—farm mortgages, (162);—homes, (134);—housing, (77);—income, (162);—land use, (97), (134), (162);—livestock, (134), (162); federal loans, 1931-35, (162);—rehabilitation prospects, relief, (162);—rural youth in, (134);—tax delinquency trends, (23), (162);—tenancy, (140), (162);—types of farming, (162). *See also* agriculture, income, relief.

CUSTOMS   A powerful determinant of behavior at Atarque, (103);—description of folk customs in the isolated villages of New Mexico, (61);—at Picuris, (159).

DANCES   Role in social organization at Atarque, (103);—Indian dances only final portions of lengthy rituals, (142);—description of typical *bailes,* (142);—listing and description of Pueblo and Navajo dances, (142);—symbolism and pageantry in Indian dances, (43);—Zuni, description and significance, (158);—institutionalized role of the dance in culture of Zuni, (13). *See also* ceremonials.

DE BACA COUNTY   Erosion, (134);—farm tenancy, (140);—fruit production, land use, (134);—tax delinquency on grazing lands, (23).

DEBT   Exploitation through use of debt has led many Spanish-speaking people to virtual peonage, (247);—the use of credit serves to tie the chili producer in the Tewa Basin to a merchant who takes his product either in payment of past debts or as a credit against future purchases. Through the use of credit and debt, the chili producer is, by and large, deprived of the right to buy at the cheapest price and sell at the dearest, (213);—in 1935-36 in the ten villages of the Tijeras Canyon area, forty rehabilitation loans totaling $11,300 were made. Of this only $2700 has been repaid 1937, (238). *See also* indebtedness, peonage.

DECIMAS   Description and examples, (25).

DEPENDENCY   Farmers in Estancia Valley depend upon local merchants for credit throughout year until harvest time, (236);—of Pueblos on outside agencies extended as a result of acculturation, (90).

DES MOINES   Population: home, car, and radio ownership: family size: income: housing: adult education: use of leisure time: books per home: magazine and newspaper subscriptions: hobbies: participation in social life: health: attitudes towards education, (75).

DIET Eating habits of early *ricos* in Albuquerque, (50) ;—largely traditional at Atarque, (103) ;—improved at El Pueblo, (84) ;— many El Pueblo families have reached adequate dietary standard, (85) ;—canning introduced at El Pueblo, (85) ;—El Pueblo, (63) ; more than half cost of food consumed at Jemez, Taos, San Ildefonso goes for cereals, meat, chili, and beans. Other purchased items include coffee, sugar, canned milk, butter, condiments, canned and dried fruits, canned vegetables, (90). *See also* food, food habits.

DIRECTED ACCULTURATION Not successful among Pueblos, (90).

DISCIPLINE Forms and methods of disciplining children at Zuni, (1).

DISEASE Behavior patterns related to treatment at Atarque, (103). *See also* health.

DISINTEGRATION Extent in rural communities in Dona Ana County, (93) ;—results from economic change in Dona Ana County, (93) ; —public assistance as a factor in, (93) ;—use of sacred designs in sand painting blankets an indication of disintegration of Navajo religious authority, (178). *See also* community disorganization, disorganization.

DISORGANIZATION At Manzano began soon after American occupation, (88) ;—causes and effects of community disorganization of Spanish-speaking communities in relation to assimilation, (248). *See also* community disorganization, disintegration.

DIVISION OF LABOR Patterns of behavior in regard to at Atarque, (103) ; —between sexes is definite and clear cut at Guadalupe, (248) ;— breakdown of family organization affecting at Sandoval, (248) ;— among Navajos, (72), (83) ;—traditional patterns disrupted by pottery production at San Ildefonso where men spend much time decorating pots for wives or female relatives, (254) ;—revolutionized at San Ildefonso by introduction of commercial pottery, (90) ; —well defined in the growing and harvesting of chili in Tewa Basin, (213).

DIXON *see* Embudo.

DOMESTICATED ANIMALS Effect of introduction on economy of Navajos, (72) ;—acquired by Indians from Spaniards, (90).

DONA ANA (community) Historical background, economic agencies, population characteristics, education, occupational status, housing, sanitation, water supply, transportation and communication, economic services, institutions, recreation, mobility, family interrelationships, (93).

DONA ANA COUNTY Accommodation important in social and cultural relations, (93) ;—agricultural development, (134) ;—agriculture, (93) ;—community relationships, (93) ;—communities, (93) ;—crops, (134) ;—dairying, (134) ;—economic life, (93) ;—importance of family in social structure, (93) ;—types of family organization, (93) ;—farm tenancy, (140) ;—history, (93) ;—housing, institutions, irrigation, (93) ;—land use, (134) ;—livestock, (134) ;—migratory labor, (92) ;—population, (93) ;—rural social organization, service centers, social disintegration, special interest groups, transportation and communication, (93). *See also* aggressive tendencies, agricultural labor, agriculture, antagonism, conflict, cooperation, cultural inertia, economic agencies, economic security, economic status, education, family, family mores, *fiestas*, gregariousness, inferiority complex, isolation, land ownership, migration, mobility, neighborhoods, occupational status, *patron-peon* complex, political organization, politics, problem areas, public assistance, religion, resettlement, self sufficiency, social control, transportation.

DREAMS As aids to Navajo diagnosis in sickness, (121), (122) ;—relation to Navajo religion, (121) ;—importance to Navajos, (72).

DRESS AND ORNAMENT Among Navajos illustrates culture change and diffusion, (72).

DRUM-MAKING Permitted as a craft at Cochiti, Jemez, Tesuque, (27) ; —decline in craft due to easier sources of income, (27) ;—history of, (27). *See also* income, marketing.

DRY CIMARRON VALLEY Agriculture, livestock, water supply, (141).

DRY FARMING Estancia Valley, (236) ;—chief occupation in San Geronimo, (136) ;—the 210 families who live on the dry farming area east of the Sandias are almost entirely dependent on a single resource, dry farm land, cultivation of which, because of uncertain rainfall, is extremely hazardous, (238) ;—growing dependence on dry farms in Spanish-speaking area, (247) ;—was begun about 1900 in upper Rio Grande watershed, (38).

DWELLINGS Evolution of types among Southwestern Indians, (165). *See also* housing.

DYES Use in early nineteenth century weaving, (6). *See also* cochineal.

ECONOMIC ADJUSTMENT Of Navajos following return from Fort Sumner, (72).

ECONOMIC AGENCIES Number and type in Dona Ana County, (93).

ECONOMIC COLLAPSE Of Navajos in American occupation period, (72).

ECONOMIC CONDITIONS In Cuba Valley, (224);—Harding County, (255);—Quay County, (115);—Quay-Curry area, (199);—Middle Rio Grande Conservancy District, (217);—Rio Grande watershed, (236).

ECONOMIC DIFFERENTIALS As a factor in regionalism in New Mexico, (171).

ECONOMIC EQUALITY Marked disequality of income at San Ildefonso as a result of commercial pottery, (90).

ECONOMIC LIFE Place of beargrass, sotol, yucca in economy of Southwestern Indians, (12);—distinction between economic life of Anglos and Spanish-Americans, (172);—Apaches formerly were on hunting and gathering level, (31);—based on livestock at Atarque, (103);—role of family in at Atarque, (103);—Cundiyo dependent on irrigated and grazing land. Income can be raised only by increase in grazing lands or increase in productivity of farm lands, (117);—Dona Ana County, (93);—money in Guadalupe comes from outside wages and occasional sales of products: goes to mail order houses, taxes, itinerant peddlers, *fiestas,* and stores in Albuquerque and Cabezon, (248);—of New Mexico Indians, (105);—one of effects of white contact on Indian culture has been a shift from subsistence to money economy, (90);—of Jicarilla Apache, (148);—in early Manzano controlled by *patrones,* (88);—of Middle Rio Grande watershed, (258);—most pressing needs of Navajos: improve present methods of herding: increase farming and farm income: extend technological education: provide more land, (83);—of Navajo group south of Gallup based on pastoral activity with rug weaving and piñon gathering important sources of income, (101);—New Mexican economy is based on bare subsistence agriculture and small scale grazing operations. Limited resources permit only a low level of livelihood. They cannot support cost of government or maintain essential public services, (176);—non-Spanish-speaking people predominate in commercial, industrial, mining activities, (141);—recent years marked by tendency for Pueblos to adopt modern machine-made goods and to discontinue production and use of handicraft articles, (90);—development of irrigation possibilities of Rio Grande watershed has not secured economic democracy nor enough income to the population dependent on the lands within the watershed. Commercial farming populations are engaged in a business enterprise with a high incidence of failure: non-commercial farming population is being rapidly converted into a wage working popu-

ECONOMIC LIFE (Continued)

lation which, considering limited labor opportunities in the area, is indicative of the inadequacy of the agricultural resources for the support of a dependent population, (223) ;—of San Geronimo, (136) ;—as late as 1858 San Ildefonso people subsisted entirely upon their land. Since then population has decreased, but needs have increased. Decrease in land fertility, loss of lands, and adoption of a commercial economy resulted in the loss of self sufficiency. To meet the need for cash, the women have developed an important commercial pottery trade in which they use, on a small scale, mass production methods. There is some income from painting. The trend is towards greater dependence on outside markets, (241) ;—of San Ildefonso firmly rooted in a flourishing pottery business dominated by women. Agriculture is declining in importance: dependency on money is increasing, (254) ;—of San Jose, (243) ;—changes in economy under which they lived, combined with periodic floods, resulted in abandonment of villages at San Marcial, (211) ;—San Miguel County, (167) ;—of Sandia Pueblo, (49) ;—economy at Sandoval on cash crop basis. Barter is rare: chief source of income is fruit, (248) ;—since 1880 nearly all families in Santa Cruz Valley have supplemented agricultural production with wage work outside the area. This resource is now nearly gone. Present economy characterized by small land holdings, opportunity of living in an adequate dwelling without cash outlay, and a persistent need for cash: about $250 per year per family of five, (227) ;—large land grants gave wealthy Spanish-Americans a type of security that caused them to be scornful of conservatism, (50) ;—of Spanish colonial New Mexico, (63) ;—economic structure of Spanish-speaking villages is simple. Wealth is concentrated in one or two families: every family owns some land and tenancy is rare. Homes are small: arable acres few. Farms approach self sufficiency: much of trading is by barter, (248) ;—economic insufficiency in Taos County demands drastic reforms, (173) ;—improvement of economic level of *Taoseño* must be coupled with improvement in education, health, civic behavior, (176) ;—because of insufficient irrigated land, the economy of Tesuque, based on agriculture, is at a low level of subsistence. The single cash product is pottery, and with the concentration on the production of saleable objects rather than on artistic ones, craftsmanship has declined. Attempts have been made to introduce doll making, mattress making, weaving, making of *fiesta* costumes and wool comforters, but none has become economically success-

ECONOMIC LIFE (Continued)

ful, (241) ;—dominant factors in economic life of Tewa Basin are: 1. Increasing press of population on dwelling resources. 2. Coming of wage labor possibilities at a time when the land could no longer support the population. 3. Coming of a market for products such as chili and fruit and its unstable character. 4. Comparative unimportance of handicrafts as a means of livelihood and their exploitation by dealers. 5. Development of extremes of wealth and large scale operations on the west side of the Rio Grande with resulting semi-feudal conditions. 6. The excessive relief load growing out of above conditions, (241) ;—economy of people of the Town of Abiquiu Grant non-commercial, sub-marginal, (206) ;—of Zuni, (13) .

ECONOMIC PROBLEMS Estancia Valley, (87) ;—Middle Rio Grande Conservancy District, (34) ;—Navajos, (131) , (262) .

ECONOMIC PROSPERITY Enjoyed by Navajos following arrival of Spanish, (72) .

ECONOMIC SECURITY Of Spanish-American farmers in Dona Ana County threatened by high irrigation costs, introduction of cotton, and commercial farming, (93) .

ECONOMIC STATUS Angostura, (93) ;—Arroyo del Agua, (123) ;—Coyote, (123) ;—of 514 Spanish-Americans in Cuba Valley, 32 per cent own no land: 41 per cent no cattle: 90 per cent no sheep, (224) ;—of Spanish-Americans in Cuba Valley affected by loss of agricultural lands and by depression, (224) ;—government aid now economic mainstay of Cuba Valley, (224) ;—of Curry County farmers, (162) ;—of Spanish-Americans in Dona Ana County lowered by land loss, (93) ;—63 per cent of families studied in Jemez area have resources insufficient to maintain them properly, (125) ;—recommendations for improving economic status of Jemez River rehabilitation area, (125) ;—Mesa Poleo, (123) ;—Middle Rio Grande Valley, (236) ;—middle and upper Rio Grande and Rio Puerco areas constitute one of nation's outstanding rural poverty areas, (226) ;—Rio Puerco, (123) ;—of Sandia Pueblo, (49) ;—of families on Sangre de Cristo Grant, (205) ;—per capita wealth consistently lower in counties with larger proportions of Spanish-speaking people, (175) ;—of upper Rio Grande watershed, (91) ;—Villanueva, (138) ;—Youngsville, (123) .

ECONOMIC STATUS—COMPARATIVE Comparison of economic levels of Anglos and Spanish-Americans in Cuba Valley, (146) ;—resources of typical Spanish-American farmer in Cuba Valley small in com-

ECONOMIC STATUS—COMPARATIVE (Continued)

parison to those of typical Anglo in same region, (224) ;—in Jemez-
Tewa area, 92 per cent of Indians and 69 per cent of Spanish-
Americans surveyed in 1935 had income from wages or relief: 50
per cent of Spanish-Americans and 20 per cent of Indians received
less than $100 during 1935: economic status of Spanish-Americans
lower than that of Indians: both are low judged by any standards,
(223) ;—Indians in Santa Clara and San Ildefonso area occupy a
superior economic position to that of Spanish-Americans in same
area. They have larger land holdings, more wage work income,
more cattle and grazing lands, are free of taxes and receive free
educational, health, and guidance services. The real competition
for land resources is not between Indian and Spanish-American,
but between both and large interests carrying on commercial grazing operations, (90) .

EDDY COUNTY Agronomy program, (134) ;—dairying, (134) ;—farm
tenancy, (140) ;—housing conditions, (77) ;—land use, livestock,
youth programs, (134) .

EDUCATION No obvious functional relationship between opportunities
for obtaining formal education and the decline of superstition and
prejudice at Alameda, Guadalupe, Sandoval, (248) ;—schools and
formal education at Alameda, Guadalupe, Sandoval do not seem
to have achieved an influence comparable to that of the church,
(248) ;—comparison of Anglo and Spanish-speaking children in
elementary grades shows that Anglos read faster and comprehend
better and that differences tend to increase in upper grades, (193) ;
—at Angostura, (93) ;—Apodaca, (241) ;—development of and
attitudes towards at Atarque, (103) ;—Berino, (93) ;—of bilinguals,
(175) ;—Cañoncito, (241) ;—attitudes towards at Capulin, Folsom,
Des Moines, (75) ;—Chamberino, (93) ;—Chimayo, (241) ;—
Cienega, (241) ;—school facilities poor, Coyote area, (123) ;—economic advancement, Coyote area, awaits raising of educational
level, (123) ;—Dixon, (241) ;—22.8 per cent of male and 41.9 per
cent of female heads of families in eight selected villages in Dona
Ana County have had no schooling, (93) ;—educational retardation
increases with age in villages studied in Dona Ana County, (93) ;
—percentage of Spanish-Americans in high school low in Dona Ana
County, (93) ;—analysis of educational system in rural Dona Ana
County, (93) ;—apathetic attitude towards education, rural areas
Dona Ana County, (93) ;—importance of in solution of social,
cultural, and economic problems in Dona Ana County, (93) ;—

EDUCATION (Continued)

school at El Cerrito poor: teaching techniques and materials ill adapted to local conditions: personnel poorly trained, attendance irregular, (108) ;–at El Pueblo must be conceived in terms of processes of socialization and agencies for raising standards of living. Should stress health, diet, farming, management, vocational techniques, and should proceed on community level, (62) ; –El Pueblo, (85) ;–Embudo, (241) ;–comparison of vocabularies of Anglo and Spanish-American high school pupils, Grant County, (94) ;–statistics for Harding County, (255) ;–of Indians deficient under present financial conditions of Indian Service, (36) ;– summary of issues and conflicting points of view in Indian education, (83) ;–principles to be followed in Indian education, (83) ;–Indian schools must consider present status of Indian culture, (83) ;–greatest reform in Indian education recently has been added emphasis on day schools on the reservation: program is handicapped somewhat by fact that day schools are taught by women, (90) ;–Indian education has not made any contribution to the restoration of Pueblo culture, largely because the Pueblos are not culture islands but are in daily contact with an economic system that has demonstrated its dominance over self-contained non-commercial economies, (90) ;–goal of present Indian education is a rural and vocational schooling to fit the pupil for a place in his own social environment, (128) ;–policies of Indian Service towards, (81) ;–Indian education poorly adapted to needs, (58) ; –Indian schools should be designed to discover Indian life and to discover to that Indian life its own unrealized needs and opportunities, (36) ;–Isleta, (119) ;–Leasburg, (93) ;–attendance poor, lack of interest in school at Manzano, (88) ;–meager educational facilities for migrant workers' children in southern New Mexico, (208) ;–statistics on education of migratory workers in New Mexico, 1937, (92) ;–educational implications of Navajo economy and culture, (83) ;–evaluation of Indian Service program for Navajos, (74) ;–need for Indian teachers in Navajo schools, (83) ; –not more than 60 per cent of Navajo children of school age are in school, (163) ;–causes of lack of interest in education among Navajos, (163) ;–Congress appealed to in 1867 for help in educating Navajos at Bosque Redondo, (73) ;–summary of differences in practices among schooled and unschooled Navajos, (83) ;– Navajo attitude towards, (131) ;–problems of among Navajos, (72) ;–Placitas, (93) ;–no public schools in New Mexico, 1860,

EDUCATIONAL RETARDATION (Continued)
Spanish-American high school pupils, Grant County, retarded seven to twelve months, (94). *See also* education.

EL BARRANCO   Part of El Pueblo community, (63).

EL CERRITO   Agriculture, culture pattern, education, family organization, history, problems, (108);—informal groupings, (109);—as a racial and cultural unit, (109). *See also* agriculture, bilingualism, cooperation, crops, education, family, honesty, inheritance, kinship, labor organization, land holdings, leadership, men, religion, self sufficiency, social institutions, women.

EL GUACHE   Statistical description covering location, population, work, land, livestock, and health, (241).

EL PUEBLO   Attitude towards acculturation, (62);—agriculture, (62); —crops, (63);—cultural resistance strong, (62);—diet, (63);—education, (62);—Farm Security Administration program, (62), (63); —health, (62), (63);—history, (63);—housing, (62), (63), (85); improvement since 1940, (85);—population, (62), (63);— rehabilitation progress in 1941, (84);—resources, (63);—sanitation, (63);—social and economic background, (63);—water supply, (62). *See also* adult education, agriculture, community consciousness, community house, cooperatives, crops, diet, education, family, health, income, land, land purchase, land tenure, land use, level of living, livestock, population, rehabilitation, sanitation, self sufficiency, suspicion, tobacco, water supply.

EL RITO   Statistical description covering location, population, work, land, livestock, health, and trade, (241).

EL VALLE   *See* Rio Pueblo District.

ELECTION LAWS   As a factor in regionalism, (171).

ELEPHANT BUTTE IRRIGATION PROJECT   Early history as private undertaking, (14).

EMBROIDERY   History of design in New Mexico. Weaving designs Indian: embroidery designs Spanish-colonial, (6).

EMBUDO   Statistical description of Embudo, Dixon, Cienega, Rinconada, Apodaca, and Cañoncito, covering location, population, land, water for irrigation, work, trade, livestock, schools, and health, (241).

EMPLOYMENT   Analysis of employment of New Mexicans, (151);— 119 employed from 125 households in Manzano, (88);—agriculture predominates as employment opportunity at Manzano,

EMPLOYMENT (Continued)

(88) ;—little or no off-season employment for migratory-casual workers in New Mexico, (92) .

EN MEDIO   *See* Chupadero.

EROSION   History of in New Mexico, (166) ;—caused by overgrazing, (144) ;—De Baca County, (134) ;—land deterioration in Guadalupe is depriving people of their only resource, (248) ;—Harding County, (134) ;—on Laguna Indian grant, (210) ;—Navajo lands, (78) ;—problem of and methods of solving, Navajo reservation, (221) ;—more than one-fourth of the state of New Mexico subject to damage by erosion, (141) ;—results from overgrazing, Rio Grande Basin, (142) ;—of thirteen million acres of range land in Rio Grande Basin above Elephant Butte, 25 per cent is in fair condition, 35 per cent badly eroded, 40 per cent excessively eroded, (141) ;—effect of on irrigation, Middle Rio Grande Valley, (142) ; —the main problem of land use in Rio Grande Valley, (144) ;— extent and effects, Rio Grande watershed, (226) ;— extent and effects, Rio Puerco watershed, (203) ;—sheet and gully erosion severe on bench lands in Tewa Basin area. Mountain lands undergoing normal erosion. Recent alluvial lands, on which agriculture is practiced, are being damaged by side cutting of main streams and through overwash from tributary streams, (241) ;—upper Puerco area characterized by excessive erosion caused by overgrazing, (225) ;—in upper Rio Grande watershed, (38) .

ESPAÑOLA   Statistical description covering location, history, population, work, trade, land, livestock, and health, for Española, Riverside, Guachepange, and San Jose, (241) .

ESPAÑOLA VALLEY   Crops, land ownership, population, relief, types of farming, wage labor, (236) . *See also* income, land use, population, relief.

ESTANCIA VALLEY   Agriculture, (87) , (141) ;—economics of bean production, (42) ;—beans as principal crop, (236) ;—climate, (87) ; —crops, (87) , (223) , (238) ;—100,000 acres in dry farming, (236) ; —farm mechanization, (223) ;—farm size, (238) ;—history, (223) ; —income, (238) ;—land ownership trend, (223) ;—land tenure, (238) ;—land use, (223) ;—livestock, (87) , (223) ;—population, (141) , (223) , (236) , (238) ;—relief, (223) , (238) ;—soils, (87);— tenancy, (223) , (238) ;—water supply, (141) . *See also* agriculture, beans, crop failure, dependency, farm labor, farm mechanization, income, land use, livestock, sharecropping, tenancy.

ETHNOBOTANY Isleta, (119);—of Southwestern Indians, (11), (12), (28), (29), (30), (31).

ETHNOCENTRICISM Analysis of as a sub-configuration in behavior patterns at Atarque, (103).

EXPENDITURES 21.5 per cent of income average spent for food among 157 Albuquerque families interviewed, (34);—at Atarque: 45 per cent for food: 12.8 per cent clothing: 10.9 per cent housing: 4.8 per cent special purchases: 10.2 per cent liquor, gambling, tobacco: 16.3 per cent all other, (103);—average yearly per capita at Atarque, $202, (103);—comparison of typical Anglo and Spanish-American family expenditures, Cuba Valley, (146);—averages for families living on five types of farms in MRGCD, (245);—per capita at Santa Clara for twenty-eight store items, (244);—Tortugas, per family for food, 1935, $193, (113). *See also* cost of living, level of living.

EXTRA COMMUNITY RELATIONS Patterns of behavior associated with at Atarque, (103).

FAIRVIEW *See* Santa Cruz.

FAMILIA CONFIGURATION Analysis of behavior at Atarque in terms of, (103).

FAMILY Importance in social structure of Dona Ana County, (93);—as agency of social control in Dona Ana County, (93);—family ties are so strong at El Cerrito that they would help defeat any governmental resettlement or rehabilitation program that did not take into account that the family unit is the larger family of grandparents, children, grandchildren, (108);—entire set of values by which El Cerrito people live are woven around family group, (108);—most instrumental element holding El Cerrito community together has been the family, (108);—at El Cerrito based on strict patriarchal organization, respect for older people, (109);—place in FSA program at El Pueblo, (63);—the basic economic and social unit of Navajos, (72);—status of Navajo women in, (72);—in social organization of Pueblos, (69);—importance and influence at San Geronimo, (136);—solidarity of in Spanish-American culture, (63).

FAMILY DISORGANIZATION At Sandoval, (248).

FAMILY LIFE Hot Springs, (263);—highly integrated at San Jose, (243).

FAMILY MORES Decreasing in power as means of social control in Dona Ana County, (93).

FAMILY ORGANIZATION   A factor in retarding assimilation, (248);—family system at Alameda, Guadalupe, Sandoval has been an isolating factor serving as a barrier to assimilation where it remains intact, (248);—an istrument of social control at Atarque, (103);—role in economic structure at Atarque, (103);—types in rural Dona Ana County, (93);—El Cerrito, (108);—in Guadalupe, people are grouped in *casas* (households) with several *casas* generally occupying a single large dwelling, (248);—a factor in integration in early Manzano, (88);—*viejo*-controlled type of family organization is breaking down at Sandoval, (248);—among Spanish-speaking people is both patrilineal and matrilineal. Organization follows a fairly rigid pattern with authority and respect definitely graded according to age groupings, (248);—at Zuni, (1).

FAMILY RELATIONSHIPS   At Angostura, (93);—behavior patterns associated with at Atarque, (103);—Berino, (93);—Chamberino, (93);—Dona Ana, (93);—kinship terms at Isleta, (152);—Leasburg, (93);—Placitas, (93);—Rodey, (93).

FAMILY SIZE   Behavior patterns in regard to at Atarque, (103);—at Bosque average 4.1. Comparison with six other resettlement communities, (112);—Capulin, Folsom, Des Moines, (75);—Manzano, average 4.52: range 1-12: median 4 (125 families studied), (88);—Tortugas, average 4.9, (113).

FARM CREDIT   Program of Rural Rehabilitation Division and FSA in Penistaja area, (224).

FARM INVESTMENT   In Clovis Project area: average $7,603 per farm ($4,982 real estate: $978 livestock: $282 feed and grain: $1,361 machinery), (220);—twenty-seven row crop farms in Quay County average $7,248, (20).

FARM LABOR   Analysis and status of and needs for in Jemez-Tewa, Rio Grande, Estancia Valley, and Mesilla Valley areas, (223);—migratory, (92);—local supply not sufficient to harvest cotton, broomcorn, peas, (92). See also agricultural labor, migratory labor, migratory workers, wage work.

FARM MECHANIZATION   About half the farmers in Estancia Valley use tractors, (223);—average value of machinery per farm including automobiles in Jemez-Tewa area less than $200, (223);—a factor in urbanization of New Mexico, (246).

FARM RESOURCES   Inadequate in upper Rio Grande Valley, (239).

FARM SECURITY ADMINISTRATION   Activities in El Pueblo, (62), (63);—half consumption groups in Penistaja area clients of FSA, (224);—

FARM SECURITY ADMINISTRATION (Continued)
$100,000 into Penistaja area, 1935-1940, (224) ;—publications of, (60), (61), (62), (63), (84), (85), (110), (113), (205), (206), (207), (208).

FARM SIZE Cotton farms, (92) ;—Estancia Valley, (238) ;—Hammond irrigation project, (196) ;—twenty-seven row crop farms, Quay County, average 924 acres, (20) ;—Sandia Park, (238) ;—13 per cent of farms in 1929 contained less than ten acres: 27 per cent less than twenty acres, (86) ;— problem of small acreage especially acute in Spanish-speaking portions of the state, (86).

FARM TENANCY *See* tenancy.

FATALISM Forced on Spanish-Americans by three hundred years of cultural stagnation, (62).

FEAR Analysis of as a pervasive configuration in Atarque behavior, (103).

FEASTS Religious feasts declining in importance in northern New Mexican villages, (164). *See also fiestas.*

FEDERAL EMERGENCY RELIEF ADMINISTRATION Expenditures in upper Rio Grande Valley during 1935-36, (212).

FEDERAL LOANS To Curry County farmers, 1931-35, (162). *See also* Farm Security Administration, rehabilitation loans, relief, Resettlement Administration, Rural Rehabilitation Division of Resettlement Administration.

FENCE LAKE Inter-community relations with Atarque, (103) ;— cultural differences between Fence Lake and Atarque, (103).

FIESTA At Santa Fe, history and description, (142).

FIESTAS Importance in behavior configurations at Atarque, (103) ;— socially significant as integrating factor in rural Dona Ana County, (93). *See also* feasts.

FIREPLACE Origin of New Mexico corner type, (6).

FLOOD CONTROL In Rio Grande Valley, (144).

FLOODS 1,700 families flooded or swamped out of valley around San Marcial between 1920 and 1937, (239) ;—floods of 1929 and 1937, added to changes in economy, led to abandonment of villages at San Marcial, (211).

FOLK BALLADS *Cuandos,* (25) ;—*inditas,* (25).

FOLK CULTURE Still strong in New Mexico, (25).

FOLK CUSTOMS Description of, (25).

FOLK DRAMA   Of Spanish-Americans affected by Anglo culture, (26) ; —has lost original purpose in New Mexico, (26). *See also* folk plays, religion.

FOLK PLAYS   Old Testament dramas in New Mexico, (25) ;—Christmas folk plays, (25) ;—secular dramatizations, (25). *See also Los Comanches, Los Moros y los Cristianos,* and *Los Pastorales.*

FOLK REMEDIES   New Mexico, (25) ;—Villanueva, (138).

FOLK SONGS   *Corridos,* (25) ;—*decimas,* (25) ;—place in New Mexican folk culture, (25). *See also alabados.*

FOLK THEATRE   Cannot remain static in New Mexico, (25). *See also* folk drama, folk plays.

FOLKLORE   European origins of New Mexico tar-baby stories, (47) ;— Indian contributions to tar-baby stories, (47) ;—European origin of Pueblo tar-baby stories, (45) ;—of Spanish-speaking New Mexicans, (46).

FOLSOM   Population: home, car, and radio ownership: family size: income: housing: adult education: use of leisure time: number of books, magazines and newspaper subscriptions per home: hobbies: participation in social life: attitudes towards education: health, (75).

FOOD   Yearly cost per family, Jemez, Taos, San Ildefonso, $175-258, (90) ;—food expenditures per family at Tortugas in 1935, $193, (113). *See also* diet, food habits.

FOOD CONSUMPTION   Bosque: $584 per family: 54.1 per cent of total value of living. Comparison with six other resettlement communities, (112). *See also* cost of living, expenditures, level of living.

FOOD HABITS   Apache use of native plants for food, (31) ;—largely traditional at Atarque, (103) ;—Bosque, (112) ;—of Navajos relatively little modified by white contact, (102) ;—use of native plants as food by Pueblo Indians has been declining since coming of Spaniards, (28) ;—Spanish importations changed food habits of Pueblos, (6) ;—yucca, sotol as foods for Indian groups, (12). *See also* diet.

FOOD PREPARATION   Indian influence on at Manzano, (88).

FOOD SHIPMENTS   Average monthly number of car loads into MRGCD, 1929-31, (34).

FOREST SERVICE   Publications, (59), (123), (124), (125), (126), (127), (209). *See also* United States Department of Agriculture, Forest Service.

FORESTS   At present no large commercial use, but are important as sources of fuel, fence posts, mine timbers in upper Rio Grande watershed, (38).

FRUIT GROWING   Declining in importance in Roswell region, (18);— grapes, apples, pears, and peaches introduced by Spanish colonials, (6).

FRUITLAND   History of as a Mormon settlement, (53).

FRUITLAND IRRIGATION DEVELOPMENT   History and present status, (131).

FUR INDUSTRY   Development in New Mexico, (151).

FURNITURE   Navajos, (72);—lacking in early Pueblos, (6);—history and development in New Mexico, (6).

GALLUP   Labor trouble at, (257). *See also* racial discrimination.

GALLUP RIOT   Description and analysis of causes, (55), (56), (188).

GAMBLING   Common among early Spanish-speaking people, (142).

GAMES   Navajos, (72). *See also* recreation.

GARAMBULLO   Part of El Pueblo community, (63).

GHOST RANCH   Statistical description covering location, population, land, livestock, game, general conditions, (241).

GOVERNMENT   Of Isleta, (119);—Nambe, (241);—Picuris, (159);—of eastern Pueblos, (69);—of western Pueblos, (69);—in pre-Spanish times Pueblo government was a theocracy with individual participation being limited to institutional channels. Set of secular officers added after appearance of Spaniards served as a front for religious hierarchy, (90);—San Felipe and Santo Domingo nomenclature, (157);—at San Ildefonso new position of importance of women in economy has not been made to conform to a pattern of government based on male dominance, (90);—San Ildefonso, (241), (254);—San Juan, (241);—Sandia, (49);—Sandoval, (248);— Santa Clara, (241);—Tesuque, (241);—the governmental scheme of the Tewa Pueblos not well known. Governmental processes and religious organizations are so closely integrated that discussion of one must include the other. Governmental organization is undergoing modification in most Pueblos, so that while all follow the same basic pattern, government varies from one to the other. The trend seems to be towards a diminishing of the importance of ceremonial and religious influences in government, (241);—Zia, (64).

GOVERNMENT ADMINISTRATION   A factor in retarding education among Spanish-speaking New Mexicans in 19th century, (177);—of Navajos, (163).

GOVERNMENT OFFICIALS   33 per cent of Spanish descent in New Mexico, 1930-32, (175).

GOVERNMENT POLICY   Towards middle Rio Grande watershed lands, (258).

GOVERNMENT PROGRAM   For Navajos, (66).

GOVERNMENTAL ORGANIZATION   In New Mexico 1821-47, 1845-50, (171).

GRANT COUNTY   Farm tenancy, (140) ;—Spanish-American children in high schools of have vocabulary handicap, (94). *See also* education, educational retardation.

GRANTS, LAND   *See* land grants.

GRAZING   De Baca County, (134) ;—privately owned grazing lands in Jemez-Tewa area in highly concentrated ownership, (223) ;—on Navajo reservation, (150) ;—overgrazing a problem of Navajos, (78) ;—overgrazing problem acute in Rio Puerco Valley, (141) ;— Rio Arriba County, (134) ;—effect of overgrazing of land in Rio Grande Basin, (142) ;—in Santa Cruz Valley there are 1,400 cattle and horses and 2,500 sheep on an area that has a carrying capacity of only 250 cattle units year long. Area around village of Santa Cruz is so overgrazed that it should be retired for a period of at least five years, (227) ;—on state owned lands, (143) ;—overgrazing prevalent on ranges of Tewa Basin area, (241) ;—carrying capacity and management plan for Tewa Basin area, (241). *See also* commercial grazing, overgrazing.

GREGARIOUSNESS   Tendency towards among Spansh-Amercans in Dona Ana County communities, (93).

GUACHEPANGE   *See* Española.

GUADALUPE   Population, community and family organization, crops, livestock, division of labor, immigration and emigration, effect of isolation on, and social change in, (248) ;—history, resources, problems, (225). *See also* acculturation, assimilation, bilingualism, division of labor, economic life, education, erosion, family organization, isolation, livestock, *patron-peon* system, political organization, poverty, social change.

GUADALUPE COUNTY   Farm tenancy, (140) ;—history, (134) ;—land use, (134) ;—management program, (134).

HACIENDA SYSTEM   Why it did not flourish in New Mexico, (103).

HACIENDAS   In early Albuquerque, (50).

HAMMOND IRRIGATION PROJECT Location, description, irrigation requirements, existing water facilities, water rights, land use, types and size of farms, crop yields, markets, land values, land ownership, (196).

HANDICRAFTS Leather work based on both Indian and Spanish tradition. First of manual crafts practiced in New Mexico, (6);—revival of at Mora, (181);—specific recommendations by New Mexico Land Use Advisory Council for increasing native skills and home industries, (133);—handicraft industries have not proved an adequate source of income in Spanish-speaking areas, (247). *See also* arts and crafts, crafts and craftsmanship.

HARDING COUNTY Educational statistics, (255);—educational program, (134);—erosion, (134);—farm tenancy, (140);—history, (255);—history of communities in, (255);—land use, (134);—political organization, (255);—population, (255);—social organization, (255);—topography, (255). *See also* agriculture.

HATCH As a community center in Dona Ana County, (93).

HEALTH Angostura, (241);—Apodaca, (241);—attitude towards illness at Atarque, (103);—Barranca, (241);—expenditures for health at Bosque compared with those of six other resettlement communities, (112);—Brady, (241);—Cañoncito, (241);—Capulin, (75);—Chamisal, (241);—Chamita, (241);—Chimayo, (241);—Chupadero, (241);—Cienega, (241);—Claro, (241);—Cordova, (241);—Cuarteles, (241);—Cundiyo, (117), (241);—Des Moines, (75);—Dixon, (241);—El Guache, (241);—1940 health program at El Pueblo, (85);—El Pueblo, (62), (63);—El Rito, (241);—El Valle, (241);—Embudo, (241);—En Medio, (214);—Española, (241);—Fairview, (241);—Folsom, (75);—Guachepange, (241); —no necessary relationship between availability of health services and health standards and practices of the people, (248);—Indian deaths from tuberculosis are few. Syphilis (9.1 per cent among 231 males tested) compares with prevalence among 1,023 Spanish-American adults tested in Mora County. Dysentery and malaria are fairly common: there is little typhoid or diphtheria, (241);—level of health among Southwestern Indians, (81);—history of government health service to Indians, (81);—Isleta, (119);—Jacona, (241);—Leyden, (241);—Llano, (241);—Llano Abeyta, (241);—Llano de los Quemadeños, (241);—Llano Layba, (241); —Los Mochos, (241);—Manzano, (88);—many migrants come to New Mexico for health reasons, (137);—Nambe, (241);—NYA examination of 'hundreds' of New Mexico youth showed: 80 per

HEALTH (Continued)

cent had never been to dentist: 65 per cent had never been to doctor: 48 per cent were in immediate need of dental care: 19 per cent needed eye refractions: 27 per cent needed tonsillectomies: 18 per cent needed special diets: 2 per cent needed immediate major surgery: 3 per cent had heart complications: 2 per cent needed treatment for social diseases, (129);—role of magic and superstition in Navajo diagnosis of sickness, (122);—development of public health nursing on Navajo reservation, (242);—Navajo, (35), (82), (163);—many New Mexicans still live in 17th century insofar as health is concerned, (176);—Ojo Sarco, (241);—Penasco, (241);—Placita, (241);—Pojoaque, (241);—public health facilities not up to national standards, (239);—Puebla, (241);—Rinconada, (241);—Rio Chama Village, (241);—Rio Oso Village, (241);—Rio Pueblo District, (241);—Riverside, (241);—Rodarte, (241); —development of sanitary facilities at San Geronimo slow, (136); —superstition still rules many health practices at San Geronimo, (136);—San Ildefonso, (241);—San Jose, (241);—Sandoval, (248); Santa Cruz, (241);—Santo Niño, (241);—Sombrio, (241);— schools should undertake health examinations in Taos County, (174);—Tierra Azul, (241);—Trampas, (241);—Tres Ritos, (241);—Vadito, (241);—Vallecito, (241);—Vallecitos, (241;)— Velarde, (241);—folk remedies at Villanueva, (138).

HERMANO MAYOR   Importance in family organization at Atarque, (103).

HIDALGO COUNTY   Farm tenancy, (140);—land inventory, (134);— livestock, (134);—population, (134);—water inventory, (134).

HILILI   Zuni dance borrowed from Acoma and Laguna, (158).

HOGANS   Advantages and disadvantages from health standpoint, (163).

HOLIDAYS   See Saints' days.

HOMESTEAD ACT   Perversion for commercial use, (258).

HOMESTEAD POLICY   Of government a factor in Anglo settlement of Rio Grande area, (90).

HONESTY   Strict code of honesty and fairness at El Cerrito does not always apply to dealings with outsiders, (108).

HOPE IRRIGATED AREA   Crops, land use, population, tax delinquency, water facilities, (197). See also land use, population, tax delinquency, water facilities.

HORSES   Navajo attitude towards reduction program, (131).

HOSPITALITY   In early Albuquerque, (191).

HOSTILITY   Anti-white sentiments growing among Navajo, (101). *See also* antagonism.

HOT SPRINGS   Family life, attitudes towards children, religion, folk tales, (263). *See also* relief.

HOUSE OF REPRESENTATIVES   Party and racial division by counties, 1913-37, (171).

HOUSEHOLD ARTS   At Villanueva, (138).

HOUSEHOLD EQUIPMENT   Of Navajos, (72).

HOUSING   More than 40 per cent of houses in New Mexico over-crowded, (239);—poor housing related to rural sanitation and infant mortality problems, (239);—Angostura, (93);— 80 per cent of 3,746 families living in five areas of Albuquerque occupied substandard dwellings, (89);—median rentals of 1,323 tenant families in five areas of Albuquerque, $8.29 per month, (89);—value of houses at Atarque, $75-$350, (103);—Berino, (93);—size and value of dwellings at Bosque compared with those of six other resettlement communities, (112);—Capulin, (75);—Chamberino, (93);—Chaves County, (77);— Cundiyo, (117);—Curry County, (77);—Des Moines, (75);—Dona Ana (community), (93);—Dona Ana County, (93);—Eddy County, (77);—improvements at El Pueblo, (62), (85);—El Pueblo, (63);—Folsom, (75);—Jemez area, (125);—Leasburg, (93);—four types of housing at Manzano, (88);—housing conditions inadequate for migratory workers in southern New Mexico, (208);—Mora County, (77);—Navajos, (72), (82);—description of typical New Mexico house, 1876, (166);—Placitas, (93);—commonest size of Pueblo home has three rooms and can be constructed for about $65 if builder supplies native materials and does labor himself.   Pueblo homes rent for average of $6 a year, (90);—Quay County, (77);—19th century Questa, (186);—Rodey, (93);—results of study of 962 farm homes in San Miguel County, (167);—San Miguel County, (77);—San Jose, (243);—Spanish colonial times, (63);—houses of thirty-seven families studied in Tortugas averaged twenty years of age, replacement value $166, (113);—Villanueva, (138).

HUNTING   Role in economy of Navajos, (72).

ILLITERACY   Seven-eighths of adult population of New Mexico illiterate, 1850, (73);—correlates .41 with bilingualism, (175);—correlation between percentage of Spanish-Americans in each county and percentage of illiterates, (171);—correlation between illiteracy and percentage of Spanish-speaking people in New Mexico population, (172);—Manzano, (88);—in 1870, 48,836 people in

ILLITERACY (Continued)

New Mexico over ten years of age could not read: 52,220 could not write, (166) ;—declining in New Mexico, (144) ;—in 1930, 13.3 per cent of people in New Mexico illiterate, (176) ;—as a factor in regionalism, (171) ;—30 per cent of population of San Geronimo cannot read either Spanish or English, (136).

INCOME   Median annual income of 2,083 families surveyed in five areas of Albuquerque $653, (89) ;—$2,750 average annual income of 332 Albuquerque families interviewed in 1930, (34) ;—range of family income at Atarque, 1936, $316 to $4,645, (103) ;—source of at Atarque, (103) ;—Bosque, (112) ;—Cañon de Jemez, (125) ;— Capulin, (75) ;—Carnuel, (238) ;—Cedar Crest, (238) ;—average farm income Clovis Project area (operator's wage and use of capital), $1,176: labor only, $871, (220) ;—typical income of Spanish-American in Cuba Valley, $400: 50 per cent derived from wage work, (224) ;—typical income of Anglo in Cuba Valley, $1,000: 26 per cent derived from wage work, (224) ;—51 per cent of 494 consumption units in Cuba Valley derive major portion of income from government assistance, (224) ;—in 1938, 27 per cent of Cuba Valley people studied had no income from agriculture, (224) ;— Cuba Valley, (146) ;—total income at Cundiyo, $4,500—about $200 per family per year. Only five families obtained more than $300, (117) ;—at Cundiyo derived from sale of crops and livestock, wage work, and relief, (117) ;—gross receipts per farm by source, Curry County, 1934, (97) ;—Curry County farmers, (162) ;—Des Moines, (75) ;—from drum-making: $167 average per year per artisan (approximately 19c per hour for time spent), (27) ;—average cash income El Pueblo, 1938, $280 per family, (63) ;—improved at El Pueblo during 1941, (84) ;—three sources in Española Valley: cash crops, sale of surplus labor, relief, (236) ;—cash income on typical farm in Estancia Valley with one hundred acres in beans has varied in past ten years from nothing to $3,900, having been under $1,000 five years out of the ten, and under $500 four years, (238) ;—specific recommendations by New Mexico Land Use Advisory Council for maintaining reasonable farm income, (133) ; —cash income from farm production in New Mexico fell 64 per cent between 1928 and 1932, (23) ;—of 31,404 farms in New Mexico in 1929, 5,670 gained less than $250, 9,950 less than $400, (86) ;—Folsom, (75) ;—of Indians, amount and sources, (105) ;— Indians from basket production in 1934: $31.25 per worker (8c per hour), (27) ;—Indians from beadwork: $29.25 per worker (7c

INCOME (Continued)

per hour), (27);—Indians from pottery, 1934: $100.56 per worker (average 14c per hour); wide variations of earnings among different Pueblos, from 7c to 25c per hour, (27);—Indians from shell and turquoise work: net earnings average 45c per hour, (27);—Indians from silversmithing: average 30c per hour, (27);—Indian tanners: average 21c per hour, (27);—Jemez River rehabilitation area, (125);—Jemez Springs, (125);—average Spanish-American farmer in Jemez-Tewa area has two acres in cash crop from which he derives approximately $75 cash annually, (223);—average income from non-relief wage work in Jemez-Tewa area $135 per family, (223);—La Cueva, (125);—La Tijera, (238);—Laguna reservation, (87);—Lower Vallecitos, (125);—probably 35,000 inhabitants of the Mesilla Valley area are dependent on family incomes under $600; 15,000 of them on incomes under $300, (223);—average value of living furnished on five types of farms in MRGCD, 1929, 1930, 1931, (245);—54 per cent of all rural consumption groups MRGCD area receive less than $100 per capita annual income, (217);—Middle Rio Grande Valley, (223);—median yearly earnings of migratory casual workers in New Mexico, 1937: $344 for unattached workers, $461 for family heads, (92);—Navajo reservation, (87), (150), (221), (240);—major sources of for Navajos, (214);—Navajos from weaving: average $61.90 per worker in 1934 (7c per hour), (27);—42.2 per cent of Navajo income is from livestock, farm, garden, and orchard: 91.88 per cent is classified as earned income, (83);—average Navajo family needs $235 a year on a trading basis for subsistence, (221); —Spanish, Anglo, and Indian painters: $729.28 average income per painter (52c per hour), (27);—Primer Agua, (238);—Pueblo weavers: $66.50 per worker average in 1934 (14c per hour), (27); —Quay County beef and sheep ranches, row crop and wheat farms, (189);—basic sources of, Rio Grande watershed: irrigated agricultural land, livestock, wage work, federal relief, (91);—average per family upper Rio Grande watershed, 1936: $650, with two thirds being below $600, (91);—San Antonio, (238);—San Antonito, (238);—marked disequality of income at San Ildefonso results from cash earned by successful potters, (90);—San Ildefonso from land, 1922, $13.11 per family, (90);—average $48.50 per month per family, San Jose, (243);—San Juan, from land, 1922, $32 per family, (90);—San Ysidro, (125);—Sandia Park, (238);—Sangre de Cristo Grant, average per family $521, (205);—per capita for farming and non-farming groups, Santa Clara, (244);

INCOME (Continued)

—Santa Fe National Forest area: average annual income per family, $301.72, (124) ;—Santa Fe National Forest area: 82 per cent of families $300 or less per year: 86 per cent, $400 or less per year: 89 per cent, $500 or less per year, (124) ;—Sedillo, (238) ;—one-third of Spanish-American farms produce less than $250 worth of products annually, (239) ;—Tesuque: from land, 1922, $16.68 per family average, (90) ;—two-thirds of the 240 families constituting the population of the ten mountain villages in Tijeras Canyon area had in 1936 cash incomes under $250. In no case did earnings from non-relief wage work exceed $480; in all but fifteen cases were under $200, (238) ;—Tortugas families live on seasonal income of $1 per day, (113) ;—average yearly cash receipts of thirty-seven Tortugas families studied, $344 (78 per cent from wages: 50 per cent of wages from relief sources) , (113) ;—cash income from crops in Town of Abiquiu Grant does not exceed $75 per year per family, (206) ;—migratory workers from upper Rio Grande area in 1920's earned about two million dollars a year. In 1930's figures dropped to about $350,000. Prospects for next ten years are that workers from this area will earn a total of about $1,300,000 a year both in and out of New Mexico, (232) ;—in upper Rio Grande area, 45 per cent of 324 families surveyed derived income from relief: 43 per cent from wages. Three-fourths of relief families received less than $100: 70 per cent of wage earners received $100 or less; 80 per cent, $200 or less, (233) ;—of 1,062 families in twenty villages in upper Rio Grande area, 64 per cent have total incomes of $600 or less; another 18 per cent incomes between $600 and $1,000, (233) ; —total income per family in upper Rio Grande area varies almost directly with income from cultivated land, (233) ;—typical family studied in upper Rio Grande area had cash income of $341, of which $336 came from sale of chili and fruit, (218) ;—estimated total income of native population of upper Rio Grande area in 1936: ten million dollars (50 per cent from cultivated land; 15 per cent from livestock; 14 per cent from relief; 21 per cent from other sources) , (233) ;—over 80 per cent of families in one group of villages in upper Rio Grande area derive income from two or more sources: 44 per cent from three or more, (223) ;—two-thirds of people in upper Rio Grande Valley have incomes under $600. Only one-tenth of six thousand farm operators receive more than $1,000 a year and only thirty-three operators receive more than $8,000 for land and livestock, (239) ;—Upper Vallecitos, (125) . See also subsistence income.

INDEBTEDNESS Average for Clovis project area, $2.96 per acre of farm land, (220). *See also* debt.

INDIAN AFFAIRS Periods in governmental management of, (81).

INDIAN ART *See* painting.

INDIAN DANCES *See* dances.

INDIAN EDUCATION *See* education.

INDIAN EMERGENCY CONSERVATION WORK Critical analysis of results of inauguration of IECW, (90), (241);—with wages paid by IECW nearly double those prevailing in the area, relief program for the Pueblos has resulted in the removal of a feeling of responsibility on the part of the individual to do community work free, has aided in the rise of a landlord class through the hiring of Spanish-Americans by the Indians on relief, and has tended to create an emergency where none existed before, (90).

INDIAN LANDS Status and extent of in New Mexico and state policy towards, (81).

INDIAN RAIDS A factor in community integration at Manzano, (88).

INDIAN SERVICE Philosophy behind educational policies, (36);— evaluation of educational program, (74);—the policies of the Indian Service in the Pueblos, insofar at least as they affect relief, education, judicial procedure, tend to hamper rather than to facilitate the process of assimilation, (90);—protest against activities of, (120). *See also* Office of Indian Affairs.

INDITAS Description of, (25).

INDIVIDUALISM Extent among Spanish-Americans, (63).

INDUSTRY Rio Puerco watershed area, (203).

INFANT MORTALITY Only thirteen New Mexico counties have an infant mortality rate under 100; eighteen have rates from 104.8 to 167. (Rate for U. S. as a whole, 51), (176);—a factor in regionalism, (171);—nearly 25 per cent at Atarque, (103);—causes of at Atarque, (103);—highest in counties inhabited by Spanish-Americans and Indians, (239);—rate among Pueblo Indians in Tewa Basin (27.9 per 100 live births) "is nearly four times as great as that for the United States at large and well over twice that of the non-Indian population of New Mexico." Comparison with Spanish-American communities in vicinity of the Pueblos indicates this high rate may be largely due to environmental conditions, (241);—not counting still births, 50 per cent at San Geronimo, (136);—correlation of plus .70 between percentage of Spanish-Americans and number of deaths per 1,000 under one year of age,

INFANT MORTALITY (Continued)

(171);—percentage of Spanish-speaking people in population correlates plus .75 with infant mortality, (172).

INFERIORITY COMPLEX   Exists among Spanish-speaking people in rural Dona Ana County, (93).

INFORMAL GROUPINGS   At El Cerrito, (109).

INFORMAL RELATIONSHIPS   Indicative of integration at Bosque Farms and Tortugas, (110).

INHERITANCE   Behavior patterns in regard to, Atarque, (103);—at Cundiyo only sons inherit land, (117);—land inherited equally by children at El Cerrito, resulting in some holdings becoming so small it is difficult to know exactly where boundaries lie, (108).

INSTITUTIONS   Angostura, (93);—Berino, (93);—Chamberino, (93);—role in social organization of Dona Ana County, (93);—Leasburg, (93);—Placitas, (93);—Rodey, (93).   See also social institutions.

INTEGRATION   Trends toward at Bosque farms, (110);—forces aiding at Bosque farms, (111);—sociometrics of Bosque farms, (111);—Spanish-American culture closely integrated in Cuba Valley, (146);—El Cerrito highly integrated and socially unified in spite of being submarginal in capacity to support its population, (108);—Navajo economic, social, and religious life highly integrated, (83);—Navajos have maintained a coherent social form while adopting a money, land-owning, competitive economy, (101). See also community organization, informal relationships.

INTER-COMMUNITY RELATIONS   Between Atarque and Zuni, Atarque and Los Pinitos, Atarque and Las Norias, Atarque and Fence Lake, (103).

INTERDEPARTMENTAL RIO GRANDE BOARD   Creation and activities, (258);—organization and purpose, (91);—reports of, (39), (168).

INTERMARRIAGE   Indians and Anglos in New Mexico, (81);—common between Indians and members of early Spanish exploring parties, (6);—between racial groups regarded with disapproval by Navajos, (83);—little in Rio Grande Valley between racial groups, (144).

INVESTMENT   See farm investment, ranch investment.

IRONWORK   Of little importance as a craft in New Mexico, (6).

IRRIGATED LAND   1.4 acres per family, Cibola National Forest area, (124);—5,200 acres under irrigation in Santa Cruz area, (235);—7.5 acres per family in Santa Fe National Forest area, (124).

IRRIGATION Alamosa River watershed area, (198);—irrigation farming, once characteristic of entire Cuba Valley, now exists only in
northern end and appears to have a brief future even there, (225);
—importance at Cundiyo, (117);—Dona Ana County, (93);—
Indian irrigation systems have been improved in last 35-40 years.
Now an ample supply of water during irrigation season except at
Tesuque and San Ildefonso. Separate information on number of
acres irrigated and irrigable both of Indian and non-Indian inhabitants of Indian grants together with material on status of
water rights for Nambe, Pojoaque, Picuris, Santa Clara, San
Ildefonso, San Juan, and Tesuque, (241);—approximately 2,437
acres can be irrigated at Manzano, (88);—Mesilla Valley, (87),
(223);—history, extent middle Rio Grande Valley, (33);—history
of in middle Rio Grande Valley, (132);—historical development,
present status, causes of recent failure in middle Rio Grande
Valley, (70);—Mora County, (134);—Mora River area, (200);—
Navajo reservation, (163);—Navajos, (83);—Ocate Creek area,
(204);—effect on Pecos Valley, (8);—Picuris, (241);—Rincon
Valley, (87);—reached peak in Rio Grande Valley in 1850, (142);
—at least 25,000 acres irrigated in Rio Grande Valley at time of
arrival of first whites, (142);—history of in Rio Grande Valley,
(144);—history, present status, Rio Puerco watershed, (203);—
primitive methods at San Geronimo borrowed from Indians,
(136);—San Juan basin, (87);—San Juan Valley, (141);—San
Miguel County, (134);—Santa Clara, (241);—waste of water due
to inadequate methods in Santa Cruz area, (202);—history of
organization and financing of Santa Cruz Irrigation District,
(229);—Tesuque, (241).

ISLETA Acculturation, (119);—arts and crafts, (119);—sketches reveal-
ing characteristics of Isletans, (16), (17);—clan system, (156);—
education, (119);—ethnobotany, (119);—government, (119);—
health, (119);—history, (119);—kinship terms, (152);—land grant
litigation, (15);—language, (119);—legends, (119);—marriage
customs, (152);—music, (119);—religion, (119);—social structure,
(119). See also acculturation, arts and crafts, ceremonials, weaving.

ISOLATION Analysis of effect on rate of social change in Alameda,
Guadalupe, Sandoval, (248);—importance in development of
behavior patterns at Atarque, (103);—breakdown of village isolation began with coming of railroads in 1880's, was accelerated by
mobilization of man power during World War I and by increased

ISOLATION (Continued)

demands for labor in 1920's, (247);—broken by draft in World War I, (19);—importance in relation to social-cultural processes in Dona Ana County, (93);—Dona Ana County communities both geographically and culturally isolated, (93);—breaking down in Dona Ana County communities, (93);—effect on Guadalupe, (248);—establishment of MRGCD broke isolation and forced much of rural population in area into a commercial situation demanding a new type of adjustment to irrigated land, (223);—a factor in the stability of Navajo culture, (102);—a limiting factor in the acculturation of rural New Mexican, (176);—a determining factor in development of Spanish-American culture, (62);—effect on Spanish-American personality, (62).

JACONA   See Pojoaque.

JACONA GRANT   History and present status of lands in, (219). See also land grants, tax delinquency.

JEFE POLITICO   Role in social organization at Atarque, (103);—role in social organization of Spanish-American communities, (248).

JEMEZ   See automobiles, cost of living, crops, diet, drum-making, self sufficiency.

JEMEZ AREA   Housing, (125).

JEMEZ PUEBLO   History of land grant litigation, (15).

JEMEZ RIVER REHABILITATION AREA   Income, income deficiency, population, recommended methods of improving economic situation, relief, resources, (125). See also agriculture, arts and crafts, economic status.

JEMEZ SPRINGS   Crops, income, population, relief, (125);—62 per cent of population needs relief, (125).

JEMEZ-TEWA AREA   Land ownership trends, land use, livestock, population analysis, relief, (223). See also agriculture, cost of living, economic status—comparative, farm labor, farm mechanization, grazing, income, land, land ownership, livestock, population, wage work.

JICARILLA APACHES   Summary of culture, (148). See also Apaches.

JUDICIAL SYSTEM   Attempt to establish Anglo judicial system at Acoma, (155).

JURIES   Regionalism as a factor in selection of, (171).

KINSHIP   Influence on visiting, borrowing, and cooperation at El Cerrito, (109);—importance among Jicarilla Apaches, (148);—role in Zuni ceremonialism, (158).

KINSHIP TERMS   Infiltration between Pueblo groups, (153).

KIRTLAND   History of as a Mormon settlement, (53).

KIVA   Significance in Indian religion, (107).

LA CUEVA   Income, income deficiency, population, relief, (125).

LA JARA   History, problems, resources, (225).

LA JOYA GRANT   History and present status of lands of, (219). *See also* land grants.

LA PERCINGUALA   Feast of at Arroyo Hondo, (164).

LA TIJERA   Statistical description covering location, population, resources, livestock, business, cash income, relief, rural rehabilitation loans, community conditions, (238).

LA VENTANA   History, problems, resources, (225).

LABOR ORGANIZATION   People of El Cerrito have no first hand experience with organized labor movements, (108);—Madrid, (188).

LABOR SUPPLY   Generally adequate in New Mexico; local supply of qualified labor not always adequate, (137);—shortage for 1937 cotton, broomcorn, pea harvests, (92).

LABOR TROUBLE   At Gallup, (55), (56), (188), (257).

LAGUNA   History, mythology, religion, traditions, (190);—land grant litigation, (15);—use of plants for medicines, (190). *See also* acculturation, ceremonials, migration, religion, tax delinquency.

LAGUNA INDIAN GRANT   Erosion on, (210). *See also* land ownership.

LAGUNA INDIAN RESERVATION   Crops, land, livestock, problems, sources of income, (87).

LAKE AVALON   Size, effects on agriculture, (8).

LAND   Cultivated acreage in Coyote area estimated sufficient to support ninety-nine of the 185 families occupying the area, (123);—a determinant of culture in the Southwest, (80);—an integral part of life in El Pueblo, (63);—for most part has not been a negotiable commodity in Jemez-Tewa area, (223);—importance in economy of middle Rio Grande Valley, (258);—effects of commercial exploitation in middle Rio Grande Valley, (258);—Navajos moving beyond legal limits of their reservation, (102);—three hundred acres per person on Navajo reservation insufficient, (35); —of Tewa area is reddish clay, quite productive when water is available. There is insufficient water for irrigation, and deforestation and overgrazing have caused heavy erosion resulting in floods that periodically destroy farm lands, (241);—irrigable lands make up about 5 per cent of upper Rio Grande watershed, (38);—

LAND (Continued)

accelerated erosion followed recent developments in upper Rio Grande watershed, (38) . *See also* land holdings, land ownership, land problems, land resources, land tenure, land use.

LAND, IRRIGATED *See* irrigated land.

LAND ECONOMY In Rio Grande watershed characterized by: scarcity of resources, declining resource base, low-income population, control of most of grazing resources by small group of commercial operators, government interest in, (226) .

LAND GRANT LITIGATION History of at Acoma, Cochiti, Isleta, Jemez, Laguna, San Felipe, Sandia, Santa Ana, Santo Domingo, Zia, (15) . *See also* Court of Private Land Claims.

LAND GRANTS Problems of ownership and fraud in connection with claims to, (160) ;—history and present status of lands in Canyon de San Diego, Cundiyo, and La Joya grants, (219) ;—Indian grants, except Zuni, guaranteed by federal government in 1848, (22) ;— tax burdens and sharp business practices by some Anglos are resulting in loss of community-owned lands by Spanish-Americans, (219) ;—present status of Manzano grant, (88) ;—history of litigation over Pueblo grants, (15) .

LAND HOLDINGS Majority of families at El Cerrito own and operate from ten to forty acres of dry-farming land plus one to four acres of irrigated land, (108) ;—half of the 2,200 farms in Taos County are six acres or less, (176) ;—land available for use in Tewa Basin under present distribution would average no more than 4.5 acres per family, (213) ;—87 per cent of 929 families in twenty villages in upper Rio Grande area own some cultivated land. One-third own two acres or less: two-thirds, six acres or less: three-fourths, ten acres or less, (233) ;—are traditionally large in Roswell region, (18) ;—three-fifths of farms in upper Rio Grande watershed have fewer than ten acres: four-fifths under twenty acres of cultivated lands, (239) . *See also* land ownership, land tenure.

LAND MANAGEMENT Navajo attitude towards, (131) .

LAND OWNERSHIP A factor in promoting traditionalism, (103) ;— Abiquiu, (241) ;—Alamosa River watershed area, (198) ;—Angostura, (241) ;—Apodaca, (241) ;—in Atarque region only 5.2 per cent of land is owned by Atarque stockmen, (103) ;—Barranca, (241) ;—Brady, (241) ;—Cañoncito, (241) ;—Cedar Crest, (238) ;— central northern New Mexico, (127) ;—Chamita, (241) ;—Chimayo, (241) ;—Chiz Community, (198) ;—Cienega, (241) ;—

LAND OWNERSHIP (Continued)

Claro, (241);—Clovis Project area, (220);—Cordova, (241);—
Cuarteles, (241);—32 per cent of 514 Spanish-American consumption units studied in Cuba Valley own no land, (146),
(224);—comparison of Spanish-American and Anglo holdings in
Cuba Valley, (146);—based on land use in early Cuba Valley,
(224);—Dixon, (241);—historical trend in Dona Ana County,
(93);—introduction of commercial farming in Dona Ana County
led to loss of land by many Spanish-American owners, (93);—
El Guache, (241);—El Rito, (241);—Embudo, (241);—65 per
cent of people of Española Valley have less than five acres per
family, (236);—holdings comparatively stable in Española Valley,
(236);—Española, (241);—trends in Estancia Valley, Jemez-Tewa
area, Mesilla Valley, Middle Rio Grande Valley, (223);—Fairview, (241);—Ghost Ranch, (241);—Guachepange, (241);—Hammond irrigation project, (196);—illegal Anglo and Spanish-American settlements on Indian land, (22);—Jacona, (241);—Spanish-
American farmer in Jemez-Tewa area owns average of 6.6 acres of
irrigated land of which two acres are in cash crop, (223);—Laguna
Indian grant, (210);—Leyden, (241);—Llano Abeyta, (241);—
Llano de los Quemadeños, (241);—Lower Vallecitos, (125);—
24.1 acres per family for 125 families studied at Manzano, (88);—
number of owners decreased in Mesilla Valley since construction
of Elephant Butte Dam, (236);—Mesilla Valley, (223);—loss of
land through high taxes in Middle Rio Grande Irrigation district,
(106);—four thousand tracts of land in MRGCD lost to Tax
Commission, (258);—Middle Rio Grande Valley, (223);—Nambe,
(241);—Navajo practices in regard to, (72);—Ocate Creek area,
(204)—Ojo Sarco, (241);—Pojoaque, (241);—Puebla, (241);—
legal controversies over Anglo encroachment on Pueblo lands,
(37);—Quay County, (115);—Rinconada, (241);—Rio Arriba
County, (239);—Rio Chama Village, (241);—Rio Grande Valley,
(144);—Rio Hondo watershed, (222);—Rio Moquino area,
(201);—Rio Oso Village, (241);—Rio Puerco watershed, (203);
—Riverside, (241);—at San Geronimo, 2.82 acres of dry land and
0.9 acres of irrigated land per capita, (136);—Anglo encroachment
reduced San Ildefonso productive acreage from 1,250 to 248, (22);
—San Jose, (241);—Sandoval County, (239);—one hundred out of
570 Santa Cruz area families are landless, (39);—Santa Cruz area,
(202), (235);—Santa Fe County, (239);—Santo Niño, (241);—
Sombrio, (241);—possession of range land by Spanish-Americans
decreasing since 1890, (61);—Spanish-speaking people rapidly

LAND OWNERSHIP (Continued)

> losing land through foreclosures and tax sales, (247);—Taos County, (239);—average holding in Tewa Basin 4.5 acres, (235); —80 per cent of families in Tewa Basin own less than eight acres of land, (235);—Tierra Azul, (241);—Trampas, (241);—Truchas, (241);—Vallecito, (241);—Velarde, (241);—Villanueva, (138). *See also* land holdings, land tenure.

LAND POLICY Of Spain, Mexico, and United States towards Pueblo Indians, (15).

LAND PROBLEMS A factor in decline of Atarque, (103);—of Navajos: increasing population, decreasing resources, (66);—Navajos (163).

LAND PURCHASE Proposed for El Pueblo experimental area, (63);— proposal for Sangre de Cristo Grant, (205);—proposal for Town of Abiquiu Grant, (206).

LAND REDUCTION Productive irrigated area in use in Middle Rio Grande district cut in half 1885-1925, (258).

LAND RESOURCES Ownership and use of in Rio Grande watershed, (226).

LAND TENURE Only one family at El Pueblo during 1940 rented all land it cultivated, (85);—Estancia Valley, (238);—56 per cent of operators own their land in lower Rio Grande area, (226);— among Navajos, (83);—among Navajos influenced by type of land, use, and social organization, (98);—only 45 per cent of land in New Mexico privately owned in 1929, (86);—Ocate Creek area, (204);—Sandia Park, (238);—interesting parallels may be drawn between the Tewa Indian system of land tenure and that of medieval Europe. Farm land is divided into narrow strips running perpendicular to irrigation ditches. Land may be acquired from parents by gift or inheritance: from a deceased spouse, a deceased child, or the community; by purchase; or through exchange. Consolidation of holdings of husband and wife is not common. Plaza, roads, grazing land, woodland are held in common. Use of land does not always follow ownership. A person with insufficient or no land may acquire part of communal holdings by petition to governor. Women do not farm land, (241);—85 per cent of operators in upper Rio Grande area own their land, (226).

LAND USE Alamosa River watershed, (198);—Arroyo del Agua, (123); —Catron County, (134);—Chaves County, (134);—80 per cent of land in Clovis Project area in crops, 19 per cent in pasture, (220); —history of, Clovis Project area, (220);—Colfax County, (134);—

LAND USE (Continued)

inadequate at San Geronimo, (136) ;—San Ildefonso, (241) ;—San Juan County, (134) ;—San Miguel County, (134) ;—history and present status, San Pedro grant, (234) ;—Sandoval County, (134) ; —4.4 per cent of Santa Cruz area used for farming, (202) ;—most farms in Santa Cruz area use between two and three acres, (39) ; —in Santa Cruz Valley centers around household type of agriculture with each family attempting to satisfy its own food needs. Area around village is badly overgrazed. Use of land for growing wheat is uneconomic, (227)·;—Santa Cruz Valley, (182) ;—intensive land use in Taos County has resulted in erosion, soil depletion, and deforestation with consequent loss of water resources, (176) ;—Taos County, (134) ;—Torrance County, (134) ;—Town of Abiquiu Grant, (206) ;—Union County, (134) ;—Valencia County, (134) ;—Villanueva, (138), (228) ;—Youngsville, (123). See also Bernalillo County.

LAND VALUE $9 to $27 per acre in Clovis Project area, (220) ;—Ocate Creek area, (204) ;—Quay County, (21) ;—Quay-Curry area, (199).

LANGUAGE   A barrier to assimilation, (248) ;—more than three-fourths of the people of New Mexico understand and speak English reasonably well, 1903, (195) ;—Indian language relationships in New Mexico, (81) ;—preservation of native languages tends to preserve native culture intact and to restrain Indians from borrowing nonmaterial traits, (90) ;—Isleta, (119) ;—95 per cent of Navajos do not speak English, (66) ;—New Mexican Spanish more archaic than that found anywhere else in the world, (248). See also Spanish language.

LAS CRUCES   As a community center in Dona Ana County, (93). See also telephone service.

LAS NORIAS   Inter-community relations with Atarque, (103).

LAW AND ORDER   Among Navajos, (163).

LAW ENFORCEMENT   Attempt to establish Anglo judicial system at Acoma, (155) .—among Navajos, (163) ;—legal control of Pueblos is in a jumbled and chaotic condition with four types of enforcement being applicable and a fifth type, extra-legal tribal courts, apparently violating the Fifth and Fourteenth Amendments, (90).

LEA COUNTY   Dry farming, (134) ;—farm tenancy, (140).

LEADERSHIP   Patterns of at El Cerrito have broken down and there is a growing tendency to look to Las Vegas and county politicians for leadership and advice, (108) ;—old pattern at El Cerrito based on age, family, ability to express oneself fluently, (108) ;—inter-

LEADERSHIP (Continued)

ference with local leadership patterns among minority groups may upset gradual development of new social and economic patterns, (83) ;—problems of among Navajos, (242) ;—importance of women in pottery business at San Ildefonso has enabled them to exercise an influence far in excess of that permitted by their traditional role, (254) ;—factional split at San Ildefonso represents a challenge to old Pueblo authorities by potters of north plaza who have converted economic dominance into political control, (90) ;— traditional leadership of Spanish-speaking communities has resided in priest, *patron,* and elders. In all cases this leadership has been institutional rather than personal. Where the pattern of institutional leadership has remained intact, it has been an important factor in retarding assimilation, (248) ;—the fundamental obstacle to effective civic leadership at Taos rests in lack of effective means of popular enlightenment on civic matters, (176) ;—not lacking among Zuni, (1) ;—existence of social ambition at Zuni, (1).

LEADERSHIP PATTERNS At Alameda, Guadalupe, Sandoval, (248).

LEASBURG History, economic agencies, population, education, occupational status, housing, sanitation, water supply, transportation, communication, economic services, institutions, recreation, mobility, family interrelationships, (93).

LEATHER WORK History of as a craft in New Mexico, (6).

LEGAL ORGANIZATION Of Middle Rio Grande Conservancy District, (65).

LEGENDS Of Isleta, (119).

LEGISLATION Federal, affecting Indians summarized, (81) ;—amendment to New Mexico Soil Conservation Act establishing range zones and farm zones, (256).

LEGISLATURE As a factor in regionalism, (171) ;—avoidance of racial issues in, (171) ;—occupational distribution, (170) ;—racial composition and political distribution, (170). *See also* House of Representatives, Senate.

LEVEL OF LIVING At Atarque by class of family, (103) ;—Bosque compared with six other resettlement projects, (112) ;—Cuba Valley, (146) ;—people conditioned to low level at El Pueblo, (63) ;—of migratory laborers in southern New Mexico, (208) ;—Pueblo houses cost about $65, rent for $6 a year. Heating and cooking done with wood; kerosene used for lamps and lanterns. Electricity, telephones, refrigeration almost unknown. Three-fourths of families surveyed had sewing machines; almost none had radio,

LEVEL OF LIVING (Continued)

washing machine. Half food cost goes for cereals, meat, chili, beans. 42-48 per cent of expenditures goes for food; costs of clothing $75-85 per family. Expenditures on feasts, health, births, deaths are moderate; for education, recreation, improvement, small. Automobiles are few and old, (90);—income of $650 per family of five (higher than two-thirds of families in upper Rio Grande area have) will permit only simplest diet, clothes in insufficient quantities, no expenditures for health, education, recreation, and no savings, (233);—typical family (four people) studied in upper Rio Grande area lives in three-room house, owns fourteen acres of irrigated land, of which only five can be used for crops. In 1935, the land produced crops for cash sales of $341 and home consumption valued at $293. Expenditures were: food, $122.15, flour and lard accounting for half the total; clothing $83.42; taxes $26; miscellaneous $60. Total value of goods used by the family was $635 of which 65 per cent went for food, 13 per cent for clothing, 8 per cent for equipment, 4 per cent for taxes, and 10 per cent for miscellaneous purposes. Level represented is comparable with that of tenant and cropper families in old South. Adequacy of diet is questionable; clothing purchases are meager; expenditures for health, recreation negligible. Yet living for this family was more ample than that of almost three-fourths of the village families in the area, (218).

LEYDEN   Statistical description covering location, population, work, health, land, livestock, for Leyden, Brady, and Claro, (241).

LIGA OBRERA   Organizational activities, (188).

LINCOLN COUNTY   Farm tenancy, (140);—crops, land use, livestock, (134).

LINGUISTIC REGIONS   Three in New Mexico, (25).

LITIGATION   *See* land grant litigation.

LIVESTOCK   Abiquiu, (241);—Angostura, (241);—Apodaca, (241);— Barranca, (241);— Bernalillo County, (134);—Brady, (241);— Cañoncito, (241);—Carnuel, (238);—Catron County, (134);—60 per cent of Chama area best suited to use by sheep, (59);—Chamita, (241);—Chaves County, (134);—Chimayo, (241);—Chupadero, (241);—Cibola National Forest, (124);—Cienega, (241);—Claro, (241);—Clovis Project area, (220);—Cordova, (241);—Cuarteles, (241);—Cuba Valley since 1848 has had extensive livestock operations, a fact largely responsible for accelerated erosion in upper Puerco, (225);—ownership of livestock in Cuba Valley widely dis-

LIVESTOCK (Continued)

tributed, (225);—development prospects in Cuba Valley not very bright. Grazing capacity estimated at 4,300 cattle yearlong; present stocking 14,500 cattle, (225);—a source of income in Cuba Valley, (146);—Cundiyo, (241);—Curry County, (162);—Dixon, (241);— Dona Ana County, (134);—Dry Cimarron Valley, (141);—Eddy County, (134);—El Guache, (241);—improvements in quality, El Pueblo, (84);—El Rito, (241);—Embudo, (241);—En Medio, (241);—Española, (241);—declining as a source of income in Estancia Valley, (223);—Estancia Valley, (87);—Fairview, (241);— Ghost Ranch, (241);—Guachepange, (241);—main cash crop at Guadalupe, (248);—Hidalgo County, (134);—domesticated animals acquired by Indians from Spanish, but never raised on same scale as that of Spaniards, (90);—Jacona, (241);—60 per cent of two hundred families surveyed in Jemez-Tewa area owned two cows or horses or less; 30 per cent totally without livestock, (223);—La Tijera, (238);—Laguna reservation, (87);—Leyden, (241);— Lincoln County, (134);—Llano Abeyta, (241);—Llano de los Quemadeños, (241);—Lower Vallecitos, (125);—Luna County, (134);—McKinley County, (134);—Mesilla Valley, (87), (223); —Middle Rio Grande Valley, (87), (223);—Mora County, (134); —Nambe, (241);—reduction of, Navajo reservation, (131), (242); Navajo reservation, (87), (150), (221), (240);—New Mexico Land Use Advisory Council recommendations regarding use of livestock for subsistence purposes and supplemental cash income, (133);—Ojo Sarco, (241);—Pecos Valley, (87);—Pojoaque, (241); —Primer Agua, (238);—Puebla, (241);—Rincon Valley, (87);— Rinconada, (241);—Rio Chama Village, (241);—Rio Hondo watershed, (222);—Rio Oso Village, (241);—Rio Puerco watershed, (203);—Riverside, (241);—Roosevelt County, (134);— San Antonio, (238);—San Antonito, (238);—San Ildefonso, (241);—San Jose, (241);—San Juan Basin, (87);—San Juan County, (134);—Sandoval County, (134);—Santa Clara, (244);— Santa Cruz, (241);—commercial operations negligible in Santa Cruz area, (39);—Santa Fe County, (134);—Santa Fe National Forest area, (124);—Sedillo, (238);—Sombrio, (241);—Santo Niño, (241);—Tierra Azul, (241);—Trampas, (241);—Truchas, (241);—68 per cent of 957 families surveyed in upper Rio Grande area owned livestock, with 80 per cent of them owning less than five cattle units, nearly 90 per cent less than ten cattle units, (233); —Vallecito, (241);—Velarde, (241);—Villanueva, (138);—Zia, (64);—Zuni reservation, (87). *See also* commercial livestock.

LIVESTOCK OWNERSHIP   55 per cent of all livestock in upper Rio Grande watershed, 1936, owned by 238 commercial operators, (258).

LIVESTOCK REDUCTION   Essential in soil erosion control program, Navajo reservation, (78);—program of among Navajos, (163);—Pueblo Indians voluntarily reduced livestock more than 50 per cent in 1935, (258).

LIVING CONDITIONS   Of migratory laborers in southern New Mexico, (208);—Santa Clara, (244). *See also* housing, level of living.

LLANO   *See* Rio Pueblo District.

LLANO ABEYTA   *See* Truchas.

LLANO DE LOS QUEMADEÑOS.   *See* Truchas.

LLANO LAYBA   *See* Rio Pueblo District.

LOCAL LABOR   Supply not adequate to harvest cotton, peas, broom-corn in New Mexico, (92);—many Spanish-Americans and Mexicans live permanently in vicinity of southern New Mexico towns, depending on wage work for a living, (208).

LOS COMANCHES   Description of, (25).

LOS MOCHOS   *See* Rio Pueblo District.

LOS MOROS Y LOS CRISTIANOS   First performed at San Juan by Oñate's group, (6).

LOS PASTORALES   Yearly production at Tortugas, (113).

LOS PINITOS   Inter-community relations with Atarque, (103).

LOWER VALLECITOS   Crops, income, income deficiency, land and live-stock ownership, (125);—population 77 per cent below subsistence standard, (125);—relief, (125).

LUNA   History of as a Mormon settlement, (53).

LUNA COUNTY   Agricultural practices, (134);—farm tenancy, (140);—home improvement, (134);—irrigation, (134);—livestock, (134);—schools, (134).

MCKINLEY COUNTY   Farm tenancy, (140);—land use, livestock, water development, (134).

MCMILLAN LAKE   Extent, effects, (8).

MADRID   Labor organization at, (188).

MAGICAL BELIEFS   *See* superstition.

MAHEDINASHA   Description of *Mahedinasha* dance at Zuni, (158).

MAÑANA CONFIGURATION   Analysis of behavior at Atarque in terms of, (103).

MANNERS   Courtesy characteristic of Spanish-Americans, (142);—Zuni etiquette, (158).

MANZANO   Economy, education, health, history, illiteracy, Indian period, *penitentes*, population, religion, social control, super-

MANZANO (Continued)

stition, (88). *See also* agriculture, courtship, crime, culture contact, disorganization, economic life, education, employment, family organization, family size, food preparation, housing, Indian raids, irrigation, land ownership, marriage, *patron-peon* system, politics, recreation, relief, religion, saints' days, superstition, *velorio,* Works Progress Administration.

MANZANO GRANT Present status of lands, (88).

MANZANO WATER COMMISSION Rules and regulations, (88).

MARKETING Half output of Indian baskets marketed locally and directly; one-fourth sold through dealers, (27);—35 per cent of Indian beadwork marketed locally, 50 per cent through dealers, (27);—10 per cent of Indian drums marketed locally, 70 per cent through dealers, (27);—Indian painting marketed through dealers on commission basis, (27);—75 per cent of Indian pottery marketed directly, 25 per cent through dealers, (27);—70 per cent of Indian shell and turquoise work marketed directly, 30 per cent handled by traders, (27);—15 per cent of Indian silver articles marketed directly, 80 per cent through dealers, (27);—65 per cent of tanned hides and moccasins marketed directly, 7 per cent through dealers, (27);—three-fourths of Pueblo woven articles marketed directly, 25 per cent through dealers, (27);—35 per cent of Navajo woven articles marketed directly, 65 per cent through dealers, (27);—specific recommendations by New Mexico Land Use Advisory Council regarding improvement in marketing conditions for New Mexico agricultural products, (133).

MARKETING PROBLEMS Of producers of farm products in MRGCD, (34).

MARRIAGE Marriage customs in early Albuquerque, (50);—patterns of behavior associated with at Atarque, (103);—at Isleta, (152);—ritual of courtship and marriage, Manzano, (88);—Navajo, (82);—importance in Navajo economy, (72);—San Felipe and Santo Domingo, (157);—courtship and marriage customs at Zuni, (13).

MARTINEZ, PADRE ANTONIO JOSE Role in early printing in Taos, (116).

MATRIARCHAL FAMILY SYSTEM Description of at Zuni, (1).

MATRILINEAL FAMILY Functioning of at Zuni, (13).

MECHANIZATION OF FARMS *See* farm mechanization.

MEDICAL SERVICE Navajo, (163).

MEDICINE SOCIETIES Comparison of Pueblo and Navajo, (252).

MEN, ROLE OF At El Cerrito less restricted than that of women, (108).

MESA POLEO Economic status, land use, resources, (123).

MESCAL   Method of preparation for food by Apaches, (31);—importance to Southwestern Indian culture, (30).

MESCALERO APACHES   Adoption of peyote influenced by contact with Anglos, (147). *See also* Apaches.

MESILLA VALLEY   Climate, (52), (87);—cotton, (223);—crops, (52), (87), (223);—farm labor, (223);—history, (52);—income, (223); —irrigation, (87), (223);—land ownership, (223);—land use, (223);—livestock, (87), (223);—migrant workers, (92), (208);— large and highly stratified population with low income level, (236); —living conditions of migrant workers, (208);—population, (223); —relief, (223);—soils, (52), (87);—tenancy, (223);—types of farming, (87), (236). *See also* commercialization, cotton, farm labor, income, land ownership, land use, migratory labor, sharecropping, tenancy.

MESQUITE   Used as food, medicine, source of decorative pigment, fuel, building material by Southwestern Indians, (11).

MESTIZO   In the New Mexico culture pattern, (25).

MEXICANOS   Suggested as term best applicable to Spanish-speaking population of New Mexico, (25).

MIDDLE CLASS   Developing among Spanish-speaking New Mexicans, (171).

MIDDLE RIO GRANDE CONSERVANCY DISTRICT   Cost of living, (245);— costs of producing crops, (245);—discussion of, (144);—economic conditions in, (132), (217);—economic problems, (34);—factors affecting economic self sufficiency, (34);—extent of, (231);—farm organization, (245);—financing, (132), (223);—food shipments into, (34);—history, (132);—income, (217);—land use, (132);— legal organization, (65);—marketing problems, (34);—organization, (223);—physical problems, (231);—purpose, (231);— sedimentation, (231);—statistics of, (132);—tax delinquency, (223);—types of farming, (217);—water shortage, (231). *See also* agriculture, cash crops, isolation, land use, population, self sufficiency, tax delinquency.

MIDDLE RIO GRANDE DISTRICT   *See* land reduction.

MIDDLE RIO GRANDE IRRIGATION DISTRICT   *See* land ownership.

MIDDLE RIO GRANDE VALLEY   Climate, (87);—crops, (87), (223);— description, (87);—economic status, (236);—effect of MRGCD on economy, (223);—history, (70);—income, (223);—irrigation, (70);—causes of irrigation failure, (70);—land ownership, (223); —land use, (223), (236);—livestock, (87), (223);—population,

MINING   Decrease in a factor in urbanization, (246).

MINIMUM LAND REQUIREMENT   In Tewa Basin a minimum of eight acres per family is necessary to produce an agricultural surplus, (235).

MISSIONARIES   Among Navajos, (163).

MOBILITY   Affects health, reduces educational opportunities, creates general unrest, (137);—Angostura, (93);—Berino, (93);—Bosque, (112);—Chamberino, (93);—Dona Ana (community), (93);— little among population of Dona Ana County villages, (93);— Guadalupe, (248);—Leasburg, (93);—Placitas, (93);—Rodey, (93).

MORA   Revival of crafts, (181).

MORA COUNTY   Dry farming, (134);—farm tenancy, (140);—flood control, (134);—housing, (77);—irrigation, (134);—livestock, (134); —range conditions, (134).

MORA RIVER AREA   Agriculture, climate, history, irrigation, land use, soils, water use, (200). *See also* population.

MORA RIVER VALLEY   Agriculture, (141);—revival of craft skills, (181); —water supply, (141).

MORA RIVER WATERSHED   *See* relief.

MORENO VALLEY   Need for migratory labor, (92).

MORMONS   History of settlement in New Mexico, (53).

MORTGAGES   Curry County farms, (162).

MOSQUERO   Historical development, (255).

MUSIC   At Isleta, (119).

MYTHOLOGY   Acoma, Laguna, (190);—of Jicarilla Apaches, (148);— Navajo, (72);—of Spanish-speaking New Mexicans, (46).

NAMBE   (community)   Statistical description covering location, population, work, trade, land, livestock, water, and health, (241).

NAMBE   (Pueblo)   Government, (241);—irrigation, irrigable land, status of water rights, (241);—description and interpretation of *Ahwanyu* ceremony, (43). *See also* irrigation.

NAMES, GEOGRAPHICAL   Derivations of Indian names near Santa Fe, (67).

NARCOTICS   Use of native plants as, by Apaches, (31).

NATIONAL FORESTS   Importance in livelihood of dependent populations of forest areas, (125).

NATIONAL YOUTH ADMINISTRATION   Justification of its program in New Mexico, (129). *See also* health.

NATURAL FORCES   Accepted by Navajos: resisted by Anglos, (83).

NAVAJO BOUNDARY ACT Analysis and criticism of, (81).

NAVAJO RESERVATION Agriculture, (87), (240);—climate, (87), (150); —crops, (87);—economic situation, (150);—grazing practices, (150);—income, (150), (221), (240);—sources of income, (87); —land status, (150), (221);—livestock, (87), (221), (240);— living conditions, (221);—location, (150);—sociological survey, (230);—soils, (87);—topography, (150);—types of farms, (87).

NAVAJO TERRITORY Accessibility, climate, vegetation, wealth, (83).

NAVAJOS Acculturation, (72);—summary of acculturation, (104);— adaptation to material aspects of Anglo culture, (102);—agricultural development, (131);—agriculture, (242);—child training, (72);—common law, (72);—cultural resistance, (102);—economic problems, (131), (262);—economy, (72);—relationship and significance of education to Navajo problem of adjusting to Anglos, (83);—attitude towards education, (131);—educational problems, (72);—Indian Service educational program for, (74);—erosion, (78);—furniture, (72);—games, (72);—governmental administration, (163);—governmental program for, (66);—health, (242); —history, (72);—household equipment, (72);—housing, (72);— major sources of income, (214);—protest against Indian Service policies, (120);—irrigation, (83);—land management, (131);— land tenure, (83);—land use, (98), (221);—law enforcement, (163);—leadership, (242);—livestock, (242);—livestock reduction program, (163);—medical service, (163);—missionaries among, (163);—mythology, (72);—overgrazing, (78);—problems of overpopulation, (78);—adjustment to pastoral life, (78);—personal development, (72);—police system, (163);—political organization, (72);—polygamy, (68);—population, (142), (163);—rehabilitation, (242);—relief, (131);—religion, (72);—resources, (142);— social relations, (72);—technology, (72);—trade, (131);—history and technique of weaving, (27);—rejection of Wheeler-Howard Bill, (242). *See also* acculturation, adjustment, adult education, agriculture, annual cycle, arts and crafts, assimilation, automobiles, basketry, case studies, ceremonial life, ceremonials, children, clans, community, conservation, costumes, crime, crop farming, cultural change, cultural efficiency, culture, disintegration, division of labor, domesticated animals, dreams, dress and ornament, economic adjustment, economic collapse, economic life, economic prosperity, education, erosion, family, food habits, grazing, health, horses, hunting, income, integration, intermarriage, isolation, land, land management, land ownership, land problem, land

NAVAJOS (Continued)

use, language, leadership, livestock, marriage, natural forces, nomadism, Office of Indian Affairs, overpopulation, personality, physical characteristics, population trends, pottery, prestige, prices, property and inheritance, range control, relief, religion, ritual, salt, self sufficiency, sheep, silverwork, skin dressing, smithery, social life, social relationships, superstition, trade, trading, trading posts, vocational education, warfare, weaving, Wheeler-Howard Bill, witchcraft.

NAVIGATION   Interference with on Rio Grande used as excuse to block early Elephant Butte Project, (14).

NEEDLEWORK   Designs adopted by Spanish-colonials from imported Chinese chests, (6).

NEGROES   10 per cent of migratory casual workers studied were Negroes, (92). *See also* population trends.

NEIGHBORHOODS   Function in social organization of Dona Ana County, (93).

NEW MEXICO AGRICULTURAL EXPERIMENT STATION   Publications, (23), (34), (86), (87), (92), (245).

NEW MEXICO ASSOCIATION ON INDIAN AFFAIRS   Activities against Bursum Bill, (22);—organization, (261).

NEW MEXICO LAND USE ADVISORY COUNCIL   *See* agriculture, handicrafts, income, livestock, marketing, range improvement, recreation.

NEW MEXICO RELIEF AND SECURITY ADMINISTRATION   Relief expenditures in upper Rio Grande Valley during 1935-36, (212).

NEW MEXICO STATE PLANNING BOARD   Publications, (81), (140), (141), (142), (143), (144).

NOMADIC LIFE   Navajo adjustment to, (79).

NOMADISM   A cause of conflict betwen Navajos and Anglos and Spanish-Americans whose lands were encroached on, (79).

OCATE CREEK AREA   Physical description, irrigation requirements, present water and land use, types of farming, crops, land ownership and tenure, population, land values, governmental subsidies, recommended land and water use, (204). *See also* agriculture.

OCCUPATIONAL STATUS   Agricultural labor, common labor, farm tenancy, and WPA have supplanted farm ownership among many Spanish-Americans in Dona Ana County, (93).

OCCUPATIONS   Abiquiu, (241);—Alameda, (248);—Angostura, (93), (241);—Apodaca, (241);—Barranca, (241);—Berino, (93);—Brady, (241);—Cañoncito, (241);—Chamberino, (93);—Chamisal, (241); —Chamita, (241);—Chimayo, (241);—Chupadero, (241);—Cie-

OCCUPATIONS (Continued)

nega, (241);—Claro, (241);—Cordova, (241);—Cuarteles, (241);—Cundiyo, (241);—Dixon, (241);—Dona Ana, (93);—El Guache, (241);—El Rito, (241);—El Valle, (241);—Embudo, (241);—En Medio, (241);—Española, (241);—Fairview, (241);—Guachepange, (241);—Jacona, (241);—Leasburg, (93);—Leyden, (241); —Llano, (241);—Llano Abeyta, (241);—Llano de los Quemadeños, (241);—Llano Layba, (241);—Los Mochos, (241); migratory casual workers in New Mexico, (92);—Nambe, (241);—Ojo Sarco, (241);—Penasco, (241);—Placita, (241);—Placitas, (93);—Pojoaque, (241);—Puebla, (241);—Rinconada, (241);—Rio Chama Village, (241);—Rio Oso Village, (241);—Rio Pueblo, (241);—Rio Pueblo District, (241);—Riverside, (241);—Rodarte, (241);—Rodey, (93);—San Ildefonso, (241);—San Jose, (241);—Santa Cruz, (241);—Santo Niño, (241);—Sombrio, (241);—San Geronimo, (136);—San Jose, (243);—Tierra Azul, (241);—Trampas, (241);—Tres Ritos, (241);—Truchas, (241);—Vadito, (241);—Vallecitos, (241);—Velarde, (241);—Villanueva, (236).

OFFICE OF INDIAN AFFAIRS Policy aims at separate economic and cultural continuance of Indians under conditions most favorable to their welfare, (128);—program of directed acculturation not successful among Pueblos. Relief wage work program has undermined self sufficiency at the same time Indian Service has attempted to foster crafts and agriculture, (90);—program among Navajos, (35);—historic trend of policies, (163);—critical comment on Pueblo policy, (58);—relief expenditures in upper Rio Grande Valley during 1935-36, (212). *See also* (244), (262), Indian Service, religion.

OJO SARCO Statistical description covering location, population, work, trade, land, livestock, and health, (241).

OLD PICACHO Historical background, economic agencies, population characteristics, education, occupational status, housing, sanitation, water supply, transportation and communication, economic services, institutions, recreation, mobility, family interrelationships, (93).

ORATORY Love of political oratory among Spanish-speaking people, (10).

ORGANIZED LABOR *See* labor organization.

OSTRICH FARMING Possibilities for New Mexico, (8).

OTERO COUNTY Crops, (134);—dry farming, (134);—farm tenancy,

OTERO COUNTY (Continued)
(140) ;—land use, (134) ;—soil conservation, (134) ;—water supply, (134) .

OVERGRAZING   The main cause of erosion, (144) ;—Navajos, (78) ;— extent in upper Rio Grande watershed, (258) . *See also* grazing.

OVERPOPULATION   One of most pressing Navajo problems, (72) ;— Navajo reservation overpopulated under present conditions, (35) ;—Navajos, (78) .

PAINTING   History of Indian painting, (27) ;—Pueblo water color painting is fairly recent, dating back only about forty years. Most Pueblo painting now being produced descends from that of Crescencio Martinez and Awatsireh (Alfonso Roybal). Art, to the San Ildefonso Indian, has usually meant more money and at least temporary freedom from farming, (241) ;—painting flourished for a time at San Ildefonso, but has now declined as a source of revenue. Formerly men's work, painting is now done by at least two women and more may take it up, (254) ;—technique of Spanish-colonial painting, (3) . *See also* crafts and craftsmanship, income.

PALLARES, JESUS   Deportation of, (188) .

PALOMAS RIVER   *See* Alamosa River watershed.

PAROCHIALISM   A factor contributing to regionalism, (171) ;—a result of geographical isolation, independent historical traditions, racial and religious differences, local and class economic interests, (169) ; —in transition stage in New Mexico, (169) .

PARTIDO CONTRACT   Sample copy of, (209) .

PARTIDO SYSTEM   History, effect on sheep industry, causes of decline, extent among Spanish-Americans and Indians, (32) ;—in 1900, 25- 50 per cent of sheep in New Mexico on *partido* basis; 3 per cent in 1940, (32) ;—legally recognized in 1882, (32) ;—not largely used by Pueblo Indians, (32) ;—seventeen owners have about 20 per cent of total stock in northern New Mexico, (126) ;—success of system due to effect of acquisitive Anglo economy upon an established, subsistence Spanish-American economy, (126) . *See also* tenant herding.

PASTORAL LIFE   Navajo adjustment to, (78) .

PASTORELA   Description of presentation at Arenal, (25) .

PATERNALISM   A sub-configuration in the behavior pattern at Atarque, (103) .

PATRON   Importance in social structure and behavior patterns at Atarque, (103) .

PATRON-PEON COMPLEX Carry-over into a system of political control in Dona Ana County, (93).

PATRON-PEON RELATIONSHIP Analysis of role in facilitating social change, (248);—carried over into political relationship, (170).

PATRON-PEON SYSTEM Strong at Alameda and Guadalupe: has broken down at Sandoval. Where it remains strong, the system is a powerful factor in resisting process of disintegration and retarding assimilation, (248);—gives Spanish-speaking people a power for resisting assimilative forces and is mainly responsible for their relative homogeneity after a century under American authority. It is also basis of their weakness in face of the agencies of regimentation, (248);—a factor in retarding assimilation, (248);—behavior patterns associated with at Atarque, (103);—social, legal, and political aspects, (171);—common in early Manzano, (88);—probable origin, (114);—in culture of rural New Mexico, (169); in economy of Spanish-colonial New Mexico, (63).

PATRONES Controlled economic life in early Manzano, (88);—influence on politics, (9).

PECOS VALLEY Climate, (87);—crops, (87);—economic problems, (87);—fertility, (8);—irrigation, (8), (87);—livestock, (87); living conditions of migrant workers, (208);—need for migratory labor, (92), (208);—soils, (87);—types of farming, (87);—water supply, (87).

PEDRO ARMENDARIZ GRANT Importance in economy of San Marcial, (211).

PENASCO See Rio Pueblo District.

PENISTAJA AREA Dry farming, early settlement, forces contributing to settlement, Farm Security Administration activities, (224). See also farm credit, Farm Security Administration, Rural Rehabilitation Division of Resettlement Administration.

PENITENTES As leaders in religious observances at Arroyo Hondo, (164);—order introduced into New Mexico by Oñate's group, (6);—as integrating and stabilizing force in isolated communities, (6);—evaluation of rites, place in cultural pattern of rural New Mexico, (7);—ceremonies described, (2);—role in local government, (2);—Good Friday ceremonies, (166);—history, membership, political influence, (171);—very influential in early Manzano, (88).

PEONAGE Exploitation through use of debt has led many Spanish-speaking people to virtual peonage, (247);—legal in New Mexico

PEONAGE (Continued)
   until 1867, (32) ;—a factor in political control in New Mexico,
   (171).

PERCHAS CREEK   *See* Alamosa River watershed.

PERSONALITY   Of early Anglo settlers, (80) ;—Anglo contrasted with
   that of Spanish-American, (54) ;—great differences in general
   attitude towards acquisition and work between Anglos and
   Spanish-speaking people, (172) ;—of Spanish-Americans at Atarque
   analyzed and explained in terms of four interrelated configurations, (103) ;—Indian pride corrupted by the tourist, (58) ;—
   personality types at Isleta, (16), (17) ;—lack of aggressiveness
   characteristic of population of Jemez River rehabilitation area,
   (125) ;—of Navajo, Pueblo, and Spanish-American characterized,
   (114) ;—Navajo, (100) ;—relationship of education to personality
   among Navajos, (83) ;—Navajo children, (83) ;—economic factors
   highly important in Navajo motivation, (101) ;—Navajo faces
   problems as an individual: Pueblo Indians meet them as a group,
   (35) ;—of Navajos, (82), (262) ;—New Mexico Indian contrasted
   with Mexican Indian, (51) ;—of Pueblo Indians, (80) ;—
   individuals at San Ildefonso are becoming less cooperative, more
   competitive. Government schools and colleges are unsettling the
   young. The Pueblo has split into two hostile factions, and the
   schism is widening rather than healing, (90) ;—introduction of
   commercial attitudes at San Ildefonso has subverted traditional
   personality. Competitive attitudes have replaced attitudes of
   cooperation, (90) ;—has disintegrated at Sandoval: drunkenness
   and fighting common: honesty is not prized: relationships between
   boys and girls increasingly freer, (248) ;—of Spanish-Americans
   influenced by isolation, (62) ;—Spanish-American's love of oratory,
   (10) ;—of early Spanish colonials, (80) ;—Spanish-speaking New
   Mexicans live in present and past, (24), (25).

PEYOTE   Use among Mescalero Apaches influenced by contact with
   Anglos, (147).

PEYOTE CULT   Description, (13).

PHILOSOPHY   Of Spanish-speaking New Mexicans, (24). *See also* social
   philosophy.

PHYSICAL CHARACTERISTICS   Comparison of Navajo and Hopi, (100).

PHYSICAL ENVIRONMENT   Pueblo region characterized by aridity, rib-
   bons of arable land along water courses, short growing season,
   invigorating climate, extensive range of elevation and life conditions, scarcity of resources, (90).

PICURIS Ceremonies, (159) ;—customs, (159) ;—government, (159) ;—
irrigation, (241) ;—religion, (159) ;—water rights, (241).

PLACITA *See* Rio Pueblo District.

PLACITAS Historical background, economic agencies, population
characteristics, education, occupational status, housing, sanitation,
water supply, transportation and communication, economic
services, institutions, recreation, mobility, family interrelationships, (93).

PLANNING Must be adapted to physiographic, social, economic, and
political divisions within the state, (172).

PLANTS Use of for medicine, Acoma and Laguna, (190) .—use of in
preparation of beverages by Apaches, (53). *See also* agave, beargrass, cactus, mescal, mesquite, narcotics, peyote, screwbean, sotol,
yucca.

POJOAQUE Irrigation, irrigable land, water rights, (241).

POJOAQUE AND JACONA Statistical description covering location, population, work, land, water for irrigation, livestock, and health,
(241).

POLICE SYSTEM Among Navajos, (163).

POLITICAL ACHIEVEMENT Of Spanish-Americans, (175).

POLITICAL ACTIVITY Of Spanish-speaking New Mexicans, (9).

POLITICAL INFLUENCE Of *penitentes*, (171).

POLITICAL MORALITY Low in rural New Mexico, (170).

POLITICAL ORGANIZATION Largely lacking in rural areas in Dona Ana
County, (93) ;—simple in Guadalupe: *jefe politico* ultimate, non-
legal source of authority, (248) ;—Harding County, (255) ;—
Navajos, (72).

POLITICAL RELATIONS In behavior patterns at Atarque, (103).

POLITICAL STATUS Pueblo Indians, (90).

POLITICAL UNITY Lacking among Spanish-Americans, (9).

POLITICS Interest in in rural Dona Ana County, (93) ;—interest in at
Manzano, (88) ;—extent of regionalism in, (171).

POLYGAMY Among Navajos, (68).

POPULATION Abiquiu, (241) ;—Alameda, (248) ;—Alamosa River
watershed area, (198) ;—detailed analysis of population developments and distribution, (151) ;—Angostura, (241) ;—Apaches,
(142) ;—Apodaca, (241) ;—Atarque, (103) ;—Barranca, (241) ;—
Berino, (93) ;—Bosque, (112) ;—Brady, (241) ;—Cañon de Jemez,
(125) ;—Cañoncito, (241) ;—Capulin, (75) ;—Carnuel, (238) ;—

POPULATION (Continued)

Cedar Crest, (238) ;—Chamberino, (93) ;—Chamisal, (241) ;—
Chamita, (241) ;—Chilili Grant, (207) ;—Chimayo, (241) ;—Chiz
Community, (198) ;—Chupadero, (241) ;—Cibola National For-
est, (124) ;—Cienega, (241) ;—Claro, (241) ;—Cordova, (241) ;—
Coyote area, (123) ;—Cuarteles, (241) ;—Cundiyo, (117), (241) ;—
Des Moines, (75) ;—Dixon, (241) ;—Dona Ana County, (93) ;—El
Guache, (241) ;—rural and village population of El Paso area about
fifty thousand with some twenty-eight thousand living on farms.
About seven thousand are in families of farm owner-operators,
twelve thousand in families of tenants and sharecroppers, and nine
thousand in those of farm laborers. Less than 40 per cent of owner-
operator farmers are Spanish-American; 80 per cent of tenant
families are Spanish-American, (223) ;—six hundred per square
mile of irrigated acreage, El Pueblo, (62) ;—El Pueblo, (63) ;—El
Rito, (241) ;—El Valle, (241) ;—Embudo, (241) ;—En Medio,
(241) ;—in Española mainly Spanish-American in residence over
three hundred years, (236) ;—Española, (241) ;—Española Valley,
(236) ;—Estancia Valley, (141), (223), (236), (238) ;—Fairview,
(241) ;—Folsom, (75) ;—Ghost Ranch, (241) ;—Guachepange,
(241) ;—Guadalupe, (248) ;—Harding County, (255) ;—Hidalgo
County, (134) ;—mostly Anglos on Hope irrigated area, (197) ;—
one-fifth of population of New Mexico in 1876, Indians, (166) ;—
twenty-five thousand Indians, 1900, (8) ;—Jacona, (241) ;—Jemez
River rehabilitation area, (125) ;—Jemez Springs, (125) ;—Jemez-
Tewa area, majority Spanish-Americans, (223) ;—La Cueva, (125) ;
—La Tijera, (238) ;—Leasburg, (93) ;—Leyden, (241) ;—Llano,
(241) ;—Llano Abeyta, (241) ;—Llano de los Quemadeños, (241) ;
—Llano Layba, (241) ;—Los Mochos, (241) ;—Lower Vallecitos,
(125) ;—Manzano, (88) ;—Mesilla Valley, (223) ;—character and
distribution, Mesilla Valley, (52) ;—MRGCD: State Planning
Board estimated Spanish-Americans comprise 80 per cent of rural
population of Bernalillo County, 81 per cent of total population of
Socorro County, 75 per cent of Valencia County, (223) ;—Middle
Rio Grande District supports densest population per cultivated
square mile in the United States, (258) ;— Middle Rio Grande
Valley, (236) ;—in Mora River area mostly rural, agricultural,
Spanish-American, (200) ; — Nambe, (241) ; — Navajos, (142),
(163) ;— in north central region of New Mexico, 11,893 families
dependent on natural resources. Under optimum conditions area
can support only 10,183 families, (127) ;—Ocate Creek area, (204) ;
—Ojo Sarco, (241) ;—Penasco, (241) ;—Placita, (241) ;—Placitas,

POPULATION (Continued))

(93);—Pojoaque, (241);—Primer Agua, (238);—Puebla, (241); —Pueblos, (142), (249);—Quay County, (115);—racial composition of New Mexico, (103);—a factor in regionalism, (171);— Rinconada, (241);—Rio Arriba County, (239);—Rio Chama Village, (241);—Rio Grande Valley, (144);—of Rio Grande watershed largely rural, agricultural, (236);—Rio Grande watershed, (226);—Rio Hondo watershed, (222);—of Rio Moquino watershed nearly 100 per cent Spanish-American, (201);—Rio Oso Village, (241); Rio Pueblo, (241);—Rio Pueblo District, (241); —Rio Puerco watershed, (203);—56 per cent of Rio Puerco watershed population Indian, (231);—Riverside, (241);—Rodarte, (241);—Rodey, (93);—San Antonio, (238);—San Antonito, (238); —San Geronimo entirely Spanish-American, (136)—of San Geronimo decreasing about 25 per cent each decade, (136);—San Ildefonso, (241);—San Jose, (241);—San Jose, 81.9 per cent Spanish-American, 1941, (243);—highly stable at San Jose, (243);— San Juan Valley, (141);—San Ysidro, (125);—Sandia Park, (238); —Sandia Pueblo dropped from three thousand in 1540 to seventy in 1936, (5);—Sandia Pueblo, (49);—Sandoval, (248);—Sandoval County, (239);—Sangre de Cristo Grant, (205);—Santa Cruz, (241);—Santa Cruz area, (39);—Santa Cruz area almost entirely Spanish-American, 90 per cent farm, (202);—Santa Fe County, (239);—Santa Fe National Forest, (124);—Santo Niño, (241);—Sedillo, (238);—Sombrio, (241);—security from Indian raids, introduction of sanitation and public health, and opportunities to earn money wages combined to bring about increased population in Spanish-speaking areas without corresponding increases in land productivity or emigration, (247);—Spanish-speaking concentrated in ten counties in which proportion of Spanish-speaking ranges from 50-95 per cent, (247);—Spanish-speaking communities represent serious local problems of overpopulation, (247);—in fifteen counties Spanish-speaking people comprise 50 per cent of population; in seven counties more than 80 per cent, (176);—Taos County, (239);— the twenty thousand Spanish-Americans in the Tewa Basin area (80-90 per cent of the total population of the area) are descendants of Spanish and Mexican immigrants who had settled the region by 1800. A majority of the people have some Indian blood, but there has been little intermarriage within the memory of the oldest inhabitants. There is considerable homogeneity among these people, and also some interesting differences which perhaps could

POPULATION (Continued)

be traced to environmental conditions. Archaic Spanish expressions, no longer heard in Spain or elsewhere in Latin America, are still being used, (241);—Tierra Azul, (241);—Trampas, (241);—trends in New Mexico, (81);—Tres Ritos, (241);—Truchas, (241);—upper Rio Grande area contains about ninety-two thousand people, including nine thousand Indians, seventy thousand Spanish-Americans, (233);—upper Rio Grande watershed in 1930 had a rural population composed of 76 per cent Spanish-Americans, 10 per cent Indians, and 14 per cent Anglos; of the urban population, about 41 per cent were Spanish-speaking, (237);—Upper Vallecitos, (125);—Vadito, (241);—Vallecito, (241);—Vallecitos, (241);—Velarde, (241);—Villanueva entirely Spanish-speaking, (228);—Villanueva, (138).

POPULATION DISTRIBUTION   Taos, Rio Arriba, Santa Fe, and Sandoval Counties, 76 per cent Spanish-American, 14 per cent Anglo, 10 per cent Indian, (239);—urban communities smaller per cent Spanish-speaking than surrounding rural areas, (141).

POPULATION TRENDS   New Mexico, past decade, (239);—Navajos rapidly increasing, (102);—Negroes in New Mexico decreasing, (141);—in next two decades Rio Grande basin must take care of thirty-five thousand natural population increase plus thirty thousand immigrants into Bernalillo County area, (142);—population at San Ildefonso slowly increasing, (254);—Indian population of Tewa Basin declined from time of Coronado until about fifteen years ago. Since that time the Tewa Pueblos, in spite of high infant mortality rates, have shown a slight increase. Spread of effective health measures may accentuate this trend, (241);—in 1850 upper Rio Grande watershed contained 6,400 Indians, 47,000 Spanish-Americans, and from 1,000 to 1,500 Anglos. Population of this region increased 153 per cent between 1850 and 1930, whereas that of the rest of the state increased 3,953 per cent. Rural population of the area increased 83 per cent in same period; that of the rest of the state increased almost 3,000 per cent, (237);—in the absence of sharp changes in birth and death rates, rural Spanish-American population of the upper Rio Grande watershed area appears likely to increase at a rapid rate, presaging more serious problems of adjustment to resources and labor opportunities than exist now. Indian population of the region may also be expected to increase, (237).

POTTERY   History of in New Mexico, (27);—the most universal craft, (27);—Navajos indifferent pottery makers, (72);—a factor in

POTTERY (Continued)

> decline of agriculture at San Ildefonso, (254) ;—at San Ildefonso pottery is upsetting agricultural values, and women potters are beginning to dominate Pueblo policies. Pottery is the basis of the village economy, being produced competitively under mass production methods, (254) ;—three conditions believed accountable for development of standardized pottery at San Ildefonso: influence of white persons who gave encouragement and advice, presence of skillful potters, need for cash, (90) ;—pottery at San Ildefonso is a culture complex which is neither the old pottery making complex of the Pueblo people nor the artistic pursuit visioned by Hewett and others. Indians do not consider pottery a medium for individualistic expression, (90) ;—history of revival of pottery at San Ildefonso, (241). *See also* crafts and craftsmanship, income, marketing.

POVERTY An important factor in retarding assimilation at Alameda, Guadalupe, Sandoval, (248) ;—the status of great masses of Spanish-speaking New Mexicans today is one of privation and want, of cultural inadequacy and bewilderment, (176) ;—a factor in delaying acculturation at Taos, (174).

PRESTIGE Personal prestige among Navajos little related to economic status, (101).

PRICES Wholesale and retail, Navajo trading posts, (262).

PRIESTHOOD Duties and status of Zuni priests, (13).

PRIMARY ELECTION LAW Delayed by racial controversy, (171).

PRIMER AGUA Statistical description covering population, resources, livestock, businesses, cash income, relief, rural rehabilitation, community conditions, (238).

PRINTING Early printing and presses in New Mexico, (116).

PROBLEM AREAS Description of areas in Dona Ana, Rio Arriba, Sandoval, Socorro, Taos counties where land resources will no longer provide a livelihood, (141) ;—classified as to cause of problem, (141).

PROPERTY Value of all types at Atarque, (103) ;—behavior patterns in regard to at Atarque, (103).

PROPERTY AND INHERITANCE Among Navajos, (72). *See also* inheritance.

PUBLIC ASSISTANCE A factor in disintegration in Dona Ana County, (93) ;—necessity for revision of policy in rural Dona Ana County, (93). *See also* relief.

PUEBLA *see* Cuarteles.

PUEBLO ART *see* art.

PUEBLO DANCES *see* dances.

PUEBLO LANDS ACT   Effect on Pueblos, (37).

PUEBLOS   Irrigation at Nambe, Pojoaque, Picuris, Santa Clara, San Juan, San Ildefonso, Tesuque, (241);—population, resources, (142). *See also* acculturation, citizenship, commercialization, economic life, food habits, government, housing, Indian Service, infant mortality, law enforcement, level of living, livestock reduction, Office of Indian Affairs, painting, population, population trends, racial history, relief, self sufficiency, weaving, and under names of individual Pueblos.

PURIFICATION RITES   Description of and significance at Zuni, (158).

QUAY COUNTY   Conservation, (134);—economic conditions, (115);—farm organization and operation, (20);—Farm Security Administration influence, (134);—farm tenancy, (140);—health, (134);—housing, (77);—land ownership, (115);—land use, (115), (134);—population, (115);—ranch organization and operation, (189);—row crop organization and operation, (20);—wheat farm organization and operation, (21). *See also* economic conditions, farm investment, farm size, income, land use, land value, ranch investment, relief.

QUAY-CURRY AREA   Topography, precipitation, economic conditions, land values, taxation, crop yields, (199). *See also* agriculture.

QUESTA   History, culture, housing, (186).

RACE PREJUDICE   A delaying factor in assimilation, (54);—analysis of causes of in New Mexico, (54);—between Mexicans and Spanish-Americans, (54);—causes of between Spanish-Americans and *Tejanos,* (103).

RACIAL ALIGNMENTS   Avoided by New Mexico legislature, (170).

RACIAL BACKGROUND   Spanish-colonials mixed with Navajos, Utes, Apaches, and Comanches, (166);—members of early Spanish exploring parties married freely among Indians, (6).

RACIAL COMPOSITION   Of Cuba Valley population, (146);—of population of New Mexico, (103).

RACIAL DIFFERENCES   A factor in delaying Americanization of Spanish-Americans, (184).

RACIAL DISCRIMINATION   Against Spanish-speaking people at Gallup, (257).

RACIAL HISTORY   Generalized physical characteristics suggest that the American Indians migrated from a common source, Asia, (90);—no uniformly characteristic physical traits among the Spanish-speaking New Mexicans. They are not a race: their bond of unity lies rather in language, religion, and other cultural traits, (248).

RADIO   Ownership and use, Capulin, Des Moines, Folsom, (75).

RAILROAD   Effect of its coming on land grant ownership controversies. (160) ;—a factor in Anglo settlement of Rio Grande area, (90) ;— effect on economy of San Jose, (243) ;—railroad wage work an important factor in economy of San Marcial. Its removal following 1929 flood was one of the main causes of the ultimate abandonment of the villages, (211); coming of railroad in 1880's changed economy of Spanish-speaking villages from subsistence to money-credit, provided wage work, increased contacts between groups, and helped increase total population, (90).

RAMAH   History of as a Mormon settlement, (53).

RAMON ABREU   Owner of first press in Santa Fe, (116).

RANCH INVESTMENT   Average investments of two sheep ranches, nineteen cattle and sheep ranches, thirty-two beef and dairy ranches, and 126 beef ranches in Quay County, (189).

RANGE   Little possibility of expansion in Coyote area, (123).

RANGE CONTROL   Navajo practice of, (83).

RANGE IMPROVEMENT   Specific recommendations by New Mexico Land Use Advisory Council, (133).

RANGE USE   Upper Rio Grande watershed 83 per cent overstocked, (91).

RAWHIDE CHESTS   Construction, varieties, and use in early New Mexico, (6).

READING   Anglo children read faster, comprehend better than Spanish-speaking, (193) ;—comparative ability in city, county, and town schools, (183) ;—Spanish-speaking pupils read progressively poorer in relation to Anglos as they proceed through school, (192) ;— Spanish-Americans show less progress in rate and comprehension than do English-speaking children, (183). *See also* education.

RECREATION   Angostura, (93) ;—among Apaches, (31) ;—Berino, (93) ; lack of facilities in Chama district due to poor roads, (59) ;—recreational developments should not be considered in Chama district if they deprive residents of grazing privileges, (59) ;—Chamberino, (93) ;—Dona Ana, (93) ;—Indian games and amusements grew out of formal ceremonies. Playing cards one of few games adopted from Anglos. Indian children's games correspond with those of Anglos, (142) ;—Leasburg, (93) ;—*corrida del gallo,* dancing, *canute, pelota, bolas, tejas, sueco* popular in 19th century Manzano, (88) ;—nearly completely lacking for migratory workers in southern New Mexico, (208) ;—specific recommendations by New Mexico

RECREATION (Continued)

Land Use Advisory Council regarding improvement in recreation facilities for rural areas, (133) ;—Placitas, (93) ;—Rodey, (93) ;—dancing major recreation at San Geronimo, (136) ;—no facilities in San Jose, (243) ;—*gallo,* dancing, feasting, communal hunting among early Spanish-American recreations, (50) ;—chief recreations of Spanish-speaking communities are *fiesta* and *baile,* together with various forms of gambling, drinking, visiting, and gossiping; children play little and have few organized games, (248) ; *chuza,* bull-baiting, cock fighting, *corrida del gallo, el coleo,* popular among Spanish-speaking people, (142) ;—in past fifty years Anglo games have been adopted by Spanish-speaking people and in some cases translated, (142) ;—a list of games played by Spanish-speaking people, (142) ;—Villanueva, (138) ;—Zia, (64) .

REGINA   Survey of history, problems, resources, (225) .

REGIONALISM   Affects all aspects of life in New Mexico, (172) ;—tends to be romantic rather than realistic, (260) ;—Southwestern universities should make themselves regional, (99) ;—New Mexico cannot remain a culture island, (40) ;—importance in New Mexico, (172) ;—must be considered in solution of cultural problems within the state, (172) —based on economic and cultural differences, (172) ;—in New Mexico, (178) .

REHABILITATION   Must be concerned with improving carrying capacity of land, stimulating individual, and modifying cultural pattern, (62) ;—critical analysis of program of Rehabilitation Division of Resettlement Administration in Cuba Valley, (225) ;—extension of credit in Cuba Valley means only extension of debt, (225) ;—rehabilitation problem of Cuba Valley can be met only by regarding it as a problem of the whole area, not a series of individual problems, (225) ;—prospects for in Curry County, (162) ;—distrust of rehabilitation program, El Pueblo, (63) ;—El Pueblo, (84) ;—land resources one of most important tools of rehabilitation, (60) ; —for Navajos, (242) ;—in Santa Cruz area must concern itself with development of new resources, improvement of land use techniques, alteration of structure of the economy. It must be conceived in terms of total economy of the area as against mere financing of individual or community enterprises, (227) ;—Santa Cruz area, (235) ;—critical analysis of activities of Resettlement Administration in Santa Cruz Valley, (227) ;—Santa Cruz Valley, (182) . *See also* rural rehabilitation.

REHABILITATION LOANS   Carnuel, La Tijera, Primer Agua, San Antonio, San Antonito, Sedillo, (238) .

RELIEF   Work relief programs influential in breaking down some of the compactness of rural communities, (108) ;—work on relief projects is drawing many natives to the towns where powerful factors operate to induce them to stay, (108) ;—17 per cent of population received relief March, 1941: 27 per cent in north central part of state, (239) ;—percentage of population receiving relief, general relief program, FERA: July 1933, 6.1 per cent; January 1934, 9.8 per cent; July 1934, 28.1 per cent; January 1935, 33.7 per cent; July 1935, 28.9 per cent, (57) ;—about $1,900 a month paid in relief wages in Alamosa River watershed area, (198) ;— approximately fifty cases state DPW relief in Alamosa River watershed area, (198) ;—little accepted at Atarque, (103) ;—Bosque, (112) ;—Cañon de Jemez, (125) ;—Carnuel, (238) ;—Cedar Crest, (238) ;—on Chilili Grant, no relief accepted up to 1940, (207) ;— 40 per cent of amount received by Cuba Valley residents from wage work in 1936 came from relief, (225) ;—about half the consumption groups in Cuba Valley received some income from relief in 1936, (225) ;— federal emergency loans averaged $151 per farm, Curry County, 1934-35, (97) ;—extent and characteristics among Curry County farmers, 1935, (162) ;—about five thousand persons in El Paso area are dependent on relief, 1,500 of them permanently, (223) ;—45 per cent of people of the Española Valley in 1936 were on relief, (236) ;—Estancia Valley, (223), (238) ;—role of relief in background of Gallup riots, (55) ;—$5,400 a month WPA wages in Hot Springs, (198) ;—a factor in decline of Indian crafts, (241) ; —Jemez River rehabilitation area, (125) ;—Jemez Springs, (125) ; —Jemez-Tewa area, (223) ;—La Cueva, (125) ;—La Tijera, (238) ; —Lower Vallecitos, (125) ;—37 per cent of 125 Manzano families studied had been on relief, (88) ;—Mesilla Valley, (223) ;—opposition to relief for migratory casual workers, (92) ;—relief payments increasing, Mora River watershed, 1941, (200) ;—New Mexico State Department of Public Welfare had 597 cases in Mora River watershed area during winter of 1940-41, (200) ;—Navajo attitude towards, (131) ;—estimated 21,000 Navajos supported by work relief, (221) ;—Primer Agua, (238) ;—with wages paid by IECW nearly double those prevailing in the area, the relief program for the Pueblos has resulted in the removal of a feeling of responsibility on the part of the individual to do community work free, has aided in the rise of a landlord class through the hiring of Spanish-Americans by the Indians on relief, and has tended to create an emergency where none existed before, (90) ;—Quay County, (115) ;—Rio Arriba County, (134) ;—WPA expenditures

RELIEF (Continued)

in Rio Grande watershed in 1936 exceeded $2,100,000, (226) :—
Rio Puerco watershed, (203) ;—San Antonio, (238) ;—San Antonito, (238) ;—forty families on relief, San Geronimo, (136) ;—
36.5 per cent of San Jose families on WPA for four years, 15.8 per
cent for five years or over, (243) ;—percentage of families on relief
in San Jose increased from 15.7 in 1936 to 45.6 in 1941, (243) ;—
40 per cent of families in San Miguel County on relief, (167) ;—
San Ysidro, (125) ;—Sandia Park, (238) ;— Sangre de Cristo Grant:
16 per cent of total yearly cash income of average family is from
relief, (205) ;—during the years 1933-39, 50 per cent of people of
Santa Cruz area depended on some form of government subsidy,
(39) ;—between 1933-39, Department of Public Welfare expenditures in Santa Cruz area averaged $50,000 yearly, (39) ;—Santa Cruz
area, (202), (235) ;—Sedillo, (238) ;—relief agencies in Taos must
relate their programs to those of established institutions capable of
attacking problem on a wider front. Formal relief alone will not
solve the problem, (176) ;—in the Tewa Basin, 65-70 per cent of
the population is on relief, (235) ;—former relief clients in Tewa
Basin now turning to rehabilitation loans, (235) ;—the relief load
of the Tewa Basin area is between 60 per cent and 70 per cent of
the people of the area and most of those not receiving relief are
indirectly depending for a livelihood on relief orders, (241) ;—by
introducing unemployment relief into an area that never depended
on wage work, the IECW dislocated the institutionalized work
pattern, artificially stimulated the economy of the Tewa Pueblos,
and set in motion forces which may result in culture deterioration
and the creation of a real emergency when the relief is withdrawn.
The IECW wage scale, well above prevailing scale for the area, is
tending to lead the Indian from craft production to wage work and
is accustoming him to a standard of living which, unaided, he will
be unable to maintain, (241) ;—nearly half the income of the 240
families comprising the ten Spanish-speaking villages of the
Tijeras Canyon area in 1936 came in the form of relief wages.
During 1935, 138 of the families received direct relief; in 1936,
ninety had WPA employment, (238) ;—one of the major sources of
income for the people of the Town of Abiquiu Grant, (206) ;—
relief totaling about $1,800,000 a year was given in 1935-36 to
about 60 per cent of rural families in upper Rio Grande area,
(233) ;—total expenditure for relief in upper Rio Grande area
during 1935-36 approximately $198 per rural family, (212) ;—analy-
sis of random 11 per cent sample of rural population of upper Rio

RELIEF (Continued)

Grande area indicates that some 60 per cent of all rural families received relief in some form in 1935 and 1936, (212);—Upper Vallecitos, (125). *See also* Bernalillo County, Cuba Valley, Federal Emergency Relief Administration, Indian Emergency Conservation Work, New Mexico Relief and Security Administration, Office of Indian Affairs, public assistance, Rural Rehabilitation Division of Resettlement Administration, Soil Conservation Service, United States Forest Service, Works Progress Administration.

RELIGION The church a factor in retarding assimilation, (248);—folk dramas a vehicle for transmitting religious ideas, (26);—two legends illustrating process by which saints are given attributes peculiar to New Mexico environment, (4);—Catholic marriages firmly established at Acoma, (155);—christening and god-parent customs at Laguna and Acoma borrowed from Spanish, (155);—Acoma, (190);—church at Alameda has proved a stabilizing influence in aiding the community to resist forces of disintegration, (248);—at Atarque an aspect of *costumbre* and *familia* configurations, (103);—a factor in community social organization at Atarque, (103);—participation in religion as shown by attendance at Bosque Farms, (110);—importance in social organization of rural communities in Dona Ana County, (93);—church plays an important part in attitudes, practices, and everyday life of people of El Cerrito. Priest is not only a spiritual leader but a source of advice on temporal matters. Integration of the individual with the church affords a barrier to disintegration, (108);—Hot Springs, (263);—Indian religion has successfully resisted impact of Christianity, (107);—pragmatic attitude of Indians towards, (6);—religious inspiration for Indian revolt of 1680, (6);—Indians but little affected by Catholicism, (58);—Isleta, (119);—Laguna, (190);—influence in early and present day Manzano, (88);—men dropping out of religious activity at Manzano, (88);—high degree of ritualization among Navajos, (72);—functional significance of among Navajos, (72);—has undergone less change than any other part of Navajo culture, (72);—half of Navajo religion concerned with curing sickness, (72);—relation of dreams to Navajo religion, (121);—use of sacred designs in sand painting blankets an indication of disintegration of Navajo religious authority, (178);—efforts to convert Navajos to Protestant religion, (68);—Navajo theology as described by Methodist Episcopal missionary, (68);—traditional feast days declining in importance in northern New Mexico villages, (164);—policy of Office of Indian Affairs one of religious

RELIGION (Continued)

tolerance, encouraging Indian religion and traditional ceremonies, (128);—Picuris, (159);—belief in Christianity superficial in Pueblos, (51);—Pueblos' faith relatively little disturbed by influences of acculturation, (107);—San Geronimo people are devout Catholics, strongly religious, (136);—spiritual and religious values of traditional ceremonials have been largely lost at San Ildefonso, (241);—declining in importance at San Jose, (243); —Sandia migrants adopted Hopi religion, (5);—after 1742, Sandia people attempted to adjust to three religions: their own, that which they learned from the Hopi, and Christianity, (5);—religion relatively unimportant in Sandia Pueblo, (5);—of Sandia Pueblo, (49);—Spanish-Americans are simple, obedient, miracle-loving believers in the most authoritative Catholicism, (166);—in Spanish colonial times, (63);—about 95 per cent of Spanish-speaking people are Catholics, (248);—attitude of Spanish-speaking people toward religious art, (6);—pagan elements still noticeable among Tortugas Catholics, (113);—participation in religion at Tortugas as shown by church attendance, (110);—Villanueva, (138);—Zia, (64);—of the Zuni, (1);—ritualized nature of Zuni religion, (13).

RELIGIOUS ART   History of in New Mexico, (6);—New Mexico *santos* a continuation of Spanish religious art, (48);—religious art flourished in New Mexico 1700-1848, (48);—highest development of Spanish colonial art reached in religious field, (3).

RESERVATIONS   History of Indian reservations in New Mexico, (81).

RESETTLEMENT   Any resettlement program must consider larger family groups, (108), (109);—recommended for inhabitants of problem areas in Dona Ana, Rio Arriba, Sandoval, Socorro, and Taos Counties, (142);—two areas in Rio Grande Valley recommended as places to resettle problem area families, (142), (144);—not desirable for Spanish-speaking communities, (141);—resettlement of surplus Spanish-speaking population not feasible because of familial and village structure, (247);—retirement of sub-marginal lands in Taos County will create resettlement problems, (174);—recommendations regarding resettlement for tenant farmers in New Mexico, (140);—not possible in Tewa Basin because of traditions and because new land is not available, (235).

RESETTLEMENT ADMINISTRATION   Policy of making loans to individual families ignores basic principles involved in rehabilitation of a people operating in a deficient economy, (227);—critical analysis of activities of in Santa Cruz Valley, (227). *See also* Rural Rehabilitation Division of Resettlement Administration.

RESOURCES   Coyote area, (123) ;—of New Mexico, (195) ;—by 1850 the agricultural resources of the upper Rio Grande watershed were supporting the maximum population they could support, (237) ;—erosion depleting those of upper Rio Grande watershed, (38) ;—Rio Hondo watershed, (222) ;—Rio Puerco, (123) ;—Santa Clara. (244) ;—Sedillo, (238) ;—one of the basic needs of Spanish-speaking people of northern New Mexico, (60) ;—Youngsville, (123) .

RINCON VALLEY   General description, climate, soils, irrigation, crops, livestock, types of farming, (87) .

RINCONADA   *see* Embudo.

RIO ANIMAS   *see* Alamosa River watershed.

RIO ARRIBA COUNTY   Crops, (134) ;—education, (134) ;—farm tenancy, (140) ;—grazing, (134) ;—land ownership, (239) ;—population, (239) ;—relief, (134) ;—schools, (134) . *See also* land ownership, land use, population distribution, problem areas, resettlement.

RIO CHAMA VILLAGE   Statistical description covering location, population, work, land, livestock, health, (241) .

RIO CUCHILLO NEGRO   *see* Alamosa River watershed.

RIO GRANDE BASIN   General description, problem areas, recommendations for resettlement of two areas, (144) ;—overgrazing, (142) .

RIO GRANDE COMPACT   History, provisions, (259) ;—principal benefits to Navajo lands, (259) ;—discussion of, (144) .

RIO GRANDE DAM AND IRRIGATION COMPANY   Attempt to build dam at Elephant Butte, (14) .

RIO GRANDE VALLEY   Flood control, (144) ;—settlements, history of cultivation and irrigation below San Marcial, (132) ;—water rights, (144) . *See also* erosion, farm labor, intermarriage, irrigation, land ownership, Middle Rio Grande Valley, resettlement, upper Rio Grande Valley, water supply.

RIO GRANDE VALLEY SURVEY COMMISSION, (70) .

RIO GRANDE WATERSHED   Economic conditions, (236) ;—economic problems, (231) ;—extent and effects of erosion, (226) ;—floods and damage, (231) ;—history, (226) , (231) ;—land use, (226) , (236) ; —overgrazing, (258) ;—physical description, (226) ;—population, (236) . *See also* economic life, income, land economy, land resources, land use, resources, Soil Conservation Service.

RIO HONDO WATERSHED   Land use and ownership, population, occupations, agriculture, livestock, general description, (222) . *See also* land ownership, land use, resources.

RIO MOQUINO AREA   *see* education, land use, population.

RIO MOQUINO WATERSHED   Crops, land ownership and use, population, water use, (201) . *See also* land ownership.

RIO OSO VILLAGE   *see* Vallecito.

RIO PUEBLO DISTRICT   Statistical description of Penasco, Llano, Chamisal, Vadito, Placita, El Valle, Vallecitos, Rodarte, Llano Layba, Rio Pueblo, Los Mochos, and Tres Ritos, covering location, population, work, trade, and health, (241) .

RIO PUERCO AREA   *see* economic status.

RIO PUERCO VALLEY   History, problems, resources, (225) . *See also* grazing.

RIO PUERCO WATERSHED   Climate, (231) ;—crops, (203) ;—description, (231) ;—economic status, (123) ;—erosion, (203) , (231) ;—flood control, (231) ;— history, (231) ;—industry, (203) ;—irrigation, (203) ;—land ownership, (203) ;—land use, (123) , (203) ;—livestock, (203) ;—population, (203) ;—relief, (203) ;—soils, (231) ;—tenancy, (203) ;—topography, (203) , (231) ;—transportation, (203) ;—water supply, (203) . *See also* agriculture, irrigation, land use, population, tenancy.

RIO SECO   *see* Alamosa River Watershed.

RITUAL   Importance in culture of Jicarilla Apaches, (148) ;—importance in Navajo culture, (72) ;—no other activity competes with ritual for time and attention of western Pueblo men, (13) . *See also* ceremonials, dances, salt gathering.

RIVERSIDE   *see* Española.

RODARTE   *see* Rio Pueblo District.

RODEY   History, economic agencies, population characteristics, education, occupational status, housing, sanitation, water supply, transportation and communication, economic services, institutions, recreation, mobility, family interrelationships, (93) .

ROOSEVELT COUNTY   Crops, (134) ;—farm tenancy, (140) ;—land use, (134) ;— livestock, (134) .

ROSEBUD   Historical development, (255) .

ROSWELL   Crops, land use, history, agriculture, (18) .

ROSWELL REGION   Decline in fruit production, (18) ;—land use, (18) . *See also* agriculture.

ROY   Historical development, (255) .

RURAL REHABILITATION   A failure in Tewa Basin, (235) .

RURAL REHABILITATION DIVISION OF RESETTLEMENT ADMINISTRATION   Of money loaned by Rural Rehabilitation Division, 39 per cent was

RURAL REHABILITATION DIVISION (Continued)
    used for direct subsistence, 13 per cent to pay back taxes, (235) ;—
    administrative philosophy of inadequate for non-commercial econ-
    omy, (235) ;—activities in Penistaja area, (224) ;—relief expendi-
    tures in upper Rio Grande Valley, 1935-36, (212) .

SAINTS' DAYS At Manzano, (88) .

SALT Navajo rituals connected with gathering of, (71) .

SALT GATHERING Navajo ritual of modified by contact with other
    tribal groups, (71) .

SAN ANTONIO Statistical description covering population, resources,
    livestock, business, cash income, relief, rural rehabilitation loans,
    community conditions, (238) .

SAN ANTONITO Statistical description covering population, resources,
    livestock, business, cash income, relief, rural rehabilitation loans,
    community conditions, (238) .

SAN FELIPE Clans, marriage customs, (157) ;—history of land grant
    litigation, (15) . *See also* shell work.

SAN GERONIMO Economic life, education, history, illiteracy, infant
    mortality, land ownership, occupations, population, relief, (136) ;
    —25 per cent population decrease each decade, (136) ;—exemplifies
    struggle of a group to maintain its individuality in a world of
    growing interdependence, (136) . *See also* dry farming, family,
    health, illiteracy, infant mortality, irrigation, land ownership, land
    use, population, recreation, relief, religion, sanitation, standard of
    living, superstition.

SAN ILDEFONSO Acculturation, (254) ;—agriculture, (254) ;—division
    of labor, (254) ;—economic life, (254) ;—government, (241),
    (254) ;—health, (241) ;—infiltration of Spanish-Americans into
    Indian grant, (241) ;—irrigation, (241) ;—land ownership and use,
    (241) ;—leadership, (254) ;—livestock, (241) ;—painting, (254) ;—
    personality, (254) ;—population, (241) ;—population trends, (254) ;
    —pottery, (254) ;—pottery and painting have become the major
    economic dependence of the Pueblo, displacing agriculture.
    Techniques are standardized. Commercialism has disrupted the
    traditional division of labor. Cooperative personality type
    being replaced by competitive type, (90) ;—religion, (254) ;—
    trade, (241) ;—water supply, (241) ;—work, (241) . *See also* accul-
    turation, agriculture, automobiles, commercialization, community
    disorganization, cost of living, crafts and craftsmanship, crops,
    diet, disorganization, division of labor, economic equality, econo-
    mic life, economic status, government, income, irrigation, land

SAN ILDEFONSO (Continued)
ownership, leadership, painting, personality, population trends, pottery, religion, self sufficiency, women.

SAN JOSE   *see* Española.

SAN JOSE (Albuquerque)   Automobile ownership, economic life, history, housing, income, occupations, population, effect of urbanization, (243). *See also* agriculture, family, income, population, railroad, recreation, relief, religion.

SAN JOSE TRAINING SCHOOL   *see* bilingualism.

SAN JUAN   Government, irrigation, water rights, (241). *See also* income, irrigation.

SAN JUAN BASIN   Description, climate, soils, crops, source and supply of irrigation water, livestock, types of farms, problems, (87).

SAN JUAN COUNTY   Crops, (134);—farm tenancy, (140);—livestock, land use, (134).

SAN JUAN RIVER   Plan to divert waters to Rio Grande basin, (259).

SAN JUAN RIVER VALLEY   Agriculture, irrigation, population, resources, (141);—center of Mormon settlement in New Mexico, (53).

SAN LUIS   History, problems, resources, (225).

SAN MARCIAL   Analysis of the causes that led to the abandonment of the San Marcial villages, (211). *See also* economic life, floods, Pedro Armendariz Grant, railroad.

SAN MARCIAL AREA   Two thousand acres of irrigated land lost to cultivation since 1929, (231);—population declining since 1929, (231).

SAN MIGUEL COUNTY   Dry farming, (134);—economic conditions, (167);—education statistics, (167);—farm tenancy, (140);—housing, (77), (167);— irrigation, (134);— land use, (134);—mineral resources, (167);—roads, (167);—social conditions, (167). *See also* agriculture, education, minerals, relief.

SAN PEDRO GRANT   Land use, (234).

SAN YSIDRO   Income, income deficiency, population, relief, sources of income, (125).

SANDIA PARK   Population, income, relief, land tenure, farm size, crops, (238).

SANDIA PUEBLO   Acculturation, architecture, ceremonies, economic life, education, government, (49);—history, (5), (49);—language, population, religion, social organization, traditions, (49);—land grant litigation, (15). *See also* acculturation, migration, population, religion.

SANDOVAL Population, history, effect of isolation on, community and family disorganization, government, crops, health, leadership patterns, (248). *See also* acculturation, assimilation, bilingualism, division of labor, economic life, education, family organization, isolation, *patron-peon* system, personality, poverty, social change.

SANDOVAL COUNTY Crops, (134);—farm tenancy, (140);—land ownership, (239);—land use, (134);—livestock, (134);—population, (239);—self sufficiency, (134). *See also* land ownership, land use, problem areas, resettlement.

SANGRE DE CRISTO GRANT Social and economic history and problems, (205). *See also* income, population, relief.

SANITATION Angostura, (93);—Berino, (93);—Chamberino, (93);—Dona Ana, (93);—El Pueblo, (63);—people at El Pueblo generally still ignorant of the most elementary sanitary improvements. Educational classes in sanitation being conducted, (85);—Leasburg, (93);—Rodey, (93);—at San Geronimo not adequate, (136);—conditions deplorable for Spanish-Americans, (60);—Zia, (64).

SANTA ANA Clan system, (156);—land grant litigation, (15). *See also* ceremonials.

SANTA CLARA Crops, expenditures, (244);—government, (241);—history, (244);—income, (244);—irrigation, (241);—livestock, living conditions, resources, (244). *See also* economic status, expenditures, income, irrigation.

SANTA CRUZ Statistical description of Santa Cruz, Sombrio, Santo Niño, and Fairview covering location, population, work, trade, land, health, livestock, (241).

SANTA CRUZ AREA Agriculture, (235);—crops, (202);—description, (39);—economic maladjustment, (202);—land ownership, (202); (235);—land tenure, (202);—land use, (202);—livestock, (202);—population, (202);—relief, (235);—resettlement failure, (235); — resources, (39); — rural rehabilitation, (235); — wage work, (235). *See also* agriculture, cooperative marketing, cooperative production, irrigated land, irrigation, land ownership, land use, population, rehabilitation, relief, wage work, water, weaving.

SANTA CRUZ IRRIGATION DISTRICT Organization and financing, (229).

SANTA CRUZ VALLEY Crops, (39);—the valley has racial and economic homogeneity, good soil, and relatively plentiful water. Yet people have not been able to sustain themselves through agricultural production for sixty years, (227);—critical analysis of activities of

SANTA CRUZ VALLEY (Continued)
Resettlement Administration, (227);—social economics, (182).
See also economic life, grazing, land use, livestock, rehabilitation.

SANTA FE COUNTY   Crops, (134);—farm planning, (134);—farm tenancy, (140);—land ownership, (239);—livestock, (134);—population, (239). *See also* land ownership, land use, population.

SANTA FE FIESTA   *see fiesta.*

SANTA FE NATIONAL FOREST   *see* commercial grazing.

SANTA FE NATIONAL FOREST AREA   Income from wages, total income,
irrigation, livestock, population, (124). *See also* income, irrigated
land.

SANTO DOMINGO   Attitude toward Anglo culture, (253);—clans, (157);
—cultural resistance, (253);—history, (253);—land grant litigation, (15);—marriage customs, (157);—social organization, (253).
See also shell work.

SANTO NIÑO   *see* Santa Cruz.

SANTOS   Analysis of their role in the behavior configurations at Atarque, (103);—history, production, cultural importance, (48);—
methods of production and value to Spanish-speaking culture, (6);
—art of *santeros* declined with coming of Anglos, (6). *See also*
religious art.

SCHOOL ATTENDANCE   Among children 7-13 at San Geronimo only 62
per cent, (136);—only three persons at San Geronimo have ever
attended high school, (136).

SCREWBEAN   Importance to Southwestern Indian culture, (11).

SEDILLO   Statistical description covering population, resources, livestock, business, cash income, relief, rural rehabilitation loans,
community conditions, (238).

SEGREGATION   Of Spanish-Americans in education, (175).

SELF SUFFICIENCY   Bosque farms produced 39.3 per cent of goods and
services consumed: comparison with six other resettlement communities, (112);—disrupted by agricultural changes in Dona Ana
County, (93);—emphasis at El Cerrito is on subsistence farming
with few families selling over ten to fifteen dollars worth of
produce a year, (108);—El Pueblo families produce an average of
69 per cent of their food, (62);—Jemez, Taos, San Ildefonso
Pueblos produce only slightly more than a third of their own food
supply, (90);—present situation in MRGCD must lead either to
the attempt to change present operators from subsistence to commercial farming, or their dispossession by a group who will carry
on commercial operations, (223);—in MRGCD, (34);—need for

SELF SUFFICIENCY (Continued)

development among Navajos, (72);—Navajos 90 per cent self sufficient in 1937, (83);—Pueblo Indians satisfy four-fifths of wants by purchase despite the fact that subsistence agriculture is supposed to be their major economic concern, (90);—factors in decline of self sufficiency in Pueblos have been declining fertility of soil, loss of land through erosion or sale, loss of opportunity to move to new land when old is exhausted, (90);—Indian Service has undermined self sufficiency with one hand while attempting to bolster it with the other, fostering crafts and agriculture at the same time it instituted a wage program which discouraged craft work and farming and increased the dependence of the Pueblos on cash, (90);—while small gardens are common, the Tewa Basin area does not subsist entirely on the foods it produces, (213);— home gardens as supplementary food supply the exception at Tortugas, (113).

SENATE Party and racial division in, by counties, 1917-39, (171).

SENIORITY A sub-configuration in the behavior patterns at Atarque, (103).

SEWAGE DISPOSAL Poorly handled in thirty-four towns studied, (141).

SHALAKO Description and significance, (158).

SHARECROPPING Widely practiced in Mesilla Valley, some in Estancia Valley. System operates much like that of large plantations in old South, (223).

SHARECROPPING, SHEEP see partido system, tenant herding.

SHEEP Made possible a change in Navajo economy, (104).

SHEEP AND GOATS Role in Navajo economy, (83).

SHEEP RAISING First sheep in New Mexico brought by Coronado. Industry started from flocks brought by Oñate, (6);—importance to Spanish-American culture, (114).

SHELL AND TURQUOISE WORK History, (27);—greatest commercial importance at Santo Domingo, San Felipe, Cochiti, (27).

SIBLINGS Relationships and behavior between at Atarque, (103).

SIERRA COUNTY Developments under AAA, (134);—central purchasing, (134);—farm tenancy, (140).

SILVERSMITHING History of among Indians, (27);—introduced by itinerant Mexican smiths; definite decline in past few years, (27). See also marketing.

SILVERSMITHS   *see* income.

SILVER WORK   Not extensive among Spanish-colonials, (6) ;—adoption by Navajos, (6) .

SKIN DRESSING   Methods and importance among Navajos, (72) .

SMITHERY   Economic importance and techniques among Navajos, (72) .

SOCIAL APATHY   Taos County, causes and results, (174) .

SOCIAL CHANGE   Analysis of effect of isolation on rate of at Alameda, Guadalupe, Sandoval, (248) ;—role of *patron-peon* relationship in facilitating, (248) . *See also* assimilation.

SOCIAL CONDITIONS   San Miguel County, (167) .

SOCIAL CONTROL   Family as an instrument of, Atarque, (103) ;—role of family in, Dona Ana County, (93) ;—role of religion in, Dona Ana County, (93) ;—at Manzano, (88) .

SOCIAL ECONOMICS   Of Santa Cruz Valley, (182) .

SOCIAL INSTITUTIONS   The family most powerful at El Cerrito, (109) . *See also* institutions.

SOCIAL LIFE   At Capulin, Des Moines, Folsom, (75) ;—patterns among Navajos, (83) ;—positive correlations between amount of clothing purchased and church attendance, Tortugas, (113) ;—community participation limited at Tortugas, (113) ;—Villanueva, (138) .

SOCIAL ORGANIZATION   Of Apaches, (31) ;—Atarque, (103) ;—Dona Ana County, (93) ;—Harding County, (255) ;—Isleta, (119) ;—of Pueblos, (69) ;—of Pueblo agriculture little affected by adoption of European crops, (90) ;—Sandia, (49) ;—Santo Domingo, (253) . *See also* clans, cooperation.

SOCIAL PATHOLOGY   Sandia, (49) .

SOCIAL PHILOSOPHY   Anglos oriented towards future, Spanish-Americans towards the past, (25) ;—Anglo and Spanish-American contrasted, (25) . *See also* philosophy.

SOCIAL RELATIONS   Of Navajos little altered by Anglo influence, (72) .

SOCIAL STATUS   Spanish-speaking population has retained psychology of peasant class, (179) ;—people of Tortugas may be considered landless proletariat, (113) ;—status by inheritance at Tortugas replaced by status based on money income and conspicuous consumption, (113) ;—the generally inferior status held by the native New Mexican is largely a result of the failure of the United States to recognize the special character of the social responsibility it assumed when it brought these people forcibly into the American society, (176) .

SOCIOMETRICS   Of Bosque Farms, (111).

SOCORRO COUNTY   Economic problems, (134) ;—farm tenancy, (140) ;—
irrigation, (23) ;—tax delinquency, (23). *See also* problem areas.

SOIL CONSERVATION SERVICE   Originated in Navajo reservation experiment, (66) ;—proposed program for Rio Grande watershed, (226) ;
—relief expenditures in upper Rio Grande Valley during 1935-36,
(212) ;—publications of, (150), (208), (210-238).

SOIL SURVEY   Of Tewa Basin, (241).

SOLANO   Historical development, (255).

SOMBRIO   *see* Santa Cruz.

SOTOL   Utilization as a source of food and fiber by Southwestern
Indians, (12).

SPANISH LANGUAGE   A factor in retarding assimilation at Alameda,
Guadalupe, Sandoval, (248) ;—arguments against making teaching compulsory in elementary schools, (149) ;—development and
deterioration in New Mexico, (25) ;—estimate of extent used in
New Mexico, (195) ;—necessity for use of interpreters in twelve
counties, (195) ;—use being discouraged in Sandoval, (248). *See
also* language.

SPANISH-SPEAKING COMMUNITY   Qualitative description of life in,
(176) ;—causes and effects of community disorganization in relation to assimilation, (248) ;—effect of coming of railroad on
economy of, (90) ;—education for Spanish-speaking communities
not well adapted to culture in which it exists. Lack of funds, poor
teachers, inflexibility of curricula result in sub-standard achievement and failure of schools to contribute to a solution of problems
of the communities, (176) ;—formal relief and service programs
of governmental agencies cannot solve problems of Spanish-speaking communities as exemplified in Taos County. Administrative
reorganization leading to inter-agency cooperation is needed
together with one comprehensive program for the whole county,
(176). *See also* culture.

SPANISH-SPEAKING PEOPLE   Political and racial history, (248).

SPANISH-SPEAKING TEACHERS   20 per cent in New Mexico, 1931-32,
(175).

SPECIAL INTEREST GROUPS   Largely lacking in social organization in
rural Dona Ana County, (93).

STANDARD OF LIVING   Any standard of living for people of San Geronimo depends on outside income, (136) ;—for Spanish-Americans
has steadily lowered, (60).

SUBSISTENCE INCOME   Minimum income for family of five, Santa Fe National Forest area, $426.25, (124).

SUICIDE   Zuni attitude towards, (13).

SUPERNATURALISM   Influence on behavior patterns at Atarque, (103); —a factor in social control at Atarque, (103).

SUPERSTITION   Influences on behavior patterns at Atarque, (103);— a factor in social control at Atarque, (103);—extensive at Manzano, (88);—Navajo use of dreams in diagnosing sickness, (122);— extent among Navajos, (72);—role in health practices, San Geronimo, (136);—prevalence among Spanish-Americans, (25);— among Spanish-speaking New Mexicans, (46).

SUSPICION   At El Pueblo towards outsiders and their programs, (63).

SYMBOLISM   Of Indian dances, (43), (80);—of Navajo dreams, (121); role in institutional life of Zuni, (13).

TALPA   *Penitente* rites at, (7).

TANNERS   *see* income.

TANNING   *see* marketing.

TANNING AND MOCCASIN MAKING   History of among Indians, (27);— decline in past few decades, (27).

TAOS   *see* acculturation, automobiles, cost of living, crops, culture, diet, economic life, education, leadership, relief, self sufficiency.

TAOS COUNTY   Declining land resources, uneven assimilation, developing caste lines and barriers, unenlightened political control, lack of native leadership, poor education, characterize Taos County, (176);—farm tenancy, (140);—land ownership, (239);—land use, (134);—livestock, (134);—population, (239);—social and economic history, (205);—water distribution, (134). *See also* adult education, agriculture, bilingualism, economic life, education, health, infant mortality, land holdings, land ownership, land use, personality, population, problem areas, resettlement, social apathy.

TAR-BABY STORIES   *see* folklore.

TAX DELINQUENCY   Alamosa River watershed, (198);—Cundiyo Grant, (219);—Curry County, (23);—12 per cent of total land area, Curry County, 1935, (97);—trends in Curry County, (162);—De Baca County, (23);—Hope irrigated area heavy until liquidated by purchase of sub-marginal lands, (197);—Hope irrigated area about 20 per cent in 1939, (197);—Jacona Grant, (219);—Laguna Grant, (219);—70 per cent in agricultural area of MRGCD, June 1937, (91);—91 per cent among non-commercial general farming operators in MRGCD, (217);—MRGCD, (223);—29.1 per cent on

TAX DELINQUENCY (Continued)
   rural lands, (231);—measures for reduction of, (23);—Socorro
   County, (23).

TAX LAWS Not fully enforced, (23).

TAXATION Quay-Curry area, (199);—analysis of tax practices in
   selected northern counties, (241).

TEACHERS 20 per cent Spanish-speaking, 1931-32, (175).

TELEPHONE SERVICE Only 7½ per cent of subscribers in Las Cruces
   are Spanish-American. Spanish-Americans form 50 per cent of
   population of the town, (93).

TENANCY 42 per cent among 3,746 families surveyed in five areas of
   Albuquerque, (89);—Catron County, (140);—Chaves County,
   (140);—Colfax County, (140);—Curry County, (140);—Curry
   County farms, (162);—De Baca County, (140);—Dona Ana
   County, (140);—Eddy County, (140);—22 per cent of farmers in
   Estancia Valley tenants, (236);—increasing in Estancia Valley,
   (223);—Estancia Valley, (238);—farm tenancy trends in New
   Mexico, (135);—role of tenancy in background of Gallup riots,
   (55);—Grant County, (140);—Guadalupe County, (140);—Hard-
   ing County, (140);—Hidalgo County, (140);—Lea County, (140);
   —Lincoln County, (140);—Luna County, (140);—McKinley
   County, (140);—increasing in Mesilla Valley, (223), (236);—one-
   third of 3,500 farms in Mesilla Valley operated by tenants, predominantly sharecroppers, (223);—Mora County, (140);—Otero
   County, (140);—Quay County, (140);—Rio Arriba County, (140);
   —not a problem in Rio Puerco watershed, (203);—Roosevelt
   County, (140);—San Juan County, (140);—San Miguel County,
   (140);—Sandoval County, (140);—Santa Fe County, (140);—
   Sierra County, (140);—Socorro County, (140);—Taos County,
   (140);—Torrance County, (140);—tenant operated farms in New
   Mexico increased from 26 per cent in 1880 to 42 per cent in 1930,
   (140);—Union County, (140);—Valencia County, (140). *See
   also* Bernalillo County.

TENANT HERDING Seventeen outfits engaged in tenant herding have
   19 per cent of total stock in their operating area and utilize 14 per
   cent of total range land of their area, (209);—system is highly
   advantageous to owners, disadvantageous to tenants, resulting in
   increasing debt and the ultimate reduction of the tenants to a state
   bordering on peonage, (209);—typical *partido* contract, (209);—in
   Cuba Valley about 45 per cent of sheep, 20 per cent of cattle, and
   20 per cent of goats are rented, (225);—tenant herding in Cuba

TENANT HERDING (Continued)

Valley bears an organic relationship to the complex series of factors which make up contemporary conditions of land use, and is but one of the various results of concentration of ownership of resources. The prospect for the Cuba Valley is one of increasing tenancy and decreasing ownership, (225) ;—analysis of practice and results in Tewa Basin, (241) ;—monopoly holdings of grazing lands have forced Tewa Basin Spanish-Americans into a system of tenant herding which brings the renter into an economic condition bordering on peonage and permits substantial profits to large scale owners from whom sheep are rented. High rentals, easy credit with high interest rates, and high prices at owners' stores serve to keep renters indebted and to prevent their accumulating sufficient resources to free them from the necessity of renting, (241)   *See also partido* system.

TESUQUE   The Community house at Tesuque is proving valuable in providing a place where new techniques can be introduced into the Pueblo with a minimum of friction. Although unable to do much for the economic life of the community, the Community house has, through its showers, laundry, cooking and sewing lessons. weaving, mattress making, become a center of influence through which the hygiene, diet, and health standards of the Pueblo are being improved and the process of adaptation and adjustment to Anglo culture made easier, (241) ;—government compared with other Pueblos, (241) ;—acres of irrigated and irrigable land, status of water rights, (241) .   *See also* drum-making, economic life, income, irrigation.

TEWA BASIN   Not suited to commercial agriculture, (235) ;—automobile ownership, (81) ;—economic and social problems, (168) ;—family size, (81) ;—housing, (81) ;—land ownership, (235) ;—land use, (81) ;—livestock, (81) ;—population, (81) ;—relief, (81) ; (235) ;— resettlement not feasible, (235) ;—failure of rural rehabilitation, (235) ;—schools, (81) ;—trade, (81) ;—water supply, (81) ;—work, (81) .   *See also* agriculture, division of labor, economic life, infant mortality, land holdings, land ownership, resettlement, rural rehabilitation, tenant herding, wage work.

TEWA BASIN AREA   *see* crops, erosion, grazing, land, relief.

TIERRA AZUL   Statistical description covering location, population, work, land, livestock, and health, (241) .

TIJERAS CANYON   *see* income, relief.

TIMBER Resources, Coyote area, adequate for support of thirty-seven families, (123).

TIME SENSE Lacking in Spanish-American personality, (103).

TIN WORK A native variant of Spanish silver work. Technique almost wholly New Mexican. Craft recently revived, (6).

TOBACCO Efforts to introduce cultivation at El Pueblo, (62);—family consumption at El Pueblo, (62).

TORRANCE COUNTY Crops, (134);—farm tenancy, (140);—land use, (134);—livestock, (134);—rural development, (134).

TORTUGAS Extent of association between families as shown by visiting, exchanging work, borrowing, (110);—cost of living, (113);—economic life, (113);—education, (113);—family size, (113);—food, (113);—history, (113);—housing, (113);—participation in religion as shown by attendance at religious organizations, (110). *See also* association, cost of living, education, food, housing, income, informal relationships, religion, self sufficiency, social life, social status.

TOWN OF ABIQUIU GRANT Economic situation, history, income, land use, relief, (206). *See also* economic status, income, land use, relief.

TRADE Abiquiu, (241);—60 per cent of Navajo accounts at traders paid in produce, 40 per cent in cash. Of the goods traded 35 per cent is wool; 35 per cent lambs; 10 per cent hides and pelts; 10 per cent piñons; 7.5 per cent rugs; 2.5 per cent hand made jewelry, (83);—status of on Navajo reservation, (131).

TRADING A factor in accelerating Navajo acculturation, (72);—in economy of Navajos, (72);—detailed study of trading with Navajos, (262).

TRADING POSTS Statistical description of among Navajos, (262).

TRADITIONS Acoma and Laguna, (190);—a powerful determinant of behavior at Atarque, (103);—Sandia, (49);—of Spanish-Americans rapidly disappearing, (164).

TRAMPAS Statistical description covering location, population, work, trade, livestock, land, water, health, (241).

TRANSPORTATION Means used by households in eight villages in Dona Ana County, (93);—Mesilla Valley, (52);—Rio Puerco watershed area, (203);—improved facilities a factor in urbanization, (246).

TRES RITOS *see* Rio Pueblo District.

TROUBADORS In early New Mexican culture, (25).

TRUCHAS Statistical description of Truchas, Llano de los Quemadeños, and Llano Abeyta covering location, population, work, trade, land,

TRUCHAS (Continued)
water, livestock, health, general economic and social conditions,
(241).

TRUCKING   About 35 per cent of chili produced in Tewa Basin trucked
to Santa Fe, Las Vegas, Raton where it is exchanged for cash or
merchandise, (213).

TURQUOISE WORK   *see* income, marketing, shell work.

TYPHOID   New Mexico death rate from typhoid almost nine times that
of Utah; four times that of Nevada, (239).

UNEMPLOYMENT   20 per cent of New Mexico workers (highest rate in
nation) unemployed, 1940, (239). *See also* relief.

UNION COUNTY   Farm tenancy, (140);—land ownership, (134);—land
use, (134).

UNIONS   No apprentice system or tradesman's unions in New Mexico
in 1803, (6).

UNITED STATES DEPARTMENT OF AGRICULTURE   Publications, (38).

UNITED STATES DEPARTMENT OF AGRICULTURE, BUREAU OF AGRICULTURAL
ECONOMICS   Publications, (20), (21), (108-110), (112), (113),
(115), (162), (189), (196-204).

UNITED STATES DEPARTMENT OF AGRICULTURE, FARM SECURITY ADMINIS-
TRATION   Publications, (60-63), (84), (85), (110), (113), (205-
208).

UNITED STATES DEPARTMENT OF AGRICULTURE, FOREST SERVICE   Relief
expenditures in upper Rio Grande Valley, 1935-36, (212);—
publications, (59), (123-127), (209).

UNITED STATES DEPARTMENT OF AGRICULTURE, SOIL CONSERVATION
SERVICE   Publications, (150), (208), (210-238).

UNITED STATES DEPARTMENT OF THE INTERIOR, OFFICE OF INDIAN
AFFAIRS   *see* Office of Indian Affairs.

UNIVERSITY OF NEW MEXICO BULLETINS   (11), (12), (28-31), (33),
(44), (71), (73), (95).

UPPER RIO GRANDE AREA   *see* income, land holdings, land tenure, level
of living, livestock, population, relief.

UPPER RIO GRANDE VALLEY   Effects of overuse on land resources, (226);
—description of physical resources, (226);—economic and social
problems, (239);—USDA recommendations for program leading
to self sufficiency, (239);—objectives of USDA program in the
Valley, (239). *See also* farm resources, income.

UPPER RIO GRANDE WATERSHED   Climate, (38);—description, (38);—
economic status, (91);—erosion, (38);—history, (38);—land re-

UPPER RIO GRANDE WATERSHED (Continued)
sources, (38) ;—overgrazing, (38) ;—vegetation, (38). *See also* livestock ownership, population trends.

UPPER VALLECITOS Income, (125).

URBANIZATION In New Mexico progressing at an accelerating rate, (246) ;—factors causing in New Mexico, (246) ;—effect on San Jose, (243).

VADITO *see* Rio Pueblo District.

VALENCIA COUNTY Agriculture, (134) ;—farm tenancy, (140) ;—land use, (134).

VALLECITO AND RIO OSO VILLAGE Statistical description covering location, population, work, land, livestock, health, (241).

VALLECITOS *see* Rio Pueblo District.

VELARDE Statistical description covering location, population, work, land, livestock, health, trade, (241).

VELORIO Description of a performance at Manzano, (88).

VILLANUEVA Agriculture, automobile ownership, early settlement, economic status, folk remedies, health, household arts, household equipment, housing, land ownership and use, (138) ;—land use, (228) ;—livestock, occupations, population, recreation, religion, sanitation, social organization, trade, (138). *See also* land use.

VIRDEN History of as a Mormon settlement, (53).

VITAL STATISTICS For Pueblo Indians, (249).

VOCABULARY Comparison of Spanish-American and Anglo high school pupils, Grant County, (94).

VOCABULARY HANDICAP *see* Grant County.

VOCATIONAL EDUCATION Summary of progress in state since 1939, (139) ;—list of schools participating in state program, (139) ;—must conform to village behavior configurations to be successful, (103) ;—objectives and accomplishments among Navajos, (163) ;—although vocational program of Indian Service was designed to prepare students for adjustment to their Pueblo environment, present location of graduates shows a majority living outside their native communities. Major careers are government service, farming, and working for native craft stores. Indications are that vocational education program for Pueblo Indians has failed to adjust graduates to Pueblo life, (90) ;—in Spanish-speaking villages, (180).

VOCATIONAL GUIDANCE Need for a program of in New Mexico, (151).

VOCATIONAL TRAINING *see* adult education, vocational education.

VOCATIONS   Development under Pueblo Indian, Spanish, Mexican, and American rule in New Mexico, (151) ;—of Pueblo Indians in prehistoric times, (151).

WAGE WORK   In 1936 only 196 out of five hundred families in Cuba Valley received no income from wage work. Labor market for the population not extensive, (233) ;—a major source of income in Cuba Valley, (146) ;—accounts for 50 per cent of income of typical Spanish-American in Cuba Valley: 25 per cent of that of Anglo, (224) ;—six thousand people in El Paso area are dependent for livelihood on permanent farm labor jobs: eleven thousand dependent on seasonal farm labor. Of the eleven thousand, five thousand are also dependent on relief, 1,500 permanently, (223) ; —in Española Valley, (236) ;—labor the only marketable surplus in Jemez-Tewa area, and for it there is but little demand, (223) ;— in Jemez-Tewa area only 32 per cent of farms hired any labor. Average expenditure per farm for labor in 1930, only $60. Average income from non-relief wage work, $135 per family, (223) ;—has always supplemented agricultural income in Santa Cruz area, (235) ; —little opportunity for in Santa Cruz area, (235) ;—since labor market collapse in 1930, cash income for Spanish-Americans in New Mexico has come mainly from relief agencies, (61) ;—chili harvesting a source of wage work in Tewa Basin, the prevailing wage being $1 a day, the season about two or three weeks, (213) ; —employment opportunities for Spanish-Americans in the upper Rio Grande area reached a peak in 1920's, declined with the depression. Available number of jobs for next ten years estimated to be 6,300; estimated annual income, $1,300,000, (232) ;—in 1920's approximately ninety workers out of every one hundred families in upper Rio Grande area found jobs; between 1930-35 number declined to about thirteen out of every one hundred families, (232) ;—since 1930 opportunities for wage work in upper Rio Grande Valley have decreased, (233) ;—a factor in decline of ceremonialism at Zuni, (158). *See also* agricultural labor, local labor, migratory labor, migratory workers.

WAGES   Rate of pay of migratory workers in cotton, broomcorn, and pea harvests, 1937, (92).

WALLPAPER   Adopted for decorative use with tinwork, (6).

WARFARE   Importance in Navajo culture, (72).

WATER FACILITIES   History and use of in Hope irrigated area, (197); —history and use of in Santa Cruz area, (197).

WATER RIGHTS No adjudication in Alamosa River watershed area, (198) ;—Hammond irrigation project, (196) ;—in Rio Grande Valley, (144).

WATER SUPPLY Dry Cimarron Valley, (141) ;—insufficient in Coyote area, (123) ;—improvement in at El Pueblo, (62) ;—decreasing in Middle Rio Grande Valley, (70) ;—Mora River area, (199) ;—Mora River Valley, (141) ;—inadequate for Rio Grande Valley, (142), (144).

WATER DIVISION Policy of on Laguna Land Grant, (210).

WEAVING Fourteen Cundiyo families do commercial weaving. Wages about $1 per ten-hour day: $70 a year, (117) ;—history of in New Mexico. Loom known before arrival of Spanish. Navajo learned from Hopi. Pueblos preferred weaving cotton to working with wool. Economics of in 18th century, (6) ;—school opened in Santa Fe in 1807 led to spread of weaving among Spanish-speaking people, (6) ;—history of among Navajos, (27) ;—Spanish influence on Navajo techniques, (27) ;—Navajos picked up weaving and developed it to a high art. In their two-faced blankets an original type of weaving was introduced shortly after 1884, (118) ;—importance in Navajo economy, (72) ;—illustrative of Navajo acculturation, (72) ;—history of in Pueblos, (27) ;—commercially important among Pueblos only at Isleta, Cochiti, and Zia, (27) ;—Pueblo methods, (27) ;—one hundred weavers in Santa Cruz area, (39) ;—effect of on economy of Spanish-speaking communities in Tewa Basin, (241) ;—at Zuni, (185). *See also* income, marketing, Navajos.

WEDDING CUSTOMS Weddings gayest of New Mexican folk customs. Engagement and actual ceremony are highly ritualized and the wedding itself is followed by a *fiesta* as elaborate as the groom's family's finances will permit, (145).

WHEELER-HOWARD ACT Ostensibly designed to grant home rule to Indians, the Act, adopted by all the Pueblos except Jemez, tends to keep them permanently subject to Office of Indian Affairs, (90) ; —home rule provisions of act meaningless as far as real Indian autonomy is concerned, (90) ;—a factor in retarding Indian assimilation, (90) ;—rejection by Navajos, (242).

WITCHCRAFT Belief in witches prevalent in early New Mexico, (50) ; —60 per cent of population of New Mexico believers in, (114) ;—comparatively minor role in Navajo culture, (72) ;—prevalence of belief among Spanish-Americans, (25) ;—description of among Spanish-speaking New Mexicans, (46) ;—at Zuni, (158).

WOMEN, ROLE OF   Women are subordinate in culture of El Cerrito, their activity limited to caring for the home, raising children, working in church affairs, (108) ;—San Ildefonso women are gradually assuming positions of dominance in community because of their economic activity in the production of pottery, (90) .

WOOL   Export from New Mexico banned in 1737, (6) ;—use of in 16th century New Mexico, (6) .

WORKS PROGRESS ADMINISTRATION   Attitude towards at Manzano, (88) ; —relief expenditures in upper Rio Grande Valley during 1935-36, (212) .

WORKS PROGRESS ADMINISTRATION, DIVISION OF SOCIAL RESEARCH   Publications, (57) , (92) , (97) , (162) , (187) , (250) , (251) .

YOUNGSVILLE   Land use, economic status, resources, and proposals for improvement, (123) .

YOUTH   Effects of depression on New Mexico rural youth, (76) .

YUCCA   Utilization as a source of food and fiber by Southwestern Indians, (12) .

ZIA   Amusements, art, crops, economic conditions, government, land, (64) ;—land grant litigation, (15) ;—location, livestock, population, recreation, religion, sanitation, (64) . *See also* weaving.

ZUNI   Inter-community relations with Atarque, (103) ;—description of institutional nature of culture, (13) ;—matriarchal family system, (1) ;—family system matrilineal, (13) ;—weaving, (185) . *See also,* beadwork, ceremonial life, ceremonials, continence, dances, discipline, economic life, *hilili,* kinship, leadership, *Mahed-inasha,* manners, marriage, personality, population, priesthood, purification rites, religion, suicide, symbolism, wage work, witchcraft.

ZUNI RESERVATION   Description, crops, livestock, types of farming, (87) .

II

SELECTED TITLES INCLUDED IN DICTIONARY-GUIDE

AN-CHE, LI (1)
Zuni: some observations and queries. *AA*, 39:62-76, 1937.
Comparison of some aspects of Zuni culture with that of the Chinese.

APPLEGATE, BETTY (2)
Los hermanos penitentes. *SR*, 17:100-07, 1931.
An account of *penitente* ceremonies based on unpublished studies of Frank Applegate.

APPLEGATE, FRANK (3)
New Mexico backgrounds. *SR*, 14:351-59, 1929.
Contrast between and comparison of Indian and Spanish colonial arts and crafts.

——— (4)
New Mexico legends. *SR*, 17:199-208, 1932.
Two legends illustrating process by which popular saints are given attributes peculiar to the New Mexico environment.

——— (5)
Sandia the tragic. *SR*, 15:310-16, 1930.
History of Sandia Pueblo since coming of *Conquistadores*.

APPLEGATE, FRANK AND AUSTIN, MARY (6)
**Spanish colonial arts.* Unpublished, illustrated manuscript on file at office of School of Inter-American Affairs. (D)
History of the various types of arts and crafts practiced in New Mexico with an account of the place of each in Spanish colonial culture.

AUSTIN, MARY (7)
The trail of the blood. *Century Magazine*, 108:35-44, May 1924.
Activities and cultural importance of *penitente* order in villages of northern New Mexico.

BARKER, ROBERT M. (8)
Reclaiming the arid Southwest. *Forum*, 33:363-71, 1902.
Rosy account of the potentialities of reclamation.

BARKER, RUTH LAUGHLIN (9)
Where Americans are "Anglos." *North American Review*, 228: 568-73, 1929.
Popular description of extent of Spanish-American influence in New Mexico.

BARKER, S. OMAR (10)
La politica. *New Mexico Quarterly*, 4:3-12, 1934.
Description of a political meeting, showing Spanish-speaking people's love of oratory.

BELL, WILLIS H. AND CASTETTER, EDWARD F. (11)
The utilization of mesquite and screwbean by the aborigines in the American Southwest. UNM Bulletin, Biological series, v. 5, no. 2, Oct. 1937.
Detailed accounts of use to which these plants have been put and their importance in Southwestern Indian culture.

BELL, WILLIS H. AND CASTETTER, EDWARD F. (Continued)   (12)
The utilization of yucca, sotol, and beargrass by the aborigines in the American Southwest. UNM Bulletin, Biological series, v. 5, no. 5, Dec. 1941.
> Methods of preparation and types of use.

BENEDICT, RUTH   (13)
*The Pueblos of New Mexico. (In her *Patterns of Culture*. Boston, Houghton Mifflin, 1934. pp. 57-129.)
> An evaluative and analytical description of the institutional culture of the Pueblo of Zuni, including some comparisons with the cultures of other non-Pueblo groups. The picture given is a simplified and somewhat idealized one describing the Pueblo culture in terms of Nietzsche's Apollonianism and emphasizing the institutional nature of Pueblo Indian behavior.

BOYD, NATHAN E.   (14)
New Mexico and statehood. Washington, Judd & Detweiler, 1902.
> Address before Committee on Territories of the House of Representatives regarding irrigation project at Elephant Butte and protesting Culberson-Stephens Bill prohibiting impounding of Rio Grande water in New Mexico.

BRAYER, HERBERT O.   (15)
Pueblo Indian land grants of the Rio Abajo, New Mexico. Albuquerque, UNM Press, 1939.
> Land policies of Spain, Mexico, and the United States in regard to Pueblo lands together with a history of the legal disputes concerning the grants of Laguna, Acoma, Isleta, Sandia, San Felipe, Santa Ana, Zia, Jemez, Santo Domingo, and Cochiti.

BROWN, MARIE HAMILTON   (16)
Tales of Isleta. *New Mexico Quarterly,* 3:9-17, 1933.
> Sketches revealing characteristics of Isletans.

————   (17)
Tales of Isleta (second series). *New Mexico Quarterly,* 4:281-90, 1934.

BROWN, R. H.   (18)
A Southwestern oasis: the Roswell region, New Mexico. *Geographical Review,* 26:610-19, 1936.
> Historical development and present use of lands near Roswell.

BURLIN, NATALIE CURTIS   (19)
A war song of the far West. *Dial,* 65:589-90, 1918.
> Attitude of Spanish-Americans towards draft in World War I.

BUTLER, CHARLES P.   (20)
Organization and operation of row crop farms in Area III, Quay County, New Mexico, 1938. USDA, BAE, n. p., 1940. Processed.
> A study of twenty-seven row crop farms in Quay County selected at random to obtain basic information in regard to farms in this area.

————   (21)
Organization and operation of wheat farms in Area II, Quay County, New Mexico, 1938. USDA, BAE, n. p., 1940. Processed.
> A study of twenty-nine farms in wheat area of Quay County.

BYNNER, WITTER   (22)
From him that hath not. *Outlook,* 133:125-27, 1923.
> Protest against Bursum Bill to legalize claims of non-Indian squatters on Indian lands.

CALLAWAY, R. P. AND COCKERILL, P. W. (23)
Tax delinquency on rural real estate in New Mexico. NMAES, Bulletin 234. State College, 1935.
> A study to determine the extent and location of rural real estate tax delinquency and to determine the most important factors responsible for increases in delinquency and for variations in amount of delinquency in various parts of the state.

CAMPA, ARTHUR L. (24)
**Mañana is today. *New Mexico Quarterly,* 9:3-11, 1939.
> Personality of Spanish-speaking New Mexican analyzed in the light of his tendency to live in the present.

———— (25)
***Our Spanish frontier.* Unpub. ms., dated 1938, in possession of the author.
> Detailed discussion of folk aspects of New Mexican culture.

———— (26)
*Religious Spanish folk drama in New Mexico. *New Mexico Quarterly,* 2:3-13, 1932.
> Effects of Anglo culture on religious Spanish folk plays.

CAMPA, ARTHUR L. AND KUIPERS, C. C. (27)
Arts and crafts of New Mexico. A survey of the present state of handicrafts in New Mexico. Unpub. study made in 1936 under auspices of FERA and NYA. (Copy of Part III, "Indian Arts and Crafts," on file at office of School of Inter-American Affairs. Parts I and II are missing.)

CASTETTER, EDWARD F. (28)
Uncultivated native plants used as sources of food. UNM Bulletin, Biological series, v. 4, no. 1, May 1935.
> Plants listed alphabetically by scientific name and grouped according to use by Pueblo Indians. Methods of preparation included.

CASTETTER, EDWARD F. AND BELL, WILLIS H. (29)
The aboriginal utilization of the tall cacti in the American Southwest. UNM Bulletin, Biological series, v. 5, no. 1, June 1937.
> Discussion of the place of tall cacti in culture of Southwestern Indians.

CASTETTER, EDWARD F., BELL, WILLIS H., AND GROVE, ALVIN R. (30)
The early utilization and distribution of agave in the American Southwest. UNM Bulletin, Biological series, v. 5, no. 4, Dec. 1938.
> Importance of agave in culture of Southwestern Indians.

CASTETTER, EDWARD F. AND OPLER, MORRIS E. (31)
The ethnobiology of the Chiricahua and Mescalero Apache. A. The use of plants for foods, beverages, and narcotics. UNM Bulletin, Biological series, v. 4, no. 5, Nov. 1936.
> A listing and discussion of the use of over one hundred plants, based on field work and the use of Indian informants.

CHARLES, RALPH (32)
Development of the partido system in the New Mexico sheep industry. Unpub. Master's thesis, UNM, 1940.
> History of the system in New Mexico with an estimate of its probable future trend.

CLARK, JOHN D. AND MAUGER, HARRY   (33)
    *The chemical characteristics of the waters of the Middle Rio
Grande Conservancy District.* UNM Bulletin, Chemistry series,
v. 2, no. 2, Aug. 1932.
> Includes irrigation history of MRGCD and detailed figures on drainage sys-
> tems and chemical characteristics of water in various parts of the valley.

COCKERILL, P. W.   (34)
    *Factors affecting the economic self-sufficiency of the Middle Rio
Grande Conservancy District.* NMAES, Bulletin 247. State College, 1937.

COLLIER, JOHN   (35)
    Navajos. *Survey,* 51:332-39, 363, 365, 1924.
> Discussion of economic and cultural status of Navajos as affected by the pro-
> gram of the Office of Indian Affairs.

————   (36)
    New policies in Indian education. *New Mexico Quarterly,* 3:202-
06, 1933.
> Statement of the philosophy behind the Indian Service education policy.

————   (37)
    The Pueblo lands. *Survey,* 65:548-49, 1931.
> Extent of Anglo encroachment on Indian lands and a statement of the result-
> ing legal tangle.

COOPERRIDER, CHARLES K. AND HENDRICKS, BARNARD A.   (38)
    *Soil erosion and stream flow on range and forest lands of the upper
Rio Grande watershed in relation to land resources and human
welfare.* USDA, Technical Bulletin 567. Washington, GPO, 1937.

CORDOVA, ANDREW   (39)
    A report on the Santa Cruz Irrigation District. Interdepartmental
Rio Grande Board, n. d. Typewritten. (Copy at library of
Interdepartmental Rio Grande Board, Albuquerque.)
> A study of the land and water resources of the Santa Cruz area, including
> recommendations for the solution of problems found.

CRICHTON, KYLE   (40)
    Cease not living. *New Mexico Quarterly,* 5:71-76, 1935.
> Impossibility and undesirability of maintaining New Mexico as a culture
> island.

CULBERT, J. T.   (41)
    Cattle industry of New Mexico. *Economic Geography,* 17:155-68,
1941.
> Discussion of necessity for reduction in numbers of cattle and improvement in
> quality to counteract over-grazing.

————   (42)
    Pinto beans in the Estancia Valley of New Mexico. *Economic
Geography,* 17:50-60, 1941.
> One-crop farming as a principal cause of unfavorable economic conditions.

DEHUFF, ELIZABETH WILLIS   (43)
    Dancing for life. *SR,* 18:360-83, 1933.
> Discussion of the symbolism and pageantry of Indian dances.

DUTTON, BERTHA AND MARMON, MIRIAM A.   (44)
    The Laguna calendar. UNM Bulletin, Anthropological series,
v. 1, no. 2, March 1936.
> Study of methods of counting days and years, together with a list of yearly
> ceremonials.

ESPINOSA, AURELIO M.   (45)
Another New Mexico version of the tar-baby story. *New Mexico Quarterly*, 3:31-36, 1933.
> Traces European origins of Pueblo version of the tar-baby folk tale.

————   (46)
New Mexican Spanish folk-lore. *JAF*, 23:395-418, 1910.
> Description of myths, superstitions, and beliefs, with a list of sixty-eight superstitions.

————   (47)
The New Mexican versions of the tar-baby story. *New Mexico Quarterly*, 1:85-104, 1931.
> Traces particular New Mexican folk tales to European sources. Three case stories included.

ESPINOSA, GILBERTO   (48)
New Mexican santos. *New Mexico Quarterly*, 6:181-89, 1936.
> History, production, and cultural importance.

FERGUSON, MARJORIE   (49)
The acculturation of Sandia Pueblo. Unpub. Master's thesis, UNM, 1931.
> A brief and rather superficial account of the more obvious aspects of acculturation at Sandia.

FERGUSSON, ERNA   (50)
From redskins to railroads. *Century Magazine*, 113:23-31, Nov. 1926.
> Life and social customs in and about Albuquerque before coming of the railroad.

————   (51)
*Indians of Mexico and New Mexico. *New Mexico Quarterly*, 4:169-73, 1934.
> Contrast between personalities of New Mexican and Mexican Indians.

FOSCUE, E. J.   (52)
The Mesilla Valley of New Mexico ... *Economic Geography*, 7:1-27, 1931.
> Description of soil, climate, historical development through Pueblo, Spanish, American pioneer, and government control periods.

FOSTER, MANNIE H.   (53)
History of Mormon settlements in Mexico and New Mexico. Unpub. Master's thesis, UNM, 1937.

GAMIO, MANUEL   (54)
*Race relations in New Mexico. (In his *Mexican Immigration to the United States*. Chicago, University of Chicago Press, 1930.)
> Analysis of causes of racial prejudices in New Mexico based on replies to twenty-seven questionnaires.

GAY, KATHERINE   (55)
Background of the Gallup riot. *Nation*, 140:511-12, 1935.
> Conditions behind race and labor troubles in Gallup.

————   (56)
Fascism enters New Mexico. *Nation*, 141:537-38, 1935.
> Trial of workers accused in Gallup riot.

GEDDES, ANNE E.   (57)
.   *Trends in relief expenditures, 1910-1935.* WPA, Division of Social
Research, Research Monograph 10. Washington, GPO, 1937.
> Includes statistics on relief expenditures in New Mexico.

GEROULD, KATHERINE FULLERTON   (58)
New Mexico and the backwash of Spain. *Harpers,* 151:199-212,
1925.
> General and somewhat impassioned criticism of New Mexico and things New
> Mexican.

GRAVES, W. L. AND STEVENSON, J. W.   (59)
*Range management plan, Chama district, Santa Fe National For-
est.* USDA, Forest Service. Unpub. ms., Albuquerque, 1940.
> Problems of administration of range resources in the Chama District, taking
> into consideration the social and economic problems of the resident Spanish-
> Americans.

GRISHAM, GLEN   (60)
*Basic needs of Spanish-American farm families in northern New
Mexico.* USDA, FSA. Albuquerque, n. d. Typewritten.
> Description of the Spanish-speaking people, together with an analysis of some
> of their most pressing needs.

_____   (61)
***El Pueblo farms.* USDA, FSA. Albuquerque, 1939. Typewritten.
> Study of the social and economic background of a Spanish-American settle-
> ment.

GRISHAM, GLEN AND MARTINEZ, JULIA H.   (62)
***El Pueblo experimental area, report, 1940.* USDA, FSA. Albuquerque, Jan. 1941. Typewritten.
> Discussion of the work of the FSA in facilitating acculturation at El Pueblo,
> together with an analysis of the social and economic problems of the Spanish-
> speaking New Mexicans and some general recommendations for alleviating
> them. The problem, as they see it, is basically one of community education.

_____   (63)
***El Pueblo farms, report, 1939.* USDA, FSA. Albuquerque, Jan.
1940. Typewritten.
> A report of the economic and social background of the New Mexicans, fac-
> tors which have contributed to their present situation, and a resume of
> the accomplishments of the FSA experimental program at El Pueblo farms.
> Presents two rather unusual points of view: that the Spanish-Americans are
> more individualistic than cooperative, and that they are not well adjusted to
> the land.

HALSETH, ODD S.   (64)
Report on the economic and social survey of the Keres Pueblo of
Zia, New Mexico. *EP,* 16:67-75, 1924.
> Rather general account of conditions at Zia in 1923. Little detail.

HARE, R. F., HAUTER, L. H., AND KOOGLER, J. G.   (65)
Economic survey and agricultural reports, 1927. Uupub. ms. on
file at office of MRGCD.
> Evaluation of the fertility of the Middle Rio Grande Valley and the benefits to
> be derived from contemplated improvements.

HARPER, ALLAN G.   (66)
.   The Indian and the land. (In *Indians and the Land.* Contribu-
tions by the Delegation of the United States, First Inter-American
Conference on Indian Life, Patzcuaro, Mexico, 1940.)
> Includes a good statement on the Navajo land problem and the steps being
> taken to remedy it.

HARRINGTON, J. P.   (67)
Old Indian geographical names around Santa Fe. *AA*, 22:341-59,
1920.
> Attempt to trace origins of some Indian geographical names.

HARWOOD, REV. THOMAS   (68)
*History of New Mexico Spanish and English missions of the
Methodist Episcopal Church from 1850 to 1910.* 2v. Albuquerque,
El Abogado Press, 1908, 1910.
> Early efforts to establish Protestant religion among Spanish-speaking New
> Mexicans and Indians.

HAWLEY, FLORENCE M.   (69)
Pueblo social organization as a lead to Pueblo history. *AA*, 39:504-
22, 1937.
> Theory of settlement of Southwest based on cultural differences between
> eastern and western Pueblos.

HEDKE, C. R.   (70)
*A report on the irrigation development and water supply of the
Middle Rio Grande Valley, New Mexico, as it relates to the Rio
Grande Compact.* Santa Fe, Rio Grande Valley Survey Commis-
sion, 1925. (Unpub. ms. on file at office of MRGCD, Albuquer-
que; typewritten copy in USDA library, Albuquerque.)
> A compact statement of historical development and present status of irriga-
> tion in the Middle Rio Grande Valley, with an analysis of the causes of recent
> irrigation failure.

HILL, WILLARD W.   (71)
Navajo salt gathering. UNM Bulletin, Anthropological series, v. 3,
no. 4, Feb. 1940.
> Legends of and rituals associated with Navajo salt gathering, and effects of
> tribal contacts on formalized patterns of behavior connected with salt gather-
> ing.

————   (72)
****An outline of Navajo history, ethnography, and acculturation.*
Unpub. ms., dated 1934, in possession of the author.
> A brief but rather complete account of degree to which Navajos have accepted
> Anglo traits, and a discussion of the particular traits accepted.

HODGIN, C. E.   (73)
The early school laws of New Mexico. UNM Bulletin, Education
series, v. 1, no. 1. [1906].
> Lists numerous requests to Congress for federal aid to education in the
> territory.

HOGNER, DOROTHY CHILDS   (74)
The Navajo Indian and education in New Mexico. *New Mexico
Quarterly*, 3:227-30, 1933.
> Evaluation of education program of Indian Service in the light of Navajo
> needs.

HOLDERNESS, DONOVAN J.   (75)
*The adaptation of the curriculum of the small high school to the
social and economic needs of the community.* Unpub. Master's
thesis, Highlands University, 1941.

HOLLINGER, E. C.   (76)
The situation of young people. NMSC, Extension Service, County
Program Planning 16. State College, 1936.
> Employment status of and possibilities for New Mexican rural youth.

HOLLINGER, E. C. AND STRONG, VEDA A.   (77)
Farm housing conditions in New Mexico. NMSC, Extension Service, County Program Reference Material 19. State College, 1936.
Results of a survey of 5,143 farm houses in six New Mexico counties.

HOOVER, J. W.   (78)
Navajo land problems. *Economic Geography,* 13:281-300, 1937.
Overpopulation, erosion, overgrazing, and governmental proposals for agricultural settlements.

———   (79)
Navajo nomadism. *Geographical Review,* 21:429-45, 1931.
Effects of geographical restrictions on Navajo nomadism.

HORGAN, PAUL   (80)
About the Southwest: a panorama of Nueva Granada. *SR,* 18:329-59, 1933.
Historical account of the Southwest with emphasis on the role of the land as a determinant of culture.

HORTON, LEO   (81)
Indian lands in New Mexico. Santa Fe, New Mexico State Planning Board, 1936. Processed.
Includes historical and statistical information on education, health, land tenure and use, governmental administration of Indians, and a summary of federal legislation affecting them.

HRDLICKA, ALES   (82)
Physical and physiological observations on the Navaho. *AA,* 2:339-45, 1900.
Contains, in addition to physiological and physical features, a brief description of Navajo culture.

HULSIZER, ALLAN LYNNE   (83)
Region and culture in the curriculum of the Navaho and the Dakota. Doctor's dissertation, Columbia University, 1940. Published.
The relationship and significance of education to the entire Indian problem of adjusting to white civilization. Includes material on influence of environment on Navajo culture, Navajo economics, social factors in Navajo life, with educational implications of each. Listed are some educational criteria based on the needs of the Navajo together with some suggested practical applications of those criteria. Suffers from a diffuseness of organization. Conclusion: education should be more closely adjusted to Indian needs.

HUNSPERGER, HENRY AND MARTINEZ, JULIA H.   (84)
Narrative of El Pueblo. USDA, FSA. Albuquerque, Jan. 1942. Typewritten.
Summary of rehabilitation progress made in 1941.

———   (85)
Narrative report of El Pueblo. USDA, FSA. Albuquerque, June 30, 1941. Typewritten.
Report on improvements in income, education, land use and conservation, tenure, housing, sanitation, food and diet, health, and group services of the El Pueblo farms.

HUNTER, BYRON, COCKERILL, P. W. AND PINGREY, H. B.   (86)
Type of farming and ranching areas in New Mexico. Part I. NMAES, Bulletin 261. State College, May 1939.
Includes a discussion of the physical, biological, and economic factors which have influenced farm and ranch development in the state.

HUNTER, BYRON, COCKERILL, P. W. AND PINGREY, H. B. (Continued) (87)
Type of farming and ranching areas in New Mexico. Part II.
NMAES, Bulletin 267.   State College, Dec. 1939.
    Detailed description of farming areas and sub-areas in New Mexico.

HURT, WESLEY ROBERT, JR.   (88)
Manzano: a study of community disorganization. Unpub. Master's
thesis, UNM, 1941.
    An analysis of historical trends in economic life, family organization, educa-
    tion, occupations, leading to conclusions that "Manzano has had a history
    characterized by a progressive community disorganization" largely due to
    "modification or disappearance of native institutions which bound the
    community together."

HUTCHINSON, CHARLES E.   (89)
The Albuquerque housing survey. *New Mexico Business Review,*
9:137-42, 1940.
    Survey of housing conditions, annual income, monthly rentals, and tenancy of
    families in five sections of Albuquerque.

––––––   (90)
***A study of processes of acculturation in the Indian Pueblos of the
Rio Grande Valley of New Mexico.* Unpub. Doctor's dissertation,
USC, 1941.   (D)
    A good study of the whole acculturation process, including material on cost
    of living and a criticism of the directed acculturation program of the Office of
    Indian Affairs.

INTERDEPARTMENTAL RIO GRANDE BOARD   (91)
Report and recommendations. Washington, Departments of Agriculture and the Interior, 1937.   Processed.
    Restatement of the basic economic and social problems of the upper Rio
    Grande Valley together with recommendations for a federal program to meet
    them.

JOHANSEN, SIGURD ARTHUR   (92)
Migratory-casual workers in New Mexico. NMAES in coopera-
tion with WPA, Division of Social Research.   Press Bulletin 870.
State College, March 1939.
    Excellent study of 235 migratory-casual worker households, including infor-
    mation on "extent of migration, characteristics of migratory-casual employ-
    ment, and personal characteristics of migratory households."

––––––   (93)
***Rural social organization in a Spanish-American culture area.*
Unpub. Doctor's thesis, University of Wisconsin, 1941.   (D)
    Purpose of the study was to find answers to these questions: "What place do
    the community, the neighborhood, the hamlet, and the village occupy in the
    social organization of the area?" (Dona Ana County) "What are the social
    institutions and agencies which play an important part in social organization
    and how are they related to the wider social organization?   What are the
    characteristics of selected hamlets and villages and of the population in these
    centers?   What are the social-cultural processes which help to explain the
    existence of unique features of social organization in the area?"

JOHNSON, LOAZ W.   (94)
A comparison of the vocabularies of Anglo-American and Spanish-
American high school pupils. *Journal of Educational Psychology,*
29:135-44, 1938.
    Study of vocabularies of Grant County children, leading to conclusion that
    Spanish-Americans have definite vocabulary handicap and are retarded from
    seven to twelve months as compared with Anglos.

JONES, VOLNEY H. (95)
A summary of data on aboriginal cotton of the Southwest. (Part VII of *Symposium on Prehistoric Agriculture*. UNM Bulletin, Anthropological series, v. 1, no. 5. Oct. 1936.)

KERCHEVILLE, F. M. (96)
Spanish and English in the American Southwest. *New Mexico School Review*, 16:24-25, Sept. 1936.
> Importance of both languages to New Mexico.

KIFER, R. S. AND STEWART, H. L. (97)
Farming hazards in the drought area. WPA, Division of Social Research, Research Monograph 16. Washington, GPO, 1938.
> Includes a survey of conditions in Curry County.

KIMBALL, SOLON T. (98)
Land tenure and land use among the Navajo. Talk delivered before 18th annual meeting, Southwestern Division, AAAS, 1938. (Typewritten copy in USDA library, Albuquerque.)

KLUCKHOHN, CLYDE (99)
The field of higher education in the Southwest. *New Mexico Quarterly*, 7:23-30, 1937.
> Argument that higher education in the Southwest should build upon the cultural and historical resources of the region.

——— (100)
Hopi and Navajo. *New Mexico Quarterly*, 3:56-64, 1933.
> Chapter from *Beyond the Rainbow*. Comparison of and contrast between characteristics of the two groups.

——— (101)
The life story of a Navaho Indian. Unpub. ms. in possession of the author.
> Actual life story in a translation of the Navajo's own words, together with an analysis of the narrative in terms of Pareto's conceptual scheme.

——— (102)
*The Navahos in the machine age. *The Technology Review*, 44:2-6, Feb. 1942.
> A study of the adaptation of the Navajos to Anglo technology.

KLUCKHOHN, FLORENCE ROCKWOOD (103)
***Los Atarqueños: a study of patterns and configurations in a New Mexico village.* 2 v. Unpub. Doctor's thesis, Radcliffe, 1941.
> An excellent explanation of group and individual behavior at Atarque in terms of one generalized principle and four basic configurations. Concludes with warning that those interested in the fate of New Mexico's Spanish-American citizens "should give consideration to the configurational structure of Spanish-American culture" because "to continue to judge *Mejicanos'* behavior and needs in terms of the radically different configurations of generalized American culture is to continue to distort them." Volume 2 includes seven hundred pages of case studies.

KUEHMSTED, ELEANOR FRIEND (104)
Navaho acculturation. Unpub. Master's thesis, USC, 1941. (D)
> Statement of the extent of acculturation of the Navajo. Contains little that is not stated elsewhere.

KUIPERS, C. C. (105)
Economic survey of the New Mexico Indian. *New Mexico Business Review*, 2:47-58, 1933.
> Sources and amounts of Indian income.

LAUGHLIN, RUTH   (106)
  Coronado's country and its people. *Survey Graphic,* 29:276-82,
  1940.
      Description of the three culture patterns of New Mexico.

LAW, GEORGE WARRINGTON   (107)
  Preface to kiva religion. *New Mexico Quarterly,* 6:203-06, 1936.
      Persistence of Indian religious values.

LEONARD, OLEN AND LOOMIS, CHARLES P.   (108)
  ***Culture of a contemporary rural community: El Cerrito, New
  Mexico.* USDA, BAE, Rural Life Studies 1. Washington, 1941.
  (D)
      Qualitative description of life at El Cerrito, including information on its
      location, history, agriculture, family and community organization, and its
      growing dependence on the outside world for help, leadership, and education.

LOOMIS, CHARLES P.   (109)
  *Informal groupings in a Spanish-American village. *Sociometry,*
  4:36-51, 1941. *Also* USDA, BAE. Washington, 1940. Processed.
      Social relationships at El Cerrito.

_____   (110)
  *Social relationships and institutions in seven new rural communi-
  ties.* USDA, FSA and BAE cooperating, Social Research Report
  XVIII. Washington, 1940.
      Sociometric study of informal social participation and participation in social
      agencies for a group of communities including Bosque Farms and Tortugas
      in New Mexico.

LOOMIS, CHARLES P. AND DAVIDSON, DWIGHT M., JR.   (111)
  Measurement of the dissolution of in-groups in the integration of
  a rural resettlement project. *Sociometry,* 2:84-94, 1939.
      Sociometric study of Bosque Farms.

_____   (112)
  *Standards of living of the residents of seven rural resettlement
  communities.* USDA, BAE, Social Research Report XI. Washington, Oct. 1938.
      Compares standards of living at Bosque with those of similar communities
      in other parts of the United States.

LOOMIS, CHARLES P. AND LEONARD, OLEN   (113)
  **Standards of living in an Indian-Mexican village and on a recla-
  mation project.* USDA, BAE and FSA, Social Research Report
  XIV. Washington, 1938.
      Sociometric study of living standards at Tortugas, New Mexico, and Tule
      Lake, California.

LUMMIS, CHARLES F.   (114)
  The land of poco tiempo. *Scribner's,* 10:760-71, 1891.
      Popular but highly informative description of characteristics of Navajos,
      Pueblo Indians, and Spanish-Americans.

MCMAINS, PAUL M.   (115)
  Land use planning in Quay County, New Mexico. USDA, BAE,
  Land Utilization Program, June 10, 1938. Processed.

MCMURTRIE, DOUGLAS C.   (116)
  Early printing in New Mexico. Unpub., undated ms. in files of
  UNM Press.
      Historical account of first printing in New Mexico with a list of early presses
      and a chronological list of New Mexico imprints, 1834-60.

MAES, ERNEST E.   (117)
   *The world and the people of Cundiyo. *Land Policy Review*, 4:8-
   14, March 1941.
          Problems of Cundiyo as typical of those of northern New Mexican Spanish-
          American villages.

MATTHEWS, WASHINGTON   (118)
   A two-faced Navaho blanket. *AA*, 2:638-42, 1900.
          Description of invention of a new type of weaving shortly after 1884.

MONTGOMERY-MCGOVERN, JANET B.   (119)
   *A general survey of Isleta Pueblo with special reference to acute
   transitional conditions. Unpub. Master's thesis, UNM, 1932.
          Some treatment of problems of acculturation.

MORGAN, J. C.   (120)
   A Navajo dissenter. *Christian Century*, 51:1379-80, 1934.
          Protest of a Navajo against federal program of keeping the Indian as he is.

MORGAN, WILLIAM   (121)
   Navajo dreams. *AA*, 34:390-405, 1932.
          Symbolism of dreams and their relation to religion.

————   (122)
   Navajo treatment of sickness. *AA*, 33:390-402, 1931.
          Relationship of dreams to diagnosis.

MORRIS, ROGER D.   (123)
   Coyote community land use plan. USDA, Forest Service.   Unpub.
   ms. dated Oct. 16, 1941. (Copy at Forest Service office, Albuquerque.)
          Study of the dependent populations of the communities of Mesa Poleo,
          Arroyo del Agua, Coyote, Lower Rio Puerco, Youngsville, and vicinity. In-
          cludes material on economic status, methods of determining area of de-
          pendency for livelihood and for drawing up an objective overall plan of
          management.

————   (124)
   A dependency study of northern New Mexico. USDA, Forest
   Service. Unpub. ms. dated 1939.   (Copy at Forest Service office,
   Albuquerque.)
          Study of the small stock owners of the communities in northern New Mexico
          and their relationship to national forest ranges. The area considered is the
          part of the Santa Fe National Forest lying east of the Rio Grande drainage.

————   (125)
   Jemez River rehabilitation area. USDA, Forest Service. Unpub.
   ms. dated April 30, 1939. (Copy at Forest Service office, Albuquerque.)
          "An attempt to outline a program of procedure which will furnish immediate
          relief and ultimately insure an independent economic status to the communi-
          ties of La Cueva, Upper Vallecitos, Lower Vallecitos, Jemez Springs, Cañon
          de Jemez, and San Ysidro."

————   (126)
   The partido system. USDA, Forest Service. Unpub. ms. dated
   1937. (Copy at Forest Service office, Albuquerque.)
          Study of the dependency situation in northern New Mexico with special
          consideration of the *partido* or share crop system of livestock operation.

MORRIS, ROGER D. AND OTHERS   (127)
   *Regional forest planning in northern New Mexico as a basis for
   national forest acquisition.* USDA, Forest Service. Unpub. ms.
   dated April 1940.   (Copy at Forest Service office, Albuquerque.)

MORRIS ROGER D. AND OTHERS (Continued)
> Study of the north-central region of New Mexico in regard to population, land ownership and use, and the possible solution of problems through enlarging national forests.

NATIONAL RESOURCES COMMITTEE   (128)
Problems of a changing population. Report of the Committee on Population Problems to the National Resources Committee. Washington, GPO, 1938. pp. 237-39, "Cultural Aspects of Indian Administration."
> Brief statement of present national policy towards Indian groups.

NATIONAL YOUTH ADMINISTRATION   (129)
NYA and New Mexican youth. NYA, Albuquerque, March 10, 1942. Typewritten.
> Brief defense of NYA activities in New Mexico with some health and education statistics.

NEUMANN, DAVID L.   (130)
Our architectural follies. *New Mexico Quarterly,* 1:211-17, 1931.
> Criticism of practice of overdoing the borrowing of architectural design from Indian and Spanish-colonial models.

NEW MEXICO ASSOCIATION ON INDIAN AFFAIRS   (131)
Urgent Navajo problems; observations and recommendations based on a recent study by the New Mexico Association on Indian Affairs. Santa Fe, August 1940.
> Short discussion of Navajo problems of land management, trade, relief, agricultural development and extension, and education, giving Navajo point of view.

NEW MEXICO HISTORICAL RECORDS SURVEY   (132)
Preliminary report, Middle Rio Grande Conservancy District (historical-statistical). Albuquerque, March 1941. Typewritten. (Copy in library of Interdepartmental Rio Grande Board, Albuquerque.)
> Historical sketch of irrigation and development in Middle Rio Grande Valley, with financial and other statistical data on the Conservancy District.

NEW MEXICO LAND USE ADVISORY COUNCIL   (133)
Preliminary report on unified agricultural program for New Mexico, 1941. NMSC, Extension Service. State College, 1941.
> Specific recommendations for meeting agricultural problems of the state.

NEW MEXICO STATE COLLEGE OF AGRICULTURE AND MECHANIC ARTS (134)
County land use and agricultural planning report for New Mexico, 1940. Processed.
> Recommendations for land use and for agricultural planning for New Mexico, by counties.

——————, EXTENSION SERVICE   (135)
Tenancy in New Mexico. County Program Planning 24. State College, 1936.
> Summary of farm tenancy trends in New Mexico.

NEW MEXICO STATE DEPARTMENT OF PUBLIC WELFARE   (136)
**San Geronimo.* n. p., n. d. Processed.
> Study of a typical Spanish-American mountain settlement which is rapidly losing population.

——————   (137)
Study of migratory labor. n. p., 1940. Processed.
> Study of migratory labor in New Mexico giving reasons for migration, occupational status of migrants, and some statistics.

NEW MEXICO STATE DEPARTMENT OF PUBLIC WELFARE (Continued)(138)
**Villanueva.* n. p., Feb. 1938. Processed.
>Qualitative description of culture of Villanueva with recommendations for
>revision of the programs of state and federal agencies working in the area.

NEW MEXICO STATE DEPARTMENT OF VOCATIONAL EDUCATION   (139)
Progress of vocational education since 1939. Santa Fe, April 1942.
Processed.
>A two-page summary of accomplishments of vocational training, together
>with a list of schools participating and the trades taught.

NEW MEXICO STATE PLANNING BOARD   (140)
Farm tenancy in New Mexico. Santa Fe, Feb. 1937. Processed.
>Evaluation of conditions of farm tenancy in New Mexico, by counties.

————   (141)
Progress report to National Resources Board. Santa Fe, April 15,
1935. Processed.
>Report of first six months' work of Planning Board.

————   (142)
Second progress report. Santa Fe, Dec. 15, 1935. Processed.
>General information on population, grazing, irrigation, water rights, recre-
>ation, economic conditions.

————   (143)
State lands. v. 1. Santa Fe, Oct. 15, 1936. Processed.
>Location, revenues from management, and status of state-owned lands.

————   (144)
Study of Rio Grande Basin. Santa Fe, Dec. 1935. Processed.
>Survey of the Rio Grande Basin, discussing climate, population, land use,
>problem areas, irrigation, water supply, and flood control.

NEW MEXICO WRITERS' PROJECT, WPA   (145)
Spanish-American wedding customs. *EP,* 49:1-6, 1942.
>Description of wedding of a fairly wealthy couple in Union County.

OBERG, KALERVO   (146)
**Cultural factors and land-use planning in Cuba Valley, New
Mexico. *Rural Sociology,* 5:438-48, 1940.
>Statement of the problems to be met in any program of planned land-use in
>the Valley.

OPLER, MORRIS EDWARD   (147)
The influence of aboriginal pattern and white contact on a recently
introduced ceremony, the Mescalero peyote rite. *JAF,* 49:143-66,
1936.
>Discovery and use of peyote among Mescalero Apaches.

————   (148)
A summary of Jicarilla Apache culture. *AA,* 38:202-23, 1936.
>Summary of culture traits, giving world conception, material culture,
>economy, attitude toward war, mythology, ritual life, kinship, death, burial,
>and underworld rites.

ORTEGA, JOAQUIN   (149)
*The compulsory teaching of Spanish in the grade schools of New
Mexico: an expression of opinion.* Albuquerque, UNM Press,
1941.
>An analysis of proposed legislation making Spanish teaching compulsory,
>and a discussion of the importance of New Mexico as a cultural link between
>the United States and Latin America.

OSBORN, M. M. AND JOHNSON, E. A. (150)
Working plan report of the grazing activities on the northern Navajo Indian reservation. Albuquerque, SCS, Dec. 10, 1930. Typewritten. (Copy in USDA library, Albuquerque.)

PANNELL, HERMAN CLAY (151)
Vocational opportunities in New Mexico. Unpub. Master's thesis, University of Colorado, 1934.
> Vocational activities of Pueblo Indians, Spanish-Americans, and Anglos. Analysis of employment possibilities, with a plan for the improvement of vocational selection.

PARSONS, ELSIE CLEWS (152)
Further notes on Isleta. *AA*, 23:149-69, 1921.
> Marriage and burial customs; birth and christening ceremonies; kinship terms.

——— (153)
The kinship nomenclature of the Pueblo Indians. *AA*, 34:377-89, 1932.
> Detailed accounts of specialized terms and how they infiltrate between groups.

——— (154)
The Laguna migration to Isleta. *AA*, 30:602-13, 1928.
> Assimilation of small infiltration of Lagunans into Isleta culture.

——— (155)
*Notes an Acoma and Laguna. *AA*, 20:162-86, 1918.
> Generalized description of cultures of the two Pueblos.

——— (156)
Notes on Isleta, Santa Ana, and Acoma. *AA*, 22:56-69, 1920.
> Clan system in the three Pueblos and the ceremonials accompanying it.

——— (157)
Notes on San Felipe and Santo Domingo. *AA*, 25:485-94, 1923.
> Development of clans, dances, marriage and burial customs, government.

——— (158)
Notes on Zuni. AAA, Memoirs, v. 4, pts. I & II. Menasha, Wisconsin, 1917.
> Description of ceremonies and list of kinship terms.

——— (159)
Picuris, New Mexico. *AA*, 41:206-22, 1939.
> Description of customs, religion, government, ceremonial calendar by an old survivor of the Pueblo.

PAULUS, LENA (160)
The private land grant problem of New Mexico. Unpub. Master's thesis, University of Pittsburgh, 1933.
> History of land grants and of the activities of the Court of Private Land Claims in regard to them.

PEARCE, T. M. (161)
Southwestern culture, an artificial or natural growth? *New Mexico Quarterly*, 1:195-209, 1931.
> A weighing of the contributions of each of the three culture groups in New Mexico to the distinctive 'New Mexican' culture.

PEVEHOUSE, H. M. (162)
Natural and economic factors affecting rehabilitation in the upper south plains of the Texas Panhandle and the high plains of eastern New Mexico (as typified by Curry County, New Mexico.) USDA, BAE and WPA Division of Social Research, Research Bulletin K-10. Washington, Dec. 1936.

PEVEHOUSE, H. M. (Continued)

> Includes material on agricultural history, type of farming, soils, topography, climate, crop yields, farm organization, income and financial progress, economic status of farmers, relief, and rehabilitation prospects for Curry County.

PHELPS-STOKES FUND   (163)

The Navajo Indian problem, an inquiry sponsored by the Phelps-Stokes Fund. New York, 1939.

> Detailed study of the present-day Navajo, covering his relations to the land, governmental administration, education, law and order, health, and missionary activity. Purpose: to ascertain and to foster trends towards better working relations between Indian Service and the Navajos.

RAEL, JUAN B.   (164)

New Mexican Spanish feasts. *California Folklore Quarterly*, 1:83-90, 1942.

> Description of religious feasts in northern New Mexican villages with observation that such ceremonies are declining in importance.

RENAUD, ETIENNE B.   (165)

Evolution of population and dwelling in the Indian Southwest. *Social Forces*, 7:263-70, 1928-29.

> Distribution and groupings of Southwest Indian population during the various periods of their prehistory and early history, and parallel evolution of their dwellings.

RIDEING, WILLIAM H.   (166)

A trail in the far Southwest. *Harper's New Monthly Magazine*, 53:15-24, June 1876.

> Describes Spanish-speaking culture in New Mexico in early 1870's.

ROBERTSON, WALTER JOYCE   (167)

Economic and social conditions of rural San Miguel County. Unpub. Master's thesis, New Mexico Normal (Highlands) University, 1934.

> Contains little that cannot be found in census reports or reports of state and county agencies.

ROGERS, VANCE   (168)

Management and development program for the Tewa Basin. Typewritten. (Revised 7-17-1940.) (Copy in library of Interdepartmental Rio Grande Board, Albuquerque.)

> Broad outline sketch of the problems of Tewa Basin area with an indication of necessary remedial measures.

RUSSELL, JOHN T. (C?)   (169)

New Mexico, a problem of parochialism in transition. *American Political Science Review*, 30:385-87, 1936.

> Factors causing parochialism and their operation in New Mexico.

RUSSELL, JOHN C.   (170)

*Racial groups in the New Mexico legislature. *Annals of the American Academy of Political and Social Science*, 195:62-71, 1938.

> Analysis of racial differences in composition of New Mexico legislature and the awareness of those differences as shown by voting alignments.

————   (171)

State regionalism in New Mexico. Unpub. Doctor's dissertation, Stanford University, 1938. (D)

> Cultural regionalism as it affects governmental and social organization, economic life, and health. Specifically studied were ethnic and cultural differences, population, the constitution, county elections, the legislature, election laws, the courts, economic ways, illiteracy, and infant mortality. The conclusion: New Mexico does present "two great and distinct regions."

RUSSELL, JOHN C. (Continued) (172)

*State regionalism in New Mexico. *Social Forces,* 16:268-72, 1937.
> Bi-culturism as a force in the economic, social, and political life of New Mexico.

SANCHEZ, GEORGE I. (173)

A brief summary of a report on the age-grade status of the rural child in New Mexico, 1931-32. New Mexico State Department of Education, Santa Fe, n. d. Processed.
> Statistical analysis showing serious retardation of children, especially in those counties with a large Spanish-speaking population.

—— (174)

**Community education in Taos County. Unpub. supplement to *Forgotten People. See* (176).
> Concrete proposals for improvement of health, educational, economic conditions in Taos County.

—— (175)

The education of bilinguals in a state school system. Unpub. Doctor's dissertation, University of California, 1934.
> Statistical study of age-grade status and educational opportunity of Anglos and Spanish-speaking children in the elementary schools of New Mexico.

—— (176)

***Forgotten people: a study of New Mexicans.* Albuquerque, UNM Press, 1940.
> A study of the present economic and cultural plight of New Mexicans in general and the inhabitants of Taos County in particular, with general proposals for the alleviation of existing conditions. The method used is that of qualitative description with a minimum of quantitative data. The role of education in any program of reform is stressed.

—— (177)

*New Mexico and acculturation. *New Mexico Quarterly Review,* 11:61-68, 1941.
> Analysis of causes of educational backwardness of New Mexicans of Spanish descent.

SAPIR, E. (178)

A Navajo sand painting blanket. *AA,* 37:609-16, 1935.
> Use of sacred designs as indication of disintegration of religious authority.

SERGEANT, ELIZABETH SHIPLEY (179)

God's country. *Nation,* 111:39-40, 1920.
> New Mexico possesses cultural resources to resist disintegrating influences of change.

SEWELL, BRICE H. (180)

A new type of school. *New Mexico School Review,* 15:49-50, Oct. 1935.
> Vocational training for Spanish-speaking villages.

—— (181)

The old skills are again being practiced in Mora Valley. *New Mexico School Review,* 16:21, Sept. 1936.
> Revival of handicraft skills under federal direction.

SHEVKY, ESHREF (182)

Rural rehabilitation in New Mexico. *New Mexico Business Review,* 5:5-9, 1936.
> Social economics and rural rehabilitation program in upper Santa Cruz Valley.

SININGER, HARLAN   (183)
New Mexico reading survey. Unpub. Master's thesis, UNM, 1930.
  Study of reading comprehension and rate in city, town, and county schools,
  showing Spanish-Americans as having consistently lower performance. Tables
  by type of school, racial group, and age.

SPERANZA, G.   (184)
The immigration peril. *World's Work,* 47:147-60, 1923.
  Statement of the viewpoint that the Spanish intelligence, character, and
  customs cannot be adapted to the Anglo-Saxon type of government.

SPIER, LESLIE   (185)
Zuni weaving technique. *AA,* 26:64-85, 1924.
  Preparation of yarn, methods of weaving.

STAPLES, BETTY   (186)
A century of mañanas. *New Mexico Quarterly,* 5:161-69, 1935.
  History and culture of Questa, New Mexico.

STECKER, MARGARET LOOMIS   (187)
*Intercity differences in costs of living in March 1935, fifty-nine
cities.* WPA, Division of Social Research, Research Monograph
12. Washington, GPO, 1937.
  Includes information on Albuquerque.

STEVENSON, PHILIP   (188)
Deporting Jesus. *Nation,* 143:67-69, 1936.
  Background of labor and Liga Obrera organization in New Mexico.

STEWART, HUGH L.   (189)
*Organization and operation of small ranches in northeastern New
Mexico, 1937.* USDA, BAE, n. d. Processed.
  Study of the operation and organization of small ranches with the aim of
  recommending ways of lowering their production costs and stabilizing their
  income.

SWANK, GEORGE R.   (190)
The ethnobotany of the Acoma and Laguna Indians. Unpub.
Master's thesis, UNM, 1932.
  Includes history of Acoma and Laguna and some material on customs, tra-
  ditions, and mythology.

THRELKELD, JAMES P.   (191)
Albuquerque from the past. *New Mexico Quarterly,* 2:283-92,
1932.
  Historical development of Albuquerque.

TIREMAN, L. S.   (192)
Reading in the elementary schools of New Mexico. *Elementary
School Journal,* 30:621-26, 1930.
  Comparison of reading abilities of Anglo and Spanish-speaking children, with
  conclusion that Spanish-speaking are most retarded.

————   (193)
Reading in the elementary schools of New Mexico. New Mexico
Education Association Papers, 44th Annual Convention, 1929.
  Results of reading survey made in 1928-29, showing differences between Anglo
  and Spanish-speaking children.

TIREMAN, L. S., BREWSTER, MELA SEDILLO, AND POOLER, LOLITA   (194)
The San Jose project. *New Mexico Quarterly,* 3:207-16, 1933.
  Statement of purposes and program of San Jose Training School.

UNITED STATES CONGRESS   (195)
Hearings on statehood bill before Committee on the Territories of the House of Representatives. Washington, GPO, 1903.
> Some discussion of number of Spanish-speaking New Mexicans and extent and use of the Spanish language.

USDA, BAE, WATER UTILIZATION SECTION, DIVISION OF LAND ECONOMICS
                                                                 (196)
Report on the Hammond project, San Juan River watershed, San Juan County, New Mexico. March 1941. Processed.
> Study to determine the feasibility of the Hammond irrigation project as a location for the resettlement of ninety families.

————, ————   (197)
Special report to the water facilities board on Hope irrigated area—Rio Peñasco. March 1939. Processed.
> An inventory of the land and water resources of the Hope irrigated area and a presentation of a plan to improve water facilities.

————, ————   (198)
Water facilities area plan for Alamosa River, Rio Cuchillo Negro, Palomas River, Rio Seco, Rio Animas, and Perchas Creek watersheds, New Mexico. Oct. 1940. Processed.
> An inventory of the land and water resources of the watersheds included, together with a plan for the more efficient utilization of those resources.

————, ————   (199)
Water facilities area plan for Quay-Curry area, New Mexico. Sept. 1940. Processed.
> Includes a description of the area, a discussion of present economic conditions, recommended land use, water facilities development, and an appraisal of value of water facilities.

————, ————   (200)
Water facilities area plan for the Mora River watershed, New Mexico. Oct. 1941. Processed.
> Study of the Mora River area showing the land and water resources and offering a plan for development and rehabilitation of water facilities to promote better utilization of existing resources.

————, ————   (201)
Water facilities area plan for the Rio Moquino watershed, New Mexico. March 1940. Processed.
> Inventory of the land and water resources of the Rio Moquino watershed and the presentation of a plan for the development of small water facilities.

————, ————   (202)
Water facilities area plan for the Rio Santa Cruz watershed, New Mexico. Feb. 1940. Processed.
> An inventory of the land and water resources of the Santa Cruz watershed and the presentation of a plan for water facilities development.

————, ————   (203)
Water facilities area plan for upper Rio Puerco watershed, Sandoval and Rio Arriba Counties, New Mexico. Oct. 1939. Processed.
> Presents "information concerning the resources of the watershed, together with recommendations pointing toward a higher and better utilization of those resources."

————, ————   (204)
Water facilities area plan for watershed of the Ocate Creek, Colfax and Mora Counties, New Mexico. Dec. 1940. Processed.

USDA, FARM SECURITY ADMINISTRATION   (205)
*Land purchase proposal for the "Sangre de Cristo Grant," Taos
County, New Mexico.* n. p., n. d. Typewritten.
> A proposal for a loan for the purchase and operation of 122,350 acres of
> grazing land, together with 6,000 acres of irrigated land to 175 families to
> supplement their small income. Some of the social and economic history,
> present problems, and general history of the grant are included.

————, ————   (206)
*Land purchase proposal for the "Town of Abiquiu Grant," Rio
Arriba County, New Mexico.* n. p., n. d. Typewritten.
> Plan for purchase of 15,803 acres of land for restoration to the former owners,
> giving some of the historical background of the area.

————, ————   (207)
*Loan proposal for the "Town of Chilili Grant," Bernalillo County,
New Mexico.* n. p., n. d. Typewritten.
> A loan proposal for the purpose of paying off a judgment against the town
> of Chilili, for the payment of delinquent taxes on all the land, giving also
> some of the historical background and economic status of families on the
> grant.

USDA, FSA AND SCS   (208)
Migratory labor in southern New Mexico. Economic Surveys
Division, 1940. Processed. (D)
> Survey of need for and conditions of migratory labor in New Mexico cotton
> producing areas.

USDA, FOREST SERVICE   (209)
**Material on the partido system.* Albuquerque, July 1937.
Processed. (D)
> Survey of tenant herding in the state showing that the system operates to the
> disadvantage of tenants. A sample *partido* contract is included.

USDA, SCS   (210)
Agronomic and farm analysis survey of Laguna Indian Grant.
1936. Processed.

————, ————   (211)
**Destruction of villages at San Marcial.* SCS Regional Bulletin
38, Conservation Economics series 11, May 1937. Processed. (D)
> The effects of periodic floods on villages at San Marcial.

————, ————   (212)
**Federal relief expenditures for labor in three sub-areas of the
upper Rio Grande watershed during 1935-36.* SCS Regional
Bulletin 41, Conservation Economics series 14, July 1937.
Processed.
> Summarizes in eight tables all available data on federal relief expenditures
> in the Jemez-Tewa, Middle Rio Grande, and Puerco areas of the upper Rio
> Grande watershed. Agencies whose expenditures are included are WPA,
> FERA, New Mexico Relief and Security Administration (federal funds only),
> Rural Rehabilitation Division of Resettlement Administration, SCS, Forest
> Service, and Indian Service.

————, ————   (213)
***Handling of a cash crop (chili).* SCS Regional Bulletin 46,
Conservation Economics series 19, July 1937. Processed. (D)
> Study of the place of chili in the agricultural economy of the Spanish-speak-
> ing communities, and of the culture complex centered around its production.

USDA, SCS (Continued) (214)

The importance of various types of income on the Navajo Reservation. SCS Regional Bulletin 30, Conservation Economics series 30, Jan. 1935. Processed. (D)
> Interrelationships of the various sources of Navajo income.

————, ———— (215)

Inventory of material on the Rio Grande watershed. Part I. SCS Regional Bulletin 34, Conservation Economics series 7, Feb. 1937. Processed.
> Analytic breakdowns under seven headings (area, type of data, intensity, sources, standard, use, and significance) of material included in Tewa Basin Study, Rural Rehabilitation in Santa Cruz, Proposals for the Santa Cruz Area, Resettlement Plan Book for the Santa Cruz-Truchas Project.

————, ———— (216)

Inventory of material on the Rio Grande watershed. Part II. SCS Regional Bulletin 35, Conservation Economics series 8, Feb. 1937. Processed.
> Same type of material as Part I (215) covering Reconnaissance Survey of Human Dependency on Resources, Human Dependency Survey, the Place of Chili in the Economy of the Tewa Basin, The Cuba Area, Study of Delinquency and Changes in Land Ownership in Middle Rio Grande Conservancy District, 1936.

————, ———— (217)

*Middle Rio Grande Conservancy District, survey of economic conditions. SCS, Division of Economic Surveys, 1940. Processed. (D)
> Types and characteristics of farms in MRGCD; analysis of consumption group income and financial problems of the district in the light of the ability of the population to pay District charges.

————, ———— (218)

***A note on the level of village livelihood in the upper Rio Grande area. SCS Regional Bulletin 44, Conservation Economics series 17, July 1937. Processed. (D)
> Case study of income and expenditures of typical Spanish-speaking family in upper Rio Grande area.

————, ———— (219)

**Notes on community-owned land grants in New Mexico. SCS Regional Bulletin 48, Conservation Economics series 21, Aug. 1937. Processed. (D)
> Survey of history and present status of lands included in Canyon de San Diego, Jacona, Cundiyo, and La Joya grants.

————, ———— (220)

Preliminary report, economic survey Clovis Project area, New Mexico, No. 9. July 1937. Processed.
> An economic and social study of the Clovis project area, giving information on agricultural conditions, type and organization of farms in the area, and the methods most commonly used on these farms.

————, ———— (221)

The problem of soil erosion on the Navajo Indian Reservation and methods being used for its solution. Typewritten. n. d.
> Includes a statement of agricultural and range resources in relation to subsistence needs and summary statistics on Navajo income and livelihood.

USDA, SCS (Continued)   (222)

Proposed conservation plan and basic data for the Rio Hondo watershed. Jan. 1941. Processed.

————, ————   (223)

***Reconnaissance survey of human dependency on resources in the Rio Grande watershed.** SCS Regional Bulletin 33, Conservation Economics series 6, Dec. 1936. Processed. (D)
> Attempts to measure dependency of people on different resources, using amount of livestock and agricultural land owned and amount of income from wage work as measures of dependency, and to describe dependency in terms of the total range of variations by consumption groups rather than in terms of averages.
> For Jemez-Tewa area includes material on population, land use, land owner-ship, labor, relief. Conclusion: any steps toward alleviating the severe con-dition of over-dependency on resources must wait on willingness and capacity of federal agencies to join in common consideration of the problems of the area.
> For Middle Rio Grande area: material on population, MRGCD, crops, labor, land use.
> Estancia area: information on history, livestock, irrigation, mechanization of farms, tenancy, crops, destruction of land resources.
> Mesilla Valley area: information on irrigation, land use, income, labor, crops, relief, tenancy. Emphasized is the effect of turning to cotton as a principal cash crop.

————, ————   (224)

***The relationship of economic and cultural factors to the land use adjustment program in Cuba Valley.** Economic Surveys Division, Region 8, Aug. 1940. Processed. (D)
> A discussion of "those social and economic factors which a planning agency should consider in carrying out a program for the physical stabilization of the region."

————, ————   (225)

***A report on the Cuba Valley.** SCS Regional Bulletin 36, Conser-vation Economics series 9, March 1937. Processed. (D)
> Survey of resources and problems of upper Puerco region, including Cuba, Regina, La Jara, Cabezon, San Luis, Guadalupe, and Casa Salazar, with dis-cussions of tenant herding, rural rehabilitation, and relief in the Cuba Valley.

————, ————   (226)

The Rio Grande watershed in Colorado and New Mexico; a report on the condition and use of the land and water resources, with a general program for soil and water conservation. Region 8, Aug. 1939. Processed. (D)
> Physical description, with information on economic status, land tenure, relief.

————, ————   (227)

****Rural rehabilitation in New Mexico.** SCS Regional Bulletin 50, Conservation Economics series 23, Dec. 1935. Processed. (D)
> Critical analysis of the work of the Resettlement Administration in the Santa Cruz River Valley. Conclusion: "Any realistic rehabilitation must be under-taken on the basis of unified action and must be conceived in terms of the total economy of the area, as against mere financing of individual or com-munity enterprises."

————, ————   (228)

***San Miguel County villages: Villanueva.** SCS Regional Bulletin 51, Conservation Economics series 24, Feb. 1938. Processed.
> A study of a typical Spanish-American village in the upper Pecos River area with special attention to land use.

USDA, SCS (Continued)   (229)
**The Santa Cruz irrigation district.* SCS Regional Bulletin 45,
Conservation Economics series 18, July 1937. Processed. (D)
> History of organization and financing of the irrigation district with an appraisal of its effects on land owners coming under the ditches.

————, ————   (230)
*Sociological survey of the Navajo Reservation; a statement of
procedure.* SCS Regional Bulletin 32, Conservation Economics
series 5, May 1936. Processed.
> Introduction to proposed series of studies of human population of Navajo Reservation, giving methods of organization and assumptions underlying the studies.

————, ————   (231)
Survey report, flood control Rio Puerco watershed, New Mexico.
Revised 1941. Processed.
> Study of the serious flood and silt producing area, taking into consideration the area, erosion, climate, vegetation, sedimentation, existing federal programs, and a plan of watershed improvement for flood control purposes.

————, ————   (232)
**Village dependence upon migratory labor in the upper Rio Grande
area.* SCS Regional Bulletin 47, Conservation Economics series
20, July 1937. Processed. (D)
> Problem posed: "To what extent may wage work in the near future contribute to the income of the rural population in the upper Rio Grande area?" Conclusion: Wage work opportunities for migratory labor are shrinking. Available number of jobs for next ten years, 6,300; estimated income, $1,300,-000. Included in this study is a summary of history, organization, and labor policy of sugar beet industry, of contract system of harvesting potatoes in the San Luis Valley of Colorado, and of labor policies of the Denver and Rio Grande Railroad with respect to Spanish-Americans from New Mexico.

————, ————   (233)
***Village livelihood in the upper Rio Grande area.* SCS Regional
Bulletin 44, Conservation Economics series 17, July 1937.
Processed. (D)
> Total income (1936) derived from four sources: land (50%), livestock (15%), relief (14%), wages (21%). 64% of families have incomes under $600. Incomes of less than $650 will provide only most meagre diet, insufficient clothing, no expenditures for health, education, recreation; no savings. Conclusion: without effective planning and action by and for the native populations, their future, even with continuing relief expenditures, is not bright.

————, ————   (234)
Work report, San Pedro Grant, Rio Grande District. 1937.
Processed.

————, ————, DIVISION OF REGIONAL PLANNING, SOUTHWEST REGION
                                                            (235)
Proposals for the Santa Cruz area, 1935. Processed.
> Criticism by SCS of the report on the Santa Cruz area by Rural Rehabilitation Division of Resettlement Administration on conditions of indebtedness and rehabilitation. Includes a plan to deal with economic and human needs of the area.

————, ————, ————   (236)
The sociological survey of the Rio Grande watershed. Dec. 1936.
Processed.
> A study of the watershed on three levels: description, the level of measurement, and the level of interpretation.

USDA, SCS, SECTION OF HUMAN SURVEYS, REGION 8 (Continued)   (237)
Population of the upper Rio Grande watershed. July 1937.
Processed. (D)
> Population and population trends in the area, broken down into figures for
> Anglos, Indians, and Spanish-Americans.

————, ————, ————   (238)
**Tijeras Canyon-Moriarty area: a report prepared for the Rural
Electrification Administration. . . May 1937. Processed. (D)*
> Includes information on population, income, relief, land tenure, farm size
> and mechanization, principal crops.

USDA, SOUTHWESTERN INTERMOUNTAIN COMMITTEE   (239)
Water, land, and people. 1942. Processed. (D)
> Study of the people of the Rio Grande Valley, their problems and the USDA
> program for the valley.

USDI, BUREAU OF INDIAN AFFAIRS   (240)
*1940 statistical summary, human dependency survey, Navajo
Reservation and grazing district 7.* Prepared by Division of Socio-
economic Surveys, Oct. 1941. Processed.
> Tabular data on income, livestock, agriculture, and consumption.

USDI, OFFICE OF INDIAN AFFAIRS   (241)
***Tewa Basin study.* Indian Land Research Unit, Office of Indian
Affairs, 1935. Processed. (D)
> Survey of the land and physical resources of the Tewa Basin region together
> with a sociological analysis of the ethnic groups living there.
> Part I includes a socio-economic study of the Tewa Pueblos covering popu-
> lation trends, health conditions, land tenure, economy, phases of the decline
> and recovery of craft skills, government, economic effects of IECW, and a
> report on the community house at Tesuque.
> Part II consists of a statistical description of life and work in twenty-seven
> Spanish-speaking villages of the Tewa area covering their history, location,
> population, work, land, livestock, health, crops, and trade.
> Part III includes a grazing survey of the area, a survey of irrigated lands at
> the Indian Pueblos, a paper on construction for the control of soil erosion,
> a paper on taxation in New Mexico, and one on sharecropping with sheep.
> Bound with the volume, but not a part of the Study, is a paper containing a
> soil survey of the Tewa Basin area.
> A limited number of copies of an atlas, illustrating the various findings of
> the Study, were prepared. One copy of the atlas, containing both maps and
> photographic materials, is on file at the USDA library, Albuquerque.

————, ————, NAVAJO SERVICE   (242)
Navajo planning and policy conference. Window Rock, Arizona,
1940. Processed.
> Includes discussion of conditions of health, leadership, livestock, rehabili-
> tation, agriculture, and reasons for rejection of Wheeler-Howard Bill.

WAGGONER, LAURA   (243)
**San Jose, a study in urbanization.* Unpub. Master's thesis, UNM,
1941.
> Study of the disintegrating influences of urbanization on the population of
> an Albuquerque suburb.

WALKER, A. L.   (244)
*An analysis of social and economic factors affecting the Indians of
the Pueblo of Santa Clara in 1936.* USDI, Office of Indian Affairs,
Credit Agent, Extension Division. Typewritten.

WALKER, A. L. AND COCKERILL, P. W.   (245)

Farm organization practices and costs of producing crops in the Middle Rio Grande Conservancy District of New Mexico. NMAES Bulletin 215. State College, 1933.

> Statistical study of economics of farming in the MRGCD by five types of farms and including material on income and expenditures of farm families in the area.

WALTER, PAUL, JR.   (246)

Rural-urban migration in New Mexico. New Mexico Business Review, 8:132-37, 1939.

> Analysis of urbanization in New Mexico, including a discussion of probable causes.

_____   (247)

**The Spanish-speaking community in New Mexico. Sociology and Social Research, 24:150-57, November-December 1939. (D)

> Brief description of the socio-economic conditions prevailing in the Spanish-speaking communities of northern and central New Mexico, summarizing and integrating many of the findings of other research projects in this field. Conclusions: assimilation problem has six phases: (1) overpopulation in Spanish-speaking communities; (2) loss of land through sale and taxes; (3) erosion; (4) growing dependence on dry farming; (5) marginal state of Spanish-speaking people isolated from their culture and attempting to compete as individuals in Anglo economic system; (6) peonage status resulting from exploitation and extension of credit. Permanent solution requires extensive regional and state planning, aiming to uncover new resources and at the same time afford protection and guidance to Spanish-speaking people as they adapt to the new economy.

_____   (248)

***A study of isolation and social change in three Spanish-speaking villages of New Mexico. Unpub. Doctor's thesis, Stanford University, 1938. (D)

> A study of the effect of isolation on social change in Guadalupe, Sandoval, and Alameda. Material gathered largely from direct observation. Contains qualitative descriptions of the social organization of each of the three communities with an evaluation of the degree of disintegration in each and the causes from which disorganization stems. Conclusions: A change in economy may start a train of alterations which may reach the very foundations of a society; assimilation cannot be a rapid process, but it must continue; each society has within itself mechanisms to facilitate adjustment to new cultures; when those mechanisms can be preserved relatively intact, assimilation is relatively painless. The stabilizing mechanisms of the villages studied are in the patron-peon relationships, the church, and the family; and upon the degree to which these institutions can be preserved depends the degree of disorganization that assimilation of these villages into the Anglo culture will bring.

WATKINS, J. H., PITNEY, E. H., AND ABERLE, S. D. B.   (249)

Vital statistics of the Pueblo Indians. American Journal of Public Health, 29:753-60, 1939.

> Population growth, distribution by age and sex, mortality. Source: Indian Service.

WEBB, JOHN N.   (250)

The migratory-casual worker. WPA, Division of Social Research, Research Monograph 7. Washington, GPO, 1937.

> Good discussion of cultural relations aspect of migratory work problem; statistics on migratory-casual workers in New Mexico.

WEBB, JOHN N. AND BROWN, MALCOLM   (251)
Migrant families. WPA, Division of Social Research, Research
Monograph 18. Washington, GPO, 1938.
> Includes statistics on migration to and from New Mexico.

WHITE, LESLIE A.   (252)
Medicine societies of the Southwest. Unpub. Doctor's thesis, University of Chicago, 1926-27.
> Comparison of medicine societies in four areas, with conclusion that flow of influence is from Navajos to Pueblos.

————   (253)
The Pueblo of Santo Domingo. AAA, Memoirs 43. Menasha, Wisconsin, 1935.
> Contains material on social organization, ceremonials, myths and tales, history, attitude towards Anglo culture.

WHITMAN, WILLIAM   (254)
*The San Ildefonso of New Mexico. (In *Seven American Indian Tribes,* edited by Ralph Linton. New York, D. Appleton-Century, 1940.)
> Follows an outline recommended by the sub-committee on acculturation of Social Science Research Council. Conclusion that community is closely integrated doubtful in view of evidence presented. Shows acceptance of Anglo material traits, rise of women to positions of dominance, place of pottery in community life, and the effect of pottery production on economic, social, and political life of the community.

WILFERTH, J. W.   (255)
An economic history of Harding County, New Mexico. Unpub. Master's thesis, New Mexico Normal (Highlands) University, 1933.
> Mainly historical sketches of the communities of Harding County, with information on political organization, economic conditions, and education.

WILLIAMS, MELVILLE C. AND PRICE, HAROLD L.   (256)
Law of the land: 1939. *Land Policy Review,* 2:30-36, July-Aug. 1939.
> Discussion of state land use legislation during the first part of 1939.

WIRIN, A. L.   (257)
Gallup goes to war. *Christian Century,* 52:639-41, 1935.
> Labor and racial discrimination at Gallup.

WOEHLKE, WALTER V.   (258)
Regional planning for Indians and Spanish Americans by the Interdepartmental Rio Grande Board. (In *Indians and the Land.* Contributions by the Delegation of the United States, First Inter-American Conference on Indian Life, Patzcuaro, Mexico, 1940.)

WOODWARD, HUGH B.   (259)
The stake of New Mexico in the waters of the San Juan. *New Mexico Business Review,* 9:127-36, 1940.
> Discussion of problems involved in diverting waters of the San Juan into the Rio Grande.

WYNN, DUDLEY   (260)
The Southwestern regional straddle. *New Mexico Quarterly,* 5:7-14, 1935.
> Criticism of point of view which hopes to preserve both Spanish and Anglo cultures without being realistic about either.

YARD, ROBERT STERLING   (261)
New Mexico aflame against two bills. *Outlook*, 133:124-25, 1923.
Protest against a bill creating a national All Year Park in New Mexico and
against Bursum Bill to legalize claims of white settlers on Indian lands.

YOUNGBLOOD, B.   (262)
Navajo trading. USDI, Office of Indian Affairs, 1935. Processed.
Detailed study of Navajo trading in relation to economy and life, with recom-
mendations for specific revisions of the regulations covering trading with the
Navajos.

ZUNSER, H.   (263)
A New Mexican village. *JAF*, 48:125-78, 1935.
Description of family relationships, attitude towards children, and religion
in Hot Springs.

III
SUPPLEMENTARY BIBLIOGRAPHIES
Bibliographies and Indexes

ALLIOT, HECTOR (264)
Bibliography of Arizona... Los Angeles, Southwest Museum, 1914.
Contains many references to New Mexico.

ANONYMOUS (265)
Bibliography of New Mexican ethnology and ethnography, 1936
and 1937. *New Mexico Anthropologist,* 2:52-62, 1938.

ASHBY, ELEANOR, COMP. (266)
*Spain and Spanish America in the libraries of the University of
California. A catalogue of books. v. 2. The Bancroft Library.*
Berkeley, 1930.

BANCROFT, HUBERT HOWE (267)
Bibliography of early New Mexican history. (In his *History of
Arizona and New Mexico, 1530-1888.* San Francisco, History Co.,
1889. pp. 19-26.)

BLOOM, LANSING B., ED. (268)
*Comprehensive index to New Mexico Historical Review, v. 1-15,
1926-1940.* Albuquerque, Historical Society of New Mexico and
UNM, 1941.

BOGARDUS, EMORY S. (268a)
The Mexican immigrant—an annotated bibliography. Los
Angeles, Council on International Relations, 1929.

BOLTON, HERBERT EUGENE (269)
*Guide to materials for the history of the United States in the
principal archives of Mexico.* Carnegie Institution, Publication
163. Washington, 1913.

CAMPA, ARTHUR L. (270)
A bibliography of Spanish folk-lore in New Mexico. Albuquerque, UNM Bulletin, Language series, v. 2, no. 3, Sept. 1930.

CASTAÑEDA, CARLOS E. AND DABBS, JACK AUTREY (271)
*Guide to the Latin American manuscripts in the University of
Texas library.* American Council of Learned Societies, Com-
mittee on Latin American Studies, Misc. Pub. 1. Cambridge,
Harvard University Press, 1939.
Some New Mexico entries.

CHAPMAN, CHARLES EDWARD (272)
*Catalogue of materials in the Archivo General de Indias for the
history of the Pacific coast and the American Southwest.* University of California Publications in History, v. 8. Berkeley, 1919.

CHAPMAN, KENNETH M., COMP. (273)
*Decorative art of the Indians of the Southwest: a list of publications
containing illustrations from basketry, costumes, and ornaments,
pottery, textiles, etc., of special value in the study of design.* Laboratory of Anthropology, General series, Bulletin 1. Santa Fe, 1934.

COOK, KATHERINE M. AND REYNOLDS, FLORENCE E. (273a)
The education of native and minority groups; a bibliography, 1923-32. USDI, Office of Education, Bulletin 12. Washington, GPO, 1933.

DOBIE, J. FRANK (273b)
Guide to life and literature of the Southwest. Austin, University of Texas Press, 1943.
Selected classified lists of materials dealing with various phases of life in the Southwest, with introductory observations for each classification.

EDWARDS, EVERETT E. (274)
Agriculture of the American Indians; a classified list of annotated historical references. 2nd ed. USDA, Biological Contributions 23. Washington, 1933. Processed.

EDWARDS, EVERETT E. AND RASMUSSEN, WAYNE D., COMPS. (275)
A bibliography on the agriculture of the American Indians. USDA Misc. Pub. 447. Washington, GPO, 1942.

FOIK, PAUL J. (276)
Survey of source materials for the Catholic history of the Southwest. *Catholic Historical Review,* n. s., 9:275-81, 1929.

GADDIS, FANNY WOODHULL (277)
A catalogue of a collection of manuscript documents relative to Southwest history, with an introduction. Unpub. Master's thesis, University of California, 1917.

GAINES, STANLEY H. (278)
Bibliography on soil erosion and soil and water conservation. USDA Misc. Pub. 312. Washington, GPO, 1938.

GRIFFIN, GRACE GARDNER (279)
Writings on American history, 1906, 1907, 1908. New York, Macmillan, 1908, 1909, 1910.

―――― (280)
Writings on American history, 1909, 1910, 1911. (In *Annual Reports* of the American Historical Association. Washington, 1911, 1912, 1913.)

―――― (281)
Writings on American history, 1918, 1919, 1920, 1921, 1922, 1923, 1924, 1925, 1926, 1927, 1928, 1929, 1930, 1931, 1932. Supplements to the *Annual Reports* of the American Historical Association. Washington, 1921, 1922, 1923, 1924, 1925, 1926, 1928, 1929, 1930, 1930, 1932, 1933, 1933, 1936, 1937.

GRIFFIN, GRACE GARDNER, LOURAINE, DOROTHY M., AND TATE, KATHERINE (282)
Writings on American history, 1933, 1934. *Annual Reports* of the American Historical Association. Washington, 1937, 1938.

HARDING, ANNE AND BOLLING, PATRICIA . (283)
Bibliography of articles and papers on North American Indian art. USDI, Indian Arts and Crafts Board. Washington, 1938. Processed.

HERZOG, GEORGE   (284)
Research in primitive and folk music in the United States.
American Council of Learned Societies, Bulletin 24. Washing-
ton, April 1936.
>   Bibliographies and lists of depositories and archives of folk music, including
>   that of the Spanish Americans and Indians of the Southwest.

HISTORICAL SOCIETY OF NEW MEXICO   (285)
*Catalogue of books in English in the library of the Society relating
to New Mexico and the Southwest.* Santa Fe, January 1910.

HODGE, FREDERICK WEBB   (286)
Bibliography of Fray Alonso de Benavides. *Museum of the Ameri-
can Indian, Heye Foundation, Indian Notes and Monographs,* v.
3, no. 1. New York, 1919.

——————   (287)
Biographical sketch and bibliography of A. F. A. Bandelier.
NMHR, 7:353-70, 1932.

HOUGH, VERA A.   (288)
The bibliography of the ethnobiology of the Southwest Indians.
Unpub. Master's thesis, UNM, 1931.

HUSTON, MAY   (289)
What to read on the American Indian; with annotations. *Mission-
ary Review of the World,* 55:461-63, 1932.

JANEWAY, W. RALPH   (289a)
Bibliography of immigration in the United States, 1900-1930.
Columbus, Ohio, H. L. Hedrick, 1934.
>   Includes Mexicans into the Southwest.

JONES, ROBERT C., COMP.   (289b)
Mexicans in the United States—a bibliography. Pan American
Union, Division of Labor and Social Information, Bibliographic
series 27. Washington, Sept. 1942. Processed.

KLUCKHOHN, CLYDE AND SPENCER, KATHERINE   (290)
A bibliography of the Navaho Indians. New York, J. J. Augustin,
1940.

LUCERO-WHITE, AURORA   (291)
Bibliography of Spanish folklore. Unpub. ms. in the files of the
New Mexico Writers' Project, Santa Fe.

LYSER, MRS. ALICE, COMP.   (292)
*Spain and Spanish America in the libraries of the University of
California. A catalogue of books. v 1. The general and depart-
mental libraries.* Berkeley, 1928.

MCKAYE, VARA L.   (293)
*A critical bibliography of certain types of the literature of New
Mexico, 1855-1929.* Unpub. Master's thesis, UNM, 1930.

MCLAUGHLIN, ANDREW C., SLADE, WILLIAM A., AND LEWIS, ERNEST D. (294)
Writings on American history, 1903. Washington, Carnegie Institution, 1905.

MAJOR, MABEL, SMITH, REBECCA, AND PEARCE, T. M.   (295)
Southwest heritage. Albuquerque, UNM Press, 1938.

MARSHALL, THOMAS MAITLAND   (296)
> *A report on certain material for the history of Arizona and New Mexico.* Unpub. Master's thesis, University of California, 1910. (Copy at New Mexico State College Library, Las Cruces.)

MOORE, ROSEBUD   (297)
> *A critical bibliography of Spanish ballads in the Spanish-American oral tradition.* Unpub. Master's thesis, Stanford, 1934-35.

MURDOCK, GEORGE PETER   (298)
> *Ethnographic bibliography of North America.* New Haven, Yale University Press, 1941.

MUSEUM OF THE AMERICAN INDIAN, HEYE FOUNDATION   (299)
> *List of publications of the Museum of the American Indian.* 7th ed. New York, March 1927. 6th ed., May 1926; 5th ed., Sept. 1925; 4th ed., March 1924; 3rd ed., Dec. 1922; 2nd ed., Sept. 1921.

PILLING, JAMES C.   (300)
> *Bibliography of the Athapascan languages.* Bureau of American Ethnology, Bulletin 14. Washington, GPO, 1892.

RAINES, LESTER   (301)
> *More New Mexico writers and writings.* Las Vegas, New Mexico Normal (Highlands) University, 1935. Processed.
>> Includes brief biographical sketches of writers.

————   (302)
> *Writers and writings of New Mexico.* Las Vegas, New Mexico Normal (Highlands) University, Department of English, 1934. Processed.
>> Includes brief biographical sketches of writers.

REED, ERIK K.   (303)
> Bibliography of the archaeology of the Jemez Mountain area. *Boletin bibliografico de antropologia americana,* 3:16-21, 1939.

————   (304)
> Bibliography of the Mimbres Valley and Mogollon culture. *Boletin bibliografico de antropologia americana,* 3:125-33, 1939.

RICHARDSON, ERNEST C. AND MORSE, ANSON ELY   (305)
> *Writings on American history, 1902.* Princeton, Princeton University Press, 1904.

RIVET, PAUL   (306)
> Bibliographie americaniste. *Societe des americanistes de Paris, Journal,* n. s., 11:677-739, 1919; 12:287-331, 1920; 13:149-68, 365-404, 1921; 14:263-96, 1922; 15:353-443, 1923; 16:461-546, 1924; 17:383-503, 1925; 18:399-531, 1926; 19:439-554, 1927.
>> History, ethnology, anthropology, and archaeology.

ROBERTSON, JAMES ALEXANDER   (307)
> *List of documents in Spanish archives relating to the history of the United States which have been printed or of which transcripts are preserved in American libraries. . .* Carnegie Institution, Publication 124. Washington, 1910.

SAUNDERS, LYLE   (307a)
> A guide to the literature of the Southwest. *New Mexico Quarterly Review,* 12:247-53, 372-79, 499-507, 1942; 13:243-255, 1943.
>> A listing of current book and periodical literature dealing with the Southwest. Reprints available at School of Inter-American Affairs, UNM.

SCHOLES, FRANCE V.   (308)
    Manuscripts for the history of New Mexico in the National Library
    of Mexico City. *NMHR*, 3:301-23, 1928.

SHEPHERD, WILLIAM ROBERT   (309)
    Guide to the materials for the history of the United States in
    Spanish archives. Carnegie Institution, Publication 91. Washing-
    ton, 1907.

TUCKER, MARY   (310)
    Books of the Southwest; a general bibliography. New York, J. J.
    Augustin, n. d.
        Includes mostly popular and well known material.

TWITCHELL, RALPH EMERSON   (311)
    Reports, documents . . . published by the United States govern-
    ment relating to New Mexico 1847-74. *EP*, 7:159-67, 1919.

———   (312)
    The Spanish archives of New Mexico; annotated and chronologi-
    cally arranged with historical, geneological, geographical, and
    other annotations. . . 2 v. Cedar Rapids, Torch Press, 1914.

USDA, BAE   (313)
    Agricultural economics bibliographies. Washington. Processed.
        Seventy-nine numbers have so far been issued in the series.

———, FOREST SERVICE   (314)
    A selected bibliography on the economics of forestry in the United
    States. Washington, October 1941. Processed.

USDI, GEOLOGICAL SURVEY   (315)
    Publications of the Geological Survey. Washington, GPO, 1942.
        Includes a listing of all geological survey materials on New Mexico—water
        supply, mineral resources, floods, etc.

———, NATIONAL PARK SERVICE   (316)
    A bibliography of national parks and monuments west of the
    Mississippi River. v. 2. Compiled at the Western Museum
    Laboratories of the National Park Service in cooperation with
    WPA and CCC. USDI, National Park Service, 1941. Processed.

USDI, OFFICE OF INDIAN AFFAIRS   (317)
    American Indian legends. Phoenix, Native American Press, 1930.

———, ———   (318)
    Indian arts and industries. Chilocco, Indian Print Shop, 1927.

———, ———   (319)
    Indian music. Chilocco, Indian Print Shop, 1928.

VAN VALKENBURGH, RICHARD F.   (320)
    Bibliography of Navajo agriculture and irrigation. USDI, Office
    of Indian Affairs, Navajo Service. Window Rock, Arizona, 1938.
    Processed.

VOEGELIN, C. F.   (321)
    Bibliography of American Indian linguistics, 1938-41. *Language*,
    18:133-39, 1942.

WAGNER, HENRY R.   (322)
    The plains and the Rockies; a bibliography of original narratives

WAGNER, HENRY R. (Continued)
of travel and adventure, 1800-1865. San Francisco, Grabhorn Press, 1937.

_____ (323)
The Spanish Southwest, 1542-1794. An annotated bibliography. Berkeley, J. J. Gillick, 1924. Same title, 2 v. Albuquerque, Quivira Society, 1937.

WINTHER, OSCAR OSBURN (323a)
The trans-Mississippi West: a guide to its periodical literature (1811-1938). Indiana University Publications, Social Science series, no. 3. Bloomington, 1942.

Pre-Spanish Period

ALEXANDER, HARTLEY B. (324)
The Pecos bull. *EP,* 39:121-24, 1935.

ALEXANDER, HUBERT G. (325)
The excavation of Jemez cave. Preliminary report. *EP,* 38:97-108, 1935.

ALEXANDER, HUBERT G. AND REITER, PAUL (326)
Report on the excavation of Jemez cave, New Mexico. UNM Bulletin, Monograph series, v. 1, no. 3, 1935.

AMERICAN SCENIC AND HISTORICAL PRESERVATION SOCIETY (327)
Aztec ruin, New Mexico, explored. *23rd Annual Report, 1918.* pp. 377-78.

_____ (328)
New discoveries in Zuni land; a Pueblo a thousand years old. *23rd Annual Report, 1918.* pp. 374-75.

AMSDEN, CHARLES A. (329)
The ancient basketmakers. Southwest Museum Leaflets 11. Los Angeles, 1939.
    San Juan region.

ANDERSON, ROBERT E. (330)
The story of extinct civilizations of the West. New York, D. Appleton, 1904.

ANONYMOUS (331)
Chettro Ketl still a riddle. *EP,* 31:29-37, 1931.

_____ (332)
Excavations at Chetro Ketl. *EP,* 33:13-20, 1932.

_____ (333)
Excavations at Tunque. *EP,* 34:193-96, 1933.

_____ (334)
The first American apartment house. *Literary Digest,* 64: 93, Jan. 3, 1920.
    Aztec ruin.

_____ (335)
Mimbres ruins, excavated by Bradfield, give clues to ancient Basket Makers. *EP,* 16:153-57, 1924.

ANONYMOUS (Continued)   (336)
    Notes on the Mimbres culture. *EP*, 12:62-63, 1922.

                                                                  (337)
    Prehistoric peoples of the Southwest. *Overland*, n. s., 52:468-71,
    1908.

                                                                  (338)
    Prehistoric pueblo Indian ruin. *Science*, n. s., 47:309-10, 1918.
        Aztec.

                                                                  (339)
    Preliminary report on the Tecolote ruin. *EP*, 34:196-98, 1933.

                                                                  (340)
    Recent finds in Chaco Canyon. *EP*, 23:485-87, 1927.

                                                                  (341)
    The story of Pecos. *EP*, 18:69-73, 1925.

ANTON Y FERRANDIZ, MANUEL   (342)
    *Antropologia de los pueblos de America anteriores al descu-
    brimiento; conferencia de D. Manuel Anton, pronunciada el dia
    19 de Mayo de 1891*. Madrid, Estab. tip. "Sucesores de Rivade-
    neyra," 1892.

ARNOLD, CHARLOTTE   (343)
    Where the mountain lions are resting. *EP*, 24:314-17, 1928.
        Stone lions of Cochiti.

ARNOLD, OREN   (344)
    A vanished empire of the Southwest. *Travel*, 58:25-29, 45, Nov.
    1931.

BANCROFT, HUBERT HOWE   (345)
    Antiquities of Arizona and New Mexico. (In *Antiquities*, v. 4 of
    The Works of H. H. Bancroft. San Francisco, A. L. Bancroft &
    Co., 1883.)

BANDELIER, ADOLPH F. A.   (346)
    *Hemenway Southwestern archaeological expedition. Contri-
    butions to the history of the Southwestern portion of the United
    States.* AIA, American series, v. 5. Cambridge, John Wilson &
    Son, 1890.

                                                                  (347)
    A report on the ruins of the Pueblo of Pecos. Papers of the AIA.
    Boston, A. Williams & Co., 1881.

BARBER, EDWIN A.   (348)
    The ancient pottery of Colorado, Utah, Arizona, and New Mexico.
    American Naturalist, 10:449-64, 1876.

                                                                  (349)
    Rock inscriptions of the 'Ancient Pueblos' of Colorado, Utah, New
    Mexico, and Arizona. *American Naturalist*, 10:716-25, 1876.

BARNES, WILL C.   (350)
    The prehistoric corn belt. *American Forestry*, 33:604-07, Oct.
    1927.

BARTLETT, KATHARINE (351)
Prehistoric Pueblo foods. *Museum of Northern Arizona, Museum Notes,* 4:1-4, Oct. 1931.

――――― (352)
A unique Pueblo II bird fetish. *AA,* 34:315-19, 1932.

――――― (353)
The utilization of maize among the ancient pueblos. (In Brand, Donald D., Ed: *Symposium on prehistoric agriculture.* UNM Bulletin, Anthropological series, v. 1, no. 5, 1936. pp. 29-34.)

――――― (354)
Why the Navajos came to Arizona. *Museum of Northern Arizona, Museum Notes,* 5:29-32, Dec. 1932.

BASTIAN, ADOLPH (355)
Die Culturlander des alten America . . . Berlin, Weidmannsche Buchhandlung, 1878-89. 3v. in 2.

BAUM, HENRY M. (356)
Pueblo and cliff dwellers of the Southwest. *Records of the Past,* 1:356-61, 1902.

BEAM, GEORGE L. (357)
Prehistoric ruin of Tsankawi. *National Geographic,* 20:807-22, 1909.

BEUCHAT, HENRI (358)
Manuel d'archeologie americaine. . . Paris, A. Picard, 1912.

BIERBOWER, S. (359)
Among the cliff and cavate dwellings of New Mexico. *Records of the Past,* 4:227-33, 1905.

BLAKE, W. P. (360)
Aboriginal turquoise mining in Arizona and New Mexico. *American Antiquarian,* 21:278-84, 1899.

――――― (361)
Racial unity of the historic and prehistoric aboriginal people of Arizona and New Mexico. *ICA, Proceedings,* 13:203-04, 1902.

BLISS, WESLEY L. (362)
A chronological problem presented by Sandia Cave, New Mexico. *American Antiquity,* 5:200-01, 1940.

BLOOM, LANSING B. (363)
The emergence of Chaco Canyon in history. *A&A,* 11:29-35, Jan. 1921.

――――― (364)
The west Jemez culture area. *EP,* 12:19-25, 1922.

BLOOM, LANSING B., BRADFIELD, WESLEY, AND CHAPMAN, KENNETH (365)
A preliminary survey of the archaeology of southwestern New Mexico. *EP,* 24:99-112, 1928.

BOWERS, GEORGE BALLARD (366)
The first farmers in America. *SW,* 59:74-82, Feb. 1930.
Cliff dwellers of the Southwest.

BRADFIELD, WESLEY   (367)
Cameron Creek Village, a site in the Mimbres area.   Santa Fe,
School of American Research, 1931.

——————   (368)
Economic resources of Chaco Canyon. *A&A*, 11:36-38, Jan. 1921.

——————   (369)
Excavations in the Sacramentos. *EP*, 27:3-6, 1929.

——————   (370)
Mimbres excavations in 1928. *EP*, 25:151-60, 1928.

——————   (371)
Preliminary report on excavating at Cameron Creek site. *EP*,
15:67-73, 1923.

——————   (372)
Summary of work on Cameron Creek site, Mimbres section. *EP*,
15:53-54, 1923.

BRAND, DONALD D.   (373)
Aboriginal trade routes for sea shells in the Southwest. *Yearbook
of the Association of Pacific Coast Geographers*, v. 4. Cheney,
Washington, 1938. pp. 3-10.

——————   (374)
The bison nomads. *NM*, 15:18-19, 37-38, March 1937.
     Evidence supporting belief that New Mexico was inhabited some ten
     thousand years ago.

——————   (375)
Prehistoric trade in the Southwest. *New Mexico Business Review*,
4:202-09, 1935.

BRAND, DONALD D., ED.   (376)
Symposium on prehistoric agriculture.   UNM Bulletin, Anthropological series, v. 1, no. 5, Oct. 1936.

BRAND, DONALD D., HAWLEY, FLORENCE M., HIBBEN, FRANK C., AND OTHERS
                                                                    (377)
Tseh So, a small house ruin Chaco Canyon, New Mexico.   UNM
Bulletin, Anthropological series, v. 2, no. 2, June 1937.

BRYAN, BRUCE   (378)
Excavation of the Galaz ruin, Mimbres Valley, New Mexico.
A&A, 32:35-42, 1931. *Also Masterkey*, 4:179-89, 221-26, 1931.

——————   (379)
The Galaz ruin in the Mimbres Valley. *EP*, 23:323-37, 1927.

BRYAN, FRANK   (380)
A review of the geology of the Clovis finds reported by Howard
and Cotter. *American Antiquity*, 4:113-30, Oct. 1938.

BRYAN, KIRK   (381)
Pre-Columbian agriculture in the Southwest, as conditioned by
periods of alluviation. *Annals of the Association of American
Geographers*, 31:219-42, 1941.

BRYAN, KIRK AND TOULOUSE, JOSEPH H., JR.   (381a)
The San Jose non-ceramic culture and its relation to a puebloan
culture in New Mexico. *American Antiquity*, 8:269-80, Jan. 1943.

BRYAN, W. A. (382)
The recent bone-cavern find at Bishop's Cap, New Mexico. *Science*, 70: 39-41, 1929.

BULLENE, EMMA F. JAY (383)
The psychic history of the cliff dwellers: their origin and destruction. Denver, Reed Pub. Co., 1905.
> Conclusion that cliff dwellers were Vikings reached as the result of psychical revelations.

BURNET, R. M. (384)
Antiquity of man in the Pecos Valley of New Mexico. *NM*, 11:24-25, 61, July 1933.

———— (385)
Recent skeletal find near Portales. *EP*, 44:80-84, 1938.

BUTMAN, CARL HAWES (386)
Stone records of the history of New Mexico. . . *Scientific American Supplement*, 74:388-89, 1912.

BYERS, D. S. (387)
Concerning Sandia Cave. *American Antiquity*, 7:408-09, 1942.

CAHILL, E. H. (388)
America has its "primitives". *EP*, 12:127-30, 1922.

CASSIDY, LOUISE LOWBER (389)
America's aboriginal corn belt. . . *Wallace's Farmer*, 51:1471, 81, Nov. 1926.
> Pueblo Indians were corn growers five thousand years ago.

CHAPIN, FREDERICK H. (390)
The land of the cliff dwellers. Boston, W. B. Clarke, 1892.

CHAPMAN, KENNETH M. (391)
An archaeological site in the Jornada del Muerto, New Mexico. *EP*, 20:118-22, March 1926.

———— (392)
The cave pictographs of the Rito de los Frijoles, New Mexico. *EP*, 4 (1) :29-31, 1917.

———— (393)
A feather symbol of the ancient Pueblos. *EP*, 23:526-40, 1927.

———— (394)
Stone wall construction in ancient Pueblos and cliff dwellings. *EP*, 23:479-85, 1927.

CHITTENDEN, NEWTON H. (395)
Pre-historic rock paintings, etchings, and pictographs in California, Arizona, and New Mexico. *Overland*, n. s., 42:106-10, 1903.

COLTON, HAROLD SELLERS (396)
Prehistoric trade in the Southwest. *Scientific Monthly*, 52:308-19, 1941.

———— (396a)
Reconstruction of Anasazi history. *American Philosophical Society, Proceedings*, 86:264-69, Feb. 10, 1943.

COOK, HAROLD J.   (397)
    Glacial age man in New Mexico. *Scientific American,* 139:38-40,
    July 1928.
        Folsom man.

——   (398)

    New geological and paleontological evidence bearing on the
    antiquity of mankind in America. *NH,* 27:240-47, 1927.
        Folsom man.

COSGROVE, C. B.   (399)
    Two kivas at Treasure Hill. *EP,* 15:19-21, 1923.

COSGROVE, HARRIET SILLIMAN AND CORNELIUS BERTON   (400)
    *The Swarts ruin; a typical Mimbres site in southwestern New
    Mexico.* Peabody Museum of American Archaeology and Eth-
    nology, Papers, v. 15, no. 1. Cambridge, 1932.

COWAN, JOHN L.   (401)
    Prehistoric apartment houses of the Southwest. *Overland,* n. s.,
    55:340-46, 1910.
        New Mexico cliff dwellers.

CRAWFORD, ROBERT P.   (402)
    America's mystery land. *Mentor,* 13:1-14, Aug. 1925.

CRIMMINS, M. L.   (403)
    Petroglyphs, pictographs and diffusion of primitive culture.
    A&A, 21:297-98, 1926.
        Chronology and migration of primitive cultures in the Southwest traced
        through petroglyphs found on a ranch at Three Rivers, New Mexico.

CUMMINGS, BYRON S.   (404)
    The ancient inhabitants of the San Juan Valley. University of
    Utah, Bulletin v. 3, no. 3. Salt Lake City, 1910.

DAVIS, EMILY CLEVELAND   (405)
    Ancient Americans: the archaeological story of two continents.
    New York, Holt, 1931.
        Contains some material on agriculture of the Pueblos.

——   (406)

    Dating the Rio Grande Pueblos. *EP,* 33:127-28, 1932.
        Tree ring calendar.

DOUGLASS, ANDREW ELLICOTT   (407)
    Dating Pueblo Bonito and other ruins of the Southwest. National
    Geographic Society, Pueblo Bonito series 1. Washington, 1935.

DOUGLASS, WILLIAM BOONE   (408)
    The land of the small house people. *EP,* 4 (2) :3-23, 1917.
        Forerunners of modern Pueblos.

——   (409)

    The shrines of the small house people. *EP,* 4 (3) :17-29, 1917.

DUFF, U. FRANCIS   (410)
    The prehistoric ruins of the Rio Tularosa. *Journal of American
    Geographical Society,* 29:261-70, 1897.

——   (411)

    Some exploded theories concerning Southwestern archaeology.
    AA, 6:303-06, 1904.

DUTTON, BERTHA P. (412)
Leyit Kin; a small house ruin, Chaco Canyon, New Mexico. Unpub. Master's thesis, UNM, 1937. *Also* UNM Bulletin, Monograph series, v. 1, no. 6, 1938.

EASTWOOD, ALICE (413)
Notes on the cliff dwellers. *Zoe*, 3:375-76, 1893.

EATON, THEODORE H., JR. (414)
Prehistoric man in the Navajo country. Berkeley, NYA, 1937.

ENOCK, C. REGINALD (415)
The cliff dwellers. (In his *The Secret of the Pacific.* New York, Scribners, 1912.)

ERWIN, A. T. (416)
A rare specimen of Zea Mays, var. Saccharta. *Science*, n. s., 79:589, June 29, 1934.
From Aztec ruin.

FEWKES, J. WALTER (417)
Ancient Pueblo and Mexican water symbol. *AA*, 6:535-38, 1904.

———— (418)
Ancient Zuni pottery. *Putnam Anniversary Volume.* New York, G. E. Stechert, 1909. pp. 43-82.

———— (419)
Animal figures on prehistoric pottery from Mimbres Valley, New Mexico. *AA*, 18:535-45, 1916.

———— (420)
Archaeological investigations in New Mexico, Colorado, and Utah. *Smithsonian Miscellaneous Collections*, v. 68, no. 1. Washington, 1917.

———— (421)
Archaeology of the lower Mimbres Valley, New Mexico. *Smithsonian Miscellaneous Collections*, 63 (10):1-53, 1914.

———— (422)
The cave dwellings of the old and the new worlds. *Smithsonian Annual Report, 1910.* Washington, 1911. pp. 613-34.

———— (423)
Designs on prehistoric pottery from the Mimbres Valley. *EP*, 15:9-13, 1923.

———— (424)
Designs on prehistoric pottery from the Mimbres Valley, New Mexico. *Smithsonian Miscellaneous Collections*, 74 (6):1-47, 1925.

———— (425)
Two types of Southwestern cliff houses. *Smithsonian Annual Report, 1919.* Washington, 1921. pp. 421-26.

FISHER, REGINALD (426)
Some geographic factors that influenced the ancient populations of the Chaco Canyon, New Mexico. A preliminary report. UNM Bulletin, Anthropological series, v. 3, no. 1. May 1934.

FOSSNOCK, ANNETTE   (427)
Pictographs and murals in the Southwest. *EP*, 39:81-90, 1935.

GAILLARD, D. D.   (428)
A gigantic earthwork in New Mexico. *AA*, o. s., 9:311-14, 1896.
Description of a prehistoric dam in the Animas Valley, Grant County.

GALLATIN, A.   (429)
Ancient semi-civilization of New Mexico, Rio Gila and its vicinity.
American Ethnological Society, Transactions II. New York, 1848.

GLADWIN, HAROLD S.   (430)
An outline of Southwestern pre-history. *Arizona Historical Review*, 3:71-87, 1930.

GRIFFIN, JEAN   (431)
Sanctuaries of the sun. *NM*, 11:20-21, 61, July 1933.
Chaco civilization.

GUTHE, CARL E.   (432)
The Pueblo ruin at Rowe, New Mexico. *EP*, 4 (4) :33-39, 1917.

HAAS, WILLIAM H.   (433)
The cliff dweller and his habitat. *Annals of the Association of American Geographers*, 16:167-215, 1926.

HALES, HENRY   (434)
Prehistoric New Mexican pottery. *Smithsonian Annual Report, 1892*. Washington, 1893. pp. 535-54.

HAMILTON, J. B.   (435)
Ancient American system for collecting water supply. *Engineering News-Record*, 110:225, Feb. 16, 1933.
Near Pueblo Bonito.

HARDACRE, EMMA C.   (436)
The cliff dwellers. *Scribner's*, 17:266-76, 1878.
Mentions Chaco Canyon, Chetro Ketl, Pueblo Bonito.

HARRINGTON, JOHN P.   (437)
Housebuilders of the desert. *A&A*, 4:299-306, 1916.
Indians of Rito de los Frijoles.

——————   (438)
Notes on the Piro language. *AA*, 11:563-94, 1909. *Also* AIA, School of American Archaeology, Papers 8. 1909.

HARRINGTON, MARK RAYMOND   (439)
Western extension of early Pueblo culture. *EP*, 20:227-31, 1926.

HAURY, EMIL W.   (440)
The age of lead glaze decorated pottery in the Southwest. *AA*, 34:418-25, 1932.

——————   (441)
Legged vessels from the Southwest. *American Antiquity*, 3:264-65, 1938.

——————   (442)
The Mogollon culture of southwestern New Mexico. Gila Pueblo. Medallion Papers 20. Globe, Arizona, 1936.

HAURY, EMIL W. (Continued)   (443)
Tree rings—the archaeologist's time-piece. *American Antiquity,*
1:98-108, Oct. 1935.
    Mentions Chetro Ketl.

HAWLEY, FLORENCE M.   (444)
The family tree of Chaco Canyon masonry. *American Antiquity,*
3:247-55, Jan. 1938.

——   (445)
Field manual of prehistoric Southwestern pottery types. UNM
Bulletin, Anthropological series, v. 1, no. 4, 1936.

——   (446)
Kokopelli, of the prehistoric Southwestern Pueblo pantheon. *AA,*
39:644-46, 1937.
    Attempt to discover significance of Kokopelli figure in Pueblo religion.

——   (447)
Prehistoric pottery pigments in the Southwest. *AA,* 31:731-54,
1929.

——   (448)
*The significance of the dated prehistory of Chetro Ketl, Chaco
Canyon, New Mexico.* Published jointly by School of American
Research and UNM. UNM Bulletin, Monograph series, v. 1, no.
1, 1934.

HAYWOOD, HELEN   (449)
El Rito de los Frijoles. *NM,* 11:24-25, 44, Nov. 1933.

HENDRY, G. W. AND BELLUE, M. K.   (450)
An approach to Southwestern agricultural history through adobe
brick analysis. (In Brand, Donald D., Ed.: *Symposium on prehistoric agriculture.* UNM Bulletin, Anthropological series, v. 1,
no. 5, 1936.)

HEWETT, EDGAR L.   (451)
Antiquities of the Jemez Plateau, New Mexico. Bureau of American Ethnology, Bulletin 32. Washington, GPO, 1906.

——   (452)
Archaeological resources of New Mexico. *EP,* 40:133-39, 1936.

——   (453)
Archaeology in the making. *EP,* 26:310-12, 1929.
    Sandia Pueblo as an example of the archaeological process.

——   (454)
Archaeology of Pajarita Park, New Mexico. *AA,* 6:629-59, 1904.

——   (455)
Archaeology of the Rio Grande Valley. *Out West,* 31:693-719,
1909.

——   (456)
The archaeology of the Southwest. *EP,* 20:78-82, 92, 93, 1926.

——   (457)
The Chaco Canyon and its monuments. Albuquerque, UNM
Press, 1936.

HEWETT, EDGAR L. (Continued)   (458)
   The excavation in Chaco Canyon, New Mexico. *EP*, 32:255-57,
   1932.

—————   (459)
   The excavations at El Rito de los Frijoles in 1909. *AA*, 11:651-73,
   1909. *Also* AIA, School of American Archaeology, Papers 10.
   1909.

—————   (460)
   Excavations at Puye in 1907. AIA, School of American Archaeology, Papers 4. 1908.

—————   (461)
   Excavations at Tyuonyi, New Mexico. *AA*, 11:434-55, 1909. *Also*
   AIA, School of American Archaeology, Papers 5. 1909.

—————   (462)
   A general view of the archaeology of the Pueblo region. *Smithsonian Annual Report, 1904*. Washington, 1905. pp. 583-605.

—————   (463)
   Les communautes anciennes dans le desert Americain. Geneve,
   Librairie Kundig, 1908.

—————   (464)
   New dates from Chaco Canyon. *EP*, 32:185-86, 1932.

—————   (465)
   The Pajaritan culture. AIA, School of American Archaeology,
   Papers 3. 1909.

—————   (466)
   Pre-hispanic frescoes in the Rio Grande Valley. AIA, School of
   American Research, Papers, n. s. 27. 1938.

—————   (467)
   Prehistoric irrigation in the Navaho desert. *Records of the Past*,
   4:323-29, 1905.

—————   (468)
   Studies on the extinct Pueblo of Pecos. *AA*, 6:426-39, 1904.

HEWETT, EDGAR L. AND TWITCHELL, R. E.   (469)
   Historic background. *A&A*, 18:195-202, 1924.
       Ancient Santa Fe.

HIBBEN, FRANK C.   (470)
   Association of man with pleistocene mammals in the Sandia
   Mountains, New Mexico. *American Antiquity*, 2:260-63, 1937.

—————   (471)
   A cache of wooden bows from the Mogollon Mountains. *American Antiquity*, 4:36-38, 1938.

—————   (471a)
   Discoveries in Sandia Cave and early horizons in the Southwest.
   American Philosophical Society, Proceedings, 86:247-54, Feb. 10,
   1943.

HIBBEN, FRANK C. (Continued) (472)

Evidences of early occupation in Sandia Cave, New Mexico and other sites in the Sandia-Manzano region. *Smithsonian Miscellaneous Collections*, v. 99, no. 23, 1941.

—— (473)

The excavation of a pre-biscuit ware ruin in the Chama Valley. *EP*, 41:48-53, 1936.

—— (474)

Excavation of the Riana ruin and Chama Valley survey. UNM Bulletin, Anthropological series, v. 2, no. 1, Jan. 1937.

—— (475)

The Gallina culture of north central New Mexico. Unpub. Doctor's dissertation, Harvard, 1940.

—— (476)

The Gallina phase. *American Antiquity*, 4:131-36, 1938.

—— (477)

Pleistocene stratification in the Sandia Cave, New Mexico. *Proceedings of the Eighth American Scientific Congress*, v. 2. U. S. Department of State. Washington, 1942.

—— (478)

Sandia man; artifacts found in basal layers of a cave. *Scientific American*, 163:14-15, July 1940.

HIGGINSON, THOMAS WENTWORTH (479)

The first Americans. *Harpers*, 65:342-55, 1882.
Pueblos.

HILTON, GRACE (480)

The castles of the Chama. *EP*, 5:51-55, 1918.
Description of area from Cumbres Pass to the Chama river.

HISTORICAL SOCIETY OF NEW MEXICO (481)

The stone idols of New Mexico. Historical Society of New Mexico, Publication 3. Santa Fe, 1896.
Description of idols belonging to the Society.

HODGE, FREDERICK WEBB (482)

Circular kivas near Hawikuh, New Mexico. *Museum of the American Indian, Heye Foundation, Contributions*, 7:9-37, 1923.

—— (483)

Excavations at the Zuni pueblo of Hawikuh in 1917. *A&A*, 7:367-79, 1918.

—— (484)

Hawikuh bonework. *Museum of the American Indian, Heye Foundation, Indian Notes and Monographs*, v. 3, no. 3. New York, 1920.

—— (485)

History of Hawikuh, New Mexico, one of the so-called cities of Cibola. Los Angeles, Southwest Museum, 1937.

HODGE, FREDERICK WEBB (Continued)   (486)
Pottery of Hawikuh. *Museum of the American Indian, Heye
Foundation, Indian Notes,* 1:8-15, 1924.

––––––   (487)
Recent excavations at Hawikuh. *EP,* 12:3-11, 1922.

––––––   (488)
Snake pens at Hawikuh. *Museum of the American Indian, Heye
Foundation, Indian Notes,* 1:111-19, 1924.

––––––   (489)
The turquoise work of Hawikuh, New Mexico. Museum of the
American Indian, Heye Foundation, Leaflet 2. New York, 1921.

HOFFMAN, FREDERICK L.   (490)
Why the cliff-dwellers vanished. *Scientific American,* 123:630,
641-42, 1920.

HOLMES, W. H.   (491)
Notes on the antiquities of Jemez Valley, New Mexico. *AA,*
7:198-212, 1905.

––––––   (492)
Pottery of the ancient Pueblos. *Bureau of American Ethnology,
4th Annual Report.* Washington, GPO, 1886.

––––––   (493)
The textile art in prehistoric archaeology. *American Antiquarian,*
8:261-66, 1886.

HOLMQUIST, ADELA   (494)
The prehistoric Southwest. *EP,* 15:35-39, 1923.

HOOTON, EARNEST ALBERT   (495)
Indians of Pecos; a study of their skeletal remains. New Haven,
Yale University Press, 1930.

HOUGH, WALTER   (496)
Ancient Pueblo subsistence. *ICA, Proceedings,* 23:67-69, 1928.

––––––   (497)
*Antiquities of the upper Gila and Salt River valleys in Arizona and
New Mexico.* Bureau of American Ethnology, Bulletin 35.
Washington, GPO, 1907.

––––––   (498)
The cliff dweller housekeeper. *American Indian Magazine,* 7:6-
10, Aug. 1920.

––––––   (499)
*Culture of the ancient Pueblos of the upper Gila River region,
New Mexico and Arizona.* United States National Museum,
Bulletin 87. Washington, GPO, 1914.

––––––   (500)
Exploration of a pit house village at Luna, New Mexico. *United
States National Museum, Proceedings,* 55:409-31, 1920.

––––––   (501)
The lead glaze decorated pottery of the Pueblo region. *AA,*
30:243-49, 1928.

HOWARD EDGAR B. (502)
The Clovis finds are not two million years old. *American Antiquity*, 5:43-51, 1939.

―――― (503)
Evidence of early man in America. *University of Pennsylvania, Museum Journal*, v. 24, nos. 2 and 3. Philadelphia, 1935.

―――― (504)
Evidence of early man in North America, based on geological and archaeological work in New Mexico. Unpub. Doctor's thesis, University of Pennsylvania, 1935.

HURST, C. T. (505)
Some interesting Mimbres bowls. *EP*, 40:37-41, 1936.

INMAN, HENRY (506)
The ruins on the Rio Pecos in New Mexico. Unpub. ms. in possession of H. C. Revercomb, Kansas City, Kansas.

JEANCON, JEAN ALLARD (507)
Archaeological investigations in the Taos Valley, New Mexico during 1920. *Smithsonian Miscellaneous Collections*, v. 81, no. 12. Washington, 1929.

―――― (508)
The Dulce ruin. *EP*, 27:161-74, 1929.

―――― (509)
Excavations in the Chama Valley, New Mexico. Bureau of American Ethnology, Bulletin 81. Washington, GPO, 1923.

―――― (510)
Explorations in Chama basin, New Mexico. *Records of the Past*, 10:92-108, 1911.

―――― (511)
Preliminary report of the excavations at Po Shu Onige, near Abiquiu. *EP*, 7:67-69, 1919.

JENKS, ALBERT ERNEST (512)
Architectural plans of geometric art on Mimbres bowls. *EP*, 33:21-64, 1932.

―――― (513)
Geometric designs on Mimbres bowls. *A&A*, 33:137-39, 1932.

―――― (514)
The significance of mended bowls in Mimbres culture. *EP*, 31:153-72, 1931.

JENNESS, DIAMOND, ED. (515)
The American aborigines, their origin and antiquity. A collection of papers by ten authors. Fifth Pacific Science Congress. Toronto, University of Toronto Press, 1933.

JUDD, NEIL MERTON (516)
Architectural evolution of Pueblo Bonito. *National Academy of Science, Proceedings*, 13:561-63, 1927.

JUDD, NEIL MERTON (Continued)   (517)
   Everyday life in Pueblo Bonito. *National Geographic Magazine*,
   48:227-62, 1925.

_____   (518)
   Prehistoric Pueblo Bonito, New Mexico. *Smithsonian Explorations and Field Work, 1927*. Washington, 1928. pp. 141-48.

_____   (519)
   Progress in the Southwest. *Smithsonian Miscellaneous Collections,*
   100. Washington, 1940. pp. 417-44.
      Statement of viewpoint that Southwestern anthropology has advanced more
      in last twenty years than ever before.

_____   (520)
   Two Chaco Canyon pit houses. *Smithsonian Annual Report,
   1922*. Washington, 1924. pp. 399-413.

_____   (521)
   The use of adobe in prehistoric dwellings of the Southwest.
   Holmes Anniversary Volume. Washington, J. W. Bryan Press,
   1916. pp. 241-52.

JULIAN, HURST R.   (522)
   Valley of the ancient Pueblos—Chaco Canyon—El Pueblo Bonito.
   NM, 11:7-9, 49-50, Oct. 1933.

KIDDER, ALFRED VINCENT   (523)
   The artifacts of Pecos. New Haven, Yale University Press, 1932.

_____   (524)
   The condition of the main Pecos ruin. *EP*, 4(1):18-21, 1917.

_____   (525)
   A design sequence from New Mexico. *National Academy of
   Science, Proceedings*, 3:369-70, 1917.

_____   (526)
   Early Pecos ruins on the Forked Lightning Ranch. *EP*, 21:275-
   83, 1926.

_____   (527)
   *An introduction to Southwestern archaeology with a preliminary
   account of the excavations at Pecos*. New Haven, Yale University
   Press, 1924.

_____   (528)
   The old North Pueblo of Pecos. *EP*, 4(1):13-17, 1917. *Also*
   AIA, School of American Archaeology, Papers 38. 1917.

_____   (529)
   A pipe of unique form from Pecos, New Mexico. *Museum of the
   American Indian, Heye Foundation, Indian Notes*, 5:293-95, 1928.

_____   (530)
   Pottery of the Pajarito plateau and of some adjacent regions in
   New Mexico. *AAA, Memoirs*, 2:407-61, 1907-15.

_____   (531)
   Prehistoric cultures of the San Juan drainage. *ICA, Proceedings*,
   19:108-13, 1917.

KIDDER, ALFRED VINCENT (Continued) (532)
The Pueblo of Pecos. *EP,* 3:43-49, 1916.

———— (533)
Ruins of the historic period in the upper San Juan Valley, New Mexico. *AA,* 22:322-29, 1920.

KIDDER, ALFRED VINCENT AND AMSDEN, CHARLES A. (534)
The pottery of Pecos. v. 1. Phillips Academy, Papers of the Southwest Expedition v. 5, 1931.

KIDDER, ALFRED VINCENT AND SHEPARD, ANNA (535)
The pottery of Pecos. v. 2. Phillips Academy, Papers of the Southwest Expedition, v. 7, 1936.

KIDDER, M. A. AND ALFRED VINCENT (536)
Notes on the pottery of Pecos. *AA,* 19:325-60, 1917.

KINNEY, CLESSON S. (537)
History of ancient irrigation in various countries. *Irrigation Age,* 33:86-89, May 1918.
    Includes material on early Indian irrigation in the Southwest.

KLUCKHOHN, CLYDE AND REITER, PAUL, EDS. (538)
Preliminary report on the 1937 excavations, Bc 50-51, Chaco Canyon, New Mexico. UNM Bulletin, Anthropological series, v. 3, no. 2, Oct. 1939.

LANGLOIS, LOUIS (539)
Les fouilles du Pueblo Bonito en 1922. *Geographie,* 41:199-200, 1924.

LAW, GEORGE WARRINGTON (540)
Ancient houses of the cliffs. *NM,* 11:12-13, 49, March 1933.
    Rito de los Frijoles.

LUCAS, F. A. (541)
A dog of the ancient Pueblos. *Science,* n.s., 5:544, 1897.

LUHRS, DOROTHY (542)
Identification and distribution of ceramic types in Rio Puerco area. Unpub. Master's thesis, UNM, 1937.

LYON, W. B. (543)
Antiquities in New Mexico. *Smithsonian Annual Report, 1871.* Washington, 1873. pp. 403-04.

MCCALL, MARION BOLANDER (544)
The archaeological station at Chaco Canyon, New Mexico. Unpub. Master's thesis, University of Pittsburgh, 1939.

MACCLARY, JOHN STEWART (545)
The first American farmers. *A&A,* 24:83-88, Sept. 1927.
    Southwestern cliff dwellers.

MCGREGOR, JOHN C. (546)
Southwestern archaeology. New York, John Wiley and Sons, 1941.

MCHARG, JOHN BRAINERD (547)
Relations of the primitive cultures of the Mississippi and the Rio Grande. *Illinois State Historical Society, Transactions,* 1926. pp. 52-64.

MAGOFFIN, RALPH VAN DEMAN   (548)
Excavations in New Mexico. *EP*, 26:163-72, 1929.

————   (549)
A thousand miles of American archaeology. *EP*, 28:61-71, 1930.
General description of Southwestern archaeological region.

MAGOFFIN, RALPH VAN DEMAN AND DAVIS, EMILY C.   (550)
Magic of spades; the romance of archaeology. New York, Henry
Holt, 1929. *Also* Garden City, Garden City Pub. Co., 1934.

MALCOLM, ROY   (551)
Archaeological remains, supposedly Navaho, from Chaco Canyon,
New Mexico. *American Antiquity,* 5:4-20, July 1939.

MARKLEY, MAX C.   (552)
Archaeology as a tool for use in predicting the permanency of
agriculture. *Science,* n.s., 86:492-93, 1937.
Explanation of disappearance of agriculture from eastern side of White
Mountain in pre-Spanish times.

MARTIN, PAUL S.   (553)
*The Su site. Excavations at a Mogollon village, western New
Mexico, 1939.* Field Museum of Natural History, Anthropological
series, v. 32, no. 1. Chicago, June 1940.

MAUZY, WAYNE   (554)
Architecture of the ancients. *NM,* 15:12-13, 35-37, Feb. 1937.
Discussion of the use of adobe in Indian architecture both before and after
Spanish conquest.

MEAD, BEN CARLTON   (555)
Netz-a-huatl's legend of the origin of the Pueblo tribes. *Panhandle
Plains Historical Review,* 7:70-78, 1934.

MERA, HARRY P.   (556)
Ceramic clues to the prehistory of north central New Mexico.
Laboratory of Anthropology, Technical series, Bulletin 8. Santa
Fe, 1935.

————   (557)
Population changes in the Rio Grande glaze-paint area. Laboratory of Anthropology, Technical series, Bulletin 9. Santa Fe,
1940.

————   (558)
A proposed revision of the Rio Grande glaze paint sequence. Laboratory of Anthropology, Technical series, Bulletin 5. Santa Fe,
1934.

————   (559)
Reconnaissance and excavation in southeastern New Mexico.
AAA, Memoirs, v. 51. Menasha, Wisconsin, 1938.

————   (560)
Some aspects of the Largo cultural phase, northern New Mexico.
American Antiquity, 3:236-43, 1938.

————   (561)
A survey of the biscuit ware area in northern New Mexico. Lab-

MERA, HARRY P. (Continued)
oratory of Anthropology, Technical series, Bulletin 6. Santa Fe, 1934.

(562)

Wares ancestral to Tewa polychrome. Laboratory of Anthropology, Technical series, Bulletin 3. Santa Fe, 1931.

MERA, HARRY P. AND STALLINGS, W. S., JR.   (563)
Lincoln black on red. Laboratory of Anthropology, Technical series, Bulletin 2. Santa Fe, 1931.

MOISE, C.   (564)
Dead cities of New Mexico. *Kansas City Review,* 5:480, 1882-83.

MOOREHEAD, WARREN KING   (565)
Explorations in New Mexico. *Phillips Academy, Department of Archaeology, Bulletin,* 3:33-53, 1906.

(566)

A narrative of exploration in New Mexico, Arizona, Indiana, etc. Andover, Mass., Andover Press, 1906.

(567)

Ruins at Aztec and on the Rio La Plata, New Mexico. *AA,* 10:255-63, 1908.

(568)

The stone age in America; an archaeological encyclopedia of the implements, ornaments, weapons, utensils, etc. of the prehistoric tribes of North America. 2 v. New York, Houghton Mifflin, 1910.

MORGAN, LEWIS H.   (569)
Description of an ancient stone Pueblo on the Animas River, New Mexico, with a ground plan. *Peabody Museum of American Archaeology and Ethnology, 12th and 13th Annual Report,* v.2, no. 3. Cambridge, 1876-79. pp. 536-56.

MORLEY, SYLVANUS GRISWOLD   (570)
The south house at Puye, New Mexico. AIA, School of American Archaeology, Papers 7. Santa Fe, 1910.

MORRIS, ANN AXTELL   (571)
Digging in the Southwest. Garden City, Doubleday Doran, 1933.
    Popular treatment of New Mexico archaeology.

MORRIS, EARL H.   (572)
Archaeological studies of La Plata district, southwestern Colorado and northwestern New Mexico. Washington, Carnegie Institution, 1939.

(573)

The Aztec ruin. AMNH, Anthropological Papers, 26. New York, 1919.

(574)

The beginnings of pottery making in the San Juan area; unfired prototypes and the wares of the earliest ceramic period. *AMNH, Anthropological Papers,* 28:125-98, 1927.

(575)

Discoveries at the Aztec ruin. *AMNH, Journal,* 17:169-79, 1917.

MORRIS, EARL H. (Continued)   (576)
 The excavation of a ruin near Aztec, San Juan County, New
 Mexico. *AA*, 17:666-84, 1915.

———   (577)
 Explorations in New Mexico. *American Museum Journal*, 17:
 461-71, 1917.

———   (578)
 Further discoveries at the Aztec ruin. *EP*, 6:18-23, 26, 1919.

———   (579)
 The place of coiled ware in Southwestern pottery. *AA*, 19:24-29,
 1917.

———   (580)
 Prehistoric Pueblo surgery. *Literary Digest*, 66:138-39, Sept. 25,
 1920.

———   (581)
 The ruins at Aztec. *EP*, 4 (3) :43-53, 1917.

MORRIS, EARL H. AND BURGH, ROBERT F.   (582)
 *Anasazi basketry. Basket maker II through Pueblo III. A study
 based on specimens from the San Juan River country.* Carnegie
 Institution, Publication 533. Washington, 1941.

NADAILLAC, MARQUIS DE   (583)
 Prehistoric America. London, Murray, 1885. *Also* New York,
 Putnam, 1884.

NELSON, C. T.   (584)
 The teeth of the Indians of Pecos Pueblo. *American Journal of
 Physical Anthropology*, 23:261-94, 1938.

NELSON, NELS C.   (585)
 Archaeology of the Tano district, New Mexico. *EP*, 7:177-83, 1919.

———   (586)
 The Aztec ruin. *EP*, 4 (3) :53-69, 1917.

———   (587)
 Chronology of the Tano ruins, New Mexico. *AA*, 18:159-80, 1916.

———   (588)
 Pueblo ruins of the Galisteo basin. AMNH, Anthropological
 Papers, v.15, pt. 1. New York, 1914.

———   (589)
 Ruins of prehistoric New Mexico. *AMNH Journal*, 13:63-81,
 1913.

———   (590)
 The Southwest problem. *EP*, 6:132-35, 1919.
   Present status of archaeological science in Southwest.

NESBITT, PAUL H.   (591)
 The ancient Mimbreños. Logan Museum, Bulletin 4. Beloit,
 Wisconsin, 1931.

———   (592)
 Starkweather ruin; a Mogollon-Pueblo site in the upper Gila area

NESBITT, PAUL H. (Continued)

of New Mexico, and affiliative aspects of the Mogollon culture.
Logan Museum, Publications in Anthropology, Bulletin 6. Beloit,
Wisconsin, 1938.

—— (593)
A stone carving in bas-relief from the upper Gila area. *American
Antiquity,* 2:264-66, 1937.

NYMEYER, ROBERT BERT (594)
Cave men of the Cornudas. *NM,* 19:22-23, 41, Jan. 1941.
    Pictographs.

ORCHARD, WILLIAM C. (595)
Fine line decoration of the ancient Southwestern pottery. *Museum
of the American Indian, Heye Foundation, Indian Notes and
Monographs,* 2:24-31, 1925.

PEABODY, CHARLES (596)
A prehistoric wind instrument from Pecos, New Mexico. *AA,*
19:30-33, 1917.

PEET, STEPHEN D. (597)
Ancient and modern pueblos compared. *American Antiquarian,*
18:333-45, 1896.

—— (598)
The cliff dwellers and pueblos. Chicago, Office of the American
Antiquarian, 1899.

—— (599)
The cliff dwellers and their works. *American Antiquarian,* 12:85-
104, 1890.

—— (600)
The relative age of the pueblos and cliff dwellings. *American
Antiquarian,* 19:100-10, 1897.

PENNSYLVANIA, UNIVERSITY OF (601)
First Americans. *University of Pennsylvania Museum Bulletin,*
6:22-25, 1936. (Article signed E.B.H.)

PEPPER, GEORGE H. (602)
Ceremonial objects and ornaments from Pueblo Bonito, New
Mexico. *AA,* 7:183-97, 1905.

—— (603)
The exploration of a burial room in Pueblo Bonito, New Mexico.
Putnam Anniversary Volume. New York, 1909. pp. 196-252.

—— (604)
Pueblo Bonito. AMNH, Anthropological Papers, v. 27. New
York, 1920.

POGUE, JOSEPH E. (605)
The aboriginal use of turquois in North America. *AA,* 14:437-66,
1912.

POOLER, LOLITA (606)
Alameda Pueblo ruins. *EP,* 47:84-88, 1940.

POWELL, J. W.   (607)
    The ancient province of Tusayan. *Scribner's*, 11:193-213, 1875.

PRENTICE, R. A.   (608)
    Were the makers of Chupadero pottery the Jumanos tribe of
    Indians? *EP*, 37:33-39, 1934.

PRINCE, L. B.   (609)
    The stone lions of Cochiti. Historical Society of New Mexico,
    Publication 4. Santa Fe, 1903. *Also Records of the Past,* 3:151-60,
    1904.

PRUDDEN, THEOPHIL MITCHELL   (610)
    A further study of the prehistoric small house ruins in the San
    Juan watershed. *AAA, Memoirs,* 5 (1) :3-50, 1918.

——   (611)
    The prehistoric ruins of the San Juan watershed in Utah, Arizona,
    Colorado, and New Mexico. *AA,* n.s., 5:224-88, 1903.

——   (612)
    Prehistoric small house ruins. *EP*, 5:18-21, 1918.
        San Juan watershed.

PUTNAM, FREDERICK W.   (613)
    The pueblo ruins and the interior tribes. *U. S. Geographical and
    Geological Survey,* 7 (2) :315-96, 1879.

READ, W. H. A.   (614)
    Ancient Aztec town in New Mexico. *American Antiquarian,* 5:65,
    1883.

REAGAN, ALBERT B.   (615)
    Additional notes on the Jemez-Zia region. *EP*, 12:120-21, 1922.
        Attempt to prove that ruins on Red Mesa were the former Zia Pueblo.

——   (616)
    Ancient cotton of the Southwest. *SW*, 56:426-29, 1927.

——   (617)
    Evidence of migration in ancient Pueblo times. *AA*, 35:206, 1933.

——   (618)
    Further notes on the archaeology of the Navajo country. *EP*, 25:3-
    26, 1928.

——   (619)
    Some notes on the archaeology of the Navajo country. *EP*, 24:334-
    46, 1928.

REED, ERIK K.   (620)
    American archaeology. *National Park Service, Region 3 Quar-
    terly,* 3:23-27, Jan. 1941.

——   (621)
    The stone lions of Cochiti and of Zuni. *National Park Service,
    Region 3 Quarterly,* 2:23, Jan. 1940.

REITER, PAUL   (622)
    The ancient Pueblo of Chetro Ketl. Unpub. Master's thesis, UNM,
    1933.

REITER, PAUL (Continued) (623)
The Jemez Pueblo of Unshagi, New Mexico. Part I. UNM Bulletin, Monograph series, v.1, no. 4, 1938. *Part II.* UNM Bulletin, Monograph series, v.1, no.5, 1938.

——— (624)
Preliminary examination of a ruin in the Rio Puerco Valley, New Mexico. *EP*, 31:414-16, 1931.

REITER, PAUL, MULLOY, WILLIAM T., AND BLUMENTHAL, E. H., JR (625)
Preliminary report of the Jemez excavations at Nanishagi, New Mexico. UNM Bulletin, Anthropological series, v.3, no.3, 1940.

REITER, WINIFRED (626)
Personal adornment of the ancient Pueblo Indians. Unpub. Master's thesis, UNM, 1933.

RENAUD, ETIENNE B. (627)
Archaeological research in northeastern New Mexico and western Oklahoma. *EP,* 27:276-79, 1929.

——— (628)
Evolution of population and dwelling in the Indian Southwest. *EP,* 26:75-88, 1929.

——— (629)
Le plus anciennes cultures prehistoriques du sud ouest americain. *Anthropologie,* 40:233-58, 1930.

——— (630)
Prehistoric cultures of the Cimarron Valley, northeastern New Mexico and western Oklahoma. *Colorado Scientific Society, Proceedings,* 12:113-50, 1929-31.

——— (631)
A summary of the prehistoric cultures of the Cimarron Valley. *EP,* 28:123-29, 1930.

——— (632)
Uncovering the first Americans. *EP,* 20:242-50, 1926.

ROBERTS, FRANK H. H., JR. (633)
Archaeological and geological investigations in the San Jon district, eastern New Mexico. *Smithsonian Miscellaneous Collections,* 103 (4), Oct. 1942.

——— (634)
Archaeology of the Southwest. *American Antiquity,* 3:3-33, July 1937.

——— (635)
Chaco Canyon masonry. *American Antiquity,* 4:60-61, July 1938.

——— (636)
The Folsom problem in American archaeology. *Smithsonian Annual Report, 1938.* Washington, 1939. pp. 531-46.

——— (637)
A prehistoric village on the Zuni reservation, New Mexico. *Smithsonian Explorations and Field Work, 1930.* pp. 177-86.

ROBERTS, FRANK H. H., JR. (Continued)   (638)
    *Shabik'eshchee village. A late basket maker site in the Chaco
    Canyon, New Mexico.* Bureau of American Ethnology, Bulletin
    92. Washington, GPO, 1929.
——   (639)
    A survey of Southwestern archaeology. *AA,* 37:1-35, 1935. *Also
    Smithsonian Annual Report, 1935.* Washington, 1936. pp. 507-35.
——   (640)
    *The village of the great kivas on the Zuni reservation, New
    Mexico.* Bureau of American Ethnology, Bulletin 111.. Wash-
    ington, GPO, 1932.

ROBINSON, THERESA G.   (641)
    Ancient Indian ruins of New Mexico. *D.A.R. Magazine,* 70:645-
    47, 1936.

ROLLINS, WARREN E.   (642)
    Pueblo Bonito. *NM,* 11:15-16, 50-52, April 1933.

RUBLE, BESSE WAYNICK   (643)
    Prehistoric apartment house. *The Family Circle,* 20:14-15, 22,
    Jan. 1942.
        Rito de los Frijoles.

RUTZ, LOUISE C.   (644)
    Pages from the Indian 'Album.' *NM,* 17:22, 46, June 1939.
        Southern New Mexico pictographs and petroglyphs.

SAFFORD, W. E.   (645)
    The isolation of ancient America as illustrated by its agriculture
    and languages. *Scientific Monthly,* 22:55-59, 1926.

SENTER, DONOVAN   (646)
    Tree rings, valley floor deposition, and erosion in Chaco Canyon.
    American Antiquity, 3:68-75, July 1937.

SHEPARD, ANNA O.   (647)
    *Rio Grande glaze paint ware; a study illustrating the place of
    ceramic technological analysis in archaeological research.* Carnegie
    Institution, Contributions to American Anthropology and His-
    tory 39. Washington, March 1942.

SHORT, JOHN T.   (648)
    *The North Americans of antiquity; their origin, migrations, and
    type of civilization considered.* New York, Harper, 1882.

SPIER, LESLIE   (649)
    An outline for a chronology of Zuni ruins. *AMNH, Anthro-
    pological papers,* 18:207-328, 1917.

SPINDEN, HERBERT J.   (650)
    The population of ancient America. *Smithsonian Annual Report,
    1929.* Washington, 1930. pp. 451-71. *Also Geographical Review,*
    18:641-60, Oct. 1928.
——   (651)
    Pueblo Bonito. *National Park Service, Region 3 Quarterly,* 1:4-6,
    Oct. 1939.

STALLINGS, W. S., JR. (652)
Dating prehistoric ruins by tree-rings. Laboratory of Anthropology, General series, Bulletin 8. Santa Fe, 1939.

―――― (653)
El Paso polychrome. Laboratory of Anthropology, Technical series 3. Santa Fe, 1931.

―――― (654)
Notes on Pueblo culture in south-central New Mexico and in the vicinity of El Paso, Texas. *AA*, 34:67-78, 1932.

STEEN, CHARLIE R. AND JONES, VOLNEY H. (655)
Prehistoric lima beans in the Southwest. *EP*, 48:197-203, 1941

STEEN, FRANK (656)
Folsom flints. *NM*, 18:20, 37-38, Feb. 1940.

STEWARD, JULIAN H. (657)
Ecological aspects of Southwestern society. *Anthropos*, 32:87-104, 1937.

STUBBS, STANLEY (658)
Preliminary report of excavations near La Luz and Alamogordo, New Mexico. *EP*, 29:3-14, 1930.

SWAN, A. M. (659)
Advent of man in New Mexico. *Southwest Magazine*, Nov. 1896.

―――― (660)
Stone circles and upright stones in New Mexico. *American Antiquarian*, July-August 1899.

SWOPE, W. D. (661)
Analysis of the prehistoric art of the Southwest. *EP*, 16:159-62, 1924.

THOBURN, JOSEPH B. (662)
Ancient irrigation ditches on the plains. *Chronicles of Oklahoma, Oklahoma Historical Society*, 9:56-62, March 1931.
    Prehistoric irrigation works in Arizona and New Mexico.

TICHY, MARJORIE FERGUSON (663)
The archaeology of Puaray, *EP*, 46:145-63, 1939.

―――― (664)
The excavation of Paa-Ko ruin. *EP*, 42:109-16, 1937.

―――― (665)
Six game pieces from Otowi. *EP*, 48:1-6, 1941.

―――― (666)
Yesterday's people. *NM*, 17:12-13, 40, 46-47, Jan. 1939.
    Pueblo origins and culture.

TITUS, W. A. (667)
The cliff ruins of the Southwest. *Wisconsin Archaeologist*, n.s, 3:82-86, 1924.

TOULOUSE, JOE H., JR. (668)
Early man in New Mexico. *EP*, 42:117-20, 1937.

―――― (669)
Early man in the Southwest. *EP*, 43:130-36, 1937.

TRUE, CLARA D.   (670)
> Shrines of a thousand years. *NM*, 16:12-13, 42, July 1938.
>> Puye cliff dwellings.

TWITCHELL, RALPH E.   (671)
> The ancient pueblo of Pecos. *Santa Fe Employees Magazine*, Oct.
> 1910.

VIVIAN, GORDON   (672)
> Excavation of a room in the Puerco ruin. *EP*, 31:416-19, 1931.

————   (673)
> The murals at Kauau. *EP*, 38:113-19, 1935.

VIVIAN, RICHARD   (674)
> *A re-study of the province of Tiguex.* Unpub. Master's thesis,
> UNM, 1932.

WALLACE, DAN   (675)
> Ancient American agriculture; the old time search for rural
> security. *Farmer*, 56:5, 17, July 16, 1938.
>> Agriculture of American Southwest in Pueblo culture period.

WALLACE, GEORGE H.   (676)
> A day in the cliff dwellings. *Land of Sunshine*, 13:23-28, June
> 1900.

WALLIS, G. A.   (677)
> Who were the prehistoric Mimbreños of New Mexico? *Scientific
> American*, 139:132-33, 1928.

WALTER, PAUL A. F.   (678)
> *The cities that died of fear.* AIA, School of American Archaeology,
> Papers 35. Santa Fe, 1916.

————   (679)
> Excavations at Hawikuh. *EP*, 5:180-84, 1918.

————   (680)
> Gran Quivera, one of the cities that died of fear. *EP*, 5:226-31,
> 1918.

WARNER, THOR   (681)
> The prehistoric man of Rio Puerco. *A&A*, 26:44-50, 1928.

————   (682)
> Rio Puerco ruins. *AA*, 30:85-93, 1928.

WATERMAN, T. T.   (683)
> Culture horizons in the Southwest. *AA*, 31:367-400, 1929.
>> Stages of culture as outlined by various authors, mainly from archaeologic
>> evidence.

WATKINS, FRANCES E.   (684)
> Prehistoric pottery of the Jemez region. *Masterkey*, 3 (5) :20-21,
> 1929.

WATSON, EDITHA L.   (685)
> Caves of the upper Gila River, New Mexico. *AA*, 31:299-306,
> 1929.

————   (686)
> Some New Mexico ruins. *EP*, 23:174-234, 1927.
>> Ruins of Gila and Mimbres Rivers, Bear Creek, and those around Pinos Altos.

WATSON, EDITHA L. (Continued) (687)
Two Mimbres River ruins. *AA*, 33:51-55, 1931.

WILSON, MRS. L. L. W. (688)
Excavations at Otowi. *EP*, 3:29-36, 1916.

_____ (689)
Hand sign or Avanyu. A note on a Pajaritan biscuit-ware motif. *AA*, 20:310-17, 1918.

_____ (690)
A prehistoric anthropomorphic figure from the Rio Grande basin. *AA*, 18:548-51, 1916.

_____ (691)
Three years at Otowi. *EP*, 5:290-94, 1918.

WISSLER, CLARK (692)
Dating our prehistoric ruins. . . *NH*, 21:13-26, 1921.

_____ (693)
Pueblo Bonito as made known by the Hyde Expedition. *NH*, 22:343-54, 1922.

_____ (694)
Report on the work at Aztec. *EP*, 6:83-84, 1919.

_____ (695)
Unearthing the secrets of the Aztec ruin. *Harpers*, 143:46-56, June 1921.

WOLFE, WILLIAM L. (696)
Archaeological report on the Hondo sites. *EP*, 31:108-12, 1931.

YEO, HERBERT W. (697)
An old ditch. *New Mexico Highway Journal*, 7:23, Aug. 1929.
Evidence to show that an irrigation ditch on Ruidoso Creek was used 2,000 years ago.

_____ (698)
Sketches concerning early irrigators and irrigation in the arid Southwest. *New Mexico Highway Journal*, 7:18, June 1929.

Apaches

ANONYMOUS (699)
Apache Indian as a road builder. *Literary Digest*, 83:25-26, Oct. 25, 1924.

_____ (700)
Prisoners of war for thirty years. *Outlook*, 99:555-56, 1911.
Government treatment of Apaches.

BARRETT, S. M., ED. (701)
Geronimo's story of his life. New York, Duffield, 1906.

BLOUNT, BERTHA (702)
The Apache in the Southwest, 1846-1886. *Southwestern Historical Quarterly*, 23:20-38, 1919.

BORDEN, W. C. (703)
The vital statistics of an Apache Indian community. *Boston Medical and Surgical Journal*, 129:5-10, July 6, 1893.

BOURKE, JOHN GREGORY   (704)
   The medicine men of the Apache. *Bureau of American Eth-*
   nology, 9th Annual Report. Washington, GPO, 1892. pp. 443-603.
      Chiricahua.

————   (705)

   Notes on Apache mythology. *JAF,* 3:209-12, 1890.
      Chiricahua.

————   (706)

   Notes upon the religion of the Apache Indians. *Folk-lore*
   (London), 2:419-54, 1891.
      Chiricahua.

BURBANK, E. A.   (707)
   Geronimo, chief of the Apaches. *The Border,* Nov. 1908.

CHARLES, TOM   (708)
   The old scouts of the Mescaleros. *NM,* 9:17-19, Aug., 1931.
      Chatto, Arnold Kinzuna, Martine, and other Apaches who served as scouts
      in the campaign against Geronimo.

CLUM, JOHN P.   (709)
   The Apaches. *NMHR,* 4:107-27, 1929.

————   (710)

   Apaches as thespians in 1876. *NMHR,* 6:76-100, 1931.

————   (711)

   Geronimo. *NMHR,* 3:1-41, 121-44, 217-64, 1928.

————   (712)

   The San Carlos Apache police. *NMHR,* 4:203-19, 1929; 5:67-92,
   1930.

COLYER, VINCENT   (713)
   Peace with the Apaches of New Mexico and Arizona. Report to
   the Board of Indian Commissioners. Washington, 1872.

COOK, WILLIAM WALLACE   (714)
   The murderous Apache. *Illustrated American,* March 28, 1896.

CRANDALL, CLINTON J.   (715)
   When Geronimo won. *New Mexico Highway Journal,* 7:12, Nov.
   1929.
      An attempt to persuade Geronimo to permit Apache children to be educated
      in government schools.

CREMONY, JOHN C.   (716)
   Life among the Apaches. San Francisco, A. Roman & Co., 1868.

DANA, R. W.   (717)
   An echo of Apache days. *Museum of the American Indian, Heye*
   Foundation, Indian Notes, 6:250-54, 1929.
      Chiricahua.

DAVIS, ANNE PENCE   (718)
   Apache debs. *NM,* 15:10-11, 40, April 1937.
      Ceremonies connected with four-day *fiesta* for adolescent Mescalero girls.

DAVIS, BRITTON   (719)
   The truth about Geronimo. New Haven, Yale University Press,
   1929.

DENVER ART MUSEUM   (720)
A Jicarilla Apache beaded cape. *DAM, Material Culture Notes,*
9:34-37, June 1939.

DOLAN, T. A.   (721)
Report of council proceedings with the Jicarilla Apache Indians.
NMHR, 4:59-71, 1929.
> Meeting between U. S. Government agent and Apaches to obtain their re-
> moval to a permanent location. Articles of agreement are included.

DORCHESTER, DANIEL   (722)
The terrible Apaches and how they gained their evil reputation.
American Methodist Magazine, Jan. 1901.

DORY, WILLIAM   (723)
The Apaches of the highlands. *SW,* 51:472-77, 1922.
> Brief account of their history since the Civil War.

——   (724)
The Mescalero Apaches' present conditions. *SW,* 51:413-19, 1922.

DOUGLAS, FREDERICK H.   (725)
Apache Indian coiled basketry. *DAM, Leaflet series,* 64:54-56,
1934.
> Jicarilla, Mescalero.

DOUGLAS, FREDERICK H. AND JEANCON, JEAN ALLARD   (726)
The Apache Indians. *DAM, Leaflet series,* 16:1-4, 1930.
> Jicarilla, Mescalero.

DUNN, WILLIAM EDWARD   (726a)
Missionary activities among the eastern Apaches. *Texas State
Historical Association Quarterly,* 15:186-200, 1911-12.

EUSTIS, ISABEL B.   (727)
History of the Chiricahua Apaches. *Lend A Hand,* 6:226-, April
1891.

FEDERAL WRITERS' PROJECT, WPA   (728)
The Apache. Arizona State Teachers College Bulletin, v. 20, no.
1. Flagstaff, Aug. 1939.
> History, daily life, handicrafts, economic life, social organization, religion.

FLANNERY, REGINA   (729)
The position of woman among the Mescalero Apache. *Primitive
Man,* 5:26-32, 1932.

FREIRE-MARRECO, BARBARA   (729a)
Two American Indians. *Sociological Review,* 4:324-37, 1911.
> Apaches.

GABBARD, T. P.   (730)
The Apache Indian. *Native American,* Oct. 17, 1900.

GATSCHET, A. S.   (731)
The Chiricahua Apache "Sun Circle." *Smithsonian Miscellaneous
Collections,* 34 (2):144-47, 1885.

GIFFORD, EDWARD WINSLOW   (732)
Apache-Pueblo culture elements; abstract. *Nature,* 147:120, 1941.

GIFFORD, EDWARD WINSLOW (Continued)   (733)
Culture element distributions: XII. Apache-Pueblo. *Anthropological Records*, v. 4, no. 1. Berkeley, 1940.

GODDARD, PLINY E.   (734)
Apache masked dances. *Holmes Anniversary Volume*. Washington, G. W. Bryan, 1916.

————   (735)
Gotal—a Mescalero Apache ceremony. *Putnam Anniversary Volume*. New York, Stechert, 1909. pp. 385-94.

————   (736)
Jicarilla Apache texts. *AMNH, Anthropological Papers* 8. New York, 1911.

————   (737)
The masked dancers of the Apache. *Holmes Anniversary Volume*. Washington, G. W. Bryan, 1916.
  Mescalero.

————   (738)
Myths and tales from the San Carlos Apaches. *AMNH, Anthropological Papers*, 24, pt. 1, 1918.

————   (739)
Myths and tales from the White Mountain Apaches. *AMNH, Anthropological Papers* 24, pt. 2, 1919.

GOODWIN, GRENVILLE   (740)
The characteristics and function of clan in a southern Athapascan culture. *AA*, 39:394-407, 1937.
  White Mountain Apaches.

————   (741)
Myths and tales of the White Mountain Apache. American Folklore Society, Memoirs, v. 33. New York, 1939.

————   (742)
The social divisions and economic life of the western Apaches. *AA*, 37:55-64, 1935.

————   (743)
The social organization of the western Apache. University of Chicago, Publications in Anthropology, Ethnological series. Chicago, 1942.

————   (744)
The southern Athapascans. *Kiva*, 4:5-10, 1938.

HALL, H. U.   (745)
Some shields of the plains and Southwest. *University of Pennsylvania, Museum Journal*, 17:37-61, 1926.
  Includes Apaches.

HALL, SHARLOT M.   (746)
Apache treatment of white captives. *Out West*, Sept. 1908.

HARRINGTON, JOHN PEABODY   (747)
The Apache and Navaho. *EP*, 27:37-38, 1929.

HARRINGTON, JOHN PEABODY (Continued)   (748)
Southern peripheral Athapaskawan origins, divisions, and migrations. *Smithsonian Miscellaneous Collections,* 100:503-32, 1940.

HILDBURGH, W. L.   (749)
Apache Indians: folklore. *Man,* 19:81-87, 1919.

HOIJER, HARRY   (750)
Chiricahua and Mescalero Apache texts. Chicago, University of Chicago Press, 1938.

———   (751)
Chiricahua loan words from Spanish. *Language,* 15:110-15, 1939.

———   (752)
The southern Athapaskan languages. *AA,* 40:75-87, 1938.

HOOVER, JAMES H.   (753)
The wrongs and the wrong doings of the Apaches. *Arizona Magazine,* Dec. 1912.

HOUGH, WALTER   (754)
Apache and Navaho fire-making. *AA,* 3:585-86, 1901.

KANE, HENRY   (755)
The Apache secret devil dance. *EP,* 42:93-94, 1937.

KENNON, L. V. W.   (756)
The case of the Chiricahuas. *North American Review,* Aug. 1890.

LA FARGE, OLIVER   (757)
Unscientific expedition. *World's Work,* 60:72-76, March 1931.

LEHMANN, HERMANN   (758)
Nine years with the Indians, 1870-79. Bandera, Texas, Frontier Times, 1927.
    Comanche and Apache.

LOCKWOOD, FRANCIS CUMMINS   (759)
The Apache Indians. New York, Macmillan, 1938.

MCCORMICK, WILFRED   (760)
Apache neighbors. *NM,* 16:18-19, 45-46, July 1938.
    History and present status.

———   (761)
Since Geronimo. *NM,* 14:19-21, 49-50, July 1936.
    Life of Jasper Kanseak, chief of Mescalero police for twenty-two years.

MACCURDY, GEORGE GRANT   (762)
A basket collection. *The Papoose,* 1 (3) :12-15, 1903.
    Apache.

MOONEY, JAMES   (763)
The Jicarilla genesis. *AA,* o. s., 11:197-209, 1898.

NICHOLAS, DAN   (764)
Mescalero Apache girls' puberty ceremony. *EP,* 46:193-204, 1939.

OPLER, MORRIS EDWARD   (765)
Adolescence rite of the Jicarilla. *EP,* 49:25-38, 1942.

———   (766)
An analysis of Mescalero and Chiricahua Apache social organi-

OPLER, MORRIS EDWARD (Continued)

zation in the light of their systems of relationship. Unpub. Doctor's thesis, University of Chicago, 1933.

(767)

Apache data concerning the relation of kinship terminology to social classification. *AA,* 39:201-12, 1937.

(768)

An Apache life-way; the economic, social, and religious institutions of the Chiricahua Indians. Chicago, University of Chicago Press, 1941.

(769)

The concept of supernatural power among the Chiricahua and Mescalero Apaches. *AA,* 37:65-70, 1935.

(770)

Dirty boy: a Jicarilla tale of raid and war. AAA, Memoirs 52. Menasha, Wisconsin, 1938.

(771)

Examples of ceremonial interchanges among Southwestern tribes. *Masterkey,* 16:77-80, 1942.

(772)

Further comparative anthropological data bearing on the solution of a psychological problem. *Journal of Social Psychology,* 9:477-83, 1938.

(773)

An interpretation of ambivalence of two American Indian tribes. *Journal of Social Psychology,* 7:82-116, 1936.

(774)

The kinship systems of the southern Athabaskan-speaking tribes. *AA,* 38:620-33, 1936.

(775)

Myths and tales of the Chiricahua Apache Indians. AAA, Memoirs 37. Menasha, Wisconsin, 1942.

(776)

Myths and tales of the Jicarilla Apache Indians. American Folklore Society, Memoirs, v. 31. New York, 1938.

(777)

An outline of Chiricahua Apache social organization. (In Eggan, F., ed.: *Social Anthropology of North American Tribes.* Chicago, University of Chicago Press, 1937. pp. 171-239.)

(778)

The sacred clowns of the Chiricahua and Mescalero Indians. *EP,* 44:75-79, 1938.

(779)

Some points of comparison and contrast between the treatment of functional disorders by Apache shamans and modern psychiatric practice. *American Journal of Psychiatry,* 92:1371-87, 1936.

OPLER, MORRIS EDWARD (Continued)   (780)
The use of peyote by the Carrizo and Lipan Apache tribes. *AA*,
40:271-85, 1938.

OPLER, MORRIS EDWARD, ED.   (781)
A Chiricahua Apache's account of the Geronimo campaign of
1886. *NMHR*, 13:360-86, 1938.

OPLER, MORRIS E. AND HOIJER, HARRY   (782)
The raid and war-path language of the Chiricahua Apache.
AA, 42:617-34, 1940.

OTIS, H. G.   (783)
The Apache race. *Overland*, 1:201-, Sept. 1868.
     (Poole's Index gives this as being by J. C. Cremony. Alliot (264) lists it
     under Otis.)

PALMER, EDWARD   (784)
Customs of the Coyotero Apaches. *Zoe*, 1:161-72, 1890.

RAFFERTY, KEEN   (785)
Mission at Mescalero. *NM*, 18:9, 30-31, Oct. 1940.

REAGAN, ALBERT B.   (786)
The moccasin game. *Indiana Academy of Science, Proceedings*,
1904. pp. 289-92.
——————   (787)
Notes on the Indians of the Fort Apache region. *AMNH,
Anthropological Papers*, 31:281-345, 1930.
     Field notes taken in 1902 and 1903 on White Mountain and San Carlos
     Apaches. Includes information on origin myth, dress, labor, food, basketry,
     agriculture, religion, medicine, ceremonies, etc.

REICH, BETTY   (788)
Apache. Unpub. ms. in files of New Mexico Writers' Project,
Santa Fe.

ROBERTS, HELEN H.   (789)
The basketry of the San Carlos Apache. *AMNH, Anthropological
Papers*, 31:121-218, 1930.

RUSSELL, FRANK   (790)
An Apache medicine dance. *AA*, o. s., 11:367-72, 1898.
     Jicarilla.
——————   (791)
Myths of the Jicarilla Apaches. *JAF*, 11:253-71, 1898.

SALZMAN, MAURICE   (792)
Geronimo, the Napoleon of Indians. *The Border*, March 1909.

SANDEMAN, JOHN J.   (793)
How I met Victorio the Apache. *Wide World Magazine*, Nov.
1901.

SANTEE, ROSS   (794)
Among the Apaches. *Century*, 109:511-15, 1925.
     Drawings, with comments.

SAPIR, E.   (795)
An Apache basket jar. *University of Pennsylvania, Museum
Journal*, 1:13-15, 1910.

SCHMITZ, O.   (796)
    Die Apachen. *Ausland,* 44:347-51, 1871.

SCHWATKA, FREDERICK   (797)
    Among the Apaches. *Century,* 34:41-52, May 1887.

SEVERANCE, MARK SIBLEY   (798)
    Checkmate to Apaches. *Old and New,* 8:702-, Dec. 1873.

SIMMS, D. HARPER   (799)
    Redskin rendezvous. *NM,* 15:14-15, 35, Sept. 1937.
        Apache games and dances.

SPRING, J. A.   (800)
    The Apache Indian. *Great Divide,* Dec. 1892.

STOLL, A. B.   (801)
    Welfare work among the Apaches. *Public Health Nurse,* 15:619-
    22, 1923.

STONE, MARGARET   (802)
    Devil dance of the Apaches. *Desert Magazine,* 5:26-29, Oct. 1942.

SULLIVAN, DON D.   (803)
    Chiricahua petroglyphs. *EP,* 4 (3) :90-91, 1917.

TASSIN, A. G.   (804)
    Among the Apaches. *Overland,* n. s., 14:322-, Sept.-Oct. 1889.

WALLACE, D.   (805)
    In the land of the Apaches. *Outing,* 57:130-43, 1910.

WATERMULDER, G. A.   (806)
    Injustice to the Apaches. *SW,* 50:131-33, 1921.

WILSON, BOURDON   (807)
    An experiment with Apache signals. *Sports Afield,* May 1898.

WOODS, BETTY   (808)
    Jicarilla fiesta. *NM,* 19:16-17, 37, 39, 41, Sept. 1941.

————   (809)
    The warriors come back. *NM,* 19:18-19, 48, 52, Aug. 1941.
        Population, health, agriculture of Apaches.

WRIGHT, HARRY ROBINSON   (810)
    In the days of Geronimo—some incidents in the Apache outbreak
    of 1885. *Pearson's,* Feb. 1905.

Navajos

ABBOTT, F. H.   (811)
    The Navajo Indians and the public domain. *LMC, Proceedings,
    2nd Session, 1913.* pp. 74-82. *Also Native American,* Jan. 17, 1914.

ABEL, THEODORA M.   (812)
    Free designs of limited scope as a personality index. *Character and
    Personality,* 7:50-63, 1938.
        Part of material based on experiments with Fort Wingate Navajos.

ABERLE, DAVID F.   (813)
    Mythology of the Navaho game stick-dice. *JAF,* 55:144-54, 1942.

ADAIR, JOHN   (814)
    The trading post in Navaho culture. Unpub. ms. dated 1937.
        Based on Ramah Navajos.

ADAMS, LUCY WILCOX (815)
Navajo men and women go to school to find out what youngsters learn. *IW,* 7:21-22, March 1940.

——— (816)
Navajos go to school. *Journal of Adult Education,* 10:149-53, 1938.
Description of program of practical vocational education.

ALLEN, PHILIPPA (817)
Whispering wind; folk-tales of the Navaho Indians, retold. Chicago, Thomas S. Rockwell Co., 1930.
Retold from Washington Matthews' Navajo legends.

ALLEY, R. D. AND PIJOAN, MICHEL (817a)
Salmonella javiana food infection. *Yale Journal of Biology and Medicine,* 15:229-39, Dec. 1942.
Among Puertocito Navajos.

AMERICAN ASSOCIATION ON INDIAN AFFAIRS (818)
Fundamentals of the Navajo problem. New York, 1941.

AMSDEN, CHARLES A. (819)
The Navaho exile at Bosque Redondo. *NMHR,* 8:31-50, 1933.

——— (820)
Navaho origins. *NMHR,* 7:193-209, 1932.
Based on early Spanish manuscripts and Navajo mythology.

——— (821)
Navajo weaving, its technic and history. Santa Ana, California, Fine Arts Press, 1934.

——— (822)
Reviving the Navajo blanket. *Masterkey,* 6:137-49, 1932.

——— (823)
When Navaho rugs were blankets. *School Arts Magazine,* 34:387-96, 1935.

ANDERSON, JOSEPH F. (824)
A study of Navajo Indian life. *Red Man,* 6:135, Dec. 1913.

ANONYMOUS (825)
The Alamos: a problem in human rehabilitation. *United Pueblos Quarterly Bulletin,* v.1, no.3, April 1940.
Puertocito Navajos.

——— (826)
Colorful fourth by Navahos. *EP,* 27:27-30, 1929.
Celebration of 4th of July in Chaco Canyon.

——— (827)
Crafts del Navajo; unique Navajo Indian trading post. *School Arts Magazine,* 30:454-55, 1931.

——— (828)
Indian basket weaving by the Navajo School of Indian basketry. Los Angeles, Whedon & Spreng, 1903.

——— (829)
The Navajo fair. *Red Man,* v.7, Dec. 1914.

——— (830)
Navajo fair. *Pan American Union, Bulletin,* 41:400-05, 1915.

ANONYMOUS (Continued)   (831)
    Navajo home life and customs. *IW,* 3:12-13, June 1, 1936.

———   (832)
    Navajo Methodist mission school. *World Outlook,* 3:23-30, Nov.
1942.

———   (833)
    Navajo property. *IW,* 5:15, April, 1938.

———   (834)
    The Navajo reservation. *Nation,* 95:96-97, Aug. 1, 1912.
        Statement of viewpoint that the Indian must be modernized and civilized.

———   (835)
    Navajo sand paintings as decorative motive. *EP,* 14:175-83, 1923.

———   (836)
    Navajos seem immune to cancer, hospital reports. *Hygeia,* 9:684,
1931.

———   (837)
    Pagans in America. *Literary Digest,* 121:17, Jan. 4, 1936.
        Brief argument for conversion of Navajos.

———   (838)
    Primitive American hand-made rugs. *Good Furniture Magazine,*
28 (1) :14-19, 1927.

———   (839)
    *Problems created by increase of Navaho population and how
they can be met.* Radio Program, Window Rock, May 2, 1939.
Processed. (Copy at Navajo Service Library, Window Rock,
Arizona.)

———   (840)
    Rapid growth of Navajo tribe becomes economic problem.
Hobbies, 46:99, Feb. 1942.

ARIZONA FEDERAL WRITERS' PROJECT, WPA   (841)
    The Navaho. Arizona State Teachers College Bulletin, v.18, no.4.
Flagstaff, 1937.

ARMER, LAURA A.   (842)
    Navaho sand-paintings. *AA,* 33:657, 1931.

———   (843)
    Sand-paintings of the Navaho Indians. *Exposition of American
Tribal Arts, Leaflets* 5:1-9, 1931.

ARNOLD, ETHEL M.   (844)
    The blanket of Chief White Antelope. *A&A,* 28:45-46, 1929.

BACKUS, MAJOR E.   (845)
    An account of the Navajoes of New Mexico. (In Schoolcraft,
Henry R.: *Historical and statistical information respecting the
history, condition, and prospects of the Indian tribes of the
United States.* Part IV. Philadelphia, Lippincott, Grambo & Co.,
1854.)

BAILEY, FLORA L.   (846)
    Navaho foods and cooking methods. *AA,* 42:270-90, 1940.

BAILEY, FLORA L. (Continued)   (847)
   Navaho motor habits. *AA*, 44:210-34, 1942.
                                                             (848)
─────
   Navaho women and the sudatory. *AA*, 43:484-85, 1941.

BANDELIER, ADOLPH F. A.   (849)
   The Navajos. *Nation*, 42:397-98, 1886.

BARBER, BERNARD   (850)
   Acculturation and messianic movements. *American Sociological Review*, 4:663-69, 1941.
      Suggests correlation between economic conditions and strength of religious influence. Navajos used for illustration.

BARRY, R.   (851)
   Redman's last stand. *Harper's Weekly*, 56:10, May 25, 1912.
      Government relations with Navajos.

BEASLEY, W. L.   (852)
   Navajo weavers and rugs. *Harper's Weekly*, 57:18, May 17, 1913.

BEDINGER, MARGERY   (853)
   Navajo Indian silver-work. Denver, Van Male, 1936.

BENHAM, J. W.   (854)
   The settlers and the Navajo Indians. *The Papoose*, May 1903.

BERRY, ROSE V. S.   (855)
   The Navajo shaman and his sacred sand-paintings. *A&A*, 27:3-16, 1929. *Also EP*, 26:23-38, 119-20, 1929.

BLACKWOOD, BEATRICE   (856)
   An anthropologist among the Navaho. *NH*, 27:223-28, 1927.
      Some physical measurements of Navajo women.

BLUNN, CECIL T.   (857)
   Improvement of the Navajo sheep. *Journal of Heredity*, 31:99-112, 1940.

BOAS, FRANZ   (858)
   Northern elements in the mythology of the Navajo. *AA*, o.s., 10: 371-76, 1897.
                                                             (859)
─────
   Zur Anthropologie der Nordamerikanischen Indianer. *Verhandlungen der Berliner Gesellschaft für Anthropologie, Ethnologie, und Urgeschichte* (Berlin), 1895. pp. 367-411.

BOURKE, JOHN GREGORY   (860)
   The early Navajo and Apache. *AA*, o.s., 8:287-94, 1895.

BOWRA, G. B.   (861)
   Glimpse of the Navajo Indian. *National Republic*, 21:22, Nov. 1933.

BOYCE, GEORGE A.   (862)
   Economic education for the Navajo Indians. USDI, Office of Indian Affairs, Navajo Service. Window Rock, 1941. Processed.

BOYCE, GEORGE A. AND FRYER, E. R.   (863)
   Dineh and government in Kaibeto District. USDI, Office of Indian

BOYCE, GEORGE A. AND FRYER, E. R. (Continued)
Affairs, Navajo Socio-economic Planning Service. Window Rock, 1939. Processed.

BOYLE, R. V.   (864)
Range management policy statement, Navaho reservation. USDA, Washington, 1935. Processed.

BREWER, JAMES, JR.   (865)
Notes on how to build a hogan. *Southwestern Monuments, Monthly Report, Supplement,* June 1936. pp. 485-88.

BRINK, L. P.   (866)
Religion of the Navahoes. *National Republic,* 22:16-18, Nov. 1934.

BROOKE, JOHN   (867)
New Mexico and the Navajo Indians. *Recreation,* May 1897. p. 341.

BROOKS, C. C.   (868)
America's last stronghold of paganism: the Navajo Indians. *Missionary Review of the World,* 58:226-30, May 1935.

BROWN, KATHERINE D.   (869)
The policy of the United States government in its relations with the Navajo Indians. Unpub. Master's thesis, UNM, 1932.

BUCKLAND, A. W.   (870)
Points of contact between Old World myths and customs and the Navajo myth entitled "The Mountain Chant." *Journal of the Royal Anthropological Institute,* 22:346-55, 1892-93.

BURGE, MORIS   (871)
The Navajos and the land—the government, the tribe, and the future. American Indian Defense Association and National Association on Indian Affairs, Bulletin 26. New York, Feb. 1937.

————   (872)
The silversmithing of the Navajos. *IW,* 2:22-25, Dec. 15, 1934.

BUSCHMANN, J. C. E.   (873)
Die Spuren der aztekischen Sprache im nordlichen Mexico und hoheren amerikanischen Norden. *Abhandlungen der Koniglichen Akademie der Wissenschaften* (Berlin) 1854, Supplement-Band, II. pp. 293-98.
Traces of Aztec language among Navajos.

BUXTON, L. H. DUDLEY   (874)
Some Navajo folktales and customs. *Folk-lore* (London), 34: 293-313, 1923.

BYNNER, WITTER   (875)
Designs for beauty. *NM,* 14:12-13, 43, Aug. 1936.
Navajo silverwork.

CALKINS, HUGH G.   (876)
National significance of the Navajo problem. Navajo Service Land Management Conference, March 2-6, 1937, Flagstaff. *Navajo School Service Bulletin* 1.

CAMPBELL, ISABEL (877)
Navajo sandpaintings. *SR*, 25:143-50, 1940.

CARPENTER, T. M. AND STEGGERDA, M. (878)
The food of present day Navajo Indians of New Mexico and Arizona. *Journal of Nutrition*, 18:297-305, 1939.
> Analyses showing energy value of Navajo diet little below that of average American.

CARR, MALCOLM (879)
Brief introduction to Navajo life. USDI, Navajo Service. Window Rock, n.d. Processed.

——— (880)
Preliminary report on the Navajo Mountain Navajo. Unpub. ms. dated 1939 on file at Navajo Central Agency, Window Rock.

——— (881)
Social and economic groupings and leadership among the Navajo. USDI, Navajo Service, Window Rock, 1939. Processed.

CARR, MALCOLM, SPENCER, KATHERINE, AND WOOLLEY, DORIANE (882)
Navaho clans and marriage at Pueblo Alto. *AA*, 41:245-57, 1939.

CASSIDY, INA SIZER (883)
Navajo weaving. *IW*, 3:41, May 1, 1936.

CHABOT, MARIA (884)
Navajo blanket weaving. *IW*, 4:6-12, Nov. 1, 1936.

——— (885)
Traditional weaving revives. *NM*, 14:24-25, 45-48, July 1936.

CHAPIN, G. (886)
A Navajo myth. *New Mexico Anthropologist*, 4:63-67, 1940.

CHAPMAN, KENNETH M. (887)
The Indian fair. *A&A*, 18:215-24, 1925.
> Includes material on Navajo silverwork.

CLARK, ANNA NOLAN (888)
Medicine man's art. *NM*, 18:20, 35-37, May 1940.
> A Navajo legend.

——— (889)
Mothers of Cebolleta. *NM*, 15:17-19, 39-40, Feb. 1937.
> Dramatic historical description of the conversion of some Navajos to Christianity.

CLARK, H. A. (890)
Conditions among the Navajo Indians. *Missionary Review of the World*, 40:917-22, Dec. 1917.

CLUTE, WILLARD N. (891)
Notes on the Navajo region. *American Botanist*, 26:39-47, 1920.

CODALLOS Y RABAL, SERGEANT MAJOR DON JOACHIN (892)
Original depositions to the superior government of the most excellent Count of Fuenclara, Viceroy, Governor, and Captain General of this New Spain. . . . upon the conversion of the pagan Indians of the Provence of Navajo to the bosom of our Holy Mother Church. (Translated in W. W. Hill: Some Navajo

CODALLOS Y RABAL, SERGEANT MAJOR DON JOACHIN (Continued)
culture changes during two centuries. *Smithsonian Miscellaneous Collections*, 100:395-415, 1940.

COLE, ELLIS P.   (893)
Navajo weaving with two- or four-harness looms. *The Weaver*, 2 (4) :11-13, 1937.

COLEMAN, NANCY R.   (894)
Navajo child health; the problem of tuberculosis and a nation's survival. National Association on Indian Affairs, Bulletin 25. New York, 1936.

COLLIER, CHARLES W.   (895)
Soil conservation in the Navajo country. *Soil Conservation*, 1:1-4, Oct. 1935.

COLLIER, JOHN   (896)
Fate of the Navajos. *Sunset*, 52:11-13, Jan. 1924.

––––––   (897)
In the depredation area of northwestern New Mexico. *IW*, 3:1-8, June 15, 1936.

––––––   (898)
Indians at work. *Survey Graphic*, 23:260-65, 297-302, June 1934.

––––––   (899)
The owners of the golden land. *Rural American*, 14:8-9. Jan. 1936.

COLTON, MARY R. F.   (900)
Wool for our Indian weavers—what shall it be? *Museum of Northern Arizona, Museum Notes*, 4:1-5, June 1932.

CONKEY, M. V.   (901)
Children of tradition. *NM*, 14:20-21, 41, 44, Nov. 1936.
    Navajo and Pueblo attitudes towards children with a description of cere-monies and activities connected with their rearing.

CONNELY, RUTH   (902)
Twelve examples of Navajo weaving, from drawings cut on lineoleum blocks. Santa Fe, New Mexico Relief Administration, 1935.

COOLIDGE, DANE   (903)
Lorenzo the Magnificent. New York, Dutton, 1925.
    Life of Lorenzo Hubbell, Sr., Navajo trader.

COOLIDGE, DANE AND MARY   (904)
The Navajo Indians. New York, Houghton Mifflin, 1930.
    Includes information on history, customs, arts, religion, governmental rela-tions.

COOPER, J. M.   (905)
Sheep management on the Navajo reservation. Navajo Service Land Management Conference, March 2-6, 1937, Flagstaff. *Navajo School Service Bulletin* 1.
    Historical development and recommendations for future improvement.

CORBETT, JOHN M.   (906)
Navajo house types. *EP*, 47:97-107, 1940.

COWAN, JOHN L. (907)
Bedouins of the American desert. *American Review of Reviews,* 45:489-90, 1912.
Economics of Navajo blanket weaving.

—— (908)
Bedouins of the Southwest. *Out West,* 35:107-16, 1912.
Discussion of blanket weaving and silver jewelry making.

—— (909)
Playing Cadmus to the Navajos. *Overland Monthly,* n.s. 58:327-33, 1911.

CRAWFORD, M. D. C. (910)
The loom in the new world. *AMNH Journal,* 16:381-, 1916.

CUMMIN, HAZEL E. (911)
Bayeta of the Navaho. *House Beautiful,* 65:644-45, 662, 664-65, 669, May 1929.

CURTIS, CHARLES A. (912)
Captured by the Navajos. New York, Harper, 1904.

CURTIS, EDWARD S. (913)
Vanishing Indian types. *Scribner's,* 39:513-29, May, 1906.
Navajo and Apache.

CURTIS, WILLIAM E. (914)
Education and morals among the Navajos and Pueblos. *American Antiquarian,* 27:259-64, 1905.

DEHUFF, ELIZABETH WILLIS (915)
Creation of the Navajos. *NM,* 11:26-27, May 1933.

—— (916)
Don't gamble. *NM,* 10:16-17, May 1932.
Navajo creation myth.

—— (917)
Giant's bones. *NM,* 10:20-22, 44, April 1932.
Navajo folklore.

—— (918)
The Navajo fire dance. *NM,* 8:10-12, 30, Feb. 1930.

—— (919)
The Navajo flood legend. *NM,* 11:18-19, 50-51, March 1933.

—— (920)
The trickster. *NM,* 10:18-19, July 1932.
A Navajo myth.

DENNIS, WAYNE (921)
Does culture appreciably affect patterns of infant behavior? *Journal of Social Psychology,* 12:305-17, 1940.
Material on infant care and behavior of infant Navajos.

DIMOCK, A. W. (922)
Among the Navaho. *Outlook,* 76:349-59, 1904.
Popular description, recommending government policy of hands off.

DIXON, MAYNARD (923)
Navajo land. *Arizona Highways,* 18:34-37, May, 1942.
Drawings and description of the land and people.

DODGE, RICHARD E. (924)
    The Navaho Indians. *Journal of School Geography,* March 1900.

DORY, WILLIAM (925)
    Navajo land. *NH,* 23:486-505, 1923.

DOUGLAS, FREDERIC H. (926)
    Navaho silversmithing. *DAM, Leaflet series,* 15, 1930.

———— (927)
    Seven Navajo pots. *DAM, Material Culture Notes,* 3:9-14, May 1937.

DUCLOS, ANTOINETTE S. (928)
    Navajo warp and woof. *Arizona Highways,* 18:10-13, Aug. 1942.
        Weaving, from sheep to blanket.

DUTTON, BERTHA P. (929)
    The Navaho wind way ceremonial. *EP,* 48:73-82, 1941.

DUXBURY, WILLIAM CROCKER (930)
    A legend of the Navajos. *Cosmopolitan,* 22:73-, Nov. 1896.

EASTERN ASSOCIATION ON INDIAN AFFAIRS (931)
    The Navajo. EAIA, Bulletin 11. New York, May 1926.

EAVES, ROYCE (932)
    Teli-Thlakai. *The Rio Grande Writer,* 1:17-20, Spring 1942.
        Navajo amusements.

EDDY, LEWIS H. (933)
    A Navajo myth. *Arizona Magazine,* Aug. 1893.

EICKEMEYER, CARL (934)
    Over the great Navajo trail. New York, J. J. Little & Co., 1900.
        Travel description.

ELDER, DOROTHY (935)
    Navajo land. *National Park Service, Region 3 Quarterly,* 3:27-30, April 1941.

ELMORE, FRANCIS H. (936)
    The ethnobotany of the Navajo. Uupub. Master's thesis, USC, 1936.

———— (937)
    Ethnobotany of the Navajo of Chaco Canyon. Unpub. research paper, USC and American School of Research. Los Angeles, 1935.

———— (938)
    Food animals of the Navajo. *EP,* 44:149-54, 1938.

EVANS, TRADER (939)
    Navajo folk lore. *Southwestern Lore,* 1 (1):10-16, 1935.

FALLS, ANNA E. (940)
    The culinary art of the Navajos. *Practical Home Economics,* 20: 349-50, 1942.

FEWKES, J. WALTER (941)
    Clay figurines made by Navaho children. *AA,* 25:559-63, 1923.

FILLMORE, J. C. (942)
    Songs of the Navajos. *Land of Sunshine,* 5:238-41, 1896.

FLOOD, FRANCIS A. (943)
I'd like to be a Navajo. *Farmer-Stockman*, 50:716, 737, 739, Dec. 15, 1937.
> Present-day agricultural conditions on Navajo reservation.

FORREST, EARLE R. (944)
Wild Navajos of the four corners. *Travel*, 42:20-23, Jan. 1924. *Also Travel*, 47:24-28, Sept. 1926.

FRANCISCAN FATHERS (945)
An ethnologic dictionary of the Navajo language. St. Michael's, Arizona, Franciscan Fathers, 1910.

———— (946)
Vocabulary of the Navajo language. St. Michael's, Arizona, Franciscan Fathers, 1912.

FREIRE-MARRECO, BARBARA (947)
Concepcion. *EP*, 14:79-81, 1923.
> Life story of a Navajo woman.

FRYER, E. R. (948)
Looking ahead. Navajo Service Land Management Conference, March 2-6, 1937, Flagstaff. *Navajo School Service Bulletin 1.*
> Summary of needed programs for Navajo reservation.

———— (949)
The Navajo Service. Navajo Service Land Management Conference, March 2-6, 1937, Flagstaff. *Navajo School Service Bulletin 1.*
> History, policies, and achievements.

———— (950)
Navajo social organization and land use adjustment. *Scientific Monthly*, 55:1403-16, Nov. 1942.

GERKEN, EDNA A. (951)
Development of a health education program; experiences with Navajo Indians. *American Journal of Public Health*, 30:915-20, 1940.

———— (952)
How the Navajos improve their health. *Childhood Education*, 18:315-18, 1942.

GILLMOR, FRANCES AND WETHERILL, LOUISA (953)
Traders to the Navajos. Boston, Houghton Mifflin, 1934.

GODDARD, PLINY E. (954)
Navaho. *Encyclopedia of Religion and Ethics*, v. 9. New York, Scribners, 1922.

———— (955)
Navajo blankets. *American Museum Journal*, 10:201-11, 1910.

———— (956)
Navajo myths, prayers, and songs, with texts and translations. *UCPAAE*, v. 5, no. 2. Berkeley, 1907.

———— (957)
Navajo texts. *AMNH, Anthropological Papers*, v. 34, pt. 1. New York, 1933.

GOODWIN, GRENVILLE (958)
A comparison of Navajo and White Mountain Apache ceremonial forms and categories. Paper read at the meeting of the Southwestern Section, AAAS, Tucson, April 22, 1940.

GRANDSTAFF, JAMES O. (959)
Wool characteristics in relation to Navajo weaving. USDA, Technical Bulletin 790. Washington, GPO, 1942.

GREGORY, HERBERT E. (960)
Geography of the Navajo country. *Annals of the Association of American Geographers,* 5:147, 1915.

—— (961)
The Navajo country. *American Geographic Society Bulletin,* 47: 561-77, 652-72, 1915.

—— (962)
*The Navajo country; a geographic and hydrographic reconnaissance of parts of Arizona, New Mexico, and Utah. USDI, Geologic Survey, Water Supply Paper 380. Washington, GPO, 1916.
> Part II contains a brief but accurate account of the natives of the Navajo country—their environment, personal characteristics, mode of living, etc.

GUERNSEY, SAMUEL J. (963)
Notes on a Navajo war dance. *AA,* 22: 304-07, 1920.

GUITERMAN, ARTHUR (964)
The star planters, a Navajo Indian legend. *The Popular Magazine,* Feb. 15, 1911.

H. R. H. (965)
The Navajo hogan survives. *EP,* 49:152-53, 1942.

HAGERMAN, H. J. (966)
Navajo Indian reservation. Report of H. J. Hagerman, special commissioner to negotiate with Indians on the status of Navajo Indian reservation land acquisitions and extensions, with specific recommendations for the outside boundaries of the reservation and of certain additional areas to be acquired for the Indians outside the reservation. Senate Doc. 64, 72nd Congress, 1st Session. Washington, GPO, 1932.

HAILE, BERARD (967)
Learning Navaho. St. Michael's Arizona, St. Michael's Press, 1942.

—— (968)
A manual of Navaho grammar. Santa Fe, Santa Fe Pub. Co., 1926.

—— (969)
The meaning of "Tusayan," a note on Navajo migrations and Pueblo names. *AA,* 19:151, 1917.

—— (970)
Navaho chantways and ceremonials. *AA,* 40:639-52, 1938.

—— (971)
Navaho country. *Franciscan Missions of the Southwest,* 10:28-38, 1922.

HAILE, BERARD (Continued) (972)
   Navaho games of chance and taboo. *Primitive Man,* 6:35-40, 1933.

────── (973)
   The Navaho land question. *Franciscan Missions of the Southwest,* 10:8-16, 1922.

────── (974)
   Navaho upward-reaching way and emergence place. *AA,* 44:407-20, 1942.

────── (975)
   A note on the Navaho visionary. *AA,* 42:359, 1940.

────── (976)
   Origin legend of the Navaho enemy way. YUPA, 17. New Haven, 1938.

────── (977)
   Racial mentality and the missionary. *Primitive Man,* 2:18-19, 1929.

────── (978)
   Religious concepts of the Navajo Indians. *American Catholic Philosophical Association, Proceedings, 10th Annual Meeting.* Washington, 1935. pp.84-98.

────── (979),
   Some cultural aspects of the Navajo hogan. USDI, Navajo Service, Window Rock, 1937. Processed.

────── (980)
   Some mortuary customs of the Navajo. *Franciscan Missions of the Southwest,* 5:29-33, 1917.

────── (981)
   Why the Navaho hogan. *Primitive Man,* 15:39-56, July-Oct. 1942.
      Religious aspects of Navajo house building.

HALL, E. T. (982)
   Navajo weaving. *Recreation,* 35:660-61, 1942.

HANCOCK, J. C. (983)
   Diseases among the Indians. *Southwestern Medicine,* 17:126, April 1933.
      Results of Wasserman tests on Navajo children.

HARRINGTON, MARK RAYMOND (984)
   Swedged Navaho bracelets. *Masterkey,* 8:183-84, 1934.

HARRIS, FERN E. (985)
   Navajo weaving. *IW,* 4:28-31, Sept. 15, 1936.

HARROLD, L. L. (986)
   Floods in the Navajo country. *Soil Conservation,* 7:172-73, 1942.

HARTMAN, LILLIAN D. (987)
   The life and customs of the Navajo women. *Wisconsin Archaeologist,* n. s., 18:100-07, 1939.

HASSELL, SANFORD W, (988)
   Navajo oddities. *NM,* 18:45, April; 41, May 1940.

HASSELL, SANFORD W. (Continued)   (989)
    A trader views the Navaho. *EP,* 48:146-47, 1941.

HAVENS, O. C.   (990)
    Transportation pioneers. *Arizona Highways,* Nov. 1938.
        Trading in Navajo country.

HAWLEY, FLORENCE M.   (991)
    Navajo night. *NM,* 20:22, 33-35, July 1942.
        Description of a night spent with a Navajo group.

HEGER, NANCY IRENE   (992)
    Before books in an Indian school. *Progressive Education,* 9:138-
    43, 1932.

HEGGIE, T. L.   (993)
    Range management for the Navajo-Hopi reservation. Navajo
    Service Land Management Conference, March 2-6, 1937, Flagstaff.
    Navajo School Service Bulletin 1.

HILL, GERTRUDE   (994)
    The art of the Navajo silversmith. *Kiva,* 2 (5) ;17-21, 1937.
                                                                    (995)
    The use of turquoise among the Navajo. *Kiva,* 4:11-14, 1938. *Also*
    Ysleta, Texas, Edwin B. Hill, 1939.

HILL, WILLARD W.   (996)
    The agricultural and hunting methods of the Navaho Indians.
    YUPA, 18. New Haven, 1938.
                                                                    (997)
    The hand trembling ceremony of the Navajo. *EP,* 38:65-68, 1935.
                                                                    (998)
    Navaho humor. Unpub. undated ms. in possession of the author.
                                                                    (999)
    Navajo pottery manufacture. UNM Bulletin, Anthropological
    series, v. 2, no. 3, 1937.
                                                                   (1000)
    Navajo rites for dispelling insanity and delirium. *EP,* 41:71-74,
    1936.
                                                                   (1001)
    Navajo use of jimson weed. *New Mexico Anthropologist,* 3:19-21,
    1938.
                                                                   (1002)
    Navaho warfare. YUPA, 5. New Haven, 1936.
                                                                   (1003)
    Reorganization report. Unpub. study in the files of USDI, Office
    of Indian Affairs, Reorganization Division. Washington, 1935.
        Contains information on Navajo history, ethnography, acculturation.
                                                                   (1004)
    Some aspects of Navajo political structure. *Plateau,* 13:23-28,
    Oct. 1940.
                                                                   (1005)
    Some Navaho culture changes during two centuries. (In Essays in

HILL, WILLARD W. (Continued)

Historical Anthropology of North America, published in honor of John R. Swanton. *Smithsonian Miscellaneous Collections,* 100: 395-415, 1940.)

——— (1006)

Stability in culture and pattern. *AA,* 41:258-60, 1939.
Navajo chants as illustrative of stable cultural elements.

——— (1007)

The status of the hermaphrodite and transvestite in Navaho culture. *AA,* 37:273-79, 1935.

HODGE, FREDERICK WEBB (1008)

The early Navaho and Apache. *AA,* o. s., 8:223-40, 1895. *Also* Washington, Judd and Detweiler, 1895.

HOFFMAN, FREDERICK L. (1009)

The Navaho population problem. *ICA, Proceedings, 23rd Session.* New York, 1930. pp. 620-32. *Also Stone and Webster Journal,* 44:650-72, 1929.

HOGNER, DOROTHY CHILDS (1010)

The Navajo rug market; what civilization is doing to one Indian hand-craft. *NM,* 12:22-23, 36, 38, Jan. 1934.
The effect of commercialization has been an increase in quantity and a deterioration of quality.

——— (1011)

Navajo winter nights. New York, T. Nelson & Sons, 1935.
Folk tales and legends.

HOGNER, NILS (1012)

Navajo art. *School Arts Magazine,* 30:465-66, 1931.

HOLDSWORTH, WILLIE (1013)

A study of the intelligence and reading ability of Navajo Indians in the ninth and tenth grades. Unpub Master's thesis, University of Texas, 1937.

HOLLISTER, U. S. (1014)

The Navajo and his blanket. Denver, the Author, 1903.

HOLMAN, H. E. (1015)

Forest resources on the Navajo reservation. Navajo Service Land Management Conference, March 2-6, 1937, Flagstaff. *Navajo School Service Bulletin 1.*

HORNER, EVA M. (1016)

Masked gods of the Navajo and their occurrence among the Pueblos and Apache. Unpub. Master's thesis, University of Chicago, 1931.

HOWARD, E. (1017)

Navajo blanket. *Ladies Home Journal,* 48:121, Dec. 1931.

HULSIZER, ALLEN (1018)

Navajo communities and secondary education. *Junior-Senior High School Clearing House,* 9:404-06, 1935.

HURT, AMY PASSMORE (1019)

Nomads of the Navajo desert. *NM,* 11:7-10, Jan. 1933.

HUYCK, MERNICE HOWE (1020)
Navajo blankets, the literature of a nomadic people. Unpub.
Master's thesis, New Mexico Normal (Highlands) University,
1930.

INDIAN RIGHTS ASSOCIATION (1021)
Effect of spoils system on Navajos. Indian Rights Association,
Publication 21. Philadelphia, 1895.

JAMES, GEORGE W. (1022)
The fire dance of the Navahoes. *Wide World Magazine*
(London), Sept. 1900. pp. 516-23.

―――― (1023)
Indian blanketry. *Outing,* 39:684-93, March 1902.

―――― (1024)
Indian blankets and their makers. *Mentor,* 10:13-28, June 1922.

―――― (1025)
The industries of the Navahoes and Mokis. *Good Health,* June
1899. pp. 315-22.

―――― (1026)
Moki and Navaho Indian sports. *Outing,* 39:10-15, Oct. 1901.

―――― (1027)
Navaho Indian blanket. *Overland,* n. s., 65:268-83, March 1915.

JAMES, MARJORIE (1028)
A note on Navajo pottery-making. *EP,* 43:85-86, 1937.

JEANCON, JEAN ALLARD AND DOUGLAS, FREDERIC H. (1029)
Indian sand-painting: tribes, techniques, and uses. *DAM, Leaflet
series* 43-44, 1932.

―――― (1030)
The Navaho Indians. *DAM, Leaflet series* 21, 1931.

―――― (1031)
Navaho spinning, dyeing, and weaving. *DAM, Leaflet series* 3,
1930.

JOHNSTON, PHILIP (1032)
My boyhood with the Navajos. *Touring Topics,* Sept. 1931.

―――― (1033)
The story of Tolchaco; a mission for the Navajos, 1900-18.
Museum of Northern Arizona, Museum Notes, 9:9-12, Aug. 1936.

JOHNSTON, W. R. (1034)
The needs of the Navajo Indians. *LMC, Proceedings, 2nd Session,
1908.* pp. 61-65.

JONES, C. IRWIN (1035)
The Navajo Indian and his ways. *New Age Magazine,* Feb. 1903.

JONES, WILFORD H. (1036)
How I make a silver Navajo ring. *IW,* 3:31, April 15, 1936.

KAY, ELEANOR (1037)
Big trouble comes—we all fight. *NM,* 19:14-15, 34-35, Oct. 1941.
War and the Navajos.

KEECH, ROY A. (1038)
Toh-Cheely. *EP,* 36:33-39, 1934.
A visit to the Navajos.

KELLY, CHARLES   (1039)
   Rain sing. *Desert Magazine,* 5:9-10, Sept. 1942.
      Reasons why the Navajo clings to his religion.

KENNARD, EDWARD A.   (1040)
   The use of native languages and cultures in Indian education.
   (In La Farge, Oliver, ed.: *The Changing Indian.* Norman, UOP,
   1942. pp. 109-115.)
      Stresses necessity for teaching Indians in their native languages. Navajo used
      as illustration.

KEUR, DOROTHY L.   (1041)
   Big Bead Mesa; an archaeological study of Navaho acculturation,
   1745-1812. Society for American Archaeology, Memoirs 1.
   Menasha, Wisconsin, 1941.

————   (1042)
   New light on Navaho origins. *New York Academy of Sciences,*
   Transactions, Section II, v. 2, no. 7. New York, 1940. pp. 182-88.

KIMBALL, SOLON T.   (1043)
   The economic need for agricultural development. Navajo
   Service Land Management Conference, March 2-6, 1937, Flag-
   staff. *Navajo School Service Bulletin* 1.

————   (1044)
   Navaho economy and environment. Paper read at meeting of
   Southwestern Section, AAAS, Tucson, April 22, 1940.

————   (1045)
   The range resource and its relation to the subsistence economy of
   the Navajo people. USDI, Navajo Service, Window Rock, n. d.
   Typewritten.

————   (1046)
   Social-economic problems. Radio address from KTGM, Window
   Rock, Oct. 25, 1938.

KIMBALL, SOLON T. AND PROVINSE, JOHN H.   (1046a)
   Navajo social organization in land use planning. *Applied Anthro-*
   pology, 1:18-25, July-Aug.-Sept. 1942.

KIRK, RUTH F.   (1047)
   The chant of Dsilyidje. *NM,* 12:14-16, 34-35, Aug. 1934.

————   (1048)
   Designs for magic. *NM,* 18:14-15, 38, Nov. 1940.
      Navajo witchcraft.

————   (1049)
   Ghosts of white medicine. *NM,* 12:10-11, 43-45, Dec. 1934.

————   (1050)
   Grandfather of the gods. *NM,* 14:28-29, 43-44, July 1936.
      Origin and present status of Navajo night chant.

————   (1051)
   In beauty it is finished. *NM,* 13:16-17, Dec. 1935.
      Navajo songs.

————   (1052)
   A letter to Clah Chee. *NM,* 12:7, 43-44, Oct. 1934.

————   (1053)
   Navajo—the people. *NM,* 16:14-15, 36-38, July 1938.
      Their origin and history.

KIRK, RUTH F. (Continued)   (1054)
    Navajo bill of fare. *NM*, 19:16-17, 37-38, June 1941.

                                                                 (1055)
    Navajo rugs. *California Art and Architecture*, Nov. 1932. pp.
    22-23, 34.

                                                                 (1056)
    Wool weights. *NM*, 12:17-18, June 1934.

KLINGER, BRUNO   (1057)
    Establishing of Navajo experiment station. USDA, Soil Con-
    servation Service, 1937.

KLUCKHOHN, CLYDE   (1058)
    Beyond the rainbow. Boston, Christopher Publishing House,
    1933.
        An account of the Southwest as experienced in extensive travel. Deals mainly
        with Navajo and Hopi.

                                                                 (1059)
    The dance of Hasjelti. *EP*, 15:187-92, 1923.

                                                                 (1060)
    Great chants of the Navajo. *Theatre Arts Monthly*, 17:639-45,
    1933.

                                                                 (1061)
    Navaho witchcraft. To be published as a paper of the Peabody
    Museum of Harvard University.

                                                                 (1062)
    Navaho women's knowledge of their song ceremonials. *EP*, 45:87-
    92, 1938.

                                                                 (1063)
    Participation in ceremonials in a Navaho community. *AA*,
    40:359-69, 1938.

                                                                 (1064)
    Patterning as exemplified in Navaho culture. (In Spier, L.;
    Hallowell, A. I.; and Newman, S. S.: *Language, culture, and
    personality; essays in memory of Edward Sapir.* Menasha, Wis-
    consin, Sapir Memorial Publication Fund, 1941.)

                                                                 (1065)
    Some personal and social aspects of Navaho ceremonial practice.
    Harvard Theological Review, 32:57-82, 1939.

                                                                 (1066)
    Theoretical bases for an empirical method of studying the acqui-
    sition of culture by individuals. *Man*, 39:98-103, 1939.
        Statement of a program for the study of Ramah Navajo children.

KLUCKHOHN, CLYDE AND WYMAN, LELAND   (1067)
    An introduction to Navajo chant practice. AAA, Memoirs 53.
    Menasha, Wisconsin, 1940.

KOCH, F. J.   (1068)
    Indians of the painted desert. *Overland*, n. s., 67:70-74, 1916.

KUTNEWSKY, F.   (1069)
    Navajo rugs hold unique place in American handicraft industry.
    Rayon, 23:31-32, Jan. 1942.

KUTNEWSKY, F. AND HOLBROOK, C.   (1070)
  Navajo rugs. *Compressed Air Magazine*, 47:6658-62, Feb. 1942.
LA FARGE, OLIVER   (1071)
  An experimental school for Indians. *Progressive Education*, 9:87-
  94, 1932.
——   (1072)
  Unscientific expedition; Navajo reservation. *World's Work*,
  60:69-73, May 1931.
LANDGRAF, JOHN   (1073)
  *Dynamic factors affecting Indian-White relations in a New
  Mexico community.* Unpub. Doctor's dissertation, Harvard Uni-
  versity. To be finished in July 1942.
LAWHEAD, H. E.   (1074)
  Teaching Navajo children to read. *Progressive Education*, 9:131-
  35, 1932.
LEFT HANDED   (1075)
  Son of Old Man Hat. New York, Harcourt Brace, 1938.
      Navajo biography recorded by Walter Dyk.
LEIGH, W. R.   (1076)
  A day with a Navajo shepherd. *Scribner's*, 71:334-42, 1922.
LEIGHTON, ALEXANDER AND DOROTHEA C.   (1077)
  Elements of psychotherapy in Navaho religion. *Psychiatry*, 4:515-
  23, 1941.
——   (1078)
  A Navaho builds a house. *NH*, 47:272-73, 1941.
      Photographic series.
——   (1079)
  A Navaho makes a blanket. *NH*, 47:274, 1941.
      Photographic series.
——   (1080)
  A Navaho makes soap. *NH*, 48:19-20, 1941.
      Photographic series.
——   (1081)
  A Navaho takes a "Turkish bath." *NH*, 48:21, 1941.
      Photographic series.
——   (1082)
  Some types of uneasiness and fear in a Navaho Indian community.
  AA, 44:194-209, 1942.
      (The Leightons are working on a handbook of introductory materials for
      Navajo Service doctors and nurses, to be published by the Office of Indian
      Affairs in the fall of 1942. They are also making "a personality study of a
      Navaho Indian" and working on a paper on sources of satisfaction among the
      Navajos, designed to be a complementary study to their one on uneasiness
      and fear.)
LETHERMAN, JONATHAN   (1083)
  Sketch of the Navajo tribe of Indians, Territory of New Mexico.
  Smithsonian 10th Annual Report. Washington, 1857. pp. 283-
  97.
LEUPP, FRANCIS ELLINGTON   (1084)
  *"Civilization's" lesson to "Barbarism"—dastardly outrage upon
  inoffensive Navajos.* Indian Rights Association, Publication 42.
  Philadelphia, 1897.

LINCOLN, J. S.   (1085)
   The dream in primitive cultures. London, Cresset Press, 1935.
LINDELY, LAWRENCE   (1086)
   Four weeks among the Navajo. *Indian Truth,* v. 14, no. 8, Nov.
   1937.
        Navajo opposition to Soil Conservation program.

————   (1087)
   The Navajos. *Indian Truth,* v. 18, no. 5, May-June 1941.
        Present economic and social problems.
LIPPS, OSCAR H.   (1088)
   History of the art of weaving among the Navajos. *Red Man,*
   7:58-63, Oct. 1914.

————   (1089)
   The Navajo and his work. *Arizona Magazine,* Dec. 1906.

————   (1090)
   The Navajos. Cedar Rapids, Iowa, Torch Press, 1909.
LOCKETT, CLAY   (1091)
   Midwives and childbirth among the Navajo. *Plateau,* 12:15-17,
   July 1939.
LOCKETT, H. CLAIBORNE   (1092)
   Navajo taboos. USDI, Navajo Service, Window Rock. Unpub.
   ms., n. d.
LUMMIS, CHARLES F.   (1093)
   The best blanket in the world. *Land of Sunshine,* 6:8-11, 1896.

————   (1094)
   Our first American jewelers. *Land of Sunshine,* 5:54-58, 1896.
LUOMALA, KATHARINE   (1095)
   Navaho life of yesterday and today. USDI, National Park Service.
   Berkeley, 1938.
        Hunting, agriculture, food, livestock.
MCCORMICK, H.   (1096)
   Through the Navaho region. *NH,* 17:473-80, 1917.
MCGINNIES, W. G.   (1097)
   General information on thirteen Navajo districts. USDA, Soil
   Conservation Service, 1937. Typewritten.
        Population, land use, range types, etc.

————   (1098)
   Stock reduction and range management. Navajo Service Land
   Management Conference, March 2-6, 1937, Flagstaff. *Navajo
   School Service Bulletin 1.*
MCGROARTY, JOHN S.   (1099)
   The Navajo. *West Coast Magazine,* Nov. 1907.
MACKENDRICK, M.   (1100)
   Mother of the Navajos: Louisa N. Wetherill. *Sunset,* 50:61-62,
   June 1923.
MARCHBANK, WILLIAM J.   (1101)
   White man's magic. *NM,* 13:18-19, Feb. 1935.
        Discussion of possibility of making the Navajo wasteland a fertile farm region.

MASON, O. T. (1102)
    Aboriginal skin dressing. *United States National Museum, Report*, 1889. pp. 574-80.

MATTHEWS, WASHINGTON (1103)
    The basket drum. *AA*, o. s., 7:202-08, 1894.
        Navajo basket making, a declining art.

—————   (1104)
    The gentile system of the Navaho Indians. *JAF*, 3:89-110, 1890.

—————   (1105)
    Marriage prohibitions on the father's side among Navajos. *JAF*, 4:78-79, 1891.

—————   (1106)
    The Mountain Chant, a Navajo ceremony; with original text and translation of songs. *Bureau of American Ethnology, 5th Annual Report*. Washington, GPO, 1887. pp. 385-467.

—————   (1107)
    Mythic dry-paintings of the Navajos. *American Naturalist*, 19:931-39, 1885.

—————   (1108)
    Mythological dry-painting of the Navajos. *Smithsonian Miscellaneous Collections*, 34 (2) :139-40, 1893.

—————   (1109)
    Myths of gestation and parturition. *AA*, 4:737-42, 1902.

—————   (1110)
    Navajo dye stuffs. *Smithsonian Annual Report, 1891*. Washington, 1893. pp. 613-15.

—————   (1111)
    Navajo gambling songs. *AA*, o. s., 2:1-20, 1889.

—————   (1112)
    A Navajo initiation. *Land of Sunshine*, 15:353-56, 1901.

—————   (1113)
    Navajo legends. Boston, Houghton Mifflin, 1897. *Also* American Folklore Society, Memoirs 5. 1897.

—————   (1114)
    Navajo myths, prayers, and songs with text and translations. *UCPAAE*, 5:21-63, 1907.

—————   (1115)
    Navajo names for plants. *American Naturalist*, 20:767-77, 1886.

—————   (1116)
    Navaho night chant. *JAF*, 14:12-19, 1901.

—————   (1117)
    Navajo silversmiths. *Bureau of American Ethnology, 2nd Annual Report*. Washington, GPO, 1883. pp. 167-78.

—————   (1118)
    Navajo weavers. *Bureau of American Ethnology, 3rd Annual Report*. Washington, GPO, 1884. pp. 371-91.

—————   (1119)
    The Navajo yellow dye. *AA*, 6:194, 1904.

MATTHEWS, WASHINGTON (Continued)   (1120)
  The night chant; a Navajo ceremony. AMNH, Memoirs, v. 6.
  New York, 1902.

——   (1121)
  Noqoilpi, the gambler; a Navajo myth. *JAF,* 2:89-94, 1889.

——   (1122)
  A part of the Navajos' mythology. *American Antiquarian,* 5:207-
  24, 1883.

——   (1123)
  The prayer of a Navajo shaman. *AA,* o. s., 1:149-71, 1888.

——   (1124)
  Serpent worship among the Navajos. *Land of Sunshine,* 9:228-35,
  1898.

——   (1125)
  Some dieties and demons of the Navajos. *American Naturalist,*
  20:841-50, 1886.

——   (1126)
  Some illustrations of the connection between myth and ceremony.
  International Congress of Anthropologists, Memoirs, 1893. pp.
  246-51.

——   (1127)
  Some sacred objects of the Navajo rites. *International Folklore
  Association, Archives,* 1:227-47, 1893.

——   (1128)
  Songs of sequence of the Navajos. *JAF,* 7:185-94, 1894.

——   (1129)
  Songs of the Navajos. *Land of Sunshine,* 5:197-201, 1896.

——   (1130)
  A study in butts and tips. *AA,* o. s., 5:345-50, 1892.

——   (1131)
  The study of ceremony. *JAF,* 10:257-63, 1897.

——   (1132)
  A study of ethics among the lower races. *JAF,* 12:1-9, 1899.

——   (1133)
  The treatment of ailing gods. *JAF,* 14:20-23, 1901.

——   (1134)
  A vigil of the gods, a Navajo ceremony. *AA,* o. s., 9:50-57, 1896.

MERA, HARRY P.   (1135)
  Banded-background blankets. Laboratory of Anthropology,
  General series, Bulletin 7. Santa Fe, 1939.

——   (1136)
  The Chinlee rug. Laboratory of Anthropology, General series,
  Bulletin 13. Santa Fe, 1942.

——   (1137)
  Navajo blankets of the "classic" period. Laboratory of Anthropology, General series, Bulletin 3. Santa Fe, 1938.

MERA, HARRY P. (Continued)   (1138)
    Navajo rugs of the crystal and two gray hills type. Laboratory of
Anthropology, General series, Bulletin 10. Santa Fe, 1940.
——————   (1139)
    Pictorial blankets. Laboratory of Anthropology, General series,
Bulletin 6. Santa Fe, 1938.
——————   (1140)
    The serrate designs of Navajo blanketry. Laboratory of Anthro-
pology, General series, Bulletin 11. Santa Fe, 1940.
——————   (1141)
    The "slave blanket." Laboratory of Anthropology, General series,
Bulletin 5. Santa Fe, 1938.
——————   (1142)
    The so-called "chief blanket." Laboratory of Anthropology,
General series, Bulletin 2. Santa Fe, 1938.
——————   (1143)
    Wedge-weave blankets. Laboratory of Anthropology, General
series, Bulletin 9. Santa Fe, 1939.
——————   (1144)
    The zoning treatment in Navajo blanket design. Laboratory of
Anthropology, General series, Bulletin 12. Santa Fe, 1940.

MILLER, EDGAR K.   (1145)
    The Indian and the trader. *Indian School Journal,* 7:11-21, June
1907.
        Trading post at Crystal Springs, New Mexico.

MILLER, WICK   (1146)
    The Navajo and his silver work. *New Mexico Highway Journal,*
8:12-14, Aug. 1930.

MINDELEFF, COSMOS   (1147)
    Aboriginal architecture in the United States. *American Geo-
graphical Society, Bulletin* 30:414-27, 1898.
        Includes discussion of Navajo and Pueblo houses.
——————   (1148)
    Houses and house dedication of the Navahos. *Scientific Ameri-
can,* 82:233-34, 1900.
——————   (1149)
    Navaho houses. *Bureau of American Ethnology, 17th Annual
Report, Part 2.* Washington, GPO, 1898. pp. 469-517.
——————   (1150)
    Navajo Indian gamblers. *Scientific American;* July 8, 1899.

MIRKOWICH, NICHOLAS   (1151)
    A note on Navajo place names. *AA,* 43:313-14, 1941.

MITCHELL, F. G.   (1152)
    *Dine Bizad: a handbook for beginners in the study of the Navaho
language.* New York, Board of National Missions of the
Presbyterian Church, 1932.
——————   (1153)
    Navaho missions. *SW,* 50:357-61, 1921.

MONSEN, FREDERICK I.   (1154)
The Navajo baby. *Sunday Magazine*, Sept. 24, 1905.

MORGAN, J. C.   (1155)
The place of the tribal council in the Navajo program. Radio
address from KTGM, Window Rock, March 7, 1939.

MORGAN, WILLIAM   (1156)
Human wolves among the Navaho. YUPA, 11. New Haven,
1936.

MOSSER, A. AND MOTYLEWSKI, S.   (1157)
From Navaho to white man's tongue. *Elementary English Review*,
16:303-06, 1939.

MUNK, J. A.   (1158)
Navajo surgery. *Journal of Eclectic Medicine*, Jan. 1906. p. 10.

MUSGRAVE, M. E.   (1159)
Distribution and utilization of flood waters. *Science*, n. s.,
82:461-62, 1935.
      For improvement of Navajo farm land.

——   (1160)
Helping the Navajos help themselves. *IW*, 4:35-39, Feb. 1, 1937.
      Soil Conservation Service program.

——   (1161)
Plant corn a foot deep. *Wallace's Farmer and Iowa Homestead*,
64:795, 803, 1939.
      Hopi and Navajo method of conserving moisture.

——   (1162)
White magic in Navajo land. *American Forests*, 43:426-31, 460,
461, 1937.
      SCS rehabilitation of Navajo lands.

NELL, A.   (1163)
Guests of the American bedouins. *Travel*, 39:5-10, June 1922.

NEUMANN, DAVID L.   (1164)
Navajo silver dies. *EP*, 35:71-75, 1933.

——   (1164a)
Navaho silversmithing survives. *EP*, 50:6-8, Jan. 1943.

——   (1165)
Navajo silverwork. *EP*, 32:102-08, 1932.

——   (1166)
Navajo weaving looks ahead. *New Mexico Quarterly*, 3:183-87,
1933.

NEW MEXICO ASSOCIATION ON INDIAN AFFAIRS   (1167)
Children of tradition. Indian art series 10. Santa Fe, 1936.
      Navajo attitudes towards children and methods of rearing.

——   (1168)
Navaho and Pueblo Indian dancing. Indian art series 9. Santa
Fe, 1936.

——   (1169)
Navaho blanket weaving. Indian art series 6. Santa Fe, 1936.

——   (1170)
Navajo silversmithing. Indian art series 7. Santa Fe, n. d.

NEWCOMB, FRANC J.   (1171)
    Doorways face the dawn. *NM*, 12:7, 40, Dec. 1934.
        Description of Navajo hogans.

_____   (1172)
    How the Navajo adopt rites. *EP*, 46:25-27, 1939.

_____   (1173)
    Mystic medicine. *NM*, 13:22, 41, Sept. 1935.
        Navajo conception of medicine and associated rituals.

_____   (1174)
    Navajo calendar. *NM*, 18:18-19, 32-34, Jan. 1940.

_____   (1175)
    The Navajo listening rite. *EP*, 45:46-49, 1938.

_____   (1176)
    Navajo omens and taboos. Santa Fe, Rydal Press, 1940.

_____   (1177)
    Navajo symbols of the sun. *New Mexico Quarterly*, 6:305-07, 1936.

_____   (1178)
    Origin legend of the Navajo Eagle Chant. *JAF*, 53:50-77, 1940.

_____   (1179)
    Small duck and the four stones. *NM*, 16:21, 44-45, July 1938.
        Navajo legend.

_____   (1180)
    Symbols in sand. *NM*, 14:24-25, 37-38, Dec. 1936. *Also* New Mexico Association on Indian Affairs, Indian art series 11. Santa Fe, n. d.

NEWELL, W. W.   (1181)
    Navaho legends. *JAF*, 9:211-18, 1896.

NEWTON, MRS. E. E.   (1182)
    The Navajo Indians. *LMC, 1st Session, 1905.* pp. 36-38.

NEWTON, ELSIE   (1183)
    Impressions of the Navahos. *SW*, 35:610-16, 1905.

NIRDLINGER, CHARLES F.   (1184)
    Moquis and Navajos. *Illustrated American*, 21:372-, 1896

OSTERMANN, LEOPOLD   (1185)
    Navajo houses. *Franciscan Missions of the Southwest*, 5:20-30, 1917.

_____   (1186)
    The Navajo Indian blanket. *Franciscan Missions of the Southwest*, 6:1-11, 1918.

_____   (1187)
    The Navajo Indians of New Mexico and Arizona. *Anthropos*, 3:859-69, 1908.

_____   (1188)
    Navajo land and language. *Echoes from the Pines*, Mid-summer 1901.

_____   (1189)
    Navajo names. *Franciscan Missions of the Southwest*, 6:11-15, 1918.

OSTERMANN, LEOPOLD (Continued)   (1190)
    The Navajo noun. *ICA, Proceedings,* 15 (2) :243-54, 1907.
                                                                 (1191)
    The Navajos. *Catholic Pioneer,* July 1905-Jan. 1906.
                                                                 (1192)
    Origin, characteristics, and costume of the Navajo Indians.
Franciscan Missions of the Southwest, 5:1-11, 1917.
                                                                 (1193)
    Silversmithing among the Navajos. *Franciscan Missions of the
Southwest,* 7:18-24, 1919.

OVERHOLT, M. E.   (1194)
    Pictures in sand. *A&A,* 34:262-65, 1933.

PAGE, GORDON B.   (1195)
    Navaho house types. *Museum of Northern Arizona, Museum
Notes,* 9:47-49, March 1937.
                                                                 (1196)
    The Navajo sweat house. *Museum of Northern Arizona, Bulletin,*
2:19-21, 1937.

PALMER, EDWARD   (1197)
    Notes on the Navajo Indians of New Mexico made in 1869. Ms.
in the library of the Peabody Museum, Harvard University.

PALMER, FRANK L.   (1198)
    The configuration pattern of Navajo culture. *EP,* 41:19-24, 1936.

PARSONS, ELSIE CLEWS   (1199)
    Navaho folk tales. *JAF,* 36:368-75, 1923.
                                                                 (1200)
    Note on a Navajo war dance. *AA,* 21:465-67, 1919.
                                                                 (1201)
    Notes on the night chant at Tuwelchedu which came to an end on
December 6, 1920. *AA,* 23:240-43, 1921.

PATTERSON, GEORGE L.   (1202)
    Navajos and their blanket-weaving industry. *New England
Magazine,* n. s., 31:64-74, Sept. 1904.

PEATFIELD, J. J.   (1203)
    A Navajo blanket. *The Californian,* Aug. 1893.

PEET, S. D.   (1204)
    The suastika and fire-worship in America. *American Antiquarian,*
26:185-92, 1904.

PEPPER, GEORGE H.   (1205)
    Ah-jih-lee-hah-neh, a Navajo legend. *JAF,* 21:178-83, 1908.
                                                                 (1206)
    Die Deckenweberei der Navajo-Indianer. *Globus,* 82:133-40, Sept.
1902.
                                                                 (1207)
    The making of a Navaho blanket. *Everybody's,* 6:33-43, 1902.
                                                                 (1208)
    Native Navajo dyes. *The Papoose,* 1:9-10, Feb. 1903.

PEPPER, GEORGE H. (Continued)   (1209)
    The Navajo Indians. *The Papoose*, Dec. 1902.
——————   (1210)
    The Navaho Indians; an ethnological study. *SW*, 29:639-44, 1900.

PERRY, R.   (1211)
    The Navajo Indian. *Native American*, Sept. 16, 1905.

PETER, W. W.   (1212)
    Land management in relation to the health of the Navajos. Navajo
    Service Land Management Conference, March 2-6, 1937, Flag-
    staff. *Navajo School Service Bulletin* 1.

PFISTER, OSKAR   (1213)
    Instinctive psychoanalysis among the Navajos. *Journal of Nervous
    and Mental Disease*, 76:234-54, 1932.

POLLOCK, FLOYD A.   (1214)
    Navajo-federal relations as a social-cultural problem. Unpub.
    Doctor's thesis, USC, 1942.

POUSMA, RICHARD H.   (1215)
    He-who-always-wins and other Navajo campfire stories. Grand
    Rapids, Michigan, Erdmans, 1934.
——————   (1216)
    Venereal disease among the Navahos. *Southwestern Medicine*,
    13:503-05, 1929.

PROVINSE, JOHN H.   (1217)
    Cultural factors in land use planning. (In La Farge, Oliver, Ed.:
    The Changing Indian. Norman, UOP, 1942. pp. 55-71.)
        Includes material on the cultures of Navajos, Pueblos, and Spanish-Ameri-
        cans in New Mexico.

R. C.   (1217a)
    Children of the wind and sun. *Arizona Highways*, 13:38, Dec.
    1942.

REAGAN, ALBERT B.   (1218)
    The influenza and the Navajo. *Indiana Academy of Science*,
    Proceedings, 1919. pp. 243-47.
——————   (1219)
    Navaho fire dance. *AA*, 36:434-37, 1934.
——————   (1220)
    Navajo sports. *Primitive Man*, 5:68-71, 1932.
——————   (1221)
    Navajos. *SW*, 57:214-18, 1928.
——————   (1222)
    Utilization of the Navajo country. *Iowa Academy of Science*,
    Proceedings, 41:215-37, 1934.

REEBEL, MOLLIE B.   (1223)
    *Navajo mountain—a community and health experiment in the
    wilderness.* National Association on Indian Affairs, Bulletin 24.
    New York, 1935.

REED, ERIK K.   (1224)
    Information on the Navaho in 1706. *AA*, 43:485-87, 1941.

REED, ERIK K. (Continued)   (1225)
    Navajo independence and acculturation. *AA*, 43:681-82, 1941.
REED, J.   (1226)
    Navajo and Pueblo Indian crafts. *Brooklyn Museum Quarterly*,
    19:67-73, April 1932.
REEVE, FRANK D.   (1227)
    The government and the Navaho, 1846-58. *NMHR*, 14:82-114,
    1939.

————   (1228)
    The government and the Navaho, 1878-83. *NMHR*, 16:275-312,
    1941.

————   (1228a)
    The government and the Navaho, 1883-1888. *NMHR*, 18:17-51,
    Jan. 1943.

REICHARD, GLADYS A.   (1229)
    Agentive and causative elements in Navajo. New York, J. J.
    Augustin, 1940.

————   (1230)
    Attitudes towards avoidance.   (In *Essays in Anthropology pre-
    sented to A. L. Kroeber.* Berkeley, 1936. pp. 265-72.)

————   (1231)
    Color in Navajo weaving. *Arizona Historical Review*, 7:19-30,
    1936.

————   (1232)
    Dezba, woman of the desert. New York, J. J. Augustin, 1939.

————   (1233)
    A few instances of cultural resistance in southwest North America.
    ICA, Proceedings, 22nd Session, Rome 1926. v. 2, pp. 289-96.

————   (1234)
    Fifty thousand sign posts. *NM*, 17:18-19, 32-33, March 1939.

————   (1235)
    Navajo medicine man; sandpaintings and legends of Miguelito.
    New York, J. J. Augustin, 1939.

————   (1236)
    Navajo shepherd and weaver. New York, J. J. Augustin, 1936.

————   (1237)
    Reunion of the tribes. *NM*, 17:9-11, 46-48, July 1939.
        A Navajo family before and during Gallup ceremonial.

————   (1238)
    Social life. (In Boas, Franz: *General Anthropology.* New York,
    Heath, 1938. pp. 409-86.)
        Some material on Navajos.

————   (1239)
    *Social life of the Navajo Indians with some attention to minor
    ceremonies.* Columbia University Contributions to Anthropology
    7. New York, 1928.

REICHARD, GLADYS A. (Continued)   (1240)
Spider woman; a story of Navajo weavers and chanters. New
York, Macmillan, 1934.
  A first-hand description of all phases of Navajo life.

—————   (1241)
The translation of two Navaho chant words. *AA*, 44:421-24, 1942.
REICHARD, GLADYS A., ED.   (1242)
Navajo texts. *AMNH, Anthropological Papers*, v. 34, Pt. 1.
New York, 1933.
REICHARD, GLADYS A. AND NEWCOMB, FRANC J.   (1243)
Sandpaintings of the Navajo shooting chant. New York, J. J.
Augustin, 1937.
REISENBERG, SIDNEY H.   (1244)
At a medicine dance of the Navajos. *Pacific Monthly*, Dec. 1906.
REITER, WINIFRED   (1245)
Desert debutantes. *NM*, 17:12-13, 36-38, April 1939.
  Description of a Navajo dance that was once a purification ceremony and is
  now only a social event.
REYNOLDS, Q.   (1246)
Meet the Navajos. *Collier's*, 97:10-11, Jan. 4, 1936.
RICKETTS, ORVAL AND MCPHEE, JOHN   (1247)
The Navajo Indians in a changing world. USDI, Navajo Service,
Window Rock, 1941. Processed.
RIORDAN, M. J.   (1248)
The Navajo Indians. *Overland Monthly*, 16:373, Oct. 1890.
ROBERTS, K. L.   (1249)
Navaho land. *Saturday Evening Post*, 197:28, Sept. 13, 1924.
ROGERS, GEORGE   (1250)
Klah the pagan. *Mentor*, 12:46-48, March 1924.
ROLLINS, WARREN E.   (1251)
Passing of the spirit dance. *EP*, 7:187-91, 1919.

—————   (1252)
The spirit of the dead (A Navajo ceremony). *EP*, 12:71-73, 1922.
RYAN, W. CARSON, JR.   (1253)
Social and educational implications of the Navajo program.
National Conference of Social Work, Proceedings, 1934. pp. 557-
63.
SALSBURY, C. G.   (1254)
Christ comes to the Navajo. *Missionary Review of the World*,
60:75-80, Feb. 1937.

—————   (1255)
Disease incidence among the Navajoes. *Southwestern Medicine*,
21:230-33, July 1937.
  Discussion of 4,826 cases admitted to Sage Memorial hospital. Statistical
  table showing incidence of various diseases included.

—————   (1256)
Medical work in Navajo land. *American Journal of Nursing*,
32:415-16, 1932.

SAPIR, EDWARD   (1257)
Internal linguistic evidence suggestive of the northern origin of the Navaho. *AA*, 38:224-35, 1936.

_____   (1258)
A linguistic trip among the Navaho Indians. Gallup *Independent*, Aug. 23, 1929.

_____   (1259)
Two Navaho puns. *Language*, 8:217-19, 1932.

SAPIR, EDWARD, ED.   (1259a)
Navaho texts. Wm. Dwight Whitney Linguistic series of Yale University, v. 8. Iowa City, Linguistic Society of America, 1942.

SAPIR, EDWARD AND SANDOVAL, ALBERT G.   (1260)
A note on Navaho pottery. *AA*, 32:575-76, 1930.

SCHLANTA, SOGHDAN A.   (1261)
A comparison of Navajo and Pueblo Indians in musical talent. Unpub. Master's thesis, UNM, 1938.

SCHOEBEL, C.   (1262)
Une expedition dans le Nouveau Mexique et l'Arizona. *Archives de la Societe Americaine de France*, n. s., 1:19-33, 1875.
Includes information on Navajos and Navajo country.

SCOTT, HUGH L.   (1263)
Testimony regarding trouble on the Navajo Reservation. Senate Document 757, 60th Congress, 2nd Session. Washington, GPO, 1909.

SENTER, DONOVAN AND HAWLEY, FLORENCE   (1264)
Hopi and Navajo child burials. *AA*, 39:131-34, 1937.

SEYMOUR, FLORA W.   (1265)
Desert domain among the Indians; Navajo Reservation. *Missionary Review of the World*, 62:448-50, 1939.

SHELTON, W. T.   (1266)
The hoe and the Navajo. *LMC, 2nd Session, 1910.* pp. 63-66.
Agriculture among the Navajos.

_____   (1267)
The Navajos. *LMC, 1st Session, 1908.* pp. 35-37.

SHEPARD, WARD   (1268)
Land problems of an expanding Indian population. (In La Farge, Oliver, Ed.: *The Changing Indian.* Norman, UOP, 1942. pp. 72-83.)
Some mention of Navajo land problems.

SHUFELDT, ROBERT W.   (1269)
Arrow release among the Navajos. *American Naturalist*, 21:784-86, 1887.

_____   (1270)
The drawings of a Navajo artist. *Magazine of American History*, 22:462-68, 1889.

_____   (1271)
Early recollections of the Navajos. *Red Man*, Jan. 1914.

SHUFELDT, ROBERT W. (Continued) (1272)
The evolution of house-building among the Navajo Indians. *United States National Museum, Proceedings,* 15:279-82, 1892.

―――― (1273)
Head-flattening as seen among the Navajo Indians. *Popular Science Monthly,* 39:535-39, 1891.

―――― (1274)
Mortuary customs of the Navajo Indians. *American Naturalist,* 25:303-06, 1891.

―――― (1275)
A Navajo artist and his notions of mechanical drawing. *Smithsonian Annual Report, 1886.* Pt. 1. Washington, 1889. pp. 240-44.

―――― (1276)
The Navaho belt weaver. *United States National Museum, Proceedings,* 14:391-93, 1891.

―――― (1277)
The Navajo tanner. *United States National Museum, Proceedings,* 11:59-66, 1888.

―――― (1278)
Notes on certain traits of infant Navajos. *Nature,* 35:346-47, 1887.

SIMEON, BROTHER (1279)
The "talking wire" among the Navajos. *Sound Waves,* April 1905.

SNOW, MILTON (1279a)
Navajo recruit. *Desert Magazine,* 6:17-18, Jan. 1943.

SPIEGELBERG, A. F. (1280)
The Navajo blanket. *Old Santa Fe,* 2:323-37, 1915.

―――― (1281)
Navajo blankets. *Out West,* 20:447-49, 1904. *Also EP,* 18:223-29, 1925.

STAPLIN, FRANK (1282)
First Navajo Indian fair. *Indian School Journal,* March 1910.

STEGGERDA, MORRIS (1283)
McAdory art test applied to Navaho Indian children. *Journal of Comparative Psychology,* 22:283-85, 1936.

STEGGERDA, MORRIS AND HILL, THOMAS J. (1284)
Incidence of dental caries among Maya and Navajo Indians. *Journal of Dental Research,* 15:233-42, 1936.

STEGGERDA, MORRIS AND MACOMBER, EILEEN (1285)
Mental and social characteristics of Maya and Navajo Indians as evidenced by a psychological rating scale. *Journal of Social Psychology,* 10:51-59, 1939.

STEPHEN, ALEXANDER M. (1286)
Hopi journal of Alexander M. Stephen, edited by Elsie Clews Parsons. Columbia University Contributions to Anthropology 23. New York, 1936.
　　Many references to Navajos.

STEPHEN, ALEXANDER M. (Continued)   (1287)
    Marriage among the Navajoes. *Our Forest Children*, 4 (4) :222,
    1890.

────   (1288)
    The Navajo. *AA*, o. s., 6:345-62, 1893.
        Environment, land tenure, architecture, family customs, arts, religion.

────   (1289)
    Navajo dress and dwelling. *Our Forest Children*, 4:222-23, 1890.

────   (1290)
    Navajo origin legend. *JAF*, 43:88-104, 1930.

────   (1291)
    The Navajo shoemaker. *United States National Museum, Pro-
    ceedings*, 11:131-36, 1888.

────   (1292)
    Notes about the Navajoes. *Canadian Indian*, 1:15-16, 1890.

STEVENS, ALDEN   (1293)
    Once they were nomads; case history of an American minority.
    Survey Graphic, 30:62-67, Feb. 1941.

STEVENSON, J.   (1294)
    Ceremonial of Hasjelti Dailjis and mythical sand-paintings of the
    Navajo Indians. *Bureau of American Ethnology, 8th Annual
    Report*. Washington, GPO, 1891. pp. 229-85.

STEVENSON, P.   (1295)
    Fire magic in the Southwest. *Travel*, 65:18-22, June 1935.
        Sacred dances and songs of the Navajo.

STEWART, O. C.   (1296)
    The Navaho wedding basket. *Museum of Northern Arizona,
    Museum Notes*, 10 (9) :25-28, 1938.

SULLIVAN, BELLE S.   (1297)
    The unvanishing Navajos. Philadelphia, Dorrance & Co., 1938.

SWAN, A. M.   (1298)
    Marriage among the Navajos. *Southwest Illustrated Magazine*,
    2:114-15, March 1896.

────   (1299)
    Some Navajo traditions and customs. *Southwest Illustrated Maga-
    zine*, 2:36-38, Feb. 1896.

TELFORD, E. P.   (1300)
    Navajo field games. *Current Literature*, 33:581-82, 1902.

TEN BROECK, P. G. S.   (1301)
    Manners and customs of the Moqui and Navajo tribes of New
    Mexico. (In Schoolcraft, Henry: *Historical and statistical infor-
    mation respecting the history, condition, and prospects of the
    Indian tribes of the United States*. . . Part 4. Philadelphia, Lip-
    pincott, 1854.)

THOMPSON, ALMON H.   (1302)
    The country and customs of the Navajo Indians. Unpub. ms. at
    New York Public Library.

TILLOTSON, WINIFRED S. (1303)
Navajo medicine man. *National Park Service, Region 3 Quarterly,*
3:11-14, July 1941.

TOWNSEND, J. G. (1304)
Indian health—past, present, and future. (In La Farge, Oliver,
Ed.: *The Changing Indian.* Norman, UOP, 1942. pp. 28-41.)
General discussion of Indian health with some mention of Navajos and
Pueblos.

TOZZER, ALFRED M. (1305)
A Navajo sand picture of the rain gods and its attendant ceremony. *ICA, Proceedings,* 13:147-56, 1902.

―――― (1306)
Note on star-lore among the Navajos. *JAF,* 21:28-32, Jan. 1908.

―――― (1307)
Notes on religious ceremonials of the Navaho. *Putnam Anniversary Volume.* New York, Stechert, 1909. pp. 299-343.

TSCHOPIK, HARRY, JR. (1308)
Navaho basketry; a study of culture change. *AA,* 42:444-62, 1940.
Comparison of present status of basketry in Ramah Navajo community with
that of the close of the 19th century.

―――― (1309)
*Navaho pottery making. An inquiry into the affinities of Navaho
painted pottery.* Peabody Museum of American Archaeology and
Ethnology, Papers, v. 17, no. 1. Cambridge, 1941.

―――― (1310)
Taboo as a possible factor involved in the obsolescence of Navajo
pottery and basketry. *AA,* 40:257-62, 1938.

UNITED STATES CONGRESS (1311)
Navaho in Arizona and New Mexico. Hearings before Senate
Sub-committee on Indian Affairs, 71st Congress, 3rd Session.
Washington, GPO, 1932.

USDI, OFFICE OF INDIAN AFFAIRS (1312)
General statement of conditions in the Navajo area. Window
Rock, Navajo Service, 1941. Processed.

VAN VALKENBURGH, RICHARD F. (1313)
Christmas legend of the Navajo. *Desert Magazine,* 6:19-23, Dec.
1942.

―――― (1314)
Dinebekeyah. USDI, Office of Indian Affairs, Navajo Service. Window Rock, 1941. Processed.

―――― (1314a)
Massacre in the mountains. *Desert Magazine,* 6:18-22, Feb. 1943.

―――― (1315)
Navajo common law. I. Notes on political organization, property
and inheritance. *Museum of Northern Arizona, Museum Notes,*
9:17-22, Oct. 1936.

―――― (1316)
Navajo common law. II. Navajo law and justice. *Museum of
Northern Arizona, Museum Notes,* 9:51-54, April 1937.

VAN VALKENBURGH, RICHARD F. (Continued)   (1317)
Navajo common law. III. Etiquette, hospitality, and justice. *Museum of Northern Arizona, Museum Notes*, 10:39-42, 1938.

────   (1318)
Notes on Navajo agriculture and irrigation. USDI, Office of Indian Affairs, Navajo Service. Window Rock, 1938. Processed.

────   (1319)
Sacred places and shrines of the Navajo. Part 2. *Plateau*, 13:6-9, July 1940.

────   (1320)
A short history of the Navajo people. USDI, Office of Indian Affairs, Navajo Service. Window Rock, 1938. Processed.

────   (1321)
Some historical aspects of the Navajo land problems. Unpub. ms. in files of Navajo Service Agency. Window Rock, 1941.

────   (1322)
Tsosi tells the story of Massacre Cave. *Desert Magazine*, 3:22-26, Feb. 1940.

VAN VALKENBURGH, RICHARD F. AND BEGAY, SCOTTY   (1323)
Sacred places and shrines of the Navajo. Part 1. The sacred mountains. *Museum of Northern Arizona, Museum Notes*, 11 (3) :29-34, 1939.

VAN VLEET, T. S.   (1324)
Legendary evolution of the Navajo Indians. *American Naturalist*, 27:69-79, 1893.

VAUGHN, A. P.   (1325)
Navajo art and craft. *Great Southwest*, Feb. 1910.

VERPLANCK, JAMES DE LANCEY   (1326)
A country of shepherds. Boston, Ruth Hill, 1934.

VESTAL, PAUL   (1327)
Field notes on the ethnobotany of the Ramah Navaho. Unpub. undated ms. at Botanical Museum, Harvard University.

WAKE, C. S.   (1328)
A Navajo origin legend. *American Antiquarian*, 26:265-71, 1904.

WALLACE, D.   (1329)
Across the Navajo desert. *Outing*, 57:398-412, 1911.

WALTON, EDA LOU   (1330)
Navaho poetry, an interpretation. *Texas Review*, 7:198-210, 1922.

────   (1331)
Navajo song patterning. *JAF*, 43:105-18, 1930.

────   (1332)
Navaho songs. *Nation*, 110:517, 1920.

────   (1333)
Navaho verse rhythms. *Poetry*, 24:40-44, 1924.

WATERS, FRANK   (1334)
Navajo Yei-bet-chai. *Yale Review*, 28:558-71, 1939.

WATKINS, FRANCES E. (1335)
Navajo Indians. I. *Masterkey*, 16:109-18, 1942.
Homeland, language, history, subsistence, shelter, costume, transportation.

——— (1336)
The Navaho. II. *Masterkey*, 16:149-56, 1942.
Crafts.

——— (1337)
The Navaho. III. *Masterkey*, 16:210-14, 1942.
Crafts.

——— (1337a)
The Navaho. IV. *Masterkey*, 17:20-24, Jan. 1943.
Social life.

——— (1338)
Two rare Navaho masks. *Masterkey*, 10:188-89, 1936.

WATSON, DON (1339)
Navahos pray for the good of the world. *Mesa Verde Notes*
(National Park Service), 7:16-18, March 1937.

WATTLES, R. J. (1340)
Sketches of Indian life; the Navajo wedding. *Overland*, n. s., 68:
170-73, 1916.

WEBER, FATHER ANSELM (1341)
The Franciscan missions among the Navajo Indians. *Franciscan
Missions of the Southwest*, 1:17-23, 1913.

——— (1342)
The Navajo Indians; a statement of facts. St. Michael's, Arizona,
Franciscan Fathers, 1914.

——— (1343)
*The Navajo Indians. Hearings Before a Sub-committee of the
Senate Committee on Indian Affairs. Part 34.* U. S. Senate, 75th
Congress, 1st Session. Washington, GPO, 1937. pp. 17553-75.

——— (1344)
Navajos on the warpath. *Franciscan Missions of the Southwest*,
7:1-18, 1918.

——— (1345)
On Navajo myths and superstitions. *Franciscan Missions of the
Southwest*, 4:38-46, 1916.

WELSH, HERBERT S. (1346)
An immediate pressing need of the Navajo Indians. Indian Rights
Association, Publication 3. Philadelphia, 1894.

——— (1347)
Navajo and other Indians on the public domain. *LMC, 2nd Session, 1913.* pp. 71-74.

——— (1348)
*Report of a visit to the Navajo, Pueblo, and Hualapais Indians of
New Mexico and Arizona.* Indian Rights Association. Philadel-
phia, 1885.

WETHERILL, FANNY (1349)
The Navaho people. *Masterkey*, 11:16-17, 1937.
An account of Navajo life and activities by a 17 year old Navajo girl.

WETHERILL, HILDA   (1350)
Trading post; letters from a primitive land. *Atlantic*, 142:289-300,
510-21, 1928.

WETHERILL, LULU W. AND CUMMINGS, BYRON   (1351)
A Navaho folk tale of Pueblo Bonito. *A&A*, 14:132-36, 1922.

WHEELWRIGHT, MARY C.   (1352)
Myth of Sontso (Big Star). Museum of Navajo Ceremonial Art,
Bulletin 2. Santa Fe, 1940.

——————   (1353)
Navajo creation myth, the story of the emergence. Museum of
Navajo Ceremonial Art, Navajo Religion series, v. 1. Santa Fe,
1942.
        As told by Hasteen Klah.

——————   (1354)
Tleji or Yehbechai myth. The House of Navajo Religion, Bulletin 1. Santa Fe, 1938.

WHITMAN, WILLIAM, 3RD   (1355)
Navaho tales. Boston, Houghton Mifflin, 1925.

WHITTEMORE, MARY   (1356)
Participation in Navajo weaving. *Plateau*, 13:49-52, 1941.

WILSON, CHARLES MORROW   (1357)
Navaho new deal. *Current History*, 48:49-51, June 1938.
        Navajo problems of population, land, and resources in the light of New Deal
        activities.

WILSON, REVEREND EDWARD F.   (1358)
The Navajo Indians. *Our Forest Children*, 3:115-17, 1890.

WILSON, THOMAS   (1359)
The swastika. *United States National Museum, Report*, 1894.
pp. 757-981.

WISSLER, CLARK   (1360)
The rebirth of the vanishing American. *NH*, 34:415-30, 1934.

WOEHLKE, WALTER V.   (1361)
The economic rehabilitation of the Navajos. *National Conference of Social Work, Proceedings*, 1934. pp. 548-56.

——————   (1362)
The new Navajo council and its significance. Radio address from
KTGM, Window Rock, Nov. 8, 1938.

——————   (1363)
Poisoning the Navajos with oil. *Sunset*, 51:11, Aug. 1923.

WOERNER, DAVIDA   (1364)
Education among the Navajo; an historical study. Unpub. Doctor's thesis, Teachers College, Columbia University, 1941.

WOODS, BETTY   (1365)
Fire dance. *NM*, 17:20-21, 40, 42, July 1939.

——————   (1366)
Navajo weavers. *NM*, 17:10-11, 37, Feb. 1939.

WOODWARD, ARTHUR (1367)
A brief history of Navaho silversmithing. Museum of Northern Arizona, Bulletin 14. Flagstaff, 1938.

WYETH, N. C. (1368)
A sheep herder of the Southwest. *Scribner's,* 45:17-21, 1909.

WYMAN, LELAND C. (1369)
The female shooting life chant; a minor Navaho ceremony. *AA,* 38:634-53, 1936.

———— (1370)
Navaho diagnosticians. *AA,* 38:236-46, 1936.

———— (1371)
Origin legends of Navaho divinatory rites. *JAF,* 49:134-42, 1936.

WYMAN, LELAND C. AND HARRIS, S. K. (1372)
Navajo Indian medical ethnobotany. UNM Bulletin, Anthropological series, v. 3, no. 5, June 1941.

WYMAN, LELAND C., HILL, W. W., AND OSANAI, IVA (1373)
Navajo eschatology. UNM Bulletin, Anthropological series, v. 4, no. 1, May 1942.

WYMAN, LELAND C. AND KLUCKHOHN, CLYDE (1374)
Navaho classification of their song ceremonials. AAA, Memoirs 50. Menasha, Wisconsin, 1938.

YOUNG, STELLA, COMP. (1375)
Navajo native dyes. USDI Office of Indian Affairs, Education Division. Washington 1940.

Pueblos

ABERLE, SOPHIE D. B. (1376)
Child mortality among Pueblo Indians. *American Journal of Physical Anthropology,* 16:339-49, 1932.

———— (1377)
Frequency of childbirth among Pueblo Indians. *Anatomical Record,* 38:1-2, 1928.

———— (1378)
Frequency of pregnancies and birth interval among Pueblo Indians. *American Journal of Physical Anthropology,* 16:63-80, 1931.

———— (1379)
Maternal mortality among the Pueblos. *American Journal of Physical Anthropology,* 18:431-35, 1934.

———— (1380)
Vital statistics of San Juan Pueblo. *Human Biology,* 12:141-87, May 1940.

ABERLE, S. D., HAWLEY, FLORENCE, AND PIJOAN, MICHEL (1380a)
Haemodynamics and vitamin status of Zia Pueblo. Unpub. ms. in possession of Dr. Pijoan, Albuquerque.

ADAMS, ANSEL EASTON (1381)
The Taos Pueblo. San Francisco, Grabhorn Press, 1930.

ADAMS, F. J.   (1382)
   The normal mental growth of Indian sub-adults; Pueblo and non-sedentary subjects. Unpub. Master's thesis, UNM, 1930.

AITKEN, BARBARA   (1383)
   Temperament in native American religion. *Journal of the Royal Anthropological Institute,* 60:1363-87, 1930.

——————   (1384)
   A Tewa craftsman—Leslie Agayo. *EP,* 17:91-97, 1924.

ALEXANDER, HARTLEY BURR   (1385)
   Field notes at Jemez. *EP,* 27:95-106, 1929.

——————   (1386)
   Pueblo Indian painting. Nice, France, C. Szwedzicki, 1932.

——————   (1387)
   Ritual dances of the Pueblo Indians. Denver, DAM, 1927.

ALLEN, F. W. AND LARSEN, H. D.   (1388)
   Heredity of agglutinogens M and N among Pueblo and Blackfeet Indians. *Journal of Immunology,* 32:301-05, 1937.

ANDERSON, ARNOLD M.   (1389)
   Picturesque Southwest—Pueblo industries. *Great Southwest Magazine,* March 1910.

ANGULO, J. DE   (1390)
   Taos kinship terminology. *AA,* 27:482-83, 1925.

ANONYMOUS   (1391)
   Acoma, our oldest inhabited settlement. *Review of Reviews,* 43:357-58, 1911.

——————   (1392)
   The All Pueblos council, a veteran confederation. *United Pueblos Quarterly Bulletin,* v. 1, no. 6, July 1940.
     History, functions, achievements of the council.

——————   (1393)
   Ancient botany of Zuni Indians. *Scientific American Supplement,* 82:197, Sept. 23, 1916.

——————   (1394)
   The animal dance at San Ildefonso. *EP,* 24:119-22, 1928.

——————   (1395)
   Are the Pueblo Indians to be robbed of their heritage? Bursum Bill. *Current Opinion,* 74:213-14, 1923.

——————   (1396)
   Canning supplants the dole. *Christian Science Monitor Magazine,* Aug. 31, 1940. p. 13.

——————   (1397)
   Comanche dance at San Ildefonso. *EP,* 10 (4) :5-7, 1921.

——————   (1398)
   Danger to the Pueblos; the Bursum Indian Bill. *SW,* 52:4-6, Jan. 1923.

——————   (1399)
   Documentary evidence in reference to the Laguna Indian Pueblo. Undated, unsigned manuscript in records of the Pueblo Lands Board, Land Agent's Office, UPA, Albuquerque.

ANONYMOUS (Continued) (1400)

From Broadway to the Pueblos. *Etude*, 41:231, 1923.
Mention of two rare Indian flutes of Pueblo origin.

——— (1401)

The green corn ceremony. *EP*, 27:48-50, 1929.
Santo Domingo.

——— (1402)

Indian census poses many problems. *United Pueblos Quarterly Bulletin*, v. 1, no. 3, April 1940.

——— (1403)

Indian rain masks. *EP*, 16:119-20, 1924.
Zuni.

——— (1404)

Indians! Indians! Indians! *Santa Fe Magazine*, 36:36-37, April 1942.
Jemez Indian dancers on a war bond selling tour.

——— (1405)

Irrigation for Tesuque Pueblo. Irrigation work on Tesuque River just completed by Federal Government. *EP*, 16:145-46, 1924.

——— (1406)

Justice for the Pueblo Indians. *Science*, n. s., 56:665-66, 1922.
Protest against the Bursum Bill.

——— (1407)

Last first Americans. *Nation*, 115:570, 1922.

——— (1408)

Lo and his lands. *The Freeman*, 8:366-67, 1923.

——— (1409)

Notes on Isleta and Sandia. *EP*, 11:114-16, 1921.
Baptism, marriage, and burial ceremonies.

——— (1410)

Occupations of a Pueblo Indian girl. *Review of Reviews*, 52:367-68, 1915.

——— (1411)

Policy of destruction. *The Freeman*, 7:172-73, 1923.
Pueblos and government administration.

——— (1412)

Pueblo handicrafts. *EP*, 18:230-32, 1925.

——— (1413)

Pueblo Indian murals. *Masterkey*, 9 (1) :25, 1935.

——— (1414)

Pueblo Indians with their backs to the wall. *Outlook*, 132:591, 1922.

——— (1415)

Pueblo land question. *SW*, 52:164-65, 1923.

——— (1416)

Pueblos' plea for justice. *Literary Digest*, 76:17, Feb. 17, 1923.
Government relations.

ANONYMOUS (Continued)   (1417)
    The rebuilding of Santa Clara. *EP*, 15:115-16, 1923.

——————   (1418)
    Report on repairs on Zia Mission. *EP*, 16:9-12, 1924.

——————   (1419)
    Santa Fe Jemez Indians tour the East in war bond and stamp drive. *Santa Fe Magazine*, 36:27-29, June 1942.

——————   (1420)
    Santo Domingo and San Felipe. *EP*, 24:427-39, 1928.
      Description of dances.

——————   (1421)
    Science and beliefs of the Tewa Indians. *Scientific American Supplement*, 82:340, 1916.

——————   (1422)
    Spring dances at the Pueblos. *EP*, 14:89, 1923.
      Description of San Felipe dance.

——————   (1423)
    Square deal for the Pueblos. *Outlook*, 133:249-50, 1923.
      Protest against Bursum Bill.

——————   (1424)
    Taos, an ancient American capital. *Review of Reviews*, 47:492-94, 1913.

——————   (1425)
    Zuni. *EP*, 27:39-40, 1929.
      Description of the people.

APPLEGATE, FRANK   (1426)
    Indian stories from the Pueblos. Philadelphia, Lippincott, 1929.

ARNIM, S. S., ABERLE, S. D., AND PITNEY, E. H.   (1427)
    A study of dental changes in a group of Pueblo children. *Journal of American Dental Association and the Dental Cosmos*, 24:478-80, 1937.

ARNOLD, CHARLOTTE   (1428)
    The dance at Nambe. *EP*, 24:26-28, 1928.

AUSTIN, MARY   (1429)
    Cults of the Pueblos. *Century*, 109:28-35, Nov. 1924.

——————   (1430)
    Days of our ancients. *Survey*, 53:33-38, 59, Oct. 1, 1924.
      Historical background of Hopi and Zuni.

——————   (1431)
    Hiawatha among the Pueblos. *EP*, 7:2-3, 1919.

——————   (1432)
    Indian art for Indians. *Survey Graphic*, 13:381-88, 1928.

——————   (1433)
    One smoke stories. *Yale Review*, n. s., 22:525-32, 1933. *Also SR*, 18:265-68, 1933; and Boston, Houghton Mifflin, 1931.

——————   (1434)
    Social and economic organization of the New Mexico Pueblo. *Progressive Education*, 9:117-21, 1932.

BAILEY, FLORENCE M.   (1435)
Some plays and dances of the Taos Indians. *NH*, 24:85-95, 1924.

BANDELIER, ADOLPH F. A.   (1436)
Documentary history of the Rio Grande Pueblos, New Mexico.
Part I, 1536-1542. *NMHR*, 4:303-35, 1929; 5:38-66, 154-85, 1930;
Part II, 1542-1581. *NMHR*, 5:240-62, 1930; Part III, 1581-1584.
NMHR, 5:333-85, 1930. *Also* AIA, School of American Archae-
ology, Papers 13. Santa Fe, 1910.

————   (1437)
Ein Brief uber Akoma: *Ausland*, 57:241-43, 1884.

————   (1438)
*Historical introduction to studies among the sedentary Indians of
New Mexico.* AIA, Papers, American series 1. Boston, 1883.

————   (1439)
Kin and clan. *NMHR*, 8:165-75, 1933.
  Social organization of Pueblos.

————   (1440)
The "Montezuma" of the Pueblo Indians. *AA*, o. s., 5:319-26,
1892.

————   (1441)
An outline of the documentary history of the Zuni tribe. *Journal
of American Ethnology and Archaeology*, v. 3, 1892.

————   (1442)
Po-se. *NMHR*, 1:335-49, 1926.
  A tale of San Ildefonso Pueblo illustrating Indian personality.

BANDELIER, ADOLPH F. A. AND HEWETT, E. L.   (1443)
Indians of the Rio Grande Valley. Albuquerque, UNM Press,
1937.

BARBER, EDWIN A.   (1444)
A comparison of the Pueblo pottery with Egyptian and Grecian
ceramics. *American Antiquarian*, 1:61-69, 1878.

————   (1445)
Notes on native American pottery. *American Antiquarian*, 8:76-
82, 1886.

————   (1446)
On the ancient and modern Pueblo tribes. *American Naturalist*,
11:453-62, 1877.

————   (1447)
Pueblo pottery. *American Naturalist*, 15:453-62, 1881.

BARKER, PEARL   (1448)
At the Acoma fiesta. *Catholic Pioneer*, July 1905.

BARTLETT, F.   (1449)
The creation of the Zuni. *Old Santa Fe*, 2:79-87, 1915.

BARTLETT, LANIER   (1450)
Slaves of the Pueblos. *Pacific Monthly*, Jan. 1907.

BARTLETT, MRS. W. H.   (1451)
The Shalako dance. *Out West*, 22:389-402, 1905.

BAYLISS, CLARA KERN   (1452)
A Tewa sun myth. *JAF*, 22:333-35, 1909.

BECKWITH, F.   (1453)
A day in Acoma. *EP*, 35:201-10, 1933.

BENEDICT, RUTH   (1454)
Eight stories from Acoma. *JAF*, 43:59-87, 1930.

————   (1455)
El hombre y la cultura. Investigacion sobre el origen de la civilizacion contemporanea tomando como punto de partida tres pueblos primitivos: Nuevo Mexico, la Isla de Dobu, y la Isla de Vancouver. Tomo I. Buenos Aires, 1939.

————   (1456)
Psychological types in the cultures of the Southwest. *23rd ICA, Proceedings, 1928.* New York, 1930. pp. 572-81.

————   (1457)
Tales of the Cochiti Indians. Bureau of American Ethnology, Bulletin 98. Washington, GPO, 1931.

————   (1458)
Zuni mythology. Columbia University Contributions to Anthropology, v. 21. New York, 1934.

BENNETT, R. W.   (1459)
Which road to the Pueblo? *NM*, 11:11-13, 52, July 1933.
    Dances.

BILLINGS, BILLIE   (1460)
Home blessing in the Zuni village. *NM*, 11:24-25, 47, Dec. 1933.

BLOOM, LANSING B.   (1461)
Another word as to "Pueblo Indians." *EP*, 26:238-39, 1929.

————   (1462)
The Pueblo people and New Mexico. *Eighth American Scientific Congress, Proceedings.* Washington, 1943. v. 9, pp. 25-32.

BOAS, FRANZ   (1463)
Abstract characteristics of Keresan folktales. *ICA, Proceedings,* 20(1):223-24, 1922.

————   (1464)
Keresan texts. American Ethnological Society, Publications, v. 8, pt. 1. New York, Stechert, 1928.

————   (1465)
Primitive art. Cambridge, Harvard University Press, 1927.
    Some reference to Pueblo pottery making and design.

————   (1466)
Tales of Spanish provenience from Zuni. *JAF*, 35:62-98, 1922.

BOKE, RICHARD L.   (1467)
Laguna Indians pin their hopes on better land use. *Soil Conservation*, 2:199-200, 1937.

BOLTON, HERBERT EUGENE   (1468)
The Jumano Indians, 1650-1771. *Texas Historical Association Quarterly*, 15:66-84, 1911.

BOURKE, JOHN GREGORY (1469)
Compilation of notes and memoranda bearing upon the use of human ordure and human urine in rites of a religious or semi-religious character among various nations. Washington, 1888.

———— (1470)
The snake dance of the Moquis of Arizona, being the narrative of a journey from Santa Fe, New Mexico, to the villages of the Moqui Indians of Arizona. . . with an account of the tablet dance of the Pueblo of Santo Domingo. New York, Scribners, 1884.

———— (1471)
The urine dance of the Zunis. *American Antiquarian Society, Proceedings,* 34:400-04, 1885.

BOWERS, GEORGE BALLARD (1472)
Zunis at home. *SW,* 60:24-27, Jan. 1931.

BRAYER, HERBERT O. (1473)
The land grants of Laguna. *Research,* 1:5-22, Dec. 1936.

———— (1474)
The Pueblo Indian land grants of the Rio Abajo. Unpub. Master's thesis, UNM, 1937. *Also* UNM Bulletin, Historical series, v. 1, no. 1, 1938.

BROOKS, FLORENCE E. (1475)
In old Acoma. *The Border,* Jan. 1909.

BUNZEL, RUTH L. (1476)
Further note on San Felipe. *JAF,* 41:592, 1928.

———— (1477)
Introduction to Zuni ceremonialism. *Bureau of American Ethnology, 47th Annual Report, 1929-30.* Washington, GPO, 1932. pp. 467-544.

———— (1478)
Notes on the katcina cult at San Felipe. *JAF,* 41:290-92, 1928.

———— (1479)
The Pueblo potter; a study of creative imagination in primitive art. New York, Columbia University Press, 1929.

———— (1480)
Zuni katcinas—an analytical study. *Bureau of American Ethnology, 47th Annual Report, 1929-30.* Washington, GPO, 1932. pp. 837-1086.

———— (1481)
Zuni origin myths. *Bureau of American Ethnology, 47th Annual Report, 1929-30.* Washington, GPO, 1932. pp. 545-609.

———— (1482)
Zuni ritual poetry. *Bureau of American Ethnology, 47th Annual Report, 1929-30.* Washington, GPO, 1932. pp. 611-835.

BUNZEL, RUTH L., ED. (1483)
Zuni texts. American Ethnological Society, Publications, v. 15. New York, Stechert, 1933.

BURBANK, E. A. (1484)
He-see-o, a Zuni belle. *Brush and Pencil,* Feb. 1905.

BURTON, HENRIETTA K.   (1485)
The reestablishment of the Indians in their Pueblo life through the revival of their traditional crafts: a study in home education. New York, Teachers College, Columbia University, 1936.
  San Ildefonso.

BUTLER, G.   (1486)
Acoma and Acoma Indians. *Catholic World,* 16:703, 1873.

BYNNER, WITTER   (1486a)
Indian earth. New York, Knopf, 1930.
    A book of poems containing excellent poetic descriptions of Pueblo dances.

BYNNER, WITTER   (1487)
Pueblo primer. *The Freeman,* 8:373-75, 1923.

CARTER, ALLEN A.   (1488)
Acoma Indian Pueblo. Unpub. ms. in files of New Mexico Writers' Project, Santa Fe.

CHABOT, MARIA   (1489)
Defense of the dance. *NM,* 14:16-17, 46-47, Oct. 1936.

CHANDLER, K. H.   (1490)
Tables and explanations derived from the Laguna sheep status report of 1931. Unpub. ms. dated Aug. 14, 1941 on file at UPA, Albuquerque.

CHAPMAN, KATE MILLER   (1491)
Sun basket dance at Santa Clara. *EP,* 18:45-47, 1925.

CHAPMAN, KENNETH M.   (1492)
The art of the bird in decorative art. *A&A,* 4:307-16, 1916.

————   (1493)
Bird forms in Zuni pottery decoration. *EP,* 24:23-25, 1928.

————   (1494)
Decorative design. New Mexico Association on Indian Affairs, Indian Art series 13. Santa Fe, n. d.

————   (1495)
Life forms in Pueblo pottery decoration. *A&A,* 13:120-22, 1922.

————   (1496)
Pottery decorations of Santo Domingo and Cochiti Pueblos. *EP,* 16:87-93, 1924.

————   (1497)
The pottery of Santo Domingo Pueblo; a detailed study of its decoration. Laboratory of Anthropology, Memoirs, v. 1. Santa Fe, 1936.

————   (1498)
Post-Spanish Pueblo pottery. *A&A,* 23:207-13, 1927.

————   (1499)
Pueblo Indian pottery. Nice, France, C. Szwedzicki, 1933.

————   (1500)
Pueblo Indian pottery of the post-Spanish period. Laboratory of Anthropology, General series, Bulletin 4. Santa Fe, 1938.

————   (1501)
Roadside shopping. *NM,* 14:20-21, 38-39, June 1936.

CHAPMAN, KENNETH M. (Continued) (1502)
The Shalako ceremony at Zuni. *EP*, 23:622-27, 1927.

CHAUVENET, BEATRICE (1503)
A Zuni shalako. *EP*, 27:299-306, 1929.

CLARK, ANNA NOLAN (1504)
The circle of seasons. *NM*, 19:18-19, 43, Jan. 1941.
Yearly round of ceremonial observances at Tesuque Pueblo.

—— (1505)
Reunion at the Place-By-The-Bridge. *NM*, 16:9-11, 40, July 1938.
Zuni ceremonials.

—— (1506)
Zuni plays. Unpub. ms. in files of New Mexico Writers' Project,
Santa Fe.

COLLIER, JOHN (1507)
American Congo. *Survey,* 50:467-76, Aug. 1923.

—— (1508)
No trespassing; the Indian bureau proposes to eject all investigators
from the reservations it rules. *Sunset,* 50:14-15, May 1923.

—— (1509)
Persecuting the Pueblos. *Sunset,* 53:50, July 1924.

—— (1510)
Plundering the Pueblo Indians. *Sunset,* 50:21-25, Jan. 1923.

—— (1511)
Pueblo lands. *Survey,* 65:548-49, Feb. 15, 1931.
Effect of Pueblo Lands Act of 1924.

—— (1512)
Pueblos' land problem. *Sunset,* 51:15, Nov. 1923.

—— (1513)
Pueblos' last stand; the Bursum Bill. *Sunset,* 50:19-22, Feb. 1923.

—— (1514)
Red Atlantis. *Survey,* 49:15-20, Oct. 1922.
Taos.

—— (1515)
Room for the Indians. *Woman Citizen,* n. s., 8:9-10, March 8,
1924.

COLLINS, G. N. (1516)
Pueblo Indian maize breeding. *Journal of Heredity,* 5:255-68,
1914.

COOK, SARAH LOUISE (1517)
The ethnobotany of the Jemez Indians. Unpub. Master's thesis,
UNM, 1930.

COSBY, E. GORDON (1518)
San Ildefonso. *Southwestern Lore,* 1:3-5, Dec. 1935.

COWAN, JOHN L. (1519)
The Pueblo of Zuni. *Overland,* n. s., 53:280-85, 1909.

CRANE, LEO (1520)
Desert drums; the Pueblo Indians of New Mexico, 1540-1928.
Boston, Little Brown, 1928.

CROSSETT, LELA   (1521)
   New Mexico Pueblo Indians as described by early explorers.
   Unpub. Master's thesis, University of California, 1928.

CUMMINGS, BYRON   (1522)
   Kivas of the San Juan drainage. *AA*, 17:272-82, 1915.

CURTIS, NATALIE   (1523)
   Pueblo poetry. *EP*, 12:95-99, 1922.

——————   (1524)
   Two Pueblo Indian grinding songs. *Craftsman*, 7:35-41, 1904.
      Acoma.

CURTIS, WILLIAM E.   (1525)
   Children of the sun. Chicago, Inter-Ocean Pub. Co., 1883.
      Zuni.

CUSHING, FRANK   (1526)
   A case of primitive surgery. *Science*, n. s., 5:977-81, 1897.

——————   (1527)
   My adventures in Zuni. *Century*, 25:191-207, Dec. 1882; 25:500-
   11, Feb. 1883. *Also* Dallas, Peripatetic Press, 1941.

——————   (1528)
   The nation of the willows. *Atlantic*, 50:362-74, 541-59, 1882.

——————   (1529)
   Outlines of Zuni creation myths. *Bureau of American Ethnology,
   13th Annual Report, 1891-92.* Washington, GPO, 1896. pp. 321-
   447.

——————   (1530)
   Primitive copper working—a study. *AA*, o. s., 7:93-117, 1894.
      At Zuni.

——————   (1531)
   A study of Pueblo pottery as illustrative of Zuni culture growth.
   Bureau of American Ethnology, 4th Annual Report, 1882-83.
   Washington, GPO, 1886. pp. 467-521.

——————   (1532)
   Zuni breadstuff. Museum of the American Indian, Heye Foundation, New York, 1920.

——————   (1533)
   Zuni fetishes. *Bureau of American Ethnology, 2nd Annual Report, 1880-81.* Washington, GPO, 1883. pp. 3-45.

——————   (1534)
   A Zuni folk tale of the underworld. *JAF*, 5:49-56, 1892.

——————   (1535)
   Zuni folk tales. New York, Putnam, 1901. *Also* New York,
   Knopf, 1931.

——————   (1536)
   The Zuni social, mythic, and religious systems. *Popular Science
   Monthly*, 21:186-92, 1882.

DALL, WILLIAM HEALEY (1537)
On masks, labrets, and certain aboriginal customs with an inquiry into the bearing of their geographical distribution. *Bureau of American Ethnology, 3rd Annual Report.* Washington, GPO, 1885. pp. 67-202.

DAVIS, WILLIAM WATTS HART (1538)
The Pueblo Indians of New Mexico. *EP,* 26:259-86, 1929.

DEHUFF, ELIZABETH WILLIS (1539)
The bear and the deer. *EP,* 31:2-4, 1931.
Taos tale.

––––––– (1540)
The fate of Yellow Corn and Blue Corn. *EP,* 16:53-55, 1924.
Taos tale.

––––––– (1541)
Fiesta foods. *NM,* 17:21, 34-36, Feb. 1939.

––––––– (1542)
Five little katchinas. Boston, Houghton Mifflin, 1930.

––––––– (1543)
Four Pueblo folk tales. *Yale Review,* n. s., 15:768-85, 1926.

––––––– (1544)
The greedy fox. *EP,* 31:20-22, 1931.
Taos tale.

––––––– (1545)
Indian glimpses. *NM,* 13:16-17, 42-43, Oct. 1935.
Anecdotes illustrating Pueblo attitudes towards health, justice, courtship and marriage, and the reasons for those attitudes.

––––––– (1546)
Indians and irony. *EP,* 22:261-64, 1927.
Pueblo Indians imitating Spanish and Anglo ways.

––––––– (1547)
Infidelity. *EP,* 31:200-01, 1931.
Taos tale.

––––––– (1548)
More Pueblo tales. *EP,* 11:140-44, 1921.
Acoma.

––––––– (1549)
Myths told by the Pueblos. *EP,* 11:86-92, 1921.

––––––– (1550)
Our unknown friends, the Pueblo Indians. *New Mexico Quarterly Review,* 11:79-88, 1941.
Pueblo behavior interpreted in the light of their basic philosophy.

––––––– (1551)
The Pojoaque giant. *NM,* 9:18-19, Dec. 1931.

––––––– (1552)
A Pueblo child's party. *EP,* 14:184, 1923.

––––––– (1553)
Pueblo myths and legends. *EP,* 11:98-99, 1921.
Zia and San Juan stories of the fate of the witch wife.

DEHUFF, ELIZABETH WILLIS (Continued)   (1554)
    The red winged hawk. *EP*, 16:51-53, 1924.
      Taos tale.

—————   (1555)
    Taytay's memories. New York, Harcourt Brace, 1924.
      Pueblo legends and folktales.

—————   (1556)
    Taytay's tales. New York, Harcourt Brace, 1922.
      Pueblo legends and folktales.

—————   (1557)
    The venomous snake girl. *EP*, 31:73-74, 1931.

—————   (1558)
    Where witches abound. *SR*, 11:253-63, 1925-26.

—————   (1559)
    Witch bears: a tale of Santo Tomas Pueblo. *SR*, 23:84-103, 1937.
                                                        (1560)
    The witches' feast is interrupted. *EP*, 45:69-73, 1938.
      Taos tale.

—————   (1561)
    The yellow house people. *EP*, 30:269-74, 1931.
      Pueblo tales.

DEHUFF, JOHN   (1562)
    The intelligence quotient of the Pueblo Indian. *EP*, 22:422-32, 1927.

DENNIS, W. AND M. G.   (1563)
    Cradles and cradling practices of the Pueblo Indians. *AA*, 42:107-15, 1940.

DENSMORE, FRANCES   (1564)
    The music of Santo Domingo Pueblo. Southwest Museum Papers 12. Los Angeles, 1938.

—————   (1565)
    Music of the Winnebago, Chippewa and Pueblo Indians. *Smithsonian Explorations and Field Work, 1930.* Baltimore, 1931. pp. 217-24.

—————   (1566)
    A resemblance between Yuman and Pueblo songs. *AA*, 34:694-700, 1932.

DIETRICH, MARGRETTA   (1567)
    Their culture survives. *NM*, 14:22-23, 45, Feb. 1936.
      Historical sketch of Pueblo painters and painting.

DISMUKE, DEWEY   (1568)
    Acoma and Laguna Indians adjust their livestock to their range. *Soil Conservation,* 6:130-32, Nov. 1940.

—————   (1569)
    Range management brings success to Isleta Indians. *Soil Conservation,* 5:34-35, 1939.

DIXON, ROLAND B.   (1570)
    The building of cultures. New York, Scribners, 1928.
      Some mention of Pueblos and Navajos.

DIXON, W. H.   (1571)
  Isleta; why the church has a wooden floor. *Scribner's*, 70:193-99,
  1921.

DONALDSON, THOMAS   (1572)
  *The Moqui Pueblo Indians of Arizona and Pueblo Indians of
  New Mexico.* Washington, U. S. Census Printing Office, 1893.

DORMAN, MARGARET   (1573)
  A study of the water-color paintings of modern Pueblo Indians.
  Unpub. Master's thesis, UNM, 1932.

DOUGLAS, FREDERIC H.   (1574)
  Acoma Pueblo weaving and embroidery. *DAM, Leaflet series,*
  89:154-56, 1939.

————   (1575)
  An embroidered cotton garment from Acoma. *DAM, Material
  Culture Notes,* 1:1-4, 1937.

————   (1576)
  Main types of Pueblo cotton textiles. *DAM, Leaflet series,* 92-93:
  166-72, 1940.

————   (1577)
  Main types of Pueblo woolen textiles. *DAM, Leaflet series,* 94-95:
  174-80, 1940.

————   (1578)
  The modern Pueblo Indian. University of Denver Radio Program
  over KOA, March 21, 1935.   (Copy in files of New Mexico
  Writers' Project, Santa Fe.)

————   (1579)
  Modern Pueblo Indian villages. *DAM, Leaflet series,* 45-46, April
  1934.

————   (1580)
  Modern Pueblo pottery types. *DAM, Leaflet series,* 53-54:10-16,
  1935.

————   (1581)
  Periods of Pueblo culture and history. *DAM, Leaflet series,* 11:
  1-4, 1930.

————   (1582)
  Pueblo Indian pottery making. *DAM, Leaflet series,* 6:1-4, 1930.

————   (1583)
  Weaving at Zuni Pueblo. *DAM, Leaflet series,* 96-97:182-87, 1940.

————   (1584)
  Weaving in the Tewa Pueblos. *DAM, Leaflet series,* 90:158-60,
  1939.

————   (1585)
  Weaving of the Keres Pueblos. *DAM, Leaflet series,* 91:162-64,
  1939.

————   (1586)
  Weaving of the Tiwa Pueblos and Jemez. *DAM, Leaflet series,*
  91, 1939.

DOUGLASS, WILLIAM BOONE   (1587)
    Notes on the shrines of the Tewa and other Pueblo Indians of New
    Mexico. *19th ICA, Proceedings.* Washington, 1915. pp. 344-78.

———   (1588)
    A world-quarter shrine of the Tewa Indians. *Records of the Past,*
    11:159-71, 1912.

DOZIER, THOMAS S.   (1589)
    Historical pageantry at Santa Clara Pueblo. *EP,* 10 (12) :3-5, 1921.

DREXLER, ALFRED, GATLIN, P., AND PIJOAN, MICHEL   (1589a)
    A study of Taos Indian school children. Unpub. ms. dated 1943,
    in possession of Dr. Pijoan, Albuquerque.

DUFOURI, J. H. (DEFOURI?)   (1590)
    New Mexico and her Pueblos. *Catholic World,* 39:72, 1884.

DUGGAN, E. V.   (1591)
    Health work among the Zuni Indians. *Public Health Nurse,* 20:
    20-22, Jan. 1928.

DUMAREST, NOEL   (1592)
    Notes on Cochiti, New Mexico. *AAA Memoirs,* v. 6, Pt. III. Lan-
    caster, Pa., 1919. pp. 141-236.
        Includes material on customs, dances, religion, myths and tales.

DUNHAM, E. C., ABERLE, S. D., FARQUAHAR, L., AND D'AMICO, M.   (1593)
    Physical status of 219 Pueblo Indian children. *American Journal
    of Diseases of Children,* 53:739-49, 1937.

DUTTON, BERTHA P.   (1594)
    Hopi dance of the Jemez Indians. *Research,* 1:70-84, 1936.

———   (1595)
    The Jemez mountain region. *EP,* 44:133-43, 1938.
        Description of Pueblos.

EGGAN, FRED   (1596)
    Social organization of the western Pueblos. Master's thesis, Uni-
    versity of Chicago, 1934.

EICKEMEYER, CARL AND LILLIAN W.   (1597)
    Among the Pueblo Indians. New York, Merriam Co., 1895.
        Travel description.

EICKHOFF, H.   (1598)
    Die Kultur der Pueblos in Arizona und New Mexico. *Studien und
    Forschungen zur Menschen- und Volkerkunde* (Stuttgart), 4:1-
    78, 1908.

ELLER, MARIAN   (1599)
    A study of drawings by Pueblo Indian children. Unpub. Master's
    thesis, UNM, 1938.

EMBREE, EDWIN ROGERS   (1600)
    Indians of the Americas. Boston, Houghton Mifflin, 1939.
        pp. 187-234, The Pueblos of the Southwest.

ESPINOSA, A. M.   (1601)
    All Souls' day at Zuni, Acoma, and Laguna. *JAF,* 31:550-52, 1918.

ESPINOSA, A. M. (Continued) (1602)
El desarrollo de la palabra Castilla en la lengua de los Indios queres de Nuevo Mejico. *Revista de Filologia Española*, 19:261-77, 1932.

——— (1603)
Miscellaneous materials from the Pueblo Indians of New Mexico. *Philological Quarterly*, 21:121-27, Jan. 1942.
Folklore materials, part in Indian languages.

——— (1604)
Pueblo Indian folk tales. *JAF*, 46:69-133, 1936.

——— (1605)
Romances españoles tradicionales que cantan y recitan los Indios de los Pueblos de Nuevo Mejico. Santander, del "Boletin de la Biblioteca Menendez y Pelayo," 1932.

ESTABROOK, EMMA FRANKLIN (1606)
Givers of life, the American Indians as contributors to civilization. Albuquerque, UNM Press, 1931.

——— (1607)
The living past. EAIA, Bulletin 12. New York, 1926.

ETTINGER, FRANCES (1607a)
The path of the snake. *The Southwest Wind*, 32:24, 33-34, Dec. 1942.
Deterioration of Pueblo population.

E-YEH-SHURE (BLUE CORN) (1608)
I am a Pueblo Indian girl. New York, William Morrow, 1939.
Personal narrative of a young Isletan.

FERGUSSON, ERNA (1609)
Crusade from Santa Fe. *North American Review*, 242:376-87, 1936.
The efforts of the Santa Fe art colony to kill the Bursum Bill and the establishment of the Pueblo Lands Board.

——— (1610)
Dancing gods; Indian ceremonials of New Mexico and Arizona. New York, Knopf, 1931.

——— (1611)
Laughing priests. *Theatre Arts Monthly*, 17:657-62, 1933.

——— (1612)
Perpetual pagans. *Scribner's*, 92:293-95, 1932.

FEWKES, J. WALTER (1613)
A comparison of Sia and Tusayan snake ceremonials. *AA*, o. s., 8:118-41, 1895.

——— (1614)
A few summer ceremonials at Zuni Pueblo. *Journal of American Ethnology and Archaeology*, 1:1-61, 1891.

——— (1615)
Pueblo culture and its relationships. *2nd Pan American Scientific Congress, Proceedings, 1915-16*, Sec. 1, v. 1. Washington, GPO, 1917. pp. 410-16.

FEWKES, J. WALTER (Continued)   (1616)
    The Pueblo settlements near El Paso. *AA*, 4:57-72, 1902.

————   (1617)
    A study of summer ceremonials at Zuni and Moqui Pueblos.
    Bulletin of Essex Institute, 22:89-113, 1890.

FISHER, REGINALD   (1618)
    Kivas of the living Pueblos. *EP*, 43:91-97, 1937.

————   (1619)
    An outline of Pueblo government.   (In Brand, D. D. and Harvey,
    Fred, Eds.: *So Live the Works of Men.* Albuquerque, UNM
    Press, 1939. pp. 147-57.)

————   (1620)
    An outline of Pueblo Indian religion. *EP*, 44:169-78, 1938.

FLEMING, HENRY CRAIG   (1621)
    Medical observations made on the Zuni Indians. *Nation's Health,*
    5:506-08, 1923.

————   (1622)
    Medical observations on the Zuni Indians. *Museum of the Ameri-
    can Indian, Heye Foundation, Contributions,* 7 (2) :39-47, 1924.

FLOOD, FRANCIS   (1623)
    Pueblos are people. *Farmer-Stockman,* 51:7, 27, Jan. 1, 1938.

FOARD, JOSEPHINE   (1624)
    The Pueblo Indian potter. *LMC, Proceedings, 1st Session, 1908.*
    pp. 14-16.

FORDE, C. D.   (1625)
    A creation myth from Acoma. *Folk-lore* (London), 41:370-87,
    1930.

FRASER, GEORGE A. H.   (1626)
    *Report on two hundred acre conflict between the Pueblo of San
    Felipe and El Ranchito purchase of the Pueblo of Santa Ana,
    October 1, 1932.* Unpub. document in the records of the Pueblo
    Lands Board, Land Agent's Office, UPA, Albuquerque.

FREELAND, HELEN   (1627)
    Ancient and modern distribution of the Pueblos. *EP*, 4 (2) :74-
    76, 1917.

FYNN, A. J.   (1628)
    *The American Indian as a product of environment, with special
    reference to the Pueblos.* Boston, Little Brown, 1907.
        Chapter 3, Pueblo lands and houses. In other chapters references to Pueblo
        food and clothing, government, education, industries, religion, dances and
        festivals.

GAASTRA, MRS. T. CHARLES   (1629)
    Santo Domingo "Bull and Horse" ceremony. *EP*, 18:67-69, 1925.

GATSCHET, ALBERT S.   (1630)
    Indian languages of the Pacific states and territories, and of the
    Pueblos of New Mexico. *Magazine of American History,* 8:254-
    64, 1882.

GATSCHET, ALBERT S. (Continued)   (1631)
Migration of the Taos Indians. *AA*, o. s., 5:191-92, 1892.

――――   (1632)
A mythic tale of the Isleta Indians. *American Philosophical Society, Proceedings*, 29:207-17, 1891.

――――   (1633)
The sun worship of Isleta Pueblo. *American Philosophical Society, Proceedings*, 29:217-19, 1891.

GEORGE, H. M.   (1634)
Among the Pueblo Indians of New Mexico. *Public Health Nurse*, 17:319-22, 1925.

GILBERT, HOPE   (1635)
Reunion at Santa Clara. *NM*, 18:14-15, 42-43, May 1940.

GILMAN, B. I.   (1636)
Zuni melodies. *Journal of American Ethnology and Archaeology*, 1:63-91, 1891.

GILPIN, LAURA   (1637)
The Pueblos: a camera chronicle. New York, Hastings House, 1942.

GLENN, NAN A.   (1638)
The probable origin of the modern Pueblos. Unpub. Master's thesis, UNM, 1938.

GODDARD, SARA ANNE   (1639)
The Zuni language as a means of interpreting Pueblo Indian culture. Unpub. Master's thesis, UNM, 1930.

GOLDFRANK, ESTHER S.   (1640)
Isleta variants: a study in flexibility. *JAF*, 39:70-78, 1926.

――――   (1641)
A note on twins. *AA*, 23:387-88, 1921.
        Comparison of Laguna with Zuni and Cochiti.

――――   (1642)
Notes on two Pueblo feasts. *AA*, 25:188-96, 1923.
        St. Joseph's Day at Laguna and St. Elizabeth's Feast at Polmati.

――――   (1643)
Social and ceremonial organizations of Cochiti. AAA, Memoirs 33. Menasha, Wisconsin, 1927.

GOLDMAN, IRVING   (1644)
The Zuni of New Mexico. (In Meade, Margaret, Ed.: *Competition and cooperation among primitive people.* New York, McGraw-Hill, 1937.)

GRAHAM, S.   (1645)
The Shalaco dance. *EP*, 15:139-40, 1923.

GRANT, BLANCHE C.   (1646)
Taos Indians. Santa Fe, New Mexican Pub. Co., 1926.

GRATTAN, H. W.   (1647)
Zuni day school shop; industrial-arts work among the Indians. *Indian Arts and Vocational Education*, 27:99-100, 1938.

GUNN, JOHN M.   (1648)
History, traditions, and narratives of the Queres Pueblos of Laguna
and Acoma. *Records of the Past,* 3:291-310, 323-44, 1904.

_____   (1649)
*Schat-chen; history, traditions, and narratives of the Queres Indians
of Laguna and Acoma.* Albuquerque, Albright and Anderson,
1917.

GUTHE, CARL E.   (1650)
Pueblo pottery-making; a study at the village of San Ildefonso.
New Haven, Yale University Press, 1925.

GWYTHER, GEORGE M. D.   (1651)
Ceremony at Acoma. *Overland Monthly,* March 1871.

HAEBERLIN, H. K.   (1652)
The idea of fertilization in the culture of the Pueblo Indians.
AAA, Memoirs, v. 3, no. 1, 1916.
> Comparison of fertility concepts of Pueblos and Navajos with those of
> Plains Indians.

HAEBERLIN, HERMANN   (1653)
Das Flachenornament in der Keramik der alten Pueblo Kultur.
Baessler-Archiv, Beitrage zur Volkerkunde, 6:1-35, 1922.

HALL, H. U.   (1654)
A buffalo robe biography. *University of Pennsylvania, Museum
Journal,* 17:5-35, 1926.

HALSETH, ODD S.   (1655)
The acculturation of the Pueblo Indians. *EP,* 18:254-68, 1925.
> A brief, general account of recent culture changes among Pueblo Indians
> and their effect on life in the Pueblos.

_____   (1656)
Primitive copyrights. *Design,* 33:188-92, 1932.
> Pueblo pottery designs.

_____   (1657)
The Pueblo Indians. *EP,* 22:238-51, 1927.

_____   (1658)
Revival of Pueblo pottery-making. *Journal of Applied Sociology,*
10:533-47, 1926. *Also EP,* 21:135-54, 1926.

HAMMOND, WILLIAM A.   (1659)
The disease of the Scythians *(Morbus Feminarum)* and certain
analogous conditions. *Journal of Neurology and Psychiatry.* 1:
339-55, 1882.
> Based on observations at Laguna.

HANDY, E. L.   (1660)
Zuni tales. *JAF,* 31:451-71, 1918.

HARD, W.   (1661)
Foreigners at Washington. *Nation,* 116:148, 1923.
> Pueblo leaders protest Bursum Bill.

HARPER, BLANCHE W.   (1662)
*Notes on the documentary history, the language, and the rituals
and customs of Jemez Pueblo.* Unpub. Master's thesis, UNM,
1929.

HARRINGTON, JOHN P. (1663)
Ambiguity in the Taos personal pronoun. *Holmes Anniversary Volume*. Washington, G. W. Bryan Press, 1916. pp. 142-56.
⸻ (1664)
A brief description of the Tewa language. *AA*, 12:497-504, 1910. *Also* AIA, School of American Archaeology, Papers 17. Santa Fe, 1910.
⸻ (1665)
The ethnogeography of the Tewa Indians. *Bureau of American Ethnology, 29th Annual Report*. Washington, GPO, 1916. pp. 29-636.
⸻ (1666)
An introductory paper on the Tiwa language. *AA*, 12:11-48, 1910. *Also* AIA, School of American Archaeology, Papers 14. Santa Fe, 1910.
⸻ (1667)
Meanings of old Tewa Indian place names. *EP*, 7:78-83, 1919.
⸻ (1668)
Studying the mission Indians of California and the Taos of New Mexico. *Smithsonian Publication 3011*, 1929. pp. 169-78.
⸻ (1669)
The Tewa Indian game of "Canute." *AA*, 14:243-86, 1912.
⸻ (1670)
Tewa relationship terms. *AA*, 14:472-98, 1912.

HARRINGTON, JOHN P. AND ROBERTS, HELEN H. (1671)
Picuris children's stories, with texts and songs. *Bureau of American Ethnology, 43rd Annual Report*. Washington, GPO, 1928. pp. 289-447.

HARRINGTON, MRS. MARK R. (1672)
My dream pot and how it came forth from Towayalane, the sacred mesa of Zuni. *Masterkey*, 2 (6) :5-13; (7) :10-15, 1929.

HARTLEY, MARSDEN (1673)
Tribal esthetic dance drama. *EP*, 6:53-55, 1919.

HAWLEY, FLORENCE M. (1674)
Pueblo of the sun (tentative title). Unpub. ms. in possession of the author.
> A study of one of the eastern Keresan Pueblos (name can be obtained from Dr. Hawley) based on several years of intimate contact. Included are discussions of Pueblo attitudes towards outsiders; government; religion, including an infiltration of the Holy Roller cult into the Pueblo; social organization; diet and food customs; child training and education; economic life; morality and authority; wedding and courtship customs.

⸻ (1675)
Pueblo politics. *NM*, 17:16-17, 34-35, Aug. 1939.

HENDERSON, ALICE CORBIN (1676)
A boy painter among the Pueblo Indians. EAIA, Bulletin 9. New York, 1925.

⸻ (1677)
Dance rituals of the Pueblo Indians. *Theatre Arts Monthly*, 7:109-15, April 1923.

HENDERSON, ALICE CORBIN (Continued)   (1678)
   Death of the Pueblos. *New Republic,* 33:11-13 Nov. 29, 1922.
      Death from starvation, poverty, and disintegration for Pueblos if Bursum Bill
      is passed.
HENDERSON, JUNIUS AND HARRINGTON, JOHN P.   (1679)
   Ethnozoology of the Tewa Indians. Bureau of American Eth-
   nology, Bulletin 56. Washington, GPO, 1914.
HERZOG, G.   (1680)
   A comparison of Pueblo and Pima musical styles. *JAF,* 49:283-417,
   1936.
HESSELDEN, ELIZABETH C.   (1681)
   Pueblo Indian costume. Unpub. Master's thesis, New Mexico
   Normal (Highlands) University, 1931.
HEWETT, EDGAR L.   (1682)
   The corn ceremony at Santo Domingo. *EP,* 5:69-76, 1918.

—————   (1683)
   Crescencio Martinez—artist. *EP,* 5:67-69, 1918.

—————   (1684)
   From barter to world trade. *EP,* 49:219-24, 1942.
      As exemplified in Santo Domingo.

—————   (1685)
   Letters on the Pueblo Indian situation. AIA, School of American
   Research, Papers, n. s., 9. Santa Fe, 1925.

—————   (1686)
   My neighbors, the Pueblo Indians. *A&A,* 16:3-24, July 1923.
   Also EP, 15:123-34, 1923.

—————   (1687)
   Native American artists. *A&A,* 13:103-12, 1922.

—————   (1688)
   On the revival of certain indigenous American arts. *22nd ICA,*
   Proceedings. Rome, 1926. pp. 549-59.

—————   (1689)
   Present condition of the Pueblo Indians. AIA, School of American Research, Papers, n. s., 10. Santa Fe, 1925. *Also EP,* 19:3-11,
   1925.

—————   (1690)
   Present status of Pueblos. *EP,* 17:227-39, 1924.

—————   (1691)
   Recent Southwestern art. *A&A,* 9:30-48, 1920.

—————   (1692)
   Religion in ancient America. *EP,* 34:157-63, 1933.

—————   (1693)
   What the government is doing for the Pueblo Indians. *A&A,* 18:
   243-44, 1924.
HEWETT, EDGAR L., HENDERSON, JUNIUS, AND ROBBINS, WILFRED W. (1694)
   The phsyiography of the Rio Grande Valley, New Mexico, in
   relation to Pueblo culture. Bureau of American Ethnology,
   Bulletin 54. Washington, GPO, 1913.

HODGE, FREDERICK WEBB (1695)
Acoma; an enchanted mesa. *Nature*, 57:450-, 1897.

(1696)
Ceremonial shields of Taos. *Museum of the American Indian, Heye Foundation, Indian Notes*, 3:95-99, 1926. *Also EP*, 20:231-34, 1926.

(1697)
The first discovered city of Cibola. *AA*, o. s., 8:142-52, 1895.
Hawikuh.

(1698)
How a Pueblo potter treated a broken handle. *Museum of the American Indian, Heye Foundation, Indian Notes*, 1:235-36, 1924.

(1699)
The Jumano Indians. *American Antiquarian Society, Proceedings*, n. s., 20:249-68, 1910.

(1700)
Laguna Indian villages, New Mexico. *AA*, o. s., 4:345-46, 1891.

(1701)
Old cradle from Taos. *Museum of the American Indian, Heye Foundation, Contributions*, 5:231-35, 1928.

(1702)
Pueblo Indian clans. *AA*, o. s., 9:345-52, 1896.

(1703)
Pueblo Indian government. *Masterkey*, 7:124-26, 1933.

(1704)
Pueblo snake ceremonials. *AA*, o. s., 9:133-36, 1896.

(1705)
Rites of the Pueblo Indians. *EP*, 18:23-28, 1925.

(1706)
War god idols of San Juan. *EP*, 23:588-89, 1927. *Also Museum of the American Indian, Heye Foundation, Indian Notes*, 4:395-400, 1927.

(1707)
A Zuni foot-race. *AA*, o. s., 3:227-31, 1890.

HODGE, GENE MEANY (1708)
The Kachinas are coming; Pueblo Indian kachina dolls with related folktales. Los Angeles, Bruce McCallister, 1936.

HODGE, Z. P. (1709)
Marie Martinez, Indian master-potter. *SW*, 62:213-15, 1933.

HOGNER, DOROTHY CHILDS (1710)
The Indian with pick and shovel. *NM*, 11:24-25, 48, Oct. 1933.
Indian Emergency Conservation Work.

HOGUE, ALEXANDER (1711)
Picturesque games and ceremonials of Indians. *EP*, 26:177-83, 1929.
Taos.

(1712)
Pueblo tribes aesthetic giants, Indian art reveals. *EP*, 24:214-18, 1928.

HOLMES, J. D.   (1713)
    Carrying water to the Indians. *NM*, 10:22-23, 41, June 1932.
        Benefits of MRGCD to Pueblos.
HORTON, CHARLES M.   (1714)
    The Pueblo Indians. *Great Southwest*, May 1907.
HOUGH, WALTER   (1715)
    Mountain peak worship of Pueblos. *EP*, 33:166-67, 1932.
————   (1716)
    Pueblo environment. An address before the Section of Anthro-
    pology, AAAS, New Orleans meeting, Dec. 29, 1905-Jan. 4, 1906.
    AAAS, Proceedings, 55:447-54, 1906.
————   (1717)
    Sacred springs in the Southwest. *Records of the Past*, 5:163-69,
    1906.
        Zuni.
HOWARD, R. G.   (1718)
    Agronomic and farm analysis survey of Isleta Indian grant. USDA,
    SCS, Dec. 1935. Typewritten. (Copy at UPA, Albuquerque.)
HRDLICKA, ALES   (1719)
    A Laguna ceremonial language. *AA*, 5:730-32, 1903.
————   (1720)
    The Pueblos: with comparative data on the bulk of the tribes of
    the Southwest and Northern Mexico. *American Journal of
    Physical Anthropology*, 20:235-460, 1935.
HUEBENER, G.   (1721)
    The green corn dance at Santo Domingo. *EP*, 45:1-17, 1938.
HURT, WESLEY R., JR.   (1722)
    Notes on the Santa Ana Indians. *EP*, 48:131-42, 1941.
        General culture, myths, dances.
INDIAN RIGHTS ASSOCIATION   (1723)
    Caring for the Pueblos. Indian Rights Association, Publication
    123. Philadelphia, 1923.
JACKSON, H. H.   (1724)
    A midsummer fete in the Pueblo of San Juan. *Atlantic*, 49:101-
    08, 1882. (Signed H. H.)
JAMES, A.   (1725)
    Home and school life of San Ildefonso Pueblo. *Visual Education*,
    5:374-76, 1924.
JAMES, AHLEE   (1726)
    Crow dance at San Ildefonso. *EP*, 18:229-30, 1925.
————   (1727)
    Tewa firelight tales. New York, Longmans Green, 1927.
————   (1728)
    Tree planting at San Ildefonso. *EP*, 18:191-92, 1925.
JAMES, GEORGE WHARTON   (1729)
    Acoma and the Enchanted Mesa. *Scientific American Supplement*,
    April 22, 1899.
————   (1730)
    With the Pueblo Indians at Acoma. *The Papoose*, July 1903.

JAMES, GEORGE WHARTON (Continued)   (1731)
  With the Zunis in New Mexico. *Overland,* n. s., 72:104-12, 254-
  60, 284-99, 1918.

JEANCON, JEAN ALLARD   (1732)
  Pueblo beads and inlay. *DAM, Leaflet series,* 30:1-4, 1931.

———   (1733)
  The Pueblo golden age. *DAM, Leaflet series* 14, 1930.

———   (1734)
  A rectangular ceremonial room. *Colorado Magazine,* 3:133-37,
  1926.
        Santa Clara.

———   (1735)
  Santa Clara and San Juan pottery. *DAM, Leaflet series* 35, 1931.

———   (1736)
  Taos notes. *EP,* 28:3-11, 1930.

JEANCON, JEAN ALLARD AND DOUGLAS, FREDERIC H.   (1737)
  Pueblo Indian clothing. *DAM, Leaflet series* 4, 1930.

———   (1738)
  Pueblo Indian foods. *DAM, Leaflet series* 8, 1930.

JENNINGS, J. D.   (1739)
  Variation of Southwestern Pueblo culture. Laboratory of Anthropology, Technical series, Bulletin 10. Santa Fe, 1940.

JOHNSON, CLIFTON   (1740)
  Life of the Pueblo. *Outlook,* 94:908-17, 1910.

———   (1741)
  Pueblo life in New Mexico. (In *Highways and Byways of the
  Rocky Mountains.* New York, Macmillan, 1910.)

JOHNSON, E. A.   (1742)
  *Working plan report of the grazing resources and activities of the
  Acoma Indian lands, New Mexico.* Unpub. ms. dated May 9,
  1931. (Copy at UPA, Albuquerque.)

———   (1743)
  *Working plan report of the grazing resources and activities of the
  Isleta Pueblo lands, New Mexico.* USDI, Indian Service, June
  20, 1931. Typewritten. (Copy at UPA, Albuquerque.)

———   (1744)
  *Working plan report of the grazing resources and activities of the
  northern Pueblo Indian lands, New Mexico.* Regional Indian
  Service Forestry Office, Albuquerque, Jan. 4, 1932. Processed.
  (Copy at UPA, Albuquerque.)
        Includes Tesuque, Pojoaque, Nambe, San Ildefonso, Santa Clara, San Juan,
        Picuris, Taos.

———   (1745)
  *Working plan report of the grazing resources and activities of the
  Sandia, San Felipe, Santo Domingo, Cochiti, Santa Ana, Zia, and
  Jemez Pueblo Indian lands, New Mexico.* Regional Indian
  Service Forestry Office, Albuquerque, Aug. 26, 1931. Processed.
  (Copy at UPA, Albuquerque.)

JONES, HESTER   (1746)
    Mythology comes to life at Zuni. *EP*, 32:57-66, 1932.

————   (1747)
    Zuni Shalako ceremony. *EP*, 30:1-10, 1931.

JONES, VOLNEY H.   (1748)
    The ethnobotany of the Isleta Indians. Unpub. Master's thesis,
    UNM, 1931.

JOUVENCEAU, A.   (1749)
    Miraculous preservation of the Pueblo of San Felipe. *Catholic
    Pioneer,* Oct. 1905.

————   (1750)
    The witches of Nambe. *Catholic Pioneer,* Sept. 1905.

KARDINER, ABRAM   (1751)
    The Zuni. (In his *The individual and his society.* New York,
    Columbia University Press, 1939.)

KATE, H. F. C. TEN   (1752)
    Zuni fetishes. *Internationales Archiv fur Ethnographie* (Leiden),
    3:118-36, 1890.

————   (1753)
    A Zuni folk tale. *JAF,* 30:496-99, 1917.

KAY, ELEANOR   (1754)
    The war priest's magic. *NM,* 20:21, 34, June 1942.
        Zuni Indians prepare for the draft.

KEECH, ROY A.   (1755)
    Christianity and the Pueblo Indians. *EP,* 34:143-46, 1933.

————   (1756)
    Green corn ceremony at the Pueblo of Zia, 1932. *EP,* 36:145-49,
    1934.

————   (1757)
    The kick-stick race at Zuni. *EP,* 37:61-64, 1934.

————   (1758)
    Life forms in Indian pottery. *New Mexico Quarterly,* 3:242-48,
    1933.
        Includes an estimate of the origin of the double thunderbird design of
        Acoma.

————   (1759)
    The Pecos ceremony at Jemez, August 2, 1932. *EP,* 36:129-34,
    1934.

————   (1760)
    Pueblo dwelling architecture. *EP,* 36:49-53, 1934.

————   (1761)
    The saline Pueblo strongholds. *EP,* 34:1-13, 1933.

————   (1762)
    Two days and nights in a Pueblo. *EP,* 35:185-95, 1933.
        Jemez.

————   (1763)
    Will the Pueblo amalgamate with the white? *EP,* 36:1-3, 1934.

KELLOGG, HAROLD   (1764)
    It's an old Indian custom. *EP*, 33:1-4, 1932.
        Dances.

KELLY, ALLEN   (1765)
    Arrested development of Cochiti. *Southwest Magazine*, June
    1896.

KENNEDY, KATHARINE   (1766)
    Poems from the Zuni. *SR*, 25:151-55, 1940.

KING, IRVING   (1767)
    Education of the Pueblo child. (In *Social aspects of education*.
    New York, Macmillan, 1912.)

KIRK, RUTH F.   (1768)
    Architecture of the ancients. *NM*, 19:14-15, 33-35, May 1941.

                                                        (1769)
    Spirits must have food. *NM*, 17:16-17, 34-36, Nov. 1939.
        Zuni fetishes.

                                                        (1770)
    Zuni hunt. *NM*, 15:16-17, 46, Nov. 1937.
        Rituals associated with hunting.

KLETT, F.   (1771)
    The Zuni Indians of New Mexico. *Popular Science Monthly*, 5:
    580-91, 1874.

KNIGHT, ERIC   (1772)
    The funny men. *NM*, 19:12-13, 33-34, June 1941.
        Zuni.

KRAUSE, FRITZ   (1773)
    Die Kultur der Pueblo-Indianer nach Ursprung und Entwicklung.
    Jahrbuch des stadtischen Museums fur Volkerkunde zu Leipzig,
    8:87, 1922.

                                                        (1774)
    Die Pueblo-Indianer. Halle, 1907.

                                                        (1775)
    Die Religion der Pueblo-Indianer. *Jahrbuch des stadtischen
    Museums fur Volkerkunde zu Leipzig*, 8:103-05, 1922.

KRIEGER, HERBERT W.   (1776)
    Aspects of aboriginal decorative art in America. *Smithsonian
    Annual Report, 1930*. pp. 519-56.
        Includes material on Pueblo art.

KROEBER, A. L.   (1777)
    The oldest town in America and its people. *American Museum
    Journal*, 16:81-85, 1916.
        Zuni.

                                                        (1778)
    Pueblo traditions and clans. *AA*, 20:328-31, 1918.

                                                        (1779)
    The speech of a Zuni child. *AA*, 18:529-34, 1916.

                                                        (1780)
    Thoughts on Zuni religion. *Holmes Anniversary Volume*. Wash-
    ington, G. W. Bryan Press, 1916. pp. 269-77.

KROEBER, A. L. (Continued)   (1781)
    Zuni culture sequences. *National Academy of Sciences, Proceedings,* 2:42-45, 1916.

—————   (1782)
    Zuni kin and clan. *AMNH, Anthropological Papers,* v. 18, pt. 2. New York, 1917.

—————   (1783)
    Zuni potsherds. *AMNH, Anthropological Papers,* v. 18, pt. 1. New York, 1916.

KUBLER, G.   (1784)
    Gran Quivira-Humanas. *NMHR,* 14:418-21, 1939.
        Identification of Gran Quivira as a Jumano Pueblo.

LA FARGE, OLIVER   (1785)
    An art that is really American. *New Mexico Highway Journal,* 9:11-12, March 1931.

LANE, D. R.   (1786)
    Church of Acoma. . . *Santa Fe Magazine,* 8:15-18, Nov. 1914.

LASSWELL, H. D.   (1787)
    Collective autism as a consequence of culture contact: notes on religious training and the peyote cult at Taos. *Zeitschrift fur Sozialforschung,* 4:232-47, 1935.

LAUGHLIN, RUTH   (1788)
    Christmas ceremonies in New Mexico. *EP,* 40:1-5, 1936.
        Pueblo dances.

LAW, G.   (1789)
    Laughing eyes of Tesuque. *Overland,* n. s., 78:47-52, Sept. 1921.

—————   (1790)
    Playing square with the Pueblo Indians. *Overland,* n. s., 77:9-20, June 1921.

LAW, GEORGE WARRINGTON   (1791)
    Santo Domingo. *NM,* 11:20-21, 45-47, Aug. 1933.
        Description of dances.

LAWRENCE, D. H.   (1792)
    The dance of the sprouting corn. *Theatre Arts Monthly,* 8:447-57, 1924.

—————   (1793)
    Indians and an Englishman. *The Dial,* 74:144-52, 1923.
        Reaction of Lawrence to his first encounter with Indians, together with his first impressions of New Mexican culture.

—————   (1794)
    Taos. *The Dial,* 74:251-54, 1923.

LEIGH, R. W.   (1795)
    Dental pathology of Indian tribes of varied environmental and food conditions. *American Journal of Physical Anthropology,* 8:179-99, 1925.
        Zuni.

LEMOS, PEDRO J.   (1796)
    The household arts of the Indian Pueblos. *School Arts Magazine,* 23:334-41, 1924. *Also EP,* 16:127-29, 1924.
        Deals particularly with pottery making.

LEMOS, PEDRO J. (Continued)   (1797)
Indian arts, Pueblo and Navajo. Worcester, Mass., Davis Press,
1932.
    Portfolio of reproductions of Indian designs.

——   (1798)
Marvellous Acoma and its craftsmen. *School Arts Magazine,* 27:
351-58, 1928. *Also EP,* 24:234-44, 1928.

——   (1799)
Zuni, the strangest art center in America. *School Arts Magazine,*
27:489-500, 1928.

LEROUX, LORETTA   (1800)
A Pueblo day school. *Childhood Education,* 18:353-56, 1942.

LEROY, J. A.   (1801)
Indian festival at Taos. *Outing,* 43:282-88, 1903.

LEWIS, FRANCES W.   (1802)
Life among the Pueblos. *SW,* Jan. 1901.

——   (1803)
The Pueblo home. *SW,* May 1901.

LINDQUIST, G. E. E.   (1804)
Pueblo Indian religion. *Missionary Review of the World,* 62:
553-54, 1939.

LINNEY, DOROTHY A.   (1805)
New Mexico's first settlers. *The Santa Fean,* 2:13-17, Summer
1942.

LINTON, RALPH M.   (1806)
Land tenure in aboriginal America. (In La Farge, Oliver, Ed.:
The Changing Indian. Norman, UOP, 1942. pp. 42-54.)
    Includes some material on land tenure among Pueblos.

LISTER, PAUL B.   (1807)
*Working plan report of the grazing resources and activities of the
Acoma Pueblo lands, New Mexico.* Survey made during Sept.
and Oct. 1935. (Copy at UPA, Albuquerque.)

——   (1808)
*Working plan report of the grazing resources and activities of the
Laguna Pueblo lands, New Mexico.* Survey made during Sept.
and Oct. 1935. (Copy at UPA, Albuquerque.)

LOWE, COSETTE CHAVEZ   (1809)
The doll maker of San Juan. *NM,* 18:20, 37, Nov. 1940.
    Regina Alvarado de Cata.

LUMMIS, CHARLES F.   (1810)
The city of the cliff. *Land of Sunshine,* 5:184-91, 1896.
    Acoma.

——   (1811)
The first American potters. *Land of Sunshine,* 7:44-50, 1897.

——   (1812)
Pueblo Indian folk-stories. New York, Century, 1910.
    (Originally issued as *The Man Who Married the Moon.*)

LUMMIS, CHARLES F. (Continued)   (1813)
A week of wonders. *Land of Sunshine*, 15:315-32, 425-37, 1901.
    Acoma.

                                                                 (1814)
The white Indian. *Land of Sunshine*, 13:8-17, 1900.
    Zuni.

LUMMIS, CHARLES F. AND OTHERS   (1815)
Three weeks in wonderland. *Land of Sunshine*, 9:111-24, 1898.
    Acoma, Enchanted Mesa.

MCCARREL, FRED   (1816)
The development of the training school. Unpub. Doctor's thesis,
George Peabody College for Teachers, 1934.
    Material on early Pueblo education by the Franciscans.

MACCLARY, JOHN STEWART   (1817)
Last of the seven cities of Cibola. *Southwestern Lore*, 2:11-16,
June 1936.
    Popular description of modern Zuni.

MCHARG, J. B.   (1818)
The lions of Cochiti. *EP*, 20:99-104, 1926.
    A "tentative bibliography for the study of the lions of Cochiti." Some text
    included.

MALKUS, ALIDA SIMS   (1819)
Those doomed Indian dances. *EP*, 14:149-52, 1923.

MANN, JESSE M.   (1820)
Range management plan for Jemez Pueblo and reservation.
USDA, SCS, Rio Grande District. Unpub. report dated March 10,
1937. (Copy at UPA, Albuquerque.)

MANNING, W. C.   (1820a)
Ancient pueblos of New Mexico and Arizona. *Harpers*, 51:327-
33, 1875.

MARCH, ELIZABETH JEAN   (1821)
A study of Zuni myths as literature. Unpub. Master's thesis,
UNM, 1942.

MARGOLD, N. R.   (1822)
The plight of the Pueblos. *Nation*, 132:121-23, 1931.
    Failure of government to halt Pueblo land losses.

MARIAGER, DAGMAR   (1823)
Some Zuni traditions. *Overland Monthly*, n. s., 8:216-18, 1886.

MARMON, MRS. WALTER K.   (1824)
The Laguna wedding gift ceremony. *EP*, 42:55-57, 1937.

MARTINEZ, DIEGO   (1825)
History of San Ildefonso. Unpub. ms. in the files of the Santa Fe
Indian School.

MARTINEZ, L. PASCUAL   (1825a)
Chispas del Valle de Taos. *Lulac News*, 7:6, July 1940.

MASON, OTIS TUFTON   (1826)
A primitive frame for weaving narrow fabric. *United States
National Museum Report*, 1899. pp. 485-511.
    Zuni.

MASON, OTIS TUFTON (Continued) (1827)
Primitive travel and transportation. *United States National Museum, Report,* 1894. pp. 237-593.
Includes material on Zuni.

MATTHEWS, WASHINGTON (1828)
Cities of the dead. *Land of Sunshine,* 12:213-21, 1900.
Zuni.

MAUZY, WAYNE (1829)
Architecture of the Pueblos. *EP,* 42:21-30, 1937.

MERA, HARRY P. (1830)
The "rain bird"; a study in Pueblo design. Laboratory of Anthropology, Memoirs, v. 2. Santa Fe, 1937.

———— (1831)
Style trends of Pueblo pottery in the Rio Grande and little Colorado cultural areas from the 16th to the 19th century. Laboratory of Anthropology, Memoirs, v. 3. Santa Fe, 1939.

MEREDITH, GRACE (1832)
Picuris Indian Pueblo. Unpub. ms. in files of New Mexico Writers' Project, Santa Fe.

———— (1833)
Sandia Indian Pueblo. Unpub. ms. in files of New Mexico Writers' Project, Santa Fe.

———— (1834)
Santa Clara Indian Pueblo. Unpub. ms. in files of New Mexico Writers' Project, Santa Fe.

METCALF, W. L. (1835)
Zuni; leaves from a sketch book. *Survey,* 53:29-32, 1924.
Drawings.

MILFORD, STANLEY JAMES (1836)
The twin war god cult of the living Pueblos. Unpub. Master's thesis, USC, 1937.

———— (1837)
The twin war god myth cycle. *EP,* 43:1-12, 19-28, 1937.

MILLER, MERTON LELAND (1838)
A preliminary study of the Pueblo of Taos, New Mexico. Doctor's dissertation, University of Chicago, 1898.
Includes material on resistance to Spaniards, linguistic relations with other Pueblos, origin of Taos people, population, land tenure, irrigation, housing, agriculture, division of labor, religion, social organization, clans, marriage, customs, traditions, myths.

———— (1839)
The Pueblo of Taos. Chicago, University of Chicago Press, 1898.

MINDELEFF, VICTOR (1840)
A study of Pueblo architecture: Tusayan and Cibola. *Bureau of American Ethnology, 8th Annual Report.* Washington, GPO, 1891. pp. 3-228.

MONSON, FREDERICK I. (1841)
Acoma, the oldest city of the western hemisphere. *Sunday Magazine,* March 20, 1904.

MOON, KARL E.   (1842)
    Taos, the Indian Pueblo. *The Burr McIntosh Monthly,* Nov.
    1909.
MOORE, ALLEN   (1843)
    Impressions of Corn Dance. *EP,* 15:77-78, 1923.
        Santo Domingo.
MORANG, ALFRED   (1844)
    Drums and dust. *Over the Turquoise Trail,* 1:21-26, Autumn
    1938.
        Literary description of rain dance at San Felipe.
MUSGRAVE, ETHEL W.   (1845)
    Indian "bread line." *NM,* 18:18-19, 40, 41, Feb. 1940.
        Pueblo bread making.
NASH, EDITH   (1846)
    Materials of fashion. *NM,* 14:22-23, 38, 39, 42, April 1936.
        Southwest Indian designs can be a source for fashionable decorative patterns.
NEW MEXICO ASSOCIATION ON INDIAN AFFAIRS   (1847)
    Architecture of the ancients. Indian Art series 12. Santa Fe, n. d.
——————   (1848)
    Booklet of reproductions of Indian paintings representing proof
    of a digression from the traditional style of Indian painting. (no
    title). Santa Fe, July 5, 1940.
——————   (1849)
    Indian pottery by the roadsides. Indian Art series 5. Santa Fe,
    n. d.
——————   (1850)
    Old art in new forms. Indian Art series 8. Santa Fe, 1936.
        Utilization of Pueblo art forms and techniques in making modern home
        furnishings.
——————   (1851)
    Pueblo Indian painting. Indian Art series 1. Santa Fe, n. d.
NOLL, ARTHUR H.   (1852)
    The Pueblo Indians. *The Dial,* 12:104-07, 1891.
ORTH, GEORGE S.   (1853)
    Report on the Pueblo of Santa Ana. House Report 70, v. 2, 40th
    Congress, 2nd Session. Washington, GPO, 1868.
OWENS, JOHN G.   (1854)
    The games of Zuni. *Popular Science Monthly,* 35:39, May 1891.
PANCOAST, C. L.   (1855)
    Last dance of the Picuris. *NH,* 18:309-11, 1918.
PARKS, MARY HITCHCOCK   (1856)
    *A free association vocabulary of Pueblo Indians in the fifth and
    sixth grades.* Unpub. Master's thesis, University of Oklahoma,
    1937.
PARSONS, ELSIE CLEWS   (1857)
    All Souls' day at Zuni, Acoma, and Laguna. *JAF,* 30:495-96, 1917.
——————   (1858)
    The antelope clan in early Keresan custom and myth. *Man,* 17:190-
    93, 1917.
        Acoma.

PARSONS, ELSIE CLEWS (Continued) (1859)
Ceremonial dances at Zuni. *EP,* 13:119-22, 1922.

———— (1860)
Ceremonial friendship at Zuni. *AA,* 19:1-8, 1917.
Three detailed case studies.

———— (1861)
Ceremonial Tewa au Nouveau Mexique et en Arizona. *Journal de la Societe des Americanistes,* (Paris), n. s., 18:9-14, 1926.

———— (1862)
Early relations between Hopi and Keres. *AA,* 38:554-60, 1936.
Tracing Hopi culture to influence of Keres.

———— (1863)
The favorite number of the Zuni. *Scientific Monthly,* 3:596-601, 1916.

———— (1864)
A few Zuni death beliefs and practices. *AA,* 18:245-56, 1916.

———— (1865)
Fiesta at Sant' Ana, New Mexico. *Scientific Monthly,* 16:178-83, 1923.

———— (1866)
Franciscans return to Zuni. *AA,* 41:337-38, 1939.

———— (1867)
Hopi and Zuni ceremonialism. AAA, Memoirs v. 39, 1933.

———— (1868)
Increase by magic—a Zuni pattern. *AA,* 21:279-86, 1919.
Winter solstice fertility ceremonial.

———— (1869)
Isleta, New Mexico. *Bureau of American Ethnology, 47th Annual Report, 1929-30.* Washington, GPO, 1932. pp. 193-466.
Population, economic and personal life, government, ceremonial organization, rituals, calendar, folk tales.

———— (1870)
The last Zuni transvestite. *AA,* 41:338-40, 1939.

———— (1871)
New Mexico folklore. Mothers and children at Laguna. *Man,* 19-20:34-38, 1919-20.

———— (1872)
New Mexico folklore. Mothers and children at Zuni, New Mexico. *Man,* 19-20:168-73, 1919-20.

———— (1873)
Notes on ceremonialism at Laguna. *AMNH, Anthropological Papers,* v. 19, pt. 4. New York, 1920.

———— (1874)
Notes on Zuni. *AAA, Memoirs,* 4:151-237, 1917.

———— (1875)
The Pueblo Indian clan in folklore. *JAF,* 34:209-16, 1921.

———— (1876)
Pueblo Indian folk-tales, presumably of Spanish provenience. *JAF,* 31:216-55, 1918.

PARSONS, ELSIE CLEWS (Continued)   (1877)
   Pueblo Indian religion. 2 v. University of Chicago, Publications
   in Anthropology, Ethnological series. Chicago, 1939.

——   (1878)
   The Pueblo of Jemez. New Haven, Yale University Press, 1925.

——   (1879)
   Reasoning from analogy at Zuni. *Scientific Monthly,* 4:365-68,
   1917.

——   (1880)
   The religion of the Pueblo Indians. *ICA, Proceedings,* 21 (1):
   140-61, 1924.

——   (1881)
   Ritual parallels in Pueblo and plains cultures, with special reference to the Pawnee. *AA,* 31:642-54, 1929.

——   (1882)
   The scalp ceremonial of Zuni. AAA, Memoirs 31. Menasha,
   Wisconsin, 1924.

——   (1883)
   The social organization of the Tewa of New Mexico. AAA,
   Memoirs 36. Menasha, Wisconsin, 1929.

——   (1884)
   Some Aztec and Pueblo parallels. *AA,* 35:611-31, 1933.

——   (1885)
   Der spanische Einfluss auf die Marchen der Pueblo-Indianer.
   Zeitschrift fur Ethnologie, 58:16-28, 1926.

——   (1886)
   Spanish elements in the Kachina cult of the Pueblos. *ICA, Proceedings,* 23:582-603, 1928.

——   (1887)
   Spring days in Zuni, New Mexico. *Scientific Monthly,* 36:49-54,
   Jan. 1933.

——   (1888)
   Taos Pueblo. General Series in Anthropology, no. 2. Menasha,
   Wisconsin, George Banta Pub. Co., 1936.

——   (1889)
   Taos tales. American Folklore Society, Memoirs, v. 34. New
   York, J. J. Augustin, 1940.

——   (1890)
   Teshlatiwa at Zuni. *Journal of Philosophy, Psychology, and
   Scientific Method,* 16:272-73, 1919.

——   (1891)
   Tewa kin, clan, and moiety. *AA,* 26:333-39, 1924.

——   (1892)
   Tewa mothers and children. *Man,* 24:148-51, 1924.

——   (1893)
   Waiyautitsa of Zuni. *Scientific Monthly,* 9:443-57, 1933.

——   (1894)
   War god shrines of Laguna and Zuni. *AA,* 20:381-405, 1918.

PARSONS, ELSIE CLEWS (Continued) (1895)
Winter and summer dance series in Zuni in 1918. *UCPAAE*, v. 17,
no. 3. Berkeley, 1922.

—————— (1896)
Witchcraft among the Pueblos: Indian or Spanish? *Man*, 27:106-
12, 125-28, 1927.

—————— (1897)
The Zuni A'doshle and Suuke. *AA*, 18:338-47, 1916.
    Use of fear of the unknown to discipline children.

—————— (1898)
Zuni conception and pregnancy beliefs. *ICA, Proceedings*, 19:
378-83, 1915.

—————— (1898a)
A Zuni detective. *Man*, 16:99-100, 1916.

—————— (1899)
Zuni inoculative magic. *Science*, n. s., 44:469-70, 1916.

—————— (1900)
The Zuni Lamana. *AA*, 18:521-28, 1916.

—————— (1901)
The Zuni Mo'lawia. *JAF*, 29:392-99, 1916.

—————— (1902)
Zuni names and naming practices. *JAF*, 36:171-76, 1923.

PARSONS, ELSIE CLEWS, ED. (1903)
Tewa tales. American Folklore Society, Memoirs, v. 19. New
York, Stechert, 1926.

PARSONS, ELSIE CLEWS AND BEALS, RALPH L. (1904)
The sacred clowns of the Pueblo and Mayo-Yaqui Indians. *AA*,
36:491-514, 1934.

PARSONS, ELSIE CLEWS AND BOAS, FRANZ (1905)
Spanish tales from Laguna and Zuni. *JAF*, 33:47-72, 1920.

PAYTIAMO, JAMES (1906)
Flaming Arrow's people. New York, Duffield, 1932.
    Acoma.

PEET, STEPHEN D. (1907)
Animal figures in American art. *American Antiquarian*, 8 (1):
1-22, 1886.
    Some material on Pueblo art.

—————— (1908)
The cross in America. *American Antiquarian*, 10:292-315, 1888.
    Material on Zuni katcinas.

—————— (1909)
Early American explorations among the Pueblos. *American
Antiquarian*, 18:228-, 1896.

—————— (1910)
The growth of symbolism: symbolism and the totem system.
American Antiquarian, 7:321-49, 1885.
    Includes material on Zuni fetishes.

PEET, STEPHEN D. (Continued)   (1911)
    The worship of the rain god. *American Antiquarian*, 16:341-56, 1894.
       Material on Zuni pottery.

PIJOAN Y SOTERAS, JOSE AND COSSIO, MANUEL BARTOLOME   (1912)
    Summa artis. v. 1. Historia general del arte de los pueblos aborigenes. Bilbao, Madrid, Espasa-Calpe, S. A., 1931.

PITNEY, ELIZABETH H.   (1913)
    Size and growth of Pueblo Indian children. Unpub. Doctor's dissertation, Yale University, 1940.

POLEY, HORACE S.   (1914)
    The ancient customs of the ancient people of Taos. *Garden of the Gods Magazine,* Dec. 1902.

POORE, HENRY R.   (1915)
    Conditions of sixteen Indian Pueblos, 1890. (In *Report on Indians taxed and Indians not taxed in the United States (except Alaska) at the eleventh census, 1890.* Washington, GPO, 1894.)

QUINTANA, C. J.   (1915a)
    San Geronimo Day. *Lulac News,* 5:28-29, Sept. 1938.
       Taos Indian *fiesta.*

REAGAN, ALBERT B.   (1916)
    All Saints' day at Jemez, New Mexico. *Indiana Academy of Science, Proceedings,* 1904. p. 287.

——   (1917)
    The corn dance at Jemez. *SW,* 44:481-84, 1915.

——   (1918)
    Dances of the Jemez Pueblo Indians. *Kansas Academy of Science, Transactions,* 23:241-72, 1906.

——   (1919)
    The Jemez Indians. *SW,* 44:343-50, 1915. *Also EP,* 4 (2) :24-72, 1917.

——   (1920)
    The masked dance at Jemez. *SW,* 44:423-27, 1915.

——   (1921)
    The Matachina dance. *Indiana Academy of Science, Proceedings,* 1904. p. 293.

——   (1922)
    Notes on Jemez ethnography. *AA,* 29:719-28, 1927.

——   (1923)
    The "Penitentes." *Indiana Academy of Science, Proceedings,* 1904. p. 294.

——   (1924)
    Some paintings from one of the estufas in the Indian village of Jemez, New Mexico. *Indiana Academy of Science, Proceedings,* 1903. pp. 201-04.

——   (1925)
    The Zia Indians. *SW,* 45:25-29, 1916.

REAGAN, JAMES B.   (1926)
    The Jemez Indians. *EP,* 16:168-73, 1924.

RED EAGLE, CHIEF JIM   (1927)
The legend of the giant cactus. *NM,* 11:6-9, 43-44, Feb. 1933.

RENAUD, ETIENNE B.   (1928)
Influence of food on Indian culture. *Social Forces,* 10:97-101, 1931.

RENEHAN, ALOIS B.   (1929)
The Pueblo Indians and their land grants; the pioneers and their families, their descendants and grantees occupying parts of the Pueblo Indian land grants in New Mexico. Albuquerque, T. Hughes, 1923.
> Reviews ancient Spanish laws affecting Pueblo Indians and their neighbors.

REUTER, B. A.   (1930)
Acoma Pueblo. Unpub. ms. in files of New Mexico Writers' Project, Santa Fe.

————   (1931)
Acoma Pueblo foods; clothing. Unpub. ms. in files of New Mexico Writers' Project, Santa Fe.

————   (1932)
Legend of the founding of Laguna Pueblo. Unpub. ms. in files of New Mexico Writers' Project, Santa Fe.

————   (1933)
Natz-Szing. Unpub. ms. in files of New Mexico Writers' Project, Santa Fe.
> Paper bread from Santa Ana and other Pueblos.

————   (1934)
Restoration of Acoma mission. *EP,* 22:79-87, 1927.

————   (1935)
The story of how a small Pueblo was annexed to Acoma. Unpub. ms. in files of New Mexico Writers' Project, Santa Fe.

————   (1936)
A story of two magicians. Unpub. ms. in files of New Mexico Writers' Project, Santa Fe.
> Acoma legend.

RILEY, L. A., 2nd.   (1937)
Repairs to the old mission at Acoma. *EP,* 18:2-9, 1925.

RISSER, ANNA   (1938)
Seven Zuni folk tales. *EP,* 48:215-26, 1941.

ROBBINS, WM. J.   (1939)
Some aspects of Pueblo Indian religion. *Harvard Theological Review,* 34:25-47, 1941.

ROBBINS, W. W., HARRINGTON, J. P., AND FREIRE-MARRECO, BARBARA (1940)
Ethnobotany of the Tewa Indians. Bureau of American Ethnology, Bulletin 55. Washington, GPO, 1916.

ROBERTS, HELEN H.   (1941)
Analysis of Picuris songs. (In Harrington, John P. and Roberts, Helen H.: Picuris children's stories with texts and songs. *Bureau of American Ethnology, 43rd Annual Report, 1925-26.* Washington, GPO, 1928. pp. 399-447.)

ROBERTS, HELEN H. (Continued)   (1942)
    Chakwena songs of Zuni and Laguna. *JAF*, 36:177-84, 1923.

——————   (1943)
    Reasons for the departure of the Pecos Indians from Jemez Pueblo.
    AA, 34:359-60, 1932.

ROBERTS, K. L.   (1944)
    First families of America. *Saturday Evening Post*, 197:23, Oct.
    18, 1924.

ROBINSON, WILLIAM W.   (1945)
    Pueblo in the sky. *Overland*, n. s., 87:265-66, 1929.
        Acoma.

ROEDIGER, VIRGINIA MORE   (1946)
    *Ceremonial costumes of the Pueblo Indians; their evolution,
    fabrication, and significance in the prayer drama.* Berkeley, Uni-
    versity of California Press, 1941.

ROLLINS, WARREN E.   (1947)
    Zuni Indian fire dance. *EP*, 5:307, 1918.

SAUNDERS, CHARLES FRANCIS   (1948)
    Ceramic art of the Pueblo Indians. *International Studio*, 41:66-
    70, Sept. 1910.

——————   (1949)
    The Indians of the terraced houses. New York, Putnam, 1912.

——————   (1950)
    Indians of the terraced houses. *Out West*, 37:301-10, 1913.

——————   (1951)
    The little world of Zuni. *Outlook*, 97:453-59, 1911.

——————   (1952)
    Save the Pueblos. *Pacific Monthly*, July 1911.

SCACHERI, M. D.   (1953)
    Bending the twig, Indian style. *Public Health Nursing*, 28:513,
    1936. *Also Scholastic*, 29:29, Oct. 1936.
        Pueblo child rearing.

SCHOLES, FRANCE V.   (1954)
    Notes on Sandia and Puaray, *EP*, 42:57-59, 1937.

SCHOLES, FRANCE V. AND MERA, HARRY P.   (1955)
    Some aspects of the Jumano problem. *Carnegie Institution
    Publication 523.* Washington, June 10, 1940. pp. 265-99.

SEDGWICK, MARY K.   (1956)
    *Acoma, the sky city; a study in Pueblo Indian history and civili-
    zation.* Cambridge, Harvard University Press, 1927.

SERGEANT, ELIZABETH S.   (1957)
    Christmas in the Pueblos. *Survey*, 51:252-56, 1923.

——————   (1958)
    Crisis in Sia Pueblo. *Scribner's*, 98:27-32, July 1935.

——————   (1959)
    Death to the golden age. *New Republic*, 35:354-57, 1923.
        Reaction of Pueblos to a letter of Commissioner Burke demanding curbing
        of Indian dances.

SERGEANT, ELIZABETH S. (Continued)   (1960)
  Plight of the Pueblos. *New Republic,* 37:121-22, 1923.
      Protest against Bursum Bill.

_____   (1961)
  Principales speak. *New Republic,* 33:273-75, 1923.
      Description of a meeting of Pueblo elders.

_____   (1962)
  Should the Pueblo Indians be American citizens? *Nation,* 112:
  588-90, 1921.

SETON, JULIA M.   (1963)
  The pulse of the Pueblo; personal glimpses of Indian life. Santa
  Fe, Seton Village Press, 1939.

SHARP, D. D.   (1964)
  Isleta. Unpub. ms. in files of New Mexico Writers' Project, Santa
  Fe.

SHEPARD, H. WARREN   (1965)
  *Report on the project for the technical improvement of Pueblo
  pottery.* Santa Fe, Laboratory of Anthropology, 1936.

SHUFELDT, R. W.   (1966)
  Examples of unusual Zunian pottery. *Records of the Past,* 9:208-
  12, 1910.

SIMS, ALIDA F.   (1967)
  Pueblo—a native American architecture. *EP,* 12:103-06, 1922.

SOMERNDIKE, J. M.   (1968)
  Shall Pueblo Indian Christians be persecuted? *Missionary Review
  of the World,* 56:427-28, 1933.

SPENCER, F. C.   (1969)
  Education of the Pueblo child. Doctor's thesis, Columbia University, 1900. *Also* New York, Macmillan, 1899.

SPENCER, ROBERT FRANCIS   (1970)
  A preliminary sketch of Keresan grammar. Unpub. Master's thesis,
  UNM, 1940.

_____   (1971)
  A sketch of Laguna land ways. *EP,* 47:214-27, 1940.

SPIER, LESLIE   (1972)
  The Pueblos since Coronado. *EP,* 47:201-04, 1940.

_____   (1973)
  Zuni chronology. *National Academy of Science, Proceedings,* 3:
  280-83, 1917.

_____   (1974)
  Zuni weaving technique. *EP,* 16:183-93, 1924.

SPINDEN, HERBERT J.   (1975)
  Characteristics of Tewa mythology. *AA,* 17:372, 1915.

_____   (1976)
  Home songs of the Tewa. *American Museum Journal,* 15:73-78,
  1915. *Also EP,* 3:42-47, 1915.

SPINDEN, HERBERT J. (Continued)   (1977)
    The making of pottery at San Ildefonso. *American Museum Journal*, 11:192-96, 1911. *Also EP*, 7:183-86, 1919.

——   (1978)
    Songs of the Tewa. New York, Exposition of Tribal Arts, 1934.

STACEY, R.   (1979)
    Some Zuni ceremonies and melodies. *Music Lovers' Calendar*, 2:54-61, 1907.

STARR, F.   (1980)
    Shrines near Cochiti. *American Antiquarian*, 22:219-23, 1900.

——   (1981)
    A study of the census of the Pueblo of Cochiti. *Davenport Academy of Sciences, Proceedings*, 7:33-45, 1899.

STEDMAN, WILFRED   (1982)
    Mudheads of Zuni. *NM*, 18:16-17, 36, Oct. 1940.

STEVENSON, MATILDA COXE   (1983)
    Ethnobotany of the Zuni Indians. *Bureau of American Ethnology, 30th Annual Report, 1908-09*. Washington, GPO, 1915. pp. 31-102.

——   (1984)
    The Sia. *Bureau of American Ethnology, 11th Annual Report, 1889-90*. Washington, GPO, 1894. pp. 3-157.

——   (1985)
    Strange rites of the Tewa Indians. *Smithsonian Miscellaneous Collections*, v. 63, no. 8, 1914. pp. 73-80.

——   (1986)
    Studies of the Tewa Indians of the Rio Grande Valley. *Smithsonian Miscellaneous Collections*, v. 60, no. 30, 1913. pp. 35-41.
        Discussion of religious beliefs and practices.

——   (1987)
    The sun and ice people among the Tewa Indians of New Mexico. *Smithsonian Miscellaneous Collections*, v. 65, no. 6, 1916. pp. 73-78.
        Coming of Spring ceremonial at San Ildefonso.

——   (1988)
    Zuni ancestral gods and masks. *AA*, o. s., 11:33-40, 1898.

——   (1989)
    Zuni games. *AA*, 5:468-97, 1903.

——   (1990)
    The Zuni Indians. *Bureau of American Ethnology, 23rd Annual Report*. Washington, GPO, 1905.
        Includes mythology, worship, calendar, festivals, history, arts, customs, games, medical practice, social organization.

STEVENSON, MRS. T. E.   (1991)
    The religious life of the Zuni child. *Bureau of American Ethnology, 5th Annual Report*. Washington, GPO, 1887. pp. 533-55.

STEVENSON, TILLY E.   (1992)
    Zuni and Zunians. Washington, 1881.

STEWART, GUY R.   (1993)
   Conservation in Pueblo agriculture. *Scientific Monthly*, 51:201-
   20, 329-40, 1940.

STIRLING, MATTHEW W.   (1994)
   Indian tribes of Pueblo land. *National Geographic*, 78:549-96,
   1940.
      A review of Pueblo history.

————   (1995)
   Origin myth of Acoma and other records. Bureau of American
   Ethnology, Bulletin 135. Washington, GPO, 1942.
      Includes material on present customs of the Pueblo.

SWIFT, LUCY G.   (1996)
   A thanksgiving feast among the first Americans. *Journal of Home
   Economics,* 19:639-41, 1927.
      Feast of Indians of Rio Grande on November 1.

TAIT, J. L.   (1997)
   Renewing an ancient empire. *Technical World Magazine,* 22:
   876-78, 1915.

THOMPSON, GILBERT   (1998)
   An Indian dance at Jemez, New Mexico. *AA,* o. s., 2:351-55, 1889.

TOOMEY, NOXEN B.   (1999)
   An outline of Keresan grammar. Publications of Hervas Laboratory of American Linguistics, Bulletin 6. St. Louis, 1914.
      Based on Acoma and Laguna.

TRAGER, G. L.   (2000)
   Days of the week in the language of Taos Pueblo. *Language,* 15:
   51-55, 1939.
      Illustrates word borrowing from Spanish.

TREGO, FRANK H.   (2001)
   Master builders of ancient America. *Travel,* 51:22-24, 49, Sept.
   1928.

TROWBRIDGE, LYDIA J.   (2002)
   Zuni. *EP,* 22:8-12, 1927.
      Description of present life as observed on several visits.

TROYER, CARLOS   (2003)
   *Indian music lecture: the Zuni Indians and their music; . . . lives,
   customs, religions, occult practices.* Philadelphia, Theo. Presser
   Co., 1913.

TRUE, CLARA D.   (2004)
   Cochiti holiday. *NM,* 18:10-11, 31-32, Oct. 1940.
      Includes the legend of the stone lions.

————   (2005)
   A legend of Sangre de Cristo. *EP,* 4 (1):2-4, 1917.

————   (2006)
   The mantle of Black Mesa. *NM,* 16:15-17, 38, April 1938.
      History of San Ildefonso.

TWITCHELL, RALPH EMERSON   (2007)
   Pueblo Indian land tenures in New Mexico and Arizona. *EP,* 12:
   31-33, 38-61, 1922.

UHLE, MAX   (2008)
Der mittelamerikanische Ursprung der Moundbuilder und Pueblo-civilisationen. *Congres international des Americanistes. Compte rendu de la 21 session. Deuxieme partie tenue a Goteborg en 1924.* Goteborg, Museum. pp. 673-98.

UNDERHILL, RUTH M.   (2009)
First penthouse dwellers of America. New York, J. J. Augustin, 1938.

USDA, SCS   (2010)
Isleta Pueblo lands range management plan. Survey made during Aug. 1935. (Copy at UPA, Albuquerque.)

USDI, OFFICE OF INDIAN AFFAIRS, NORTHERN PUEBLOS AGENCY   (2011)
Annual reports, statistical and narrative sections, 1920-35. (Copies at UPA, Albuquerque.)
> Includes data on population, health, schools, agriculture, industries, economic conditions, law and order.

————, ————, SOUTHERN PUEBLOS AGENCY   (2012)
Annual reports, statistical and narrative sections, 1919-35. (Copies at UPA, Albuquerque.)
> Includes data on population, economic status, agriculture, disease, health, industries, schools, and forestry.

————, ————, UNITED PUEBLOS AGENCY   (2013)
Agronomic report on the Acoma reservation. Unpub. ms., UPA, 1941. (Copy at UPA, Albuquerque.)
> Includes data on crops, acreages, yields, production.

————, ————, ————   (2014)
Agronomic report on the Jemez reservation. Unpub. ms., UPA, 1941. (Copy at UPA, Albuquerque.)
> Data on crops, acreages, yields.

————, ————, ————   (2015)
Agronomic report on the Laguna reservation. Unpub. ms., UPA, 1941. (Copy at UPA, Albuquerque.)
> Data on crops, acreages, yields.

————, ————, ————   (2016)
Agronomic report on the Zuni Reservation. Unpub. ms., UPA, 1941. (Copy at UPA, Albuquerque.)
> Data on crops, acreages, yields.

————, ————, ————   (2017)
Agronomic survey, Jemez Pueblo Grant. Unpub. ms., UPA, 1941. (Copy at UPA, Albuquerque.)
> Soil survey of six areas on the Jemez Pueblo grant.

————, ————, ————   (2018)
Annual reports, 1936 to date. (Copies at UPA, Albuquerque.)
> Includes data on disease, land area, population, births, marriages, deaths, crops, livestock, agricultural income, arrests and offenses, law and order, and land tenure.

————, ————, ————   (2019)
Dry farming problems on Indian reservations under the jurisdiction of the United Pueblos Agency. Unpub. ms., UPA, 1941. (Copy at UPA, Albuquerque.)

USDI, OFFICE OF INDIAN AFFAIRS, UNITED PUEBLOS AGENCY (Continued)
(2020)
Dry-land or flood-irrigation farming on lands under the juris-diction of the United Pueblos Agency. Unpub. report, UPA, 1941. (Copy at UPA, Albuquerque.)

————, ————, ————,   (2021)
Pueblo stockman and farmer. UPA periodical publication, November 1940 to January 1942. (Copies at UPA, Albuquerque.)
Information on agriculture and livestock raising among Pueblos.

————, ————, ————,   (2022)
United Pueblo Quarterly Bulletin. UPA periodical publication, October 1939 to date. Processed. (Copies at UPA, Albuquerque.)
General information on Pueblo affairs.

————, ————, ZUNI AGENCY   (2023)
Annual statistical reports, 1931-35. (Copies at UPA, Albuquerque.)
Data on population, health, agriculture, and industries.

VAN STONE, MARY R.   (2024)
The Matachina dance. *EP,* 38:10-12, 1935.

————   (2025)
Songs of the Indians. *EP,* 48:149-54, 1941.

WALLACE, SUSAN E.   (2026)
Among the Pueblos. *Atlantic,* 46:215-25, 1880.
Brief review of Pueblo history to American occupation.

————   (2027)
The land of the Pueblos. Troy, N. Y., Nims and Knight, 1889.
History, laws, and customs of the Pueblos interspersed with information on the Apaches, Indian pottery, Mexican house building, Indian and Spanish-American legends, and other topics.

WARNER, LOUIS H.   (2028)
Laguna is a modern Pueblo. *National Republic,* 19:16-17, July 1931.

WATKINS, J. H., PITNEY, E. H., AND ABERLE, S. D. B.   (2029)
Vital statistics of the Pueblo Indians. *American Journal of Public Health,* 29:753-60, 1939.

WATSON, EDITHA L.   (2030)
The cult of the mountain lion. *EP,* 34:95-109, 1933.

————   (2031)
The one-line technique. *A&A,* 34:227-34, 1933.

WELTFISH, GENE   (2032)
White-on-red pottery from Cochiti Pueblo. *AA,* 33:263-64, 1931.

WHITE, A. E.   (2033)
Pueblo titles; with reply by J. Collier. *Survey,* 55:702-04, 1926.
Letter discussing provisions of Pueblo Lands Bill, called by Collier in his reply "an achievement of inaccuracy."

WHITE, LESLIE A.   (2034)
The Acoma Indians. *Bureau of American Ethnology, 47th Annual Report, 1929-30.* Washington, GPO, 1932. pp. 17-192.

WHITE, LESLIE A. (Continued)   (2035)
    Ancient Indians and modern Pueblos. *Hobbies* (Buffalo Society
    of Natural Sciences), 8 (6) :3-19, 1927.

——————   (2036)
    A comparative study of Keresan medicine societies.   *23rd ICA,
    Proceedings, 1928.* New York, 1930. pp. 604-19.

——————   (2037)
    The cultivation of cotton by Pueblo Indians of New Mexico.
    Science, 94:162, Aug. 15, 1941.

——————   (2038)
    An ethnological study of the Pueblo of Acoma. Doctor's disserta-
    tion, University of Chicago, 1927.

——————   (2039)
    Further data on the cultivation of tobacco among the Pueblo
    Indians. *Science,* 96:59-60, July 17, 1942.
        Attempt to trace the origin of the cultivation of *nicotiana rustica* by Pueblos.

——————   (2040)
    The impersonation of saints among the Pueblos. *Michigan
    Academy of Science, Papers,* 27, (Pt. 4) :559-64, 1942.

——————   (2041)
    Nicotiana rustica cultivated by Pueblo Indians. *Science,* 94:64-
    65, July 18, 1941.
        A species of tobacco not previously known to have been grown by Pueblos.

——————   (2042)
    The Pueblo of San Felipe. AAA, Memoirs 38. Menasha, Wis-
    consin, 1932.
        History, political organization, clan system, ceremonial cults, dances.

——————   (2043)
    The Pueblo of Santa Ana, New Mexico. AAA, Memoirs 60, 1942.

——————   (2044)
    Summary report of field work at Acoma. *AA,* 30:559-68, 1928.

WILLIAMS, J. HENRYETTE   (2045)
    Bah-Tah-Ko. *NM,* 11:15-17, 47, Oct. 1933.
        Indian legend of the founding of Taos.

WILLIAMSON, TEN BROECK   (2046)
    The Jemez yucca ring basket. *EP,* 42:37-39, 1937.

WILSON, FRANCIS C.   (2047)
    The Pueblo Indians of New Mexico. *LMC, Proceedings,* 1st
    Session, 1911. pp. 17-24.

WILSON, OLIVE   (2048)
    The survival of an ancient art. *A&A,* 9:24-29, 1920.
        Making of Tewa pottery.

WINSHIP, GEORGE PARKER   (2049)
    Acoma, sky city. *EP,* 22:38-43, 1927.
        Description of the rock, the people, and the Pueblo. Compiled from Charles
        F. Lummis' *Land of Poco Tiempo.*

WITTFOGEL, KARL A. AND GOLDFRANK, ESTHER S.   (2049a)
    Some aspects of Pueblo mythology and society. *JAF,* 56:17-30,
    Jan.-March. 1943.

WOODS BETTY (2050)
Feast day guests. *NM*, 16:14-15, 41, Nov. 1938.
Pueblo feasts.

——— (2051)
Mixed gods. *NM*, 20:12-13, March 1942.
Religious mixture of Sandia Pueblo following migration to Hopi.

——— (2052)
Salt harvest. *NM*, 18:14-15, 34, Oct. 1940.
Zuni.

——— (2053)
Wagons to Laguna. *NM*, 17:16-17, 33, Sept. 1939.
Celebration of St. Joseph's festival.

WOODWARD, A. (2054)
A modern Zuni pilgrimage. *Masterkey*, 6:44-51, 1932.

YARROW, H. C. (2055)
Medical facts relating to the Zuni Indians of New Mexico. *Rocky Mountain Medical Review*, 1:192-94, 1880-81.

Indians, General

ABEL, ANNIE HELOISE, ED. (2056)
Indian affairs in New Mexico under the administration of William Carr Lane. *NMHR*, 16:206-32, 328-58, 1941.

ADAIR, JOHN (2057)
Silversmiths of the Southwest. New York, J. J. Augustin, 1940.

ALEXANDER, HARTLEY BURR (2058)
L'art et la philosophie des Indiens de l'Amerique du nord. Paris, Editions Ernest Leroux, 1926.

——— (2059)
The rain cloud in Indian myth. *EP*, 21:314-19, 1926.
Comparison with Greek mythology.

ALLEN, FRED W. AND SCHAEFER, WALDEMAR (2060)
The distribution of the human blood groups among the Navajo and Pueblo Indians of the Southwest. UNM Bulletin, Biological series, v. 4, no. 2, 1935.

AMERICAN INDIAN DEFENSE ASSOCIATION (2061)
American Indian life. Bulletin 25. Washington, 1934.

AMMON, SOLOMON R. (2062)
History and present development of Indian schools in the United States. Unpub. Master's thesis, USC, 1935.

AMSDEN, CHARLES (2063)
Arts and crafts of the Southwestern Indians. *Masterkey*, 15:74-80, 1941.

——— (2064)
The loom and its prototypes. *AA*, 34:216-35, 1932.
Historical development of the loom among the Indians.

ANONYMOUS (2065)
Ethnological work in the Southwest. *Nation*, 102:473-74, 1916.
Resume of previous twenty-five years of progress in the field of Southwestern ethnology, with an evaluation of results in terms of its contribution to an understanding of Indian life.

ANONYMOUS (Continued)   (2066)
    Indian art in the Southwest. *EP*, 15:171-73, 1923.

                                                                       (2067)
    Indians of the Southwest: from an English point of view. *The Touchstone*, 6:241-43, 1920. *Also EP*, 8:34-35, 1920.

                                                                       (2068)
    Native tribes of New Mexico. *All the Year Round*, 21:468, 493, 517, 1869.

                                                                       (2069)
    1940 Indian decennial census completed. *United Pueblos Quarterly Bulletin*, v. 1, no. 6, July 1940.

                                                                       (2070)
    Recommendation for educational program. *EP*, 25:214-18, 1928.
        For Indians.

ASPLUND, R. F.   (2071)
    New Mexico and the Indian problem. EAIA, Bulletin 20. New York, April 1930.

AUSTIN, MARY   (2072)
    The American rhythm; studies and reexpressions of Amerindian songs. Boston, Houghton Mifflin, 1930.

                                                                       (2073)
    Indian poetry. (In *Introduction to American Indian art.* Pt. II. New York, Exposition of Indian Tribal Arts, 1931.)
        Includes poetry of Pueblos.

                                                                       (2074)
    Medicine songs. *Everybody's*, 21:413-15, Sept. 1914.

BACON, LUCY   (2075)
    Indian independence through tribal arts. *NM*, 10:11-13, 44, Jan. 1932.

BAILEY, VIRGINIA   (2076)
    Indian music of the Southwest. *EP*, 44:1-3, 1938.

BALL, SYDNEY H.   (2077)
    The mining of gems and ornamental stones by American Indians. Bureau of American Ethnology, Bulletin 128. Washington, GPO, 1941.
        Includes some discussion of mining by New Mexico Indians.

BANCROFT, HUBERT HOWE   (2078)
    Myths and languages. San Francisco, History Co., 1886.
        Includes those of New Mexico Indians.

                                                                       (2079)
    The native races. San Francisco, A. L. Bancroft Co., 1883.
        Chapter 5 of v. 1 deals with customs, dress, living conditions, agriculture, weapons, implements of New Mexico Indians.

BANDELIER, ADOLPH F. A.   (2080)
    Final report of investigations among the Indians of the Southwestern United States, carried on mainly in the years 1880 to 1885. 2 v. AIA, Papers, American series, v. 3-4. Cambridge, John Wilson & Son, 1890-92.

BARBER, BERNARD   (2081)
Messianic movements in primitive societies, a phase in the process of acculturation. Honors thesis on file in the Department of Sociology, Harvard University.

BARBER, EDWIN A.   (2082)
A brief review of native American pottery. *ICA Proceedings,* 4:323-34, 1881.

BARNARD, M. A. AND GARTH, T. R.   (2083)
The will temperament of Indians. *JAP,* 11:512-18, 1927.

BARNES, NELLIE   (2084)
Indian choral songs. *SR,* 13:481-90, 1928.

————   (2085)
On the age of American Indian songs. *SR,* 18:186-89, 1933.

BAUCH, LLOYD   (2086)
Educational service for Indians. The Advisory Committee on Education, Staff Study 18. Washington, GPO, 1939.

BEALS, RALPH   (2087)
Preliminary report on ethnography of the Southwest. Berkeley, UCP, 1935.

BEATTY, WILLARD W.   (2088)
La educacion de los Indios en los Estados Unidos. Washington, National Indian Institute, USDI, 1942.

————   (2089)
Indian education in the United States. *IW,* v. 8, no. 8, April 1940.

————   (2090)
Training Indians for the best use of their own resources. (In La Farge, Oliver, Ed.: *The Changing Indian.* Norman, UOP, 1942. pp. 128-38.)
> Urges vocational training to develop skills already possessed by Indians. Little direct mention of New Mexico.

BELL, W. A.   (2091)
On the native races of New Mexico. *Journal of the Ethnological Society of London,* n. s., I, session 1868-69. pp. 222-49.

BENEDICT, RUTH   (2092)
Concept of the guardian spirit in North America. AAA, Memoirs 29. Menasha, Wisconsin, 1923.

BENT, CHARLES   (2093)
Indian tribes of New Mexico. (In Schoolcraft, Henry R.:*Historical and statistical information respecting the history, condition, and prospects of the Indian tribes of the United States.* Part I. Philadelphia, Lippincott, 1854.)

BERRY, ROSE V. S.   (2094)
American inter-tribal Indian art. *A&A,* 32:147-59, 1931.

BIXLER, RAYMOND WALTER   (2095)
Some Indian contributions to American civilization. Unpub. Master's essay, Columbia University, 1924.

BLACKMAR, FRANK WILSON   (2096)
  The American Indian and status. *Sociology and Social Research,*
  14:221-32, 1930.

————   (2097)
  Social assimilation of the American Indians. *Journal of Educational Sociology,* 3:7-19, Sept. 1929.

BOAS, FRANZ   (2098)
  Anthropology and modern life. New York, Norton, 1932.
      Some material on Southwestern Indians.

————   (2099)
  Handbook of American Indian languages. Bureau of American
  Ethnology, Bulletin 40. Washington, GPO, 1911. Part I, pp. 85-
  158, Athapascan, by Pliny E. Goddard.

————   . (2100)
  *The mind of primitive man; a course of lectures delivered before
  the Lowell Institute, Boston, Massachusetts, and the National University of Mexico, 1910-11.* New York, Macmillan, 1931.
      Some material on Southwestern Indians.

BOURKE, JOHN GREGORY   (2101)
  The laws of Spain in their application to the American Indian.
  AA, o. s., 7:193-201, 1894.

BRENNECKE, NINA DE   (2102)
  Metal work designed from motifs of the American Indian. *EP,*
  30:33-35, 1931.
      Zuni and Apache designs included.

BREWER, ISAAC W.   (2103)
  Tuberculosis among the Indians of Arizona and New Mexico.
  New York Medical Journal, 84:981-83, Nov. 17, 1906.

BRINTON, DANIEL G.   (2104)
  *The myths of the new world, a treatise on the symbolism and myth-
  ology of the red race of America.* Philadelphia, David McKay,
  1905.
      Some mention of Pueblo and Navajo myths.

BROWNELL, CHARLES DE WOLF   (2105)
  The Indian races of North and South America. . . New York, H.
  E. and S. S. Scranton, 1853.

————   (2106)
  The tribes of the 35th parallel. *Harper's New Monthly Magazine,*
  17:448-67, 1858.
      Description of Indians encountered by Whipple & Ives expedition, 1853. In-
      cludes Zuni, Navajos.

BUILDING AMERICA   (2107)
  Our minority groups. I. The American Indian. *Building
  America,* v. 7, no. 4, Jan. 1942.

BURLIN, NATALIE CURTIS   (2108)
  *The Indians' book; an offering by the American Indians of Indian
  lore, musical and narrative, to form a record of songs and legends
  of their race.* New York, Harper, 1907.

BURSEY, JOSEPH (2109)
Reviving the art of the weavers. *NM*, 11:22-24, 44-46, May 1933.

BUSCHMANN, J. C. E. (2110)
Die Verwandtschafts-Verhaltnisse der athapaskischen Sprachen.
v. II. Berlin, *Abhandlungen der Koniglichen Akademie der Wissenschaften*, 1862. pp. 195-252.
Relationships between Athapascan languages.

——— (2111)
Die Volker und Sprachen Neu-Mexico's und der Westseite des
britischen Nordamerika. Berlin, *Abhandlungen der Koniglichen
Akademie der Wissenschaften*, 1857. pp. 209-404.
People and languages of New Mexico.

BUTTREE, JULIA M. (2112)
The rhythm of the Red Man, in song, dance, and decoration. New
York, A. S. Barnes, 1930.

CHABOT, MARIA (2113)
Heritage from the ancients. *NM*, 14:22-23, 35-37, March 1936.
Basketmakers of the Southwest.

CHAPMAN, KENNETH M. (2114)
Indian pottery. (In *Introduction to American Indian art.* Part
II. New York, Exposition of Indian Tribal Arts, 1931.)
Includes discussion of pottery of Zuni, Acoma, Cochiti, San Ildefonso.

CHESKEY, JANE (2115)
Indian music of the Southwest. *Kiva*, 7 (3) :9-12, 1941.

CLARK, S. P. (2116)
Lessons from Southwestern Indian agriculture. AAES, Bulletin
125. Tucson, 1928. pp. 229-52.

CLARK, WILLIAM P. (2117)
The Indian sign language. Philadelphia, Hammersley, 1885.

COLLIER, JOHN (2118)
Accursed system. *Sunset*, 52:15-16, June 1924.
Government relations with Indians.

——— (2119)
America's treatment of her Indians. *Current History Magazine
of the New York Times*, 18:771-81, 1923.

——— (2120)
Amerindians; problems in psychic and physical adjustment to a
dominant civilization. *Pacific Affairs*, March 1929. pp. 116-22.

——— (2121)
Indians come alive. *Atlantic*, 170:75-81, Sept. 1942.
Some information on recent governmental policies towards Mescalero and
Jicarilla Apaches, Acomas, and Navajos.

——— (2122)
Indians, inc. *Survey*, 63:519-23, 1930.
Some discussion of tenor of government's relations with Pueblos and Navajos.
Mainly a criticism of allotment system.

——— (2123)
The order relating to Indian religious liberty. USDI, Navajo
Service. Window Rock, n. d. Processed.

COOLIDGE, MARY R.   (2124)
   The rainmakers; Indians of Arizona and New Mexico. Boston,
   Houghton Mifflin, 1929.

COPE, LEONA   (2125)
   Calendar of the Indians north of Mexico. *UCPAAE*, v. 16, no. 4.
   Berkeley, 1919.

CORLETT, WILLIAM THOMAS   (2126)
   *The medicine man of the American Indian and his cultural back-
   ground.* Springfield, Illinois, Charles C. Thomas, 1935.
        Acoma and Navajo.

CRANE, LEO   (2127)
   Indians of the enchanted desert. Boston, Little Brown, 1925.
        Generalized account of everyday life of Southwestern desert Indians. Mostly
        concerned with Arizona, but contains some material on Navajos which is
        applicable to New Mexico.

CRIMMINS, M. L.   (2128)
   The Aztec influence on the primitive culture of the Southwest.
   Texas Archaeological and Paleontological Society, Bulletin, 4:32-
   39, Sept. 1932.

CULIN, STEWART   (2129)
   American Indian games. *AA*, 5:58-64, 1903.
        Includes Zuni games.

——————   (2130)
   Games of the North American Indians. *Bureau of American Ethnology, 24th Annual Report, 1902-03.* Washington, GPO, 1907.
   pp. 3-846.

CURTIS, EDWARD S.   (2131)
   The North American Indian. 20 v. Cambridge, Harvard University Press, 1907-30.
        v. 1 The Apache.   The Jicarillas.   The Navaho.
        v. 17.   The Tewa.   The Zuni.

CURTIS, NATALIE   (2132)
   Our native craftsmen. *EP*, 7:51-53, 1919.
        Includes Navajo and Pueblo craftsmen.

DEHUFF, ELIZABETH WILLIS AND GRUNN, HOMER   (2133)
   From desert and Pueblo. Boston, Ditson, 1924.
        Indian songs and music.

DEHUFF, JOHN D.   (2134)
   How shall we educate the Indian? *EP*, 13:59-64, Sept. 1922.

DELLENBAUGH, FREDERICK S.   (2135)
   *The North Americans of yesterday; a comparative study of North
   American Indian life, customs, and products, on the theory of
   the ethnic unity of the race.* New York, Putnam, 1901.

DENHARDT, ROBERT M.   (2136)
   The Indian acquires the horse. *Western Horseman*, 2:13, 24, Nov.-
   Dec. 1937.

DENNIS, WAYNE   (2137)
   Infant reaction to restraint: an evaluation of Watson's theory. *New
   York Academy of Sciences, Transactions*, Series II, v. 2, no. 7, 1940.
        Some material on reaction of Navajo and Pueblo children to cradleboard
        binding.

DENNIS, WAYNE AND MARSENA G.   (2138)
  The effect of cradling practices upon the onset of walking in Hopi
  children. *Journal of Genetic Psychology*, 56:77-86, 1940.
    Some mention of walking ages of Navajo, Santa Clara, San Ildefonso, and San
    Juan children.

DENSMORE, FRANCES   (2139)
  The American Indians and their music. New York, Women's
  Press, 1926.
    Some mention of New Mexico Indians.

————   (2140)
  The study of Indian music in the 19th century. *AA*, 29:77-86,
  1927.
    Some reference to Zuni music.

D'HARNONCOURT, RENE   (2141)
  Indian arts and crafts and their place in the modern world. (In
  La Farge, Oliver, Ed.: *The changing Indian.* Norman, UOP,
  1942. pp. 144-57.)
    Suggestions for developing arts and crafts market. Little direct mention of
    New Mexico Indians.

DIXON, MABEL EASTMAN   (2142)
  Methods of dyeing among the aboriginal tribes of America.
  Unpub. Master's essay, Columbia University, 1924.

DODGE, RICHARD IRVING   (2143)
  *Our wild Indians; thirty-three years personal experience among
  the red men of the great West.* Hartford, Worthington, 1882.

DORSEY, GEORGE A.   (2144)
  Indians of the Southwest. Chicago, Santa Fe Railway Passenger
  Dept., 1903.

DOUGLAS, FREDERIC H.   (2145)
  American Indian tobacco; varieties, cultivation, methods of
  use. *DAM, Indian Art leaflet* 22, 1931.

————   (2146)
  Pottery of the Southwestern tribes. *DAM, Leaflet series,* 69-70:
  74-80, 1935.

————   (2147)
  Southwestern twined, wicker, and plaited basketry. *DAM, Leaflet
  series* 99-100:194-99, 1940.

————   (2148)
  Tribes of the Southwest. *DAM, Leaflet series,* 55:1-4, 1933.

DOUGLAS, FREDERIC H., ED.   (2149)
  Indian design series; a series of 130 plates with explanatory notes.
  Denver, DAM, 1933-34.

DRAKE, SAMUEL GARDNER   (2150)
  The aboriginal races of North America. New York, Hurst & Co.,
  1880.
    Includes Navajos and Apaches "who live in New Mexico."

————   (2151)
  Biography and history of the Indians of North America. New York,
  Collins, Hannay & Co., 1834. *Also* Boston, Mussey, 1851.

DRAPER, WILLIAM R.   (2152)
   The Indian as a farmer. *Harper's Weekly*, 45:725-, July 20, 1901.

―――   (2153)
   Indian dances of the Southwest. *Outing*, 37:659-66, March 1901.

DUTTON, DEWEY ALVA   (2154)
   *A study of the application of intelligence tests to the Indians of
   the Southwest.* Unpub. Master's thesis, University of Denver, 1931.
         Pueblos and Navajos from Albuquerque and Santa Fe Indian Schools.

EASTERN ASSOCIATION ON INDIAN AFFAIRS   (2155)
   The American Indian—a national obligation. EAIA, Bulletin 19.
   New York, Jan. 1930.

―――   (2156)
   Indian dances. EAIA, Bulletin 3. New York, Jan. 1924.

―――   (2157)
   Industrial conditions among the Indians of New Mexico. EAIA,
   Bulletin 14. New York, May 1927.

―――   (2158)
   Modernizing an old system. EAIA, Bulletin 22. New York, March
   1931.
         Indian administration.

―――   (2159)
   The problem of Indian administration. (*A summary of the Meriam report.*) EAIA, Bulletin 16. New York, Nov. 1928.

―――   (2160)
   Trachoma among the Indians. EAIA, Bulletin 10. New York, Dec.
   1925.

EASTMAN, CHARLES A.   (2161)
   Indian today; the past and the future of the first American. Garden City, Doubleday Page & Co., 1915.
         Information on governmental relations, health, education, arts, written
         from Indian point of view.

EATON, COLONEL J. H.   (2162)
   Description of the true state and character of the New Mexican
   tribes. (In Schoolcraft, Henry R.: *Historical and statistical information respecting the history, conditions, and prospects of the
   Indian tribes of the United States.* Part IV. Philadelphia, Lippincott, 1854.)

ELMORE, FRANCIS H.   (2163)
   The shaman and modern medicine. *EP*, 42:39-46, 1937.

EVANS, BESSIE AND MAY G.   (2164)
   American Indian dance steps. New York, A. S. Barnes, 1931.

FARIS, C. T.   (2165)
   The Indian as a wool grower. *National Wool Grower*, 15:23-25,
   Nov. 1925.

FARRAND, LIVINGSTON   (2166)
   Basis of American history, 1500-1900. New York, Harper, 1904.
         Chapter 12 contains information on social organization and history of South-
         western Indian tribes.

FEWKES, J. WALTER, ED.   (2167)
A journal of American ethnology and archaeology: Hemenway Southwestern Archaeological Expedition. 5v. Boston, Houghton Mifflin, 1891-1908.

FEWKES, J. WALTER AND MINDELEFF, CHARLES   (2168)
Indian tribes of the Southwest; antiquities, arts and habits of modern and extinct races. Western Magazine, 14:230-33, 1919; 15:4-7, 61-64, 1920.

FLOOD, FRANCIS   (2169)
Farming, a way of life. Farmer-Stockman, 50:663, 672, Nov. 15, 1937.
> Indian agriculture in the Southwest.

————   (2170)
First farmers of America. Farmer-Stockman, 50:631, 658, Nov. 1, 1937.
> Present lands of Navajo, Hopi, and Pueblos.

FOLEY, BROTHER RUDOLPH X.   (2171)
The origins of the Indian reorganization act of 1934. Unpub. Doctor's dissertation, Fordham University, 1937.

FORREST, EARLE R.   (2172)
Missions and Pueblos of the old Southwest; their myths, legends, fiestas, and ceremonials. 2v. Cleveland, Clark, 1929.

FOSTER, T. S.   (2173)
Travels and settlements of early man; a study of the origins of human progress. London, Ernest Benn Ltd., 1929.
> Some material on Pueblos.

FRIEDERICI, GEORG   (2174)
Scalping in America. Smithsonian Annual Report, 1906. Washington, 1907. pp. 423-38.

GARTH, T. R.   (2175)
The intelligence of full blood Indians. JAP, 9:382-89, 1925.

GATSCHET, A. S.   (2176)
Zwolf Sprachen aus dem Sudwesten Nordamerikas. Weimar, 1876.
> Includes Navajo, Isletan, and Jemez languages.

GERMANN, FRANK E. E.   (2177)
Ceramic pigments of the Indians of the Southwest. EP, 20:222-26, 1926. Also Science, n. s., 63:480-82, 1926.

GESSNER, ROBERT   (2178)
Massacre: a survey of today's American Indian. New York, Jonathan Cape, 1931.
> Protest against government's treatment of Indians. Chapter 23, Pueblos.

GIFFORD, E. W.   (2179)
Indian basketry. (In Introduction to American Indian Art. Part II. New York, Exposition of Indian Tribal Arts, 1931.)
> Apache and Pueblo basketry included.

————   (2180)
Pottery-making in the Southwest. UCPAAE, 23:353-73, 1928.

GODDARD, PLINY E. (2181)
Assimilation to environment as illustrated by Athapascan peoples. *15th ICA, Proceedings,* Quebec, 1906. v. 1, pp. 337-59.

———— (2182)
Indians of the Southwest. New York, AMNH, 1913.
Chapter 2, Pueblo dwellers.

———— (2183)
Native dwellings of North America. *NH,* 28:191-203, 1928.
Includes San Ildefonso, San Juan, Santa Clara, and Navajo.

———— (2184)
Pottery of the Southwestern Indians. *AMNH, Guide Leaflet series,* 73:1-30, 1928.

———— (2185)
Similarities and diversities within Athapascan linguistic stocks. *ICA, Proceedings,* 23 (2) :489-94, 1926.

GOODRICH, SAMUEL GRISWOLD (2186)
History of the Indians of North and South America. Boston, Bradbury, Soden & Co., 1844.

GRINNELL, GEORGE BIRD (2187)
The Indians of today. New York, Duffield, 1911.

———— (2188)
The story of the Indian. New York, Appleton, 1895.

GROVE, ALVIN R. (2189)
The aboriginal utilization of mescal in the American Southwest. Unpub. Master's thesis, UNM, 1938.

HAECKEL, J. (2190)
Das Mutterrecht bei den Indianer-stammen im sudwestlichen Nordamerika. *Zeitschrift fur Ethnologie* (Berlin) 68:227-49, 1936.
Predominance of women in Southwestern societies.

HAINES, FRANCIS (2191)
Where did the Plains Indians get their horses? *AA,* 40:112-17, 1938.
Evidence that they came from Santa Fe.

HARMON, G. D. (2192)
Sixty years of Indian affairs, political, economic, diplomatic, 1789-1850. Chapel Hill, University of North Carolina Press, 1941.

HARPER, ALLAN G. (2192a)
Las tierras de los indios en los Estados Unidos. Washington, National Indian Institute, USDI, 1943.

HARPER, ALLAN G., COLLIER, JOHN, AND MCCASKILL, JOSEPH C. (2193)
Los indios de los Estados Unidos. Washington, National Indian Institute, USDI, 1942.

HARRINGTON, IRIS L. (2194)
An English foundation for Indians. *New Mexico School Review,* 11:8-9, Dec. 1931.
Discusses necessity for basing English instruction upon things familiar to the Indian.

HARRINGTON, JOHN P. (2195)
Studying the Indians of New Mexico and California. *Smithsonian Explorations and Field Work, 1930.* Baltimore, 1931. pp. 187-94.

HAUGHT, B. F. (2196)
Mental growth of the Southwestern Indian. *JAP,* 18:137-42, 1934.

HAURY, EMIL (2197)
Some Southwestern pottery types. Gila Pueblo, Medallion Papers 19. Globe, Arizona, 1936.

HENDERSON, ALICE CORBIN (2198)
Modern Indian painting. (In *Introduction to American Indian art.* Part II. New York, Exposition of Indian Tribal Arts, 1931.)
> Includes Navajo, Pueblo.

—— (2199)
A plea for the study of Indian culture. *EP,* 15:91-92, 1923.
> Necessity for awakening the public to the values of Indian culture.

HENDERSON, ROSE (2200)
Indian art in the Southwest. *International Studio,* 78:109-12, Nov. 1923.

—— (2201)
Indian painters of the Southwest. *SW,* 59:214-22, 1930.

—— (2202)
Modern Indian craftsmen. *SW,* 61:409-13, 1932.

—— (2203)
Primitive basis for modern architecture. *Architectural Record,* 54: 188-96, Aug. 1923.

HERRICK, JOHN (2204)
La agricultura de los indios en los Estados Unidos. Washington, National Indian Institute, USDI, 1942.

HESSELDEN, ELIZABETH C. (2205)
Indian silver of the Southwest. *Design,* 32:101-03, 118-19, 1930.

HEWETT, EDGAR L. (2206)
The Indian ceremonies. *A&A,* 18:207-14, 1924. *Also EP,* 17:109-24, 1924.
> Religious life of the Pueblos is the key to their whole existence.

HITTELL, THEODORE H. (2207)
The seven cities of Cibola. *The Californian,* Feb. 1880.

HODGE, FREDERICK WEBB (2208)
Handbook of American Indians north of Mexico. 2 parts. Bureau of American Ethnology, Bulletin 30. Washington, GPO, 1907.
> A descriptive list of the tribes, stocks, settlements, including biographies of Indians of note, sketches of their history, archaeology, manners, arts, customs, and institutions.

—— (2209)
How old is Southwestern Indian silverwork? *EP,* 25:224-32, 1928.

HOFFMAN, FREDERICK L. (2210)
Medical problems of our Indian population. EAIA, Bulletin 6. New York, 1925.

HOFFMAN, W. J.   (2211)
Native American blanket-making. *Monthly Illustrator*, 4:114-,
April 1895.

————   (2212)
The practice of medicine and surgery by the aboriginal races
of the Southwest. *Medical and Surgical Reporter*, 40:157-60,
1879.

HOLDER, A. B.   (2213)
The bote: description of a peculiar sexual perversion found
among North American Indians. *New York Medical Journal*, 50:
623-25, 1889.

HOLDER, CHARLES F.   (2214)
Indian granaries. *Scientific American*, 89:263, Oct. 10, 1903.

HOLFORD, C. N.   (2215)
Oriental resemblances in New Mexico. *Kansas City Review*,
4:602-, 1881.

HOOPES, ALBAN W.   (2216)
*Indian affairs and their administration: with special reference to
the far West, 1849-60.* Philadelphia, University of Pennsylvania
Press, 1932. *Also* Doctor's thesis, University of Pennsylvania, 1933.

HOOVER, J. W.   (2217)
House and village types of the Southwest as conditioned by aridity.
Scientific Monthly, 40:237-49, 1935.

HORNBAKER, HORACE WAYNE   (2218)
*A historical study of the use of color in the decorative arts of the
Indians of New Mexico, Arizona, and Colorado.* Unpub. Master's
thesis, USC, 1940.

HOWARD, JOSEPHINE THEO   (2219)
The mechanical aptitudes of Indian boys of the Southwest. Unpub.
Master's thesis, George Washington University, 1940.

HRDLICKA, ALES   (2220)
Diseases of the Indians, more especially of the Southwestern
United States and northern Mexico. *Washington Medical Annals*,
4:372-82, 1905-06.

————   (2221)
On the stature of Indians of the Southwest and of northern Mexico. *Putnam Anniversary Volume.* New York, Stetchert, 1909. pp.
405-26.

————   (2222)
*Physiological and medical observations among the Indians of the
southwestern United States and northern Mexico.* Bureau of
American Ethnology, Bulletin 34. Washington, GPO, 1908.

HUCKEL, J. F., ED.   (2223)
American Indians: first families of the Southwest. Kansas City,
Fred Harvey, 1920.

HURT, WESLEY R., JR.   (2224)
   The drawing ability of children; a comparison of two groups of
   Indian and Spanish-American students. *EP*, 48:42-48, 1941.

HUTTON, A. G.   (2225)
   Indian administration in New Mexico and Arizona. Unpub.
   report in Navajo Service archives. (Navajo Service Library at
   Window Rock unable to locate, June 1942.)

INDIAN AFFAIRS   (2226)
   Periodical publication of the American Association on Indian
   Affairs, 1933-38, containing articles on Indian problems.

INDIAN EDUCATION   (2227)
   Fortnightly letter of the Education Division, Office of Indian
   Affairs, since September 15, 1937.

INDIAN RIGHTS ASSOCIATION   (2228)
   Annual reports, 1883 to date.
         Include information on New Mexico Indians.

────────   (2229)
   Tour of observation among Indians in . . . New Mexico. Indian
   Rights Association, Publication 18. Philadelphia, 1894.

INDIAN TRUTH   (2230)
   Monthly publication of the Indian Rights Association since
   December 15, 1882.
         Includes numerous references to New Mexico Indians.

INDIANS AT WORK   (2231)
   Monthly news sheet of Indian activities, published by Office of
   Indian Affairs since August 15, 1933.

JAEGER, ELLSWORTH   (2232)
   Indians of the Southwest. *Royal Canadian Institute, Proceedings,*
   Ser. 3, v. 2, 1937. pp. 35-42.
         Travel description.

JAMES, GEORGE WHARTON   (2233)
   Aboriginal American homes. *Craftsman,* 8:459-71, 640-49, 781-
   95, 1905.

────────   (2234)
   Indian baskets and how to make Indian and other baskets. Pasadena, the Author, 1903.

────────   (2235)
   Indian blankets and their makers. Chicago, McClurg, 1920.

────────   (2236)
   The Indians of the Painted Desert region. Boston, Little Brown,
   1903.

────────   (2237)
   What the white race may learn from the Indian. Chicago, Forbes
   & Co., 1908.

JEANCON, JEAN ALLARD   (2238)
   Indian music of the Southwest. *EP,* 23:438-47, 1927.

JEANCON, JEAN ALLARD AND DOUGLAS, FREDERIC H.   (2239)
Southwestern Indian dwellings. *DAM, Leaflet series* 9, 1930.

JOHNSTON, W. R.   (2240)
Indians on the public domain in Arizona and New Mexico; their
relation to the community and state. *LMC, Proceedings,* 2nd session, 1913. pp. 64-70.

JONES, VOLNEY H.   (2241)
An ancient food plant of the Southwest and plateau regions. *EP,*
44:41-52, 1938.
> Indian millet.

JUDSON, KATHARINE BERRY   (2242)
Myths and legends of California and the old Southwest. Chicago,
McClurg, 1912.

KAPPLER, CHARLES J.   (2243)
Indian affairs, laws, and treaties. Senate Document 319, 58th Congress, 2nd Session. Washington, GPO, 1904.

KATE, HERMAN TEN   (2244)
Observations sur les Indiens du Nouveau-Mexique et du Colorado. *Bulletin de la Societe d'Anthropologie de Paris,* 6:801-07,
1883.

KENNEDY, BRICE MORRIS   (2245)
The Indian in Southwestern fiction. *Research,* 1:212-25, 1937.

KENNEDY, MRS. ELLA   (2246)
The Indian in Southwestern fiction. Unpub. Master's thesis,
UNM, 1938.

————   (2247)
The Indian school in Indian fiction. *Research,* 3:55-61, 1939.

KINNEY, J. P.   (2248)
*A continent lost—a civilization won: Indian land tenure in
America.* Baltimore, Johns Hopkins Press, 1937.

KIRCHOFF, P.   (2249)
Versuch einer Gliederung der Sudgruppe des Athapaskischen.
ICA, Proceedings, 24:258-63, 1930.
> Athapascan language groupings.

KIRK, RUTH F.   (2250)
Indian traders. *NM,* 16:12-13, 34-36, Dec. 1938.

————   (2251)
When Indians dance. *NM,* 19:11-12, 45-46, July 1941.
> Gallup ceremonial.

KISSELL, MARY LOIS   (2252)
Indian weaving. (In *Introduction to American Indian Art.* Part
II. New York, Exposition of Indian Tribal Arts, 1931.)
> Includes Navajo and Pueblo weaving.

KLUCKHOHN, CLYDE   (2253)
Myths and rituals: a general theory. *Harvard Theological Review,* 35:45-79, 1942.

KROEBER, A. L. (2254)
Cultural and natural areas of native North America. *UCPAAE*,
v. 38, 1939.
  pp. 32-48: Southwest.

—————— (2255)
Heredity, environment, and civilization; factors controlling human
behavior as illustrated by the natives of the southwestern United
States. *Scientific American Supplement*, 86:210-12, 1918.

—————— (2256)
Native culture of the Southwest. *UCPAAE*, 23:375-98, 1928.

KUIPERS, CORNELIUS C. (2257)
Contemporary Indian adjustments. *New Mexico Business Review*,
4:129-36, 1935.

—————— (2258)
The new deal for the Indian. *New Mexico Business Review*,
2:101-06, 1933.
  An economic survey of the New Mexico Indian, including information on
  population, government agencies, missions, agriculture, handicrafts, and
  sources of income.

—————— (2259)
Results of an intelligence test based on Indian culture. Unpub.
Master's thesis, UNM, 1934.

LABARRE, WESTON (2260)
The peyote cult. YUPA 19. New Haven, 1938. Also Doctor's
dissertation, Yale University, 1937.

LA FARGE, OLIVER (2261)
The American Indian's revenge. *Current History*, 40:163-68, May
1934.
  Indian dependency on the government resulting from Wheeler-Howard Bill.

—————— (2262)
As long as the grass shall grow. New York, Alliance, 1940.
  Present situation of the Indians under the Office of Indian Affairs.

—————— (2263)
Plastic prayers, dances of the Southwestern Indians. *Theatre Arts
Monthly*, 14:218-24, 1930.

LA FARGE, OLIVER, ED. (2264)
The changing Indian. Norman, UOP, 1942.
  Problems of Indians and Indian administration discussed by experts in Indian
  affairs.

LA FARGE, OLIVER AND BURGE, MORIS (2265)
Various articles on Indian affairs included in monthly news letter of the American Association on Indian Affairs. Letters 2, 8,
9, 10, 17, 21, 22, 24, 26, 27, 29 deal with Navajo and Pueblo
Indians.

LEE, BURTON J. (2266)
Cancer among the Indians of the Southwest. *Boletin de la Liga
Contra el Cancer, Edicion Social*, (Habana), 1:234-41, 1930.

—————— (2267)
The incidence of cancer among the Indians of the Southwest.
Surgery, Gynecology, and Obstetrics, 50:196-99, 1930.

LEUPP, FRANCIS ELLINGTON   (2268)
    Failure of the educated American Indian. *Appleton's Magazine*,
    v. 7, May 1906.

————   (2269)
    The Indian and his problem. New York, Scribners, 1910.

————   (2270)
    Notes on a summer tour among the Indians of the Southwest.
    Philadelphia, Indian Rights Association, 1907.

LIEN, ARNOLD J.   (2271)
    The acquisition of citizenship by the native American Indians.
    Washington University (St. Louis) Studies, Humanistic series,
    13 (1):121-79, 1925.

LINDQUIST, G. E. E.   (2272)
    *The red man in the United States; an intimate study of the social,
    economic, and religious life of the American Indian*. New York,
    Doran, 1923.

LINTON, RALPH   (2273)
    The significance of certain traits in North American maize
    culture. *AA*, 26:345-49, 1924.

————   (2274)
    Use of tobacco among North American Indians. Field Museum of
    Natural History, Anthropology leaflet 15. Chicago, 1924.

LORIMER, FRANK   (2275)
    Observations on the trend of Indian population in the United
    States. (In La Farge, Oliver, Ed.: *The changing Indian*. Norman,
    UOP, 1942. pp. 11-18.)
        Only incidental mention of New Mexico Indians.

LOWIE, ROBERT H.   (2276)
    American Indian dances. *American Museum Journal*, 15:95-102,
    March 1915.
        Some material on San Ildefonso.

LUMMIS, CHARLES F.   (2277)
    Indian education. *Land of Sunshine*, 12:28-30, 1899; 12:90-94,
    178-80, 244-46, 1900.

————   (2278)
    The Indian problem. *Land of Sunshine*, 11:139-47, 207-13, 263-
    68, 333-35, 1899.
        Government administration.

————   (2279)
    A new Indian policy. *Land of Sunshine*, 15:457-64, 1901.
        Government administration.

————   (2280)
    The Southwestern wonderland. *Land of Sunshine*, 4:204-13, 1896.
        Description of the Indians.

MCCASKILL, JOSEPH C. AND MCNICKLE, D'ARCY   (2281)
    *La politica de los Estados Unidos sobre los gobiernos tribales y
    las empresas comunales de los indios*. Washington, National
    Indian Institute, USDI, 1942.

MACGREGOR, FRANCES COOKE (2282)
Twentieth century Indians. New York, Putnam, 1941.
> Brief account of present cultural, economic, and social status of Indians, including those of New Mexico.

MACGREGOR, GORDON (2283)
Indian education in relation to the social and economic background of the reservation. (In La Farge, Oliver, Ed.: *The changing Indian.* Norman, UOP, 1942. pp. 116-27.)
> Little direct mention of New Mexico Indians although much of the discussion is applicable to their situation.

MCKENZIE, FAYETTE AVERY (2284)
The Indian in relation to the white population of the United States. Columbus, Ohio, The Author, 1908. *Also* Doctor's thesis, University of Pennsylvania.
> Includes information on Indian status, education, schools, citizenship.

MCKINNEY, LILLIE G. (2285)
History of the Albuquerque Indian School . . . Unpub. Master's thesis, UNM, 1934.

MCKITTRICK, MARGARET (2286)
Indian boarding schools. EAIA, Bulletin 17. New York, 1928.

MACLEOD, WILLIAM CHRISTIE (2287)
The American Indian frontier. New York, Knopf, 1938.
> A study of the effect of European civilization on the Indians of America. Includes material on Indian origins, economic life, numbers, political and social organization, health, and inter-cultural relations.

MCNICOL, DONALD M. (2288)
The Amerindians . . . New York, Stokes, 1937.

MASON, GREGORY (2289)
Columbus came late. New York, Century, 1931.

MASON, OTIS TUFTON (2290)
Cradles of the American aborigines. *National Museum, Annual Report, 1886-87.* Washington, GPO, 1889.

——— (2291)
Indian basketry; studies in a textile art without machinery. 2 v. Garden City, Doubleday Page, 1904.

——— (2292)
North American bows, arrows, and quivers. *Smithsonian Annual Report, 1893.* Washington, 1894.

——— (2293)
Women's share in primitive culture. New York, Appleton, 1894.
> Includes information on Navajo women as weavers, Pueblo women as potters.

MATSON, JESSIE AND DOUGLAS, FREDERIC H. (2294)
Indian vegetable dyes. Part I. *DAM, Leaflet series* 63, 1934; Part II, *DAM, Leaflet series* 71, 1936.

MATTHEWS, WASHINGTON (2295)
Ichthyophobia. *JAF,* 11:105-12, 1898.
> Fish taboos of Navajo, Apache, and Zuni.

MAUZY, WAYNE (2296)
Santa Fe's native market. *EP,* 40:65-72, 1936.
> Indian arts and crafts.

MERA, HARRY P. (2297)
Chupadero black on white. Laboratory of Anthropology, Technical series, Bulletin 1. Santa Fe, 1931.

MERIAM, LEWIS (2298)
The problem of Indian administration. Baltimore, Johns Hopkins Press, 1928.

MESERVE, CHARLES F. (2299)
A tour of observation among Indians and Indian schools in Arizona, New Mexico, Oklahoma, and Kansas. Philadelphia, Indian Rights Association, 1894.

MOFFETT, T. C. (2300)
Indians of Arizona and New Mexico. *Native American,* April 29, 1905.

MOON, CARL (2301)
Indians of the Southwest; a collection of one hundred photographs taken among the tribes and villages of Oklahoma, New Mexico, and Arizona. 4 v. Pasadena, C. Moon, 1936.

MOON, KARL E. (2302)
American Indians of the Southwest. *Century,* 74:923-27, Oct. 1907.
　　　Photographs.

MOOREHEAD, WARREN KING (2303)
The American Indian in the United States, period, 1850-1914 . . . the present condition of the American Indian; his political history and other topics: a plea for justice. Andover, Massachusetts, Andover Press, 1914.

MORRISON, RUTH (2304)
Indian legends. Pamphlet, n. p., n. p., n. d. (Copy in Museum library, Santa Fe.)

MOUNTIN, JOSEPH W. AND TOWNSEND, J. G. (2305)
Observations on Indian health problems and facilities. U. S. Public Health Service, Bulletin 223. Washington, GPO, 1936.

NATIONAL ASSOCIATION ON INDIAN AFFAIRS (2306)
Contemporary Southwestern Indian arts and crafts. Bulletin 23. New York, Jan. 1935.

NATIONAL RESOURCES BOARD (2307)
Indian land tenure, economic status, and population trends. (Part 10 of the Supplementary Report of the Land Planning Committee.) Washington, GPO, 1935.

NEUBERGER, RICHARD L. (2308)
The American Indian enlists. *Asia and the Americas,* 42:628-31, Nov. 1942.

NEW MEXICO ASSOCIATION ON INDIAN AFFAIRS (2309)
Basket making among the Indians of the Southwest. Indian Art series 2. Santa Fe, 1936.

———— (2310)
Indian dress. Indian Art series 4. Santa Fe, 1936.

NEW MEXICO ASSOCIATION ON INDIAN AFFAIRS (Continued) (2311)
Indian embroidery. Indian Art series 3. Santa Fe, 1936.

———— (2312)
New Mexico Indians; a pocket handbook. Santa Fe, 1941.

NEW MEXICO HIGHLANDS UNIVERSITY, DEPARTMENT OF ENGLISH (2313)
The relation of the Indian ceremonials to medieval drama. Las
Vegas, 1931.

NEWCOMB, MRS. FRANCES L. (2314)
Description of the symbolism of a sand-painting of the sun. (In
Introduction to American Indian art. Pt. II. New York, Expo-
sition of Indian Tribal Arts, 1931.)

NEWHERNE, R. E. L. (2315)
Peyote. Lawrence, Kansas, Haskell Institute, 1925.

NORRIS, THEODORE (2316)
*The aboriginal utilization of the small cacti in the American
Southwest.* Unpub. Master's thesis, UNM, 1939.

NUSBAUM, AILEEN (2317)
The four last evils. *Over the Turquoise Trail,* 1:29-31, Autumn
1938.
    Folklore.

OGLESBY, CATHARINE (2318)
Modern primitive arts of Mexico, Guatemala, and the Southwest.
New York, McGraw-Hill, 1939.

OLSON, WALTER O. (2319)
Progress in Indian education. Address delivered at School for the
Rio Grande Valley, UNM, April 27-May 1, 1942. To be published
by School of Inter-American Affairs in *Proceedings of the School for
the Rio Grande Valley.*
    Historical resume with some discussion of objectives and methods.

OTIS, RAYMOND (2320)
Indian art of the Southwest. Santa Fe, 1931.

PALMER, EDWARD (2321)
Food products of North American Indians. USDA, *Report of the
Commissioner of Agriculture, 1870.* Washington, GPO, 1871. pp.
404-28.

———— (2322)
Manufacture of pottery by the Indians. *American Naturalist,* 8:
245-46, 1874.

———— (2323)
Notes on Indian manners and customs. *American Naturalist,* 12:
308-13, 1878.

———— (2324)
Plants used by Indians of the United States. *American Naturalist,*
12:593-606, 646-55, 1878.

PARSONS, ELSIE CLEWS (2325)
Relations between ethnology and archaeology in the Southwest.
American Antiquity, 5:214-20, 1940.

PARSONS, ELSIE CLEWS, ED.   (2326)
   American Indian life, by several of its students.   New York, H.
   W. Huebsch Inc., 1922.

PAUL, HATTIE BELLE   (2327)
   The Garces reports on the Southwestern Indians.   Unpub. Master's
   thesis, University of California, 1917.

PETER, W. W.   (2328)
   The land's health—basis for a people's health.   *IW*, v. 4, no. 20,
   June 1937.

PETERS, J. HENRY   (2329)
   Dyeing, spinning and weaving by the Camanches, Navajoes, and
   other Indians of New Mexico.   (In Beach, William W., Ed.: *The
   Indian Miscellany.*   Albany, J. Munsell, 1877.)

PETERSON, WILLIAM M.   (2330)
   Indian education.   *New Mexico Journal of Education*, 8:57-58,
   Jan. 1912.
        Includes data on number of schools and enrollment in New Mexico.

PETRULLO, VINCENZO   (2331)
   Peyotism as an emergent Indian culture.   *IW*, v. 8, no. 8, April
   1940.

POSEY, WILLIAM CAMPBELL   (2332)
   Trachoma among the Indians of the Southwest.   *Journal of American Medical Association*, 88:1618-19, 1927.

PRIEST, LORING B.   (2333)
   *The reformation of the American Indian policy of the United
   States, 1865-87.*   Unpub. Doctor's thesis, Harvard University, 1937.
——————   (2334)
   *Uncle Sam's stepchildren: the reformation of United States Indian
   policy.*   New Brunswick, Rutgers University Press, 1942.

PRUDDEN, THEOPHIL MITCHELL   (2335)
   On the great American plateau.   New York, Putnam, 1906.

RADIN, PAUL   (2336)
   The story of the American Indian.   New York, Liveright, 1934.
        Chapter 10.   From cliffs to Pueblos.

REAGAN, ALBERT B.   (2337)
   Sketches of Indian life and character. *Kansas Academy of Science,
   Transactions*, 21:207-15, 1908.

REED, ERIK K.   (2338)
   Indians don't stay home.   *National Park Service, Region 3
   Quarterly*, 3:8-9, Oct. 1941.

REEVE, FRANK D.   (2339)
   Federal Indian policy in New Mexico, 1858-80.   *NMHR*, 12:218-
   69, 1937; 13:14-62, 146-91, 261-313, 1938.   *Also* Doctor's dissertation, University of Texas, 1937.

RENAUD, ETIENNE B.   (2340)
   Fabrication de la ceramique Indienne du sud-ouest des Etats-Unis.
   Journal de la Societe des Americanistes (Paris), n. s., 17:101-17,
   1925.

RENAUD, ETIENNE B. (Continued)   (2341)
   Notes sur le ceramique Indienne du sud-ouest des Etats-Unis.
   Journal de la Societe des Americanistes (Paris), n. s., 17:85-99,
   1925.

RISTER, CARL COKE   (2342)
   *Border captives; the traffic in prisoners by southern Plains Indians,
   1835-1875.* Norman, UOP, 1940.
      Little direct mention of New Mexico Indians.

ROBERTS, HELEN H.   (2343)
   Indian music from the Southwest. *NH*, 27:257-65, 1927.
      Apache and Navajo songs.

ROBINSON, H. F.   (2344)
   Uncle Sam and the Indian. *EP*, 5:55-57, 1918.
      Review of U. S. Indian policy.

ROGERS, SAM L.   (2345)
   Indian population in the United States and Alaska, 1910. USDC,
   Bureau of the Census. Washington, GPO, 1915.

ROSE, WINIFRED   (2346)
   A study of achievement of Indians. Unpub. Master's thesis, Denver University, 1931.
      Based on Albuquerque Indian School.

ROSS, NANCY WILSON   (2347)
   The Indian way of life. Undated pamphlet published by the
   National Gallery of the American Indian emphasizing the im-
   portance of preserving Indian culture.

RUSH, EMMY MATT   (2348)
   Indian legends. *EP*, 32:137-54, 1932.

RYAN, W. CARSON AND BRANDT, ROSE K.   (2349)
   Indian education today. *Progressive Education*, 9:81-86, Feb.
   1932.

SALOMON, JULIAN HARRIS   (2350)
   The book of Indian crafts and Indian lore. New York, Harper,
   1928.

SCHERMERHORN, JOHN F.   (2351)
   Report respecting the Indians inhabiting the western parts of the
   United States. *Massachusetts Historical Society Collections*, 2nd
   series, 2:1-45, 1814.

SCHMITT, PAUL N.   (2352)
   *A study showing that traditional grade classifications in Indian
   schools of the Southwest is impracticable and misleading.* Unpub.
   Master's thesis, University of Kansas, 1936.

SCHOOLCRAFT, HENRY ROWE   (2353)
   *Archives of aboriginal knowledge. Containing all the original
   papers laid before Congress respecting the history, antiquities,
   language, ethnology, pictography, rites, superstitions, and mythology of the Indian tribes of the United States.* Philadelphia, Lippincott, 1860.

SCHOOLCRAFT, HENRY ROWE (Continued)   (2354)
Historical and statistical information respecting the history, con-dition, and prospects of the Indian tribes of the United States. 6 v. Philadelphia, Lippincott, 1851-60.

                                                                (2355)
The Indian tribes of the United States: their history, antiquities, customs, religion, arts, languages, traditions, oral legends, and myths. Edited by Francis S. Drake. 2 v. Philadelphia, Lippincott, 1884.

SENDERS, ROSELLA   (2356)
Indian history in the making. *IW*, 8:23-26, April 1941.

SERGEANT, ELIZABETH S.   (2357)
A new deal for the Indian. *New Republic,* 95:151-54, 1938.
    Accomplishments of Office of Indian Affairs.

                                                                (2358)
Red man's burden. *New Republic,* 37:199-201, 1924.
    Criticism of Indian Service.

SETON, ERNEST THOMPSON, COMP.   (2359)
The gospel of the red man; an Indian bible. Garden City, Double-day Doran, 1936.
    Indian mythology and religion.

SEYMOUR, FLORA WARREN   (2360)
Indians today. New York, Benjamin Sanborn & Co., 1926.

                                                                (2361)
Our Indian land policy. *Journal of Land and Public Utility Eco-nomics,* 2:93-108, Jan. 1926.

                                                                (2362)
The story of the red man. New York, Longmans Green, 1929.
    General history of Indians, including Pueblos, Apache, Navajos.

                                                                (2363)
Thunder over the Southwest. *Saturday Evening Post,* 211:23, 71-72, 74, 76, April 1, 1939.
    Opposition to policies based on Indian Reorganization Act.

SEYMOUR, FLORA WARREN AND AUSTIN, MARY   (2364)
Our Indian problem: debate. *Forum,* 71:273-88, 1924.

SHAFFER, ELIZABETH   (2365)
Three R's for the redman. *NM*, 20:10-11, Feb. 1942.
    Activities and accomplishments of government schools.

SIDES, DOROTHY SMITH   (2366)
Decorative art of the Southwestern Indians. Santa Ana, California, Fine Arts Press, 1936.

SLOAN, JOHN AND LA FARGE, OLIVER   (2367)
Introduction to American Indian Art. New York, Exposition of Indian Tribal Arts, 1931.
    Discussion of painting, basketry, weaving, beadwork, pottery, jewelry, sculpture.

SMITH, DAMA MARGARET   (2368)
Indian tribes of the Southwest. Stanford University Press, 1933.

SMITH, OWEN DALE (2369)
A comparison of the performances of full-blooded Indians, seden-tary and nomadic, on achievement and on language and non-language intelligence tests. Unpub. Master's thesis, University of Denver, 1932.
> Based on Santa Fe and Albuquerque Indian Schools.

SNYDER, EVERT ALBERT (2370)
Primitive uses of pine among the Indians of the American South-west. Unpub. Master's thesis, UNM, 1940.

SPINDEN, HERBERT J. (2371)
Fine art and the first Americans. (In *Introduction to American Indian art.* Pt. II. New York, Exposition of Indian Tribal Arts, 1931.)
> Includes Pueblo arts.

――――― (2372)
Indian artists of the Southwest. *International Studio,* 95:49-51, Feb. 1930.

――――― (2373)
Indian dances of the Southwest. *American Museum Journal,* 15: 103-15, 1915.

――――― (2374)
Indian symbolism. (In *Introduction to American Indian art.* Pt. II. New York, Exposition of Indian Tribal Arts, 1931.)
> Pueblos included.

STALLINGS, ALICE R. (2375)
Indian dress. *NM,* 14:18-19, 48-49, May 1936.

STEECE, HENRY M. (2376)
Corn culture among the Indians of the Southwest. *NH,* 21:414-24, 1921. *Also Indian School Journal,* 22:9-19, Oct. 1922.

STEVENS, ALDEN (2377)
Whither the American Indian? *Survey Graphic,* 29:168-74, 1940.
> Appraisal of Indian affairs under John Collier.

STEVENSON, HELEN FLORENCE (2378)
Counting systems of North American Indians. Unpub. Master's thesis, UNM, 1940.

STEVENSON, JAMES (2379)
Illustrated catalogue of the collections obtained from the Indians of New Mexico and Arizona in 1879. *Bureau of American Eth-nology, 2nd Annual Report, 1880-81.* Washington, GPO, 1883. pp. 307-465.

STILES, HELEN E. (2380)
Pottery of the American Indians. New York, Dutton, 1939.

STRONG, ESTHER B. (2381)
Wardship in American Indian administration. Unpub. Doctor's dissertation, Yale University, 1941.

STRONG, W. D. (2382)
An analysis of Southwestern society. *AA,* 29:1-61, 1927.
> Comparison of Southwestern peoples from developmental and historic point of view. Few direct references to New Mexico.

SWANTON, JOHN R.   (2383)
The social organization of American tribes. *AA*, 7:663-73, 1905.
Includes Pueblos, Navajo, Apache.

THAYER, JAMES B.   (2384)
A people without law. *Atlantic*, 67:540-51, 676-87, 1891.
Discussion of legal status of Indians, with a plea for citizenship rights. Little mention of New Mexico Indians.

TOWNSEND, J. G.   (2385)
Disease and the Indian. *Scientific Monthly*, 47:479-95, 1938.
Historical review of health activities of Indian Service.

TSCHOHL, L. F.   (2386)
Indian art of the Southwest. Albuquerque, U. S. Indian Vocational School, n. d. Processed.

TURNER, WILLIAM W.   (2387)
The aborigines of New Mexico and the surrounding regions. *American Ethnological Society, Transactions,* v. 3, Pt. 1, 1909. pp. 159-66.

UNDERHILL, RUTH M.   (2388)
Southwest Indians; an outline of social and ceremonial organization in New Mexico and Arizona. Outline of lectures delivered at Santa Fe Indian School in summer of 1934. [Issued by U. S. Office of Education, 1934.] Processed.

UNITED STATES CONGRESS   (2389)
Condition of the Indian tribes. Report of the Joint Special Committee. Senate report 156, 39th Congress, 2nd Session. Washington, GPO, 1867.

————, SENATE COMMITTEE ON INDIAN AFFAIRS   (2390)
Survey of conditions of the Indians in the United States. Hearings. . . . *70th-74th Congress.* 35 parts. Washington, GPO, 1929-39.

USDI, BOARD OF INDIAN COMMISSIONERS   (2391)
Annual Reports to the Secretary of the Interior, 1869 to date.

USDI, COMMISSIONER OF INDIAN AFFAIRS   (2392)
Annual Reports, 1824 to date.

USDI, OFFICE OF INDIAN AFFAIRS   (2393)
Annual Reports, United States Indian School, Santa Fe. (Copies 1920-27 on file at UPA, Albuquerque.)

————, ————   (2394)
General data concerning Indian reservations. Washington, GPO, 1930.

————, ————   (2395)
Indians, yesterday and today. Educational Division. Washington, GPO, 1941.

————, ————   (2396)
Primitive agriculture of the Indians. Bulletin 1. [Washington] 1921. Processed.

VALLIANT, GEORGE   (2397)
Indian arts in North America. New York, Harper, 1939.

VAN STONE, MARY R.   (2398)
　　Songs of the Indians. *EP*, 48:149-54, 1941.

VIAULT, ELSIE ROSINE   (2399)
　　*Maize, its cultivation and preparation as a food by the Indians of
　　the Southwest and the area east of the Mississippi.* Unpub.
　　Master's essay, Columbia University, 1921.

WALKER, FRANCIS A.   (2400)
　　The Indian question. Boston, J. R. Osgood & Co., 1874.

WALTER, PAUL A. F.   (2401)
　　Meat. *New Mexico Conservationist*, 1:4-6, 26, Dec. 1927.
　　　　Relation of Indian quest for food to religious philosophy.

WALTON, EDA LOU AND WATERMAN, T. T.   (2402)
　　American Indian poetry. *AA*, 27:25-52, 1925.

WARNER, H. J.   (2403)
　　Notes on the results of trachoma work by the Indian Service in
　　Arizona and New Mexico. *Public Health Reports*, 44:2913-20,
　　1929.

WATERMAN, T. T.   (2404)
　　North American Indian dwellings. *Smithsonian Annual Report,
　　1924.* Washington, 1925. pp. 461-85.

——————   (2405)
　　Ornamental designs in Southwestern pottery. *Museum of the
　　American Indian, Heye Foundation, Indian Notes*, 7:497-521,
　　1930.

WATKINS, FRANCES E.   (2406)
　　*Crafts and industries of the American Indian women of California
　　and the Southwest.* Doctor's dissertation, USC, 1941-42.

WESTLAKE, INEZ B.   (2407)
　　American Indian designs. Philadelphia, Perleberg, 1925-30.

WHITENER, H. C.   (2407a)
　　The number system of three Southwestern Indian tribes. *The
　　Pentagon*, 2:15-19, Fall 1942.
　　　　Apache, Navajo, Acoma.

WILLOUGHBY, CHARLES C.   (2408)
　　Indian masks. (In *Introduction to American Indian art*. Pt. II.
　　New York, Exposition of Indian Tribal arts, 1931.)
　　　　Includes Pueblos.

WISE, JENNINGS CROPPER   (2409)
　　A plea for the Indian citizen of the United States. Washington,
　　GPO, 1926.

——————   (2410)
　　*The red man in the new world drama. A politico-legal study with
　　a pageantry of American Indian history.* Washington, Roberts,
　　1931.
　　　　Some material on Geronimo and the Apaches.

WISSLER, CLARK   (2411)
　　*The American Indian; an introduction to the anthropology of the
　　new world.* New York, Oxford University Press, 1938.

WISSLER, CLARK (Continued)   (2412)
American Indian saddles, borrowed, together with other features
of horse culture from the Spanish colonization, in the first half of
the sixteenth century. *American Museum Journal,* 16:496-99,
Dec. 1916.

———   (2413)
The Indian and the horse. *American Indian Magazine,* 7:20-26,
Aug. 1920.

———   (2414)
Indian beadwork. *AMNH, Guide leaflet series 50.* New York,
1919.

———   (2415)
Indian costumes in the United States. *AMNH, Guide leaflet
series 63.* New York, 1926.

———   (2416)
*Indians of the United States: four centuries of their history and
culture.* New York, Doubleday Doran, 1940.

———   (2417)
The lore of the demon mask. *NH,* 28:339-52, 1928.
  Includes Navajos, Pueblos.

———   (2418)
Riding gear of North American Indians. *AMNH, Anthropological Papers,* v. 17, Pt. 1. New York, 1916.

WOEHLKE, WALTER V.   (2419)
The battle for grass. *Saturday Evening Post,* 206:10, 11, 79, 80, 81,
84, Nov. 25, 1933.
  Fight against erosion on Southwestern Indian lands.

WOODARD, M. L.   (2420)
When tom- toms beat at Gallup. *NM,* 11:22-23, 49-50, July 1933.
  Ceremonial dances.

Spanish-Colonial and Mexican Periods

ADAMS, ELEANOR B. AND SCHOLES, FRANCE V.   (2421)
Books in New Mexico, 1598-1680. *NMHR,* 17:226-70, 1942.

AITKEN, BARBARA   (2422)
Folk-history and its raw material. *NMHR,* 6:376-82, 1931.

AITON, ARTHUR S. AND REY, AGAPITO   (2423)
Coronado's testimony in the Viceroy Mendoza Residencia.
NMHR, 12:288-329, 1937.

ANONYMOUS   (2424)
Altar pieces from the Llano Quemado. *EP,* 28:95-97, 1930.

———   (2425)
The first community theater and playwright in the United States.
EP, 16:83-87, 1924.
  Performances of plays written by Captain Don Marcos Farfan de los Godos.

ANONYMOUS (Continued)   (2426)
A New Mexican episode in 1748; some unpublished history. *Land of Sunshine*, 8:74-78, 1898.
    Uprising of Pecos Pueblo against Spanish.

────────   (2427)
Spanish colonization in New Mexico. *EP*, 7:60-62, 1919.

ARMIJO, ISIDORO, TR.   (2428)
Information communicated by Juan Candelaria, resident of this villa de San Francisco Xavier de Alburquerque. *NMHR*, 4:274-97, 1929.
    History of the incorporation of the villa de Alburquerque.

ARNOLD, CHARLOTTE   (2429)
The mission of San Diego de Jemez. *EP*, 28:118-22, 1930.

ARTEAGA Y S., ARMANDO   (2430)
Fray Marcos de Niza y el descubrimiento de Nuevo Mexico. *Hispanic American Historical Review*, 12:481-89, 1932.

AUDET, FRANCIS J.   (2431)
Les Canadiens au Nouveau-Mexique. *Societe de Geographie de Quebec, Bulletin*, 17:139-63, 1923.
    Journey to New Mexico by Canadians in 1739.

AYER, MRS. EDWARD E., TR.   (2432)
Memorial of Fray Alonso de Benavides on New Mexico, 1630. *Land of Sunshine*, 13:277-90, 337-40, 345-58, 419-20, 435-44, 1900; 14:39-51, 137-48, 227-32, 1901. *Also* Chicago, Lakeside Press, 1916.

BAILEY, JESSIE BROMILOW   (2433)
Diego de Vargas and the reconquest of New Mexico. Albuquerque, UNM Press, 1940. *Also* (by Jessie Elizabeth Bromilow), Doctor's thesis, USC, 1936.
    Relations between Conquistadores, colonists, and Indians.

BALDWIN, PERCY M.   (2434)
Fray Marcos de Niza and his discovery of the Seven Cities of Cibola. *NMHR*, 1:193-223, 1926. *Also* Historical Society of New Mexico, Publications in History, v. 1, 1926.

BANCROFT, GEORGE   (2435)
History of the United States of America from the discovery of the continent to 1789. New York, Appleton, 1883.
    v. 1 *The Spaniards in the United States.*

BANDELIER, ADOLPH F. A.   (2436)
Alvar Nuñez Cabeza de Vaca. . . *Magazine of Western History*, 4:327-36, 1886.

────────   (2436a)
The discovery of New Mexico. *NMHR*, 4:28-44, 1929.

────────   (2437)
Discovery of New Mexico by Fray Marcos. *Magazine of Western History*, 4:659-, 1886.

────────   (2438)
The gilded man. New York, D. Appleton, 1893.

BANDELIER, ADOLPH F. A. (Continued)   (2439)
    New Mexican Spanish antiquities. *Nation*, 48:265-66, 1889.

─────   (2440)
    Quivira. *Nation*, 49:348-49, 365-66, 1889.

BANDELIER, ADOLPH F. A., ED.   (2441)
    *The journey of Alvar Nuñez Cabeza de Vaca and his companions
    from Florida to the Pacific, 1528-1536; translated from his own
    narrative by Fanny Bandelier, together with the report of Father
    Marcos of Nizza and a letter from the Viceroy Mendoza. . .* New
    York, Allerton Book Co., 1905.

BARBER, RUTH KERNS   (2442)
    Indian labor in the Spanish colonies. *NMHR*, 7:105-42, 233-72,
    311-47, 1932. *Also* Historical Society of New Mexico, Publications
    in History, v. 6. Santa Fe, 1932.

BARREIRO, ANTONIO   (2443)
    Ojeada sobre Nuevo Mejico. Puebla, Mexico, J. M. Campos, 1832.

BARTH, A. W.   (2444)
    New notes on El Morro. *A&A*, 34:146-56, 1933.

─────   (2445)
    The Nieto inscription on El Morro. *Hispanic American Historical
    Review*, 14:352-54, 1934.

BENAVIDES, ALONSO DE   (2446)
    Memorial on New Mexico in 1626. *New York Public Library
    Bulletin*, 3:417-28, 481-99, 1899. J. G. Shea, Tr.

BERRY, J. M.   (2447)
    Indian policy of Spain in the Southwest, 1783-95. *Mississippi
    Valley Historical Review*, 3:462-77, 1917.

BISHOP, MORRIS   (2448)
    The odyssey of Cabeza de Vaca. New York, Appleton, 1933.

BISHOP, WILLIAM HENRY   (2449)
    Old Mexico and her lost provinces. New York, Harper, 1883.

BLACKMAR, FRANK WILSON   (2450)
    Spanish colonization in the Southwest. Baltimore, Johns Hopkins
    Press, 1890.

─────   (2451)
    Spanish institutions of the Southwest. Baltimore, Johns Hopkins
    Press, 1891.
        History, social and political life of the Southwest under Spanish rule.

BLOOM, LANSING B.   (2452)
    Alburquerque and Galisteo, 1706. *NMHR*, 10:48-50, 1935.

─────   (2453)
    Beginnings of representative government in New Mexico. *EP*,
    12:74-78, 1922.

─────   (2454)
    The Chihuahua highway. *NMHR*, 12:209-16, 1937.

BLOOM, LANSING B. (Continued) (2455)
Early bridges in New Mexico. AIA, School of American Research, Papers, n. s., 7. Santa Fe, 1925. *Also EP,* 18:163-82, 1925.

—— (2456)
Early vaccination in New Mexico. Historical Society of New Mexico, Publication 27. Santa Fe, 1924.

—— (2457)
A glimpse of New Mexico in 1620. *NMHR,* 3:357-89, 1928.

—— (2458)
New Mexico under Mexican administration, 1821-46. *Old Santa Fe,* 1:3-49, 131-75, 236-87, 348-85, 1913-14.

—— (2459)
Oñate's exoneration. *NMHR,* 12:175-92, 1937.

—— (2460)
The royal order of 1620. *NMHR,* 5:288-98, 1930.
     Translation of an order from the royal audencia of Mexico to the governor of New Mexico (among others) pertaining to division of authority between church and state.

—— (2461)
A trade invoice of 1638. *NMHR,* 10:242-48, 1935.

—— (2462)
The Vargas encomienda. *NMHR,* 14:366-417, 1939.

—— (2463)
When was Santa Fe founded? *NMHR,* 4:188-94, 1929.

—— (2464)
Who discovered New Mexico? *NMHR,* 15:101-32, 1940.
     Discussion leading to conclusion that Coronado was the true "discoverer" of New Mexico.

BLOOM, LANSING B., ED. (2465)
Barreiro's Ojeada sobre Nuevo Mexico. *NMHR,* 3:73-96, 145-78, 1928. *Also* Historical Society of New Mexico, Publications in History, v. 5. Santa Fe, 1929.

—— (2466)
A campaign against the Moqui Pueblos under Governor Phelix Martinez. . . 1716: annotated by Ralph E. Twitchell and now edited. *NMHR,* 6:158-226, 1931.

—— (2467)
Fray Estevan de Perea's relacion. *NMHR,* 8:211-35, 1933.

BLOOM, LANSING B. AND MITCHELL, LYNN B. (2468)
The chapter elections of 1672. *NMHR,* 13:85-119, 1938.
     Mission at San Diego de los Jemez (Franciscan).

BOLTON, HERBERT EUGENE (2469)
Athanase de Mezieres and the Louisiana-Texas frontier, 1768-80. 2 v. Cleveland, Clark, 1914.
     Only incidental mention of New Mexico.

—— (2470)
The black robes of New Spain. *Catholic Historical Review,* 21:257-82, 1935.

BOLTON, HERBERT EUGENE (Continued)   (2471)
   The Spanish borderlands. New Haven, Yale University Press, 1921.
      Chapters 1-4, The early explorers. Chapter 6, General history of New Mexico.

BOLTON, HERBERT EUGENE, ED.   (2472)
   Spanish exploration in the Southwest, 1542-1706. New York, Scribners, 1916.
      Includes a section on exploration and settlement of New Mexico.

BOLTON, HERBERT EUGENE AND MARSHALL, THOMAS M.   (2473)
   The colonization of North America, 1492-1783. New York, Macmillan, 1936.
      Deals in part with Spanish colonization of New Mexico.

BOYCE, MARJORIE GRAY   (2474)
   Franciscan complaints against the governmental officials of New Mexico, 1760-1790; translation of original documents with introduction and notes. Unpub. Master's thesis, University of California, 1924.

BRACKENRIDGE, HENRY MARIE   (2475)
   Early discoveries by Spaniards in New Mexico, containing an account of the castles in Cibola and the present appearance of their ruins. Pittsburgh, Henry Miner, 1857.

BREBNER, JOHN BARTLET   (2476)
   The explorers of North America, 1492-1806. New York, Macmillan, 1933.

BUDLONG, ROBERT R.   (2477)
   Inscription rock. *National Park Service, Region 3 Quarterly,* 2: 33-36, July 1940.

CAMPA, ARTHUR L.   (2478)
   The churchmen and the Indian languages of New Spain. *Hispanic American Historical Review,* 11:543-50, 1931.

CARNEY, JAMES, JR.   (2479)
   Some aspects of Spanish colonial policy. Unpub. Doctor's dissertation, Duke University, 1938.

CARROLL, H. BAILEY, AND HAGGARD, J. VILLASANA, TRS.   (2480)
   Three New Mexico chronicles. Albuquerque, Quivira Society (UNM Press) , 1942.
      Includes Exposicion of Don Pedro Bautista Pino, 1812; the Ojeada of Lic. Antonio Barreiro, 1832; and the additions by Don Jose Agustin de Escudero, 1849.

CASTAÑEDA, CARLOS E.   (2481)
   Spanish trail blazers in New Mexico and Texas. Paper presented at 8th American Scientific Congress, Washington, May 1940.

CASTAÑEDA, PEDRO DE NAGERA   (2482)
   The narrative of the expedition of Coronado. New York, Scribners, 1907.

CHAVES, AMADO   (2483)
   The defeat of the Comanches in 1716. Historical Society of New Mexico, Publications in History, v. 8. Santa Fe, 1906.

CHEETHAM, F. T. (2484)
El camino militar. *NMHR*, 15:1-11, 1940.
> History of Santa Fe-Taos military road.

COMAN, KATHERINE (2485)
Economic beginnings of the far West. New York, Macmillan, 1925.
> v. 1 pp. 30-66. New Mexico explored by the Spanish
> v. 2 pp. 75-93. The Santa Fe trade.

COUES, ELLIOTT, ED. AND TR. (2486)
On the trail of a Spanish pioneer; the diary and itinerary of Francisco Garces, 1775-76. New York, Harper, 1900.

CUEVAS, MARIANO (2487)
Historia de los descubrimientos antiguos y modernos de la Nueva España, escrita por el conquistador Baltasar de Obregon, año de 1584. Mexico, Departamento Editorial de la Sria. de Educacion Publica, 1924.

DAVIS, WILLIAM WATTS HART (2488)
The Spanish conquest of New Mexico. Doylestown, Pa. 1869.

DAY, A. GROVE (2489)
Coronado's quest. Berkeley, UCP, 1940.

DEFOURI, REV. JAMES H. (2490)
The martyrs of New Mexico; a brief account of the lives and deaths of the earliest missionaries in the territory. Las Vegas, Revista Catolica Printing Office, 1893.

DEHUFF, ELIZABETH WILLIS (2491)
On the borderline of history. *EP*, 46:64-68, 1939.
> Some stories of the conquest of New Mexico.

DELESTRY, EDMOND L. (2492)
The fabled cities of Cibola; relation of the remarkable and fruitless expeditions of Coronado in the years 1528-1539. *Western Magazine*, 13:72-75, 108-11, 158-62, 198-201, 1919; 14:10-14, 51-55, 96-100, 142-46, 186-90, 1919.

DELLENBAUGH, FREDERICK SAMUEL (2493)
Breaking the wilderness; the story of the conquest of the far West from the wanderings of Cabeza de Vaca to the first descent of the Colorado by Powell. New York, Putnam, 1905.

DOWNING, M. B. (2494)
San Jose de Acoma. *Catholic World*, 108:784-94, March 1919.
> Historical sketch of Acoma church.

DUNN, W. E. (2495)
Spanish reaction against the French advance toward New Mexico, 1717-1727. *Mississippi Valley Historical Review*, 2:348-62, 1915.

DUNNE, MARIE (2496)
Thirty families and a priest. *NM*, 15:24-25, 52, Jan. 1937.
> Founding and early history of Albuquerque.

EDSALL, BESSIE   (2496a)
Social and economic life of the last century of the Spanish regime in the northern province known as New Mexico. University of Wisconsin, 1931.

ENGELHART, FATHER ZEPHYRIN   (2497)
El Yllustre señor Xamuscado. *Southwestern Historical Quarterly*, 29:296-300, 1926.

ESPEJO, ANTONIO DE   (2498)
New Mexico . . . otherwise the voiage of Anthony of Espeio . . . Lancaster, Pennsylvania, Lancaster Press, 1928.

ESPINOSA, JOSE MANUEL   (2499)
Crusaders of the Rio Grande; the story of Don Diego de Vargas and the reconquest and refounding of New Mexico. Chicago, Institute of Jesuit History, 1942.

——   (2500)
Diego de Vargas and the re-conquest of New Mexico, 1691-1704. Doctor's dissertation, University of California, 1935.

——   (2501)
Legend of Sierra Azul, with special emphasis upon the part it played in the reconquest of New Mexico. *NMHR*, 9:113-58, 1934.

——   (2502)
Recapture of Santa Fe, New Mexico, by the Spaniards, December 29-30, 1693. *Hispanic American Historical Review*, 19:443-63, 1939.

——   (2503)
The virgin of the reconquest of New Mexico. *Mid-America*, 18 (n. s. 7) :79-87, 1936.

ESPINOSA, JOSE MANUEL, ED. AND TR.   (2503a)
Account of the first Jesuit missionary journey across the plains to Santa Fe. *Mid-America*, 9:51-62, 1938.

ESPINOSA, JOSE MANUEL, TR.   (2504)
First expedition of Vargas into New Mexico, 1692. Albuquerque, UNM Press, 1940.

FOIK, PAUL J.   (2505)
Early explorers of the Southwest. *Mid-America*, 12 (n. s. 1) : 199-211, 1930.

——   (2506)
Fray Juan Padilla; proto-martyr of the United States and Texas. *Mid-America*, 13:132-40, 1930.

——   (2507)
The martyrs of the Southwest. *Illinois Catholic Historical Review*, 11:27-55, 1928.

FOLMER, HENRI   (2508)
Contraband trade between Louisiana and New Mexico in the 18th century. *NMHR*, 16:249-74, 1941.

FORDYCE, KENNETH   (2509)
A hard trail into New Mexico. Unpub. ms. in files of New Mexico
Writers' Project, Santa Fe.
    Coming of the Spanish.

FORTIER, ALCEE AND FICKLEN, JOHN R.   (2510)
Central America and Mexico. Philadelphia, George Barrie's Sons,
1907.
    pp. 463-97, exploration and conquest of New Mexico and Arizona.

FRANCIS, J. D.   (2511)
The first "tour of the Southwest", Coronado, Alarcon, Dias,
Cardenas, Tovar. *California History Nugget,* 4:15-21, 1934.

FREYTAS, FATHER NICHOLAS DE   (2512)
*The expedition of Don Diego Dionisio de Peñalosa, from Santa
Fe to the river Mischipi and Quivera in 1662.* New York, J. G.
Shaw, 1882.

GARDNER, ALBERT F.   (2512a)
French penetration into New Mexico, 1739-1754. Doctor's thesis,
University of California, 1939.

GHENT, W. J.   (2513)
The early far West; a narrative outline, 1540-1850. New York,
Longmans Green, 1932.

GILBERT, HOPE   (2514)
Battle of Black Mesa. *NM,* 18:16-17, 33-34, Dec. 1940.
    Indian resistance to De Vargas.

GREENE, A. R.   (2515)
Old Spanish mines in New Mexico. *Kansas City Review,* 5:179-,
1882-83.

GUSINDE, MARTIN   (2516)
Ein zweites Memorial del Fray Alonso de Benavides aufge-
funden. *Mitteilungen der anthropologischen Gessellschaft in
Wien,* 60 (2, 3):186-90, 1930.

HACKETT, CHARLES WILSON   (2517)
*The causes for the failure of Otermin's attempt to reconquer
New Mexico, 1681-82.* New York, Macmillan, 1917.

————   (2518)
New light on (Don) Diego de Peñalosa: proof that he never
made an expedition from Santa Fe to Quivira and the Mississippi River in 1662. *Mississippi Valley Historical Review,* 6:
313-35, 1919.

————   (2519)
Otermin's attempt to reconquer New Mexico, 1681-82. *Old Santa
Fe,* 3:44-84, 103-32, 1916.

————   (2520)
Retreat of the Spaniards from New Mexico in 1680 and the
beginnings of El Paso. *Southwestern Historical Review,* 16:
137-276, 1912. *Also Southwestern Quarterly,* 16:259-77, 1912.

HACKETT, CHARLES WILSON (Continued)   (2521)
Revolt of the Pueblo Indians of New Mexico in 1680. *Texas State Historical Association Quarterly*, 15:93-147, 1911.

──────   (2522)
The uprising of the Pueblo Indians of New Mexico, 1680-1682. Doctor's thesis, University of California, 1917.

HACKETT, CHARLES WILSON, ED.   (2523)
Historical documents relating to New Mexico, Nueva Viscaya and approaches thereto, to 1773. Washington, Carnegie Institution, Publication 330. v. 1, 1923; v. 2, 1926; v. 3, 1937.

──────   (2524)
New Spain and the Anglo-American West. . . 2 v. Los Angeles, Privately Printed, 1932.
> v. 1 deals with northward advance of the frontiers of New Spain; v. 2, with the Anglo-American westward movement.

HALE, EDWARD E.   (2525)
Coronado's discovery of the Seven Cities. *American Antiquarian Society, Proceedings*, 1:236-41, 1881.

HALLENBECK, CLEVE   (2526)
Spanish missions of the old Southwest. New York, Doubleday, 1926.

HAMMOND, GEORGE P.   (2527)
The conviction of Don Juan de Oñate, New Mexico's first governor. (In Hackett, Charles, W., Ed.: *New Spain and the Anglo-American West.* Los Angeles, Privately Printed, 1932. v. 1, pp. 67-79.)

──────   (2528)
The desertion of Oñate's colony from New Mexico. *North Dakota University Quarterly Journal*, 15:154-67, 1925.

──────   (2529)
Don Juan de Oñate and the founding of New Mexico. *NMHR*, 1:42-77, 99, 156-92, 291, 292-323, 445-47, 1926; 2:37-66, 134-74, 1927. *Also* Historical Society of New Mexico, Publications in History, v. 2. Santa Fe, 1927.

──────   (2530)
Oñate a marauder? *NMHR*, 10:249-70, 1935.

──────   (2531)
Oñate's appointment as governor of New Mexico. *NMHR*, 13:241-54, 1938.

──────   (2532)
The Zuniga journal, Tucson to Santa Fe; the opening of a Spanish trade route, 1788-95. *NMHR*, 6:40-65, 1931. *Also* Historical Society of New Mexico. Santa Fe, 1931.

HAMMOND, GEORGE P. AND DONNELLY, THOMAS C.   (2533)
The story of New Mexico; its history and government. Albuquerque, UNM Press, 1936.

HAMMOND, GEORGE P. AND REY, AGAPITO, TRS. AND EDS. (2534)
Expedition into New Mexico by Antonio de Espejo, 1582-83; as revealed in the journal of Diego Perez de Luxan, a member of the party. Quivira Society, Publications in History, v. 1. Los Angeles, 1929.

——— (2535)
The Gallegos relation of the Rodriguez expedition, 1581-82. *NMHR*, 2:239-68, 334-62, 1927. *Also* Historical Society of New Mexico, Publications in History, v. 4. Santa Fe, 1927.

——— (2536)
Narratives of the Coronado expedition. Albuquerque, UNM Press, 1940.

——— (2537)
New Mexico in 1602; Juan de Montoya's relation of the discovery of New Mexico. Quivira Society Publications, v. 8. Albuquerque, UNM Press, 1938.

——— (2538)
Obregon's history of 16th century explorations in western America entitled Chronicle, commentary or relation of the ancient and modern discoveries in New Spain, New Mexico, and Mexico, 1584. Los Angeles, Wetzel, 1928.

HANKE, LEWIS U. (2539)
Theoretical aspects of the Spanish discovery, exploration and administration of America. Unpub. Doctor's dissertation, Harvard University, 1936.

HAYNES, HENRY W. (2540)
Early explorations in New Mexico. (In Winsor, Justin, Ed.: *Narrative and critical history of America.* Boston, Houghton Mifflin, 1884. v. 2, pp. 473-504.)

HESLEY, ETTIS MIRIAM (2541)
The New Mexico mission in the middle 18th century. Unpub. Master's thesis, University of California, 1922.

HEWETT, EDGAR L. (2542)
Hispanic monuments. *NM*, 16:14-17, 51-54, Aug. 1938. *Also EP*, 45:53-67, 1938, and AIA, School of American Research, Papers, n. s., 28. Santa Fe, 1938.

HILL, JOSEPH J. (2543)
The old Spanish trail; a study of Spanish and Mexican trade and explorations northwest from Mexico to the Great Basin and California. *Hispanic American Historical Review*, 4:444-73, 1921.

HODGE, FREDERICK WEBB (2544)
French intrusion towards New Mexico in 1695. *NMHR*, 4:72-76, 1929.

——— (2544a)
Pueblo names in the Oñate documents. *NMHR*, 10:36-47, 1935.

——— (2545)
The six cities of Cibola, 1581-1680. *NMHR*, 1:478-88, 1926.

HODGE, FREDERICK WEBB, ED.   (2546)
A Virginian in New Mexico, 1773-74. *NMHR*, 4:239-72, 1929.

HODGE, FREDERICK WEBB AND LEWIS, THEODORE H., EDS.   (2547)
Spanish explorers in the Southwestern United States, 1528-1543
. . . New York, Scribners, 1925.
> Original narratives of Cabeza de Vaca, de Soto, and Castañeda's narrative of Coronado's expedition.

HORGAN, PAUL   (2548)
The habit of empire. Santa Fe, Rydal Press, 1938.
> Oñate's expedition.

HUGHES, ANNE E.   (2549)
The beginnings of Spanish settlement in the El Paso district.
University of California, Publications in History, 1:295-392, 1914.

HULL, DOROTHY   (2550)
Castaño de la Sosa's expedition into New Mexico in 1590. Master's thesis, University of California, 1916. *Also Old Santa Fe*, 3: 307-32, 1916.

JAMES, W. W.   (2551)
Quarai, a Spanish mission. *D. A. R. Magazine*, 70:640-42, 1936.

JAMESON, J. FRANKLIN   (2552)
Spanish explorers in the southern United States. New York, Scribners, 1907.

JAMESON, J. FRANKLIN, ED.   (2553)
Spanish exploration in the Southwest. New York, Scribners, 1916.

JOHNSON, WILLIAM HENRY   (2554)
Pioneer Spaniards in North America. Boston, Little Brown, 1903.

JONES, HESTER   (2555)
Uses of wood by the Spanish colonists in New Mexico. *NMHR*, 7:273-91, 1932.

JONES, O. GARFIELD   (2556)
Local government in the Spanish colonies. *Southwestern Historical Quarterly*, 19:65-91, 1915.

JONES, PAUL A.   (2557)
New Mexico and Kansas linked in history. *EP*, 28:88-91, 1930.
> Coronado's expedition.

————   (2558)
Quivira. Wichita, McCormick-Armstrong, 1929.
> Coronado's expedition.

KEARNEY, LELIA   (2558a)
French intrusion into New Mexico after the Pueblo revolt of 1680. Master's thesis, Catholic University, 1939.

KELLY, HENRY W.   (2559)
Franciscan missions of New Mexico, 1740-60. *NMHR*, 15:345-68, 1940; 16:41-69, 148-83, 1941. *Also* Historical Society of New Mexico, Publications in History, v. 10. Albuquerque, 1942.

KELLY, JOHN T.   (2560)
Story of La Gran Quivira. *The Earth*, Feb. 1909.

KEYES, CHARLES R.   (2561)
    Precursor of the Santa Fe trail. *EP*, 5:38-40, 1918.
        Coronado.
KIRKPATRICK, F. A.   (2562)
    The Spanish conquistadores. London, Black, 1934.
KYLE, CLARA ETHEL   (2563)
    The re-conquest of New Mexico, 1680-1698. Unpub. Master's
    thesis, University of California, 1926.
LAUBER, ALMON WHEELER   (2564)
    *Indian slavery in colonial times within the present limits of the
    United States.* New York, Columbia University Press, 1913.
        Includes material on Indian slavery among Spaniards.
LAWRENCE, ELEANOR   (2565)
    Mexican trade between Santa Fe and Los Angeles, 1830-48.
    California Historical Society Quarterly, 10:27-39, 1931.
————   (2565a)
    *Trade in Spanish horses on the Anglo-Spanish border in North
    America.* Doctor's thesis, University of California, 1931.
LEON, CAPITAN ALONSO DE Y SANCHEZ DE ZAMORA, GENERAL FERNANDO
                                                           (2566)
    *Historia de Nuevo Leon, con noticias sobre Coahuila, Tejas,
    y Nueva Mexico.* Mexico, Ch. Bouret; Madrid, Victoriano Suarez,
    1909.
LOPEZ DE GAUNA, MARTIN   (2567)
    Instructions for Don Pedro de Peralta, Governor and Captain
    General of New Mexico, in the place of Don Juan de Oñate.
    EP, 24:466-73, 1928.
LOWERY, WOODBURY   (2568)
    *The Spanish settlements within the present limits of the United
    States, 1513-1561.* New York, Putnam, 1901.
LUMMIS, CHARLES F.   (2569)
    The autograph cliff, El Morro. *Land of Sunshine*, 5:101-05,
    1896.
————   (2570)
    The cities that were forgotten. *Scribner's*, 13:466-77, 1893.
        Myths and legends about Quivira.
————   (2571)
    The ghost of the Quivira. *Land of Sunshine*, 5:222-26, 1896.
————   (2572)
    A New Mexican sheep king. *Land of Sunshine*, 11:197-98, 1899.
        Juan de Oñate.
————   (2573)
    The Spanish pioneers and the California missions. Chicago, Mc-
    Clurg, 1936.
        Chapters 3, 4, and 7 deal with New Mexico.
MAAS, OTTO   (2574)
    Documentos sobre las misiones de Nuevo Mejico. *Archivo Ibero-
    Americano*, (Madrid), 20:145-76, 195-209, 1923; 21:96-113, 369-
    84, 1924; 32:76-108, 226-50, 368-85, 1929; 33:81-111, 1930.

MAAS, OTTO (Continued)   (2575)
Die ersten Versuche einer Missionierung und Kolonisierung
Neumexikos. *Ibero-amerikanisches Archiv, Ibero-amerikanisches
Institut*, 6:345-78, 1933.

MAAS, OTTO, ED.   (2576)
*Misiones de Nuevo Mejico; documentos del Archivo general de
Indias (Sevilla) publicados por primera vez y anotados.* I. Madrid,
Imprenta Hijos de T. Minuesa de los Rios, 1929.

————   (2577)
*Viajes de misioneros franciscanos a la conquista del Nuevo
Mexico* . . . Sevilla, Imprenta de San Antonio, 1915.

MCMURTRIE, DOUGLAS C.   (2578)
The beginning of printing in New Mexico. *American Printer*,
89 (5) :45-46, 1929.

————   (2579)
The history of early printing in New Mexico. *NMHR*, 4:372-
409, 1929.

————   (2580)
El payo de Nuevo Mejico. *NMHR*, 8:130-38, 1933.

MARTINEZ, L. PASCUAL   (2580a)
Rev. Antonio Jose Martinez. *Lulac News*, 5:3-6, Sept. 1938.

MAYER, BRANTZ   (2581)
*Mexico; Aztec, Spanish, and Republican: . . . with a view of
the ancient Aztec empire and civilization . . . and notices of New
Mexico and California.* Hartford, S. Drake & Co., 1851.

MAYFIELD, THOMAS, JR.   (2582)
Education in New Mexico during the Spanish and Mexican
periods. *Research*, 2:99-106, 1938.

MECHAM, JOHN LLOYD   (2583)
Antonio de Espejo and his journey to New Mexico. *Southwestern
Historical Quarterly*, 30:114-38, 1926.

————   (2584)
The martyrdom of Father Juan de Santa Maria. *Catholic Historical Review*, 6:308-21, 1920.

————   (2585)
The Rodriguez expedition into New Mexico, 1581-82. Master's
thesis, University of California, 1917.

————   (2586)
The second Spanish expedition to New Mexico. *NMHR*, 1:265-
91, 371, 478, 1926.

————   (2587)
Supplementary documents relating to the Chamuscado-Rodri-
guez expedition. *Southwestern Historical Quarterly*, 29:224-31,
1926.

MEYER, REV. THEODOSIUS   (2588)
St. Francis and the Franciscans in New Mexico. Santa Fe, Historical Society of New Mexico, 1926.

MILLER, MAMIE RUTH TANQUIST (2589)
Pueblo Indian culture as seen by the early Spanish explorers.
USC, School of Research, Studies 18, Social Science series 21.
Los Angeles, 1941.

MONTOYA, JUAN DE (2590)
Relacion del descubrimiento del Nuovo Mexico . . . Roma,
Bartholame Bonfadino, 1602. (Americana series, Photostat repro-
ductions by the Massachusetts Historical Society, no. 249. Boston
1930.)

MORFI, FRAY JUAN AGUSTIN (2591)
Viaje de indios y diario del Nuevo Mexico. Mexico, Antigua
libreria Robredo de J. Porrua e Hijos, 1935.

MORGAN, LEWIS H. (2592)
Seven cities of Cibola. *North American Review,* 108:457, 1869.

MORROW, W. W. (2593)
Spanish and Mexican private land grants. San Francisco, Bancroft, Whitney Co., 1923.

MUNTSCH, ALBERT (2594)
The Pueblo culture and the Franciscans. *Fortnightly Review,*
(St. Louis), 37:101-02, 1930.

NASATIR, A. P. (2595)
Jacques Clamorgan: colonial promoter of the northern border
of New Spain. *NMHR,* 17:101-12, 1942.

NELSON, AL. B. (2596)
Juan de Ugalde and the Rio Grande frontier, 1777-90. Unpub.
Doctor's thesis, University of California, 1937.

NESBITT, PAUL H. (2597)
When Spaniards settled—1598. *Chronicles of Oklahoma, Oklahoma Historical Society,* 9:287-99, 1931.

OCARANZA, FERNANDO (2598)
*Establecimientos Franciscanos en el misterioso reino de Nuevo
Mexico.* Mexico, 1934.

O'GORMAN, JOHN J. (2599)
The Franciscans in New Mexico in the sixteenth century. *Ecclesiastical Review,* 81:244-70, 1929.

O'NEILL, KATE NEVIN (2600)
The Oñate expedition into New Mexico. Unpub. Master's thesis,
University of California, 1923.

O'ROURKE, THOMAS P. (2601)
A study of the "Memorial of Fray Alonso de Benavides." *American Catholic Historical Society of Philadelphia, Record,* 39:239-
59, 1928.

PALM, RUFUS A., JR. (2602)
New Mexico schools from 1581-1846. Unpub. Master's thesis,
UNM, 1930.

PARRISH, RANDALL (2603)
*The great plains; the romance of western American exploration,
warfare, and settlement, 1527-1870.* Chicago, McClurg, 1907.

PATTERSON, J. C. (2603a)
The extension of the Santa Fe trade with Mexico. American
University, 1939.

PEET, STEPHEN D. (2604)
Spanish and American explorations. *American Antiquarian,* 20:
143-68, 1898.

PEREA, FRAY ESTEVAN DE (2605)
Truthful report of Fray Estevan de Perea on New Mexico, 1632-33.
Land of Sunshine, 15:357-62, 465-69, 1901.

PIÑO, PEDRO BAUTISTA (2606)
*Exposicion sucinta y sencilla de la provincia del Nuevo Mexico;
hecha por su disputado en cortes.* . . . Cadiz, Impr. del Estado-
Mayor-General, 1812.

——— (2607)
*Noticias historicas y estadisticas de la antigua provincia del Nuevo
Mexico* . . . Mexico, Imprenta de Lara, 1849.

PRIESTLEY, HERBERT INGRAM (2608)
Jose de Galvez, visitory general of New Spain, 1765-71. Doctor's
dissertation, University of California, 1917. *Also* University of
California Publications in History, v. 5. Berkeley, 1916.

PRINCE, L. BRADFORD (2609)
Early Pueblo Indian missions in New Mexico. *ICA, Proceedings,*
19:506-14, 1915.

——— (2610)
*Historical sketches of New Mexico from the earliest records to the
American occupation.* Kansas City, Ramsey, Millett, & Hudson,
1883.

——— (2611)
Spanish mission churches of New Mexico. *Journal of American
History,* 9:513-61, 1915.

RAINES, LESTER (2612)
Slavery. Unpub. ms. in files of New Mexico Writers' Project,
Santa Fe.
    Indian slavery in the Southwest.

RAMONA, M. (2613)
The ecclesiastical status of New Mexico, 1680-1875. *Catholic Historical Review,* n. s., 8:525-68, 1929.

READ, BENJAMIN MAURICE (2614)
*Chronological digest of the "Documentos ineditos del archivo de
las Indias."* Albuquerque, Albright and Anderson, 1914.

——— (2615)
In Santa Fe during the Mexican regime. *NMHR,* 2:90-97, 1927.

REED, ERIK K. (2616)
History of Quarai. Santa Fe, National Park Service, 1940.

REED, ERIK K. (Continued) (2617)
Southwestern Indians in Coronado's time. *National Park Service, Region 3 Quarterly,* 2:22-27, July 1940.

RICHMOND, IRVING BERDINE (2618)
The Spanish conquerors, a chronicle of the dawn of empire overseas. New Haven, Yale University Press, 1920.

RIORDAN, M. J. (2619)
Footprints of the Spanish padres in New Mexico and Arizona. Los Angeles, The Tidings Co., 1900.

ROBERTS, EDWARDS (2620)
With the invader: glimpses of the Southwest. San Francisco, S. Carson & Co., 1885.

ROLLINS, WARREN E. (2621)
Where history began in the great Southwest. *EP,* 6:117-19, 1919.

ROMERO, CECIL V., ED. (2621a)
Apologia of Presbyter Antonio J. Martinez. *NMHR,* 3:325-46, 1928.

SALPOINTE, JEAN BAPTISTE (2622)
Soldiers of the cross. Notes on the ecclesiastical history of New Mexico, Arizona, and Colorado. Banning, California, St. Boniface's Industrial School, 1898.

SARIÑANA Y CUENCA, YSIDRO (2623)
The Franciscan martyrs of 1680. Historical Society of New Mexico, Publications 7. Santa Fe, 1906.

SAUER, CARL O. (2624)
The credibility of the Fray Marcos account. *NMHR,* 16:233-43, 1941.

—— (2625)
The discovery of New Mexico reconsidered. *NMHR,* 12:270-87, 1937.

SCHOLES, FRANCE V. (2626)
Church and state in New Mexico, 1610-1650. *NHMR,* 11:9-76, 145-78, 283-94, 297-349, 1936; 12:78-106, 1937. *Also* Historical Society of New Mexico, Publications in History, v. 7. Santa Fe, 1937.

—— (2627)
Civil government and society in New Mexico in the 17th century. *NMHR,* 10:71-111, 1935.

—— (2628)
Documents for the history of the New Mexican missions in the 17th century. *NMHR,* 4:45-58, 195-201, 1929.

—— (2629)
The first decade of the Inquisition in New Mexico. *NMHR,* 10:195-241, 1935.

—— (2630)
History of the Inquisition in the Southwest. Doctor's thesis, Harvard University, 1942.

SCHOLES, FRANCE V. (Continued)   (2631)
     Notes on the Jemez missions in the 17th century. *EP*, 44:61-71, 93-
     102, 1938.

——   (2632)
     Problems in the early ecclesiastical history of New Mexico. *NMHR*,
     7:32-74, 1932.

——   (2633)
     The supply service of the New Mexico missions in the 17th cen-
     tury. *NMHR*, 5:93-155, 186-209, 386-404, 1930.

——   (2634)
     Troublous times in New Mexico, 1659-70. *NMHR*, 12:134-74,
     380-452, 1937; 13:63-84, 1938; 15:249-68, 369-417, 1940; 16:15-40,
     184-205, 313-27, 1941. *Also* Historical Society of New Mexico,
     Publications in History, v. 11. Santa Fe, 1942.

SHALLENBERGER, MRS. IVAH   (2635)
     La historia de la Nueva Mexico, by Gaspar de Villagra; a synthesis.
     Unpub. Master's thesis, UNM, 1936.

SHEA, JOHN GILMARY   (2636)
     *History of the Catholic Church in the United States in colonial
     days, 1521-1763.* New York, Edward O. Jenkins' Sons, 1886.

——   (2637)
     *History of the Catholic missions among the Indian tribes of the
     United States, 1529-1854.* New York, Edward Dunigan and Brother,
     1855.

SIGUENZA Y GONGORA, DON CARLOS DE   (2638)
     *The Mercurio Volante; an account of the first expedition of Don
     Diego de Vargas into New Mexico in 1692.* Quivira Society, Pub-
     lications in History, v. 3.   Los Angeles, 1932.

SIMPSON, JAMES HERVEY   (2639)
     Coronado's march in search of the "seven cities of Cibola" and dis-
     cussion of their probable location. *Smithsonian Annual Report,
     1869.* Washington, 1871.

SPELL, LOTA M.   (2639a)
     Music in the Southwest. *The Musicale* (Dallas), April, May, 1929.

——   (2640)
     Music teaching in New Mexico in the 17th century. *NMHR*,
     2:27-36, 1927.

SULLIVAN, ELLA C. AND LAGLE, ALFRED ERNEST   (2641)
     The story of the old Spanish missions of the Southwest. Chicago,
     Lyons & Carnahan, 1927.

TERNAUX-COMPANS, H.   (2642)
     *Voyages, relations et memoires originaux pour servir a l'histoire de
     la decouverte de l'Amerique. Commentaires D'Alvar Nuñez
     Cabeca de Vaca.* Paris, Arthus Bertrand, Libraire-editeur, 1837.

TERNAUX-COMPANS, H. (Continued) (2643)
Voyages, relations et memoires originaux pour servir a l'histoire de la decouverte de l'Amerique. Relation et naufrages L'Alvar Nuñez Cabeca de Vaca. Paris, Arthus Bertrand, Libraire-editeur, 1837.

———————— (2644)
Voyages, relations et memoires originaux pour servir a l'histoire de la decouverte de l'Amerique. Relation du voyage de Cibola, entrepris en 1540. Paris, Arthus Bertrand, Libraire-editeur, 1838.

THOMAS, ALFRED B. (2645)
Antonio de Bonilla and Spanish plans for the defense of New Mexico. (In Hackett, C. W., ed.: *New Spain and the Anglo-American West.* Los Angeles, Privately printed, 1932. v. 1, pp. 183-209.)

———————— (2646)
The first Santa Fe expedition, 1792-93. *Chronicles of Oklahoma, Oklahoma Historical Society,* 9:195-208, 1931.

———————— (2647)
Governor Mendinueta's proposals for the defense of New Mexico, 1772-78. *NMHR,* 6:21-39, 1931.

THOMAS, ALFRED B., ED. (2647a)
An anonymous description of New Mexico, 1818. *Southwestern Historical Quarterly,* 33:50-74, 1929-30.

THOMAS, ALFRED B., ED. AND TR. (2648)
After Coronado; Spanish exploration of New Mexico, 1696-1727. Documents from the archives of Spain, Mexico, and New Mexico. Norman, UOP, 1935.

———————— (2649)
Forgotten frontiers; a study of the Spanish Indian policy of Don Juan Bautista de Anza, governor of New Mexico, 1777-87. Norman, UOP, 1932.

———————— (2650)
Teodoro de Croix and the northern provinces of New Spain, 1776-83. Norman, UOP, 1941.

TOULOUSE, JOSEPH H., JR. (2651)
The mission of San Gregorio de Abo. *EP,* 45:103-07, 1938.

———————— (2652)
San Gregorio de Abo mission. *EP,* 47:49-58, 1940.

TRUE, C. A. (2652a)
Influence of Spain on the cattle industry in the colonial period. Texas Christian University, 1931.

TRUE, CLARA D. (2653)
The valley of Oñate. *NM,* 16:12-13, 54, 56, Aug. 1938.
Discovery and settlement of Española valley.

TWITCHELL, RALPH EMERSON (2654)
Captain Don Gaspar de Villagra, author of the first history of the conquest of New Mexico. Historical Society of New Mexico. Publication 28. Santa Fe, 1924. *Also EP,* 17:208-20, 1924.

TWITCHELL, RALPH EMERSON (Continued)   (2655)
Colonel Juan Baptista de Anza. Historical Society of New Mexico, Publication 21. Santa Fe, 1918.

――――   (2656)
The Pueblo revolt of 1696; extracts from a journal of De Vargas. *Old Santa Fe,* 3:333-73, 1916.

――――   (2657)
The royal palace at Santa Fe two hundred years ago. *A&A,* 7:33-34, 1918.

――――   (2658)
Spanish colonization and the founding of ciudades and villas in the time of Juan de Oñate. *New Mexico Bar Association Minutes, 32nd Annual Session.* Albuquerque, Aug. 1918. pp. 27-43.

――――   (2659)
Spanish colonization in New Mexico in the Oñate and de Vargas periods. Historical Society of New Mexico, Publication 22. Santa Fe, 1919.

TYLER, DANIEL   (2660)
A concise history of the Mormon Battalion in the Mexican war, 1846-47. Salt Lake City, 1881.

VALLETTE, MARC F.   (2660a)
Work of the Spanish friars on the American continent in the 16th century. *American Catholic Quarterly Review,* 43:133-50, 1918.

VAN VALKENBURGH, RICHARD F.   (2661)
Astaelakwa, house of the vanished. *Desert Magazine,* 5:18-21, April 1942.
> Story of the Spanish conquest of an ancient Pueblo.

VARGAS, DIEGO DE   (2662)
Pueblo revolt of June 4, 1696. AIA, School of American Archaeology, Papers 36. Santa Fe, 1917.

VAUGHAN, JOHN HENRY   (2663)
A preliminary report on the archives of New Mexico. *American Historical Association, Annual Report, 1909.* Washington, 1911.

VELEZ DE ESCALANTE, FRAY SILVESTRE   (2664)
Letter of the Father Fray Silvestre Velez de Escalante, written April 2, 1778. *Land of Sunshine,* 12:247$\frac{1}{2}$50, 305-14, 1900.

VILLA-SEÑOR Y SANCHEZ, JOSEPH ANTONIO DE   (2665)
Teatro Americano, descripcion general de los reynos y provincias de la Nueva España. 2 v. Mexico, Imprenta de la viuda de D. J. Bernardo de Hogal, 1746-48.

VOGEL, CLAUDE L., ED.   (2666)
Franciscan history of North America. The Franciscan Educational Conference, v. 18, no. 18. Washington, 1936.

VOLLMAR, EDWARD   (2666a)
The Jesuits in the Colorado-New Mexico frontier. Doctor's thesis, St. Louis University, 1939.

WAGNER, HENRY R. (2667)
Fray Marcos de Niza. *NMHR*, 9:184-227, 1934.

WALTER, PAUL A. F. (2668)
Inscription rock or El Morro. *EP*, 5:213-17, 1918.

―――― (2669)
New Mexico mission churches. *EP*, 5:116-23, 1918.

―――― (2670)
Peña Blanca and the early inhabitants of the Santa Fe valley. *EP*, 3:17-41, 1915.

WEBB, WALTER PRESCOTT (2671)
The great plains. Boston, Ginn & Co., 1931.
Includes some material on the early explorers.

WEEKS, STEPHEN BEAUREGARD (2672)
The Spaniards in the South and Southwest ... *Southern Historical Association, Publications*, 6:241-52, 1902.

WENTWORTH, EDWARD N. (2673)
The advent of sheep in New Mexico *New Mexico Stockman*, 4:2, Oct. 1939.

WESTSTEYEN, LELA MARGARET (2674)
The expansion of the land grant system under the last two Mexican governors. Unpub. Master's thesis, USC, 1937.

WILLIS, W. G. (2675)
The lost mines of Father La Cruz. Las Cruces, Bronson Ptg. Co., 1939.
Mesilla Valley history and legend.

WINSHIP, GEORGE PARKER (2676)
The Coronado expedition, 1540-42. *Bureau of American Ethnology, 14th Annual Report, 1892-93.* Washington, GPO, 1896. Pt. 1, pp. 329-613.

―――― (2677)
The story of Coronado. *Land of Sunshine*, 9:53-65, July 1898.

―――― (2678)
Why Coronado went to New Mexico in 1540. *American Historical Association, Annual Report, 1894.* Washington, 1895. pp. 83-92.

WINSHIP, GEORGE PARKER, ED. (2679)
The journey of Coronado, 1540-42, from the city of Mexico to the buffalo plains of Texas, Kansas, and Nebraska, as told by himself and his followers. New York, Allerton Book Co., 1924.

―――― (2680)
The journey of Francisco Vasquez de Coronado, 1540-42, as told by Pedro de Castañeda, Francisco Vasquez de Coronado, and others. San Francisco, Grabhorn Press, 1933.

WORCESTER, DONALD E. (2681)
The beginnings of the Apache menace of the Southwest. *NMHR*, 16:1-14, 1941.

―――― (2682)
Early Spanish accounts of the Apache Indians. *AA*, 43:308-12, 1941.

WRIGHT, ALICE   (2683)
  Jornada del muerto. *NM*, 15:18, 40, Sept. 1937.

WRIGHT, R. R.   (2684)
  Negro companions of the Spanish explorers. *AA*, 4:217-28, 1902.

WUTHENAU, A. VON   (2685)
  The Spanish military chapels in Santa Fe and the reredos of Our
  Lady of Light. *NMHR*, 10:175-94, 1935. *Also* Historical Society
  of New Mexico, 1935.

WYLLYS, RUFUS KAY   (2686)
  The Spanish missions of the Southwest. *Arizona Historical Review*, 6 (1) :27-37, 1935.

WYNKOOP, FRANK M.   (2687)
  Journey of conquest. *NM*, 18:17-19, 59-60, 62, June 1940.
    Coronado.

ZARATE SALMERON, FRAY GERONIMO DE   (2688)
  Relacion of events in California and New Mexico from 1528-1626.
  Tr. by C. F. Lummis. *Land of Sunshine*, 11:336-46, 1899; 12:39-
  48, 104-13, 180-87, 1900.

American Frontier Period

ABBOTT, JOHN S. C.   (2689)
  Kit Carson, the pioneer of the West. New York, Dodd Mead, 1875.

ABEL, ANNIE HELOISE, ED.   (2690)
  The journal of John Greiner. *Old Santa Fe*, 3:189-243, 1916.

ABERT, LIEUTENANT J. W.   (2691)
  *Report of Lieutenant J. W. Abert of his examination of New
  Mexico in the years 1846-47*. Senate Exec. Doc. 23, 30th Congress,
  1st Session. Washington, GPO, 1848.

AIMARD, GUSTAVE   (2692)
  The trail hunter; a tale of the far West. London, Ward & Lock,
  1861.

ALLEN, KENNETH   (2693)
  March of the Mormons. *NM*, 19:20-21, 38-39, Nov. 1941.

ALLEN, R. S.   (2694)
  A summary of the history of Pinos Altos. Silver City, Enterprise
  Press, 1889.

ALPERS, GERTRUDE   (2695)
  New Mexico interlude. *NM*, 20:18, 31-32, Oct. 1942.
    Life of Mrs. Henry Tinson of London on the Maxwell Grant about 1871.

ANDERSON, ALEXANDER DWIGHT   (2696)
  *The silver country, or the great Southwest; a review of the mineral
  and other wealth. . . of the former kingdom of New Spain*. New
  York, Putnam, 1877.

ANDERSON, GEORGE BAKER   (2697)
  A New Mexico baron. *Out West*, 26:15-22, 1907.
    Maxwell land grant.

ANDERSON, GEORGE BAKER (Continued)   (2698)
A new Mexico baron, Charles Beaublen. *Santa Fe Magazine*, 4:65-68, Aug. 1910.

ANDERSON, HATTIE M.   (2699)
Mining and Indian fighting in Arizona and New Mexico, 1858-61. *Panhandle-Plains Historical Review*, 1:67-115, 1928.
  Memoirs of Hank Smith.

——   (2700)
With the Confederates in New Mexico. *Panhandle-Plains Historical Review*, 2:65-97, 1929.
  Continuation of memoirs of Hank Smith.

ANDERSON, J. B.   (2701)
A history of the Mogollon mining district, New Mexico. Unpub. Master's thesis, UNM, 1939.

ANDERSON, LATHAM   (2702)
Canby's campaign in New Mexico, 1861. *Magazine of History*, 3:141-48, 1906.

ANDERSON, ROBERT   (2703)
An artillery officer in the Mexican war, 1846-47. New York, Putnam, 1911.

ANDREWS, MYRTLE   (2704)
Flurries of fortune. *NM*, 15:16-17, 40-41, Dec. 1937.
  Cerrillos since territorial days.

ANONYMOUS   (2705)
American expedition into New Mexico, 1841. *Hogg's Instructor*, 5:229, 243, 1850.

——   (2706)
The conquest of Santa Fe. *EP*, 13:152-54, 1922.

——   (2707)
Destruction of Spanish and Mexican archives in New Mexico by United States officials. Santa Fe, 1870.
  Copy in Bancroft Library, University of California.

——   (2708)
Early commerce with Santa Fe. *Santa Fe Magazine*, 4:29-32, May 1910.

——   (2709)
Folklore and folkways. Unpub. ms. in files of New Mexico Writer's Project, Santa Fe.
  Cowboys.

——   (2710)
Kendall's Santa Fe expedition. *Living Age*, 1:346-49, 1844.

——   (2711)
Overland from Cincinnati to Santa Fe in 1865. *American Catholic Historical Society of Philadelphia, Record*, 44:375-78, 1933.

——   (2712)
The Santa Fe trail. *Land of Sunshine*, 8:185-86, 1898.

——   (2713)
Travels in New Mexico. *Western Monthly Review*, 2:597, 649, 1829.

ANONYMOUS (Continued)   (2714)
   Vilojen and his Boers in New Mexico. *Collier's*, 45:13-14, April 9,
   1910.

ANTONY, BROTHER CLAUDIUS   (2715)
   Kit Carson, Catholic. *NMHR*, 10:323-36, 1935.

ARNY, W. F. M.   (2715a)
   *Memorial to his excellency Andrew Johnson, Honorable E. M.
   Stanton, and Lieutenant General U. S. Grant by the citizens of the
   Territory of New Mexico. . . Santa Fe, 1866.*
       Protest against Indian depredations signed by more than 2,000 New Mexicans,
       presented to Congress by J. Francisco Chaves.

————   (2715b)
   *Report on the Apache and Navaho Indians of Abiquiu Indian
   Agency, to President Grant.* Rio Arriba County (Tierra Ama-
   rilla?) , Sept. 23, 1869.

ATHERTON, LEWIS E.   (2715c)
   Disorganizing effects of the Mexican war on the Santa Fe trade.
   Kansas Historical Quarterly, 6:115-23, 1937.

AUBRY, F. X.   (2716)
   Aubry's journey from California to New Mexico. *The Western
   Journal and Civilian*, 11 (n. s. 5) :84-96, 1853.

BAIRD, G. W.   (2717)
   General Miles' Indian campaigns. *Century*, 42:351-70, July 1891.

BANCROFT, HUBERT HOWE   (2718)
   Popular tribunals. San Francisco, History Co., 1887.
       Chapter 36. Popular tribunals of Arizona, New Mexico, and Mexico.

BANDELIER, ADOLPH F. A.   (2719)
   New Mexico; why it does not flourish. *Nation*, 42:70, 1886.
       System of land tenure blamed.

BARNES, F. E.   (2720)
   Santa Fe trail of yesterday and today. *Mentor*, 16:18-22, 52, Sept.
   1928.

BARTLETT, JOHN RUSSELL   (2721)
   *Personal narrative of explorations and incidents in Texas, New
   Mexico, California, and Chihuahua, connected with the United
   States and Mexican Boundary Commission, during the years 1850-
   51, 1852, and 1853* . . . 2 v. New York, Appleton, 1856.

BARTLETT, KATHARINE   (2722)
   The Navajo wars, 1823-70. *Museum of Northern Arizona, Museum Notes*, 8:33-37, Jan. 1936.

BAYNE, EVELYN   (2723)
   The silver era. *NM*, 16:14-15, 43-44, June 1938.
       Life in and around Silver City in late 1800's.

BEADLE, JOHN HANSON   (2724)
   The undeveloped West or five years in the territories . . . 2 v.
   Philadelphia, National Pub. Co., 1873.

————   (2725)
   Western wilds and the men who redeem them. Cincinnati, Jones
   Brothers & Co., 1878.

BEALE, EDWARD F.   (2726)
    Report of superintendent of wagon road from Fort Defiance to the Colorado River. House Exec. Doc. 124, 35th Congress, 1st Session. Washington, GPO, 1858.
        Exploration up Rio Grande to Albuquerque, then to Zuni. Camels were used.

———   (2727)
    Report relating to the construction of a wagon road from Fort Smith to the Colorado River. House Exec. Doc. 42, 36th Congress, 1st Session. Washington, GPO, 1860.

BECHDOLT, FREDERICK RITCHIE   (2728)
    Giants of the old West. New York, Century, 1930.

———   (2729)
    Tales of the old-timers. New York, Century, 1924.

BEERS, HENRY P.   (2730)
    Military protection of the Santa Fe trail to 1843. *NMHR,* 12:113-33, 1937.

BELKNAP, HELEN O.   (2731)
    The church on the changing frontier; a study of the homesteader and his church. New York, Doubleday, 1922.
        Includes a study of Union County.

BELL, OLIVE W.   (2732)
    The fabulous frontier. *NM,* 16:23, 41, 42, June 1938.

BELL, W. A.   (2733)
    New tracks in North America; a journal of travel and adventure whilst engaged in the survey for a southern railroad to the Pacific Ocean during 1867-1868 . . . 2 v. New York, Scribners, 1869.

BENDER, A. B.   (2734)
    Frontier defense in the territory of New Mexico, 1846-53. *NMHR,* 9:249-72, 1934.

———   (2735)
    Frontier defense in the territory of New Mexico, 1853-61. *NMHR,* 9:345-73, 1934.

———   (2736)
    Government explorations in the territory of New Mexico, 1846-59. *NMHR,* 9:1-32, 1934.

———   (2737)
    Military posts in the Southwest, 1848-60. Santa Fe, Historical Society of New Mexico, 1941.

BEWLEY, MARY   (2738)
    Indians of New Mexico in the Civil War. Unpub. Master's thesis, UNM, 1938.

———   (2739)
    A resume of the pre-civil war Indian situation in New Mexico. *Research,* 3:33-41, Jan. 1939.

BIEBER, RALPH P.   (2740)
Some aspects of the Santa Fe trail, 1848-80. *Chronicles of Oklahoma, Oklahoma Historical Society,* 2:1-8, March 1924. *Also Missouri Historical Review,* 18:158-66, Jan. 1924, and *Southern Magazine,* 2:19-20, 46, 1935.

———   (2741)
The Southwestern trails to California in 1849. *Mississippi Valley Historical Review,* 12:342-75, 1925.

BIEBER, RALPH P., ED.   (2742)
Exploring Southwestern trails; the journal of Philip St. George Cooke (1846), Lieut. W. H. C. Whiting (1849), Francis Xavier Aubry (1853), and others. Glendale, Clark, 1938.

———   (2743)
Letters of William Carr Lane, 1852-54. *NMHR,* 3:179-203, 1928.

———   (2744)
The papers of James J. Webb, Santa Fe merchant, 1844-61. *Washington University (St. Louis) Studies, Humanistic series,* 11 (2): 255-305, 1924.

BINKLEY, WILLIAM CAMPBELL   (2745)
New Mexico and the Texan-Santa Fe expedition. *Southwestern Historical Quarterly,* 27:85-107, 1923.

———   (2746)
The question of Texan jurisdiction in New Mexico under the United States, 1848-50. *Southwestern Historical Quarterly,* 24:1-38, 1920.

———   (2747)
Reports from a Texan agent in New Mexico, 1849. (In Hackett, Charles W., Ed.: *New Spain and the Anglo-American West.* Los Angeles, Privately Printed, 1932. v. 2, pp. 157-83.)

———   (2748)
Texan efforts to establish jurisdiction in New Mexico, 1836-50. Unpub. Master's thesis, University of California, 1918.

BLAKE, FORRESTER   (2749)
Riding the mustang trail. New York, Scribners, 1918.
Account of a trail drive of wild horses from New Mexico to Oklahoma.

BLAZER, A. N.   (2750)
Beginnings of an Indian war. *NM,* 16:22-23, 39-40, Feb. 1938.
Events immediately preceeding uprising by Victorio and his Mescalero Apaches in 1881.

———   (2751)
Blazer's mill. *NM,* 16:20, 48-49, Jan. 1938.
Description of life in the late 19th century in an isolated sawmill located in Tularosa region.

BLISS, CHARLES R.   (2752)
The new West. New Mexico. Boston, F. Wood, 1879.

BLOOM, LANSING B.   (2753)
The death of Jacques D'Eglise. *NMHR,* 2:369-79, 1927.
French adventurer murdered in New Mexico early in 19th century.

BLOOM, LANSING B. (Continued) (2754)
Ledgers of a Santa Fe trader. *EP*, 14:133-36, 1923.
Manuel Alvarez who operated in New Mexico about 1824.

BLOOM, LANSING B., ED. (2755)
Bourke on the Southwest. *NMHR*, 8:1-30, 1933; 9:33-77, 159-83, 273-89, 375-435, 1934; 10:1-35, 271-322, 1935; 11:77-122, 188-207, 217-82, 1936; 12:41-77, 337-79, 1937; 13:192-238, 1938.
Edited version of Bourke's notebooks.

———— (2755a)
A group of Kearny letters. *NMHR*, 5:17-37, 1930.

BOGGS, WILLIAM M. (2756)
Bent's Fort, Kit Carson, the far West, and life among the Indians. . . . Denver, Privately printed, 1930. Edited and annotated by LeRoy Hafen.

BONNER, T. D., ED. (2757)
The life and adventures of James P. Beckwourth. New York, Knopf, 1931.
Chapter 34 includes information on Taos insurrection and Indian troubles in New Mexico.

BOULDIN, EDNA (2758)
Frontier garrison. *NM*, 15:22-23, 37, Oct. 1937.
Fort Selden.

BOURKE, JOHN GREGORY (2759)
On the border with Crook. New York, Scribners, 1892.
Narrative of the campaigns against Geronimo.

BOX, MICHAEL JAMES (2760)
Captain James Box's adventures and explorations in New and Old Mexico. . . . New York, J. Miller, 1869.

BRADLEY, GLENN DANFORD (2761)
The story of the Pony Express . . . Chicago, McClurg, 1913.

———— (2762)
The story of the Santa Fe. Boston, Badger, 1920.

———— (2763)
Winning the Southwest; a story of conquest. Chicago, McClurg, 1912.

BRANCH, E. DOUGLAS (2764)
The cowboy and his interpreters. New York, Appleton, 1926.

———— (2765)
The hunting of the buffalo. New York, Appleton, 1929.

———— (2766)
Westward: the romance of the American frontier. New York, Appleton, 1930.

BRAYER, HERBERT O. (2767)
To form a more perfect union—the lives of Charles and Mary Clark from their letters 1847-71. Albuquerque, UNM Press, 1941.

BREAKENRIDGE, WILLIAM A.   (2768)
  Helldorado; bringing the law to the mesquite. Boston, Houghton
  Mifflin, 1928.

BRENT, MRS. CARLOTTA   (2769)
  Early days in Lincoln County. Unpub. ms. in files of New Mexico Writers' Project, Santa Fe.

——   (2770)
  Lincoln County history. Unpub. ms. in files of New Mexico
  Writers' Project, Santa Fe.

BREWER, SALLY P., ED.   (2771)
  The long walk to Bosque Redondo as told by Peshlakai Etsedi.
  Museum of Northern Arizona, Museum Notes, 9:55-62, 1937.

BREWERTON, GEORGE D.   (2772)
  Incidents of travel in New Mexico. *Harper's New Monthly Magazine,* 8:577-96, 1854.

——   (2773)
  *Overland with Kit Carson; a narrative of the old Spanish trail in
  '48.* New York, Coward-McCann, 1930.

BRIGGS, LLOYD VERNON   (2774)
  Arizona and New Mexico, 1882; California, 1886; Mexico, 1891.
  Boston, Privately Printed, 1932.

BRININSTOOL, EARL ALONZO, ED.   (2775)
  Trailing Geronimo. Los Angeles, Gem Pub. Co., 1920.

BROADHEAD, G. C.   (2775a)
  The Santa Fe trail. *Missouri Historical Review,* 4:309-19, 1909-10.

BROCKETT, L. P.   (2776)
  Our western empire or the New West beyond the Mississippi. . .
  Philadelphia, Bradley, Garretson & Co., 1882.

BROOME, BERTRAM   (2777)
  The Kid's tomorrow. *NM,* 11:18-19, 55-56, July 1933.
      Billy the Kid.

BROPHY, MRS. KATHLEEN   (2778)
  The language of the Santa Fe trader. Unpub. Master's thesis,
  UNM, 1932.

BROTHERS, MARY HUDSON   (2779)
  Meeting of the gun fighters. *NM,* 16:14, 40, Feb. 1938.
      Pat Garrett and Billy the Kid.

——   (2780)
  Pecos pioneer. Albuquerque, UNM Press, 1943.
      Biography of Bell Hudson in the days of the Chisum Trail.

BROWN, WILLIAM HORACE   (2781)
  *The glory seekers; the romance of the would-be founders of empire
  in the early days of the great Southwest.* Chicago, McClurg, 1906.

BURDETT, CHARLES   (2782)
  Life of Kit Carson, the great western hunter and guide. Philadelphia, John E. Potter [1869].

BURDETT, CHARLES (Continued)   (2783)
The life of Kit Carson. . . with an account of various expeditions
to the far West. New York, Perkins Book Co., 1902.

BURNEY, DUDLEY H.   (2784)
The Indian policy of the United States government from 1870 to
1906, with special reference to land tenure. Unpub. Doctor's dissertation, Stanford University, 1937.

BURNS, JAMES A.   (2785)
Caviar to the general. Unpub. ms. in files of New Mexico Writers'
Project, Santa Fe.
   Story of the first trip southwest of George Bandreath, D. C. Pittman, and
   James Whitcomb Riley.

BURNS, WALTER NOBLE   (2786)
Saga of Billy the Kid. New York, Doubleday, 1926.

BURTON, ESTELLE BENNETT   (2787)
The Taos rebellion. Old Santa Fe, 1:176-209, 1913.

————   (2788)
Volunteer soldiers of New Mexico and their conflicts with Indians
in 1862 and 1863. Old Santa Fe, 1:386-419, 1914.

BURTON, H. T.   (2789)
A history of the J. A. ranch. Southwestern Historical Quarterly,
31:330-35, 1928.

CALHOUN, JAMES S.   (2790)
The official correspondence of James S. Calhoun while Indian
agent at Santa Fe and Superintendent of Indian Affairs in New
Mexico, 1849-52. Edited by A. H. Abel. Washington, GPO, 1915.

CALVIN, ROSS   (2791)
How Main Street became the big ditch. Soil Conservation, 2:102-
05, 1936.
   Results of Silver City flood, 1895.

CANTON, FRANK M.   (2792)
Frontier trails; the autobiography of Frank M. Canton. Boston,
Houghton Mifflin, 1930.

CARLETON, JAMES HENRY   (2793)
Business letters from the Apache country. Business Historical
Society Bulletin, 3:1-6, Feb. 1929.

————   (2794)
Diary of an excursion to the ruins of Abo, Quarra, and Grand
Quivira, in New Mexico, under the command of Major James
Henry Carleton, U. S. A. Smithsonian 9th Annual Report.
Washington, 1855. pp. 296-316.

————   (2795)
Ruins of New Mexico. Western Journal, 14:185, 1855.

————   (2796)
Tour through New Mexico in 1846. Western Journal, 1:363,
1848.

CARNES, SISTER MARY LOYOLA   (2797)
The American occupation of New Mexico. Unpub. Master's thesis, University of California, 1922.

CARROLL, DECLAN F.   (2798)
The sisters of Loretto, pioneer educators. Unpub. Master's thesis, University of Kentucky, 1937.

CARROLL, HORACE B.   (2799)
The route of the Texan-Santa Fe expedition. Unpub. Doctor's dissertation, University of Texas, 1935.

CARROLL, HORACE BAILEY, ED.   (2800)
The journal of Lieut. J. W. Abert from Bent's Fort to St. Louis in 1845. Panhandle-Plains Historical Society, v. 14. Canyon, Texas, 1941.

CARSON, CHRISTOPHER   (2801)
Kit Carson's autobiography. Edited by Milo Milton Quaife. Chicago, Donnelley & Sons, 1935.

———   (2802)
Kit Carson's own story as dictated to Col. and Mrs. D. C. Peters about 1856-57. Santa Fe, Museum of New Mexico, 1926.

CARTER, ALLEN A.   (2803)
Desperadoes. Unpub. ms. in files of New Mexico Writers' Project, Santa Fe.

CARTERET, J.   (2803a)
A fortune hunter: or, the Old Stone Corral. A narrative of the Santa Fe trail. Cincinnati, 1888.

CASON, INA WILSON   (2804)
The Bent brothers on the frontier. Unpub. Master's thesis, UNM, 1939.

CAUGHEY, JOHN WALTON   (2805)
Early federal relations with New Mexico. Unpub. Master's thesis, University of California, 1926.

CHAMPLIN, N. HARRY   (2806)
The Beefsteak trail. *NM,* 18:9-11, 42-43, March 1940.
   Trailing cattle from ranch to railroad.

CHAPMAN, ARTHUR   (2807)
Cowboy war. *Outing,* 58:498-506, 1911.
   Lincoln County war.

———   (2808)
A cowboy war in New Mexico. *Santa Fe Magazine,* 6:65-72, Nov. 1912.
   Lincoln County war.

———   (2809)
The Pony Express. New York, Putnam, 1932.

CHAPMAN, MANVILLE   (2810)
Pioneer headquarters. *NM,* 15:18-19, 39-40, June 1937.
   Founding of Raton.

CHARLES, TOM   (2811)
Apache battleground. *NM*, 19:16-17, 38, 40, April 1941.
Dog Canyon.

CHEETHAM, F. T.   (2812)
The first term of the American Court in Taos, New Mexico.
NMHR, 1:23-41, 1926.

————   (2813)
Kit Carson. *NMHR*, 1:375-399, 1926.

CHITTENDEN, HIRAM MARTIN   (2814)
*American fur trade of the far West: a history of the pioneer trad-
ing posts and early fur companies of the Missouri Valley and the
Rocky Mountains and of the overland commerce with Santa Fe.*
3 v. New York, Harper, 1902. *Also* New York, Pioneer Press,
1935.

CLANCY, FRANK W.   (2815)
Reminiscences of territorial days. *New Mexico Bar Association,
Minutes, 32nd Annual Session, Clovis, September 1919.* pp. 47-
60.

CLARK, ANNA NOLAN   (2816)
He blazed the trail. *NM*, 19:21-23, 38-40, Feb. 1941.
Richens Lacy Wootton.

CLARK, E. P.   (2817)
Twenty-two years ago. *Nation*, 62:337, 1896.
Reasons why New Mexico was not sooner admitted as a state.

CLIFFORD, J.   (2818)
An officer's wife in New Mexico. *Overland Monthly*, 4:152, 1870.

CLUM, JOHN P.   (2819)
Apache misrule—a bungling agent sets the military arm in motion.
NMHR, 5:138-53, 221-39, 1930.
Apache outbreaks in 1877.

————   (2820)
Santa Fe in the '70's. *NMHR*, 2:380-86, 1927.

CLUM, WOODWORTH   (2821)
Apache agent, the story of John P. Clum. Boston, Houghton
Mifflin, 1936.

COE, GEORGE W.   (2822)
Frontier fighter. Boston, Houghton Mifflin, 1934.

COFFEY, FREDERIC A.   (2822a)
Some general aspects of the Gadsden treaty. *NMHR*, 8:145-64,
1933.

COLEMAN, MAX   (2823)
Life of a desperado. *SR*, 16:484-95, 1930-31.
Account of W. C. (Bronco Bill) Brown, illustrating sense of honor of western
"bad men."

COLLIER, H. P.   (2824)
Camp Maddox. Unpub. ms. in files of New Mexico Writers'
Project, Santa Fe.

COLLIER, H. P. (Continued)   (2825)
Cooney's tomb. Unpub. ms. in files of New Mexico Writers'
Project, Santa Fe.
    Story of a miner killed in 1880 by Indians.

————   (2826)
San Francisco Plaza, Catron County. Unpub. ms. in files of New
Mexico Writers' Project, Santa Fe.

COMBS, FRANKLIN   (2827)
Combs' narrative of the Santa Fe expedition in 1841. *NMHR*,
5:305-14, 1930.

CONARD, HOWARD LOUIS   (2828)
"Uncle Dick" Wootton. Chicago, Dibble, 1890.

CONNELLEY, WILLIAM ELSEY   (2829)
*Doniphan's expedition and the conquest of New Mexico and Cali-
fornia.* Topeka, the Author, 1907.

————   (2830)
*The war with Mexico, 1846-47; Doniphan's expedition, and the
conquest of New Mexico and California.* Kansas City, Privately
Printed, 1907.

————   (2831)
Wild Bill and his era; the adventures of James Butler Hickock.
New York, Pioneer Press, 1933.

CONNELLY, GOV. HENRY   (2831a)
*The first annual message of Governor Connelly, delivered before
the legislative assembly of the Territory of New Mexico.* Santa Fe,
Gazette Office, 1861.
    Includes information on Indian troubles, mining, manufacturing, laws, agri-
    culture, etc.

COOK, JAMES H.   (2832)
The art of fighting Indians. *American Mercury*, 23:170-79, 1931.

————   (2833)
*Fifty years on the old frontier; as a cowboy, hunter, scout, and
ranchman.* New Haven, Yale University Press, 1923.

————   (2834)
Longhorn cowboy. Edited by Howard R. Driggs. New York, Putnam, 1942.

COOK, JAMES M.   (2835)
Lane of the Llano. Edited by T. M. Pearce. Boston, Little Brown,
1936.

COOK, JOHN R.   (2836)
*The border and the buffalo; an untold story of the Southwest
plains* . . . Topeka, Crane & Co., 1907.

COOKE, PHILIP ST. GEORGE   (2837)
The conquest of New Mexico and California . . . New York, Putnam, 1878.

————   (2838)
A journal of the Santa Fe trail. Edited by William E. Connelley.
Mississippi Valley Historical Review, 12:72-98, 227-55, 1925.

COOKE, PHILIP ST. GEORGE (Continued) (2839)
A winter's work of a captain of dragoons. *Magazine of American History*, 18:510-17, 1887.

COOLIDGE, DANE (2840)
Fighting men of the West. New York, Dutton, 1932.
    Biographies of Charles Goodnight, John Chisum, Clay Allison, and others.

COTTRELL, DOROTHY (2841)
Texas reprisals against New Mexico in 1843. Unpub. Master's thesis, UNM, 1934.

COUES, ELLIOTT, ED. (2842)
The expedition of Zebulon Montgomery Pike to the headwaters of the Mississippi River through Louisiana Territory, and in New Spain during the years 1805-07. 3 v. New York, Harper, 1895.

———— (2843)
The journal of Jacob Fowler; an adventure from Arkansas through the Indian territory, Oklahoma, Kansas, Colorado, and New Mexico to the sources of the Rio Grande. New York, Harper, 1898.

COWAN, JOHN L. (2844)
The Santa Fe trail. *Overland*, n. s., 62:317-26, 1913.

COX, ISAAC JOSLIN (2845)
Opening the Santa Fe trail. *Missouri Historical Review*, 25:30-66, Oct. 1930.

COX, JAMES (2846)
Historical and biographical record of the cattle industry and the cattlemen of Texas and adjoining territory. St. Louis, Woodward & Tiernan, 1895.

COZZENS, SAMUEL (2847)
The marvellous country, or three years in Arizona and New Mexico. Boston, Lee & Shepard, 1876.

———— (2848)
Voyage dans le Nouveau-Mexique. Paris, Garnier Freres, 1876.

CRAWFORD, EDITH L. (2849)
Billy the Kid. Unpub. ms. in files of New Mexico Writers' Project, Santa Fe.

———— (2850)
Billy the Kid's gun. Unpub. ms. in files of New Mexico Writer's Project, Santa Fe.

———— (2851)
Early days in Lincoln County. Unpub. ms. in files of New Mexico Writers' Project, Santa Fe.

———— (2852)
Pioneer story. Unpub. mss. in files of New Mexico Writers' Project, Santa Fe.
    Several mss. dealing with life in Lincoln County during the time of Billy the Kid.

———— (2853)
Reminiscences of Billy the Kid. Unpub. ms. in files of New Mexico Writers' Project, Santa Fe.

CRAWFORD, EDITH L. (Continued)   (2854)
Story of Billy the Kid. Unpub. ms. in files of New Mexico Writers'
Project, Santa Fe.

CRICHTON, KYLE   (2855)
Law and order, ltd. Santa Fe, Santa Fe Pub. Co., 1928.
    Life of Elfego Baca.

————   (2856)
Zeb Pike. Scribner's, 82:462-67, 1927.

CRIMMINS, M. L.   (2857)
The battle of Val Verde. NMHR, 7:348-52, 1932.

————   (2858)
Fort Fillmore. NMHR, 6:327-33, 1931.

CRUSE, THOMAS   (2859)
Apache days and after. Edited by Eugene Cunningham. Caldwell,
Idaho, Caxton Printers, 1942.
    History of campaigns against Apaches of Arizona and New Mexico in 1870's
    and 1880's.

CUNNINGHAM, EUGENE   (2860)
Triggernometry, a gallery of gunfighters. Caldwell, Idaho, Caxton
Printers, 1941.

CUTTS, JAMES MADISON   (2861)
The conquest of California and New Mexico by the forces of the
United States in the years 1846 and 1847. Philadelphia, Carey &
Hart, 1847.

DALY, H. W.   (2861a)
The Geronimo campaign. Arizona Historical Review, 3 (2) :26-44,
1930-31.

DARGAN, MRS. LENA   (2862)
James S. Calhoun in New Mexico. Unpub. Master's thesis, UNM,
1932.

DOBIE, J. FRANK   (2863)
Billy the Kid. SR, 14:314-20, 1929.

DOMENECH, EM., ABBE   (2864)
Reminiscences of Fort Defiance, New Mexico, 1860. Journal of
the Military Service Institution of the United States, 4:90-92, 1883.

DONNELL, F. S.   (2865)
When Las Vegas was the capital of New Mexico. NMHR, 8:265-
72, 1933.

————   (2866)
When Texas owned New Mexico to the Rio Grande. NMHR, 8:
65-75, 1933.

DOSCH, ARNO   (2867)
Kit Carson, the great American. Pacific Monthly, March 1908.

DOWNEY, FAIRFAX DAVIS   (2868)
Indian-fighting army. New York, Scribners, 1941.
    History of Indian wars in Western U. S. from 1865-1915.

DRIGGS, HOWARD ROSCOE (2869)
Westward America. New York, Putnam, 1942.
> Pictorial history of the development of the West including material on the Santa Fe trail.

DRUMM, STELLA M., ED. (2870)
Down the Santa Fe trail and into Mexico; the diary of Susan Shelby Magoffin, 1846-47. New Haven, Yale University Press, 1926.

DUFFUS, R. L. (2871)
The Santa Fe trail. New York, Longmans Green, 1930.

DUNBAR, SEYMOUR (2871a)
History of travel in America. New York, Tudor Pub. Co., 1937.
> Includes information on travel over the Santa Fe trail.

DUNN, J. P., JR. (2872)
Massacres of the mountains; a history of the Indian wars of the far West. New York, Harper, 1886.

DUNNE, MARIE (2873)
Advance of empire. NM, 15:14-15, 60, Aug. 1937.
> Kearny's entrance into Santa Fe.

EDWARDS, FRANK S. (2874)
A campaign in New Mexico with Colonel Doniphan ... Philadelphia, Carey & Hart, 1847.

EDWORDS, CLARENCE E. (2875)
Camp-fires of a naturalist. New York, Appleton, 1893.
> Travel description.

ELLIOTT, RICHARD SMITH (2876)
Notes taken in sixty years. St. Louis, R. P. Studley & Co., 1883.
> Writer was a member of Doniphan's expedition.

ELLIS, EDWARD SYLVESTER (2877)
The life and times of Christopher Carson, the Rocky Mountain scout and guide. New York, Beadle & Co., 1861.

———— (2878)
The round up, or Geronimo's last stand. Philadelphia, Winston, 1908.

ELLISON, MRS. EDITH NICHOLL (2879)
Little experiences of a ranchwoman. *Nineteenth Century and After,* 70:950-59, 1911.

EMERY, W. M. (2880)
Church as a stable. Unpub. ms. in files of New Mexico Writers' Project, Santa Fe.
> Freighters hid their horses from Indians in a church at Pecos.

———— (2881)
Early day Folsom. Unpub. ms. in files of New Mexico Writers' Project, Santa Fe.

———— (2882)
Indians and sheepmen. Unpub. ms. in files of New Mexico Writers' Project, Santa Fe.

EMORY, WILLIAM HENSLEY   (2883)
   *Notes of a military reconnaissance from Fort Leavenworth, in
   Missouri, to San Diego, California, including part of the Arkansas,
   del Norte, and Gila rivers, 1846-47.* House Exec. Doc. 41, 30th
   Congress, 1st Session. Washington, GPO, 1848.
——————   (2884)
   Reconnaissance in New Mexico and California. Senate Exec. Doc.
   7, 30th Congress, 1st Session. Washington, GPO, 1847.
ESPINOSA, JOSE MANUEL, ED.   (2885)
   Memoir of a Kentuckian in New Mexico, 1848-84. *NMHR*, 13:
   1-13, 1938.
       Judge Samuel Ellison.
FALCONER, THOMAS   (2886)
   Letters and notes on the Texan-Santa Fe expedition, 1841-42 . . .
   New York, Dauber and Pine, 1930.
FARRAND, MAX   (2887)
   *The legislation of Congress for the government of the organized
   territories of the United States, 1789-1895.* Newark, Wm. A. Baker,
   1896.
FAVOUR, ALPHEUS H.   (2888)
   Old Bill Williams, mountain man. Chapel Hill, University of
   North Carolina Press, 1936.
FESSLER, W. JULIAN, ED.   (2889)
   Jacob Fowler's journal. *Chronicles of Oklahoma, Oklahoma His-
   torical Society,* 8:181-88, June 1930.
FILLMORE, MILLARD   (2890)
   Message on affairs in New Mexico. Senate Exec. Doc. 74, 31st
   Congress, 1st Session. Washington, GPO, 1850.
——————   (2891)
   Message on New Mexico and Texas. House Exec. Doc. 85, 31st
   Congress, 1st Session. Washington, GPO, 1850.
FORDYCE, KENNETH   (2892)
   Cheese and butter for Santa Fe. Unpub. ms. in files of New Mex-
   ico Writers' Project, Santa Fe.
       Business enterprise of an early family.
——————   (2893)
   The Clifton House. Unpub. ms. in files of New Mexico Writers'
   Project, Santa Fe.
       The story of a Raton Hotel.
——————   (2894)
   Crime did not pay in '73. Unpub. ms. in files of New Mexico
   Writers' Project, Santa Fe.
——————   (2895)
   Early crimes and tragedies in northern New Mexico. Unpub. ms.
   in files of New Mexico Writers' Project, Santa Fe.
——————   (2896)
   The law in their hands. Unpub. ms. in files of New Mexico
   Writers' Project, Santa Fe.
       Crime and mob violence, Raton.

FORDYCE, KENNETH (Continued)   (2897)
    The naming of Cimarron. Unpub. ms. in files of New Mexico
    Writers' Project, Santa Fe.

_____   (2898)
    Northern New Mexico in 1870. Unpub. ms. in files of New Mex-
    ico Writers' Project, Santa Fe.

_____   (2899)
    Northern New Mexico's bad man and his gang. Unpub. ms. in
    files of New Mexico Writers' Project, Santa Fe.
        Black Jack Ketchum.

FOREMAN, GRANT   (2900)
    Advancing the frontier, 1830-60. Norman, UOP, 1933.

_____   (2901)
    Antoine Leroux, New Mexico guide. *NMHR,* 16:367-77, 1941.

_____   (2902)
    Indians and pioneers; the story of the Southwest before 1830.
    New Haven, Yale University Press, 1930.

_____   (2903)
    *Marcy and the gold seekers; the journal of Captain R. B. Marcy
    with an account of the gold rush over the southern route.* Norman,
    UOP, 1939.

_____   (2904)
    Pioneer days in the early Southwest. Cleveland, Clark, 1926.

FOREMAN, GRANT, ED.   (2905)
    *A pathfinder in the Southwest: the itinerary of Lieutenant A. W.
    Whipple* . . . Norman, UOP, 1941.

FOWLER, W.   (2905a)
    *Women of the American frontier: history of the heroism, pri-
    vations, captivities, lives, and deaths of pioneer mothers.* Hartford,
    1878.
        Includes some New Mexican experiences.

FRENCH, WILLIAM   (2906)
    Some recollections of a western ranchman, New Mexico, 1883-99.
    New York, Stokes, 1928.
        Silver City region.

FRESQUE, CLARA   (2907)
    Billy the Kid. Unpub. ms. in files of New Mexico Writers' Pro-
    ject, Santa Fe.

FROST, JOHN   (2908)
    *The Mexican War and its warriors; comprising a complete history
    of all the operations of the American armies in Mexico* . . . New
    Haven, H. Mansfield, 1849.

_____   (2909)
    Thrilling adventures among the Indians . . . Philadelphia, J. W.
    Bradley, 1849.

FULTON, MAURICE G.   (2910)
    Clay Allison. *SR,* 15:192-215, 1930.

FULTON, MAURICE G., ED.   (2911)
*Diary and letters of Josiah Gregg: Southwestern enterprises, 1840-
47.* Norman, UOP, 1941.

GALLOWAY, TOD B.   (2912)
Private letters of a government official in the Southwest. *Journal
of American History,* 3:541-54, 1909.
  John Greiner.

GANAWAY, LOOMIS MORTON   (2913)
New Mexico and the sectional controversy, 1846-61. Unpub.
Doctor's dissertation, Vanderbilt University, 1941. *Also NMHR,*
18:113-47, 1943.

GARBER, PAUL   (2914)
The Gadsden Treaty. Philadelphia, University of Pennsylvania
Press, 1923.

GARRARD, LEWIS HECTOR   (2915)
Wah-to-yoh and the Taos trail. Oklahoma City, Harlow Pub. Co.,
1927.
     Early western travel.

GARRETT, PAT F.   (2916)
The authentic life of Billy the Kid. New York, Macmillan, 1927.

GIANINI, CHARLES A.   (2917)
Manuel Lisa. *NMHR,* 2:323-33, 1927.
     An early Missouri trader.

GIBSON, GEORGE RUTLEDGE   (2918)
Journal of a soldier under Kearny and Doniphan, 1846-47. Edited
by Ralph Bieber. Glendale, Clark, 1935.

GILBERT, E. W.   (2919)
The exploration of western America, 1800-1850. Cambridge, Harvard University Press, 1933.

GOLDER, FRANK ALFRED   (2920)
*The march of the Mormon battalion from Council Bluffs to Cal-
ifornia.* Taken from the journal of Henry Standage. New York,
Century, 1928.

GOODNIGHT, CHARLES   (2921)
Pioneer days in the Southwest. Guthrie, Oklahoma, State Capital
Co., 1909.

GOODWIN, CARDINAL   (2922)
*The trans-Mississippi West (1803-1853); a history of its acqui-
sition and settlement.* New York, Appleton, 1922.

GRANT, BLANCHE C.   (2923)
One hundred years ago in old Taos. Taos, the Author, 1925.

GRANT, BLANCHE C., ED.   (2924)
Kit Carson's own story. Taos, the Author, 1926.

GREENBIE, SYDNEY   (2925)
Furs to furrows; an epic of rugged individualism. Caldwell, Idaho,
Caxton Printers, 1939.
     Some mention of fur trapping in New Mexico.

GREENE, J. EVARTS   (2926)
   The Santa Fe trade; its route and character. Worcester, Massachusetts, Press of Charles Hamilton, 1893.

GREGG, JOSIAH   (2927)
   Commerce of the prairies; the journal of a Santa Fe trader . . .
   2v. Cleveland, Clark, 1905. *Also* Dallas, Southwest Press, 1933.

GRINNELL, GEORGE BIRD   (2928)
   *Beyond the old frontier; adventures of Indian fighters, hunters,
   and fur-traders.* New York, Scribners, 1913.

————   (2929)
   Trails of the pathfinders. New York, Scribners, 1911.
      Sketches of pioneer characters including Pike and Fremont.

GUINN, J. M.   (2930)
   Camel caravan of the American desert. *Historical Society of
   Southern California, Annual Publications,* 5:146-51, 1901.

GWYTHER, G.   (2931)
   An Indian reservation; the story of Fort Sumner. *Overland
   Monthly,* 9:123-34, 1873.

HAFEN, LEROY   (2932)
   The overland mail, 1849-69. Cleveland, Clark, 1926.

HAFEN, LEROY, ED.   (2932a)
   The W. M. Boggs manuscript about Bent's Fort, Kit Carson, the
   far West, and life among the Indians. *Colorado Magazine,* 7:45-69,
   1930.

HAFEN, LEROY AND GHENT, W. J.   (2933)
   *Broken Hand, the life story of Thomas Fitzpatrick, chief of the
   mountain men.* Denver, Old West Pub. Co., 1931.

HAFEN, LEROY AND RISTER, CARL COKE   (2934)
   *Western America; the exploration, settlement, and development
   of the region beyond the Mississippi.* New York, Prentice-Hall,
   1941.

HALEY, J. EVETTS   (2935)
   Charles Goodnight, cowman and plainsman. Boston, Houghton
   Mifflin, 1936.

————   (2936)
   Driving a trail herd. *SR,* 18:384-403, 1932-33.
      Cattle driving experiences of Charles Goodnight.

————   (2937)
   Horse thieves. *SR,* 15:317-32, 1930.
      Lincoln County war.

————   (2938)
   Pastores del Palo Duro. *SR,* 19:279-94, 1933-34.
      Cattle and sheep conflicts between Charles Goodnight and Mexican authori-
      ties in New Mexico.

HARDY, R.   (2939)
   *Travels in the interior of Mexico (Colorado, Arizona, New
   Mexico, and Lower California) in 1825-28.* London, H. Colburn
   & R. Bentley, 1829.

HARPER, CARL (2940)
Building the Santa Fe Railroad through the south plains. *West Texas Historical Association Yearbook*, 11:73-92, 1935.

HARR, JOHN L. (2941)
The ante-bellum Southwest, 1815-61. Unpub. Doctor's dissertation, University of Chicago, 1941.

HARRIS, MRS. CAROLINE (2941a)
The history of the captivity and providential release of Mrs. Caroline Harris who was taken prisoner with her husband and others by the Comanche Indians while emigrating to Texas . . . Rochester, 1848.
> Mrs. Harris and her companions were held in New Mexico.

HARVEY, CHARLES M. (2942)
The story of the Santa Fe trail. *Atlantic*, 104:774-85, 1909.
> Includes some material on first contacts between Anglos and Spanish-Americans in New Mexico.

HAWTHORNE, HILDEGARDE (2943)
Ox-team miracle; the story of Alexander Majors. New York, Longmans Green, 1942.

HAYES, A. A. (2944)
New Colorado and the Santa Fe trail. New York, Harper, 1880.

———— (2945)
The New Mexican campaign of 1862; a stirring chapter of our late Civil War. *Magazine of American History*, 15:171-84, 1886.

———— (2946)
Santa Fe trail. *Harper's New Monthly Magazine*, 61:185-96, 1880.

HEAP, G. H. (2947)
Central route to the Pacific from the Mississippi to California. Journal of the expedition of F. E. Beale and G. H. Heap, from Missouri to California in 1853. Philadelphia, Lippincott, 1854.

HENDRICKS, GEORGE (2948)
The bad man of the West. San Antonio, Naylor, 1941.
> Includes stories of some New Mexico outlaws.

HENDRON, J. W. (2949)
The old Lincoln County court house. *EP*, 46:1-18, 1939.

HESS, JOHN W. (2950)
John W. Hess with the Mormon Battalion. *Utah Historical Quarterly*, 4:47-55, 1931.

HEWLETT, WILLIAM JOSEPH (2951)
Life of the Right Reverend Joseph P. Machebeuf, D.D., pioneer priest of Ohio, pioneer priest of New Mexico, pioneer priest of Colorado, vicar apostolic of Colorado and Utah, and first bishop of Denver. Pueblo, Franklin Press, 1908.

HIGGINS, CHARLES A. (2952)
New guide to the Pacific coast, Santa Fe route. Chicago, Rand McNally, 1896.

HILL, JOSEPH J. (2953)
Ewing Young in the fur trade of the far Southwest, 1822-1834. *Oregon Historical Quarterly*, 24:1-34, 1923.

———— (2954)
Unknown expedition to Santa Fe in 1807. *Mississippi Valley Historical Review*, 6:560-62, 1920.

HITCHCOCK, ETHAN ALLAN (2955)
A traveller in Indian territory. Cedar Rapids, Torch Press, 1930.

HOBBS, JAMES (2956)
Wild life in the far West; personal adventures of a border mountain man . . . Hartford, Wiley, Waterman & Eaton, 1872.

HODGES, CARRIE L. (2957)
Tales of old timers; the staked plains. Unpub. ms. in files of New Mexico Writers' Project, Santa Fe.

———— (2958)
Tales of old times. Unpub. ms. in files of New Mexico Writers' Project, Santa Fe.

HOLCER, LOLA MAY AND MILLER, FLORA LILLIAN (2959)
The bridge of life. Topeka, Crane & Co., 1915.
    Memoirs of life in and about Socorro.

HOOPES, ALBAN W., ED. (2960)
Letters to and from Abraham G. Mayers, 1854-57. *NMHR*, 9: 290-335, 1934.

HORGAN, PAUL (2961)
The prairies revisited; a re-estimation of Josiah Gregg. *SR*, 26: 145-66, 1941.

HORN, SARAH ANN (2961a)
An authentic and thrilling narrative of the captivity of Mrs. Horn and her two children, with Mrs. Harris, by the Comanche Indians and the murder of their husbands and traveling companions. Cincinnati, the Author, 1851.
    Mrs. Horn was held captive in New Mexico from April 1836 to the autumn of 1837.

HOUGH, EMERSON (2962)
Billy the Kid. *Everybody's*, Sept. 1901.

———— (2963)
Kit Carson. *Outing*, 45:480-86, Jan. 1905.

———— (2964)
The passing of the frontier; a chronicle of the old West. New Haven, Yale University Press, 1921.

———— (2965)
The story of the outlaw . . . New York, Outing Pub. Co., 1907.
    Includes material on Lincoln County war.

———— (2966)
The way to the West. Indianapolis, Bobbs-Merrill, 1903.
    Lives of early Americans, including Kit Carson.

HOWARD, O. O.   (2967)
My life and experiences among our hostile Indians. Hartford, A. D. Worthington & Co., 1907.

HOWE, HENRY   (2968)
Historical collections of the great West. Cincinnati, Henry Howe, 1873.
  pp. 373-376, historical and descriptive sketch of New Mexico.

————   (2969)
The times of rebellion in the West. Cincinnati, Howe's Subscription Book Concern, 1867.

HOYT, HENRY F.   (2970)
A frontier doctor. Boston, Houghton Mifflin, 1929.

HUGHES, JOHN T.   (2971)
Doniphan's expedition, account of conquest of New Mexico, General Kearny's overland expedition to California, Doniphan's campaign against the Navajos, his unparalleled march on Chihuahua and Durango and operations of General Price at Santa Fe. Senate Doc. 608, 63rd Congress, 2nd Session. Washington, GPO, 1914.

————   (2972)
Doniphan's expedition; containing an account of the conquest of New Mexico. Cincinnati, J. A. and U. P. James, 1848-1850.

HULBERT, ARCHER BUTLER, ED.   (2973)
Southwest on the turquoise trail: the first diaries on the road to Santa Fe. Denver, The Stewart Commission of Colorado College and the Denver Public Library, 1933.

HUMFREVILLE, J. LEE   (2974)
Twenty years among our savage Indians. Hartford, Hartford Pub. Co., 1897.

HUMPHRIES, KEITH   (2975)
They watered at Cummings. *NM*, 17:21-23, 42, 44, Aug. 1939.
  History of Fort Cummings.

HUNSAKER, WILLIAM J.   (2976)
Lansford W. Hastings' project for the invasion and conquest of Arizona and New Mexico for the southern confederacy. *Arizona Historical Review*, 4 (2) :5-12, 1931.

HUNT, A. E. AND CLARK, ANNA NOLAN   (2977)
Far horizons. *NM*, 15:22-23, 42-43, May 1937.
  Account of John Clancy, one of first cattle and sheep men, who established a ranch near Alamogordo.

HURD, C. W.   (2978)
Origin and development of the Santa Fe trail. *Santa Fe Magazine*, 15:17-27, Sept. 1921.

HUSSEY, JOHN ADAM   (2978a)
The New Mexico-California caravan of 1847-1848. *NMHR*, 18: 1-16, Jan. 1943.

HYDE, ALBERT E. (2979)
The old regime in the Southwest; the reign of the revolver in
New Mexico. *Century*, 63:690-701, 1902.
"Wild West" description of frontier conditions in 1880's.

INGERSOLL, ERNEST (2980)
*The crest of the continent; a record of a summer's ramble in the
Rocky Mountains and beyond.* Chicago, R. R. Donnelley & Sons,
1885.

———— (2981)
La villa real de Santa Fe. *Harper's New Monthly Magazine*, 60:
667-82, 1880.

INMAN, HENRY (2982)
The old Santa Fe trail . . . New York, Macmillan, 1897.

———— (2983)
Tales of the trail; short stories of western life. Topeka, Crane &
Co., 1917.

IRWIN, GENERAL B. J. D. (2984)
The Apache Pass fight. *Infantry Journal*, April 1928.

JACKSON, ANDREW (2984a)
The fur trade, and inland trade to Mexico. Washington, 1832.
Contains original accounts of Indian depredations on Santa Fe trail.

JACKSON, ANDREW (2985)
Message on trade with New Mexico. Senate Doc. 46, 21st Congress,
1st Session. Washington, GPO, 1830.

JAMES, THOMAS (2986)
Three years among the Mexicans and Indians. St. Louis, Missouri
Historical Society, 1916.

JAYNE, R. H. (2987)
On the trail of Geronimo. New York, Hurst & Co., n. d. *Also*
New York, American Publishers Corp., 1889.

———— (2988)
Through Apache land. St. Paul, Price-McGill Co., 1893.

JOHNSON, EMMET E. (2989)
New Mexico in the war of the rebellion, 1860-61. Unpub. Master's
thesis, New Mexico Normal (Highlands) University, 1934.

JOHNSON, WILLARD (2990)
The good old days. *SR*, 10:66-72, July 1925.

JOHNSTON, ABRAHAM ROBINSON, EDWARDS, MARCELLUS BALL,
AND FERGUSON, PHILIP G. (2991)
Marching with the army of the West, 1846-48. Edited by Ralph
P. Bieber. Glendale, Clark, 1936.

JONES, DANIEL W. (2992)
Forty years among the Indians. Salt Lake City, Juvenile Instructor Office, 1890.

JONES, HESTER   (2993)
Report on historical investigations at Crownpoint. Ms. dated August 1933 on file at Department of History, UNM.
> Interviews with three old Navajos who remembered Bosque Redondo and Fort Sumner.

———   (2994)
The Spiegelbergers and early trade in New Mexico. EP, 38:81-89, 1935.

JORDAN, MILDRED   (2995)
Geronimo's raid. Unpub. ms. in files of New Mexico Writers' Project, Santa Fe.

KEARNY, THOMAS   (2996)
Kearny and Kit Carson . . . NMHR, 5:1-16, 1930.

KELSEY, D. M.   (2997)
History of our wild West and stories of pioneer life . . . Chicago, Charles C. Thompson Co., 1901.

KENDALL, GEORGE WILKINS   (2998)
Narratives of the Texan-Santa Fe expedition. Chicago, Donnelley & Sons, 1929. Also New York, Harper, 1844.

KIMBALL, MARIE BRACE   (2999)
The passing of a frontier fort; account of life among the Navajo Indians at Fort Wingate, New Mexico, in the middle of the nineteenth century. Journal of American History, 17(1):21-29, 1923.

KING, CHARLES   (3000)
Campaigning with Crook. New York, Harper, 1890.

KING, FRANK M.   (3001)
Wranglin' the past. Los Angeles, Haynes Corp., 1935.

LAKE, STUART N.   (3002)
Wyatt Earp, frontier marshall. Boston, Houghton Mifflin, 1931.

LANE, WILLIAM   (3003)
Letters of William Carr Lane, 1852-54. Santa Fe, Historical Society of New Mexico, 1928.

LAUGHLIN, RUTH   (3004)
Flight from Santa Fe. NM, 15:22-23, 40, Dec. 1937.
> Pueblo rebellion in the 1830's.

LAUMBACH, VERNA   (3005)
Las Vegas before 1850. NMHR, 8:241-64, 1933.

LAUT, AGNES CHRISTINA   (3006)
Pilgrims of the Santa Fe. New York, Stokes, 1931.

LEE, JOHN THOMAS, ED.   (3007)
New found letters of Josiah Gregg, Santa Fe trader and historian. American Antiquarian Society, Proceedings, n. s. 40(2):47-68, 1930.

LESLIE, LEWIS B., ED.   (3008)
Uncle Sam's camels; the journal of May Humphreys Stacey, supplemented by a report of Edward Fitzgerald Beale (1857-58). Cambridge, Harvard University Press, 1929.

LIVINGSTON, CARL (3009)
Cattle on the drift. *NM*, 11:18-20, 44-46, Oct. 1933.
Early days in the cattle industry in New Mexico.

LLOYD, EVERETT (3010)
Law west of the Pecos; the story of Roy Bean. San Antonio, Naylor Co., 1941.

LOCKETT, H. CLAIBORNE (3011)
Along the Beale trail. A photographic account of wasted range land based on the diary of Lt. E. F. Beale, 1857. Lawrence, Kansas, Haskell Institute, 1940.

LOCKWOOD, FRANK R., ED. (3012)
Apaches and longhorns: the reminiscences of Will C. Barnes. Los Angeles, Ward Ritchie Press, 1941.

LOEW, O. (3013)
Lieutenant G. M. Wheeler's zweite expedition nach Neu Mexiko und Colorado. *Petermanns Mitteilungen, Erganzungshefte* (Gotha), 22:209-11, 1876.

LOGAN, ROBERT R. (3014)
Early banking in New Mexico. *New Mexico Business Review,* 9:199-214, 1940.

LOWE, PERCIVAL G. (3015)
Five years a dragoon ('49 to '54); and other adventures on the great plains. Kansas City, Franklin Hudson Pub. Co., 1906.

LOYOLA, SISTER MARY (3016)
The American occupation of New Mexico, 1821-52. *NMHR,* 14: 34-75, 143-99, 230-86, 1939. *Also* Historical Society of New Mexico, Publications in History, v. 8. Albuquerque, 1939.

——— (3017)
New Mexico as a factor in the westward movement. *American Historical Association, Pacific Coast Branch, Proceedings, 1930.* pp. 174-84.

LYNN, BRIGHT (3018)
Government land. Unpub. ms. in files of New Mexico Writers' Project, Santa Fe.
Tales of early settlers.

——— (3019)
Wetherill's death. Unpub. ms. in files of New Mexico Writers' Project, Santa Fe.
Killing of a settler by the Indians.

MCCALL, GEORGE A. (3020)
Report of the Secretary of War communicating Colonel McCall's report in relation to New Mexico. Senate Exec. Doc. 26, 31st Congress, 2nd Session. Washington, GPO, 1850.
Conditions in New Mexico, 1849-50.

MCCLENDON, R. EARL (3021)
Daniel Webster and Mexican relations: the Santa Fe prisoners. *Southwestern Historical Quarterly,* 36:288-311, 1933.

MCCORMICK, WILFRED (3022)
The burro freighters. *NM*, 11:20-21, Feb. 1933.

MCCOY, JOSEPH G. (3023)
Historic sketches of the cattle trails of the West and Southwest.
Washington, Rare Book Shop, 1932. *Also* Ralph P. Bieber, Editor,
Glendale, Clark, 1940.

MCELROY, ROBERT MCNUTT (3024)
The winning of the far West. New York, Putnam, 1914.

MCINTYRE, JOHN T. (3025)
In the Rockies with Kit Carson. Philadelphia, Penn Pub. Co.,
1913.

MCKEE, JAMES COOPER (3026)
*Narrative of the surrender of a command of United States forces
at Fort Fillmore, New Mexico.* New York, n. p., 1881. *Also* Boston,
J. A. Lowell & Co., 1886.

MCKENNA, JAMES A. (3027)
*Black range tales; chronicling sixty years of life and adventure
in the Southwest.* New York, Wilson-Erickson, 1936.

MCKINNAN, BESS (3028)
The toll road over Raton Pass. *NMHR*, 2:83-89, 1927.

MCMURTRIE, DOUGLAS C. (3029)
Some supplementary New Mexican imprints, 1850-60. *NMHR*, 7:
165-75, 1932.

MACOMB, J. N. (3030)
*Report of the exploring expedition from Santa Fe, New Mexico,
to the junction of the Grand and Green Rivers of the great Colorado of the West, in 1859.* Engineer Department, U. S. Army.
Washington, GPO, 1876.

MAJORS, ALEXANDER (3031)
Seventy years on the frontier. Chicago, Rand McNally, 1893.

MALIN, JAMES C. (3032)
Indian policy and westward expansion. University of Kansas,
Humanistic studies, v. 2, no. 3. Lawrence, 1921.

MANNING, BERTHA BALLARD (3033)
Child friend of Billy the Kid. Unpub. ms. in files of New Mexico
Writers' Project, Santa Fe.

MANNING, WILLIAM R. (3034)
Diplomacy concerning the Santa Fe road. *Mississippi Valley Historical Review*, 1:516-31, 1915.

MANYPENNY, GEORGE W. (3034a)
Our Indian wards. Cincinnati, 1880.
Military campaigns against the Indians, including those of New Mexico.

MARCY, RANDOLPH B. (3035)
The prairie traveller; a hand-book for overland expeditions . . .
London, Trubner & Co., 1863. *Also* New York, Harper, 1861.

MARCY, RANDOLPH B. (Continued) (3036)
Report on the route from Fort Smith to Santa Fe. House Exec.
Doc. 45, 31st Congress, 1st Session. Washington, GPO, 1850.
——— (3037)
Thirty years of army life on the border . . . New York, Harper,
1866.

MARSHALL, THOMAS MAITLAND (3038)
Commercial aspects of the Texas-Santa Fe expedition. *Southwest-
ern Historical Quarterly,* 20:242-59, 1917.
——— (3039)
St. Vrain's expedition to the Gila in 1826. *Southwestern Historical
Quarterly,* 19:251-60, 1916.

MARTINEZ, REYES N. (3040)
The first phonograph. Unpub. ms. in files of New Mexico Writers'
Project, Santa Fe.
The first phonograph brought to Taos.

MAURY, GENERAL DABNEY H. (3041)
*Recollections of a Virginian in the Mexican, Indian, and Civil
wars.* New York, Scribners, 1894.

MAUZY, WAYNE (3042)
Western stage coach days. *EP,* 39:33-42, 1935.

MAXWELL, GRANT (3043)
Course of empire. *NM,* 16:18-19, 34, 36, 38, Oct. 1938.
Taking over of Mesilla by the U. S.
——— (3044)
Sentinels on the frontier. *NM,* 18:13-15, 39, 41-42, Sept. 1940.
Report of Col. Mansfield on early New Mexico, the forts, the people, some
customs and problems.

MAYFIELD, THOMAS J., JR. (3045)
*The development of the public schools in New Mexico between
1848 and 1900.* Unpub. Master's thesis, UNM, 1938.

MAZZANOVICH, ANTON (3046)
Trailing Geronimo. Los Angeles, Gem Pub. Co., 1926.

MEADER, JOHN R. (3047)
Little wars of the republic. *Americana,* v. 6, pt. 15, 1910.
The revolt in New Mexico.

MELINE, JAMES FLORANT (3048)
*Two thousand miles on horseback; a summer tour to the plains,
the Rocky Mountains, and New Mexico.* New York, Catholic Pub.
Co., 1873.

MERK, FREDERICK, ED. (3049)
*Fur trade and empire; George Simpson's journal 1824-25, together
with accompanying documents.* Harvard Historical Studies, v. 31.
Cambridge, 1935.

METHVIN, REV. J. (3049a)
Andele, or the Mexican-Kiowa captive: life among the Indians.
Louisville, 1899.
Adventures of Andres Martinez, captured by Mescaleros near Las Vegas and
sold to the Kiowa.

MEYERCORD, MADELINE   (3050)
Oliver Loving, pioneer drover of Texas. *SR*, 21:261-77, 1936.

MILES, NELSON A.   (3051)
Personal recollections and observations of General Nelson A. Miles . . . Chicago, Werner, 1896.

MILLER, CHARLES DE WITTE   (3052)
New Mexico during the Civil War. Unpub. Bachelor's thesis, NMSC, 1906.

MOLLHAUSEN, BALDWIN   (3053)
Diary of a journey from the Mississippi to the coasts of the Pacific. London, Longman, Brown, Green, Longman, & Roberts, 1858.

MONTOYA, SAMUEL   (3054)
A buffalo hunt. Unpub. ms. in files of New Mexico Writers' Project, Santa Fe.

MOORE, RICHARD ROY WOODS   (3055)
The role of the Baron de Bastrop in the Anglo-American settlement of the Spanish Southwest. Unpub. Master's thesis, University of Texas, 1932.

MOREHOUSE, GEORGE P.   (3056)
An historical trail through the American Southwest. *Journal of American History*, 3:461-70, 1909.

MOSLEY, MRS. BENTON   (3057)
Captain Arrington at Ranger Lake. Unpub. ms. in files of New Mexico Writers' Project, Santa Fe.
     Discovery of the lake.

——————   (3058)
A last steal: pioneer story. Unpub. ms. in files of New Mexico Writers' Project, Santa Fe.

——————   (3059)
Our predecessors; Indians of the plains. Unpub. ms. in files of New Mexico Writers' Project, Santa Fe.

MOTE, O. S.   (3060)
Reminiscent of the frontier days of Raton, New Mexico. *Santa Fe Magazine*, 7:61-62, Oct. 1913.

MUMEY, NOLIE   (3061)
The life of Jim Baker, 1818-98; trapper, scout, guide, and Indian fighter. Denver, World Press, 1931.

NEVINS, ALLAN   (3062)
Fremont, the world's greatest adventurer. 2 v. New York, Harper, 1928.

NICKOLL, EDITH M.   (3063)
Observations of a ranch woman in New Mexico. New York, Macmillan, 1898.

NUSBAUM, MARK E. (3064)
Tom-toms and tomahawks. *NM*, 11:20-21, 47, Dec. 1933.
Old Fort Selden.

O'CONNOR, THOMAS F., ED. (3064a)
Narratives of a missionary journey to New Mexico in 1867. *Mid-America*, 8:63-67, 1937.

OGLE, RALPH H. (3065)
Federal control of the western Apaches, 1848-86. *NMHR*, 14:309-45, 1939; 15:12-71, 188-248, 269-335, 1940. *Also* Doctor's dissertation, Columbia, 1940 and Historical Society of New Mexico, Publications in History, v. 9. Albuquerque, UNM Press, 1940.

O'NEIL, JAMES B. (3066)
They die but once. New York, Knight Publications, 1935.
Biography of Jeff Ake, Southwestern pioneer.

OTERO, MIGUEL (3066a)
The Indian depredations in the Territory of New Mexico. Washington, 1859.

—— (3067)
My life on the frontier. New York, Press of the Pioneers, 1935-39.

—— (3068)
My nine years as governor of the Territory of New Mexico, 1897-1906. Albuquerque, UNM Press, 1940.

—— (3069)
The real Billy the Kid. New York, Rufus Wilson Inc., 1936.

OWENS, SISTER MARY L. (3070)
The history of the sisters of Loretto in the trans-Mississippi West ... Unpub. Doctor's dissertation, St. Louis University, 1935.

OWENS, SISTER M. LILLIANA (3071)
Joseph Projectus Machebeuf. *NMHR*, 12:193-203, 1937.
Pioneer New Mexican priest.

—— (3072)
Our Lady of Light Academy, Santa Fe. *NMHR*, 13:129-45, 1938.

PACIFIC RAILROAD SURVEYS (3073)
Reports of explorations and surveys to ascertain the most practicable and economical route for a railroad from the Mississippi River to the Pacific Ocean, made under the direction of the Secretary of War, 1853-56. 12 v. Washington, GPO, 1855-60.
Considerable information on conditions in New Mexico included.

PANCOAST, C. L. (3074)
Naming towns on the New Mexico division. *Santa Fe Magazine*, 4:33-37, July 1910.

PARKE, J. G. (3075)
Report of explorations ... from Dona Ana to the Pima villages.
Serial set 792, Document 91. Washington, GPO, 1855.

PARKER, SAMUEL (3076)
Journal of an exploring tour beyond the Rocky mountains.
Ithaca, New York, Mack, Andrus & Woodruff, 1844.

PARKER, WILLIAM THORNTON   (3077)
   Annals of old Fort Cummings, New Mexico, 1867-68. Northamp-
   ton, Massachusetts, the Author, 1916. *Also* Northampton, Gazette
   Printing Co., 1925.

PARSONS, EDWARD   (3078)
   Recollections of my life in New Mexico during the eighties.
   Santa Fe Magazine, 14:23-31, May 1920.

PATTERSON, W. L.   (3079)
   A mine for two barrels of water. Unpub. ms. in files of New
   Mexico Writers' Project, Santa Fe.

————   (3080)
   The old Barber House. Unpub. ms. in files of New Mexico Writers' Project, Santa Fe.
         Story of Mrs. Susan Barber, cattle queen of New Mexico.

PATTIE, JAMES O.   (3081)
   The personal narrative of James O. Pattie of Kentucky. Edited by
   Timothy Fling. Chicago, Donnelley, 1930.

PAXON, F. L.   (3082)
   The cow country. *American Historical Review,* 22:65-82, 1916.

————   (3083)
   History of the American frontier, 1763-1893. Boston, Houghton
   Mifflin, 1924.

————   (3084)
   The last American frontier. New York, Macmillan, 1930.
         Includes a chapter on the Santa Fe trail.

PEABODY, O. W. B.   (3085)
   Kendall's expedition to Santa Fe. *North American Review,* 60:
   196, 1845.

PELZER, LOUIS   (3086)
   *The cattlemen's frontier; a record of the trans-Mississippi cattle
   industry from oxen trains to pooling companies, 1850-90.* Glendale, Clark, 1936.

PERRINE, FRED S.   (3087)
   Military escorts on the Santa Fe trail. *NMHR,* 2:175-93, 269-
   304, 1927.

————   (3088)
   Uncle Sam's camel corps. *NMHR,* 1:434-44, 1926.

PETERS, DEWITT C.   (3089)
   Kit Carson's life and adventures from facts narrated by himself.
   Hartford, Dustin, Gilman & Co., 1875.

————   (3090)
   Life and adventures of Kit Carson. New York, Clark & Co., 1863.

————   (3091)
   Pioneer life and frontier adventures. Boston, Estes and Lauriat,
   1881.
         Kit Carson.

PETTIS, GEORGE H. (3092)
The California column. Historical Society of New Mexico, Publication 11. Santa Fe, 1908.

───── (3093)
Carson's fight with the Comanches at Adobe Walls. Historical Society of New Mexico, Publication 12. Santa Fe, 1908.

PEYTON, JOHN LEWIS (3094)
The adventures of my grandfather. London, J. Wilson, 1867.

PIKE, ZEBULON MONTGOMERY (3095)
An account of expeditions to the sources of the Mississippi . . . and a tour through the interior parts of New Spain, 1807. Edited by E. Coues. New York, 1895.

───── (3096)
Exploratory travels through the western territories of North America . . . London, Paternoster Row, 1811. *Also* Denver, Lawrence & Co., 1889.

───── (3097)
Southwestern expedition of Zebulon M. Pike. Edited by M. M. Quaife. Chicago, Donnelley, 1925.

POE, JOHN W. (3098)
The death of Billy the Kid. New York, Houghton Mifflin, 1933.

POE, SOPHIE A. (3099)
Buckboard days. Caldwell, Idaho, Caxton Printers, 1936.

POPE, JOHN (3100)
Report of exploration of a route for the Pacific railroad, near the 32nd parallel of north latitude from the Red River to the Rio Grande. Washington, GPO, 1854.

PORTER, HENRY M. (3101)
Pencilings of an early western pioneer. Denver, World Press, 1929.

POTTER, COLONEL JACK (3102)
Cattle trails of the old West. Clayton, New Mexico, Laura R. Krehbiel, 1935.

───── (3103)
Lead steer and other tales . . . Clayton, New Mexico, Leader Press, 1939.

POTTER, COLONEL JACK AND HODGES, CARRIE L. (3104)
Dragging a big loop. Unpub. ms. in files of New Mexico Writers' Project, Santa Fe.

POWELL, H. M. T. (3105)
The Santa Fe trail to California, 1849-52. Edited by Douglas S. Watson. San Francisco, Book Club of California, 1931.

POWERS, STEPHEN (3106)
Afoot and alone; a walk from sea to sea . . . Hartford, Columbian Book Co., 1872.

PRINCE, L. BRADFORD AND IRWIN, J. N.   (3106a)
  Claims to statehood. *North American Review*, 156:346-58, 1893.
RABER, CHARLES   (3107)
  Personal recollections of life on the plains from 1860-68. *Kansas State Historical Society, Collections*, 16:316-41, 1925.
RAGSDALE, KATHERINE   (3108)
  The old R. M. Gilbert ranch. Unpub. ms. in files of New Mexico Writers' Project, Santa Fe.
      A stage station during Lincoln County war.

————   (3109)
  Pioneer story: Billy the Kid. Unpub. ms. in files of New Mexico Writers' Project, Santa Fe.
RAINE, WILLIAM MACLEOD   (3110)
  Famous sheriffs and western outlaws. Garden City, Doubleday Doran, 1929.
RAINE, WILLIAM MACLEOD AND BARNES, WILL C.   (3111)
  Cattle. Garden City, Doubleday Doran, 1930.

————   (3112)
  Cattle, cowboys, and rangers. New York, Grosset, 1930.
      Originally published under title *Cattle.*
RAINES, LESTER   (3113)
  The laxative of the stranger. Unpub. ms. in files of New Mexico Writers' Project, Santa Fe.
      How early settlers discouraged the visits of begging Indians.
————   (3114)
  A wild horse hunt. Unpub. ms. in files of New Mexico Writers' Project, Santa Fe.
RANCK, J. E.   (3114a)
  Petition for recovery of property taken or destroyed by the Apache Indians on the Rio Azul in 1869. Washington, 1891.
READ, BENJAMIN MAURICE   (3115)
  Perils of the Santa Fe trail in its early days, 1822-52. EP, 19:206-11, 1925.
REDFIELD, GEORGIA B.   (3116)
  Battle at Blazer's Mill. Unpub. ms. in files of New Mexico Writers' Project, Santa Fe.

————   (3117)
  Outlaw shooting in old Lincoln. Unpub. ms. in files of New Mexico Writers' Project, Santa Fe.
REICH, BETTY   (3118)
  Indian tricks and early life of Billy the Kid. Unpub. ms. in files of New Mexico Writers' Project, Santa Fe.

————   (3119)
  Pioneer stories. Unpub. ms. in files of New Mexico Writers' Project, Santa Fe.
      Attacks by Geronimo and his band of Apaches.

REMINGTON, FREDERIC (3120)
Pony tracks. New York, Harper, 1895.
Travel description.

RENCHER, GOV. A. (3120a)
Indian disturbances in the Territory of New Mexico . . . Washington, 1860.
Twelve reports, covering period from Jan. 3, 1858 to Nov. 10, 1860, on depredations by Comanches, Navajos, Utes.

RHODES, MAY D. (3121)
Frontier memoir. NM, 20:22, 37-38, Aug. 1942.
Nursing in Tularosa.

RICHARDSON, RUPERT NORVAL (3122)
The Comanche barrier to south plains settlement; a century and a half of savage resistance to the advancing white frontier. Glendale, Clark, 1933.

RICKETTS, ORVAL (3123)
Frontier Farmington. NM, 20:20, 37, 39, Sept. 1942.

RIDEING, WILLIAM H. (3124)
A-saddle in the wild West. New York, Appleton, 1879.

RIPPY, J. FRED (3125)
Boundary of New Mexico and the Gadsden Treaty. *Hispanic American Historical Review,* 4:715-42, 1921.

——— (3125a)
The Indians of the Southwest in the diplomacy of the United States and Mexico, 1848-1853. *Hispanic American Historical Review,* 2:363-96, 1919.

——— (3125b)
The negotiation of the Gadsden Treaty. *Southwestern Historical Quarterly,* 27:1-26, 1923-24.

——— (3125c)
A ray of light on the Gadsden Treaty. *Southwestern Historical Quarterly,* 24:235-42, 1920-21.

RISTER, CARL COKE (3126)
Harmful practices of Indian traders of the Southwest, 1865-76. *NMHR,* 6:231-48, 1931. *Also* Santa Fe, Historical Society of New Mexico, 1931.

——— (3127)
Outlaws and vigilantes of the southern plains, 1865-85. *Mississippi Valley Historical Review,* 19:537-54, 1933.

——— (3128)
Southern plainsmen. Norman, UOP, 1938.

——— (3129)
Southwestern frontier, 1865-81; an history of its development and disappearance. Cleveland, Clark, 1928.

ROBERTS, B. H. (3130)
The Mormon Battalion; its history and achievements. Salt Lake City, Deseret News, 1919.

ROBINSON, JACOB S.   (3131)
Journal of the Santa Fe expedition under Colonel Doniphan.
Princeton, Princeton University Press, 1932.

ROLLINS, PHILIP ASHTON   (3132)
*The cowboy; his equipment and his part in the development of
the West.* New York, Scribners, 1936.

ROTHROCK, JOSEPH TRUMBULL   (3133)
Notes on Colorado-New Mexico; notes on economic botany. U. S.
War Department, Geographic Survey of the Western 100th Meri-
dian, Report, v. 6. Washington, GPO, 1878.

ROWLAND, BUFORD, ED.   (3134)
Report of the Commissioners on the road from Missouri to New
Mexico, October 1827. *NMHR,* 14:213-29, 1939.

RUFFNER, E.   (3135)
*Report relative to lines of communication between southern
Colorado and northern New Mexico.* House Exec. Doc. 172, 44th
Congress, 1st Session. Washington, GPO, 1876.

RUXTON, GEORGE F. A.   (3136)
Adventures in Mexico and the Rocky Mountains. London, J.
Murray, 1847 and 1849. *Also* New York, Harper, 1848.

——   (3137)
In the old West. New York, Macmillan, 1924. *Also* New York,
Outing, 1915.
    A series of trapper stories including a number of references to New Mexico.

——   (3138)
Wild life in the Rocky Mountains . . . New York, Outing, 1916.

RYUS, WILLIAM H.   (3139)
The second William Penn . . . Kansas City, F. T. Riley, 1913.
    Santa Fe trail in the '60's.

SABIN, EDWIN LEGRAND   (3140)
Kit Carson days, 1809-1868. 2 v. New York, Pioneer Press, 1935.

SAGE, RUFUS B.   (3141)
Scenes in the Rocky Mountains. Philadelphia, Carey & Hart, 1847.

——   (3142)
*Wild scenes in Kansas and Nebraska, the Rocky Mountains, Ore-
gon, California, New Mexico, Texas, and the grand prairies . . .*
Philadelphia, G. D. Miller, 1855.

SAMPSON, F. A., ED.   (3142a)
Santa Fe trail: M. M. Marmaduke journal. *Missouri Historical
Review,* 6:1-10, 1911-12.

SANTEE, J. F.   (3143)
The battle of La Glorieta pass. *NMHR,* 6:66-75, 1931.

SCHOOLCRAFT, HENRY ROWE   (3144)
*Personal memoirs of a residence of thirty years with the Indian
tribes of the American frontiers: with brief notices of passing
events, facts, and opinions, 1812-42.* Philadelphia, Lippincott,
1842.

SCHOOLCRAFT, HENRY ROWE (Continued) (3145)
Western scenes and reminiscences: together with thrilling legends and traditions of the red man of the forest; to which is added several narratives of adventures among the Indians. Auburn, New York, Derby & Miller, 1853.

SCURRY, W. R. (3146)
Military operations along the Rio Grande. *Southern Historical Society, Papers,* 18:318, 1887.

SEGALE, SISTER BLANDINA (3147)
At the end of the Santa Fe trail. Columbus, Ohio, Columbian Press, 1932.
    Journal of a Sister of Charity in Santa Fe and Albuquerque in 1880's.

SEYMOUR, FLORA WARREN (3148)
Indian agents of the old frontier. New York, Appleton-Century, 1941.

SHUTZ, MR. (3149)
Billy the Kid and Lincoln County war days. Unpub. ms. in files of New Mexico Writers' Project, Santa Fe.

SIMPSON, J. H. (3150)
Journal of a military reconnaissance from Santa Fe, New Mexico, to the Navajo country made with troops under command of Brevet Lieutenant Colonel John M. Washington ... Senate Exec. Doc. 64, 31st Congress, 1st Session. Philadelphia, Lippincott, 1852.

———— (3151)
Narrative of a tour in the Navaho country in 1849. *Minnesota Historical Society, Annals.* St. Paul, 1852.

———— (3152)
Report of an expedition into the Navajo country in 1849. Senate Doc. 64, 31st Congress, 1st Session. Washington, GPO, 1850.

———— (3153)
The route from Fort Smith to Santa Fe. House Exec. Doc. 45, 31st Congress, 1st Session. Washington, GPO, 1850.

SIMPSON, MRS. R. T. F. (3154)
Frontier life and characters: Old man Saunderson. Unpub. ms. in files of New Mexico Writers' Project, Santa Fe.

———— (3155)
Pioneer history and reminiscences. Unpub. ms. in files of New Mexico Writers' Project, Santa Fe.
    San Juan Basin.

———— (3156)
Reminiscences of Mr. Joe Prewitt. Unpub. ms. in files of New Mexico Writers' Project, Santa Fe.
    Early history of Farmington.

SINCLAIR, JOHN L. (3157)
Major Murphy's mansion. *NM,* 19:20-21, 41-42, July 1941.
    History of Lincoln County, including the war.

SIRINGO, CHARLES A. (3158)
History of Billy the Kid. n. p., the Author, 1920.

SITGREAVES, CAPTAIN CHARLES L.   (3159)
   Report of an expedition down the Zuni and Colorado Rivers.
   Senate Exec. Doc. 64, 32nd Congress, 2nd Session. Washington,
   GPO, 1850.

SLIGH, J. E.   (3160)
   Lincoln County war. *Overland,* n. s., 52:168-74, 1908.

SMITH, JANET   (3161)
   Pioneer stories. Unpub. ms. in files of New Mexico Writers' Project, Santa Fe.
        Santa Fe in Bishop Lamy's time.

SMITH, WILBUR   (3162)
   The amigo of Billy the Kid. *NM,* 11:26-27, 47-48, April 1933.

SMITHSON, J. VERNON   (3163)
   Billy the Kid's grave. Unpub. ms. in files of New Mexico Writers'
   Project, Santa Fe.

————   (3164)
   De Baca County history. Unpub. ms. in files of New Mexico
   Writers' Project, Santa Fe.
        Billy the Kid.

————   (3165)
   Old timer's tales. Unpub. ms. in files of New Mexico Writers'
   Project, Santa Fe.
        Migratory families in New Mexico about 1907.

SPENCER, LILLIAN WHITE   (3166)
   Bright arrow. Unpublished biography of Ouray, chief of the Utes.
   Ms. at UNM Press.
        History of Colorado and northern New Mexico from the Indian point of
        view, 1850-90.

SPIEGELBERG, MRS. WILLIE   (3167)
   A pioneer bride. *EP,* 29:188-90, 1930.
        Description of life in Santa Fe in the '80's.

STEELE, JAMES W.   (3168)
   Among the New Mexicans. *Kansas Magazine,* 1:105-12, Feb. 1872.

————   (3169)
   Frontier army sketches. Chicago, Jansen, McClurg & Co., 1883.
        Border life in Texas and New Mexico.

STEERE, EDWARD   (3170)
   Fort Union; its economic and military history. Unpub. ms. in
   files of the National Park Service, Santa Fe.

STEPHENS, F. F., ED.   (3170a)
   Major Alphonso Wetmore's diary of a journey to Santa Fe, 1828.
   Missouri Historical Review, 8:177-97, 1913-14.

STORRS, AUGUSTUS   (3170b)
   *Answers of Augustus Storrs of Missouri, to certain queries upon
   the origin, present state, and future prospect of trade and inter-
   course between Missouri and the internal provinces of Mexico.*
   Washington, 1825.
        Account of an expedition to Santa Fe and of the situation in New Mexico.

STRAHORN, CARRIE ADELL (3171)
Fifteen thousand miles by stage. New York, Putnam, 1911.

STRATTON, ROYAL B. (3172)
Life among the Indians; or the captivity of the Oatman girls.
San Francisco, Grabhorn Press, 1935.

TAYLOR, ZACHARY (3173)
Message of the President on California and New Mexico. House
Exec. Doc. 17, 31st Congress, 1st Session. Washington, GPO,
1850.

———— (3174)
Message on New Mexico. Senate Exec. Doc. 60, 31st Congress, 1st
Session. Washington, GPO, 1850.

THAYER, WILLIAM MAKEPEACE (3175)
Marvels of the new West. Norwich, Connecticut, Henry Bill Pub.
Co., 1887.

THOMAS, ALFRED B., ED. (3176)
Documents bearing upon the northern frontier of New Mexico,
1818-19. *NMHR*, 4:146-77, 1929. *Also* Santa Fe, Historical Society of New Mexico, 1929.
> Revealing interest taken by Spanish officials in activities of Americans in New
> Mexico.

———— (3177)
The Yellowstone River, James Long, and Spanish reaction to
American intrusion into Spanish dominions, 1818-19. *NMHR*,
4:164-77, 1929.

THOMAS, CYRUS (3178)
*The agricultural and pastoral resources of southern Colorado and
northern New Mexico, condensed from the official report of
Professor Cyrus Thomas, forming part of the report of the Geolo-
gical Survey made to the Secretary of the Interior in 1871.*
London, J. King & Co., 1872.

THOMPSON, ALBERT W. (3179)
Clay Allison, extinguisher of bad men. Unpub., undated ms. in
files of UNM Press.

———— (3180)
I helped raise the Rough Riders. *NMHR*, 14:287-99, 1939.

———— (3181)
In Major Long's footsteps; expedition of 1820. Clayton, New
Mexico, Citizen Publishing Co., 1919.

———— (3182)
Insurrection at Taos. *NM*, 20:18, 30-31, April 1942.

———— (3183)
The story of early Clayton, New Mexico. Clayton, Clayton News,
1933.

THOMPSON, JESSE EDWARD (3184)
Overland staging on the 32nd parallel route in the '50's. *Overland
Monthly*, n. s. 12:289-, Aug., Sept. 1888.

THOMPSON, W. A.   (3185)
Ruins of forts on the Santa Fe trail. *EP*, 12:93-94, 1922.

THOMPSON, WILLIAM   (3186)
On the warpath with Kit Carson. *Lippincott's Monthly Magazine*, 57:555-, April 1896.

THWAITES, REUBEN GOLD, ED.   (3187)
Early western travels, 1748-1846; a series of annotated reprints of some of the best and rarest contemporary volumes of travel, descriptive of the aborigines and social and economic conditions in the middle and far West during the period of early American settlement. 30 v. Cleveland, Clark, 1904.

TIPTON, WILL M.   (3188)
The prince of imposters. *Land of Sunshine*, 8:107-18, 161-70, 1898.
    James Addison Reavis.

TITTMANN, EDWARD D.   (3189)
By order of Richard Campbell. *NMHR*, 3:390-98, 1928.
    Law enforcement in Dona Ana County.

————   (3190)
Confederate courts in New Mexico. *NMHR*, 3:347-56, 1928.

————   (3191)
The first irrigation lawsuit. *NMHR*, 2:363-68, 1927.
    Dispute between Acoma and Laguna in 1855 for water rights.

————   (3192)
The last legal frontier. *NMHR*, 2:219-27, 1927.
    The gradual dominance of English common law over the civil code of Spain in New Mexico.

TOTTY, MRS. FRANCES   (3193)
Billy the Kid. Unpub. ms. in files of New Mexico Writers' Project, Santa Fe.

————   (3194)
Early days in Lincoln County. Unpub. ms. in files of New Mexico Writers' Project, Santa Fe.

————   (3195)
Early days in the Southwest. Unpub. ms. in files of New Mexico Writers' Project, Santa Fe.
    Billy the Kid, Caesar Brock, and others.

TOTTY, MRS. W. C.   (3196)
Billy the Kid. Unpub. ms. in files of New Mexico Writers' Project, Santa Fe.

TWITCHELL, RALPH EMERSON   (3197)
The Confederate invasion of New Mexico, 1861-62. *Old Santa Fe*, 3:5-43, 1916.

————   (3198)
Historical sketch of Governor William Carr Lane. Historical Society of New Mexico, Publication 20. Santa Fe, 1917.

————   (3199)
The history of the military occupation of the Territory of New Mexico from 1846 to 1851, by the Government of the United States. Denver, Smith-Brooks Co., 1909.

TWITCHELL, RALPH EMERSON (Continued) (3200)
The story of the conquest of Santa Fe, New Mexico, and the building of old Fort Marcy. Historical Society of New Mexico, Publication 24. Santa Fe, 1923.

UNITED STATES CONGRESS (3201)
Indian disturbances in the State of New Mexico. House Exec. Doc. 24, 36th Congress, 2nd Session. Washington, GPO, 1861.

——— (3202)
Report on military and Indian affairs. House Exec. Doc. 2, 32nd Congress, 1st Session. Washington, GPO, 1851.
v. 2, pt. 1, pp. 125-36, deals with New Mexico.

VADEN, CLAY W. (3203)
Sadie Orchard, one of New Mexico's women stage drivers. Unpub. ms. in files of New Mexico Writers' Project, Santa Fe.
Hillsboro and vicinity.

VALDEZ, ISMAEL (3204)
Billy the Kid. Unpub. ms. in files of New Mexico Writers' Project Santa Fe.
Blowing up a Fort Sumner store.

VAN CLEAVE, EVRET (3205)
Credit on the Santa Fe trail: business pioneering in Pueblo regions. *Credit and Financial Management*, 41:16-17, Oct. 1939.

VAN TRAMP, JOHN C. (3206)
Prairie and Rocky Mountain adventures or life in the West. Columbus, Ohio, Gilmore & Segner, 1866.

VAN VALKENBURGH, RICHARD (3207)
Captain Red Shirt. *NM*, 19:28, 44-45, July 1941.
Henry Dodge, Navajo agent, killed by Apaches, 1856.

——— (3208)
Kit Carson's calling card. *NM*, 18:12, 37, 39. Sept. 1940.
Incidents in war against the Navajos.

VANDEGRIFT, F. L. (3209)
The old Santa Fe trail. *The Earth*, May 1907.

VESTAL, STANLEY (3210)
Expedition for conquest. *NM*, 16:18-19, 41-42, Jan. 1938.
Kearny's conquest of New Mexico.

——— (3211)
Imitating the Indian. *SR*, 15:444-51, 1930.

——— (3212)
Kit Carson, the happy warrior of the old West. Boston, Houghton Mifflin, 1928.

——— (3213)
Mountain men. Boston, Houghton Mifflin, 1937.
Chapter XIII: Pueblo revolt. Chapter XIV: Taos reconquered.

——— (3214)
Old Santa Fe trail. Boston, Houghton Mifflin, 1939.

VIGIL, JOSE (3214a)
Jose de la Cruz Vigil vs. the Mescalero Apache Indians. n. p., n. d.
Depredations by Apaches with some material on their history.

VINEYARD, HAZEL   (3215)
Trails of the trouper; a historical study of the theater in New Mexico from 1880-1910. Unpub. Master's thesis, UNM, 1941.

VISCHER, WILLIAM LIGHTFOOT   (3216)
A thrilling and truthful history of the Pony Express. Chicago, Rand McNally, 1908.

VOLLMAR, EDWARD   (3216a)
Donato Gasparri, New Mexico-Colorado mission founder. *Mid-America,* 9:96-102, 1938.

WALKER, CHARLES S.   (3217)
Causes of the Confederate invasion of New Mexico. *NMHR,* 8:76-97, 1933.

————   (3218)
Confederate government in Dona Ana County, as shown in the records of the Probate Court, 1861-62. *NMHR,* 6:253-302, 1931.

WALLACE, J. F. AND FRICKEL, GENEVIEVE INGRAM   (3219)
Deep trails in the old West. Unpub. ms. in possession of Mrs. H. B. Frickel, Wichita, Kansas.
> Reminiscences of J. F. Wallace as a cowboy in New Mexico and Texas in 1870's.

WALTER, PAUL A. F.   (3220)
The coming of the railroad. *EP,* 39:2-5, 1935.

————   (3221)
Diary of Sylvester Davis, with introduction. *NMHR,* 6:383-416, 1931.

————   (3222)
The first civil governor of New Mexico under the Stars and Stripes. *NMHR,* 8:98-129, 1933.
> Gov. Charles Bent.

————   (3223)
Governor William Carr Lane. *EP,* 5:35-38, 1918.

WARD, MARGARET B. AND CLARK, ANNA NOLAN   (3224)
Portrait of a pioneer. *NM,* 16:24-25, 37-41, Aug. 1938.
> Story of the Todhunter family.

WARNER, LOUIS H.   (3225)
Archbishop Lamy, an epoch maker. Santa Fe, New Mexican Pub. Co., 1936.

————   (3226)
The Kearny code. *NM,* 13:26, 41, 42. July, 1935.

WASSON, JOSEPH   (3227)
The Southwest in 1880. *NMHR,* 5:263-87, 1930.

WATTS, JOHN S.   (3227a)
Indian depredations in New Mexico [and Arizona]. Washington, Privately Printed, 1858.
> Apaches, Navajos, Utes.

WEBB, JAMES JOSIAH   (3228)
Adventures in the Santa Fe trade. Cleveland, Clark, 1931.

WEBB, JAMES JOSIAH (Continued) (3229)
Adventures in the Santa Fe trade, 1844-47. *NMHR,* 6:313-16, 1931.

——— (3230)
Journal of a Santa Fe trader. Glendale, Clark, 1931.

WEIGHTMAN, R. H. (3231)
Communication of R. H. Weightman. Senate Exec. Doc. 76, 31st Congress, 1st Session. Washington, GPO, 1850.
  Memorial of New Mexico legislature setting forth grievances and asking Congress for their correction.

WELLMAN, PAUL ISELY (3232)
Death in the desert. New York, Macmillan, 1935.
  The fifty year's war for the Southwest, 1822-86.

WHEELER, GEORGE MONTAGUE (3233)
Report upon the geographic surveys west of the 100th meridian, in charge of First Lieutenant George M. Wheeler. 7 v. and 1 supplement. Washington, GPO, 1875-89.

WHEELER, W. E. (3234)
The Indians fight at Loving. Unpub. ms. in files of New Mexico Writers' Project, Santa Fe.

WHIPPLE, A. W., EWBANK, THOMAS, AND TURNER, WILLIAM (3235)
Report upon the Indian tribes. Part 3 of the report of explorations for a railway route near the 35th parallel of north latitude, from the Mississippi River to the Pacific Ocean, by Lieutenant A. W. Whipple and Lieutenant J. C. Ives. Senate Exec. Doc. 78, 32nd Congress, 2nd Session. Washington, GPO, 1856.

WHITE, G. M. (3236)
First election in Portales, New Mexico. Unpub. ms. in files of New Mexico Writers' Project, Santa Fe.

WHITE, LESLIE A., ED. (3237)
Lewis H. Morgan's journal of a trip to southwestern Colorado and New Mexico, June 21 to August 7, 1878. *American Antiquity,* 8:1-26, July 1942.

WILSON, BROWNLOW (3238)
Frontier ranches. *NM,* 15:20-21, 41-43, June 1937.
  History of cattle industry in Colfax County.

WILSON, GORGONIO (3239)
Billy the Kid story. Unpub. ms. in files of New Mexico Writers' Project, Santa Fe.

WILSON, NEIL C. (3240)
Treasure express; epic days of the Wells-Fargo. New York, Macmillan, 1936.

WILSON, RUFUS ROCKWELL (3241)
Out of the West. New York, Press of the Pioneers, 1933.

WISLIZENUS, A. (3242)
Memoir of a tour to northern Mexico, connected with Colonel Doniphan's expedition in 1846 and 1847. Senate Misc. Pub. 26, 30th Congress, 1st Session. Washington, Tippin & Streeper, 1848.

WISTER, OWEN   (3243)
  Redmen and white. New York, Harper, 1896.

WOOD, STANLEY   (3244)
  Over the range to the Golden Gate; a complete tourist's guide. . .
  Chicago, Donnelley & Sons, 1891.

WOOD, JUDGE WILLIAM A.   (3245)
  General Sterling Price; insurrection in New Mexico, 1846-47.
  Magazine of American History, 18:333-35, 1887.

WOODS, HENRY   (3246)
  *Fort Union; the history of New Mexico's most famous military
  fort.* Unpub. ms. in files of National Park Service, Santa Fe.

WOODWARD, ARTHUR   (3247)
  Adventuring to Santa Fe. *NMHR,* 17:288-93, 1942.

WOODWARD, ARTHUR, ED.   (3248)
  Benjamin David Wilson's observations on early days in California
  and New Mexico. *Historical Society of Southern California, Annual Publication,* 16 (1) :74-150, 1934.

WOOTEN, MATTIE LLOYD, ED.   (3249)
  Women tell the story of the Southwest. San Antonio, Naylor Co.,
  1940.

WPA, WRITERS' PROJECT   (3250)
  Lords of the old West. Chicago, A. Whitman, 1942.
        Story of the buffalo.

WYMAN, WALKER D.   (3251)
  Bullwhacking: a prosaic profession peculiar to the great plains.
  NMHR, 7:297-310, 1932.

————   (3252)
  F. X. Aubry: Santa Fe freighter, pathfinder, and explorer.
  NMHR, 7:1-31, 1932.

————   (3253)
  Freighting; a big business on the Santa Fe trail. *Kansas Historical
  Quarterly,* 1:17-27, 1931.

————   (3253a)
  The military phase of Santa Fe freighting, 1846-1865. *Kansas
  Historical Quarterly,* 1:415-28, 1931-32.

WYNKOOP, FRANK M.   (3254)
  He led the way. *NM,* 16:17-19, 36-38, Dec. 1938.
        Kit Carson.

Spanish-Americans and Mexicans

ALLWELL, PATRICK J.   (3255)
  Mexican immigration into the United States. Unpub. Master's
  thesis, University of Missouri, 1928.
        Includes some material on immigration into New Mexico.

AMERICAN GEOGRAPHICAL SOCIETY   (3256)
  Memorial volume of the transcontinental excursion of 1912. New
  York, 1915.
        Mention of the population and Spanish atmosphere of New Mexico.

ANONYMOUS   (3257)
    Alabado del sanctuario. *EP*, 34:33-39, 1933.
       Spanish-American Christmas custom stemming from colonial days.

—————   (3258)
    Los hermanos penitentes. *EP*, 8:3-20, 1920.

—————   (3259)
    Increase of Mexican population in the United States, 1920 to
1930. *Monthly Labor Review*, 37:46-48, July 1933.
       Statistics by regions and states.

—————   (3260)
    New Mexico family names: the name of "Chaves". *EP*, 22:112-16,
1927.
       Traced to Spanish origin.

—————   (3261)
    Results of admission of Mexican laborers under departmental
orders for employment in agricultural pursuits. *Monthly Labor
Review*, 11:221-23, Nov. 1920.

—————   (3262)
    Spanish folk customs. Unpub. mss. in files of New Mexico Writers'
Project, Santa Fe.
       Christmas, Feast of the Magi, St. John's Day, Holy Innocent's Day, New
       Year's Day.

—————   (3263)
    What do we speak? *EP*, 13:130-31, 1922.
       Influence of Spanish language on English usage in New Mexico.

APPLEGATE, FRANK   (3264)
    New Mexican sketches. *Yale Review*, 21:376-92, 1932.
       Tales illustrating personality of Spanish-speaking New Mexicans.

—————   (3265)
    Spanish colonial arts. *EP*, 29:329-32, 1930.
       Furniture, *santos*, etc. Their origin in Spain and transplantation to New
       Spain.

—————   (3266)
    Spanish colonial arts. *Survey*, 66:156-57, 1931.

AUSTIN, MARY   (3267)
    Catholic culture in our Southwest. *Commonweal*, 8:510-12, 544-
46, 572-75, 1928.

—————   (3268)
    Folk plays of the Southwest. *Theatre Arts Monthly*, 17:599-610,
1933.

—————   (3269)
    Mexicans and New Mexico. *Survey*, 66:141-44, 187-90, 1931.
       The influence of Mexican immigration since 1598 on New Mexican cul-
       ture, and an evaluation of cultural elements of the Indian and Spanish
       New Mexicans.

—————   (3270)
    New Mexican Spanish. *Saturday Review of Literature*, 7:930, June
27, 1931.
       Letter answering Oliver La Farge's charge of incorrect Spanish grammar
       in *Starry Adventure*.

AUSTIN, MARY (Continued)   (3271)
New Mexico folk poetry. *EP,* 7:146-50, 1919.

——   (3272)
Rimas infantiles of New Mexico. *SR,* 16:60-64, Oct., 1930.
     An attempt to show through children's poetry that the *poblanos* of Spanish
     New Mexico have a strong mixture of native Indian strain from Mexico.

——   (3273)
Spanish-colonial furnishings in New Mexico. *Antiques,* 23:46-49,
1933.

——   (3274)
Spanish manuscripts in the Southwest. *SR,* 19:402-09, July 1934.
     Discussion of songs, plays, folk tales, proverbs collected by Mary Austin
     and A. L. Campa.

BACA, DON MANUEL C. DE   (3275)
*Historia de Vicente Silva, sus cuarenta bandidos, sus crimenes y
retribuciones.* Las Vegas, La Voz del Pueblo, 1896.

——   (3276)
The history of Vicente Silva and his forty bandits. Las Vegas,
Spanish-American Pub. Co., n. d.

BACA, M.   (3277)
Gabriel Sandoval. Unpub. ms. in files of New Mexico Writers'
Project, Santa Fe.
     Folk tale of his murder.

BACH, M.   (3278)
Los Pastores. *Theatre Arts Monthly,* 24:283-88, 1940.

BAMFORD, EDWIN F.   (3279)
The Mexican casual problem in the Southwest. *Journal of Applied Sociology,* 8:363-71, July 1924.

BARKER, RUTH LAUGHLIN   (3280)
Caballeros. New York, Appleton-Century, 1935.
     Spanish elements in the culture of Santa Fe.

——   (3281)
The craft of Chimayo. *EP,* 28:161-73, 1930.
     Blanket weaving.

——   (3282)
New Mexico witch tales. *Texas Folklore Society, Publications,*
10:62-70, 1932.

BATCHEN, LOU SAGE   (3283)
Folk tales. Unpub. ms. in files of New Mexico Writers' Project,
Santa Fe.
     La Madera; The good samaritan of La Madera; La cita de las brujas; El
     misterio; El hombre alegre; Felicia the witch; The story of la curandera.

——   (3284)
Gold fever in Ojo de la Casa. Unpub. ms. in files of New Mexico
Writers' Project, Santa Fe.
     Mining story.

——   (3285)
El indio viejo. Unpub. ms. in files of New Mexico Writers' Project, Santa Fe.
     Folk customs: wakes, *rezador,* prayers for the dying.

BATCHEN, LOU SAGE (Continued)   (3286)
  Madrecita piedad. Unpub. ms. in files of New Mexico Writers'
  Project, Santa Fe.
      Folk belief in village of Placitas.

_____   (3287)
  Mining stories from Las Placitas; legend of Montezuma Mine.
  Unpub. ms. in files of New Mexico Writers' Project, Santa Fe.

_____   (3288)
  An old native custom: la curandera. Unpub. ms. in files of New
  Mexico Writers' Project, Santa Fe. ·

_____   (3289)
  El Pelon y la Pelona. Unpub. ms. in files of New Mexico Writers'
  Project, Santa Fe.
      Folk tales.

BERG, MANUEL   (3290)
  Folk tales. Unpub. mss. in files of New Mexico Writers' Project,
  Santa Fe.
      The good child and the bad; The hunter; The magic ointment; The twisted
      neck and the black cat.

_____   (3291)
  New Mexico witchcraft. Unpub. ms. in files of New Mexico Writers' Project, Santa Fe.

BLACKMAN, ROBERT D.   (3292)
  The language handicap of Spanish-American children. Unpub.
  Master's thesis, University of Arizona, 1940.

BLOCH, LOUIS   (3293)
  Facts about Mexican immigration before and since the quota
  restriction laws. *Journal of the American Statistical Association,*
  24:50-60, March 1929.
      Breakdown of statistics into states and areas.

BOGARDUS, EMORY S.   (3294)
  The Mexican immigrant. (In *Essentials of Americanization.* Los
  Angeles, Jessie Ray Miller, 1923. pp. 264-71.)

_____   (3295)
  The Mexican immigrant and segregation. *American Journal of
  Sociology,* 36:74-80, July 1930.

_____   (3296)
  The Mexican in the United States. Los Angeles, USC Press, 1934.

BOHANNAN, CHARLES D.   (3297)
  Report on survey of Chacon, New Mexico, community. Made
  under the direction of Prof. C. D. Bohannan, Vice-Dean, School
  of Agriculture, NMSC, August 1927, under the auspices of the
  Board of National Missions of the Presbyterian Church of the
  U. S. A. (Unpub. ms. at the New York office of the Board.)
      A social and economic study.

BOKE, RICHARD L.   (3298)
  Roots in the earth. *New Mexico Quarterly Review,* 11:25-36, 1941.
      Scenario of the movie.

BOULDIN, EDNA   (3299)
  Flames across the hills. *NM,* 15:14-15, Dec. 1937.
    Tortugas Christmas celebration.

BOURKE, JOHN GREGORY   (3300)
  Customs of the Rio Grande. *Land of Sunshine,* 5:168-69, Sept.
  1896.

────   (3301)
  The folk-foods of the Rio Grande Valley and of northern Mexico.
  JAF, 8:41-71, 1895.

────   (3302)
  Notes on the language and folk usages of the Rio Grande Valley.
  JAF, 9:81-115, 1896.
    Information on dress, jewelry, houses, food, courtship and marriage, church
    customs, *penitentes,* amusements.

────   (3303)
  Popular medicine, customs, and superstitions of the Rio Grande.
  JAF, 7:119-46, 1894.

BRESETTE, LINNA E.   (3304)
  Mexicans in the United States. Washington, National Catholic
  Welfare Conference, 1930.

BREWSTER, MELA SEDILLO   (3305)
  *New Mexico weaving and the practical vegetable dyes from
  colonial times.* Unpub. Master's thesis, UNM, 1935.

────   (3306)
  *A practical study of the use of the natural vegetable dyes in New
  Mexico.* UNM Bulletin, San Jose Training School series, v. 2,
  no. 2, 1937.

BROWN, LORIN W.   (3307)
  Compadres y comadres. Unpub. ms. in files of New Mexico Writers' Project, Santa Fe.
    Folk customs, relation and duties of godparents.

────   (3308)
  Comparison of Agua Fria and San Rafael versions of Los Pastores.
  Unpub. ms. in files of New Mexico Writers' Project, Santa Fe.

────   (3309)
  Dia de los inocentes. Unpub. ms. in files of New Mexico Writers'
  Project, Santa Fe.
    Spanish sorrowing and redemption customs.

────   (3310)
  Folk tales. Unpub. ms. in files of New Mexico Writers' Project,
  Santa Fe.
    Witch story; Chilili; Secrets of the Guadalupes; Treasure of New Mexico
    (translation of a document of 1650); The pet magpie; El Inocente; The
    witch doctor; How San Cristobal got its name; Tia Lupe; The Priest's
    cats; Un angelito; Jesus Cristo a caballo; The lion and the man.

────   (3311)
  Nuestra Señora de los Dolores. Unpub. ms. in files of New Mexico
  Writers' Project, Santa Fe.
    Folk custom.

BROWN, LORIN W. (Continued) (3312)
San Luis Gonzaga. Unpub. ms. in files of New Mexico Writers'
Project, Santa Fe.
<blockquote>Feast of the patron saint of the dance.</blockquote>

_____ (3313)
Santa Ines del Campo. Unpub. ms. in files of New Mexico Writers'
Project, Santa Fe.
<blockquote>Patron saint of outdoor people.</blockquote>

_____ (3314)
Se volco la olla. Unpub. ms. in files of New Mexico Writers'
Project, Santa Fe.
<blockquote>Origin of use of face powder.</blockquote>

BRYAN, SAMUEL (3315)
Mexican immigrants in the United States. *Survey,* 28:726-30,
Sept. 1912.

BURNS, JAMES A. (3316)
School days in old Taos. Unpub. ms. in files of the New Mexico
Writers' Project, Santa Fe.

_____ (3317)
Spanish customs. Unpub. ms. in files of New Mexico Writers'
Project, Santa Fe.
<blockquote>Naming of Spanish boys when born on certain days.</blockquote>

BUSHEE, ALICE H. (3318)
Spanish influence in the Southwest. *Hispania,* 6:148-57, 1923.

BUTTS, ONNA BARRETT MILLS (3319)
The history of Los Pastores of Las Cruces, New Mexico. Unpub.
Master's thesis, USC, 1936.

CAMPA, ARTHUR L. (3320)
Chili in New Mexico. *New Mexico Business Review,* 3:61-63,
1934.
<blockquote>Its role in food habits and economy of Spanish-speaking New Mexicans.</blockquote>

_____ (3321)
Los Comanches; a New Mexican folk drama. UNM Bulletin,
Language series, v. 7, no. 1, April 1942.

_____ (3322)
*The folk poetry of New Mexico; a comparative study of Hispanic
traditional ballads and folk songs in New Mexico.* To be published by UNM Press.

_____ (3323)
New Mexican Spanish folk tales. Unpub. Master's thesis, UNM,
1930.

_____ (3324)
The New Mexican Spanish folktheater. *Southern Folklore Quarterly,* 5:127-31, 1941.

_____ (3325)
Sayings and riddles in New Mexico. UNM Bulletin, Language
series, v. 6, no. 2, Sept. 1937.

CAMPA, ARTHUR L. (Continued)   (3326)
Spanish folklore in New Mexico. *New Mexico School Review,*
9:22, Nov. 1929.
> Stresses necessity for taking steps to preserve New Mexican folklore.

――――   (3327)
The Spanish folksong in the Southwest. UNM Bulletin, Language
series, v. 4, no. 1, Nov. 1933.

――――   (3328)
Spanish religious folk theatre in the Spanish Southwest. UNM
Bulletin, Language series v. 5, no. 1, Feb. 1934; v. 5, no. 2, June
1934.

――――   (3329)
Today's troubadors. *NM,* 14:16-17, 49-50, Sept. 1936.

CAMPA, ARTHUR L., ED.   (3330)
New Mexico folkways. Unpub. ms. in files of UNM Press.
> Indian, Spanish, and English folk songs, dances, drama, and stories.

CARTER, ALLEN A.   (3331)
The legend of Tome. Unpub. ms. in files of New Mexico Writers'
Project, Santa Fe.

CASAVANTES, OCTAVIO   (3332)
Mañana melody. *NM,* 13:14-15, 39, Dec. 1935.
> History of the guitar and its importance in Spanish-American culture of
> New Mexico.

CASEY, PEARLE R.   (3333)
Chimayo, the ageless village. *Southwestern Lore,* 1:12-13, March
1936.
> Popular description of the village including remarks on the weaving
> industry.

CASSIDY, INA SIZER   (3334)
Saint Michael stops at Socorro. Unpub. ms. in files of New Mexico
Writers' Project, Santa Fe.

CHAPIN, GENEVIEVE   (3335)
Chair waltz. Unpub. ms. in files of New Mexico Writers' Project,
Santa Fe.
> Folk dance.

――――   (3336)
Folk tales. Unpub. mss. in files of New Mexico Writers' Project,
Santa Fe.
> No calamity like a bad neighbor; Buried treasure; Stories of San Isidro
> and of the Indians of New Mexico.

――――   (3337)
Penitentes. Unpub. ms. in files of New Mexico Writers' Project,
Santa Fe.

――――   (3338)
Spanish proverbs. Unpub. ms. in files of New Mexico Writers'
Project, Santa Fe.

CHEETHAM, F. T.   (3339)
San Geronimo fiesta. *New Mexico Highway Journal,* 7:20-21, 34,
Aug. 1929.

CHEYNEY, S. AND CANDLER, M.   (3340)
Santos: an enigma of American native art. *Parnassus*, 7:22-24,
May 1935.

CLARK, ANNA NOLAN   (3341)
Art of the loom. *NM*, 16:9-11, 35-36, Nov. 1938.
History of Santa Fe weaving.

_____   (3342)
Goodbye to gloom. *NM*, 15:11-13, 54, Aug. 1937.
Santa Fe fiesta.

CLARK, JOE M.   (3343)
Chile for health. *NM*, 19:14-15, 46-47, Sept. 1941.

CLARK, VICTOR S.   (3344)
Mexican labor in the United States. Bureau of Labor, Bulletin
78. Washington, GPO, Sept. 1908.
General discussion of occupations, social conditions.

CLARKE, WALTER   (3345)
Impressions of Mora. *Public Health Nursing*, 26:636-42, 1934.

COAN, MARY W.   (3346)
La corrida del gallo—at Galisteo. *NM*, 11:15-16, 49-50, Dec. 1933.
Amusements at a *fiesta*.

_____   (3347)
Handicraft arts revived. *NM*, 13:14-15, 52, Feb. 1935.
Activities of N. M. State Dept. of Trade and Industrial Education leading
to opening of native market in Santa Fe.

_____   (3348)
*The language difficulty in measuring the intelligence of Spanish-
American students*. Unpub. Master's thesis, UNM, 1927.

COLLINS, HENRY HILL, JR.   (3349)
America's own refugees. Princeton, Princeton University Press,
1941.
Mexicans.

CONDON, DAVE   (3350)
Montezuma, *NM*, 20:12, 32, Nov. 1942.
History of school near Las Vegas, now a seminary for Mexican Catholics.

COSTALES, DIONISIO   (3351)
Spanish games in New Mexico. Unpub. Master's thesis, UNM,
1937.

CUNNINGHAM, BLANCHE   (3352)
A little leche, please. *The Rio Grande Writer*, 1:50-57, Spring
1942.
Dialogues tending to reveal Spanish-American personality.

CURTIS, FAYETTE S., JR.   (3353)
El conejo. *EP*, 6:195-203, 1919.
A Spanish-American drama.

_____   (3354)
Spanish arms and armor in the Southwest. *NMHR*, 2:107-33, 1927.

_____   (3355)
Spanish folk-poetry of the Southwest. *SR*, 10:68-73, Jan. 1925.

CURTIS, FAYETTE S., JR. (Continued)   (3356)
Spanish songs of New Mexico. *Texas Folklore Society, Publications,* 4:18-29, 1925.
> Music included.

DAVIS, WILLIAM WATTS HART   (3357)
The Spaniards in New Mexico. *American Historical Association, Papers,* 3 (1):164-76, 1888. *Also* Doylestown, Pa., 1888.

DEHUFF, ELIZABETH WILLIS   (3358)
Cookery as of old. *NM,* 11:13-14, 45-46, Feb. 1933.
> New Mexican Spanish cookery.

———   (3359)
People of the soil. *NM,* 18:26-27, 44, 46, 48, June 1940.
> Description of rural Spanish-American New Mexicans.

DE LAITTRE, KARL   (3360)
The Mexican laborer and you. *Nation's Business,* 18:44, 104, 106, 108, 110, Nov. 1930.
> Importance of Mexican immigrant in development of the Southwest.

DE LONG, MRS. ELEANOR   (3361)
Superstitions of a mountain town. Unpub. ms. in files of New Mexico Writers' Project, Santa Fe.

DE MIRELES, JOVITA GONZALES   (3362)
Latin Americans. (In Brown, Francis J. and Roucek, Joseph S., Eds.: *Our racial and national minorities; their history, contributions, and present problems.* New York, Prentice-Hall, 1937. pp. 497-509.)
> General social conditions, problems of assimilation. Some mention of New Mexico.

DONNELLY, THOMAS C.   (3363)
The Spanish-speaking American—his political education. Address given at School for the Rio Grande Valley, UNM, April 27-May 1, 1942. To be published by School of Inter-American Affairs in *Proceedings of the School for the Rio Grande Valley.*
> Includes a proposal for the establishment of state scholarships for gifted New Mexican boys and girls so that potential leaders will not be denied opportunities for development.

DRAKE, E. L.   (3364)
Albuquerque and vicinity. Unpub. ms. in files of New Mexico Writers' Project, Santa Fe.
> Folklore and legends.

DUNTON, NELLIE   (3365)
Old Spanish embroidery designs. *School Arts Magazine,* 42 (3): 88, Nov. 1942.

———   (3366)
The Spanish colonial ornament. Philadelphia, Perleberg, 1935.

EGGAN, FRED AND PIJOAN, MICHEL   (3366a)
Some problems in the study of food and nutrition. *America Indigena,* 3:9-22, Jan. 1943.
> Based on cultural backgrounds and physical conditions of Spanish-Americans and Indians.

EGGAN, FRED; PIJOAN, MICHEL; SIEGEL, MORRIS; KING, MARGUERITE; AND
GOUBAUD, ANTONIO (3367)
*Food patterns and body economy in two Spanish-American com-
munities.* To be published by School of Inter-American Affairs.
Nutritional studies of Cundiyo and Cañon de Taos.

EMERY, W. M. (3368)
Christmas day in Clayton. Unpub. ms. in files of New Mexico
Writers' Project, Santa Fe.
Spanish-American customs.

ENGLEKIRK, JOHN E. (3369)
Notes on the repertoire of the New Mexican Spanish folktheater.
Southern Folklore Quarterly, 4:227-37, 1940.

ESPINOSA, AURELIO M. (3370)
Los Comanches. UNM Bulletin, Language series, v. 1, no. 1, Dec.
1907.

——— (3371)
Comparative notes on New Mexican and Mexican Spanish
folktales. *JAF,* 27:211-31, 1914.

——— (3372)
Estudios sobre el español de Nuevo Mejico. Faculdad de Filosofia
y Letras de la Universidad de Buenos Aires, Instituto de Filologia.
Buenos Aires, 1930.

——— (3373)
The field of Spanish folklore in America. *Southern Folklore
Quarterly,* 5:29-35, 1941.

——— (3374)
New Mexican Spanish folklore. *JAF,* 23:395-481, 1910; 24:397-
444, 1911; 26:97-122, 1913; 27:105-47, 1914; 28:315-52, 1915;
29:505-35, 1916.

——— (3375)
Spanish folklore in New Mexico. *NMHR,* 1:135-55, 1926.

——— (3376)
The Spanish language in New Mexico and southern Colorado.
Historical Society of New Mexico, Publication 16. Santa Fe,
1911.

——— (3377)
Speech mixture in New Mexico. (In Stephens, H. Morse and
Bolton, Herbert: *The Pacific Ocean in history.* New York, Mac-
millan, 1917.)

——— (3378)
Studies in New Mexican Spanish. UNM Bulletin, Language series,
v. 1, no. 2, Dec. 1909.

——— (3379)
Traditional Spanish ballads in New Mexico. *Hispania,* 15:89-102,
1932.

ESPINOSA, CARMEN (3380)
Fashions in filigree. *NM,* 17:22-23, 43, Sept. 1939.
History of filigree jewelry in New Mexico.

ESPINOSA, CARMEN (Continued)   (3381)
Untitled, undated ms. on *santos*. In possession of the author,
Santa Fe.

ESPINOSA, GILBERTO   (3382)
*The curate of Taos; the story of the life of Padre Antonio Jose
Martinez and of his times.* Undated ms. at UNM Press.

———   (3383)
New Mexico santos. *NM,* 13:9-11, 43, March; 22-23, 36-37, April;
24-25, May 1935.

ESPINOSA, GILBERTO, TR.   (3384)
Los Comanches. *New Mexico Quarterly,* 1:133-46, 1931.

ESPINOSA, JOSE MANUEL   (3385)
Spanish folk tales from New Mexico. American Folklore Society,
Memoirs, 30. New York, 1937.

ESPINOSA, REGINALDO   (3386)
Canute. *NM,* 11:16-17, 46-48, May 1933.
    Indian-Spanish game.

FERGUSSON, ERNA   (3387)
Mexican cook book. Santa Fe, Rydal Press, 1924.

———   (3388)
New Mexico's New Mexicans. *Century,* 116:437-44, 1928.

———   (3389)
Taos sketches. *SR,* 17:188-98, Jan. 1932.
    Sketches illustrating personality of Spanish-speaking people.

FICKINGER, PAUL L.   (3390)
*A study of certain phases of the language problem of Spanish-
American children.* Unpub. Master's thesis, UNM, 1930.

FISH, RUTH G.   (3390a)
Relics of the days of the dons. *Lulac News,* 7:18-19, Oct. 1940.
    Martinez Placita, Taos.

FISHER, REGINALD   (3391)
Hispanic people of the Rio Grande: a statement of a program of
research being planned in the conservation of human resources.
EP, 49:157-62, 1942.
    Includes a brief summary of current socio-economic status of Spanish-
    speaking New Mexicans.

———   (3392)
Notes on the relation of the Franciscans to the Penitentes. *EP,*
48:263-71, 1941.

FORDYCE, KENNETH   (3393)
Easter and Christmas celebrations in New Mexico. Unpub. ms.
in files of New Mexico Writers' Project, Santa Fe.

———   (3394)
Pioneer customs. Unpub. ms. in files of New Mexico Writers'
Project, Santa Fe.
    Northern New Mexico.

———   (3395)
Pioneer Mexican woman. Unpub. ms. in files of New Mexico
Writers' Project, Santa Fe.

FORDYCE, KENNETH (Continued)   (3396)
Las posadas. Unpub. ms. in files of New Mexico Writers' Project,
Santa Fe.
    Spanish customs observed in New Mexico at Christmas.

————   (3397)
Spanish crosses. Unpub. ms. in files of New Mexico Writers'
Project, Santa Fe.
    Spanish-American prayer crosses.

————   (3398)
Spanish-American customs. Unpub. ms. in files of New Mexico
Writers' Project, Santa Fe.
    Funerals: Days of the innocents; Feast of St. Anthony at San Antonio Arriba;
    How flies can be chased out of a house.

FOSTER, THORA ALICE LUTE   (3399)
The folklore of the Mesilla Valley, a contribution to the folklore
of New Mexico. Unpub. Bachelor's thesis, NMSC, 1904.

GALARZA, ERNEST   (3400)
Life in the United States for Mexican people. Out of the experience of a Mexican. National Conference of Social Work, Proceedings, 1929. Chicago, 1930. pp. 399-404.

GAMIO, MANUEL   (3401)
The Mexican immigrant—his life story. Chicago, University of
Chicago Press, 1931.
    Autobiographic documents of Mexicans in the United States.

————   (3402)
Number, origin, and geographic distribution of the Mexican
immigrants in the United States. Institute of Pacific Relations,
1929. Processed.

————   (3403)
Preliminary survey of the antecedents and conditions of the
Mexican immigrant population in the United States and the
formation of a program for a definite and scientific study of the
problem. New York, Social Science Research Council, 1928.

————   (3404)
Quantitative estimate of sources and distribution of Mexican
immigration into the United States. Mexico, D. F., Talleres
Graficos, 1930.

GARTH, THOMAS R.   (3405)
A comparison of the intelligence of Mexican and mixed and full
blood Indian children. Psychological Review, 30:388-401, 1923.

————   (3406)
The intelligence of Mexican school children. School and Society,
27:791-94, 1928.

GIBSON, MARY ELLEN   (3407)
Some important problems in teaching Spanish-culture children.
Unpub. Master's thesis, Texas College of Arts and Industry, 1940.

GONZALEZ, JENNIE M.   (3408)
Christmas in New Mexico. Lulac News, 4:11-12, Dec. 1937.

GOSS, ARTHUR (3409)
Nutrition investigations in New Mexico in 1897. USDA, Bulletin
54. Washington, GPO, 1898.
<small>Includes a dietary study of a Spanish-speaking family with an income of
less than $100 a year.</small>

GRAY, EDWARD D. MCQUEEN (3409a)
*Un recurso nacional en Nuevo Mexico aun no desarrollado; lo
desarrollaremos?* UNM Bulletin, Sociological series, v. 1, no. 3,
1912.

———— (3410)
Spanish language in New Mexico; a national resource. UNM Bulletin, Sociological series, v. 1, no. 2, 1912.

GWIN, J. B. (3411)
Back and forth to Mexico. *Survey,* 39:9-10, Oct. 1917.

———— (3412)
Immigration along our Southwest border. *Annals of the American
Academy of Political and Social Science,* 93:126-30, Jan. 1921.

HAGUE, ELEANOR, TR. (3413)
Spanish-American folk-songs. *JAF,* 24:323-31, 1911. *Also* American Folklore Society, Memoirs, v. 10, 1917.

HALLENBECK, CLEVE AND WILLIAMS, JUANITA H. (3414)
Legends of the Spanish Southwest. Glendale, Clark, 1938.

HALSETH, ODD S. (3415)
The crucifixion. *EP,* 27:298, 1929.

———— (3416)
New Mexico Santos—El angel de la guarda. *EP,* 25:434-35, 1928.

———— (3417)
New Mexico Santos—Nuestra Señora de los Dolores. *EP,* 25:274-
75, 1928.

———— (3418)
New Mexico Santos—San Ignacio de Loyola. *EP,* 25:414-15, 1928.

———— (3419)
New Mexico Santos—San Juan Nepomoceno. *EP,* 25:186-87, 1928.

———— (3420)
New Mexico Santos—San Miguel, Arcangel. *EP,* 25:294-95, 1928.

———— (3421)
Nuestra Señora de Guadalupe. *EP,* 27:246, 1929.

———— (3422)
Nuestra Señora del Carmen. *EP,* 25:314-15, 1928.

———— (3423)
Our lady of Guadalupe. *EP,* 26:69-70, 1929.

———— (3424)
Reina del Cielo. *EP,* 27:296, 1929.

———— (3425)
San Antonio de Padua. *EP,* 25:374-75, 1928.

———— (3426)
San Cristobal. *EP,* 27:130, 1929.

———— (3427)
San Francesco d'Asis. *EP,* 27:158, 1929. Also *EP,* 27:210, 1929.

HALSETH, ODD S. (Continued) (3428)
    San Gregorio. *EP*, 26:203, 1929.

––––– (3429)
    San Jose. *EP*, 26:200, 1929.

––––– (3430)
    San Lazaro Mendigo. *EP*, 26:94, 1929.

––––– (3431)
    San Mateo. *EP*, 27:90, 1929.

––––– (3432)
    San Pedro Apostolo. *EP*, 25:222-23, 1928.

––––– (3433)
    San Rafael, San Miguel, San Gabriel. *EP*, 26:74, 1929.

––––– (3434)
    San Ramon Nonnato. *EP*, 25:394-95, 1928.

––––– (3435)
    Santa Liberada. *EP*, 27:2, 1929.

––––– (3436)
    La Santisima Trinidad. *EP*, 27:94, 1929.

––––– (3437)
    Santo Niño de Atocha. *EP*, 26:130, 1929.

––––– (3438)
    Santos of the Southwest. *EP*, 25:436-39, 1928.

––––– (3439)
    Women saints. *EP*, 37:17-23, 1934.

HANDMAN, MAX S. (3440)
    Economic reasons for the coming of the Mexican immigrant.
    American Journal of Sociology, 35:601-11, Jan. 1930.

HANNA, AGNES K. (3441)
    Social services on the Mexican border. *National Conference of
    Social Work, Proceedings, 1935.* Chicago, 1935. pp. 692-702.

HARROUN, MRS. W. S. (3442)
    The plumed knight. *EP*, 4 (3) :11-17, 1917.
        Spanish-American folktale.

HASSAUREK, F. (3443)
    Four years among Spanish-Americans. London, Sampson Low,
    Son and Marston, 1868.

HAUGHT, B. F. (3444)
    The language difficulty of Spanish-American children. *JAP*, 15:
    92-95, Feb. 1931.

HAWLEY, FLORENCE M. (3445)
    Beyond Taos. *NM*, 19:14-15, 37-39, July 1941.

HAWLEY, FLORENCE AND PIJOAN, MICHEL (3446)
    The Spanish-American school. Unpub. ms. in possession of Dr.
    Pijoan, Albuquerque.

HELLER, C. A. (3446a)
    Regional patterns of dietary deficiency; Spanish-Americans of New
    Mexico. *Annals of the American Academy of Political and Social
    Science*, 225:49-51, Jan. 1943.

HENDERSON, ALICE CORBIN   (3447)
Brothers of light—the Penitentes of the Southwest. New York, Harcourt Brace, 1937.

HENRIQUEZ UREÑA, PEDRO, ED.   (3448)
El español en Mejico, los Estados Unidos y la America Central. Buenos Aires, Instituto de Filologia, Universidad de Buenos Aires, Biblioteca de Dialectologia Americana, v. 4, 1937. *Also Revista Cubana,* 11:147-60, 1937. (Includes Hill, E. C.: El español de Nuevo Mejico.)

HIDALGO, ERNESTO   (3449)
La proteccion de mexicanos en los Estados Unidos. Mexico, Secretaria de Relaciones Exteriores, 1940.

HILL, E. C.   (3450)
New Mexican Spanish. Modern Language Association, Publications, v. 21, no. 3, 1906.

HINOJOS, ROSARIO O.   (3451)
Folk tales. Unpub. mss. in files of New Mexico Writers' Project, Santa Fe.
> The brownies and the old woman; The old hermit; The murder of Tomas Martinez.

———   (3452)
Old time wedding customs. Unpub. ms. in files of New Mexico Writers' Project, Santa Fe.

HOLBROOK, C.   (3452a)
Pedro's land; Spanish-speaking people of New Mexico. *Compressed Air Magazine,* 47:6890-94, Nov. 1942.

HOLT, ALFRED MOSS   (3453)
Dietary study of a Mexican family and a study of the protein factor for beef. Unpub. Master's thesis, NMSC, 1898.

HOME MISSIONS COUNCIL   (3454)
Notes for report of commission on international and interracial factors in the problem of Mexicans in the United States. New York, 1926.

HOOVER, G. E.   (3455)
Our Mexican immigrants. *Foreign Affairs,* 8:99-107, 1929.
> New Mexico cited as an example of failure of Mexican immigrants to assimilate into Anglo culture.

HURT, WESLEY R., JR.   (3456)
Buffalo hunters. *NM,* 19:9, 35-36, Nov. 1941.
> Hunting methods used by Spanish-Americans.

———   (3457)
Indian influence at Manzano. *EP,* 46:245-54, 1939.

———   (3458)
Spanish-American superstitions. *EP,* 47:193-201, 1940.

———   (3459)
Witchcraft in New Mexico. *EP,* 47:73-83, 1940.

JARAMILLO, CLEO M.   (3460)
Cuentos del hogar. El Campo, Texas, Citizen Press, 1939.
> Spanish-American fairy stories.

JARAMILLO, MRS. CLEOFAS M.   . (3461)
    Shadows of the past. Santa Fe, Seton Village Press, 1942.
        Folklore.

JOHANSEN, SIGURD   (3462)
    The social organization of Spanish-American villages. *South-western Social Science Quarterly,* 23:151-59, Sept. 1942.
        Location, type of buildings, economic and social conditions, education, co-operation, disintegration.

JOHNSON, J. B.   (3463)
    The Allelujahs: a religious cult in northern New Mexico. *SR,* 22:131-39, Jan. 1937.

JOHNSON, JAMES WOOD   (3464)
    Spanish America in the Southwest. *Travel,* 80:13-17, 30, Nov. 1942.
        Popular description of Spanish-American culture of New Mexico.

JONES, HESTER   (3465)
    The fiesta of San Geronimo at Taos. *EP,* 31:300-02, 1931.

———   (3466)
    New Mexico embroidered bedspreads. *EP,* 37:97-104, 1934.

KEECH, ROY A.   (3467)
    Children sing in New Mexico. Clarenden, Texas, Clarenden Press, 1941.
        Spanish-American children's songs.

KERCHEVILLE, F. M.   (3468)
    A preliminary glossary of New Mexican Spanish. UNM Bulletin, Language series, v. 5, no. 3, 1934.

KIKER, VESTA   (3469)
    Fiesta at Taos. *NM,* 17:20, 39, Sept. 1939.

KLUCKHOHN, FLORENCE R.   (3470)
    The participant-observer technique in small communities. *American Journal of Sociology,* 46:331-43, 1940.
        Explanation of one of the techniques used to gather material for the study of Los Atarqueños (103).

KNOTT, SARAH GERTRUDE   (3471)
    North of the border; folk festivals of the Southwest. *Survey Graphic,* 29:338-43, 1940.

KOMADINA, TONIA A.   (3472)
    The Spanish folksong in New Mexico. Unpub. Master's thesis, UNM, 1934.

KROMER, JANET SMITH   (3473)
    Witchcraft in Ranchos de Albuquerque. Unpub. ms. in files of New Mexico Writers' Project, Santa Fe.

LAUMBACH, VERNA   (3474)
    Spanish houses. *NM,* 11:20-21, Nov. 1933.

LEIS, WARD WILLIAM   (3475)
    The status of education for Mexican children in four border states. Unpub. Master's thesis, USC, 1932.

LENOIR, PHIL   (3476)
   The hermit of Las Vegas. *Texas Folklore Society, Publications,*
   10:124-26, 1932.

LEONARD, OLEN E.   (3477)
   *The role of the land grant in the social organization and social
   processes of a Spanish-American village in New Mexico.* Unpub.
   Doctor's thesis, Louisiana State University, 1943.
        Based on El Cerrito.

LEYBA, ELY   (3478)
   The church of the twelve apostles. *NM,* 11:19-21, 47-52, June
   1933.
        At Trampas.

LINTHICUM, JOHN BUREN   (3479)
   *The classification of Spanish-American beginners in an Albu-
   querque public school.* Unpub. Master's thesis, USC, 1929.

LOOMIS, CHARLES P.   (3480)
   The development of planned rural communities. *Rural Sociology,*
   3 (4):385-409, 1938.
        Study of the development of an integrated social structure in seven re-
        settlement communities including Bosque Farms and, for purposes of
        comparison, Tortugas.

————   (3481)
   *Wartime migration from the rural Spanish-speaking villages of
   New Mexico.* USDA, BAE, Nov. 24, 1942. Processed. *Also Rural
   Sociology,* 7:384-95, Dec. 1942.
        Statistical treatment of migration from twenty-four New Mexican villages
        showing an average migration of 45 per cent of males between ages 15-65.

LOOMIS, CHARLES P. AND NELLIE H.   (3482)
   Skilled Spanish-American war-industry workers from New Mexico.
   USDA, BAE, Nov. 24, 1942. Processed.
        Of 3500 Spanish-Americans graduated from New Mexico's Vocational Train-
        ing program nearly two-thirds are now located on west coast earning
        average monthly wage of $148.

LOWE, COSETTE CHAVEZ   (3483)
   Dos reales de ay! *NM,* 17:26, 35-37, Aug. 1939.
        Folk tale.

————   (3484)
   Hallowed ground. *NM,* 19:24, 52, Aug. 1941.
        Chimayo legends.

————   (3485)
   El Pelon. *NM,* 16:40, 42, Nov. 1938.
        Folk tale.

LUCERO, ANTONIO   (3486)
   In days of yore (homely virtues of the Spanish-Americans.) *EP,*
   1:1, 3, Jan. 1914.

LUCERO-WHITE, AURORA   (3487)
   El bautismo. Unpub. ms. in files of New Mexico Writers' Project,
   Santa Fe.
        Baptism customs.

————   (3488)
   Casorios. Unpub. ms. in files of New Mexico Writers' Project,
   Santa Fe.
        Wedding customs.

LUCERO-WHITE, AURORA (Continued)   (3489)
    Coloquios de Los Pastores de Las Vegas. Unpub. Master's thesis,
New Mexico Normal (Highlands) University, 1932. *Also* unpub.
ms. in files of New Mexico Writers' Project, Santa Fe.

    ————   (3490)
    The corrido and other poetic compilations of New Mexico.
Unpub. ms. in files of New Mexico Writers' Project, Santa Fe.

    ————   (3491)
    Fiestas in New Mexico. Unpub. ms. in files of New Mexico
Writers' Project, Santa Fe.
        Small village folk and *fiesta* customs.

    ————   (3492)
    Folk dances of the Spanish colonials of New Mexico. Santa Fe,
Santa Fe Press, 1937.

    ————   (3493)
    Folkways. *NM,* 18:16-17, 38-39, Feb. 1940.
        New Mexican Spanish-American and Indian.

    ————   (3494)
    Folkways and fiestas. *NM,* 18:18-19, 44, March 1940.

    ————   (3495)
    Los Moros y Cristianos. Unpub. ms. in files of New Mexico
Writers' Project, Santa Fe.

    ————   (3496)
    Los Pastores. Unpub. ms. in files of New Mexico Writers' Pro-
ject, Santa Fe.

    ————   (3497)
    The Penitentes. Unpub. ms. in files of New Mexico Writers'
Project, Santa Fe.
        Laws, activities, and history.

    ————   (3498)
    Sones puramente nuevo mejicanos. Unpub. ms. in possession of
the author.
        Transcription of twelve unrecorded New Mexican tunes.

    ————   (3499)
    Spanish folklore of New Mexico. Unpub. ms. in files of New
Mexico Writers' Project, Santa Fe.
        History, poetry, *corridos,* romances.

    ————   (3500)
    El velorio. Unpub. ms. in files of New Mexico Writers' Project,
Santa Fe.
        Place of *alabados* in New Mexican folk life.

LUCERO-WHITE, AURORA, COMP.   (3501)
    The folklore of New Mexico. v. 1, Santa Fe, Seton Village Press,
1941. v. 2. unpub. ms. in possession of the author.

LUMMIS, CHARLES F.   (3502)
    An American passion play. *Land of Sunshine,* 4:255-65, 1896.
        Penitentes' ceremonies.

LYNN, BRIGHT   (3503)
    The church bells of processions. Unpub. ms. in files of New
Mexico Writers' Project, Santa Fe.
        Spanish religious customs.

LYNN, BRIGHT (Continued)   (3504)
Costume of the Spanish dons and ladies of the 18th century.
Unpub. ms. in files of New Mexico Writers' Project, Santa Fe.

————   (3505)
Folk beliefs. Unpub. ms. in files of New Mexico Writers' Project,
Santa Fe.

————   (3506)
Folk tales. Unpub. ms. in files of New Mexico Writers' Project,
Santa Fe.
> God helps those who help themselves; The Witches; Sylvestre; The witch of
> old town; The three treasurers; The smoke from which you never return;
> Fearless John; The seven brothers; Marquita la linda; So powerful thou art
> thou hast broken my legs; The four friends; The rat and the ant; St. Peter
> loses the keys of Heaven; The three princesses; Riddles; Your fame is
> greater than your beauty; The bewitched one; Tujuyana; Doloritas; John
> of the Cadenillas; The donkey of St. Benedict; The fortune teller; Enri-
> quito; Asusena; The gloves; Give me my ear; Aparisada; John of Calais;
> Big's suicide; The man who went in search of our Lord; The three negroes;
> Griselda; The little red ant; The rabbit and the toad; Constancia; Billy
> Green; Don't count your chickens before they hatch; Three bags of money;
> The three old women; Aunt Gabriel; El hombre; The enchanted princesses;
> Isabel; The man who owed everybody; The three sisters; The man who
> fooled a village; El Gangozo; The simple old man; Tu que andas parado;
> Good buñuelitos; The promise; The child; The little old lady; Francisquita;
> The bird man.

————   (3507)
A New Mexico pageant of costume. Five unpub. mss. in files of
New Mexico Writers' Project, Santa Fe.
> Old Spanish-American costumes, Oñate and later.

————   (3508)
Peon, vaquero, ranchero, and caballero. Unpub. ms. in files of
New Mexico Writers' Project, Santa Fe.
> Costume and customs.

MCCLUE, JOHN E.   (3509)
The story of the history and outgrowth of the penitente cult.
Unpub. ms. in files of New Mexico Writers' Project, Santa Fe.

MCCOMBS, VERNON MONROE   (3510)
From over the border. New York, Council of Women for Home
Missions, 1925.
> Mexican immigration.

MCGINNIS, JOHN H.   (3511)
Cities and towns of the Southwest: III. Taos. *SR*, 13:36-47, Oct.
1927.

MCGREGOR (PSEUD.)   (3512)
Our Spanish-American fellow citizens. *Harper's Weekly*, 58:6-8,
1914.

MCLEAN, ROBERT N.   (3513)
Goodbye, Vicente! *Survey*, 66:182-83, 195, May 1931.
> The problem of Mexican immigrants.

————   (3514)
The Mexican return. *Nation*, 135:165-66, 1932.

MCLEAN, ROBERT N. (Continued) (3515)
Mexican workers in the United States. *National Conference of Social Work, Proceedings, 1929.* Chicago, 1930. pp. 531-38.

——— (3516)
Tightening the Mexican border. *Survey,* 64:28-29, 54-56, April 1930.

MACMILLAN, JAMES (3517)
Fifteen New Mexico santos. Santa Fe, Libros Escogidos, 1941.

MCSPADDEN, GEORGE (3518)
Some semantic and philological facts of the Spanish spoken in Chilili, New Mexico. Unpub. Master's thesis, UNM, 1934. *Also* UNM Bulletin, Language series, v. 5, no. 3, 1934.

MCWILLIAMS, CAREY (3519)
Employment problems of the Spanish-speaking groups. Address given at School for the Rio Grande Valley, UNM, April 27-May 1, 1942. To be published by School of Inter-American Affairs in *Proceedings of the School for the Rio Grande Valley.*
Deals mainly with situation in California, with some mention of the problems of New Mexico.

——— (3519a)
The forgotten Mexican. *Common Ground,* 3:65-78, Spring 1943.
A condensation of a chapter from a forthcoming book.

MANGRAVITE, PEPPINO (3520)
Saints and a death angel. *Magazine of Art,* 33:160-65, 1940.
Interpretive description of New Mexican *santos.*

MANUEL, H. T. (3521)
The educational problem presented by the Spanish-speaking child of the Southwest. *School and Society,* 40:692-95, 1934. *Also National Education Association, Addresses and Proceedings.* Washington, 1934.

MAREAU, HELENE, HAUSKINS, EUNICE, AND LUCERO-WHITE, AURORA (3522)
Folk dances of the Spanish colonials of New Mexico. n. p., the Authors, 1937.

MARTINEZ, FILEMON T. (3522a)
Conservation and purification of the Spanish language. *Lulac News,* 5:13-18, Nov. 1938.

MARTINEZ, PAUL G. (3523)
Los Comanches, a play celebrated yearly. Unpub. ms. in files of New Mexico Writers' Project, Santa Fe.

——— (3524)
Teaching English to Spanish-speaking Americans in New Mexico. *New Mexico School Review,* 13:22-23, Sept. 1933.

MARTINEZ, REYES N. (3525)
Balse de cadena. Unpub. ms. in files of New Mexico Writers' Project, Santa Fe.
Folk dance.

MARTINEZ, REYES N. (Continued)   (3526)

By sunset. Unpub. ms. in files of New Mexico Writers' Project, Santa Fe.
> A Spanish-American borrowing custom.

_____   (3527)

Candles by the highway. Unpub. ms. in files of New Mexico Writers' Project, Santa Fe.
> *Penitentes.*

_____   (3528)

Community spirit preserved by some religious and social customs. Unpub. ms. in files of New Mexico Writers' Project, Santa Fe.
> Religious customs observed in Taos.

_____   (3529)

The cuna. Unpub. ms. in files of New Mexico Writers' Project, Santa Fe.
> Folk dance.

_____   (3530)

Curious practices. Unpub. ms. in files of New Mexico Writers' Project, Santa Fe.
> Superstitious beliefs of Spanish-Americans.

_____   (3531)

Curious practices and curious beliefs. Unpub. ms. in files of New Mexico Writers' Project, Santa Fe.
> *Penitente* beliefs and customs.

_____   (3532)

Delousing. Unpub. ms. in files of New Mexico Writers' Project, Santa Fe.
> Folk custom.

_____   (3533)

Entertainment of the past. Unpub. ms. in files of New Mexico Writers' Project, Santa Fe.
> *Los titeres* (puppet shows).

_____   (3534)

Fiddle and heel. Unpub. ms. in files of New Mexico Writers' Project, Santa Fe.
> Folk dance.

_____   (3535)

Folk stories. Unpub. mss. in files of New Mexico Writers' Project, Santa Fe.
> Prophecy, murder, and bloody execution; The raid on the granary; A holdup after midnight; El mal hijo; Story of the river of the golden waters; The tree that sings; The bird that talks; The bells on Ute Mountain; Unmasked; The lodge house of the dead; Death makes a hit; El senador; The chimney; Pillows in the windows; The lucky fisherman; El cuento de la mariposa.

_____   (3536)

Foods of the Southwest. Unpub. ms. in files of New Mexico Writers' Project, Santa Fe.

_____   (3537)

El gallo. Unpub. ms. in files of New Mexico Writers' Project, Santa Fe.
> How people announce a dance in a village.

MARTINEZ, REYES N. (Continued)   (3538)
    Gypsy caravans. Unpub. ms. in files of New Mexico Writers'
Project, Santa Fe.
        Arrival of gypsy caravan at small villages.

                                                                   (3539)
    Meager contributions: Spanish customs. Unpub. ms. in files of
New Mexico Writers' Project, Santa Fe.
        Feast of San Roque.

                                                                    (3540)
    Native customs and celebrations: Saint John's day. Unpub. ms.
in files of New Mexico Writers' Project, Santa Fe.
        Taos County.

                                                                    (3541)
    Native group dances. Unpub. ms. in files of New Mexico Writers'
Project, Santa Fe.

                                                                     (3542)
    Native Spanish-American customs. Unpub. ms. in files of New
Mexico Writers' Project, Santa Fe.
        New Year's customs.

                                                                    (3543)
    Native winter pastimes. Unpub. ms. in files of New Mexico
Writers' Project, Santa Fe.
        Spanish-American games.

                                                                    (3544)
    Odd religious practices. Unpub. ms. in files of New Mexico Writ-
ers' Project, Santa Fe.
        Penitentes.

                                                                    (3545)
    An old religious custom: Valerse a la Ave Maria. Unpub. ms.
in files of New Mexico Writers' Project, Santa Fe.

                                                                    (3546)
    Queer beliefs. Unpub. ms. in files of New Mexico Writers' Pro-
ject, Santa Fe.

                                                                    (3547)
    Rural weddings. Unpub. ms. in files of New Mexico Writers'
Project, Santa Fe.
        Spanish-American courtship and marriage procedure.

                                                                    (3548)
    Sheep herders galore. Unpub. ms. in files of New Mexico Writers'
Project, Santa Fe.
        Penitentes in northern New Mexico village.

                                                                    (3549)
    Social life. Unpub. ms. in files of New Mexico Writers' Project,
Santa Fe.
        Games and entertainment.

                                                                    (3550)
    Societies—severity—corruption. Unpub. ms. in files of New Mexico
Writers' Project, Santa Fe.
        Organizations and societies in villages; folk customs.

                                                                    (3551)
    Spanish folk songs and poems. Unpub. mss. in files of New Mexico
Writers' Project, Santa Fe.

MARTINEZ, REYES N. (Continued)   (3552)
Spanish folkways. Unpub. ms. in files of New Mexico Writers'
Project, Santa Fe.
    Native group dances.

————   (3553)
Spanish quadrille. Unpub. ms. in files of New Mexico Writers'
Project, Santa Fe.

————   (3554)
The weaver of Talpa. Unpub. ms. in files of New Mexico Writers'
Project, Santa Fe.
    Description of a Taos County weaver.

MEHRENS, HAROLD E.   (3555)
Los Pastores, a survival of medieval drama. Unpub. Master's thesis, New Mexico Normal (Highlands) University, 1931.

MIERA, GILBERT E.   (3556)
Today is fiesta. *NM*, 18:22-23, 44, June 1940.
    Coronado *fiesta* at Moquino.

MILLER, PEARL CHERRY   (3557)
Mexican cookery. Unpub. Bachelor's thesis, NMSC, 1904.
    Diet and mode of living in New Mexico.

MONTALBO, PHILIP J.   (3557a)
Our rights. *Lulac News,* 5:3-5, Feb. 1938.
    Protest that Spanish-Americans do not have rights guaranteed under Treaty
    of Guadalupe Hidalgo.

MONTOYA, PEDRO AND SENTER, DONOVAN   (3558)
Pedro of Taos. Unpub. ms. in possession of Mr. Senter, Albuquerque.
    Observations on Spanish-American and Anglo cultures in New Mexico by
    a Taoseño who was born into the one and has succeeded in adapting him-
    self to the other. The point of view is non-technical and non-academic,
    but the attitude of the Spanish-American to the encroaching Anglo is
    clearly portrayed. The narrative is in Mr. Montoya's own words as recorded
    by Mr. Senter.

MOORE, REVEREND FRANK L.   (3559)
The penitentes of New Mexico. New York, Congregational Home
Mission Society, n. d.

MORRILL, D. B.   (3560)
The Spanish language problem. *New Mexico Journal of Education,* 14:6-7, May 1918.
    Need for Spanish-speaking children to learn Spanish in elementary schools.

————   (3561)
Teaching the Spanish-American child. *New Mexico Journal of
Education,* 13:8, 10-11, April 1917.
    Protest against teaching Spanish-speaking primary children only in English.

MOYA, BENJAMIN S.   (3562)
*Superstitions and beliefs among the Spanish-speaking people of
New Mexico.* Unpub. Master's thesis, UNM, 1940.

MULKY, CARL   (3563)
Tuberculosis in the Spanish population of New Mexico. *Southwestern Medicine,* 25:165-66, 1941.

MUNRO, EDWIN C. (3564)
The nativity plays of New Mexico. Unpub. Master's thesis, UNM, 1940.

MURDOCH, ALLAN (3565)
Looms of the mountains. *The Santa Fean,* 2:7-9, Summer 1942.
Hand-weaving in northern New Mexico.

NMSC, EXTENSION SERVICE (3566)
Historic cookery from the land of poco tiempo. Extension Circular 161, May 1939.

NEW MEXICO STATE DEPARTMENT OF TRADE AND INDUSTRIAL
EDUCATION (3567)
Spanish colonial painted chests. Santa Fe, 1937. Processed.

NEW MEXICO STATE DEPARTMENT OF VOCATIONAL EDUCATION (3568)
New Mexico colonial embroidery. Santa Fe, 1935. Processed.

——— (3569)
Tin craft in New Mexico. Santa Fe, 1937. Processed.

NEW MEXICO WRITERS', MUSIC, AND ART PROJECTS, WPA (3570)
The Spanish-American song and game book. New York, A. S. Barnes, 1942.

NEW MEXICO WRITERS' PROJECT, WPA (3571)
Alabados. Unpub. collection of more than a hundred *alabados* in files of the New Mexico Writers' Project, Santa Fe.

——— (3572)
Folk plays. Unpub. mss. in the files of New Mexico Writers' Project, Santa Fe.
Various versions of *Los Pastores, Los Moros y los Cristianos, Los Comanches,* and *Los Tres Reyes.*

——— (3573)
Indian, Spanish, and cowboy dances. Unpub. mss. in files of New Mexico Writers' Project, Santa Fe.
Native group dances, *Balse de cadena,* the *Cuna,* Spanish Quadrille, Fiddle and heel, by Reyes Martinez; *Chiquiau,* by N. Howard Thorp; Chair waltz by Genevieve Chapin.

——— (3574)
Spanish folk sayings, riddles, etc. Unpub. mss. in files of New Mexico Writers' Project, Santa Fe.

——— (3575)
Spanish songs and poems. Unpub. mss. in files of New Mexico Writers' Project, Santa Fe.

——— (3576)
Superstitions of the Spanish people. Unpub. ms. in files of New Mexico Writers' Project, Santa Fe.

NEWCOMB, REXFORD (3577)
Spanish colonial architecture in the United States. New York, J. J. Augustin, 1937.
Includes drawings, photographs, measurements, word descriptions of types found in New Mexico.

OTERO, ADELINA   (3578)
My people. *Survey,* 66:149-51, 1931.
        Practical education for the Spanish-speaking Americans and the need to incor-
        porate their arts and crafts into the public school curriculum.

OTERO-WARREN, NINA   (3579)
The clown of San Cristobal. *Survey Graphic,* 24: 16-18, 1935.
        Folk tales of Spanish colonials.

—————   (3580)
Folk tales of the saints. Unpub. ms. in possession of the author.

—————   (3581)
Old Spain in our Southwest. New York, Harcourt Brace, 1936.
        The influence of Spain in New Mexico culture as seen in the day by day
        activities and legends.

—————   (3582)
Spanish Christmas customs. Unpub. ms. in files of New Mexico
Writers' Project, Santa Fe.

OTIS, RAYMOND   (3583)
Medievalism in America. *New Mexico Quarterly,* 6:83-90, 1936.
        History and activities of *penitentes.*

PAGE, MRS. DOROTHY   (3584)
*Performance of Spanish-American children on verbal and non-
verbal intelligence tests.* Unpub. Master's thesis, UNM, 1931.

PHELPS, CARRIE PADON   (3585)
The primitive Mexican home in New Mexico. Unpub. Bachelor's
thesis, NMSC, 1913.
        Furnishings, foods, dress, customs, domestic arts.

PIJOAN, MICHEL, ELKIN, C. A. AND WARREN, ROBERTA   (3586)
*Contrast study in body economy in two Spanish-American vil-
lages.* Unpub. ms. in possession of Dr. Pijoan, Albuquerque.

POOLER, LOLITA H.   (3587)
Cuentos populares españoles de Nuevo Mejico, recojidos. Unpub.
Bachelor's thesis, UNM, 1930.

—————   (3588)
Las posadas. Unpub. ms. in files of New Mexico Writers' Project,
Santa Fe.
        Religious folk drama.

RAEL, JUAN B.   (3589)
Alternate forms in speech of the individual. *Studies in Philology,*
36:664-70, 1939.
        Peculiarities of speech observed in the Spanish-speaking people of northern
        New Mexico and southern Colorado.

—————   (3590)
Cuentos españoles de Colorado y de Nuevo Mejico (Segunda
serie) . *JAF,* 55:1-93, 1942.

—————   (3591)
The theme of the theft of food by playing godfather in New Mexican folklore. *Hispania,* 20:231-34, 1937.

RAINES, LESTER   (3592)
A corrida del gallo at San Jose. Unpub. ms. in files of New Mexico Writers' Project, Santa Fe.

RAINES, LESTER (Continued)   (3593)
La costumbre de la Comida Crusada. Unpub. ms. in files of New
Mexico Writers' Project, Santa Fe.

――――   (3594)
The day of the Manuels. Unpub. ms. in files of New Mexico
Writers' Project, Santa Fe.
 Folk custom honoring all men named Manuel.

――――   (3595)
Early life in Questa. Unpub. ms. in files of New Mexico Writers'
Project, Santa Fe.
 Folk customs.

――――   (3596)
Early settlers of Llano Quemado. Unpub. ms. in files of New
Mexico Writers' Project, Santa Fe.

――――   (3597)
Folk stories. Unpub. ms. in files of New Mexico Writers' Project,
Santa Fe.
 The captive shepherd boy.

――――   (3598)
Lost mines. Unpub. ms. in files of New Mexico Writers' Project,
Santa Fe.
 Lost mine in the Zuni mountains; a folk legend.

――――   (3599)
Los oremus. Unpub. ms. in files of New Mexico Writers' Project,
Santa Fe.
 Custom of Spanish-American children to ask for gifts on Christmas day.

――――   (3600)
Pablo Candelarias of Tinaja. Unpub. ms. in files of New Mexico
Writers' Project, Santa Fe.
 Account of the first settlers of Tinaja.

――――   (3601)
A roulette player. Unpub. ms. in files of New Mexico Writers'
Project, Santa Fe.
 An unusual trade that took place near Taos.

――――   (3602)
Spanish-American festivals and dramas. Unpub. ms. in files of
New Mexico Writers' Project, Santa Fe.

RAPP, MRS. I. H.   (3603)
Los Pastores is gem of miracle plays. *EP,* 11:151-63, 1921.

REAM, GLEN O.   (3604)
A study of Spanish-speaking pupils in Albuquerque High School.
Unpub. Master's thesis, Yale University, 1930.
 Statistical study leading to conclusion that Spanish-speaking pupils do as
 well as Anglos.

REBOLLEDO, ANTONIO   (3605)
Teaching of Spanish in elementary grades. *New Mexico School
Review,* 19:2-3, March 1940.
 Plea for development of bilingualism in the grades.

REDFIELD, GEORGIA B.   (3606)
Spanish folk customs. Unpub. ms. in files of New Mexico Writers'
Project, Santa Fe.
 Religious, social, and other customs of Spanish-Americans in Roswell.

REDFIELD, ROBERT (3607)
   Antecedents of Mexican immigration to the United States. *American Journal of Sociology*, 35:433-38, Nov. 1929.
      Summary of Dr. Manuel Gamio's findings regarding settlement of Mexicans in the United States.

REINDORP, REGINALD (3608)
   The New Mexican decima. Unpub. Master's thesis, UNM, 1933.

REUTER, B. A. (3609)
   Governor Donaciano Vigil's ancestors. Unpub. ms. in files of New Mexico Writers' Project, Santa Fe.

———— (3610)
   The private life of Donaciano Vigil. Unpub. ms. in files of New Mexico Writers' Project, Santa Fe.

———— (3611)
   Will of Donaciano Vigil. Unpub. ms. in files of New Mexico Writers' Project, Santa Fe.

REYNOLDS, ANNIE (3612)
   The education of Spanish-speaking children in five Southwestern states. USDI, Office of Education, Bulletin 11. Washington, GPO, 1933.

ROMERO, CECIL V. (3613)
   Notes on New Mexican Spanish. *EP*, 24:290-95, 1928.

———— (3614)
   Spanish in New Mexico. *EP*, 24:286-87, 1928.

———— (3615)
   A unique American chronicle. *EP*, 24:154-65, 1928.
      The Spanish heritage as found in New Mexico.

ROSS, J. C. (3616)
   Industrial education for the Spanish-speaking people. *New Mexico Journal of Education*, 7:19-21, Feb. 1911.
      Industrial education as a factor in economic assimilation.

ROSS, P. (3617)
   Village of many blessings; a fragment of colonial Spain in New Mexico. *Travel*, 64:35-37, 46, Feb. 1935.
      Chimayo.

ROUSSEAU, MRS. EDNA (3618)
   Is the Spanish-American child handicapped on account of language difficulties? *New Mexico Education Association, Papers, 44th Annual Convention, 1929.*
      Affirmative answer with reasons.

RUSINOW, IRVING (3619)
   A camera report on El Cerrito, a typical Spanish-American community in New Mexico. USDA, BAE, Misc. Pub. 479. Washington, 1942.

———— (3620)
   Spanish-Americans in New Mexico. *Survey Graphic*, 27:95-99, 1938.
      Photographs of Santa Cruz Valley people.

SABIN, EDWIN LEGRAND (3621)
   Mucha fiesta in the Southwest. *Overland*, n. s., 64:426-36, 1914.

SAFONOVA, LUDMILA (3622)
The Russian icon at San Miguel church. *EP*, 35:17-19, 1933.

SANCHEZ, A. M. (3623)
The Spanish-speaking child and the English language. *New Mexico Educational Association Journal and Proceedings, 22nd Annual Meeting, 1907.*

SANCHEZ, GEORGE I. (3624)
The age-grade status of the rural child in New Mexico, 1931-32. New Mexico State Department of Education, Educational Research Bulletin v. 1, no. 1, Nov. 1932.
    Gives degree of retardation of rural school children by counties.

——— (3625)
Group differences and Spanish-speaking children. *JAP*, 16:549-58, 1932.

——— (3626)
Scores of Spanish-speaking children. *Pedagogical Seminary and Journal of Genetic Psychology*, 40:223-31, 1932.

——— (3627)
The Spanish-speaking American: helping him to help himself. Address given at School for the Rio Grande Valley, UNM, April 27-May 1, 1942. To be published by School of Inter-American Affairs in *Proceedings of the School for the Rio Grande Valley.*
    Underlines the need for fitting adult and other education programs to the existing culture base of the Spanish-speaking American.

——— (3628)
A study of the scores of Spanish-speaking children on repeated tests. Unpub. Master's thesis, University of Texas, 1931.

SANTIBAÑEZ, ENRIQUE (3629)
Ensayo acerca de la inmigracion mexicana en los Estados Unidos. San Antonio, Clegg Co., 1930.

SCHRIEKE, B. (3630)
Mexicans and Indians. (In his *Alien Americans.* New York, Viking Press, 1936. pp. 46-69.)
    General discussion. Some mention of New Mexico.

SEDILLO, MELA (3631)
Art without a name. *New Mexico School Review*, 21:6, Jan. 1942.
    Place of crafts in New Mexico life.

——— (3632)
Mexican and New Mexican folk dances. Albuquerque, UNM Press, 1938.

——— (3633)
New Mexico and its dance. *Educational Dance*, 3:7-9, 1940.

SENA, JOSE D. (3634)
The chapel of Don Antonio Jose Ortiz. *NMHR*, 13:347-59, 1938.

——— (3635)
Christmas customs in Spanish-speaking lands. Unpub. ms. in files of New Mexico Writers' Project, Santa Fe.

SENTER, DONOVAN (3636)
Human geography of the Manzano area, New Mexico. Unpub. ms. on file in Department of Anthropology, UNM.

SENTER, DONOVAN (Continued)   (3637)
    *The pilgrims came late. (Tentative title.) Unpub. ms. in posses-
    sion of Mr. Senter, Albuquerque.
        A detailed study of the culture of northern New Mexico Spanish-American
        villages with an appraisal of the degree of acculturation which has taken
        place in several of the communities of the region. Included are discussions of
        agricultural methods and customs, ceremonial and ritual life, house con-
        struction, diet and food habits, economic life, land ownership conflicts, history
        and present status of land grants, cultural changes caused by declining
        resources, religion, social organization, the patron system, family organization,
        child training, marriage, birth and death customs, methods and processes of
        social control, education, arts and crafts, superstition and witchcraft, costumes,
        music, games, plays, entertainments, santos. Numerous case histories are
        used to illustrate the various processes of acculturation. One chapter is
        devoted to a comparison of the Spanish-Americans of New Mexico with the
        Mexicans of El Paso and Southern California. (Received too late to be in-
        cluded in Dictionary-Guide.)

SHARP, D. D.   (3638)
    San Antonio fiesta. Unpub. ms. in files of New Mexico Writers'
    Project, Santa Fe.
        Village celebration.

SHAURT, HARRY E.   (3639)
    Oñate comes back. NM, 11:25-27, 47-49, Aug. 1933.
        Española celebration.

SHONTZ, ORFA JEAN   (3640)
    The land of "poco tiempo." A study in Mexican family relation-
    ships in a changing social environment. The Family, 8:74-79,
    May 1927.

SIEGEL, MORRIS AND KING, MARGUERITE   (3641)
    *The food economy of Cundiyo, a Spanish-American village in New
    Mexico. (In Eggan, Fred, Pijoan, Michel, Siegel, Morris, King,
    Marguerite, and Goubaud, Antonio. Food patterns and body
    economy in two Spanish-American communities. To be published
    by School of Inter-American Affairs.)
        Although centered primarily around the sociology of food, this is an excel-
        lent study of the entire cultural picture of Cundiyo, including the degree to
        which it has been modified in recent years by contacts with Anglo civilization.
        Preceding the detailed treatment of the production, preservation, preparation,
        and consumption of foods in Cundiyo, is a general discussion of the village
        and of its economy. The relationship of food and food habits to the entire
        cultural pattern is stressed.

SIFUENTES, FERNANDO   (3642)
    Comparative study of New Mexican and Mexican popular songs.
    Unpub. Master's thesis, UNM, 1940.

SIMPICH, FREDERICK   (3643)
    Along our side of the Mexican border. National Geographic, 56:
    61-80, July 1920.

SIMPSON, EDNA   (3644)
    New Mexico adds another interest. New Mexico Quarterly, 5:16-
    19, 1935.
        Description of Red River passion play.

SLAYDEN, JAMES L.   (3645)
    Some observations on Mexican immigration. Annals of the Amer-
    ican Academy of Political and Social Science, 93:121-26, Jan. 1921.

STEPHENSON, ERNST   (3646)
   The potters of La Luz. *NM*, 15:20-21, April 1937.

STORM, DAN   (3646a)
   The pastor and the serpent. *Texas Folklore Society, Publications*,
   15:122-33, 1939.
      Two serpent tales of a New Mexican shepherd translated into English.

STORM, O. P.   (3647)
   Teaching Spanish-American children how to speak, read, and write
   English. *New Mexico School Review*, 17:26-27, May 1938.

STOWELL, JAY S.   (3648)
   The near side of the Mexican question. New York, Home Missions
   Council, 1921.
      Southwest, social conditions.

———   (3649)
   A study of Mexicans and Spanish-Americans in the United States.
   New York, Home Missions Council, 1920.

STURGES, VERA L.   (3650)
   Mexican immigrants. *Survey*, 46:470-71, July 1921.
      Conditions at Customs House, El Paso.

TAYLOR, C. B.   (3651)
   Mexican penitentes of New Mexico. *Everybody's* 10:501-, 1904.

TAYLOR, CARL N.   (3652)
   Agony in New Mexico. *Today*, 5:3-4, 20, Feb. 1936.
      Penitente rites.

TAYLOR, HARRY FRANKLIN   (3653)
   The musical abilities of Spanish-American children. Unpub. Master's thesis, Denver University, 1934.

TAYLOR, M. C.   (3654)
   Retardation of Mexican children in the Albuquerque schools.
   Unpub. Master's thesis, Stanford University, 1927.

TAYLOR, PAUL S.   (3655)
   Mexican labor in the United States; migration statistics IV. *University of California Publications in Economics*, 12:23-50, 1934.
      Includes a discussion of Mexican population in New Mexico.

———   (3656)
   Mexicans north of the Rio Grande. *Survey*, 66:135-40, 197, 200-02,
   205, 1931.
      Review of social and economic status of Mexican immigrants into the South-
      west.

———   (3657)
   Some aspects of Mexican immigration. *Journal of Political Economy*, 38:609-15, Oct. 1930.
      General with some mention of Southwestern agriculture and industry.

———   (3658)
   Songs of the Mexican migration. (In Dobie, J. Frank, Ed.: *Puro
   Mexicano*. Austin, Texas Folklore Society, 1935.)

TEJADA, SIMEON   (3659)
   Acertijos. Unpub. ms. in files of New Mexico Writers' Project,
   Santa Fe.
      Folk riddles.

TEJADA, SIMEON (Continued)   (3660)
  Folk and fairy tales. Unpub. mss. in files of New Mexico Writers'
  Project, Santa Fe.
    Periwig and his horse; The most beautiful maiden; The tale of the sick
    woman; A fortune teller by accident; La rana y la culebra; An old maid's
    prayer; Virtue and evil; Paloma blanca; The priest and the drunkard.

TELLES, ELIAS W.   (3661)
  *A critical study of the Spanish picaresque novel and a comparison
  of the picaresque elements with certain phases of New Mexican
  folklore.* Unpub. Master's thesis, UNM, 1937.

THOMSON, CHARLES A.   (3662)
  The man from next door. *Century,* 111:275-82, Jan. 1926.
    Economic and social background of the problem of Mexican immigration into
    the Southwest.

————   (3663)
  Mexicans—an interpretation. *National Conference of Social
  Work, Proceedings, 1928.* Chicago, 1929. pp. 499-503.
    Habits, customs, etc.

THORP, N. HOWARD   (3664)
  Chiquiau—a Spanish dance. Unpub. ms. in files of New Mexico
  Writers' Project, Santa Fe.

————   (3665)
  A wedding feast. Unpub. ms. in files of New Mexico Writers'
  Project, Santa Fe.

TIREMAN, L. S.   (3666)
  Discovery and use of community resources in the education of
  Spanish-speaking pupils. *National Education Association, Depart-
  ment of Rural Education, Yearbook, 1939.* pp. 72-85.

————   (3667)
  New Mexico tackles the problem of the Spanish-speaking child.
  Journal of Education, 114:300-01, 1931.

TIREMAN, L. S., DIXON, NEWELL, AND CORNELIUS, VERA   (3668)
  Vocabulary acquisition of Spanish-speaking children. *Elementary
  English Review,* 12:118-19, 144, 1935.

TIREMAN, L. S. AND WOODS, V. E.   (3669)
  Aural and visual comprehension of English by Spanish-speaking
  children. *Elementary School Journal,* 40:204-11, 1939.

TRUJILLO, J.   (3670)
  Spanish refranes and riddles of the Southwest. Unpub. Master's
  thesis, UNM, 1933.

TRUJILLO, JOSE AND RAFAELITA   (3671)
  History of the settlement of El Llano. Unpub. ms. in files of New
  Mexico Writers' Project, Santa Fe.

UNDERWOOD, MARION   (3672)
  Survivals of Spanish influence in the Southwest. Unpub. Master's
  thesis, University of California, 1919.

UNITED STATES BUREAU OF THE CENSUS   (3673)
  Population of Spanish mother tongue: 1940. Washington, GPO,
  1942.

VALDEZ, FELIX D. (3673a)
Reminiscences of pioneer Taoseños. *Lulac News*, 6:23-24, Sept. 1939.

VAN STONE, MARY R. (3674)
El niño perdido. *EP*, 34:163-65, 1933.
Folk drama.

———— (3675)
Los pastores; excerpts from an old Christmas play of the Southwest as given annually by the Griego family, Santa Fe, New Mexico. Cleveland, Gates Press, 1933.

VAN STONE, MARY R. AND SIMS, E. R. (3676)
Canto del niño perdido. *Texas Folklore Society, Publications*, 11: 48-89, 1933.

VINCENT, HENRIETTA H. (3677)
A study of performance of Spanish-speaking pupils on Spanish tests. Unpub. Master's thesis, New Mexico State Teachers College, 1933.

WAGNER, HENRY R. (3678)
New Mexico Spanish press. *NMHR*, 12:1-40, 1937.
Its history and development.

WALL, SISTER M. MATTHIAS (3679)
Contributions to New Mexico folklore. Unpub. Master's thesis, New Mexico Normal (Highlands) University, 1932.

WARNER, LOUIS H. (3680)
Conveyance of property, the Spanish and Mexican way. *NMHR*, 6:334-59, 1931.

———— (3681)
Old town of Santa Cruz. *National Republic*, 18:20-21, July 1930.
———— (3682)
Wills and hijuelas. *NMHR*, 7:75-89, 1932.

WATERS, LAWRENCE LESLIE (3683)
Transient Mexican agricultural labor. *Southwestern Social Science Quarterly*, 22:49-66, June 1941.

WATTERS, MARY (3684)
The penitentes: a folk observance. *Social Forces*, 6:253-56, 1927-28.

WENHAM, EDWARD (3685)
Spanish-American silverware in New Mexico. *International Studio*, 99:31-33, July 1931.

WEST, E. H. (3686)
The right of asylum in New Mexico in the 17th and 18th centuries. *Hispanic American Historical Review*, 8:357-91, 1928.
Historical development of right of asylum since Grecian times with thirty-two cases illustrating strength of the custom in New Mexico.

WHITAKER, ARTHUR P. (3687)
The Spanish contribution to American agriculture. *Agricultural History*, 3:1-14, Jan. 1929.
A systematic account of the transplanting of Spanish agriculture to America.

WHITMAN, WALT (3688)
The Spanish element in our nationality. *EP*, 5:164-65, 1918.

WILDER, MITCHELL A.   (3688a)
Religious folk art in New Mexico. *Bulletin of the Art Institute of Chicago,* 37:20-22, Feb. 1943.

――――   (3689)
Santos: the religious folk art of New Mexico. To be published early in 1943 by the Taylor Museum of the Colorado Springs Fine Arts Center.
> This study is a first report on the Taylor Museum collection, serving both as a Museum catalogue and as a contribution based on research studies in the field of New Mexican religious art being carried on at the Taylor Museum. The text includes a layman's introduction to the Spanish-American background and a classification of *bultos* from the standpoint of regional styles and technology. Sixty-four full page plates, based largely on *santos* from the Taylor Museum collection and with captions by Edgar Breitenbach relating New Mexican forms to the better known religious art of Europe, will be included.

――――   (3690)
Santos and bultos in New Mexico. *Design,* 43:16, April, 1942.

WILLIAMS, A. D.   (3691)
Spanish-colonial furniture. Milwaukee, Bruce Pub. Co., 1941.

WOODS, BETTY   (3692)
The blonds of Vallecito. *NM,* 20:10, 30, Oct. 1942.
> Blond Spanish-Americans are descendants of the *conquistadores.*

WOODS, CLEE   (3692a)
He found his glory hole in his own front yard. *Desert Magazine,* 6:11-13, Jan. 1943.
> Life of a New Mexican Spanish-American miner and sheepherder.

WOODWARD, DOROTHY   (3693)
The penitentes of New Mexico. Unpub. Doctor's thesis, Yale University, 1935. (To be published by Yale University Press, 1943.)
> A historical study of the *penitentes* in New Mexico based on the Spanish culture background of medieval Spain as it was carried into the northern frontier country in the 16th and 17th centuries. Some consideration is given to the modification of the societies due to the dominance of the Anglo culture which came in the 19th century and to the development of the creative arts in New Mexico.

WOOLFORD, WITHERS   (3694)
Revival of the native crafts. *NM,* 9:24-26, Sept. 1931.

WPA, WRITER'S PROJECT   (3695)
San Antonio's day. *EP,* 48:242-45, 1941.
> *Fiesta* at San Antonio, N. M.

――――   (3696)
San Ysidro's day in Cordova. *EP,* 48:239-42, 1941.

――――   (3697)
Spanish-American baptismal customs. *EP,* 49:59-61, 1942.
> San Miguel County.

ZEPHYRIN, FATHER   (3698)
Father Zephyrin and the penitentes. *EP,* 8:73-74, 1920.

Fiction and Drama

ALLEN, HERVEY (3699)
Anthony Adverse. New York, Farrar & Rinehart, 1933.
Part of setting in New Mexico.

ANDERSON, MAXWELL (3700)
Night over Taos. New York, Samuel French, 1932.
Drama based on Taos insurrection.

ARMER, LAURA A. (3701)
Waterless mountain. New York, Longmans Green, 1931.
Navajo setting.

AUSTIN, MARY (3702)
Starry adventure. Boston, Houghton Mifflin, 1931.
New Mexico setting.

BANDELIER, ADOLPH F. A. (3703)
The delight makers. New York, Dodd Mead, 1916.
Rito de los Frijoles setting.

BARTLETT, FLORENCE (3704)
Gloria Crucis (An historical pageant). *EP,* 4 (1):32-66, 1917.

BECKER, MARY L. (3704a)
Golden tales of the Southwest. New York, Dodd Mead, 1939.

BERGMANN, CHARLES (3705)
The McSween affair. Unpub. radio play in files of New Mexico
Writers' Project, Santa Fe.
Based on a Billy the Kid incident.

BIRNEY, HOFFMAN (3706)
Eagle in the sun. New York, Putnam, 1935.
Santa Fe setting.

BRINKERHOFF, HENRY (3707)
Nah-nee-ta; a tale of the Navajos. Washington, Soule, 1886.

BRUMFIELD, D. (3708)
The way of a Spanish man with a Tigua maid: a story of the Spanish conquistadores. *Out West,* 37:334-39, 1913.

BURR, ANNA ROBESON (3709)
Golden quicksand; a novel of Santa Fe. New York, D. Appleton,
1936.

CANNON, CORNELIA JAMES (3710)
The fight for the Pueblo. Boston, Houghton Mifflin, 1934.

CARR, LORRAINE (3711)
Mother of the Smiths. New York, Macmillan, 1940.
Taos County setting.

CASSIDY, ELLIOT (3712)
A Southwestern romance. Unpub. radio play in files of New
Mexico Writers' Project, Santa Fe.
About Billy the Kid.

CASSIDY, ELLIOT AND PADDOCK, WILLIAM FRED (3713)
Billy Bonney, the Kid. Unpub. ms. in files of New Mexico
Writers' Project, Santa Fe.
Three-act play.

CATHER, WILLA   (3714)
    Death comes for the archbishop. New York, Knopf, 1927.
        Bishop Lamy and his times.

CHAMPNEY, ELIZABETH W.   (3715)
    Great grandmother's girls in New Mexico, 1670-80. Boston, Estes
    & Lauriat, 1888.
        Fictionized version of events leading up to Pueblo uprising.

CHAVEZ, ANGELICO   (3716)
    New Mexico triptych. Paterson, New Jersey, St. Anthony's Guild
    Press, 1940.
        New Mexico setting.

CLARK, ANNA NOLAN   (3717)
    The chief's pants. Unpub. radio play in files of New Mexico
    Writers' Project, Santa Fe.

COMFORT, WILL LEVINGTON   (3718)
    Apache. New York, Dutton, 1936.

COOLIDGE, DANE   (3719)
    Under the sun. New York, Dutton, 1926.

CORLE, EDWIN   (3720)
    Burro Alley. New York, Random House, 1938.
        Santa Fe setting.

————   (3721)
    People on the earth. New York, Random House, 1937.
        Navajo setting.

DNEH BI'KIS (REV. WILLIAM GOUDBERG)   (3722)
    The upward trail. Grand Rapids, Erdmans, 1935.
        Navajo setting.

DUFFUS, R. L.   (3723)
    Jornada. New York, Covici-Friede, 1935.

ELLIS, A.   (3723a)
    Sunshine preferred. Boston, Houghton Mifflin, 1934.
        New Mexico setting.

ELLISON, MRS. EDITH NICHOLL   (3724)
    The upward trail. New York, Rowland & Ives, 1928.

FENN, G. M.   (3725)
    In the wilds of New Mexico. New York, John W. Lovell, n. d.

FERGUSSON, HARVEY   (3726)
    Followers of the sun; a trilogy of the Santa Fe trail. New York,
    Knopf, 1936.

FOREMAN, L. L.   (3727)
    Don Desperado. New York, Dutton, 1941.
        Santa Fe trail period.

FOSTER, JOSEPH O'KANE   (3728)
    In the night did I sing. New York, Scribners, 1942.
        Taos setting.

GILLMOR, FRANCES   (3729)
    Fruit out of rock. New York, Duell, Sloan & Pearce, 1940.

————   (3730)
    Windsinger. New York, Milton Balch & Co., 1930.
        Navajo setting.

GRANT, BLANCHE C.   (3731)
Doña Lona. New York, Wilfred Funk, 1941.

HALL, DONALD J.   (3732)
Perilous sanctuary. London, G. G. Harrap & Co., 1937.
    Jemez setting.

HAWTHORNE, HILDEGARDE   (3733)
Lone rider. New York, Longmans Green, 1934.

HOGNER, DOROTHY CHILDS   (3734)
Santa Fe caravans. New York, T. Nelson & Sons, 1937.

HORGAN, PAUL   (3735)
*From the royal city of the Holy Faith of St. Francis, being five
accounts of life in that place. . .* Santa Fe, Rydal Press, 1936.

———   (3736)
No quarter given. New York, Harper, 1935.
    Santa Fe setting.

HOW, LOUIS   (3737)
The penitentes of San Rafael. Indianapolis, Bowen-Merrill Co.,
1900.

INMAN, HENRY   (3738)
A pioneer from Kentucky; an idyl of the Raton range. Topeka,
Crane & Co., 1898.

JANIVER, THOMAS   (3739)
Santa Fe's partner. New York, Harper, 1907.

———   (3740)
Stories of old New Spain. New York, Appleton, 1898.

KUIPERS, CORNELIUS C.   (3741)
Chant of the night. Grand Rapids, Zondervan Pub. Co., 1934.
    Zuni setting.

———   (3742)
Deep snow. Grand Rapids, Zondervan Pub. Co., 1934.

LADD, HORATIO   (3743)
Chunda, a story of the Navajos. New York, Easton & Mains, 1906.

LA FARGE, OLIVER   (3744)
All the young men. Boston, Houghton Mifflin, 1935.

———   (3745)
The enemy gods. Boston, Houghton Mifflin, 1929.

———   (3746)
Laughing boy. Boston, Houghton Mifflin, 1929.

———   (3747)
Sparks fly upward. Boston, Houghton Mifflin, 1931.

LARKIN, MARGARET   (3748)
El Cristo. New York, Samuel French, 1926.
    A play.

LAURITZEN, JONREED   (3748a)
Arrows into the sun. New York, Knopf, 1943.
        Novel of Navajo and Mormon country depicting conflict between ways of the
        Anglo and the Indian.

LEHMAN, P. E.   (3748b)
  Blood of the West. New York, Macaulay, 1934.
    New Mexico setting.

LUCERO-WHITE, AURORA   (3749)
  Kearny takes Las Vegas. Unpub. radio play in files of the New Mexico Writers' Project, Santa Fe.

MCGEE, MRS. MAYNOR D.   (3750)
  Milestones. Chicago, M. A. Donohue & Co., 1926.

MALKUS, ALIDA SIMS   (3751)
  Caravans to Santa Fe. New York, Harper, 1928.

————   (3752)
  The dragonfly of Zuni. New York, Harcourt Brace, 1928.

————   (3753)
  Stone knife boy. New York, Harcourt Brace, 1933.

MEANS, FLORENCE CRANNELL   (3753a)
  Adella Mary in old New Mexico. Boston, Houghton Mifflin, 1939.

————   (3754)
  In old New Mexico. Boston, Houghton Mifflin, 1939.
    Taos-Santa Fe trail.

————   (3755)
  Shadow over wide ruins. Boston, Houghton Mifflin, 1942.

MEINE, FRANKLIN, ED.   (3756)
  Tall tales of the Southwest. New York, Knopf, 1930.

MOON, CARL   (3757)
  Flaming arrow. New York, Stokes, 1927.

NASSOUR, SARAH A.   (3758)
  Skin of gods (Hycette). Los Angeles, Sutton House, 1938.
    Jemez setting.

ONION, CHARLES C.   (3759)
  The end of an outlaw. Unpub. radio play in files of the New Mexico Writers' Project, Santa Fe.
    Billy the Kid.

OTIS, RAYMOND   (3760)
  Fire in the night. New York, Farrar & Rinehart, 1934.

RAINE, WILLIAM MACLEOD   (3761)
  A daughter of the dons; a story of New Mexico today. New York, G. W. Dillingham, 1941.

REAGAN, ALBERT B.   (3762)
  Don Diego; or the Pueblo Indian uprising of 1680. New York, Alice Harriman, 1914.

RHODES, EUGENE MANLOVE   (3763)
  The come on. New York, Grossett & Dunlap, 1920.

————   (3764)
  Desire of the moth. New York, Grossett & Dunlap, 1925.

————   (3765)
  Good men and true. New York, Grossett & Dunlap, 1920.

RHODES, EUGENE MANLOVE (Continued)   (3766)
   Hit the line hard. New York, Grossett & Dunlap, 1920.

————   (3767)
   Once in the saddle. Boston, Houghton Mifflin, 1927.

————   (3768)
   Paso por aqui. Boston, Houghton Mifflin, 1927.

————   (3769)
   Peñalosa. Santa Fe, Writers' Editions, 1934.

————   (3770)
   The proud sheriff. Boston, Houghton Mifflin, 1935.

————   (3771)
   Stepsons of light. Boston, Houghton Mifflin, 1921.

————   (3772)
   Trusty knaves. Boston, Houghton Mifflin, 1933.

RICHTER, CONRAD   (3773)
   Early Americana. New York, Knopf, 1936.
     Short stories; Southwestern setting.

RYAN, MRS. MARAH ELLIS   (3774)
   Flute of the gods. New York, Stokes, 1909.

SABIN, EDWIN LEGRAND   (3775)
   The rose of Santa Fe. Philadelphia, Jacobs, 1923.

SANTEE, ROSS   (3776)
   Men and horses. New York, Century, 1926.
     Short stories; Southwestern setting.

SCARBOROUGH, DOROTHY   (3777)
   The wind. New York, Harper, 1925.

SWANSON, N. H.   (3777a)
   The phantom emperor. New York, Putnam, 1934.
     Historical novel partly New Mexico setting.

UNDERHILL, RUTH M.   (3778)
   Hawk over whirlpools. New York, J. J. Augustin, 1940.

VESTAL, STANLEY   (3779)
   'Dobe walls; a story of Kit Carson's Southwest. Boston, Houghton
   Mifflin, 1929.

WATERS, FRANK   (3780)
   The man who killed the deer. New York, Farrar & Rinehart,
   1942.

————   (3781)
   People of the valley. New York, Farrar & Rinehart, 1941.

WEADOCK, JACK   (3782)
   Dust of the desert; plain tales of the desert and the border. New
   York, Appleton, 1936.

WELLMAN, PAUL ISELY   (3783)
   Bronco Apache. New York, Macmillan, 1936.
     Pueblo setting.

General

ABERLE, SOPHIE D. (3784)
Health problem of the valley. Address delivered at School for the Rio Grande Valley, UNM, April 27-May 1, 1942. To be published by School of Inter-American Affairs in *Proceedings of the School for the Rio Grande Valley.*
Particular reference to health history of the Pueblos.

ACKERMAN, R. E. (3785)
Trends in illiteracy in New Mexico. Unpub. Master's thesis, UNM, 1933.

ADAMS, QUINCY D. (3786)
Progress of the New Mexico Bar. (In *Report of the Proceedings, Annual meeting of the State Bar of New Mexico, Albuquerque, August 1934.* pp. 49-57.)

ADAMS, R. L. (3787)
The farm mortgage situation with special reference to the eleven western states. *Journal of Farm Economics,* 14:605-14, 1932.

ADAMS, RAMON F. (3788)
Cowboy lingo. Boston, Houghton Mifflin, 1936.

ADAMS, ROMANZO (3789)
Public range lands—a new policy needed. *American Journal of Sociology,* 22:324-51, 1916.

ADAMS, THELMA (3790)
A study of cowboy diction, with a glossary of terms. Unpub. Master's thesis, UNM, 1931.

ALIANZA (3790a)
Monthly publication of the Alianza Hispano Americana containing articles giving Spanish-American viewpoint on social and economic problems of New Mexico.

ALLEMAN, HERBERT NEGLEY (3791)
The investigation of some building materials adapted to New Mexico. Unpub. Bachelor's thesis, NMSC, 1909.

ALLEN, JULES VERNE (3792)
Cowboy lore. San Antonio, Naylor, 1933.

ALLEN, KENNETH (3793)
Cow country bonanza. *NM,* 17:20, 32, Feb. 1939.
Manganese dioxide in De Baca County.

———— (3794)
Fiesta. *NM,* 20, 9-13, Aug. 1942.
Santa Fe.

ALLISON, IRL LESLIE (3795)
Through the years. Montezuma College Press, Montezuma, New Mexico, 1928.
Experiences of a college professor in New Mexico.

ALVIS, BERRY NEWTON (3796)
Settlement and economic development of Union County, New Mexico. Unpub. Master's thesis, University of Colorado, 1934.

AMERICAN MEDICAL ASSOCIATION (3797)
Hospital service in the United States. Annual publication, 1921–
date.
> Complete statistical data on hospitals in New Mexico.

AMERICAN SCENIC AND HISTORIC PRESERVATION SOCIETY (3798)
New museum at Santa Fe. *23rd Annual Report, 1918.* pp. 366-74.
> Includes a historical summary of Southwestern archaeology.

AMISON, E. ANNE (3799)
One day in the field. *New Mexico Health Officer,* 10:19-22, Sept.
1942.
> Registration field agent in Rio Arriba County.

ANDERSON, ARNOLD M. (3800)
The native New Mexican. *Great Southwest,* Sept. 1909.

ANDERSON, C. A. (3801)
Compilation of appraisal data, properties, etc., covering the Middle Rio Grande Conservancy District. Unpub. ms. dated April 23,
1931. (Copy at MRGCD office, Albuquerque.)

———— (3802)
General data relative to the district. Unpub. ms. dated February
19, 1929. Rev. April 20, 1931. (Copy at MRGCD office, Albuquerque.)

ANDERSON, D. R. (3803)
Adventures in New Mexico. *Public Health Nurse,* 19:346-47, July
1927.

———— (3804)
Why New Mexico nurses cooperate in maternity and infancy
work. *American Journal of Public Health,* 16:473-75, 1926.
> Discusses some problems in field of nursing in New Mexico.

ANDERSON, GEORGE BAKER (3805)
The conquest of the desert. *Out West,* 25:109-24, 1906.
> Spanish and American irrigation in Rio Grande Valley.

———— (3806)
History of New Mexico; its resources and people. 2 v. Los Angeles,
Pacific States Pub. Co., 1907.

———— (3807)
The land of Shalam; the colony of the Faithists, New Mexico.
Out West, 25:414-, 1906.

ANDERSON, R. A. (3808)
A study of vocational opportunities in Albuquerque. *Research,*
2:59-63, June 1938. *Also* unpub. Master's thesis, UNM, 1938.

ANDERSON, WILLIAM A. (3809)
*School changes and economies made in New Mexico during the
school years 1930-31 and 1931-32.* Unpub. Master's thesis, Denver University, 1933.

ANGELINO, HENRY R. (3810)
A study of shoplifting. Unpub. Master's thesis, UNM, 1942.
> In Albuquerque.

ANONYMOUS   (3811)
Art in New Mexico. *EP,* 16:137-40, 1924. *Also EP,* 10:11-14, June
15, 1921.

──────   (3812)
A Bostonian finds a new home (Albuquerque). *Out West,* 26:
81-90, 1907.

──────   (3813)
Comparison of public health activities between New Mexico and
Arizona. *Southwestern Medicine,* 10:312-13, July 1926.

──────   (3814)
Delinquent taxes and the new tax collection law. *New Mexico
Tax Review,* 2:3-6, June 1917.
          Tax delinquencies by counties.

──────   (3815)
Diphtheria in New Mexico. *Southwestern Medicine,* 11:38, Jan.
1927.
          80 per cent reduction in number of cases between 1920-1926.

──────   (3816)
Irrigacion economica en Nuevo Mexico. *La Hacienda,* 35:36, Jan.
1940.

──────   (3817)
Nambe, a community school. n. p., n. p., May 1, 1939.
          Description of experimental program at Nambe.

──────   (3818)
National recovery road program provides winter employment.
NM, 11:34, Nov. 1933.
          Includes some employment statistics.

──────   (3819)
New Mexico mission architecture. *EP,* 10:14-16, April 15, 1921.

──────   (3820)
1937 state legislation for control of soil erosion. *Journal of Land
and Public Utility Economics.* 14:210-17, 1938.

──────   (3821)
Old chest found in mountain cave. *EP,* 12:142-43, 1922.
          Spanish-American chest.

──────   (3822)
Proud and loyal state; reply to Henry Wray. *North American
Review,* 208:487-93, 1918. *See* (4834)

──────   (3823)
Public health in New Mexico. *Southwestern Medicine,* 9:362,
Sept. 1925.
          Review of accomplishments of Bureau of Public Health during previous six
          years.

──────   (3824)
Rural industry in New Mexico. *Dublin Review,* 114:177-, 1894.

──────   (3825)
Small pox in New Mexico. *Southwestern Medicine,* 10:127,
March 1926.

ANONYMOUS (Continued)   (3826)
> Social hygiene activities, 1932. *Journal of Social Hygiene,* 19:83-84, Feb. 1933.

(3827)
> *Sons of Indians. What they have been and what they are becoming under new dispensation.* Albuquerque, Daily Democrat, n. d.

(3828)
> The story of old Santa Fe. *EP,* 10 (4) :2-4, 1921.

(3829)
> A trip to Jemez. *EP,* 11:15-23, 1921.

(3830)
> Two more undeveloped states. *Review of Reviews,* 41:268-70, 1910.
>> Arizona and New Mexico.

(3831)
> Typhoid in New Mexico. *Southwestern Medicine,* 11:511, Nov. 1927.
>> Prevalence in northern New Mexico ascribed to infected wells.

APPLEGATE, FRANK   (3832)
> If you buy antiques. *New Mexico Highway Journal,* 7:25-26, 34, April 1929.
>> Blankets, *santos,* chests, etc.

ARMER, LAURA   (3833)
> *Southwest.* New York, Longmans Green, 1935.
>> A literary interpretation of the Southwest.

ARMIJO, ANTHONY   (3834)
> *A survey of the . . . merit system commission in New Mexico.* Unpub. Master's thesis, UNM, 1941.

ARMY OFFICER (PSEUD.)   (3835)
> *Who are the New Mexicans?* Pamphlet in Bancroft Library, University of California.

ARNOLD, CHARLOTTE   (3836)
> On the trail of the ancients. *EP,* 23:50-104, 1927.
>> Gossipy description of sights and celebrities of New Mexico.

ARNOLD, OREN   (3836a)
> *Wild life in the Southwest.* Dallas, Banks, Upshaw & Co., 1936.

ARNOLD, OREN AND HALE, JOHN P.   (3837)
> *Hot irons, heraldry of the range.* New York, Macmillan, 1940.
>> The story of brands and branding.

ARNY, W. F. M.   (3838)
> *Interesting items regarding New Mexico: its agricultural, pastoral, and mineral resources, people, climate, soil, scenery.* Santa Fe, Manderfield & Tucker, 1873.

ASPLUND, JULIA BROWN   (3839)
> New Mexico State Library Extension Service, first annual report. *EP,* 29:213-22, 1930.
>> Includes listing of libraries, volumes, circulation.

ASPLUND, R. F.   (3840)
> *New Mexico in the great war.* Chapter 4. Civilian attitudes. *NMHR,* 1:120-34, 1926.

AUSTIN, MARY   (3841)
Education in New Mexico. *New Mexico Quarterly,* 3:217-21,
1933.
> The three cultural groups in New Mexico have distinct educational needs
> which should be developed separately.

───   (3842)
Indian detour. *Bookman,* 68:653-58, Feb. 1929.
> Implications of New Mexico land and culture for American art.

───   (3843)
The land of journey's ending. New York, Century, 1924.
> Panoramic comments on the land and people of New Mexico, covering a large
> segment of both time and space. Some of the chapters have been published
> separately.

───   (3844)
Life at Santa Fe. *South Atlantic Quarterly,* 31:263-71, 1932.

───   (3845)
Rural education in New Mexico. UNM Bulletin, Training School
series, v. 2, no. 1, 1931.

───   (3846)
Santa Fe's community theatre. *EP,* 6:26-27, 1919.

───   (3847)
Sources of poetic influence in the Southwest. *Poetry,* 43:152-63,
1933.

AVANT, LOUIS   (3848)
*The history of Catholic education in New Mexico since the Amer-
ican occupation.* Unpub. Master's thesis, UNM, 1940.

B. G. K.   (3848a)
Taos and its artists. *Lulac News,* 6:19-22, Sept. 1939.

BACA, F. F.   (3848b)
New Mexico's need of leaders. *Lulac News,* 6:17, Sept. 1939.

BACON, LUCY   (3849)
Turquoise. *NM,* 11:14-16, 53, March 1933.
> Description of turquoise mines and sources of petrified wood and ways in
> which Indians have used both.

BAILEY, HENRY TURNER   (3850)
Instruction in the fine and manual arts in the United States. USDI,
Bureau of Education, Bulletin 6. Washington, GPO, 1909.
> Includes New Mexico.

BAILEY, VERNON   (3851)
Life zones and crop zones of New Mexico. USDA, Bureau of Biological Survey, North American Fauna 35. Washington, GPO,
1913.

───   (3852)
Mammals of New Mexico. USDA, Bureau of Biological Survey,
North American Fauna 53. Washington, GPO, 1931.

BAIRD, ENID   (3853)
Average general relief benefits, 1933-1938. WPA, Division of Research and Division of Statistics. Washington, GPO, 1940.
> Includes statistics on family size, direct and work relief, and amount received
> per family for New Mexico.

BALDWIN, PERCY M.   (3854)
A historical note on the boundaries of New Mexico. *NMHR*,
5:116-37, 1930.

——   (3855)
The 1940 census and legislative reapportionment in New Mexico.
New Mexico Quarterly Review, 11:37-50, 1941.
    Suggests reorganization of representation.

——   (3856)
A short history of the Mesilla Valley. *NMHR*, 13:314-24, 1938.

BANCROFT, HUBERT HOWE   (3857)
History of Arizona and New Mexico, 1530-1888. San Francisco,
History Co., 1889.

BANDELIER, ADOLPH F. A.   (3858)
*The journals of Adolphe Francis Alphonse Bandelier during the
years 1886-1889.* . . . New York, Press of the Pioneers, 1934.

BANNER, ROY AND MAES, ARTHUR   (3859)
The justice of peace courts in Bernalillo County, New Mexico.
Research, 1:99-112, 1937.

BARBER, M. A. AND FORBRICH, L. R.   (3860)
Malaria in the irrigated regions of New Mexico. *Public Health
Reports*, 48:610-23, 1933.

BARELA, FRED   (3861)
*The relation between scholastic achievement and economic status
as shown by parental occupation.* Unpub. Master's thesis, UNM,
1936.

——   (3862)
Scholastic achievement, economic status, and the New Deal. *New
Mexico Business Review*, 5:251-56, 1936.
    Study of correlation between scholastic achievement and socio-economic status
    of English- and Spanish-speaking graduates of Albuquerque High School,
    1933-35.

BARKER, R. M.   (3863)
The economics of cattle ranching in the Southwest. *Review of
Reviews*, 25:305-13, 1901.

BARKER, RUTH LAUGHLIN   (3864)
Club-women. *SR*, 12:154-58, 1927.
    Arguments for making Santa Fe "The Cultural Center of the Southwest" by
    establishing Women's Club center there.

BARKER, S. OMAR   (3865)
The hungry loop. *NM*, 16:16-17, 42, 44, Oct. 1938.
    The art of roping, and the various animals on which it has been tried from
    jackrabbits to camels.

——   (3866)
New-old houses of Santa Fe. *Overland*, n. s., 82:403-04, 1924.

——   (3867)
Sagebrush Spanish. *NM*, 20:18-19, 32-33, Dec. 1942.
    Corruption of Spanish terms commonly used in the Southwest.

BARNES, WILL C.   (3868)
The story of the range. USDA, Forest Service. Washington, GPO,
1926.

BARTLETT, JOHN RUSSELL   (3869)
Dictionary of Americanisms; a glossary of words and phrases usually regarded as peculiar to the United States. Boston, Little Brown, 1877.

BAXTER, SYLVESTER   (3869a)
The father of the Pueblos. *Harpers,* 65:72-91, 1882.

BEDINGER, MARGERY   (3870)
New Mexico: a great library opportunity. *Library Journal,* 52: 351-53, 1927.

BEHRINGER, FREDERICK D.   (3871)
The legal status of local government in New Mexico. *Research,* 2:81-94, June 1938.

—————   (3872)
New Mexico municipalities. *New Mexico Business Review,* 6:85-101, 1937.

—————   (3873)
New Mexico municipalities and county consolidation in New Mexico. UNM, Dept. of Government and Citizenship, Public Affairs series 1, 1937.

BENTLEY, HAROLD WOODMANSEE   (3874)
A dictionary of Spanish terms in English. New York, Columbia University Press, 1933.

BERNARD, EDWARD M.   (3875)
History of the Christian brothers' educational work in New Mexico. Unpub. Master's thesis, New Mexico Normal (Highlands) University, 1930.

BERNSTEIN, HARRY   (3876)
Spanish influence in the United States. Economic aspects. *Hispanic American Historical Review,* 18:43-65, Feb. 1938.

BEVERIDGE, ALBERT J.   (3877)
Speech in Senate of the United States, Feb. 6, 1905. Washington, GPO, 1905.
        Argument for uniting Arizona and New Mexico as a single state on the grounds that Spanish people would assimilate better if surrounded by Anglos.

BIBO, NATHAN   (3878)
The making of Albuquerque. *Santa Fe Magazine,* 17:55-56, Jan. 1923.

BIGGERS, CHESTER A.   (3879)
Flood damages for the Pecos River watershed from Alamogordo Dam, New Mexico, to Givrin, Texas, for the flood of September 1941. USDA, SCS, January 15, 1942. (Copy in USDA Library, Albuquerque.)

BLACK, HELEN   (3880)
New Mexican melodrama. *Nation,* 119:181-82, 1924.
        The career of Carl Magee.

BLOODGOOD, DEAN W.   (3881)
Water resources of New Mexico that might be utilized for irrigation purposes. NMAES, Press Bulletin 406, State College, 1922; and Press Bulletin 511, State College, 1926. Processed.

BLOOM, LANSING B. (3882)
Early weaving in New Mexico. *NMHR*, 2:228-38, 1927.

————— (3883)
The governors of New Mexico. *NMHR*, 10:152-57, 1935.

————— (3884)
New Mexico in the great war. Chapter 1. The breaking of the storm. *NMHR*, 1:1-15, 1926. Chapter 8. To the colors. *NMHR*, 1:419-33, 1926.

BLOOM, LANSING B., ED. (3885)
New Mexico in the great war. Historical Society of New Mexico, Publications in History, v. 2. Santa Fe, 1927.

BLOOM, LANSING B. AND DONNELLY, THOMAS C. (3886)
New Mexico history and civics. Albuquerque, UNM Press, 1933.

BLOOM, MAUD MCFIE (3887)
Childhood memories of the Rio Grande in flood. *NMHR*, 16:359-65, 1941.

BLUMENSCHEIN, ERNEST L. (3888)
Origin of the Taos art colony. *EP*, 20:190-93, 1926.

BOHANNAN, CHARLES D. (3889)
The present status of attempts at improvement of instruction in land grant colleges. State College, NMSC, 1927.

BONNER, H. R. (3890)
Statistics of public high schools, 1917-18. USDI, Bureau of Education, Bulletin 19. Washington, GPO, 1920.
    Includes New Mexico.

————— (3891)
Statistitics of state school systems, 1917-18. USDI, Bureau of Education, Bulletin 11. Washington, GPO, 1920 .
    Includes New Mexico.

BOTKIN, C. W. AND SMITH, E. C. (3892)
Effect of irrigation waters and cropping on the nutrients and exchangeable bases of desert soils. NMAES, Bulletin 292. State College, 1942.

BOTTS, MRS. MARGARET (3893)
Las Vegas in 1890, through the Daily Optic. Unpub. Master's thesis, UNM, 1939.

BOULDIN, EDNA (3894)
Gift of the river. *NM*, 15:9-11, 34, Feb. 1937.
    Rio Grande irrigation project.

BOWDEN, A. O. (3895)
The qualifications of the teachers of New Mexico. *School and Society*, 30:818-24, 1930.

BOYD, JAMES V. (3896)
Early schools of Dona Ana County, New Mexico. Unpub. Master's thesis, NMSC, 1941.

BOYD, NATHAN (3897)
Commentary on Secretary Root's memorandum in re The Elephant Butte Dam Project. Published by stockholders of Rio Grande Dam and Irrigation Co., n. d.

BOYLES, DAVID HARDEN   (3898)
   *A study of the teacher placement bureau of the University of New
   Mexico from 1929-1938.* Unpub. Master's thesis, UNM, 1940.

BRANSCUM, ARVEL   (3899)
   *A survey of commercial subjects taught in the high schools of New
   Mexico.* Unpub. Master's thesis, Texas Technological College,
   1940.

BRATTON, SAM G.   (3900)
   New Mexico, mythology, tradition, history. Senate Doc. 147, 71st
   Congress, 2nd Session. Washington, GPO, 1930.

BRAYER, HERBERT O.   (3901)
   Living history: El Morro National Monument, New Mexico. n. p.,
   n. p., April 1940. Processed.

———   (3902)
   *The lost cities of New Mexico; a tour for the social science teachers
   of the Albuquerque schools.* n. p., n. p., [1939]. Processed.

BREVOORT, ELIAS   (3903)
   New Mexico; her natural resources and attractions . . . Published and printed by Elias Brevoort, Santa Fe, 1874.

BRIGGS, F. A.   (3904)
   Land tenure is Southwestern problem. *Farm and Ranch,* 51 (18) :
   3, 14, 1932.

BROOKS, H. H.   (3905)
   *The international aspects of the Rio Grande project, Texas and
   New Mexico.* Las Cruces, n. p., 1923.

BROWN, CHARLES E.   (3906)
   Some phases of rural education in New Mexico. Unpub. Master's
   thesis, UNM, 1929.

BROWN, FRANCES R.   (3907)
   The Spanish had a name for them. *NM,* 20:14, 29-30, Oct. 1942.
       Spanish names for New Mexico mountains.

BROWN, RALPH H.   (3908)
   The Roswell region, New Mexico. *Annals of the Association of
   American Geographers,* 26:43-44, 1936.

BROWNE, W. A.   (3909)
   Agriculture in the Llano Estacado. *Economic Geography,* 13:155-
   74, 1937.

———   (3910)
   The Llano Estacado: a geographic interpretation. Unpub. Doctor's thesis, George Peabody College for Teachers, 1936.

BROWNFIELD, A. D.   (3911)
   The effect of government land purchases on county finances. *New
   Mexico Business Review,* 9:36-43, 1940.

BRUCE, J. CLARK   (3912)
   *International relations as a high school subject: including a study
   of New Mexico high schools.* Unpub. Master's thesis, University
   of Colorado, 1934.

BRUCE, RICHARD A. (3913)
School enrollment in New Mexico, including comparisons with United States and other states. Unpub. Master's thesis, UNM, 1935.

BRYAN, KIRK (3914)
Flood water farming. *Geographical Review,* 19:444-56, 1929.
Includes contrast between Indian and Spanish farming and some material on dry farming in New Mexico.

—————— (3915)
Historic evidence on changes in the channel of Rio Puerco, a tributary of Rio Grande in New Mexico. *Journal of Geology,* 36:265-82, 1928.

BRYAN, KIRK AND POST, GEORGE M. (3916)
Erosion and control of silt on the Rio Puerco, New Mexico. Report to the Chief Engineer, MRGCD, Oct. 1927. (Typewritten copy at USDA Library, Albuquerque.)

BRYAN, KIRK AND ROBINSON, H. F. (3917)
Erosion and sedimentation on the Zuni watershed, New Mexico. *American Geological Society Bulletin,* 39:158-59, 1928.

BRYAN, O. M. (3918)
Climate and diseases of New Mexico. *Chicago Medical Examiner,* v. 6, 1865.

BUCHANAN, JOHN VICTOR (3919)
Education in New Mexico during the territorial period (1850-1912). Unpub. Master's thesis, University of Kentucky, 1933.

BUCK, CARL E. (3920)
Health survey of the state of New Mexico. New Mexico State Department of Public Health, unpub. ms. dated 1934.

BUER, ETHEL (3921)
Development of home economics in New Mexico. Unpub. Master's thesis, Colorado State College, 1940.

BURSEY, JOSEPH A. (3922)
Baa, baa, black sheep. *NM,* 18:12-13, 38, Jan. 1940.
Sheep raising.

—————— (3923)
Horses of the Southwest. *NM,* 11:10-12, 36-37, Sept. 1933.

—————— (3924)
Minerals of New Mexico. *NM,* 11:22-25, Jan. 1933.

BUTCHER, F. M. (3925)
Crop and livestock loans at 5½ per cent interest. *Financing of Farming,* 8:2-3, April 1934.

BUTTERWORTH, JULIAN E. (3926)
The county superintendent in the United States. USDI, Office of Education, Bulletin 6. Washington, GPO, 1932.
Includes New Mexico.

BUVENS, MARGARET S. (3927)
The admission of New Mexico as a state. Unpub. Bachelor's thesis, NMSC, 1918.

BYNNER, WITTER   (3928)
   Santa Fe and the club-women. *SR*, 12:153-54, 1927.
     Arguments against making Santa Fe "the Cultural Center of the Southwest"
     by establishing a women's club there.

BYNUM, HUBERT EARL   (3929)
   Inequalities of educational opportunity in New Mexico. Unpub.
   Master's thesis, USC, 1937.

CALKINS, FRED H.   (3930)
   *Report of the value of a certain type of supplementary material in
   teaching of American history to native Spanish-speaking pupils in
   the 5th grade.* Unpub. Master's thesis, UNM, 1930.

CALKINS, HUGH G.   (3931)
   Erosion control on the Navajo reservation. *The Land, Today and
   Tomorrow,* 2:19-23, 1935.

————   (3932)
   Man and gullies. *New Mexico Quarterly Review,* 11:69-78, 1941.

CALLAWAY, R. P.   (3933)
   Cooperative cotton ginning in New Mexico, 1938-39 season.
   NMAES, Press Bulletin 896. State College, Feb. 1940. Processed.

————   (3934)
   *Organization and operation of New Mexico cooperative cotton gin
   associations.* NMAES Bulletin 293. State College, May 1942.

CALVIN, ROSS   (3935)
   The history of the upper Gila region in Arizona and New Mexico.
   USDA, SCS, 1935. Processed.

————   (3936)
   In praise of desert. *NM,* 11:13-14, 50-51, Dec. 1933.

————   (3937)
   *Sky determines; an interpretation of the Southwest. New York,
   Macmillan, 1934.

CAMPA, ARTHUR L.   (3938)
   Piñon as an economic and social factor. *New Mexico Business Review,* 1:144-47, 1932.

CAMPBELL, E. C. AND KIBBY, L. P.   (3939)
   Educational organization and reorganization in New Mexico.
   School and Society, 34:59-62, 1931.

CAMPBELL, R. S.   (3940)
   Plant succession and grazing capacity on clay soils in southern New
   Mexico. *Journal of Agricultural Research,* 43:1027-51, 1931.

CANALES, J. T.   (3940a)
   Albuquerque. *Lulac News,* 5:20, 21, Oct. 1938.
     Brief historical sketch.

————   (3940b)
   Santa Fe. *Lulac News,* 5:35-36, Nov. 1938.
     The center of Spanish-American culture in New Mexico.

————   (3940c)
   Taos. *Lulac News,* 5:8-9, Dec. 1938.
     Brief description.

CARLISLE, MRS. ROSE JEANNE (3941)
A Southwestern dictionary . . . Unpub. Master's thesis, UNM, 1939.

CARMAN, E. A., HEATH, H. A., AND MINTO, JOHN (3942)
Special report on the history and present condition of the sheep industry in the United States. House Misc. Doc. 105, 52nd Congress, 2nd Session. Washington, GPO, 1892.

CARR, HARRY (3943)
The West is still wild. New York, Houghton Mifflin, 1933.

CARRINGTON, PAUL M. (3944)
The climate of New Mexico, nature's sanitorium for consumptives. *New York Medical Journal,* July 6, 1907.

CARROLL, NITA WRIGHT (3945)
The adventures and travels of a young California girl through Arizona and New Mexico. *Western Ladies' Magazine,* Feb. 1904.

CARSON, PAUL K. (3946)
Industrial welfare work at Dawson. *Southwestern Medicine,* 10: 486-89, 1926.

CARTER, DIANA B. (3947)
Potsherds and their significance. *EP,* 32:89-101, 1932.

CARTER, GAIL S. (3948)
Address of welcome to School for the Rio Grande Valley. To be published by School of Inter-American Affairs in *Proceedings of the School for the Rio Grande Valley.*
Stresses the role of New Mexico in inter-American relations.

CARTER, GENEVIEVE WILEY (3949)
Juvenile delinquency in Bernalillo County. *Research,* 1:45-69, Dec. 1936. *Also* Unpub. Master's thesis, UNM, 1936.

CARTER, JOHN, JR. (3950)
Crop production in northeastern New Mexico under severe soil-blowing conditions. NMAES, Bulletin 243. State College, 1936.

―――― (3951)
Dry farming investigation in northeastern New Mexico. NMAES Bulletin 191. State College, 1931.

CASE, T. S. (3952)
The old in New Mexico. *Kansas City Review,* 4:502, 1881.

CATON, J. W. (3953)
The organization and legislative activities of the New Mexico Education Association. Unpub. Master's thesis, UNM, 1938.

CHARLES, RALPH (3954)
Land of mañana. *Land Policy Review,* 1:9-11, Nov.-Dec., 1938.
Cuba-Rio Puerco land purchase project.

―――― (3955)
New Mexico report of the extent and character of desirable adjustment in rural land use and the most effective means of obtaining such adjustment. Ms. submitted by New Mexico Land Planning Consultant to National Resources Board, Sept. 1934.

CHARLES, RALPH (Continued)   (3956)
    *Report covering three of the Indian submarginal land purchase
    projects.* NMSC, June 1935. Typewritten. (Copy on file at Na-
    tional Resources Committee Library.)

CHASE, C. M.   (3957)
    The editor's run in New Mexico and Colorado . . . Lyndon, Ver-
    mont, C. M. Chase, 1882.
        Travel description.

CHASE, LEWIS NATHANIEL   (3958)
    The doctor of Santa Fe. *Out West,* 25:380-82, 1906.

CHASE, STUART   (3959)
    *Rich land, poor land; a study of waste in the natural resources of
    America.* New York, Whittlesey House, 1936.
        Some information on erosion in New Mexico.

CHAVEZ, ADOLFO PABLO   (3960)
    A study of the school hot lunch program in New Mexico. Unpub.
    Master's thesis, UNM, 1941.

CHENEY, M. M.   (3961)
    Recreation development in the Southwest. *Journal of Forestry,*
    28:629-31, 1930.

CLARK, JOHN D.   (3962)
    New Mexico must 'come back.' *New Mexico Quarterly,* 5:21-26,
    1935.
        Need for conservation and development of chemical industries.

CLARK, VAN D.   (3963)
    *NYA educational, vocational, and recreational survey of Valencia
    County.* NYA, 1936. Processed.

CLARKE, WALTER   (3964)
    Syphilis in New Mexico. Santa Fe, New Mexico Tuberculosis
    Association, 1934.

CLEAVELAND, AGNES MORLEY   (3965)
    No life for a lady. Boston, Houghton Mifflin, 1941.

————   (3966)
    Titan of the range. *NM,* 19:16, 37, Dec. 1941.
        Ray Morley.

CLEVER, CHARLES P.   (3967)
    *New Mexico: her resources; her necessities for railroad communi-
    cation with the Atlantic and Pacific states; her great future.* Wash-
    ington, McGill & Witherow, 1868.

COAN, CHARLES F.   (3968)
    County boundaries of New Mexico. *Southwestern Political Science
    Quarterly,* 3:252-86, 1922.

————   (3969)
    A history of New Mexico . . . 3 v. Chicago, American Historical
    Society, 1925.

————   (3970)
    A shorter history of New Mexico. 2 v. Ann Arbor, Edwards
    Brothers, 1928.

COCHRANE, LEON JOHN (3971)
A social survey of Dona Ana County. Unpub. Bachelor's thesis, NMSC, 1915.
> Economic, social, religious, and educational conditions.

COCKERILL, P. W. (3972)
Agricultural problems peculiar to the Rio Grande Valley. Address given at School for the Rio Grande Valley, UNM, April 27-May 1, 1942. To be published by the School of Inter-American Affairs in *Proceedings of the School for the Rio Grande Valley.*
> A realistic appraisal of the agricultural situation in the Valley and of the prospects for the future.

COCKERILL, P. W. AND CALLAWAY, R. P. (3973)
Economics of the production and marketing of apples in New Mexico. NMAES Bulletin 242. State College, 1936.

COCKERILL, P. W. AND WALKER, A. L. (3974)
Progress report on production costs of New Mexico vegetables. NMAES Press Bulletin 623. State College, 1931. Processed.
> Press bulletins 624, 625, 627, 628, 658, 659, 669, 671, 672, give costs for individual fruits and vegetables.

—— (3975)
A two-year analysis of farm organization practices in the Middle Rio Grande Conservancy District. NMAES Bulletin 196. State College, 1931.

COHEN, FELIX S. (3975a)
Derecho indigena: contribucion española al sistema legal de los Estados Unidos. Washington, National Indian Institute, 1942.

COLQUITT, EDNA BOULDIN (3976)
Cash crop. *NM,* 18:12-13, 36, Oct. 1940.
> Pecan orchards.

—— (3977)
New Mexico's cantaloupe patch. *NM,* 17:23, 46, June 1939.
> Mesilla Valley.

CONLEE, CARL S. (3978)
The history, past income, and probable trends of the New Mexico permanent common school fund. Unpub. Master's thesis, UNM, 1931.

CONNOR, L. G. (3979)
A brief history of the sheep industry in the United States. 2 v. and supplement. American Historical Association, Annual Report, 1918.
> v. 1, pp. 89-197 deals with New Mexico.

CONWAY, T. F. (3979a)
The bilingual problem in the schools of New Mexico. *Alianza,* 36:13,17, Feb. 1942.

COOK, KATHERINE M. (3980)
Supervision of rural schools. USDI, Bureau of Education, Bulletin 10. Washington, GPO, 1922.
> Includes New Mexico.

COOPERRIDER, C. K. AND HENDRICKS, BARNARD A. (3981)
Erosion on the upper Rio Grande. *Science,* 84:203, 1936.

CORDOVA, ANDREW R.   (3982)
The effect of government land purchases on the tax structure of
three New Mexico counties. *New Mexico Business Review*, 8:3-10,
1939.
> Santa Fe, Sandoval, Rio Arriba.

CORLEY, VAUGHN   (3983)
*New Mexico ranges grouped in areas according to the rate of
stocking capacity with recommended adjustments based on nutritional requirements of livestock.* Unpub. Master's thesis, NMSC,
1937.

COTTRELL, BEATRICE   (3984)
Senate action on the omnibus statehood bill of 1902. Unpub. Master's thesis, UNM, 1939.

COWAN, JOHN L.   (3985)
America's oldest and oddest capital. *Overland*, n. s., 53:169-74,
1909.
> Santa Fe.

————   (3986)
Two more stars for Old Glory. *Pacific Monthly*, Sept. 1909.

CRAFTS, EDWARD C. AND GLENDENING, GEORGE E.   (3987)
How to graze blue grama on Southwestern ranges. USDA Leaflet
215. Washington, GPO, 1942.

CRAIL, F. H.   (3988)
Some problems that confront practitioners in New Mexico. *Southwestern Medicine*, 13:379-82, Sept. 1929.
> Problems in medical care caused by isolation.

CREECY, CARSON HENRY   (3989)
A history of the public schools of Raton, New Mexico. Unpub.
Master's thesis, UNM, 1941.

CROMWELL, O. E.   (3990)
Agriculture along the Rio Grande. *Overland Monthly*, 9:551-,
May 1887.
> Status of agriculture in New Mexico with forecast of "bigger and better."

CRONIN, FRANCIS D. AND BEERS, HOWARD W.   (3991)
Areas of intense drought distress, 1930-36. WPA, Division of Social
Research, Research Bulletin, series 5, no. 1. Washington, GPO,
1937.
> Material on rainfall, crop and cattle conditions, pasture, federal aid, and types
> of farming in New Mexico.

CROOK, ALICE M.   (3992)
Cowboy's dictionary. Unpub. ms. in files of New Mexico Writers'
Project, Santa Fe.

————   (3993)
No priority on adobe. *NM*, 20:18, 34, Nov. 1942.

CULLEY, JACK   (3994)
Cow horses. *NM*, 19:17-19, 34-36, Dec. 1941.

CULLEY, JOHN H.   (3995)
Cattle, horses, and men. Los Angeles, Ward Ritchie Press, 1940.
> Anecdotal delineation of New Mexico ranch life of last four or five decades.

CULMER, FREDERIC A. (3996)
Marking the Santa Fe trail. *NMHR,* 9:78-93, 1934.

CUMMINS, JOHN F. (3997)
Educational trend in New Mexico public schools from 1890-1900 to 1929-1930 inclusive ... Unpub. Master's thesis, UNM, 1937.

CUNNIFF, M. G. (3998)
Last of the territories. *World's Work,* 11:108-19, Jan. 1906.
Social and political situation in New Mexico in 1906.

CUNNINGHAM, JONATHAN ROY (3999)
A political biography of Bronson M. Cutting. Unpub. Master's thesis, UNM, 1940.

CURRIE, BARTON WOOD (4000)
The transformation of the Southwest through the legal abolition of gambling. *Century,* 75:905-10, April 1908.
Effects of 1908 law against gambling in Territory of New Mexico.

CURRIER, CHARLES E. (4001)
The effect of government land purchases on the tax structure of two counties in New Mexico. *New Mexico Business Review,* 8: 167-72, 1939.
Valencia and Sandoval.

CURRY, ALBERT S. (4002)
Production of pinto beans under dry farming and irrigation on experimental plots in the Estancia Valley of New Mexico during 1926 and 1927. NMAES, Press Bulletin 550. State College, 1928. Processed.

―――― (4003)
Results of irrigation treatments on Acala cotton grown in the Mesilla Valley, New Mexico. NMAES Bulletin 220. State College, 1934.

CURRY, GENN (4004)
Americanization of the great Southwest—Arizona and New Mexico are ready for statehood and the duties of statehood. *Journal of American History,* 2:205-07, 1908.

CURTIS, F. S., JR. (4005)
The influence of weapons on New Mexico history. NMHR, 1: 324-34, 1926.

CUSTER, GEORGE E. (4006)
Ranch and farm contacts in New Mexico. *U. S. Dept. of Labor, Employment Service News,* 5:17, 1938.

CUTLER, VERA (4007)
The relation between attendance and achievement in the third grade of San Jose School. Unpub. Master's thesis, UNM, 1936.

DALE, EDWARD E. (4008)
The range cattle industry. Normon, UOP, 1930.

DANBURG, WALTER M. (4009)
New Mexico in the great war. Chapter 3. The state council of defense. *NMHR,* 1:103-20, 1926.

DARGAN, MARION (4010)
New Mexico's fight for statehood, 1895-1912. *NMHR*, 14:1-33, 121-42, 1939; 15:133-87, 1940; 16:70-103, 1941; 18:60-96, 1943.

DAVIES, LAURA A. (4011)
An Indian painter of the West. *EP*, 13:65-69, 1922.
Henry Sharp, Taos.

DAVIS, ARTHUR CADMUS (4012)
Status of the classroom teacher in Taos County. Unpub. Master's thesis, UNM, 1942.
Salary, tenure, experience, and education.

DAVIS, WILLIAM WATTS HART (4013)
El Gringo, or New Mexico and her people. New York, Harper, 1857.

DAWSON, JOSEPH MARTIN (4014)
Keeping up with culture in Texas and the Southwest. *Social Forces*, 10:176-83, 1931.

DEBLER, E. B. AND WALKER A. W. (4015)
Rio Grande. Unpub. ms. dated Aug. 1924 at office of MRGCD.
Study of the water supply demand for the Rio Grande project.

DE BOER, S. R. (4016)
Resettlement in the mountain states. *Planner's Journal.* 2:155-56, 1936.

DEFFENBAUGH, W. S. AND KEESECKER, W. W. (4017)
State boards of education and chief state school officers. USDI, Office of Education, Bulletin 6, Monograph 1, 1940. Washington, GPO, 1941.
Includes New Mexico.

DEFOURI, REV. JAMES H. (4018)
Historical sketch of the Catholic Church in New Mexico. San Francisco, McCormick, 1887.

DEHUFF, JOHN D. (4019)
History of the Santa Fe fiesta. *New Mexico Highway Journal,* 7:18-19, Aug. 1929.

—————— (4020)
The Santa Fe fiesta. *NMHR,* 6:323-25, 1931.

DELANEY, P. (4021)
Frontiering in an automobile. *Outing,* 43:131-35, 1903.

DENNIS, MARY E. (4022)
Plants and animals used as sources of dye, paint, and skin dressing in the Southwest. Unpub. Master's thesis, UNM, 1939.

DEPEW, CHAUNCEY M. (4023)
Speech of Chauncey M. Depew in the Senate of the United States Feb. 11, 12, 13, 17, 1903.
Arguments against admission of New Mexico to statehood, including a number of references to Spanish-speaking people.

DIETRICH, MARGRETTA (4024)
Old art in new forms. *NM,* 14:26-27, 56, Sept. 1936.
Indian and Spanish designs used for Anglo gadgets.

DILLON, R. C. (4025)
New Mexico: an undeveloped empire. *Southern California Business,* Nov. 1927.

DILLS, LUCIUS (4026)
Roswell: some facts and observations relative to its settlement and early growth. Roswell, Chaves County Archaeological and Historical Society, 1933.

DIMOCK, A. W. (4027)
Wild West show. *Harper's Weekly,* 50:1746-48, 1906.
New Mexico Territorial Fair.

DINGUS, CHARLES (4028)
Valley of the windmills. *NM,* 17:12, 13, 37, Dec. 1939.
Portales Valley irrigation.

DIXON, W. H. (4029)
Westward hoboes; ups and downs of frontier motoring. New York, Scribners, 1922.

DOBIE, J. FRANK (4030)
Apache gold and Yaqui silver. Boston, Little Brown, 1939.
Legends of prospecting and lost mines.

———— (4031)
Coronado's children; tales of lost mines and buried treasures of the Southwest. Dallas, Southwest Press, 1930.

———— (4032)
The longhorns. Boston, Little Brown, 1941.

DOMENECH, EM., ABBE (4033)
Seven years' residence in the great deserts of North America. 2 v. London, Longman, Green, Longman, & Roberts, 1860.
Travel description.

———— (4034)
Voyage pittoresque dans les grands deserts du nouveau monde. Paris, Morizot, Libraire-Editeur, 1862.

DONNELL, P. S. (4035)
Historical report of the Middle Rio Grande Conservancy District. Unpub. ms. dated 1926 on file at office of MRGCD.

DONNELLY, THOMAS C. (4036)
The absentee voter problem in New Mexico. UNM, Dept. of Government and Citizenship, Public Affairs series 2, 1938.

———— (4037)
Features essential to a voters' registration law in New Mexico. UNM, Dept. of Government and Citizenship, Public Affairs series 4, 1939.

———— (4038)
Government action in the valley—accomplishments and possibilities. Address given at School for the Rio Grande Valley, UNM, April 27-May 1, 1942. To be published by School of Inter-American Affairs in *Proceedings of the School for the Rio Grande Valley.*
A resume of the social and economic problems of the valley and of the governmental programs for alleviating them.

DONNELLY, THOMAS C. (Continued)   (4039)
The making of the New Mexico constitution. I. Constitutional conventions in the period from 1848 to 1910; their history and significance. *New Mexico Quarterly Review*, 11:452-62, 1941.

————   (4040)
The Constitutional Convention of 1910. *New Mexico Quarterly Review*, 12:435-49, Nov. 1942.

————   (4041)
The New Mexico special election of 1937 on constitutional amendments. *New Mexico Business Review*, 7:164-69, 1938.

————   (4042)
Public health administration in New Mexico. UNM Bulletin, Political Science series, v. 1, no. 2, May 1938.

DONNELLY, THOMAS C., ED.   (4043)
Rocky mountain politics. Albuquerque, UNM Press, 1940.

DONNELLY, THOMAS C. AND SWAYNE, JAMES   (4044)
The labor record of political parties in New Mexico. *New Mexico Business Review*, 5:227-36, 1936.

DORSEY, S. W.   (4045)
Land stealings in New Mexico. *North American Review*, 145: 396, 1887.

DOUTHIRT, C. H.   (4046)
Report on pneumonia control program, 1941-42. *New Mexico Health Officer*, 10:15-19, Sept. 1942.

DOW, HIRAM M.   (4047)
Oil—600,000,000 barrels. *NM*, 16:22-23, 43-44, Aug. 1938.

DOWNING, MARGARET R.   (4048)
Christmas in the Rio Grande country. *Catholic World*, 110:344-54, Dec. 1919.

DRAKE, SAMUEL ADAMS   (4049)
The making of the great West, 1512-1883. New York, Scribners, 1887.

DUNCAN, CATHERINE WATKINS   (4050)
The separate elementary schools for Negroes in the state of New Mexico. *Research*, 2:113-20, July 1938.

————   (4051)
A study and evaluation of the separate elementary schools for Negroes in the state of New Mexico. Unpub. Master's thesis, UNM, 1938.

DUNLAP, LON   (4052)
The Pecos Valley. *NM*, 17:9-11, 43-44, Oct. 1939.
          Historical development.

DUNTON, W. HERBERT   (4053)
The painters of Taos. *EP*, 13:45-46, Aug. 15, 1922.

EARP, J. R.   (4054)
Administrative practice in the West. *American Journal of Public Health*, 26:761-63, 1926.

EASTERN ASSOCIATION ON INDIAN AFFAIRS (4055)
Public health nurses—New Mexico. EAIA, Bulletin 18. New York,
Nov. 1929.

——— (4056)
The Rio Grande River—friend or foe. EAIA, Bulletin 50. New
York, April 1928.

ECCLES, LEONIE SEABROOK (4057)
*A survey of the preparation in Spanish of the elementary grade
teachers in New Mexico.* Unpub. Master's thesis, UNM, 1939.

EDWARDS, WILLIAM H. (4058)
Politics and higher education in New Mexico. *Bulletin of American Association of University Professors,* 28:452-64, Oct. 1942.

ELLIOTT, EDWARD C. (4059)
*State school systems: legislation and judicial decisions relating
to public education, October 1904-October 1906.* USDI, Bureau
of Education, Bulletin 3, 1906. Washington, GPO, 1907. *Same,
October 1906-October 1908.* USDI, Bureau of Education, Bulletin
7, 1908. Washington, GPO, 1909; *Same, October 1908-October
1909.* USDI, Bureau of Education, Bulletin 2, 1910. Washington,
GPO, 1910.

ELLISON, MRS. EDITH NICHOLL (4060)
The desert and the rose. Boston, Cornhill, 1921.
   Travel and description with emphasis on New Mexico agriculture.

ELY, ALBERT G. (4061)
The excavation and repair of Quarai mission. Unpub. Master's
thesis, UNM, 1935. *Also EP,* 39:133-44, 1935.

EMBREE, EDWIN ROGERS (4062)
*Cultural relations in the Rio Grande Valley; the national setting
of the problem.* Address delivered at School for the Rio Grande
Valley, UNM, April 27-May 1, 1942. To be published by the
School of Inter-American Affairs in *Proceedings of the School for
the Rio Grande Valley.*
   A general discussion of the status of minorities in the American scene.

EMERY, W. M. (4063)
A day on the roundup. Unpub. ms. in files of New Mexico Writers' Project, Santa Fe.

ENLOE, E. L. (4064)
New Mexico school laws. Unpub. Master's thesis, UNM, 1930.

ESCUDERO, CARLOS (4065)
Taos . . . by any name. *NM,* 18:20-21, 43-44, March 1940.
   Founding and historical development.

ESPINOSA, AURELIO M. (4065a)
A new classification of the Tar-Baby story on the basis of two
hundred and sixty-seven versions. *JAF,* 56:31-37, Jan.-March,
1943.

ESPINOSA, GILBERTO (4065b)
An opportunity for New Mexico and the Spanish Southwest.
Lulac News, 6:8-10, Jan. 1939.
   Coronado Cuarto Centennial.

ESQUIVEL, JOHN A.   (4065c)
Latin-American true clean sportsmanship recognized. *Lulac News,*
5:10-11, Feb. 1938.

ETTINGER, FRANCES   (4065d)
Feliz navidad. *The Southwest Wind,* 32:23, 30, Dec. 1942.
Reactions of a priest to his first Christmas in a Pueblo.

EVENDEN, EDWARD S., GAMBLE, GUY C., AND BLUE, HAROLD C. (4066)
Teacher personnel in the United States. USDI, Office of Education, Bulletin 10, 1933. v. 2. Washington, GPO, 1935.
Includes New Mexico.

EXNER, M. J. AND CLARKE, WALTER   (4067)
A census of cases of syphilis and of gonorrhea under medical care in New Mexico. *Southwestern Medicine,* 19:241-43, July 1935.

FALLS, ANNA E.   (4068)
The place of private and church schools in the education of the state. Unpub. Master's thesis, UNM, 1929.

FARM CREDIT ADMINISTRATION   (4069)
The story of wool. Episodes 3 and 4, Radio Broadcast series. Washington, 1940. Processed.
Sheep industry in New Mexico.

FAUNCE, HILDA   (4070)
Desert wife. Boston, Little Brown, 1934.
Trading post contacts with Navajo and Hopi.

FAXON, R. H.   (4071)
Raton: gateway. *NM,* 15:13-15, 43, June 1937.
History and development of the town.

FEDERAL EMERGENCY RELIEF ADMINISTRATION   (4072)
Conditions determining residence and settlement for persons seeking relief—Nevada, New Hampshire, New Jersey, New Mexico. FERA, Division of Research, Statistics, and Finance. [Washington,] Jan. 1935. Processed.

————   (4073)
Monthly reports, June 1933 through June 1936. Contain statistical data on relief payments and programs in the various states, including New Mexico.

————   (4074)
Rural problem areas survey reports. No. 42. The short grass, winter wheat areas, Roosevelt County, New Mexico. FERA, Division of Research, Statistics, and Finance. Washington, GPO, 1934.
Relief and rehabilitation survey.

FEDERAL SECURITY AGENCY   (4075)
Public assistance, 1940. FSA, Social Security Board, Bureau of Public Assistance. Washington, GPO, 1940.
Statistics for New Mexico.

FEDERAL WORKS AGENCY   (4076)
First annual report, 1940. Washington, GPO, 1940. *Second annual report, 1941.* Washington, GPO, 1941.
Includes statistics for New Mexico.

FEDERAL WRITERS' PROGRAM, WPA (4077)
New Mexico; a guide to the colorful state. New York, Hastings
House, 1940.
> Includes information on land, history, language, agriculture, industry, folk-
> lore, religion, education, literature, music, architecture, and art.

FELTER, WILLIAM (4078)
Blossom land. *NM*, 15:39, March 1937.
> San Juan country.

FENNEMAN, N. M. (4079)
Physiography of the western United States. New York, McGraw-
Hill, 1931.
> Chapters 1, 2, 7, 8 touch on New Mexico.

FERGUSON, F. E. (4080)
A study of school transportation costs in New Mexico. Unpub.
Master's thesis, Colorado Agricultural College, 1933.

FERGUSSON, ERNA (4081)
The Anglo-Saxon element. Address delivered at School for the
Rio Grande Valley, UNM, April 27-May 1, 1942. To be published
by School of Inter-American Affairs in *Proceedings of the School
for the Rio Grande Valley.*
> Role of the Anglos in the New Mexican cultural pattern.

—————— (4082)
From rodeo to Rotary. *Century*, 113:199-207, Dec. 1926.
> Albuquerque immediately following coming of the railroad.

—————— (4083)
Our Southwest. New York, Knopf, 1940.
> History, description, manners and customs, language, industries.

—————— (4084)
Tearing down the West. *Yale Review*, n. s., 25:331-43, 1935.
> History of spoliation of New Mexico through introduction of livestock by
> Spaniards.

FERGUSSON, HARVEY (4085)
Out where the bureaucracy begins. *Nation*, 121:112, 1925.
> Influence of federal agencies in New Mexico; general low level of New Mexico
> politics.

—————— (4086)
Rio Grande. New York, Knopf, 1933.
> The story of the Rio Grande Valley.

FERGUSSON, HARVEY B. AND CLANCY, F. W. (4087)
Making of a constitution. UNM Bulletin, Sociological series, v. 1,
no. 1, 1910.

FETTER, THEODORE A. (4088)
Southwestern freight rates. Boston, Christopher Pub. House, 1934.

FINGER, CHARLES J. (4089)
Adventure under sapphire skies. New York, Morrow, 1931.
> Chapter 3. New Mexico. Travel description.

—————— (4090)
*Footloose in the West; an account of a journey to western Colo-
rado, California, and New Mexico.* New York, Morrow, 1932.

FIOCK, L. R.   (4091)
*The functioning of a completed irrigation project as illustrated by
the development and operation of the Rio Grande irrigation project.* USDA, SCS, 1934. Typewritten. (Copy in USDA Library,
Albuquerque.

FISHER, REGINALD   (4092)
A sketch of climates and natural regions of New Mexico. *EP,*
46:263-70, 1939.

FISHER, REGINALD AND HEWETT, E. L.   (4093)
Mission monuments of New Mexico. Albuquerque, UNM Press,
1943.

FITE, ARRA BURTON   (4094)
The Irish potato in the Mesilla Valley. Unpub. Master's thesis,
NMSC, 1924.

————   (4095)
*Preliminary report on the growing and marketing of fresh toma-
toes in New Mexico.* NMAES, Bulletin 157. State College, 1927.

FITZPATRICK, ELMER GRANT   (4096)
Reclamation of alkali land in the Mesilla Valley of New Mexico.
Unpub. Bachelor's thesis, NMSC, 1926.

FLECK, MARTIN   (4097)
Notes on the origin and development of Zea Mays. Unpub. Master's thesis, UNM, 1939.

FLEMING, B. P. AND WHITFIELD, C. J.   (4098)
Possibilities of vegetative restoration on the Gila. *The Land, Today and Tomorrow,* 2:15-17, April 1935.

FLETCHER, JOEL E. AND BEUTNER, E. L.   (4099)
*Erodibility investigations on some soils of the upper Gila water-
shed.* USDA, Technical Bulletin 794. Washington, GPO, 1941.

FOGHT, HAROLD W.   (4100)
Efficiency and preparation of rural school teachers. USDI, Bureau
of Education, Bulletin 49, 1914. Washington, GPO, 1915.
    Includes New Mexico.

FOLLANSBEE, R. AND DEAN, H. J.   (4101)
Water resources of the Rio Grande basin, 1888-1913. U. S. Geological Survey, Water Supply Paper 358. Washington, GPO, 1915.

FOLSOM, JOSIAH C.   (4102)
Workmen's compensation acts and agricultural laborers. USDA,
BAE, *Agricultural Situation,* 21:9-10, 1937.
    Includes information on New Mexico's act.

FORDYCE, KENNETH   (4103)
Cowboy music. Unpub. ms. in files of New Mexico Writers' Project, Santa Fe.

FORREST, LEO   (4104)
*Budgets and expenditures for school purposes in Curry County
New Mexico, 1935-36.* Unpub. Master's thesis, UNM, 1938.

FOSTER, L. AND CLEVELAND, W. H. (4105)
Range cow maintenance on yucca and sotol. NMAES, Bulletin
114. State College, 1918.

FOX, P. S. (4106)
Districting New Mexico for sanitation. *American Journal of Public Health,* 29:910-11, 1929.

―――― (4107)
Flood relief in New Mexico. *Southwestern Medicine,* 14:546-47,
1930.

FRENCH, JAMES A. (4108)
Surface water supply of New Mexico, 1888-1917. Albuquerque,
Albright and Anderson, 1918.

FROST, MAX (4109)
The resources, development, and prospects of a great territory.
Santa Fe, New Mexico Bureau of Immigration, 1895.
Information on mining, agriculture, irrigation, markets, land titles.

FROST, MAX, ED. (4110)
New Mexico; its resources, geography, and geological condition.
Santa Fe, New Mexico Bureau of Immigration, 1890.

FROST, MAX AND WALTER, PAUL A. F. (4111)
*Land of sunshine. A handbook of the resources, products, indus-
tries, and climate of New Mexico.* Santa Fe, New Mexican Pub.
Co., 1904. *Also* Santa Fe, New Mexico Bureau of Immigration,
1906.

―――― (4112)
Santa Fe county . . . Santa Fe, New Mexico Bureau of Immigra-
tion, 1906.
Resources, attractions.

FROTHINGHAM, ROBERT (4113)
Trails through the golden west. New York, McBride, 1932.
Travel description.

FULTON, MAURICE G. AND HORGAN, PAUL (4114)
*New Mexico's own chronicle; three races in the writings of four
hundred years.* Dallas, Banks, Upshaw, 1937.
Material taken from original sources to illustrate the development of New
Mexico.

GAINES, NEWTON (4115)
Some characteristics of cowboy songs. *Texas Folklore Society, Publications,* 7:145-54, 1928.

GALLAGHER, THOMAS C. (4116)
Costs of schools in New Mexico in relation to size. Unpub. Master's thesis, UNM, 1934.

GALLOWAY, BERNICE (4117)
*A study of the artistic abilities of natively Spanish-speaking chil-
dren and natively English-speaking children.* Unpub. Master's
thesis, UNM, 1939.

GANNETT, LEWIS S. (4118)
Sweet land. New York, Doubleday Doran, 1934.
Travel description.

GARCIA, GUS C.   (4118a)
Lulac and the English language. *Lulac News*, 5:29-30, Nov. 1938.
Stresses need of Spanish-Americans to learn English.

GARCIA, REV. JOSE   (4118b)
La gente del pais. *Lulac News*, 7:7-8, 26, July 1940.
People of Taos.

————   (4118c)

Symphony in mud. *Lulac News*, 6:9-12, Sept. 1939.
St. Francis Church, Ranchos de Taos.

GARCIA, ZEBEDEO   (4119)
New Mexico state common school funds, sources and distribution.
Unpub. Master's thesis, UNM, 1939.

GATES, E.   (4120)
Stealing a border town. *Cosmopolitan*, 45:577-87, 1908.

GAUMNITZ, WALTER H.   (4121)
Salaries and salary trends of teachers in rural schools. USDI, Bureau of Education, Bulletin 6. Washington, GPO, 1929.
Includes New Mexico.

————   (4122)

The smallness of America's rural high schools. USDI, Office of Education, Bulletin 13. Washington, GPO, 1930.
Includes New Mexico.

GAUT, GERTRUDE FLINN   (4123)
The relative efficiency of the direct methods of teaching the English vocabulary to Spanish-speaking children of kindergarten age. Unpub. Master's thesis, New Mexico Normal (Highlands) University, 1930.

GERBER, C. W.   (4124)
Summary of malarial control work in Dona Ana County, New Mexico. *Southwestern Medicine*, 15:370-75, Aug. 1931.

GHENT, W. J.   (4125)
The centenary of the Santa Fe trail. *Outlook*, 140:517-19, 1925.

GILBERT, F. DE B.   (4126)
New Mexican diets. *Journal of Home Economics*, 34:668-69, Nov. 1942.

GILBERT, HOPE   (4127)
Padre of the Camino Real. *NM*, 18:12-13, 34-35, Feb. 1940.

GLADSON, ROY TAYLOR   (4128)
Needs for high school consolidation in Curry County. Unpub. Master's thesis, New Mexico Normal (Highlands) University, 1932.

GLEASON, LYMAN W.   (4129)
The valley of opportunity. *NM*, 15:28-29, Jan. 1937.
Rio Grande Valley.

GLEAVES, LEO L.   (4130)
An evaluation of the health and physical education programs in the secondary schools of New Mexico. Unpub. Master's thesis, UNM, 1941.

GOAD, EDGAR F. (4130a)
Historical sketch of the University of New Mexico. *Lulac News,* 4:8-9, Dec. 1937.

———— (4131)
A study of the life of Adolph Francis Alphonse Bandelier with an appraisal of his contributions to American anthropology and related sciences. Unpub. Doctor's dissertation, USC, 1939.

GOETZ, OTTO (4132)
Caballo treasure. *NM,* 18:14-15, 35, 37-38, March 1940.
  Hidden treasure legend.

GONZALES, JENNIE M. (4132a)
Shall Spanish be taught in the elementary schools of New Mexico. *Lulac News,* 7:6, Oct. 1940.

GONZALES, M. C. (4132b)
Lulac was first in the effort to stem foreign anti-American propaganda. *Lulac News,* 5:27, Nov. 1938.

GRAHAM, STEPHEN (4133)
In quest of El Dorado. Boston, Appleton, 1923.
  Book III. New Mexico.

GRANT, BLANCHE C. (4134)
Taos today. Taos, the Author, 1925.

———— (4135)
When old trails were new: the story of Taos. New York, Press of the Pioneers, 1934.

GRAY, W. S. AND MONROE, RUTH (4136)
The reading interests and habits of adults. New York, Macmillan, 1929.
  Newspaper and book circulation in New Mexico.

GREAVES, GORDON (4137)
Mr. Peanut goes to war. *NM,* 20:16-17, 32, May 1942.
  Effect of war on Portales Valley crop.

GREELY, ADOLPHUS WASHINGTON (4138)
Report on the climatology of the arid regions of the United States with reference to irrigation. House Exec. Doc. 287, 61st Congress, 2nd Session. Washington, GPO, 1891.

GREER, RICHARD R. (4139)
Origins of the foreign-born population of New Mexico during the territorial period. *NMHR,* 17:281-87, 1942.

GREGGERSON, HERB (4140)
On with the dance. *NM,* 18:20-21, 45-47, Sept. 1940.
  Southwestern square dances.

GRIGGS, GEORGE (4141)
History of the Mesilla Valley or the Gadsden purchase. Mesilla, New Mexico, the Author, 1930.

GUTIERREZ, RUDOLPHO (4141a)
Adult education. *Lulac News,* 6:15-16, Feb. 1939.
  For Spanish-Americans in New Mexico.

HAGERMAN, H. J.   (4142)
The attitude of the Taxpayers' Association to public health work. *Southwestern Medicine,* 10:394-96, Sept. 1926.
   Public health service should aim at meeting community needs rather than providing individual relief.

———   (4143)
Matters relating to the administration and removal of Henry J. Hagerman, Governor of New Mexico 1906-07. Printed for private circulation, 1908.

HAINES, HELEN   (4144)
History of New Mexico from the Spanish conquest to the present time, 1530-1890. New York, New Mexico Historical Pub. Co., 1891.

HALL, DONALD J.   (4145)
Enchanted sand: a New Mexican pilgrimage. New York, Morrow, 1933.
   Travel description.

HALSETH, ODD S.   (4146)
Fieldwork at Gran Quivira. *EP,* 21:223-26, 1926.

HARDY, ERLE L., OVERPECK, J. C., AND WILSON, C. P.   (4147)
Precipitation and evaporation in New Mexico. NMAES, Bulletin 269. State College, 1939.

HARGER, C. M.   (4148)
Our two new states. *Outlook,* 97:165-76, 1911.

HARPER, ALLAN G.   (4149)
The war and cultural relations in the Rio Grande Valley; the inter-American setting. Address given before School for the Rio Grande Valley, UNM, April 27-May 1, 1942. To be published by School of Inter-American Affairs in *Proceedings of the School for the Rio Grande Valley.*
   The importance of New Mexican Spanish-Americans and Indians in inter-American relations.

HARPER, ALLAN G., CORDOVA, ANDREW, AND OBERG, KALERVO   (4150)
Man and resources in the Middle Rio Grande Valley. Albuquerque, UNM Press, 1943.
   A summary statement of the social and economic problems of the valley with suggestions for their solution.

HARPER, WILLIAM   (4151)
A history of New Mexico election laws. Unpub. Master's thesis, UNM, 1927.

HARRINGTON, E. R.   (4152)
Bean valley. *NM,* 18:16-17, 36-37, Nov. 1940.
   Estancia Valley.

———   (4153)
Geological chart of New Mexico. *NM,* 19:17, Feb. 1941.
   Resources of the state.

———   (4153a)
The Pecos . . . river of romance. *NM,* 21:7-9, 29, 30, Jan. 1943.

———   (4154)
Rio Grande. *NM,* 17:12-13, 45-47, Sept. 1939.
   Irrigation and flood control.

HARRIS, D. V. AND HEADLEY, R. D. (4155)
Work report, detailed soil and erosion survey, Isleta Pueblo grant, Rio Grande District. USDA, SCS, 1936. Processed.

HARRIS, GERTRUDE (4156)
At the end of the Santa Fe trail. *NM*, 11:10-13, 45-46, June 1933.

—— (4157)
Sketches of old Santa Fe. *NM*, 11:26-28, 48, July; 24-26, 48, Sept., 1933.

HARVEY, HUGH (4158)
Range survey San Luis, Cabezon, Guadalupe, and Casa Salazar. USDI, UPA, 1938. Typewritten. (Copy at USDA Library, Albuquerque.)

HARVEY, LUCIA M. (4159)
The Miami ranch of Springer, New Mexico. *The Earth*, Feb. 1908.

HAUTER, L. H. (4160)
Economics of crop production on the Elephant Butte Irrigation Project. NMAES, Extension Circular 97. State College, 1928.

—— (4161)
Milk production on the Elephant Butte Irrigation Project. NMAES, Extension Circular 99. State College, 1929.

—— (4162)
Sheep and cattle on southern New Mexico irrigated farms. NMAES, Extension Circular 98. State College, 1928.

HAUTER, L. H. AND HUNTER, BYRON (4163)
Estimated returns from operating an 80-acre Mesilla Valley farm under eight different plans in 1932. A method of determining what to produce. NMAES, Extension Circular 124. State College, 1933.

HAUTER, L. H., WALKER, A. L., AND WELLS, O. V. (4164)
A five-year economic study of 125 farms in Curry and Roosevelt Counties, New Mexico. NMAES, Bulletin 186. State College, 1930

—— (4165)
Production requirements, costs, and returns from dry land farming in eastern New Mexico. NMAES Bulletin 187. State College, 1930.

—— (4166)
Selecting the most profitable system of dry-land farming in eastern New Mexico. NMAES, Bulletin 188. State College, 1931.

HAWLEY, FLORENCE (4167)
Yes, we have no old apples. *NM*, 14:16, Aug. 1936.
Manzano orchards no earlier than 1800.

HEARD, DWIGHT B. (4168)
Why Arizona opposes union with New Mexico. *World Today*, 10:409-18, April, 1906.

HEBART, GRACE RAYMOND (4169)
The pathbreakers from river to ocean; the story of the great West from the time of Coronado to the present. Glendale, Clark, 1932.

HELLBUSH, C. E.   (4170)
New Mexico tries irrigated pastures. *Western Farm Life,* Sept.
15, 1942.

HELLER, C. A.   (4171)
Education in nutrition as part of the maternal health program.
American Journal of Public Health, 32:1021-24, Sept. 1942.
    In New Mexico.

HEMING, H. B.   (4172)
Facts about the Las Vegas Grant. *The Earth,* Oct. 1907.

HENDERSON, ALICE CORBIN   (4173)
New Mexico in the great war. Chapter 5. The women's part.
NMHR, 1:231-45, 1926.

HENDERSON, MARY   (4174)
Historical sketch of Latter Day Saints settlements in New Mexico.
Unpub. ms. in Historical Records Survey files, Albuquerque.

HENDERSON, ROSE   (4175)
Architecture of the Southwest. *EP,* 16:19-22, 1924.
    Evolution from Pueblo and mission architecture.

———   (4176)
Little journeys in America. Dallas, Southern Pub. Co., 1923.
    One chapter on the Southwest.

HEPLER, ROBERT D.   (4177)
William Watts Hart Davis in New Mexico. Unpub. Master's
thesis, UNM, 1941.

HERBST, GEORGE F.   (4178)
Extra-curricular activities, their status in New Mexico. Unpub.
Master's thesis, New Mexico Normal (Highlands) University,
1930.

HERNANDEZ, A. S.   (4178a)
Taos and the Carson National Forest. *Lulac News,* 5:13-14, Sept.
1938.

HERRING, H. C.   (4179)
Study in red, white, and New Mexico. *Christian Century,* 41:1331-
32, 1924.

HERRING, LOUIS B.   (4180)
*A comparison of property values with assessed valuation in Albu-
querque and vicinity.* Unpub. Master's thesis, UNM, 1934.

HEWETT, EDGAR L.   (4181)
Address at the opening of the new museum at Santa Fe. *EP,*
4 (4) :71-75, 1917.

———   (4182)
New Mexico in the great war. Chapter II. The cost and the gain.
NMHR, 2:21-26, 1927.

———   (4183)
Preservation of American antiquities; progress during the last year;
needed legislation. *AA,* 8:109-14, 1906.

———   (4184)
The proposed "National Park of the Cliff Cities." *EP,* 3 (3) :50-56,
1916.

HEWETT, EDGAR L. (Continued)   (4185)
Santa Fe in 1926. *EP*, 4 (1) :23-27, 1917.

——   (4186)
The Southwest: yesterday and tomorrow. *EP*, 10 (6) :6-11, 1921.

HEWETT, EDGAR L. AND MAUZY, WAYNE L.   (4187)
Land marks of New Mexico. Albuquerque, UNM Press, 1940.

HIBBARD, BENJAMIN HORACE   (4188)
History of public land policy. New York, Macmillan, 1924.

HIGGINS, CHARLES A.   (4189)
To California over the Santa Fe trail. Chicago, ATSF Railway
Co., 1915.

HILL, DAVID S.   (4190)
The new conquest of the Southwest. UNM Bulletin, Political Science series, v. 1, no. 1, 1925.
    Colorado River compact.

HILL, R. M.   (4191)
Basic economic and social data for the Southwest region. USDA,
SCS Region 6, Albuquerque, Aug. 1942. (Copy at USDA Library,
Albuquerque.)

HILL, ROBERT T.   (4192)
*An estimate of the resources and possible revenues of the Armen-
dariz grants, New Mexico.* Washington, 1893.

HINES, ELSIE RAY   (4193)
History of education in New Mexico. Unpub. Bachelor's thesis,
NMSC, 1911.

HINES, FRED PHILIP   (4194)
The development of education in De Baca County, New Mexico.
Unpub. Master's thesis, University of Texas, 1940.

HINTON, RICHARD JOSIAH   (4195)
*Irrigation in the United States, being a second edition of Misc.
Doc. 15, 49th Congress.* Washington, GPO, 1890. (No. 928,
Part 6, Senate select committee on irrigation and reclamation of
arid lands.)

——   (4196)
*A report on irrigation and the cultivation of the soil thereby with
physical data, condition and progress within the United States for
1891.* 4 Parts. Senate Exec. Doc. 41, 52nd Congress, 1st Session.
Washington, GPO, 1893.

HITE, OLIVE ENNIS   (4197)
A mystery of old Albuquerque. *The Southwest Magazine*, Feb.
1890.

HOBBS, HULDA R.   (4198)
Bandelier in the Southwest. *EP*, 47:121-36, 1940.

HOBLIT, O. B.   (4199)
New Mexican picture. *Overland*, n. s., 71:491-92, 1918.

HOCHMUTH, H. R. AND OTHERS   (4200)
Sheep migration in the Intermountain Region. USDA, Circular
624. Washington, GPO, 1942.

HODGE, FREDERICK WEBB   (4201)
   The verification of a tradition. *AA*, o. s., 10:299-302, 1897.
      Evidence that Enchanted Mesa was once occupied.

HOGNER, DOROTHY CHILDS   (4202)
   Westward, high, low, and dry. New York, Dutton, 1938.
      Travel description.

HOGREFE, HARRY L.   (4203)
   Eighth grade objectives and testing those objectives in New Mexico. Unpub. Master's thesis, UNM, 1930.

——————   (4204)
   Unit costs in public education. *New Mexico Business Review,*
   9:78-83, 1940.
      Statistics by counties.

HOGUE, ALEXANDER   (4205)
   History and romance of Villa Real de Santa Fe. *EP,* 26: 42-52,
   1929.

HOGUE, ALEXANDRE (ALEXANDER?)   (4206)
   Land of little churches. *EP,* 26:204-12, 1929.
      Taos and vicinity.

HOLBROOK, CAREY   (4207)
   Great goats. *NM,* 16:20-21, 40, Oct. 1938.
      Development of a goat ranch near Albuquerque.

——————   (4208)
   More ambitious acres. *NM,* 17:12-13, 33, Nov. 1939.
      Rio Grande Valley.

HOLLING, HOLLING CLANCY   (4209)
   New Mexico made easy with words of modern syllables. Chicago,
   Rockwell F. Clancy Co., 1923.

HOLLINGER, EDWIN CONDIT   (4210)
   The effect of population and occupation shifts on rural life.
   NMSC, Extension service. State College, 1935. Processed.

——————   (4211)
   Farm economics in the farm home. NMSC, Extension Service,
   County Program Planning 18. State College, 1936.

——————   (4212)
   Studies in land economics in New Mexico. Unpub. Master's
   thesis, NMSC, 1929.

HOLMES, GEORGE K.   (4213)
   Wages of farm labor. U. S. Bureau of Statistics, Bulletin 99. Washington, GPO, 1912.
      Includes New Mexico.

HOOD, WILLIAM R.   (4214)
   Important state laws relating to education in 1922 and 1923.
   USDI, Bureau of Education, Bulletin 2. Washington, GPO, 1925.
      Includes New Mexico.

——————   (4215)
   Legal provisions for rural high schools. USDI, Bureau of Education, Bulletin 40, 1924. Washington, GPO, 1925.
      Includes New Mexico.

HOOD, WILLIAM R. (Continued)   (4216)
State laws relating to education enacted in 1918 and 1919. USDI,
Bureau of Education, Bulletin 30, 1920. Washington, GPO, 1921.
    Includes New Mexico.

——————   (4217)
State laws relating to education enacted in 1920 and 1921. USDI,
Bureau of Education, Bulletin 20. Washington, GPO, 1922.
    Includes New Mexico.

HORTON, LEO   (4218)
Potash production and marketing. Santa Fe, State Planning Board,
1937. Processed.

HOSEA, R. G.   (4219)
*Floods in the Rio Grande through the Middle Valley and a detailed
study of the flood of September 21, 23, 1929.* Unpub. undated ms.
at office of MRGCD, Albuquerque.

——————   (4220)
The Middle Rio Grande Conservancy District. *New Mexico Highway Journal,* 7:6-9, May 1929.

——————   (4221)
Report on irrigation in the Rio Grande Valley. Unpub. undated
ms. at office of MRGCD, Albuquerque.
    Includes a history of settlement and irrigation and a report on status of
    existing water rights in the Valley.

——————   (4222)
Rio Grande development projects in New Mexico. *Engineering
News,* 98:400-01, March 10, 1927.

——————   (4223)
The Rio Grande flood of August 13, 1929. Unpub. undated ms.
at office of MRGCD, Albuquerque.

HOUGH, EMERSON   (4224)
Story of the cowboy. New York, Appleton, 1897.

HOWELL, C. H.   (4225)
A description of the district and the construction of its works.
Unpub. undated ms. at office of MRGCD, Albuquerque.

HUBBELL, D. S., GARDNER, J. L., AND SHERMAN, G. L.   (4226)
*Soil and water conservation investigation progress report on Mexi-
can Springs, 1934-39.* USDA, SCS. Washington, 1941. Processed.

HUDDLESTON, RUTH B.   (4227)
New Mexico—la tierra de mañana. *Public Health Nursing,* 29:421-
24, 1937.

HUFF, RAYMOND   (4228)
*Development and operation of the county unit system in New Mex-
ico.* Unpub. Master's thesis, University of Colorado, 1930.

HUGHES, DOROTHY L.   (4229)
*Pueblo on the mesa; the first fifty years at the University of New
Mexico.* Albuquerque, UNM Press, 1939.

HUGHES, MARIE M.   (4230)
*Teaching a standard English vocabulary with initial reading in-
struction.* Santa Fe, New Mexico State Department of Education,
1932.

HUMBLE, C. W. AND VICKERS, G. S   (4231)
   Economic survey of the dairies of the Mesilla Valley. Unpub.
   Bachelor's thesis, NMSC, 1917.

HUNT, GEORGE R.   (4232)
   *A study of the intra-county distribution of certain budgeted cur-
   rent expenditures in New Mexico public schools.* Unpub. Master's
   thesis, UNM, 1940.

HUNTER, MARY   (4233)
   Modern painters of Santa Fe. *SR,* 13:401-06, 1928.

HURT, AMY PASSMORE   (4234)
   All in a nutshell. *NM,* 11:16-18, 46-47, June 1933.
      Piñon industry.

HURT, WESLEY R., JR.   (4235)
   Ruins that defy time. *NM,* 18:16, 43-44, Sept. 1940.
      Quarai.

————   (4236)

   Shadows of the past. *NM,* 18:21, 37-38, May 1940.
      History of Chilili.

HUTCHINS, WELLS A.   (4236a)
   The community acequia: its origin and development. *Southwestern Historical Quarterly,* 31:261-84, 1927-28.

ICKES, ANNA W.   (4237)
   Mesa land: the history and romance of the American Southwest.
   Boston, Houghton Mifflin, 1933.

INGERSOLL, ERNEST   (4238)
   La Villa Real de Santa Fe. *Harpers,* 60:667-82, April 1880.

INTERNATIONAL BOUNDARY COMMISSION   (4239)
   *Flow of the Rio Grande and tributary contributions from San
   Marcial, New Mexico to Gulf of Mexico, 1940.* Water Bulletin
   10. Washington, GPO, 1941.

————   (4240)

   *Report of the Commission upon the survey and remarking of the
   boundary between the United States and Mexico, west of the Rio
   Grande, 1891-96.* 2 Parts. Washington, GPO, 1898.

JACKSON, MARGARET MERLE   (4241)
   *The training of high school English teachers in Texas and New
   Mexico.* Unpub. Master's thesis, New Mexico State Teachers Col-
   lege, 1932.

JACKSON, MILI   (4242)
   Libraries in New Mexico. Santa Fe, State Planning Board, Sept.
   15, 1936. Processed.

JAMES, A. E.   (4243)
   Municipal school costs and achievements in New Mexico. *New
   Mexico Tax Review,* 1:3-8, March 1916.
      Analysis of municipal school costs and their relation to attendance.

————   (4244)

   Rural school costs and achievements in New Mexico. *New Mexico
   Tax Review,* 1:18-23, Feb. 1916.
      Daily cost per pupil by counties.

JAMES, GEORGE WHARTON (4245)
Mission—pueblo architecture of New Mexico. *Overland*, n. s., 73: 382-88, 1919.

—— (4246)
New Mexico, the land of the delight makers. Boston, Page Co., 1920.
Its history, people, land.

—— (4247)
Reclaiming the arid West. New York, Dodd Mead, 1917.

JAMES, WILL (4248)
The American cowboy. New York, Scribners, 1942.

—— (4249)
Lone cowboy. New York, Scribners, 1930.

JEBENS, ARTHUR B. AND ENGELBERT, ERNEST (4250)
1941 summary of outstanding federal and state legislation affecting rural land use. USDA, BAE. Washington, June 1942. Processed.
Includes New Mexico.

JOHANSEN, SIGURD (4251)
Migratory-casual workers in New Mexico. (In Brown, Malcolm and Cassmore, Orin: *Migratory cotton pickers in Arizona.* WPA, Division of Research. Washington, 1939.)

—— (4252)
New Mexico's place in United States population. NMAES, Press Bulletin 926. State College, 1941.

—— (4253)
The population of New Mexico; its composition and changes. NMAES, Bulletin 273. State College, 1940.

—— (4254)
Population trends in New Mexico. NMAES, Press Bulletin 869. State College, 1939. Processed.

—— (4255)
Recent population changes in New Mexico. NMAES, Press Bulletin 931. State College, 1941.

JOHNSON, CLAUDE E. (4256)
The municipal government of the city of Las Vegas, New Mexico, for the year 1909. Unpub. Master's thesis, New Mexico Normal (Highlands) University, 1935.

JOHNSON, D. W. (4257)
To the Manzano salt lakes. *Out West*, 16:367-76, 1902.

JOHNSON, E. DANA (4258)
New Mexico's first state automobile. *NMHR*, 11:1-8, 1936.

JOHNSON, WILLIAM TEMPLETON (4259)
The archaic architecture of New Mexico. *American Institute of Architecture Journal*, 7:65-70, 1919.

—— (4260)
Bell towers and capitals. *Survey*, 66:158-59, 1931.
Mission architecture of the Southwest.

—— (4261)
The Santa Fe of the future. *EP*, 3 (3):11-31, 1916.

JONES, FAYETTE ALEXANDER   (4262)
    Epitome of the economic geology of New Mexico. Santa Fe, New Mexico Bureau of Immigration, 1908.

—————   (4263)
    The mineral resources of New Mexico. New Mexico School of Mines, Mineral Resource Survey, Bulletin 1. Socorro, 1915.

—————   (4264)
    New Mexico mines and minerals . . . Santa Fe, New Mexican Printing Co., 1904.

JONES, S. A.   (4265)
    Melrose, Roosevelt County, New Mexico. *The Earth,* March 1908.

JONES, VOLNEY H.   (4265a)
    A native Southwestern tea plant. *EP,* 49:272-80, Dec. 1942.

JONSON, CARL R.   (4266)
    A study of the Spanish-American Normal School at El Rito. Unpub. Master's thesis, UNM, 1939.

JORDAN, HARRY J.   (4267)
    The activity of home financing agencies in New Mexico. *New Mexico Business Review,* 9:172-77, 1940.

JULIAN, G. W.   (4268)
    Land stealings in New Mexico. *North American Review,* 145:17, 1887.

—————   (4269)
    Redemption of New Mexico. *Magazine of Western History,* 10: 238-, 1889.

KALBACH, L. A., AND NEAL, A. O.   (4270)
    Organization of state departments of education. USDI, Bureau of Education, Bulletin 46, 1920. Washington, GPO, 1921.
        Includes New Mexico.

KAY, ELEANOR   (4271)
    Gems galore. *NM,* 17:18-19, 41-43, Sept. 1939.
        Precious stones in New Mexico.

KEESECKER, WARD W.   (4272)
    Legal status of Bible reading and religious instruction in public schools. USDI, Office of Education, Bulletin 14. Washington, GPO, 1930.
        Includes New Mexico.

—————   (4273)
    A review of education legislation 1937-38. USDI, Office of Education, Bulletin 16. Washington, GPO, 1939.

KEITH, GENTRY   (4274)
    Crossroads. *NM,* 18:21, 35-37, Feb. 1940.
        Historical development of Belen.

—————   (4275)
    Peaceful village. *NM,* 17:16-17, 42-43, June 1939.
        Tome.

KELEHER, JULIA AND CHANT, ELSIE RUTH   (4276)
    The padre of Isleta. Santa Fe, Rydal Press, 1940.
        Life and accomplishments of Father Docher.

KELEHER, ROBERT F., ED. (4277)
Resources and opportunities of the Middle Rio Grande Valley.
UNM Bulletin, Economics series, v. 2, no. 3, 1935.

KELEHER, W. A. (4278)
Law of New Mexico land grant. Santa Fe, Historical Society of
New Mexico, 1929.

———— (4279)
The Maxwell land grant; a New Mexico item. Santa Fe, Rydal
Press, 1942.

KENNAMER, L. G. (4280)
Cattle ranch in New Mexico. *Journal of Geography,* 22:153-60,
1923.

KENYON, WILLIAM S. (4281)
Report on land claims in New Mexico. House Report 321, 36th
Congress, 1st Session. Washington, GPO, 1903.

KERR, J. W. (4282)
Public health administration in New Mexico. *Public Health
Reports,* 33:1976-95, 1918.

KIKER, VESTA (4283)
The kingdom of Colfax. *NM,* 15:22-23, 45, June 1937.
History and development of Colfax County.

KLUCKHOHN, CLYDE (4284)
To the foot of the rainbow. New York, Century, 1927.
A tale of 2,500 miles of wandering on horseback through the Southwest.

KNEE, ERNEST (4285)
Santa Fe, New Mexico. New York, Hastings House, 1942.
Photographs illustrating phases of culture of Santa Fe and vicinity.

KOEHLER, A. (4286)
New Mexico, the land of opportunity. Albuquerque, n. p., 1915.
Resources and attractions.

KOOGLER, CLAIR VANE (4287)
Transportation of school children in New Mexico. Unpub.
Master's thesis, New Mexico Normal (Highlands) University,
1934.

KREHBIEL, LAURA R. (4288)
Red River valley. *NM,* 16:26-27, 40, 41, Jan. 1938.
Historical development of Red River and vicinity.

KRICH, ARON AND GAROFFOLO, VINCENT (4289)
Regionalism and politics. *New Mexico Quarterly,* 6:261-69, 1937.
Regionalism as a cover for social and economic exploitation.

KRUSE, HORACE W. (4290)
*Americanizing an industrial center. An account of the experience
and procedure in the towns of the St. Louis, Rocky Mountain, and
Pacific Company in Colfax County, New Mexico.* Raton, St.
Louis, Rocky Mountain, & Pacific Co., 1920.

KUBLER, GEORGE C. (4291)
*The religious architecture of New Mexico in the colonial period
and since the American occupation.* Contributions of the Colorado Springs Fine Arts Center, Taylor Museum, 1940.

LADD, HORATIO O.   (4292)
  The story of the states; the story of New Mexico. Boston, Lothrop,
  1891.

LANDERS, G. V.   (4293)
  *A study of the training, experience, tenure, and salaries of the high
  school teachers of New Mexico.* Unpub. Master's thesis, New
  Mexico Normal (Highlands) University, 1933.

LANDERS, MARIE W.   (4294)
  *A study of the training, experience, tenure, and salaries of ele-
  mentary teachers of New Mexico.* Unpub. Master's thesis, New
  Mexico Normal (Highlands) University, 1931.

LANTZ, EDITH M.   (4295)
  Dehydration of green chili at home. NMAES, Press Bulletin 955.
  State College, Sept. 1942.

LARKIN, A. S.   (4296)
  Between two machines. *Woman Citizen,* n. s., 10:13, Nov. 1925.

LARKIN, MARGARET   (4297)
  Singing cowboy; a book of western songs. New York, Knopf, 1931.

LARSON, OLAF F.   (4298)
  Farm population mobility in the southern great plains. *Social
  Forces,* 18:514-20, 1940.

LASKY, SAMUEL G. AND WOOTTON, THOMAS PELTIER   (4299)
  The metal resources of New Mexico and their economic features.
  New Mexico School of Mines, Bulletin 7. Socorro, 1933.

LAUT, AGNES CHRISTINA   (4300)
  The conquest of our western empire. New York, McBride, 1927.

————   (4301)
  How irrigation is making good. *Review of Reviews,* 46:457-61,
  1912.
          Roswell region and Pecos valley.

————   (4302)
  Through our unknown Southwest . . . New York, McBride, 1913.
          Travel description.

LAWRENCE, D. H.   (4303)
  New Mexico. *Survey,* 66:153-55, 1931.
          Religious-esthetic interpretation of New Mexico environment.

LEE, W. T.   (4304)
  *Water resources of the Rio Grande Valley in New Mexico and their
  development.* U. S. Geological Survey, Water Supply Paper 188.
  Washington, GPO, 1907.

LEOPOLD, LUNA B.   (4305)
  Areal extent of intense rainfalls, New Mexico and Arizona. USDA,
  SCS, 1942. Processed. (Copy at USDA Library, Albuquerque.)
  Also American Geophysical Union, Transactions, 1942. Pt. 2, pp.
  558-63.

————   (4306)
  Characteristics of high rainfall in New Mexico and Arizona.
  USDA, SCS, 1942. Processed. (Copy at USDA Library, Albu-
  querque.)

LIGON, J. STOKLEY   (4307)
Conservation—hope of the Southwest. *NM*, 11:22-24, 42, 44, Aug. 1933.

———   (4308)
Wild life of New Mexico. Santa Fe, New Mexican Ptg. Co., 1927.

LINDER, ROBERT L.   (4309)
Life span of business in Albuquerque, New Mexico. *New Mexico Business Review*, 8:31-35, 1939.

LINNEY, CHARLES E., GARCIA, FABIAN, AND HOLLINGER, E. C.   (4310)
Climate as it affects crops and ranges in New Mexico. NMAES Bulletin 182. State College, 1930.

LITCHFIELD, E.   (4311)
Vocational choices of Clovis, New Mexico, high school graduates according to intelligence and occupational levels of their parents. Unpub. Master's thesis, UNM, 1936.

LITTLE, ELBERT L., JR.   (4312)
Profit in piñon nuts. *NM*, 16:12-13, Feb. 1938.

LIVELY, C. E. AND TAEUBER, CONRAD   (4313)
Rural migration in the United States. WPA, Division of Social Research, Research Monograph 19. Washington, 1939.
        Includes New Mexico.

LIVINGSTON, CARL   (4314)
Secrets of the Guadalupes. *New Mexico Highway Journal*, 7:6-9, January; 9-11, 20, March; 15, April 1929.

LOGAN, ROBERT R.   (4315)
Notes on New Mexico banking. *New Mexico Quarterly Review*, 11:200-10, 1941.

LOMAX, JOHN A.   (4316)
Cowboy songs and other frontier ballads. New York, Macmillan, 1919.

LOMAX, P. S.   (4317)
Significant results of Missouri and New Mexico commercial education surveys. *School Review*, 26:73-84, Feb. 1918.

LONG, HANIEL   (4318)
Piñon country. New York, Duell, Sloan, & Pearce, 1941.

LONG, WILLIAM S.   (4318a)
Importance of irrigation to New Mexico and Arizona. *American Catholic Quarterly Review*, 43:330-39, 1918.

LOOMIS, CHARLES P.   (4319)
Informal social participation in the planned rural communities. *Sociometry*, 2:1-37, 1939.
        Studies of Bosque Farms and Tortugas.

———   (4320)
Social organization of Tortugas Indian village. Unpub. ms. in possession of the author.

LOOMIS, CHARLES P. AND LEONARD, OLEN   (4321)
Standard of living of the residents of seven rural resettlement communities. Summarized in *Monthly Labor Review*, 48:105-07, 1939.
        Includes Bosque Farms and Tortugas.

LORD, RUSSELL   (4322)
   To hold this soil. USDA, Misc. Pub. 321. Washington, 1938.
    Soil conservation and erosion.

LOTTRITZ, J. MARTIN   (4323)
   Lure of lost mines. *NM,* 15:12-13, 38-39, Oct. 1937.

LOVE, CLARA M.   (4324)
   History of the cattle industry in the Southwest. *Southwestern Historical Quarterly,* 19:370-99; 20:1-18, 1916.

LOWE, ROBERT C.   (4325)
   State public welfare legislation. WPA, Division of Research, Research Monograph 20. Washington, GPO, 1939.
    Includes New Mexico.

LOWE, ROBERT C. AND HOLCOMBE, JOHN L.   (4326)
   Legislative trends in public relief and assistance, December 31, 1929 to July 1, 1936. WPA, Division of Social Research, Research Bulletin, Series 3, no. 2. Washington, GPO, 1936.
    Includes New Mexico.

LUCKETT, G. S.   (4327)
   Health work in New Mexico is five years old. *Nation's Health,* 6:745-46, 1924.

LUHAN, MABEL DODGE   (4328)
   Circus in Taos. *Over the Turquoise Trail,* 1:10-18, Autumn 1938.
    Description of the visit of a circus to the village of Taos.

———   (4329)
   Edge of Taos desert; an escape to reality. New York, Harcourt Brace, 1937.

———   (4330)
   Winter in Taos. New York, Harcourt Brace, 1935.

LULAC NEWS   (4330a)
   Monthly publication of the League of United Latin-American Citizens containing articles giving Spanish-American viewpoint on social and economic problems of New Mexico. 1934-date.

LUMMIS, CHARLES F.   (4331)
   King of the broncos and other stories of New Mexico. New York, Scribners, 1918.

———   (4332)
   Land of poco tiempo. New York, Scribners, 1913.
    Cultural description of New Mexico.

———   (4333)
   Mesa, cañon, and pueblo. New York, Century, 1925.
    Travel description. A revision of *Some strange corners of our country.*

———   (4334)
   New Mexico David and other stories and sketches of the Southwest. New York, Scribners, 1905.

———   (4334a)
   Santa Fe—the capital of our romance. *Lulac News,* 5:3-5, June 1938.

———   (4335)
   Some strange corners of our country. New York, Century, 1906.
    Travel description.

LUMMIS, CHARLES F. (Continued)   (4336)
  A tramp across the continent. New York, Scribners, 1908.
    Travel description.

LUNA, MAX L.   (4336a)
  Vocational training . . . *Lulac News,* 6:27, Sept. 1939.
    Taos County vocational school.

LUSK, DON   (4337)
  Bonanzas. *NM,* 16:19-21, 44-45, June 1938.
    Grant County mining.

LUSK, MRS. G.   (4338)
  Standards for teachers in New Mexico. *School and Society,* 33:
  583, 1931.

MCALLISTER, DOROTHY   (4339)
  The Santa Fe fiesta. *EP,* 11:78-81, 1921.

MCBRIDE, R. E.   (4340)
  Dona Ana County in New Mexico. Santa Fe, New Mexico Bureau
  of Immigration, 1908.
    Resources and attractions.

MCCANN, FRANKLIN T.   (4341)
  *The growth of the tourist court in the United States, and its re-
  lationship to the urban development of Albuquerque, New
  Mexico.* Denison University Bulletin, v. 42, no. 2 (*Journal of the
  Scientific Laboratories,* v. 37.) Granville, Ohio, April 1942. pp.
  51-66.

MCCANNE, D. J.   (4342)
  In and around old Fort Sumner. *The Earth,* Feb. 1909.

MCCLANAHAN, MURIEL H.   (4343)
  *Aspects of Southwestern regionalism in the prose works of Mary
  Austin.* Doctor's dissertation, University of Pittsburgh, 1941.

MCCLENAHAN, P. E.   (4344)
  Las Cruces: the crosses. *Americana,* 5:292-97, 1910.

————   (4345)
  Reminiscences of Southwest America. *Journal of American
  History,* 2:669-73, 1908.

MCCORMICK, WILFRED   (4346)
  Acres of wealth. *NM,* 16:21-23, 35-36, April 1938.
    State lands.

————   (4347)
  Anchors away. *NM,* 19:9-11, 38-39, June 1941.
    German prison camp at Fort Stanton.

————   (4348)
  Black manna. *NM,* 15:9-11, 36, Sept. 1937.
    Oil at Hobbs.

————   (4349)
  From gamble to cinch. *NM,* 15:12-13, 39-40, Nov. 1937.
    Farming near Roswell.

————   (4350)
  The magic of water. *NM,* 17:22-23, 41-42, Oct. 1939.
    Pecos Valley.

MCCORMICK, WILFRED (Continued)   (4351)
Riches in royalties. *NM*, 15:9-11, 42, Oct. 1937.
<small>Oil in New Mexico.</small>

MCCRACKEN, GLEN F.   (4352)
A comparative study of certain objective factors of the Protestant and the public high schools of New Mexico. Unpub. Master's thesis, UNM, 1939.

MCDOUGAL, CLAUDE   (4353)
Sex and cultural differences on New Mexico state test of academic achievement. Unpub. Master's thesis, UNM, 1939.

MCDOWELL, ARCHIE   (4354)
The opposition to statehood within the territory of New Mexico, 1888-1903. Unpub. Master's thesis, UNM, 1940.

MCFIE, MAUDE ELIZABETH   (4355)
A history of the Mesilla Valley. Unpub. Bachelor's thesis, NMSC, 1903.

MCILHARGEY, A. L.   (4356)
Indian and Mexican jewelry. *Great Southwest*, May 1907.

MCKELWAY, A. J.   (4357)
Social principles of the new state constitutions. *Survey*, 25:610-12, 1911.

MCKINLEY, FRANK ROBERT   (4358)
The teaching and integration of health and physical education in the secondary schools of New Mexico. Unpub. Master's thesis, New Mexico Normal (Highlands) University, 1932.

MCMILLAN, MYRTLE   (4359)
History of the growth of education in Las Vegas, New Mexico. Unpub. Master's thesis, New Mexico Normal (Highlands) University, 1935.

MCPARLIN, THOMAS A.   (4360)
Notes on the history and climate of New Mexico. *Smithsonian Annual report, 1877.* Washington, 1878. pp. 321-48.

MADDOX, CHARLES   (4361)
The statehood policy of Senator Albert J. Beveridge, 1901-11. Unpub. Master's thesis, UNM, 1938.

MAES, ERNEST E.   (4362)
The labor movement in New Mexico. *New Mexico Business Review*, 4:137-40, 1935.

MAHONEY, TOM   (4363)
The Columbus raid. *SR*, 17:161-71, 1932.

MANGUS, A. R.   (4364)
Rural regions of the United States. WPA, Division of Research. Washington, GPO, 1940.
<small>Population, level of living, farm labor, land values.</small>

MANIRE, L. Z.   (4365)
A school survey of Lea County, New Mexico. Unpub. Master's thesis, UNM, 1931.

MARTIN, WALTER H.   (4366)
A proposed system for apportionment of school money from state funds. Unpub. Master's thesis, UNM, 1930.

MARTINEZ, F. T. (4366a)

New Mexico Lulac councils. *Lulac News,* 4:3-4, Dec. 1937.

MARTINEZ, J. B. (4366b)

Taos history. *Lulac News,* 5:20-21, Sept. 1938.

MARTINEZ, RUTH C. MILLER (4367)

The supervisory program in Taos County. *New Mexico School Review,* 16:15-17, Nov. 1936.
An effort to improve Taos County education.

MATTHIESSEN, F. O. (4368)

The New Mexican workers' case. *New Republic,* 82:361-63, 1935.
Background of the Gallup riot.

MAXWELL, GRANT (4369)

New Mexico grows. *NM,* 16:13-15, 47, Jan. 1938.
Review of present day life in the state.

MEADE, FRANCIS (4370)

La Mesilla. *Americana,* 4:514-18, 1909.

MEEKER, R. L. (4371)

Review of water supply, irrigated areas, etc. Rio Grande basin above Fort Quitman. Unpub. ms. dated 1924 on file at office of MRGCD, Albuquerque.

MELUGIN, ROY (4372)

A history of teacher certification in New Mexico. Unpub. Master's thesis, UNM, 1940.

MERRILL, WILLIAM STETSON (4373)

Bandelier; archaeologist of our Southwest. *Mid-America,* 12 (n. s. 1) :291-95, 1930.

MERSFELDER, LOUIS CALHOUN (4374)

Cowboy-fisherman-hunter; true stories of the great Southwest. Kansas City, Brown-White-Lowell Press, 1941.

MEWBORNE, R. G. (4375)

Tobacco as a new industry for New Mexico. Santa Fe, New Mexico State Planning Board, 1936.

MILLER, C. D. (4376)

The irrigation resources of New Mexico. Santa Fe, n. p., 1911.

MING, F. ERIC (4377)

Inequalities in educational opportunities among the children of Roosevelt County, New Mexico, as shown by inequalities in the distribution of school funds during the period 1923-33. Unpub. Master's thesis, New Mexico Normal (Highlands) University, 1932.

MOISE, C. (4378)

New Mexico and old Mexico. *Potter's American Monthly,* 17:193, 1881.

MONAHAN, A. C. (4379)

Organization of state departments of education. USDI, Bureau of Education, Bulletin 5. Washington, GPO, 1915.
Includes New Mexico.

MONTOYA, A.   (4380)
The consolidated schools of Bernalillo County, New Mexico.
USDI, Bureau of Education, Rural School Leaflet 22.   Washington, GPO, 1924.

MONTOYA, RAMITOS   (4381)
Treasure. Unpub. ms. in files of New Mexico Writers' Project, Santa Fe.
   Treasure buried near Roy and at Fort Union.

MOON, WILLARD W.   (4382)
History of education in Quay County. Unpub. Master's thesis, UNM, 1941.

MOORE, C. C.   (4383)
Discussion of the MRGCD as a source of water supply for desert land entries. Unpub. undated ms. on file at office of MRGCD, Albuquerque.

MOOREFIELD, C. H.   (4384)
Roads lead as job providers. *NM,* 11:34, Feb. 1933.
   Employment possibilities of highway construction and maintenance.

MOREHEAD, HENRY C.   (4385)
Teacher selection practices in New Mexico. Unpub. Master's thesis, UNM, 1932.

MORGAN, ELISABETH LEE   (4386)
Brief sketches of regional tales of western New Mexico. Unpub. Master's thesis, New Mexico Normal (Highlands) University, 1935.

MORGAN, HENRY   (4387)
A brief history of Roosevelt County, New Mexico. Unpub. Master's thesis, UNM, 1938.

MORGAN, W. D.   (4388)
Where 16th century customs linger. *Bureau Farmer,* 5:5, April 1930.
   Primitive New Mexico farming.

MOSK, SANFORD A.   (4388a)
The influence of tradition on agriculture in New Mexico. *Journal of Economic History.* Dec. 1942, Supplement. pp. 34-51.

————   (4389)
Tradition and agricultural development in New Mexico. Paper presented at 2nd Annual Meeting of Economic History Association, Williams College, Sept. 4-5, 1942.

MOSLEY, MRS. BENTON   (4390)
Blizzard happenings. Unpub. ms. in files of New Mexico Writers' Project, Santa Fe.
   Tall stories of south plains area.

MOWAT, JEAN   (4391)
The artist in the Southwest. *EP,* 20:194-200, 1926.

MOYERS, ROBERT ARTHUR   (4392)
A history of education in New Mexico. Unpub. Doctor's thesis, George Peabody College for Teachers, 1941.

MOZLEY, LOREN (4393)
The Taos moderns. *SR*, 14:370-76, 1929.

MULLENDORE, D. L. (4394)
The farmer and stockman now helps himself to credit. *Financing of Farming*, 9:1, July 1934.

MULLINS, R. J. (4395)
A plan for state support of public schools in New Mexico. Unpub. Master's thesis, University of Colorado, 1930.

MUNK, JOSEPH AMASA (4396)
Activities of a life-time. Los Angeles, Times-Mirror Press, 1924.

—— (4397)
Southwest sketches. New York, Putnam, 1920.

MURRAY, MARION (4398)
Art in the Southwest. *SR*. 11:281-93, 1926.

MURRAY, T. B. (4399)
Oldest part of America. *Catholic World*, 149:415-22, July 1939.

MUSEUM AND LABORATORY OF ANTHROPOLOGY (4400)
Preliminary statement of ad interim executive committee of the Museum and Laboratory of Anthropology to the members of the Board of Trustees. November 1927.
Includes articles of incorporation.

MUSGRAVE, ETHEL W. (4401)
Christmas in the land of enchantment. *NM*, 15:12-13, 36-38, Dec. 1937.
At Santa Fe.

NASSIMBENE, R. (4402)
Age of WPA workers November 1937. WPA, Division of Social Research. Washington, GPO, 1938.
Statistics for New Mexico.

NATIONAL EDUCATION ASSOCIATION (4403)
The efforts of the states to support education. Research Bulletin, v. 14, no. 3. Washington, May 1936.
Includes New Mexico.

NATIONAL RESOURCES COMMITTEE (4404)
Farm tenancy. Report of the President's committee. Washington, GPO, Feb. 1937.
Contains statistics on farm tenancy in New Mexico.

—— (4405)
The Rio Grande joint investigation in the upper Rio Grande Basin . . . 1936-37. 2 v. National Resources Committee, Regional Planning, Part 6. Washington, GPO, 1938.
A comprehensive study of the water resources of the Rio Grande Basin.

NATIONAL RESOURCES PLANNING BOARD (4405a)
Industrial development. National Resources Planning Board, Mountain States Region. Washington, GPO, Dec. 1942.

—— (4406)
The Pecos River joint investigation in the Pecos River basin in New Mexico and Texas, 1939-41. 3 v. June 1941. Processed.

NATIONAL RESOURCES PLANNING BOARD (Continued)   (4407)
   Tax delinquency and rural land-use adjustment. Subcommittee
   on Tax Delinquency of the Land Committee of the National Resources Planning Board, Technical Paper 81. Washington, Sept.
   1942.
      Includes MRGCD.

NEAL, JOE W.   (4407a)
   *The United States policy with respect to the entry of Mexicans
   into the United States.* Master's thesis, University of Texas, 1939.

NEALE, MRS. P. E.   (4408)
   Shalam colony. *New Mexico School Review,* 19:8-9, April 1940.

NEASHAM, AUBREY   (4409)
   Save the ruins. *National Park Service, Region 3 Quarterly,* 2:29-
   33, Jan. 1940.

——   (4410)
   The Southwest. *National Park Service, Region 3 Quarterly,* 3:29-
   35, Jan. 1941.
      Settlement, mining, homesteading, cattle industry.

NEEL, GEORGE M.   (4411)
   Surface water supply of New Mexico, 1888-1925. Santa Fe, State
   Engineer Department, 1926.

NEEL, GLADYS   (4412)
   History of Albuquerque. Unpub. Master's thesis, UNM, 1928.

NELSON, ETHELYN G.   (4413)
   Camp life in New Mexico. *EP,* 4 (4) :19-32, 1917.

NELSON, MARGARET W.   (4414)
   Commercial subjects in the high schools of New Mexico. Unpub.
   Master's thesis, UNM, 1938.

NEUFFER, H. C.   (4415)
   Rio Grande joint investigation. Unpub. undated ms. at office of
   MRGCD, Albuquerque.

NEW MEXICO BUREAU OF IMMIGRATION   (4416)
   Bernalillo County, New Mexico. Santa Fe, 1901.
      Agricultural and mineral resources.

——   (4417)
   Farming by irrigation in New Mexico. Santa Fe, 1897.

——   (4418)
   Ho! to the land of sunshine. Santa Fe, 1907.
      Public land by counties, and laws under which it could be obtained.

——   (4419)
   The mines of New Mexico. Santa Fe, 1896.

——   (4420)
   San Juan County, New Mexico. Santa Fe, 1908.
      Physical description, resources.

NEW MEXICO HIGHLANDS UNIVERSITY   (4421)
   Rural education in New Mexico. New Mexico Normal (Highlands) University, Bulletin 113. Las Vegas, 1934.

NEW MEXICO HISTORICAL RECORDS SURVEY (4422)
Directory of churches and religious organizations in New Mexico. Albuquerque, July 1940. Processed.

——— (4423)
Guide to the public vital statistics records in New Mexico. Albuquerque, March 1942. Processed.

——— (4424)
Index to "Final report of investigations among the Indians of the southwestern United States carried on mainly in the years from 1880 to 1885 by A. F. Bandelier." Albuquerque, June 1942. Processed.

——— (4425)
Inventory of county archives of Bernalillo County, no. 1. Albuquerque, Sept. 1938. Processed.

——— (4426)
Inventory of county archives of Colfax County, no. 4. Albuquerque, Dec. 1937. Processed.

——— (4427)
Inventory of county archives of Dona Ana County, no. 7. Albuquerque, Nov. 1940. Processed.

——— (4428)
Inventory of county archives of Eddy County, no. 8. Albuquerque, May 1939. Processed.

——— (4429)
Inventory of county archives of Grant County, no. 9. Albuquerque, April 1942. Processed.

——— (4430)
Inventory of county archives of Hidalgo County, no. 12. Albuquerque, [1941]. Processed.

——— (4431)
Inventory of county archives of Luna County, no. 15. Albuquerque, April 1942. Processed.

——— (4432)
Inventory of county archives of Mora County, no. 17. Albuquerque, Nov. 1941. Processed.

——— (4433)
Inventory of county archives of Otero County no. 18. Albuquerque, Oct. 1939. Processed.

——— (4434)
Inventory of county archives of Sandoval County, no. 23. Albuquerque, Jan. 1939. Processed.

——— (4435)
Inventory of county archives of San Miguel County, no. 24. Albuquerque, Feb. 1941. Processed.

——— (4436)
Inventory of county archives of Sierra County, no. 26. Albuquerque, June 1942. Processed.

NEW MEXICO HISTORICAL RECORDS SURVEY (Continued)   (4437)
    Inventory of county archives of Torrance County, no. 29. Albuquerque, April 1939. Processed.

——   (4438)
    Inventory of county archives of Union County, no. 30. Albuquerque, June 1940. Processed.

——   (4439)
    Inventory of county archives of Valencia County, no. 31. Albuquerque, Sept. 1940. Processed.

——   (4440)
    Inventory of federal archives in the states. Series XIII, no. 30. The Civil Works Administration. Albuquerque, Dec. 1940. Processed.

——   (4441)
    Inventory of federal archives in the states. Series V, no. 30. The Department of Justice. Albuquerque, 1940. Processed.

——   (4442)
    Inventory of federal archives in the states. Series VII, no. 30. The Department of the Navy. Albuquerque, July 1940. Processed.

——   (4443)
    Inventory of federal archives in the states. Series III, no. 30. The Department of the Treasury. Albuquerque, 1941. Processed.

——   (4444)
    Inventory of federal archives in the states. Series IV, no. 30. The Department of War. Albuquerque, Dec. 1940. Processed.

——   (4445)
    Inventory of federal archives in the states. Series II, no. 30. The Federal Courts. Albuquerque, April 1941. Processed.

——   (4446)
    Inventory of federal archives in the states. Series XII, no. 30. The Veterans' Administration. Albuquerque, Oct. 1940. Processed.

NEW MEXICO LAND PLANNING CONSULTANT   (4447)
    Report on extent and character of desirable adjustment in rural land use. NMSC, May 20, 1935. Typewritten. (Copy in Library of National Resources Committee.)
        For 1934 report *see* (3955)

NEW MEXICO SECRETARY OF STATE   (4448)
    The New Mexico Blue book. Biennial publication, 1913-date.

NEW MEXICO SPECIAL REVENUE COMMISSION   (4449)
    Report 1920. Santa Fe, 1920.
        Review of tax system.

——   (4450)
    Report of hearings . . . Santa Fe, August 16-20, 1920. Albuquerque, Central Printing Co., 1920.
        On taxation of agriculture and grazing lands.

NEW MEXICO STATE BOARD FOR VOCATIONAL EDUCATION   (4451)
Outline of work being done by the various bureaus, organizations, and agencies interested in the development of agriculture in New Mexico. Vocational Education Bulletin 6. Santa Fe, 1922.

――――   (4452)
Revised plans for vocational education in New Mexico under the provisions of the Smith-Hughes act . . . Vocational Education Bulletin 4. Santa Fe, 1919.

NEW MEXICO STATE COLLEGE   (4453)
New Mexico bi-monthly agricultural planning digest. State College, Dec. 1941-date. Processed.
News and notes on planning programs, farm labor, community activities, and social studies.

―――― EXTENSION SERVICE   (4454)
Economic survey and conference Elephant Butte irrigation district, February 1927. Outline reports and summary of recommendations. State College, 1927. Processed.

――――, ――――   (4455)
New Mexico agricultural outlook for 1940. Extension Circular 167. State College, 1939. Similar information for other years in Circulars 160, 146, 135, 134, 127, 125.
Includes information on farm family living.

――――, ――――   (4456)
Statistical data for the state of New Mexico, by counties. County Program Planning 4. State College, 1936.
Contains much the same information as the Census of Agriculture.

NEW MEXICO STATE COMMISSIONER OF PUBLIC LANDS   (4457)
Annual reports of state and territorial commissioners, 1900-date.

NEW MEXICO STATE DEPARTMENT OF PUBLIC HEALTH   (4458)
Vital statistics in New Mexico. *New Mexico Health Officer,* July 1942.

NEW MEXICO STATE DEPARTMENT OF PUBLIC WELFARE   (4459)
Relief statistics. Monthly compilation. Santa Fe, January 1937-date. Processed.

NEW MEXICO STATE DEPARTMENT OF VOCATIONAL EDUCATION   (4460)
General information, vocational training for defense workers. Santa Fe, n. d. Processed.

――――   (4461)
Report of vocational education program for defense workers at Albuquerque, Clayton, Clovis, Hobbs, Santa Fe high schools, New Mexico Highlands University, and New Mexico State College. Santa Fe, May 1942. Processed.

NEW MEXICO STATE EMPLOYMENT SECURITY COMMISSION   (4462)
Annual reports to the Governor, 1937-date.

NEW MEXICO STATE ENGINEER   (4463)
Biennial reports, state and territorial engineers, 1908-date.

――――   (4464)
Reports on the surface water supply of New Mexico, 1911-date.

NEW MEXICO STATE PARK COMMISSION AND UNIVERSITY OF NEW MEXICO
(4465)
New Mexico park, parkway, and recreational area plan. Feb. 1940. Processed.
> Prepared with cooperation of National Park Service. Includes material on population and culture of the state. (Copy at National Park Service, Santa Fe.)

NEW MEXICO STATE PLANNING BOARD (4465a)
The post-war years in New Mexico. Santa Fe, 1943.

———— (4466)
Preliminary report to the national resources board. Santa Fe, Dec. 15, 1934. Typewritten.
> Discussion of land grants, homestead acts, reclamation, problem areas, and publicly owned lands.

———— (4467)
A survey of illiteracy in New Mexico. Santa Fe, 1936. Processed.

———— (4468)
Third progress report. Summary of work. Santa Fe, June 15, 1936. Typewritten.

———— (4469)
Wind erosion. Progress report to National Resources Board. Santa Fe, 1935. Processed.

NEW MEXICO TERRITORIAL GOVERNOR (4470)
Reports to the Secretary of the Interior, 1878-1911.

NEW MEXICO WRITERS' PROJECT, WPA (4471)
Unpub. mss. of tall tales; cowboy, Spanish, and Indian folk dances; folk tales; folk ways; folk customs; and cowboy songs and poems, by various authors in files of the Project at Santa Fe.

NEWELL, F. H. (4472)
Government reclamation in New Mexico. *The Earth,* 5:18-19, Sept. 1908.

NEWELL, F. H., COMP. (4473)
Proceedings of the first conference of engineers of the reclamation service. USDI, Geological Survey, Water Supply & Irrigation Paper 93. Washington, GPO, 1904.

NICHOLL, M. (4474)
New Mexico. *Cornhill Magazine,* 82:251-, 1900.

NOFTZER, LEE J. (4475)
Distribution system, Tucumcari Project, New Mexico. *Reclamation Era,* 31:125-26, April 1941.
> Description of general plan for irrigating and draining the arable and irrigable land of the Tucumcari area.

NORTHROP, STUART A. (4476)
Minerals of New Mexico. UNM Bulletin, Geological series, v. 6, no. 1, 1942.

———— (4477)
Terms from the Spanish. *American Speech,* 12:79-81, 1937.
> Topographic terms.

NYLANDER, J. H. (4478)
Subject combinations prevalent in the teaching programs of teachers in New Mexico high schools. Unpub. Master's thesis, UNM, 1937.

NYMEYER, ROBERT BERT (4479)
Riches from below. *NM,* 17:12-15, 49, Oct. 1939.
Extractive industries of New Mexico.

OESTREICH, W. C. (4480)
The Middle Rio Grande Conservancy District and the flood menace of the Rio Grande. Unpub. ms. dated April 15, 1938 on file at office of MRGCD, Albuquerque.

OLDEN, SARAH EMILIA (4481)
Little slants at western life; a note book of travel and reflection. New York, Harold Vinal Ltd., 1927.

O'LEARY, JOHN (4481a)
Behind the firing line. *NM,* 21:7-9, 34-36, March 1943.
Activities in Grant County in war time.

ORTEGA, JOAQUIN (4481b)
Economic aspects of the Pan American policy of the United States. Address delivered before the History Conference at the Coronado Congress, Albuquerque, Aug. 12, 1940 and before a conference at the University of Iowa. Unpub. ms. in possession of the author.
Contains allusions to the role of the Hispanic Southwest in inter-American relations.

———— (4482)
New Mexico interlude, 1934. Unpub. ms. in possession of the author, UNM, Albuquerque.
A discussion of Spanish psychology, the character of New Mexican land and people, and the potential role of educational institutions in improving cultural relations.

———— (4483)
New Mexico's opportunity; a message to my fellow New Mexicans. Albuquerque, UNM Press, 1942.
Discussion of the social and economic problems of the state.

———— (4484)
Proposal for the foundation in the Laboratory of Anthropology at Santa Fe of a village of Hispanic folklore and popular arts and crafts. October 1942. Processed.
A discussion of the Hispanic arts and crafts of New Mexico, their possible development through the foundation of the Village with its school of arts and crafts, the creation of a Museum of Hispanic arts and crafts and a Repository of Design, and of a research program in the field of Hispanic arts and crafts.

O'SEASNAIN, B. P. (4485)
Santa Fe and the Southwest. *Catholic World,* 119:465-76, 1924.

OSTERMANN, LEOPOLD (4486)
Franciscans in the wilds and wastes of the Navajo country. *St. Anthony's Messenger,* Feb. 1901-Nov. 1902.

OVERPECK, J. C. (4487)
Corn production in New Mexico. NMAES Bulletin 166. State College, 1928.

PACHECO, LEONIDES   (4487a)
Education in New Mexico. *Lulac News,* 5:9, Sept. 1938.

PALMER, R. S.   (4488)
The marketing of fresh fruits and vegetables in the vicinity of Albuquerque. Unpub. Master's thesis, UNM, 1935.

PARKER, NEUMAN R.   (4489)
Survey of the municipal government of the city of Las Vegas, New Mexico for the year 1908. Unpub. Master's thesis, New Mexico Normal (Highlands) University, 1931.

PARKS, CHARLES E.   (4490)
The lure of old Santa Fe. *EP,* 11:123-31, 1921.

PARR, V. V., COLLIER, G. W., AND KLEMMEDSON, G. S.   (4491)
Ranch organization and methods of livestock production in the Southwest. USDA, Technical Bulletin 68. Washington, GPO, 1928.

PARSONS, FRANCIS   (4492)
A time of preservation. Boston, Stratford Co., 1935.
Travel description.

PATTON, F. H.   (4493)
Courts of New Mexico hear both Spanish and English. *State Government,* 11:62, March 1938.

PAYNTER, ELIZABETH ANN   (4494)
Educational requirements of commercial teachers in the Southwest. Unpub. Master's thesis, New Mexico Normal (Highlands) University, 1933.

PEARCE, THOMAS M.   (4495)
The beloved house. Caldwell, Idaho, Caxton Printers, 1940.
Biography of Mary Austin.

——   (4496)
Cartoon guide to New Mexico. New York, J. J. Augustin, 1939.

——   (4497)
The English language in the Southwest. *NMHR,* 7:210-32, 1932.

——   (4498)
Mary Austin and the pattern of New Mexico. *SR,* 22:140-48, 1937.

——   (4499)
The Southwestern word box. *New Mexico Quarterly,* 2:263-68, 1932.
Some probable origins of the words "Amerind," "Anglo-American," "gringo," "greaser."

——   (4500)
Trader terms in Southwestern English. *American Speech,* 16:179-86, 1941.

PEARCE, THOMAS M. AND HENDON, TELFAIR   (4501)
America in the Southwest; a regional anthology. Albuquerque, UNM Press, 1933.

PECK, WALTER E.   (4502)
Gasoline prairie schooner. *Scribner's,* 44:197-203, 1908.
Travel description.

PEIXOTTO, ERNEST C.   (4503)
Our Hispanic Southwest. New York, Scribners, 1916.

PERSINGER, CLARK E.   (4504)
Advantages and disadvantages of the mixed method of choosing
county officials. *EP*, 12:87-91, 1922.
    In New Mexico.

PETERS, LEROY S.   (4505)
New Mexico medicine. *New Mexico Quarterly Review*, 11:322-
29, 1941.

PETERSON, C. S., COMP.   (4506)
Representative New Mexicans. Denver, C. S. Peterson, 1912.
    Biographies of over 400 prominent New Mexicans.

PETERSON, FRANKLIN C.   (4507)
*The distribution of the tax dollar in McKinley County, New
Mexico, for the fiscal year 1930-31.* Unpub. Master's thesis, New
Mexico Normal (Highlands) University, 1931.

PETTET, ZELLMER R.   (4508)
*Irrigation of agricultural lands, New Mexico. Enterprises, areas,
works and equipment, capital invested, and maintenance and
operation cost, with statistics for counties and drainage basins.*
USDI, Bureau of the Census. Washington, GPO, 1942.

PETTY, HAZEL   (4509)
The facilities of high school libraries in New Mexico. Unpub.
Master's thesis, UNM, 1942.

PHILIBERT, SISTER MARY   (4510)
Christmas in New Mexico. *Commonweal*, 27:233-34, 1937.

PHILLIPS, FRANK M.   (4511)
Statistics of city school systems, 1925-26. USDI, Bureau of Education, Bulletin 32, 1927. Washington, GPO, 1928.
    Includes New Mexico.

————   (4512)
Statistics of public high schools, 1921-22. USDI, Bureau of Edu-
cation, Bulletin 7. Washington, GPO, 1924; *Same, 1923-24,* USDI,
Bureau of Education, Bulletin 40, 1925. Washington, GPO,
1926; *Same, 1925-26.* USDI, Bureau of Education, Bulletin 33.
Washington, GPO, 1927.
    Includes New Mexico.

————   (4513)
Statistics of state school systems, 1922-23. USDI, Bureau of Edu-
cation, Bulletin 31, 1924. Washington, GPO, 1925; *Same, 1923-24,*
USDI, Bureau of Education, Bulletin 42, 1925. Washington,
GPO, 1926; *Same, 1924-25,* USDI, Bureau of Education, Bulletin
13. Washington, GPO, 1927; *Same, 1925-26,* USDI, Bureau of
Education, Bulletin 39. Washington, GPO, 1927.
    Includes New Mexico.

PIJOAN, MICHEL   (4513a)
Nutritional and constitutional factors as related to body economy.
Albuquerque, U. S. Indian Service, May 1942. Processed.

PIJOAN, MICHEL (Continued)   (4514)
Nutritional factors as they relate to the health problem in the Rio Grande Valley. Address given at School for the Rio Grande Valley, UNM, April 27-May 1, 1942. To be published by School of Inter-American Affairs in *Proceedings of the School for the Rio Grande Valley.*
> Effects of food habits of Spanish-Americans in northern counties on their general health status and on their receptivity to the processes of acculturation.

PIJOAN, MICHEL AND EGGAN, FRED   (4515)
Some aspects of the study of nutrition. To be published in *American Anthropologist.*
> Discussion of the relation of individual body economy to culture, based on observations at Cundiyo and Cañon de Taos. Stresses necessity of relating any programs for the improvement of nutrition to the existing culture pattern.

PIJOAN, MICHEL AND ELKIN, C. A.   (4516)
Studies of vitamin C containing foods in New Mexico diets. Unpub. ms. in possession of Dr. Pijoan, Albuquerque.

PINGREY, H. B.   (4517)
Cattle and lamb feeding costs and returns in the southern irrigated valleys of New Mexico, 1938-39. NMAES, Press Bulletin 884. State College, 1939. Processed.

————   (4518)
Costs and returns from cattle feeding in the southern irrigated valleys of New Mexico, 1937-38. NMAES, Press Bulletin 862. State College, 1938. Processed.

————   (4519)
Income and expense of sheep ranches in southeastern New Mexico, 1941. NMAES, Press Bulletin 954. State College, Aug. 1942.

————   (4520)
Lamb feeding in the irrigated valleys of southern New Mexico. NMAES, Bulletin 285. State College, Nov. 1941.

————   (4521)
Physical and financial organization of stock ranches in southeastern New Mexico, 1938. NMAES, Press Bulletin 892. State College, 1940. Processed.

POND, ASHLEY   (4522)
New Mexico in the great war. Chapter 10. At the front. *NMHR,* 2:17-21, 1927.

POPEJOY, THOMAS L.   (4523)
Analysis of the causes of bank failures in New Mexico, 1920-25. Master's thesis, UNM, 1929. *Also* UNM Bulletin, Economics series, v. 1, no. 1, 1931.

POUND, LOUISE   (4524)
The Southwestern cowboy songs and the English and Scottish popular ballads. *Modern Philology,* 11:195-207, 1913.

POWELL, E. A. (4525)
The end of the trail; the far West from New Mexico to British Columbia. New York, Scribners, 1915.
> Chapter 1, New Mexico: the people, religion, climate, desert; Chapter 2, description of a trip to Acoma.

POWER, MARJORIE (4525a)
Oil at Hobbs, New Mexico. *The Historian*, 1:54-49, Winter 1938.

PRICE, HUGH (4526)
A history of the New Mexico Normal University, 1893-1931. Unpub. Master's thesis, New Mexico Normal (Highlands) University, 1932.

PRIEST, KENNETH F. (4527)
Public water supplies of New Mexico. Unpub. Master's thesis, UNM, 1937.

PRINCE, L. B. (4528)
Admission of New Mexico as a state. *North American Review*, 156:346, 1893.

――― (4529)
A concise history of New Mexico. Cedar Rapids, Torch Press, 1912.

――― (4530)
New Mexico's struggle for statehood; sixty years of struggle to obtain self government. Santa Fe, New Mexican Printing Co., 1910.

PRISON INDUSTRY REORGANIZATION ADMINISTRATION (4531)
The prison labor problem in New Mexico. Washington 1938. Processed.

PROCTOR, R. (4532)
Reports relative to the treatment of certain Apache Indians. Senate Exec. Doc. 88, 51st Congress, 1st Session. Washington, GPO, 1890.

PROVINSE, JOHN H. (4533)
Cultural factors in land use planning. USDI, Bureau of Indian Affairs, 1941. Processed.
> Includes material on Spanish-Americans of Rio Grande and Pecos valleys.

――― (4534)
The work of the human surveys branch. Navajo Service Land Management Conference, March 2-6, 1937, Flagstaff. *Navajo School Service Bulletin 1.*
> Discussion of a socio-economic survey of the Navajo reservation giving methods used and a few results.

PULLEN, CLARENCE (4535)
New Mexico; its geography, scenes, and peoples. American Geographic Society, Bulletin 1, 1887.

QUESENBERRY, G. R. (4536)
Moisture conservation in New Mexico. *Extension Service Review*, 2:69, May 1931.

RAEL, J. P. (4536a)
The primitive hamlet. *Lulac News*, 7:23, July 1940.
> Questa, New Mexico.

RAEL, JUAN B.   (4536b)
Associative interference in New Mexican Spanish. *Hispanic Review*, 7:324-36, 1939.

RAGSDALE, KATHERINE   (4537)
Cowboys and their customs. Unpub. ms. in files of New Mexico Writers' Project, Santa Fe.

RAINE, WILLIAM MACLEOD   (4538)
The government Indian school as a promoter of civilization. *World Today*, May 1903.

RAINES, LESTER   (4539)
Buried treasure. Unpub. ms. in files of New Mexico Writers' Project, Santa Fe.

RAK, MARY KIDDER   (4540)
Border patrol. Boston, Houghton Mifflin, 1938.

RAND, FRANK C., JR.   (4541)
The land of enchantment in war. *The Santa Fean*, 2:18-20, Summer 1942.

RAYMER, ROBERT GEORGE   (4542)
The development of Christianity in the Southwest. *Methodist Quarterly Review*, 76:69-98, 1927.

READ, BENJAMIN MAURICE   (4543)
Historia ilustrada de Nuevo Mexico. Santa Fe, Compania Impresora del Nuevo Mexicano, 1911.

————   (4544)
History of education in New Mexico. Santa Fe, 1911.

————   (4545)
Illustrated history of New Mexico, translated from the second Spanish edition, revised and corrected. Santa Fe, New Mexican Printing Co., 1912.

————   (4546)
A treatise on the disputed points of the history of New Mexico. Santa Fe, B. M. Read, 1919.

REBOLLEDO, ANTONIO   (4547)
El cuarto centenario de Coronado y Nuevo Mexico. *Hispania*, 22:354-56, 1939.

————   (4548)
Meditaciones en un centenario. *Hispania*, 18:437-40, 1935.
Founding of Las Vegas.

————   (4549)
Objectives of the New Mexico Spanish research project. *New Mexico Quarterly Review*, 12:25-30, 1942.

REED, R. J.   (4550)
The Villa raid on Columbus, New Mexico. *Research*, 1:181-93, Aug. 1937.

REEVE, FRANK D.   (4551)
History of the University of New Mexico. Unpub. Master's thesis, UNM, 1928.

REEVE, FRANK D (Continued)   (4552)
  The old University of New Mexico at Santa Fe. *NMHR*, 8:201-
  10, 1933.

REEVES, M.   (4553)
  In the wake of the flood. *Survey*, 44:657-58, 1920.
      Red Cross activities during a flood in Socorro County.

REID, J. T.   (4554)
  A new concept of adult education in rural areas. Address given
  at School for the Rio Grande Valley, UNM, April 27-May 1,
  1942. To be published by the School of Inter-American Affairs
  in the *Proceedings of the School for the Rio Grande Valley.*
      Activities and accomplishments of the Taos County Project.

RENAUD, STEPHEN   (4555)
  Au Nouveau-Mexique. *Nouvelle-France* (Quebec), 9:88-90, 180-
  84, 229-34, 280-84, 323-31, 374-78, 421-24, 516-23, 1910.
      Missionary travel.

RHODES, MAY D.   (4556)
  Hired man on horseback. Boston, Houghton Mifflin, 1938.
      Life of Eugene M. Rhodes.

RICH, JOHN L.   (4557)
  Recent stream trenching in the desert of southwestern New
  Mexico. *Annals of the Association of American Geographers,*
  1:135, 1911.

———   (4558)
  Recent stream trenching in the semi-arid portion of southwestern
  New Mexico, a result of removal of vegetation cover. *American
  Journal of Science*, 32:237-45, 1911.

RICHARDSON, RUPERT NORVAL AND RISTER, CARL COKE, EDS.   (4559)
  *The greater Southwest . . . from Spanish conquest to twentieth
  century.* Glendale, Clark, 1934.
      Economic, social, and cultural development of New Mexico.

RIPPLE, L. W.   (4560)
  *Experience, tenure, salaries, and professional rating of teachers
  in North Central Association secondary schools in New Mexico.*
  Unpub. Master's thesis, UNM, 1933.

RITCH, W. G.   (4561)
  Aztlan: the history, resources, and attractions of New Mexico.
  Boston, D. Lothrop, 1885.

———   (4562)
  Illustrated New Mexico. 5th ed. Santa Fe, New Mexico Bureau
  of Immigration, 1885.

———   (4563)
  Santa Fe. Topeka, Crane & Co., 1885.

ROBBINS, ROY M.   (4564)
  Our landed heritage; the public domain, 1776-1936. Princeton,
  Princeton University Press, 1942.

ROBERTS, MRS. BONNIDELL   (4565)
  *Character types of the Southwest as delineated in New Mexico
  fiction.* Unpub. Master's thesis, UNM, 1932.

ROBERTS, FRANK H. H.   (4566)
New Mexico in the great war. Chapter 2. The war executive. *NMHR,* 1:15-23, 99, 1926.

ROBERTS, FRANK H. H. AND TWITCHELL, RALPH EMERSON   (4567)
History and civics of New Mexico. Albuquerque, Charles Ilfeld, 1914.

ROBERTS, K. L.   (4568)
Fruits of the desert. *Saturday Evening Post,* 197:19, Oct. 4, 1924.

ROBINSON, WILLIAM H.   (4569)
Under turquoise skies. New York, Macmillan, 1928.
> Travel description.

ROCKWELL, JOHN A.   (4570)
Compilation of Spanish and Mexican law in relation to mines and titles to real estate. v. 1. New York, John S. Voorhies, 1851.

ROGERS, B. A.   (4571)
Community activities and requirements of public school teachers in New Mexico. Unpub. Master's thesis, UNM, 1937.

ROOSEVELT, THEODORE   (4572)
A book-lover's holidays in the open. New York, Scribners, 1916.
> Description and travel.

ROWALT, E. M.   (4573)
Soil defense of range and farm lands in the Southwest. USDA, Misc. Pub. 338. Washington, GPO, 1939.

ROWLEY, MARGARET ARNER   (4574)
In the ancient town of Santa Fe. *The Earth,* July 1907.

ROYCE, CHARLES C.   (4575)
Indian land cessions in the United States. *Bureau of American Ethnology, 18th Annual Report, 1896-97.* Washington, GPO, 1899. Part 2, pp. 521-997.

RURAL REHABILITATION COMMITTEE OF VALENCIA COUNTY   (4576)
Committee report. Unpub. undated ms. on file at office of MRGCD, Albuquerque.

RUSH, MYRTLE   (4577)
A study of chain grocery stores in Albuquerque, New Mexico. Unpub. Master's thesis, UNM, 1931.

RYAN, E.   (4578)
American Southwest. *Dublin Review,* 182:122-33, 1928.

SAHD, S. P.   (4579)
Geography of Tijeras-Cerrillos region. Unpub. Bachelor's thesis, UNM, 1937.

SAINT, J. E.   (4580)
Tax problems in New Mexico. *National Tax Association, Proceedings, 13th Session, 1920.* pp. 331-41.

ST. MICHAEL'S COLLEGE   (4581)
Seventy-five years of service, 1859-1934. Santa Fe, 1934.

SANCHEZ, GEORGE I.   (4582)
Bilingualism. Address given at School for the Rio Grande Valley,
UNM, April 27-May 1, 1942. To be published by School of
Inter-American Affairs in *Proceedings of the School for the Rio
Grande Valley.*
> The deeper implications and issues of the language problem in New Mex-
> ico as they affect cultural relations in general and education in particular.

——————   (4583)
Bilingualism—a social economic emergency. Santa Fe, New Mexico State Department of Education, n. d. Processed.

——————   (4584)
Bilingualism and mental measures. *JAP,* 78:765-72, 1934.

——————   (4585)
Bilingualism and mental measures; a word of caution. Santa Fe,
New Mexico State Department of Education, June 1, 1934. Pro-
cessed.

——————   (4586)
*The equalization of educational opportunity—some issues and
problems.* UNM, Bulletin, Educational series, v. 5, no. 1, 1939.

——————   (4587)
The implications of a basal vocabulary to the measurement of
ability of bilingual children. *Journal of Social Psychology,* 5:395-
402, 1934.

——————   (4588)
The state public school equalization fund in law and practice.
New Mexico Business Review, 8:11-20, 1939.

SAUNDERS, CHARLES FRANCIS   (4589)
Finding the worthwhile in the Southwest. New York, McBride,
1928.

SAUNDERS, LYLE   (4589a)
Economic problems of the Middle Rio Grande Valley. *Alianza,*
36:6, 16, Feb. 1943.

SAUNDERS, SALLY   (4590)
Santa Fe's new conquistadores. *Outlook,* 155:607-09, 1930.
> Santa Fe as an art center.

SCOTT, DUNCAN   (4591)
SCS helps New Mexico farmers to repair flood damage. *Soil Conservation,* 8:114-15, Nov. 1942.
> Lincoln County.

SENA, JOSE D.   (4592)
Archives in the office of the cadastral engineer at Santa Fe. *EP,*
36:113-21, 1934.

SENA, MARIE ISABEL   (4592a)
A bit of Santa Fe and its fiesta. *Lulac News,* 6:43, May 1939.

SERGEANT, ELIZABETH S.   (4593)
The Indian goes to war. *New Republic,* 107:708-09, Nov. 30,
1942.

SERGEANT, ELIZABETH S. (Continued)   (4594)
New Mexico, a relic of ancient America. *Nation,* 117:577-79, 1923. *Also* in Gruening, Ernest, Ed.: *These United States.* New York, Boni and Liveright, 1924.

SEYFRIED, J. E.   (4595)
Analysis of New Mexico state school laws. Unpub. Master's thesis, UNM, 1928.

——   (4596)
Illiteracy trends in New Mexico. UNM Bulletin, Education series, v. 8, no. 1, 1934.

SEYMOUR, FLORA WARREN   (4597)
Land titles in the Pueblo Indian country. *American Bar Association Journal,* 10:36-41, 1924.

SHAFFER, E. H.   (4598)
Editorials, judges, and jails. *New Republic,* 39:353-54, 1924.

SHAMBERGER, MRS. ELIZABETH STRONG   (4599)
A thirty year educational history of Albuquerque, New Mexico. Unpub. Master's thesis, UNM, 1928.

SHAW, ALBERT   (4600)
Should Arizona and New Mexico be admitted. *Review of Reviews,* 22:652-53, Dec. 1900.

SHAW, M. M.   (4601)
Witchery of western towns. *Overland,* 56:480-82, 1910.

SHELLY, PAUL C.   (4602)
The status of music in the high schools of New Mexico. Unpub. Master's thesis, New Mexico State Teachers' College, 1934.

SHEPHERD, W. G.   (4603)
How Carl Magee broke Fall's New Mexico ring. *World's Work,* 48:29-40, May 1924.

SHEVKY, ESHREF   (4604)
The middle Rio Grande situation. *New Mexico Business Review,* 7:43-46, 1938.
> Stresses necessity for physical control of the valley before expansion of irrigation projects is made.

SIMMS, D. HARPER   (4605)
Dust bowlers get a third chance. *Land Policy Review,* 4:11-14, 1941.
> Fight against wind erosion at Fence Lake.

SIMONS, KATHERINE   (4606)
New Mexico, el camino real. *Phi Delta Gamma Journal,* 7:75-78, June 1942.
> Excellent summary statement of problems and potentialities of New Mexico.

——   (4606a)
Street names of Albuquerque. *American Speech,* 17:209-10, Oct. 1942.

SINCLAIR, JOHN L.   (4607)
Bronc peelers. *NM,* 17:18-19, 32-33, Feb. 1939.
> Horse breaking and training.

SINCLAIR, JOHN L. (Continued) (4608)
Chuck wagon chow. *NM*, 16:14-15, 34, March 1938.

—— (4609)
Little town of heart's desire. *NM*, 18:18-19, 39, Dec. 1940.
White Oaks.

—— (4610)
On the hoof. *NM*, 17:26-27, 42-43, Oct. 1939.
History of cattle raising in Lincoln County.

—— (4611)
Shepherds on horseback. *NM*, 15:19-21, 35, Sept. 1937.

—— (4612)
Spinning them fancy. *NM*, 18:12-13, 32, May 1940.
Cowboy roping.

—— (4613)
Vaquero lingo. *NM*, 15:20-21, 38-39, Dec. 1937.
Influence of Spanish culture on language used in cattle industry.

SLUGA, MARY E. (4614)
The political life of Thomas Benton Catron. Unpub. Master's
thesis, UNM, 1941.

SMITH, J. RUSSELL (4615)
The doomed valley of the upper Rio Grande—an example of
regional suicide. *Annals of the Association of American Geographers,* 29:94-95, 1939.

SMITHSON, J. VERNON (4616)
Folk customs in Curry County. Unpub. ms. in files of New Mexico Writers' Project, Santa Fe.

SMYTHE, WILLIAM E. (4617)
Conquest of arid America. New York, Macmillan, 1911.

SNYDER, CHARLES M. (4618)
To quiet title to lands within Pueblo Indian land grants. House
Report 787, 68th Congress, 1st Session. Washington, GPO, 1921.

SOCIAL SECURITY BOARD (4619)
Annual reports, 1936-date.
Statistical data by states of all programs included in the Board's field of
activity.

—— (4620)
Social Security Bulletin. Monthly publication containing statistical data on relief, employment, unemployment compensation . . .
by states. From 1938 to date.

———, BUREAU OF RESEARCH AND STATISTICS (4621)
Tabular summary of statistics of public assistance. Bureau report
1. Washington, GPO, 1938.
Includes statistics for New Mexico by counties.

———, —— (4622)
*Trends in public assistance 1933-39; data on old age assistance,
aid to dependent children, aid to the blind, and general relief,
by states, 1936-39, and by counties, December 1939.* Bureau report 8. Washington, GPO, 1940.
Includes New Mexico.

SOMMERS, HERBERT J.   (4623)
  Infant mortality in rural and urban areas. *Public Health Reports,*
  57:1494-1501, Oct. 2, 1942.
        Includes New Mexico.

SORRELL, VERNON G.   (4624)
  State and local taxation with special reference to New Mexico
  problems. UNM Bulletin, Economics series, v. 2, no. 1, 1932.

SORRELL, VERNON G. AND STUART, J. R.   (4625)
  County consolidation in New Mexico. UNM Bulletin, Economics series, v. 2, no. 2, 1934.

SOTOMAYOR, FRANCISCO   (4626)
  Extra curricular activities in the private Catholic secondary
  schools of New Mexico. Unpub. Master's thesis, UNM, 1940.

SPENCER, D. C. AND OTHERS   (4627)
  The sheep industry. USDA, Yearbook. Washington, GPO, 1923.

SPIEGELBERG, FLORA   (4628)
  Tribute to Archbishop Lamy of New Mexico. *EP,* 36:22-25, 1934.

SPIESS, JAN   (4629)
  Feudalism and Senator Cutting. *American Mercury,* 33:371-74,
  Nov. 1934.

SPRINGER, F.   (4630)
  Dedicatory words at opening of the Santa Fe art museum. *A&A,*
  7:5-7, 1918.

SQUIER, EPHRAIM GEORGE   (4631)
  New Mexico and California. The ancient monuments and the
  aboriginal semi-civilized nations . . . with an abstract of the
  early Spanish explorations and conquests in those regions . . .
  The American Review 8 (n. s. 2) :503-28, 1848.

STANDLEY, PAUL C.   (4632)
  Some useful native plants of New Mexico. *Smithsonian Annual*
  Report, 1911. Washington, 1912. pp. 447-62.

STEPHENSON, WAYMON A.   (4633)
  The free textbook movement in New Mexico. Unpub. Master's
  thesis, UNM, 1939.

STEVENSON, PHILIP   (4634)
  Santa Fe, a study in integrity. *New Mexico Quarterly,* 3:125-32,
  1933.
        Effect of successive waves of culture on life in Santa Fe.

STEVER, THERESA MILLER   (4635)
  Statutes concerning public school teachers in New Mexico, 1848-
  1939. Unpub. Master's thesis, NMSC, 1940.

STEWART, GUY R. AND DONNELLY, MAURICE   (4635a)
  Soil and water economy in the Pueblo Southwest. *Scientific*
  Monthly, 56:31-44, Jan., 134-44, Feb. 1943.

STEWART, H. C.   (4636)
  The Soil Conservation Service activities in the Southwest. *New*
  Mexico Business Review, 7:176-86, 1938.

STINNETT, RUFUS M. (4637)
Utilization of high school buildings in Socorro County, New Mexico. Unpub. Master's thesis, UNM, 1939.

STIRRAT, MAY (4638)
The Francisco Villa raid on Columbus, New Mexico. Unpub. Master's thesis, UNM, 1935.

STOES, KATHERINE E. (4639)
Early history of Dona Ana county. *Rio Grande Farmer* (Las Cruces), 1932.

STORMS, J. ROY (4640)
Trends in subjects offered and pupils registered in those subjects in New Mexico high schools. Unpub. Master's thesis, UNM, 1938.

STORMS, WALTER W. (4641)
The story of New Mexico briefly told. Terre Haute, Indiana, Inland Pub. Co., 1897.

STRONG, R. L. (4642)
Distinctive agricultural areas in New Mexico. USDA, SCS, 1936. Typewritten.
Data on climate, erosion, types of agriculture, topography, and major soils for nine areas in New Mexico.

STUART, RAYMOND (4643)
A plan for the consolidation of counties in New Mexico. Unpub. Master's thesis, UNM, 1932.

STUART, WALTER S. (4644)
The parent-teacher association in New Mexico. Unpub. Master's thesis, New Mexico Normal (Highlands) University, 1934.

STUBBS, STANLEY (4645)
Survey of Governador region, preliminary report of general characteristics of the Upper San Juan area of Rio Arriba County in New Mexico. *EP,* 29:75-79, 1930.

STUMPH, ROY C. (4646)
History of the referendum in New Mexico. Unpub. Master's thesis, UNM, 1941.

SULLIVAN, MAUD D. (4647)
Old roads and new highways in the Southwest. *NMHR,* 10:143-49, 1935.

SULLY, JOHN M. (4648)
The story of the Santa Rita Copper Mine. *Old Santa Fe,* 3:133-49, 1916.

SUNDT, J. R. (4649)
Nursing on the frontier in our great Southwest. *Public Health Nurse,* 18:70-72, Feb. 1926.

SWANK, STELLA M. (4650)
Academic achievement and intelligence of graduates of the University of New Mexico. Unpub. Master's thesis, UNM, 1932.

SWAYNE, JAMES B. (4651)
A survey of the economic, political, and legal aspects of the labor problem in New Mexico. Unpub. Master's thesis, UNM, 1936.

SWEENEY, RAYMOND P.   (4652)
Sources, annual revenue, and apportionment of New Mexico current common school fund from 1923-24 to 1933-34. Unpub. Master's thesis, UNM, 1935.

SWEET, ERNEST A.   (4653)
Interstate migration of tuberculous people: its bearing on the public health with special reference to the states of New Mexico and Texas. Reprint 269. *Public Health Reports*, April 9, 16, 23, 1915.

SWIFT, FLETCHER HARPER   (4654)
State policies in public school finance. USDI, Bureau of Education, Bulletin 6. Washington, GPO, 1922.
Includes New Mexico.

SWIFT, FLETCHER HARPER AND ZIMMERMAN, BRUCE LEWIS   (4655)
State school taxes and school funds and their apportionment. USDI, Bureau of Education, Bulletin 29, 1928. Washington, GPO, 1929.

TAEUBER, CONRAD AND TAYLOR, CARL C.   (4656)
The people of the drought states. WPA, Division of Social Research, Research Bulletin, series 5, no. 2. Washington, GPO, 1937.
Some general information on settlement and migration in New Mexico.

TAEUSCH, CARL F.   (4657)
The Rio Grande Valley in a world at war. Address given at School for the Rio Grande Valley, UNM, April 27-May 1, 1942. To be published by School of Inter-American Affairs in *Proceedings of the School for the Rio Grande Valley.*
Historical summary of culture contacts in the Valley with an appraisal of its role in present-day inter-American relations.

TALBOT, M. W.   (4658)
Range watering places in the Southwest. USDA, Bulletin 1358. Washington, GPO, 1926.

TALBOT, WINTHROP   (4659)
Adult illiteracy. USDI, Bureau of Education, Bulletin 35. Washington, GPO, 1916.
Includes New Mexico.

TAOS COUNTY PROJECT   (4660)
First annual report, July 1, 1940-June 30, 1941. UNM Bulletin, Catalog series, v. 54, no. 7, 1941.

————   (4661)
Staff meeting minutes. July 1940-date. Mimeographed twice monthly.

TAPPAN, JULIA B. AND RAYMOND, ANNE   (4662)
Land—the first line of defense; a manual for community leaders. USDA, SCS, Education Division. Albuquerque, 1942. Unpublished.

TATE, NORVELL   (4663)
A brief history of Curry County, New Mexico. Unpub. Master's thesis, UNM, 1934.

TAYLOR, LYTTON R.   (4664)
The economic status of the New Mexico farmer. Unpub. Bachelor's thesis, NMSC, 1917.

TERRELL, SYLVIA   (4665)
Burros. *The Rio Grande Writer,* 1:21-22, Spring 1942.

TETREAU, E. D.   (4666)
Profile of farm wage rates in the Southwest. *Rural Sociology,* 4: 36-42, 1939.

THOMA, FRANCISCO DE   (4667)
Historia popular de Nuevo Mexico, desde su descubrimiento hasta la actualidad. New York, American Book Co., 1896.

THOMAS, CHESTER A.   (4668)
Bandelier's centennial. *National Park Service, Region 3 Quarterly,* 2:26-31, April 1940.

THOMAS, DOROTHY E.   (4669)
The final years of New Mexico's struggle for statehood, 1907-12. Unpub. Master's thesis, UNM, 1940.

THOMAS, HELEN LEONA   (4670)
The occupational training of high school pupils. Unpub. Master's thesis, UNM, 1940.

THOMPSON, JAMES WESTFALL   (4670a)
A history of livestock raising in the United States, 1607-1860. USDA, Agricultural History series, no. 5. Washington, Nov. 1942.
Chapter 7: The Spanish Southwest and California.

THOMPSON, MERRELL E. AND DOVE, CLAUDE D.   (4671)
A comparison of physical achievement of Anglo and Spanish-American boys in junior high school. *The Research Quarterly,* 13:341-46, Oct. 1942.

THORP, N. HOWARD   (4672)
A chuck wagon supper. Unpub. ms. in files of New Mexico Writers' Project, Santa Fe.

———   (4673)
Following the flocks. *NM,* 14:9-11, 36-37, Nov. 1936.
Sheep raising.

———   (4673a)
Songs of the cowboys. Boston, Houghton Mifflin, 1921.

———   (4674)
Tales of the chuck wagon. Santa Fe, New Mexican Pub. Co., 1926.
Cowboy yarns.

THORPE, JAMES R.   (4675)
The town of Santa Fe, New Mexico; the Bishop's Lodge, Santa Fe. Santa Fe, n. p., 1921.

THURMAN, RUTH   (4675a)
Here's health. *NM,* 21, 17-19, March 1943.
History of Fort Bayard, now a Veterans' hospital.

TICHY, MARJORIE FERGUSON   (4676)
In the footsteps of Coronado. *NM,* 16:16-17, 35-37, March 1938.
Visit to the Tiguex towns.

TICHY, MARJORIE FERGUSON (Continued)   (4677)
Observations on the mission uncovered at Puaray. *EP*, 41:63-66, 1936.

TILDEN, FREEMAN   (4678)
Harnessing the Rio Grande. *World's Work*, 59:73-76, Aug. 1930.
    Elephant Butte Dam.

TINSLEY, J. D.   (4679)
Dry farming in New Mexico. Santa Fe, New Mexico Bureau of Immigration, 1909.

TIPTON, A. S.   (4680)
Conserving flood waters in New Mexico. *Irrigation Age*, 32:22-23, 27, Dec. 1916.

TIPTON, R. J.   (4681)
Resume of the problem concerning the Rio Grande above Fort Quitman, Texas. USDA, SCS, Jan. 1935. Typewritten.

TIREMAN, L. S. AND WATSON, MARY   (4682)
La comunidad: report of Nambe community school, 1937-42. Albuquerque, UNM Press, 1942.
    A report on a five-year educational experiment in a Spanish-speaking community.

TOLLE, VERNON   (4683)
Budgetary procedure in the municipal and other independent school units of New Mexico. Unpub. Doctor's dissertation, University of California, 1938.

————   (4684)
Report of the Belen, New Mexico, school survey. Unpub. Master's thesis, UNM, 1929.

TOMBS, JOHN   (4685)
New health law and the department of health of New Mexico. *National Conference of Social Work, Proceedings, 1920*. pp. 188-91.

TOTTY, MRS. FRANCES   (4686)
Buried money on the Mimbres. Unpub. ms. in files of New Mexico Writers' Project, Santa Fe.

TOWNSHEND, R. B.   (4687)
Last memories of a tenderfoot. New York, Dodd Mead, 1926.
    Travel description.

————   (4688)
The tenderfoot in New Mexico. New York, Dodd Mead, 1924.

TREGO, FRANK H.   (4689)
Boulevarded old trails in the great Southwest. New York, Greenberg, 1929.
    Travel description.

TROWBRIDGE, LYDIA J.   (4690)
To Taos and back. *EP*, 5 (2) :28-32, 1918.

TRUE, CLARA D.   (4690a)
The Española country. *Lulac News*, 6:14, 16, Sept. 1939.

TRUE, CLARA D. (Continued)   (4691)
Forgotten capital. *NM*, 16:10-11, 41, March 1938.
History of Santa Fe.

TUPPER, M.   (4692)
Maternal and infant hygiene in New Mexico. *Public Health Nurse*, 14:191-94, 1922.

TWITCHELL, RALPH EMERSON   (4693)
Leading facts of New Mexico history. 2 v. Cedar Rapids, Torch Press, 1911-12.

———   (4694)
Old Santa Fe; the story of New Mexico's ancient capital. Santa Fe, New Mexican Pub. Co., 1925.

UNITED STATES CONGRESS   (4695)
Equitable distribution of the waters of the Rio Grande. Senate Doc. 229, 55th Congress, 2nd Session. Washington, GPO, 1898.

———   (4696)
Report of the special committee of the United States Senate on the irrigation and reclamation of arid lands. Washington, GPO, 1890.
v. 3, Rocky Mountain region and the great plains.

———   (4697)
A report on the western range—a great but neglected natural resource. Senate Doc. 199, 74th Congress, 2nd Session. Washington, GPO, 1936.

———, HOUSE COMMITTEE ON AGRICULTURE   (4698)
New Mexico relief. Hearings . . . 68th Congress, 1st Session, on Senate Joint Resolution 52 for relief of the drought-stricken farm areas of New Mexico, March 28, 1924. Washington, GPO, 1924.

———, HOUSE COMMITTEE ON WAYS AND MEANS   (4699)
Return of cattle from Mexico. Hearings . . . House Joint Resolution 325, 68th Congress, 2nd Session. Washington, GPO, 1925.
Includes information on cattle loans in New Mexico.

———, HOUSE SELECT COMMITTEE TO INVESTIGATE THE INTERSTATE

MIGRATION OF DESTITUTE CITIZENS   (4700)
Interstate migration. Hearings . . . 76th Congress, 3rd Session pursuant to House Resolution 63 and 491. Washington, GPO, 1940-41.
Part V, *Oklahoma City hearings, Sept. 19, 20, 1940* contains statements by Edwin R. Henson on migration problems in the southern great plains, and Virginia Higgins, New Mexico Department of Public Welfare, on migrant labor in New Mexico.

———, SENATE COMMITTEE ON AGRICULTURE AND FORESTRY   (4701)
Relief of the drought-stricken farm areas of New Mexico. Hearings . . . 68th Congress, 1st Session on Senate Joint Resolution 52. Washington, GPO, 1924.

USDA, AGRICULTURAL ADJUSTMENT ADMINISTRATION   (4702)
New Mexico farm and range conservation program, 1939. Washington, 1940. Processed.

USDA, BAE   (4703)
Floods in the Rio Grande watershed, Colorado and New Mexico during May and June 1941. Aug. 1941. Processed.

————, ————   (4704)
Preliminary examination report, runoff and waterflow retardation and soil erosion prevention for flood control, Rio Grande watershed above El Paso. Berkeley, Sept. 1941. Processed.

————, ————   (4705)
Water facilities operations guidance report for the Canadian River basin, New Mexico. Water Utilization Planning Service, Feb. 1942. Processed.

————, FSA   (4706)
Western cattle and sheep areas. Circular C-103, Sept. 1936.

————, FIELD COORDINATING COMMITTEE   (4707)
Program of watershed management and conservation, Pecos River watershed. Feb. 1941. Processed.
         Includes some material on land use and ownership.

————, FIELD FLOOD-CONTROL COORDINATING COMMITTEE   (4708)
Preliminary examination report, runoff and waterflow retardation and soil-erosion prevention for flood-control purposes, Gila River watershed (Arizona and New Mexico). 1941. Processed.

————, FOREST SERVICE   (4709)
National forest facts, Southwestern region. March 1, 1942.
         Statistical tables for New Mexico and Arizona.

————, ————   (4710)
National forests of New Mexico. Washington, GPO, n. d.
         Descriptive and statistical data.

————, ————   (4711)
Range management plans for nine working circles in Santa Fe National Forest. Unpub. mss. dated 1924-40, in files of Forest Service, Albuquerque.

————, SCS   (4712)
Annual report, Mesilla area, fiscal year 1940. Typewritten. (Copy at USDA Library, Albuquerque.)
         Report on conservation practices, surveys made, efforts for public education in conservation methods.

————, ————   (4713)
Annual report, Middle Pecos area, fiscal year 1940. Typewritten. (Copy at USDA Library, Albuquerque.)

————, ————   (4714)
Annual report, Middle Rio Grande area, fiscal year 1940. Typewritten. (Copy at USDA Library, Albuquerque.)
         Includes discussion of inter-agency cooperation, land and ranges made available to Indians and Spanish-Americans, development of forestry, and developments in water engineering.

————, ————   (4715)
Annual report, Navajo district. June 30, 1936. (Copy at USDA Library, Albuquerque.)
         Iucludes a statement of SCS objectives.

usda, scs (Continued)   (4716)
Annual report of the Navajo project. Part II, 1935. (Copy at
USDA Library, Albuquerque.)
    Includes a statement of present situation and objectives of SCS.

————, ————   (4717)
Annual report, San Juan area, fiscal year 1940. Typewritten.
(Copy at USDA Library, Albuquerque.)
    Includes a report on surveys made.

————, ————   (4718)
Annual report, Southwest region, 1941-42. Albuquerque, 1942.
(Copy at USDA Library, Albuquerque.)

————, ————   (4719)
*Conservation—land classification survey report, Middle Rio
Grande Conservation District lands.* May 1940. (Copy at USDA
Library, Albuquerque.)

————, ————   (4720)
*District program and work plan for Salado Soil Conservation
District, Catron, Socorro, and Valencia Counties, New Mexico.*
Albuquerque, June 1942. Processed. (Copy at USDA Library,
Albuquerque.)

————, ————   (4721)
High water at San Marcial, preliminary report. May 16, 1937.
(Copy at USDA Library, Albuquerque.)

————, ————   (4722)
Memorandum on research and planning in the Navajo area.
SCS, Division of Regional Planning, May 1935. (Copy at USDA
Library, Albuquerque.)

————, ————   (4723)
*Preliminary report of floods of Rio Hondo and tributaries, May
28 to June 1, 1937.* SCS, Rio Grande District, n. d. (Copy at
USDA Library, Albuquerque.)

————, ————   (4724)
*Program and work plan for the Lindrith Soil Conservation Dis-
trict, Rio Arriba and Sandoval Counties, New Mexico.* Albuquerque, June 1942. Processed. (Copy at USDA Library, Albuquerque.)

————, ————   (4725)
*Program and work plan for the Luna Soil Conservation District,
Catron County, New Mexico.* Albuquerque, April 1942. Pro-
cessed. (Copy at USDA Library, Albuquerque.)

————, ————   (4726)
*Program and work plan for Pojoaque Soil Conservation District,
Santa Fe County, New Mexico.* Albuquerque, Aug. 10, 1942.
(Copy at USDA Library, Albuquerque.)

————, ————   (4727)
*Program and work plan for the Sedillo Soil Conservation District,
Bernalillo, Santa Fe, and Sandoval Counties, New Mexico.* Albuquerque, May 1942. Processed. (Copy at USDA Library, Albuquerque.)

USDA, SCS (Continued)   (4728)
*Progress report of the Navajo soil and water conservation exper-
iment station, Mexican Springs, New Mexico, 1934-39.* Processed. (Copy at USDA Library, Albuquerque.)

————, ————   (4729)
*Report on silt in the Rio Grande above Elephant Butte reser-
voir, 1937, 1938, 1939.* SCS, Region 8, Section of Watershed and
Project Planning, 1939. Typewritten. (Copy at USDA Library,
Albuquerque.)

————, ————   (4730)
*A report on the Rio Grande watershed, with special reference to
soil conservation problems.* November 1936. Typewritten. (Copy
at USDA Library, Albuquerque.)

————, ————   (4731)
Soil conservation practices and results in the Southwest. March
1, 1942. Processed. (Copy at USDA Library, Albuquerque.)

————, ————   (4732)
The Southwest region, annual report, fiscal year 1939-40. Processed. (Copy at USDA Library, Albuquerque.)

————, SOIL EROSION SERVICE   (4733)
Report of the committee on irrigation, 1934. (Copy at USDA
Library, Albuquerque.)

USDI   (4734)
Report of the Secretary of the Interior, 1891-92. House Exec.
Doc., 52nd Congress, 1st Session. Washington, GPO, 1892.
    pp. 378-84, report of the surveyor-general of New Mexico; pp. 133-35, ma-
    terial on private land claims in New Mexico.

————, BUREAU OF EDUCATION   (4735)
Illiteracy in the United States. Bureau of Education, Bulletin
20. Washington, GPO, 1913.
    Includes New Mexico.

————, ————   (4736)
Index to the reports of the Commissioner of Education, 1867-1907.
Bureau of Education, Bulletin 7. Washington, GPO, 1909.
    A guide to educational material on New Mexico.

————, ————   (4737)
Public and private high schools. Bureau of Education, Bulletin
22. Washington, GPO, 1912.
    Includes New Mexico.

————, ————   (4738)
The rural junior high school. Bureau of Education, Bulletin
28, 1928. Washington, GPO, 1929.
    Includes New Mexico.

————, ————   (4739)
Statistics for public high schools, 1919-20. Bureau of Education,
Bulletin 37, 1922. Washington, GPO, 1923.
    Includes New Mexico.

USDI, BUREAU OF EDUCATION (Continued) (4740)
Statistics of public, society and school libraries having 5,000 volumes and over in 1908. Bureau of Education, Bulletin 5. Washington, GPO, 1909.
Includes New Mexico.

————, BUREAU OF RECLAMATION (4741)
Rio Grande federal reclamation project, New Mexico-Texas. Washington, GPO, 1936.

————, OFFICE OF EDUCATION (4742)
Annual reports of the Commissioner of Education, 1867-date.
Include some material on education in New Mexico.

————, ———— (4743)
Biennial surveys of education. (1916-18—1934-36 included in Bulletin series of Office of Education. 1938-40 survey, a separate publication including some material for 1936-38 period.)
Statistical data on education in New Mexico.

————, ———— (4744)
Statistics of public, society, and school libraries, 1929. Office of Education, Bulletin 37, 1930. Washington, GPO, 1931.
Includes New Mexico.

————, SECRETARY OF THE INTERIOR (4745)
Annual reports, 1849-date.

UNITED STATES EXTENSION SERVICE (4746)
Cushioning the wind in New Mexico. Farms aided by emergency program to control wind erosion. *United States Extension Service Review,* 7:133-34, 1936.

UNITED STATES GREAT PLAINS COMMITTEE (4747)
The future of the great plains. Washington, GPO, 1936. *Also* House Doc. 144, 75th Congress, 1st Session. Washington, GPO, 1937.

UNIVERSITY OF NEW MEXICO (4748)
The San Jose Training School. UNM Bulletin, Training School series, v. 1, no. 1, 1930; v. 1, no. 2, 1931.
Program and activities of the school.

————, SPECIAL FACULTY COMMITTEE (4749)
Taxation and governmental reorganization for New Mexico. *New Mexico Business Review,* 3:1-43, 1934.
Includes: Governmental reorganization, by A. S. White; The property tax, by Tom L. Popejoy; A broader tax base, by Vernon G. Sorrell; and Public education, by J. E. Seyfried.

UPCHURCH, M. L. AND HILL, LEON W. (4750)
Administration and management of public land in New Mexico. USDA, BAE. Amarillo, 1942. Processed.

UPDEGRAFF, HARLAN (4751)
Teachers' certificates issued under general state laws and regulations. USDI, Bureau of Education, Bulletin 18. Washington, GPO, 1911.
Includes New Mexico.

UTTERBACK, THOMAS E. (4752)
Summary progress report for 1941; quantity and quality of flood run-off in the semi-arid Southwest. USDA, SCS, Feb. 1, 1942. (Copy at USDA Library, Albuquerque.)

VALENCIA, F. (4752a)
March onward Lulac soldiers. *Lulac News,* 5:7-8, Feb. 1938.
Toward a solution of Spanish-Americans' social and economic problems.

VALLIANT, MAUDE DRAKE (4753)
The history of the railroads of the Southwest. Unpub. Master's thesis, Columbia University, 1932.

VAN ARSDALE, JONATHAN (4754)
Railroads in New Mexico. *Research,* 2:3-16, Dec. 1937.

VAN CLEAVE, MARJORIE (4755)
Vegetative changes in the Middle Rio Grande Conservancy District. Unpub. Master's thesis, UNM, 1936.

VAN DEVANTER, D. W. (4756)
The proposed national monument at Manuelito, New Mexico. *American Antiquity,* 5:223-25, 1940.

VAUGHAN, JOHN HENRY (4757)
History and government of New Mexico. NMSC, 1927.

VESELY, FRANK (4758)
Public lands in New Mexico. *NM,* 11:10-12, 49-52, May; 24-26, June; 16-17, 50, July 1933.

VESTAL, STANLEY (4759)
Short grass country. New York, Duell, Sloan & Pearce, 1942.
Mostly Oklahoma and Texas. Contains some general material on life in New Mexico.

VIERRA, C. (4760)
New Mexico architecture. *A&A,* 7:37-49, 1918.

———— (4761)
Our native architecture in its relation to Santa Fe. AIA, School of American Archaeology, Papers 39. Santa Fe, 1917. *Also EP,* 4 (1) :5-11, 1917.

VILLAGRA, GASPAR PEREZ DE (4762)
History of New Mexico. Quivira Society Publications in History, v. 4. Los Angeles, 1933.

VILLARD, R. L. (4763)
Desirability of state-adopted textbooks for New Mexico high schools. Unpub. Master's thesis, UNM, 1936.

VIVIAN, GORDON (4764)
The excavation of Bandelier's Puaray. *EP,* 37:153-59, 1934.

———— (4765)
Restoring Rinconada. *EP,* 41:89-97, 1936.

THE VOCATIONAL NEWS (4766)
Periodical publication of the New Mexico Department of Vocational Education, containing news of training programs.

WAGGONER, W. H. (4767)
New livestock credit agency needed. *Producer*, 14:28-29, Feb. 1933.

WALKER, A. L. (4768)
Farm organization studies in Curry and Roosevelt Counties. NMAES Press Bulletin 581. State College, 1929. Processed.

—— (4769)
Farmers' cooperation in New Mexico, 1925-26. NMAES Bulletin 164. State College, 1927.

—— (4770)
Important factors in New Mexico range cattle production. NMAES Press Bulletin 523. State College, 1927. Processed.

—— (4771)
Indications of the cost of cotton production in the Mesilla Valley, 1925. NMAES Press Bulletin 515. State College, 1926. Processed.

WALKER, A. L. AND COCKERILL, P. W. (4772)
A preliminary report on 113 farms in the Middle Rio Grande Conservancy District. NMAES Press Bulletin 608. State College, 1930.

WALKER, A. L. AND CURRY, ALBERT S. (4773)
The status of land and capital in the Elephant Butte Irrigation District. *Journal of Land and Public Utility Economics*, 4:75-84, 1928.
> History of irrigation in the region up to building of the Dam; legislative activities, construction, capital involved, effect of Dam on land settlement and farm production in Mesilla Valley.

WALKER, A. L. AND LANTOW, J. L. (4774)
A preliminary study of 127 New Mexico ranches in 1925. NMAES Bulletin 159. State College, 1927.

WALKER, A. L., LANTOW, J. L., AND PICKERELL, K. P. (4775)
Economics of sheep production in western New Mexico. NMAES Bulletin 204. State College, 1932.

WALLER, C. E. (4776)
Plans and personnel of the recently created New Mexico State Board. *American Journal of Public Health*, 9:783, 1919.

WALTER, PAUL A. F. (4777)
First meeting of the New Mexico Educational Association. *NMHR*, 2:67-82, 1927.

—— (4778)
New Mexico in the great war. Chapter 6. The press and public opinion. *NMHR*, 1:245-64, 1926. Chapter 7. Art drama and literature in war service. *NMHR*, 1:400-19, 1926. Chapter 9. Life in camp and cantonment. *NMHR*, 2:3-16, 1927.

—— (4779)
A New Mexico Lourdes. *EP*, 3 (2) :1-28, 1916.

—— (4780)
Octaviano Ambrosio Larrazolo. *NMHR*, 7:97-105, 1932.

WALTER, PAUL A. F. (Continued)   (4781)
    The St. Francis murals at Santa Fe, New Mexico. *EP*, 5:323-26, 1918.

————   (4782)
    The Santa Fe-Taos art movement. *A&A*, 4:330-38, 1916.

————   (4783)
    Ten years after: an appraisal of L. Bradford Prince. *NMHR*, 7:371-76, 1932.

————   (4784)
    William Hayes Pope; the first federal district judge of New Mexico. *EP*, 4 (1) :109-22, 1917.

WALTER, PAUL, JR.   (4785)
    Notes on a trip to Jemez. *EP*, 29:206-13, 1930.
      Historical background of Jemez country.

————   (4786)
    The press as a source in the study of social problems. Unpub. Master's thesis, UNM, 1933.

WALTER, PAUL, JR. AND SAXTON, MARVIN   (4787)
    Social pathology of New Mexico. UNM Bulletin, Sociological series, v. 2, no. 3, 1936.

WATSON, MORRIS P.   (4788)
    The people of New Mexico. *Outlook*, 73:341-44, 1903.

WELLMAN, PAUL ISELY   (4789)
    The trampling herd. New York, Carrick & Evans, 1939.
      Cattle industry.

WELLS, CARVETH   (4790)
    Best of the West—New Mexico. *NM*, 11:11-13, 40, Aug. 1933.
      Travel description.

WEST, GUY A.   (4791)
    Racial attitudes among teachers of New Mexico. Chico, California State Teachers College, 1934.

WESTERGAARD, WALDEMAR   (4792)
    Senator Bard and the Arizona-New Mexico statehood controversy. *Southern California Historical Society, Publication* 11, part 2, 1919. pp. 9-17.

WHITE, O. P.   (4793)
    Cutting free. *Collier's*, 94:24-, Oct. 27, 1934.
      Political influence of Senator Cutting.

————   (4794)
    Low the poor Indian; greedy stockmen and politicians in New Mexico's no man's land. *Collier's*, 99:16-17, Feb. 6, 1937.

————   (4795)
    Membership in both clubs. *American Mercury*, 25:182-89, Feb. 1932.
      Senator Cutting's political activities.

WHITEMAN, LAURA M.   (4796)
    Economic and social status of wards in state welfare home for girls, Albuquerque, New Mexico. Unpub. Master's thesis, UNM, 1941.

WHITING, LILIAN (4797)
The land of enchantment. Boston, Little Brown, 1906.
Travel description.

WILBAR, A. P. (4798)
Private land claims in New Mexico. Exec. Doc. 57, 36th Congress, 2nd Session. Washington, GPO, 1861.

WILLIAMS, AGNES (4799)
Mexican words used by English-speaking inhabitants of the Mesilla Valley. Unpub. Bachelor's thesis, NMSC, 1894.

WILLIAMS, BURTON T. (4800)
Tenure and turnover of public school teachers in New Mexico. Unpub. Master's thesis, UNM, 1937.

WILLOUGHBY, ROY (4801)
The range cattle industry in New Mexico. Unpub. Master's thesis, UNM, 1933.

WILLS, L. (4802)
Isolated New Mexico. *Public Health Nurse,* 14:291-93, 1922.

WILSON, BROWNLOW (4803)
Open range. *NM,* 16:26-27, 42-43, June 1938.
Ranch life in southwestern New Mexico.

———— (4804)
The waste of natural resources. *American Cattle Producer,* 18: 3-7, 21, April 1937.
By overgrazing and erosion.

WILSON, C. P. (4805)
Forty-five year precipitation record at State College, New Mexico. NMAES Press Bulletin 832. State College, 1937. Processed.

WILSON, C. P., NEALE, P. E., PARKER, K. W., AND WATENPAUGH, H. N. (4806)
Soil and rainfall conservation in New Mexico. NMAES Bulletin 238. State College, 1936.

WILSON, EDMUND (4807)
Enchanted forest. *New Republic,* 68:290-94, 1931.
Description of Bellamy, New Mexico.

———— (4808)
New Mexico notes. *New Republic,* 68:202-04, 1931.
Satiric description of Anglo types who attend Indian dances.

WILSON, GLENN THOMPSON (4809)
Financial support of the Otero County schools. Unpub. Master's thesis, USC, 1934.

WILSON, GRACE BARKER (4810)
A study of pupil elimination in the public high schools of San Juan County, New Mexico. Unpub. Master's thesis, UNM, 1940.

WILSON, H. T. (4811)
Historical sketch of Las Vegas, New Mexico. Chicago, n. p., n. d.

WINSHIP, A. E. (4812)
New Mexico: third of a millenium—half a century—a decade. *National Magazine* (Boston), 18:723-25, 1903.
Educational progress.

WINSOR, JUSTIN   (4813)
Narrative and critical history of America. 2 v. Boston, Houghton Mifflin, 1884-89.
  Includes material on history of New Mexico.

WISSLER, CLARK   (4814)
New Mexico's great heritage. *EP,* 6:146-51, 154-55, 1919.

WISTRAND, P. H.   (4815)
Rio Grande. *The Santa Fean,* 2:10-12, Summer 1942.
  History of the river.

WOEHLKE, WALTER V.   (4816)
New day in New Mexico. *Sunset,* 46:21-24, June 1921.
  Economic conditions.

WOOD, CHARLIE H.   (4817)
The relation between the size and the cost of operation of county schools in New Mexico. Unpub. Master's thesis, New Mexico Normal (Highlands) University, 1932.

WOOD, KATHERINE D.   (4818)
Urban workers on relief. Part II. The occupational characteristics of workers on relief in 79 cities, May 1934. WPA, Research Monograph IV. Washington, GPO, 1936.
  Includes Albuquerque.

WOODS, BETTY   (4818a)
Better than gold. *NM,* 21:16, 36, March 1943.
  History of Steeple Rock, ghost town in Grant County.

————   (4819)
He man's town. *NM,* 19:12-13, 37-38, April 1941.
  Historical development of Reserve, New Mexico.

————   (4820)
Play town. *NM,* 19:20-21, 42, Jan. 1941.
  History of Tyrone, New Mexico .

————   (4821)
Stagecoach town. *NM,* 20:10-11, 31-32, Dec. 1942.
  Story of Mowry City, an abandoned town in southwest New Mexico.

WOODWARD, DOROTHY AND FETH, JACK   (4822)
New Mexico; land of enchantment. Senate Doc. 91, 77th Congress, 1st Session. Washington, GPO, 1941.

WOOLFORD, WITHERS   (4823)
Modernism in New Mexico. *New Mexico Highway Journal,* 7:21, April 1929.

WOOTON, E. O.   (4824)
Factors affecting range management in New Mexico. USDA, Bulletin 211. Washington, GPO, 1915.

————   (4825)
The range problem in New Mexico. NMAES Bulletin 66. State College, 1908.

————   (4826)
The relation of land tenure to the use of the arid grazing lands of the Southwestern states. USDA, Bulletin 1001. Washington, GPO, 1922.

WOOTON, E. O. (Continued) (4827)
Settler's progress in dry land farming in eastern New Mexico.
USDA, BAE, Circular 4. Washington, GPO, 1927.

WOOTON, E. O. AND STANDLEY, PAUL C. (4828)
Description of new plants preliminary to a report upon the
flora of New Mexico. *Contributions from the United States National Herbarium*, v. 16, pt. 4. Washington, 1913. pp. 109-96.

WORKS PROGRESS ADMINISTRATION (4829)
Report on progress of the WPA program, December 1937. Washington, GPO, 1938; *Same, June 30, 1938;* Washington, GPO, 1938;
Same, June 30, 1939. Washington, GPO, 1939; *Same, June 30,
1940.* Washington, GPO, 1940; *Same, June 30, 1941.* Washington, GPO, 1941.
    Includes relief statistics for New Mexico.

————, DIVISION OF SOCIAL RESEARCH (4830)
Areas of intense drought distress 1930-36. Research series 5, no. 1.
Washington, GPO, 1937.
    Includes New Mexico.

————, ———— (4831)
Inter-city differences in the cost of living. Research series 1, no. 20.
Washington, GPO, 1936.
    Includes Albuquerque.

————, ———— (4832)
*Usual occupations of workers eligible for works program em-
ployment in the United States, January 15, 1936.* Washington,
GPO, Jan. 1937.
    Includes separate statistics for New Mexico.

————, ———— (4833)
*Workers on relief in the United States in March 1935; a census
of usual occupations.* Washington, GPO, Jan. 1937.
    Statistics for New Mexico.

WRAY, HENRY (4834)
America's unguarded gateway. *North American Review,* 208:312-
15, 1918.
    Charges that New Mexico is controlled by *penitentes* loyal to Mexico.

WRIGHT, ALICE (4835)
Tubers and goobers. *NM,* 16:9-11, 41, Feb. 1938.
    Portales Valley farming.

YEO, HERBERT W. (4836)
*Preliminary report on flood conditions during April and May
1937 in the vicinity of San Marcial, New Mexico.* USDA, SCS.
Processed. (Copy in USDA Library, Albuquerque.)

———— (4837)
*Report on surveys, examinations, and investigations made near
San Marcial, New Mexico during 1936, 1937, 1938.* USDA, SCS,
Rio Grande District, Region 8, Rio Grande Survey. Processed.
(Copy in USDA Library, Albuquerque.)

YEO, HERBERT W. (Continued)   (4838)
Report on the rains of August 29-30, 1935 in Las Cruces and vicinity and the flood resulting therefrom. USDA, SCS. Processed. (Copy in USDA Library, Albuquerque.)

——————   (4839)
The San Juan irrigation project. *New Mexico Highway Journal,* 7:20, Nov. 1929.

ZARATE-SALMERON, G. DE   (4840)
Relating all the things that have been seen and known in New Mexico. *Land of Sunshine,* 11:337-56, 1899; 12:39-48, 104-13, 180-87, 1900.

ZIGROSSER, CARL   (4841)
Prints in the Southwest. *SR,* 26:188-202, 1941.
    Art prints.

IV

ADDENDA

Bibliographies and Indexes

DEGOYLER, E. L. (4842)
Compleat collector: New Mexicana. *Saturday Review of Literature*, 25:29-30, May 16, 1942.

LOMAX, ALAN AND COWELL, SIDNEY ROBERTSON (4843)
American folksong and folklore: a regional bibliography. New York, Progressive Education Association, 1942.

MICHIGAN HISTORICAL RECORDS SURVEY (4844)
Check list of New Mexico imprints and publications, 1784-1786. Inventory of American Imprints, No. 25, 1942. Processed.

NEW MEXICO HISTORICAL RECORDS SURVEY (4845)
Unpub. index to *El Palacio,* on file at UNM Library.

SAUNDERS, LYLE (4846)
Spanish-speaking Americans and Mexican-Americans in the United States. New York, Bureau for Intercultural Education, 1944.

———— (4847)
A guide to the literature of the Southwest. *New Mexico Quarterly Review,* 13:116-25, 1943; 14:115-22, 1944.
See also (307a).

STECK, FRANCIS BORGIA (4848)
A tentative guide to historical materials on the Spanish borderlands. Philadelphia, Catholic Historical Society, 1943. Part VI: New Mexico and Arizona, 1581-1846.

Pre-Spanish Period

ANONYMOUS (4849)
Ancient New Mexicans; excavations at a Mogollon village. *Scientific American,* 168:274, June 1943.

ARMAGNAC, ALDEN P. (4850)
Cave machine helps find the first American. *Popular Science,* 140:125-28, March 1942.
Popular account of excavation at Sandia Cave.

BARBER, E. A. (4851)
Ancient Pueblos. *American Naturalist,* 12:526-, 606-, 1878.

BULLEN, ADELAIDE K. AND RIPLEY P. (4852)
A Pueblo cave site at Tres Piedras, New Mexico. *American Antiquity,* 8:57-64, July 1942.

DICK, HERBERT W. (4853)
Alluvial sites of central New Mexico. *New Mexico Anthropologist,* 6-7:19-22, Jan.-Feb.-March 1943.

ELMORE, FRANCIS H. (4854)
Great sanctuary. *Desert Magazine,* 5:23, Oct. 1942.
Description of a shrine in Chaco Canyon.

FARMER, MALCOLM F.   (4855)
    Navaho archaeology of Upper Blanco and Largo canyons, northern
    New Mexico. *American Antiquity*, 8:65-79, July 1942.

FEWKES, J. WALTER   (4856)
    A ruined pueblo in New Mexico. *American Geographical Society
    Bulletin*, 34:217-, 1902.

FLINN, MARJORIE CRAMER   (4857)
    *A preliminary survey of mammalian bone implements of the Ana-
    sazi region.* Unpub. Master's thesis, UNM, 1940.

GILBERT, HOPE   (4858)
    Pecos ruin. *NM*, 20:12-13, 33-34, Dec. 1942.

HALL, EDWARD TWITCHELL, JR.   (4859)
    Early stockaded settlements in the Governador, New Mexico.
    Columbia University Studies in Archaeology and Ethnology, v. 2,
    no. 1, 1943.
        Description of excavations with sections on pottery, textiles, and cranial
        material. Marginal Anasazi development from Basketmaker III to Pueblo I
        times.
────   (4860)
    Recent clues to Athapascan prehistory in the Southwest. *AA*, 46:
    98-105, Jan.-March 1944.

HARRINGTON, E. R.   (4861)
    The four corners country. *NM*, 21:7-9, 32, 33, Oct. 1943.
        Brief material on Chaco ruins.

HART, F.   (4862)
    Some antiquity in America. *Arena*, 24:175-, 1900.

HIBBEN, FRANK C. AND DICK, HERBERT W.   (4863)
    A Basketmaker III site in Canyon Largo, New Mexico. *American
    Antiquity*, 9:381-85, April 1944.

HOWARD, EDGAR B.   (4864)
    Folsom and Yuma problems. *Proceedings of the American Philo-
    sophical Society*, 86:255-59, Feb. 10, 1943.

HURT, WESLEY R., JR.   (4865)
    Folsom and Yuma points from the Estancia Valley, New Mexico.
    American Antiquity, 7:400-02, April 1942.

JONES, VOLNEY H.   (4866)
    Was tobacco smoked in the Pueblo region in pre-Spanish times?
    American Antiquity, 9:451-56, April 1944.

LANGE, CHARLES H., JR.   (4867)
    *The Evans site: a contribution to the archaeology of the Gallina
    region, northern New Mexico.* Unpub. Master's thesis, UNM,
    1941.

MARTIN, PAUL S.   (4868)
    *The Su site. Excavations at a Mogollon village, western New
    Mexico, second season, 1941.* Field Museum of Natural History,
    Anthropological series, v. 32, no. 2. Chicago, Feb. 1943.
        See (553).

MERA, H. P. (4869)
Jaritas rock shelter, northeastern New Mexico. *American Antiquity,* 9:295-301, Jan. 1944.

MORRIS, EARL H. (4870)
Adobe bricks in a pre-Spanish wall near Aztec, New Mexico. *American Antiquity,* 9:434-38, April 1944.

PRICE, W. ARMSTRONG (4871)
The Clovis site: regional physiography and geology. *American Antiquity,* 9:401-07, April 1944.

REED, ERIK K. (4872)
Abandonment of the San Juan region. *EP,* 51:61-74, April 1944.
By the Anasazi.
——— (4873)
The problem of protohistoric Picuries. *EP,* 50:65-68, March 1943.

RENAUD, ETÏENNE B. (4874)
Indian stone enclosures of Colorado and New Mexico. University of Denver, Archaeological series, 2nd paper. Denver, 1942.
——— (4875)
Reconnaissance work in the upper Rio Grande Valley, Colorado and New Mexico. University of Denver, Archaeological series, 3rd paper. Denver, 1942.
——— (4876)
The Rio Grande points. *Southwestern Lore,* 8:33-36, Dec. 1942.

SCHULTZ, C. B. (4877)
Some artifact sites of early man in the great plains and adjacent areas; work done by the field parties of the University of Nebraska State Museum since 1937. *American Antiquity,* 8:242-49, Jan. 1943.

TANNER, CLARA LEE (4878)
Life forms in prehistoric pottery of the Southwest. *The Kiva,* 8: 26-32, May 1943.

Apaches

BANDELIER, ADOLPH F. A. (4879)
Apache outbreak, 1885. *Nation,* 43:208-, 1886.

BOURKE, JOHN G. (4880)
Gentile system of the Apaches. *JAF,* 3:111-, 1890.

GRIFFIN, FRED M. (4881)
Under five flags. *NM,* 21:18, 33-34, July 1943.
Hosteen Magoosh, Mescalero Apache chief.

HOIJER, HARRY (4882)
Pitch accent in the Apachean languages. *Language,* 19:38-41, Jan. 1943.

LUPAN, N. (4883)
An Apache dance. *Outing,* 22:189-, 1893.

NICHOLSON, A. (4884)
Last of the Apache scouts. *Country Gentleman,* 113:15-, March 1943.

OPLER, MORRIS EDWARD   (4885)
    The Jicarilla Apache ceremonial relay race. *AA*, 46:75-97, Jan.-
March 1944.

–––––   (4886)
    Navaho shamanistic practices among the Jicarilla Apache. *New
Mexico Anthropologist*, 6-7:13-18, Jan.-Feb.-March 1943.

Navajos

ABBOTT, CHUCK   (4887)
    The Navajo squaw dance. *Arizona Highways*, 19:8-11, June 1943.

BAXTER, SYLVESTER   (4888)
    Dances of the Navajo Indians. *American Architect*, 28:22-, 1889.

CARLSON, RICHARD   (4889)
    The Navajo and his land. *Arizona Highways*, 19:24-27, June 1943.

–––––   (4890)
    The Navajo goes to market. *Arizona Highways*, 19:36-37, June
1943.

CASSIDY, INA SIZER   (4891)
    Quincy Tahoma, Navajo. *NM*, 22:40, 50, Jan. 1944.

DUTTON, BERTHA P.   (4892)
    Navajo creation myth. *EP*, 49:145-52, July 1942.

HAILE, BERARD   (4893)
    Origin legend of the Navaho flintway; text and translation. Uni-
versity of Chicago Publications in Anthropology, Linguistic series.
Chicago, 1943.

HIGGINS, HELEN   (4894)
    Navajo warriors. *NM*, 21:12-13, 33, 34, Oct. 1943.

HILL, W. W.   (4895)
    Navaho humor. General series in Anthropology, no. 9. Menasha,
Wisconsin, George Banta Pub. Co., 1943.
       Same as (998).

–––––   (4896)
    The Navaho Indians and the ghost dance of 1890. Unpub. ms.
in possession of the author. To be published in *American Anthropologist.*

HILL, W. W. AND DOROTHY   (4897)
    The legend of the Navajo eagle-catching way. *New Mexico An-
thropologist*, 6-7: 31-36, April-May-June 1943.

–––––   (4898)
    Two Navajo myths. *New Mexico Anthropologist*, 6-7:111-14, July-
Aug.-Sept.- 1943.

HUFF, CHARLES   (4899)
    The wind that talks. *Compressed Air Magazine*, 48:7120-21, Aug.
1943.
       Use of radio on Navajo reservation.

HURT, WESLEY R., JR.   (4900)
Eighteenth century Navaho hogans from Canyon de Chelly National Monument. *American Antiquity*, 8:89-104, July 1942.

LEMOS, PEDRO   (4901)
Sand painting. *School Arts*, 43:81, Nov. 1943.

MERA, H. P.,   (4902)
Navajo twilled weaving. Laboratory of Anthropology, Bulletin 14. Santa Fe, 1943.

MILLER, JOSEPH   (4903)
The Navajo in literature. *Arizona Highways*, 19:28-33, June 1943.

NEWCOMB, FRANC J.   (4904)
The price of a horse. *New Mexico Quarterly Review*, 13:194-99, Summer 1943.
   Navajo legend.

OAKES, MAUD   (4905)
Where the two came to their father; Navaho war ceremonial. Bollingen Series I. New York, Pantheon Books, 1943.

REICHARD, GLADYS A.   (4906)
Good characters in myth: the Navajo sun god. *JAF*, 56:141-43, April 1943.

————   (4907)
Human nature as conceived by the Navajo Indians and their use of ritual. *Review of Religion*, 7:353-60, May 1943.

RICHARDSON, CECIL   (4908)
Charlie Day. *Arizona Highways*, 18:38-39, Oct. 1942.
   Story of an old Navajo told by an Indian trader.

SCHEVILL, MARGARET ERWIN   (4909)
Navajo ritual poetry. Unpub. Master's thesis, University of Arizona, 1942.

STEWART, JAMES M.   (4910)
The Navajo Indian at war. *Arizona Highways*, 19:20-23, 43, June 1943.

TADLOCK, JAMES A.   (4911)
Navajos respond to nation's need. *Manpower Review*, 10:7-8, April 1943.

VAN VALKENBURGH, RICHARD   (4912)
Blood revenge of the Navajo. *Desert Magazine*, 6:19-23, Oct. 1943.
————   (4913)
The gods walked up there. *Desert Magazine*, 7:5-10, Dec. 1943.
————   (4914)
Henry Chee Dodge, chief of the Navajo nation. *Arizona Highways*, 19:5-7, June 1943.
————   (4915)
I saw the Red Ant Chant. *Desert Magazine*, 6:5-7, July 1943.
————   (4916)
Mission to Ch'ool'i'i. *Desert Magazine*, 5:5-8, July 1942.
   Navajo medicine on El Governador.

WATKINS, FRANCES E. (4917)
    The Navaho. V. *Masterkey*, 17:77-81, May 1943.
        Social life (continued).

——— (4918)
    The Navaho. VI. *Masterkey*, 17:136-40, July 1943.
        Social life (continued).

——— (4919)
    The Navaho. VII. *Masterkey*, 17:168-72, Sept. 1943.
        Religion. *See also* (1335) - (1337a).

——— (4920)
    The Navaho. Southwest Museum Leaflets, no. 16, 1943.

WYMAN, LELAND C. AND BAILEY, FLORA L. (4921)
    Navaho girl's puberty rite. *New Mexico Anthropologist*, 6-7:3-12,
    Jan.-Feb.-March 1943.

——— (4922)
    *Navaho upward-reaching way: objective behavior, rationale, and
    sanction.* UNM Bulletin, Anthropological series, v. 4, no. 2, May
    1943.

Pueblos

AMERICAN ASSOCIATION ON INDIAN AFFAIRS (4923)
    Flooding the Pueblos. News-Letter, no. 27, Nov. 25, 1941.

——— (4924)
    Pueblos and flood control. News-Letter, no. 29, March 25, 1942.

ANONYMOUS (4925)
    Acoma, New Mexico. *American Architect*, 16:258-, 1884.

——— (4926)
    Animal forms in Zuni pottery. *Science*, 6:266-, 1885.

——— (4927)
    Art of potters. *NM*, 21:14-15, July 1943.
        Julian and Maria Martinez.

——— (4928)
    The arts of the Pueblos. *Design*, 43:14, April 1942.

——— (4929)
    Dam threatens Pueblos. *Life*, 15:104-10, Nov. 29, 1943.

——— (4930)
    F. H. Cushing at Zuni. *American Architect*, 11:56-, 121-, 1881.

——— (4931)
    Pottery making—Indian style. *Popular Science*, 143:94-95, Oct.
    1943.

——— (4932)
    Pottery making in the Southwest. *Design*, 45:6-7, Dec. 1943.

——— (4933)
    St. Jerome's day with the Pueblo Indians. *Lippincott's Magazine*,
    30:113-, 1882.

——— (4934)
    That Pueblo threat. *Masterkey*, 17:193, Sept. 1943.
        Indian protests against proposed Rio Grande dam.

——— (4935)
    Zuni religion. *Science*, 11:136-, 1887.

ATA, TE (4936)
The creation of an Indian jar. *NM*, 51:180-85, April 1943.
Julian and Maria Martinez.

BARBER, E. A. (4937)
Pueblo Indians. *American Naturalist*, 11:591-, 1877.

BAXTER, SYLVESTER (4938)
Cushing's discoveries among the Zuni Indians. *American Architect*, 11:195-, 1881; 12:195-, 1882.

—— (4939)
Pilgrimage of Zuni Indians to Boston. *Century*, 2:526-, 1882.

—— (4940)
Zuni revisited. *American Architect*, 13:124-, 1882.

BURCH, TILLIE (4941)
In the Pueblo kitchen. *NM*, 22:18,34, March 1944.

BYNNER, WITTER (4942)
Threat to the Pueblo Indians. *Asia and the Americas*, 43:560, Sept. 1943.

CARTER, O. C. S. (4943)
Acoma, New Mexico. *Journal of the Franklin Institute*, 162:449-, 1906.

CUSHING, FRANK (4944)
Habitations of the Pueblo Indians. *American Architect*, 21:103-, 1886.

DENNIS, WAYNE AND RUSSELL, R. W. (4945)
Piaget's questions applied to Zuni children. *Child Development*, 11:181-87, 1940.

FILLMORE, J. C. (4946)
Music of Zuni. *Music*, 5:39-, 1893.

GWYTHER, G. (4947)
Pueblo Indians. *Overland Monthly*, 6:260-, 1870.

HAWLEY, FLORENCE; PIJOAN, MICHEL; AND ELKIN, C. A. (4948)
An inquiry into food economy and body economy in Zia Pueblo. *AA*, 45:547-56, Oct.-Dec. 1943.

INGERSOLL, E. (4949)
Chimney corners in Zuni. *Monthly Illustrator*, 3:251-, 1895.

JAMES, GEORGE WHARTON (4950)
A pilgrimage to some scenes of Spanish occupancy in our Southwest. *Review of Reviews*, 20:51-59, 1899.

KIRK, RUTH F. (4951)
Introduction to Zuni fetishism. *EP*, 50:117-29, June; 146-59, July; 183-98, Aug.; 206-19, Sept.; 235-45, Oct. 1943.

—— (4952)
Zuni fetish worship. *Masterkey*, 17:129-35, July 1943.

LEMOS, PEDRO (4953)
Zuni hunt fetishes. *School Arts*, 43:86-87, Nov. 1943.

LUMMIS, CHARLES F.   (4954)
Acoma, New Mexico, ancient city of the Queres. *California Illustrated Magazine,* 1:31-, 1891.

————   (4955)
The Indian who is not poor. *Scribners,* 12:361-72, 1892.

————   (4956)
The pyramids of Taos. *Land of Sunshine,* 6:141-, 1896.

MARIAGER, DAGMAR   (4957)
A Zuni genesis. *Overland Monthly,* n.s., 13:383-, 1888.

MASON, OTIS TUFTON   (4958)
Prayer-burying by Zuni Indians. *Science,* 8:24-, 1886.

MERA, H. P.   (4959)
Pueblo Indian embroidery. Laboratory of Anthropology, Memoirs, v. 4. Santa Fe, 1943.

MINDELEFF, COSMOS   (4960)
Pueblo architecture. *American Architect,* 56:19-, 59-, 1896; 57:31-,
87-, 1896.

MINDELEFF, VICTOR   (4961)
Origin of Pueblo architecture. *Science,* 9:593-, 1886.

OBER, F. A.   (4962)
Acoma, New Mexico. *American Architect,* 29:65-, 1889.

PEET, S. D.   (4963)
Beginnings of Pueblo architecture. *American Antiquarian,* 21:
327-, 1899.

————   (4964)
Discovery of the Pueblo Indians. *American Antiquarian,* 17:339-,
1895.

————   (4965).
Ethnic styles in American architecture. *American Antiquarian,*
24:19-, 61-, 1902.

————   (4966)
Great houses and fortresses of the Pueblo Indians. *American
Antiquarian,* 20:315-, 1898.

————   (4967)
Pueblos and Pueblo architecture. *American Antiquarian,* 20:
143-, 1898.

PILLSBURY, DOROTHY L.   (4968)
Christmas trail to the sky city. *Desert Magazine,* 7:11-13, Dec.
1943.
        Acoma.

POWELL, L. W.   (4969)
Pueblo Indians. *Potter's American Monthly,* 10:226-, 1877.

PRICE, E. D.   (4970)
Pueblo Indians. *Sunday Magazine,* 17:436-, 1888.

REED, ERIK K.   (4971)
Southern Tewa Pueblos in the historic period. *EP,* 50:254-64, 276-
88, 1943.

ROBERTS, E.   (4972)
Festival of Pueblo Indians. *Overland Monthly*, n.s., 3:337-, 1883.

RUSSELL, R. W.   (4973)
Spontaneous and instructed drawing of Zuni children. *Journal of Comparative Psychology*, 35:11-15, Feb. 1943.

SNEDDEN, GENEVA SISSON   (4974)
Docas, Indian of Santa Clara. Boston, D. C. Heath & Co., 1942.

STONE, MARGARET   (4975)
Blue Water—artist of Tesuque. *Desert Magazine*, 7:9-14, Feb. 1944.

————   (4976)
Toli goes back to Laguna. *Desert Magazine*, 7:12-16, Nov. 1943.

STRETTELL, A.   (4977)
Festival of Pueblo Indians. *Macmillan's Magazine*, 47:21-, 1882. *Also Eclectic Magazine*, 100:684-, 1882.

TRAGER, GEORGE L.   (4978)
The kinship and status terms of the Tiwa languages. *AA*, 45:557-71, Oct.-Dec. 1943.

————   (4979)
The language of Taos Pueblo. Maitre Phonetique, no. 56, 1936.

WEST, RICHARD S.   (4980)
Rain dance. *The Rio Grande Writer*, 1:62-63, Spring 1942.

WHITE, LESLIE A.   (4981)
New material from Acoma. Bureau of American Ethnology, Anthropological Papers, no. 32. Washington, GPO, 1943.

WILDER, MITCHELL A.   (4982)
Architectural revival in the Southwest; churches in New Mexico built by Pueblo Indians. *Liturgical Arts*, 11:2-4, Nov. 1942.

WILLIAMSON, TEN BROECK   (4983)
The Pueblo canes. *NM*, 21:10-11, 35, Dec. 1943.

WILTON, ANNA K.   (4984)
Zuni pottery making. Unpub. Master's thesis, UNM, 1943.

WOODS, BETTY   (4985)
The drum maker of Cochiti. *Desert Magazine*, 5:11-14, Jan. 1942.

Indians, General

ANONYMOUS   (4986)
Inter-tribal Indian ceremonial at Gallup. *Design*, 43:17, April, 1942.

BEALS, RALPH L.   (4987)
Masks in the Southwest. *AA*, 34:166-68, Jan.-March, 1932.

BEATTY, WILLARD W. AND YOUNG, ROBERT W.   (4988)
La educacion bilingue en las escuelas para indigenas de los Estados Unidos. *America Indigena*, 2:39-42, Oct. 1942.
Includes material on teaching of Navajo language.

BOULTON, L. C.   (4989)
Recent recordings in the Southwest. *Music Teachers National
Assn. Proceedings,* 1940. pp. 128-31.

BULLEN, RIPLEY P.   (4990)
Corn goddess or phalli? *American Antiquity,* 9:448-49, April 1944.

BUTCHER, HAROLD   (4991)
Our Indians demand their rights. *Travel,* 81:23-25, 32, 34, Sept.
1943.

CARTER, GEORGE FRANCIS   (4992)
Agricultural geography of the Southwest Indians. Unpub. Doctor's
thesis, University of California, 1943.

CASTETTER, E. F.   (4993)
Early tobacco utilization and cultivation in the American Southwest. *AA,* 45:320-25, April 1943.

COHEN, FELIX S.   (4994)
Handbook of federal Indian law. Washington, USDI, Office of
the Solicitor, 1942.

CURTIS, EDWARD S.   (4995)
The North American Indian. Cambridge, Mass., Harvard University Press, 1908. 20v.
     V. 16. The Tiwa, The Keres.

DEN HOLLANDER, A. N. J.   (4996)
De Peyote—cultus der Noord-Amerikaansche Indianen. *Mensch
Maatschij,* 35:17-29, 123-31, 1935.

D'HARNONCOURT, RENE   (4997)
El arte del indio en los Estados Unidos. Washington, National
Indian Institute, 1943.

DIETRICH, MARGRETTA   (4998)
Braves on the warpath. *NM,* 21:14-15, 29-30, June 1943.

HODGE, FREDERICK WEBB   (4999)
Coral among Southwestern Indians. *Masterkey,* 17:99-102, May
1943.

HOIJER, HARRY   (5000)
Phonetic and phonemic change in the Athapascan languages.
Language, 18:218-20, July 1942.

HUSCHER, BETTY H. AND HAROD, A   (5001)
Athapascan migration via the intermountain region. *American
Antiquity,* 8:80-88, July 1942.

HUTCHINSON, CHARLES   (5002)
Cultural adjustment aims in Indian education. Unpub. ms. in
possession of author.

KAY, ELEANOR   (5003)
Gathering of the tribes. *NM,* 20:9-13, 37, July 1942.
    Gallup Ceremonial.

KIRK, RUTH F.   (5004)
Dances for war . . . and peace. *NM,* 21:9-13, 28, July 1943.
    Gallup Ceremonial.

LANGE, CHARLES H., JR.   (5005)
Tiponi, or corn goddess symbols. *American Antiquity,* 9:446-48,
April 1944.

LINTON, RALPH   (5006)
Nativistic movements. *AA*, 45:230-40, 1943.

MERA, H. P.   (5007)
An outline of ceramic developments in southern and southeastern New Mexico. Laboratory of Anthropology, Technical series, Bulletin 11. Santa Fe, July 1943.

MORICE, A. G.   (5008)
The great Dene race. *Anthropos,* 1:229-78, 483-509, 695-730, 1906; 2:1-34, 181-96, 1907.

SHEPARD, WARD   (5009)
La conservacion de las tierras indigenas en los Estados Unidos. Washington, National Indian Institute, 1942.

STRONG, W. D.   (5010)
An analysis of Southwestern society. Doctor's thesis, University of California, 1926.

WHITE, LESLIE A.   (5011)
Punche: tobacco in New Mexico history. *NMHR,* 18:386-93, Oct. 1943.

Spanish-Colonial and Mexican Periods

ADAMS, ELEANOR B.   (5012)
Two colonial New Mexico libraries. *NMHR,* 19:135-67, April 1944.

BARTLETT, KATHARINE   (5013)
Notes upon the routes of Espejo and Farfan to the mines in the 16th century. *NMHR,* 17:21-36, Jan. 1942.

BLOOM, LANSING B.   (5014)
Martin Amador and Mesilla Valley history. *NMHR,* 17:178-80, April 1942.

CORLE, EDWIN   (5015)
There's something about a soldier. *Virginia Quarterly Review,* 19:575-92, Autumn 1943.
    The search for Cibola.

FARNUM, MABEL   (5016)
The seven golden cities. Milwaukee, Bruce Pub. Co., 1943.
    Fray Marcos de Niza and the conquest of the Spanish Southwest.

HAMMOND, GEORGE P.   (5017)
New light on the Coronado expedition, 1540-1542. *Proceedings of the Eighth American Scientific Congress, 1940.* v. 9, pp. 33-34.

LUMMIS, CHARLES F.   (5018)
An episode in 1748. *Land of Sunshine,* 8:74-, 126-, 1897.

POSTLETHWAITE, W. W.   (5019)
Indians and Spaniards in the Southwest, 1540-1700. *Southwestern Lore,* 8:48-52, March 1943.

STECK, FRANCIS BORGIA   (5020)
Education in Spanish North America during the 16th century. *Catholic Educational Review,* 41:3-19, Jan. 1943.

UNIVERSITY OF NEW MEXICO   (5021)
New Mexico archives. Arzobispos. Mexico, 18th century.
> Photostated material from the Archivo general nacional de Mexico pertaining
> to the history of the Southwest. University has v. 7, pts. 1-2.

──────   (5022)
New Mexico archives. Audiencia de Mexico. [Seville, Archivo
general de Indias, 1580-1805.]
> Photostated material from the Archivo general de Indias pertaining to the
> history of the Southwest. University has vols. 1-29; 35-37; 42; 47; 48; 50, pts.
> 1-5; 51; 53, pts. 1-3; 66-68; 71-73; 82-83; 92-93; 95-110; 112-114; 117; 120-125;
> 128-129; 131; 132; 135; 136; 139-143; 153; 156; 158; 163; 167; 168; 170; 172;
> 203-207; 209-217; 223-224; 226-228; 231; 232; 235; 258; 270; 274-277; 279;
> 280; 284-287; 294; 296; 297; 304; 306; 308; 310-312; 317; 320; 348; 376; 377;
> 379; 469; 471; 521; 523; 526; 559; 561; 563; 566; 567; 569; 616; 617; 636; 683;
> 701; 722; 1064, pt. 1; 1065-1074; 1076-1080; 1082-1084; 1086; 1088; 1091-1095;
> 1097-1103; 1117; 1216-1217; 1254-1256; 1841; 1843-1844; 1846-1849; 1912; 1913;
> 2347; 2525; 2531; 2532; 2606; 2730; 2732; 2734-2736; 2739; 3171; 3172; 3174;
> 3186; 3187; 3189; 3191-3196.

──────   (5023)
New Mexico archives. Audiencia de Santo Domingo. [Seville, Archivo general de Indias, 1539-1759?]
> Photostated material from the Archivo general de Indias pertaining to the
> history of the Southwest. University has vols. 203-204, 2545, 2562.

──────   (5024)
New Mexico archives. Biblioteca nacional. [Mexico, 1580-1855?]
> Photostated material from the Biblioteca nacional de Mexico pertaining to
> the history of the Southwest. University has vols. 1-10, 23, 27, 28, 36, 37, 41,
> 57, 58, 65, 69, 70, 72.

──────   (5025)
New Mexico archives. Californias. [Mexico, 1634-1829.]
> Photostated material from the Archivo general nacional de Mexico pertaining
> to the history of the Southwest. University has vols. 2, pts. 1-2; 9, pts. 1-2;
> 12, pts. 1-2; 13, pts. 1-2; 16, pts. 1-2; 18; 21; 24; 29; 31; 33; 35; 36; 39; 40;
> 41; 45-47; 48, pt. 2; 49, pt. 1; 51; 61; 65; 66; 69; 71-75.

──────   (5026)
New Mexico archives. Civil. Mexico.
> Photostated material from the Archivo general nacional de Mexico pertaining
> to the history of the Southwest. University has vols. 511, 1362-1363.

──────   (5027)
New Mexico archives. Contratacion. [Seville, Archivo general de
Indias, 1535-1650?]
> Photostated material from the Archivo general de Indias pertaining to the
> history of the Southwest. University has vols. 5009; 5429; 5536; 5787.

──────   (5028)
New Mexico archives. Documents. [Albuquerque, 1685-1820.]
> Photostated material from the New Mexico territorial archives, New Mexico
> State Museum, Santa Fe. University has nos. 1-1049, 1055-2277, 2281-2453,
> 2455-2573, 2576-2736, 2738-2950.

──────   (5029)
New Mexico archives. Escribania de camara. [Seville, Archivo
general de Indias, 1525-1760.]
> Photostated material from the Archivo general de Indias pertaining to the
> history of the Southwest. University has vols. 239, 380A, 960.

──────   (5030)
New Mexico archives. Guadalajara. [Seville, Archivo general de
Indias, 1543-1821?]
> Photostated material from the Archivo general de Indias pertaining to the
> history of the Southwest. University has vols. 1-2; 3, pts. 1-3; 4-6; 12-14; 18;

UNIVERSITY OF NEW MEXICO (continued)   (5030)

20; 28, pts. 1-5; 29; 33-35; 37-38; 40; 47; 48; 51; 55; 57; 63; 69-87; 89;
109; 110; 114-115; 116, pts. 1-2; 117-119; 138-144; 147, pts. 1-9; 151, pts. 1-7;
152, pts. 1-4; 204; 206, pts. 1-2; 209; 230; 235; 236; 252; 278; 281, pts. 1-7; 423;
561.

————   (5031)

New Mexico archives. Historia. [Mexico, 1538-1812.]

Photostated material from the Archivo general nacional de Mexico pertaining
to the history of the Southwest. University has vols. 2, pts. 1-2; 3, pts. 1-2; 16;
18; 20; 24; 25, pts. 1-3; 26, pts. 1-3; 27, pts. 1-3; 28, pts. 1-2; 29, pts. 1-2; 37,
pts. 1-5; 38, pts. 1-3; 39, pts. 1-4; 41; 43; 52, pts. 1-2; 62; 72; 95; 97, pts. 1-2;
295, pts. 1-2; 298, pts. 1-2; 299; 393; 394.

————   (5032)

New Mexico archives. Indiferente. [Seville, Archivo general de
Indias, 1526-1787?]

Photostated material from the Archivo general de Indias pertaining to the
history of the Southwest. University has vols. 7; 9; 18; 20-22; 29; 35; 36; 415;
416; 737; 744; 747; 748; 761; 782; 786; 819.

————   (5033)

New Mexico archives. Inquisicion. Mexico, circa 1500-1900.

Photostated material from the Archivo general nacional de Mexico pertaining
to the history of the Southwest. University has vols. 268; 304; 312; 316; 318;
342; 345; 356; 363; 365; 366; 369; 372; 380; 385; 388; 421; 425; 467; 471; 486;
502; 507, pts. 1-6; 520; 522; 529; 540; 551; 582; 583; 586, pts. 1-2; 587, pts. 1-2;
593, pts. 1-2; 594, pts. 1-3; 595; 596, pts. 1-2; 598; 600; 601; 604; 608; 610; 611;
616; 629; 666; 680; 701; 710; 735; 758; 826; 830; 832; 849; 862; 872; 890; 892;
902; 913; 926; 932; 941; 950; 952; 1049; 1153, pts. 1-2; 1210; 1250; 1257; 1322;
1353; 1370; 1382; 1398; 1406; 1430; 1443; 1461; 1462; 1468; 1551.

————   (5034)

New Mexico archives. Justicia. [Mexico, 1821-1887.]

Photostated material from the Archivo general nacional de Mexico pertaining
to the history of the Southwest. University has vols. 1, pts. 1-2; 124; 125; 129;
138; 159; 181-183; 185.

————   (5035)

New Mexico archives. Justicia. [Seville, Archivo general de Indias, 1536-1552.]

Photostated material from the Archivo general de Indias pertaining to the
history of the Southwest. University has vols. 336; 339, pts. 1-8.

————   (5036)

New Mexico archives. Miscellany. [Albuquerque, 1821-1846.]

Photostated material from the New Mexico territorial archives, New Mexico
State Museum, Santa Fe. University has vols. 1821-1846.

————   (5037)

New Mexico archives. Misiones. [Mexico, 1779-1820.]

Photostated material from the Archivo general nacional de Mexico pertaining
to the history of the Southwest. University has vols. 14, pts. 1-3; 25, pts. 1-3;
26, pts. 1-3; 27, pts. 1-5.

————   (5038)

New Mexico archives. Museo nacional. [Mexico, 18th century.]

Photostated material from manuscripts in the Museo Nacional, Mexico, pertaining to the history of the Southwest.

————   (5039)

New Mexico archives. Oficio de Soria. Mexico, 1758-1820.

Photostated material from the Archivo general nacional de Mexico pertaining
to the history of the Southwest. University has v. 8.

UNIVERSITY OF NEW MEXICO (continued) (5040)
New Mexico archives. Patronato. [Seville, Archivo general de
Indias, 1493-1703?]
> Photostated material from the Archivo general de Indias pertaining to the
> history of the Southwest. University has vols. 20, pts. 1-2; 21, pts. 1-3; 22,
> pts. 1-8.

——— (5041)
New Mexico archives. Provincias internas. Mexico, 1691-1830.
> Photostated material from the Archivo general nacional de Mexico pertaining
> to the history of the Southwest. University has vols. 14; 22; 24; 29; 30; 34,
> pts. 1-2; 35, pt. 1; 36, pts. 1-4; 37, pts. 1-4; 65, pts. 1-4; 67; 73, pts. 1-2; 102,
> pts. 1-3; 103, pts. 1-2; 112, pts. 1-3; 120, pts. 1-2; 121, pts. 1-2; 122; 128, pts.
> 1-2; 129; 154; 161, pts. 1-2; 166; 169; 183, pts. 1-2; 193, pts. 1-2; 250, pts. 1-2.

——— (5042)
New Mexico archives. Reales cedulas y ordenes. [Mexico, 1609-
1821.]
> Photostated material from the Archivo general nacional de Mexico pertaining
> to the history of the Southwest. University has vols. 2; 3; 5; 8; 10-23; 24; 26;
> 28-32; 34; 35; 108; 153; 195.

——— (5043)
New Mexico archives. Tierras. Mexico.
> Photostated material from the Archivo general nacional de Mexico pertaining
> to the history of the Southwest. University has vols. 3268, pts. 1-3; 3283, pts.
> 1-4; 3286, pts. 1-4.

——— (5044)
New Mexico archives. Tierras: civil. Mexico.
> Photostated material from the Archivo general nacional de Mexico pertaining
> to the history of the Southwest. University has v. 426.

WALTER, PAUL A. F. (5045)
The forgotten Cristobal de Oñate. *NMHR*, 18:429-33, Oct. 1943.

WHITNEY, ALFRED F. (5046)
The bearing of junipers on the Espejo expedition. *Plateau*, 15:21-
23, Oct. 1942.

American Frontier Period

ANONYMOUS (5047)
Apache captives. *Lend a Hand*, 5:163-, 1890.

——— (5048)
Boundary line between Texas and New Mexico. *Science*, n.s., 15:
184-, 1901.

——— (5049)
A fight with Navajo Indians. *Chamber's Journal*, 71:238-, 1894.

——— (5050)
A tour through New Mexico in 1846. *Western Journal and Civilian*, 1:363-, 1848.

BARNES, WILL C. (5051)
In the Apache country. *Overland Monthly*, n.s., 9:172-, 1886.

BLOOM, LANSING B., ED. (5052)
The Rev. Hiram Walter Read, Baptist missionary to New Mexico.
NMHR, 17:113-47, April 1942.

BROOKS, JUANITA (5053)
The Mormon battalion. *Arizona Highways*, 19:38-40, 42, May
1943.

BROTHERS, MARY HUDSON   (5054)
Frontier rations. *NM*, 21:17, 35, Nov. 1943.
  Mogollon region in the 1890's.

BYERS, MINNIE HOBBS   (5055)
The nesters. *NM*, 21:12, 34-35, April 1943.
  Pioneers in Hobbs area.

CASE, T. S.   (5056)
An excursion in New Mexico. *Kansas City Review*, 4:419-, 1881.

COPE, E. D.   (5057)
Wheeler's survey of New Mexico. *American Naturalist*, 9:49-,
1875.

ELSTON, ALLAN VAUGHN   (5058)
Guns on the Cimarron. Philadelphia, Macrae-Smith, 1943.
  Trip of Johnnie Cameron to Santa Fe in 1873.

FORT, LEWIS D.   (5059)
Tenderfoot days. *NM*, 21:16, 33-34, Jan. 1943.
  In and around Las Vegas.

GANAWAY, LOOMIS MORTON   (5060)
New Mexico and the sectional controversy, 1846-1861. *NMHR*,
18:113-47, April; 205-46, July; 325-48, Oct. 1943; 19:55-79, Jan.
1944.

JOHNSTON, PHILIP   (5061)
The battle at Canyon Padre from the Navajo's point of view.
Plateau, 14:57-63, April 1942.

LEEPER, RUTH A.   (5062)
St. Louis in the Santa Fe trade. Unpub. Master's thesis, UNM,
1938.

LIVINGSTON, CARL   (5063)
School days of the New Mexico frontier. *New Mexico School
Review*, 23:4-6, April 1944.

LUMMIS, CHARLES F.   (5064)
The Santa Fe trail. *Land of Sunshine*, 8:185-, 1897.

MARIAGER, DAGMAR   (5065)
Camp and travel in New Mexico. *Overland Monthly*, n.s., 16:347-,
1890.

MENDIVIL, J.   (5066)
A ride with the Apaches. *Overland Monthly*, 6:341-, 1870.

PUMPELLY, R.   (5067)
Mining adventure in New Mexico. *Putnam's Monthly Magazine*,
14:494- 1869.

RUSSELL, MRS. HAL   (5068)
Memoirs of Marian Russell. *Colorado Magazine*, July 1943.
  Life in Santa Fe in the 1850's.

SHINN, C. H.   (5069)
Spanish plots in the old Southwest. *Overland Monthly*, n.s., 1:
569-, 1883.

SONNICHSEN, CHARLES L. (5070)
Roy Bean, law west of the Pecos. New York, Macmillan Co., 1942.

STEVENS, MONTAGUE (5071)
Meet Mr. Grizzly. Albuquerque, UNM Press, 1944.
Old timer's reminiscences of western New Mexico.

STRUTT, ERIC (5072)
Camel caravan. Catholic Digest, July 1942.

TAPY, AUDREY T. (5073)
Las Vegas, 1890-1900; a frontier town becomes cosmopolitan. Unpub. Master's thesis, UNM, 1943.

WARREN, CHARLES MARQUIS (5074)
Only the valiant. New York, Macmillan Co., 1943.

Spanish-Americans and Mexicans

ABERLE, SOPHIE D. AND PIJOAN, MICHEL (5075)
The health problems of Taos and its environs. Albuquerque, June 10, 1942. Processed. (Copy on file at School of Inter-American Affairs.)

AGNEW, EDITH (5076)
Rural riddles. NM, 21:23, Aug. 1943.

BANDINI, H. E. (5077)
Our Spanish-American families. Overland Monthly, n.s., 26:9-, 1895.

BARKER, VIRGIL (5078)
Santos and signs: likenesses and contrasts. Magazine of Art, 36: 129-31, April 1943.

BOOTH, MARY (5079)
Pattern of the centuries. NM, 21:10-11, 32-33, April 1943.
Taos county.

BOYD E. (5080)
Antiques in New Mexico. Products of craftsmanship in the Spanish Southwest. Antiques, 44:58-62, Aug. 1943.

BUILDING AMERICA (5081)
Our minority groups. II. Spanish-speaking people. Building America, 8:130-59, Feb. 1943.

BUTCHER, HAROLD (5082)
Recreating a Spanish mission. Travel, 80:20-21, 34, March 1943.
At Peña Blanca.

CARROLL, CHARLES D. (5083)
Miguel Aragon, a great santero. EP, 50:49-64, March 1943.

COORDINATOR OF INTER-AMERICAN AFFAIRS (5084)
Conference of field representatives and project associates on the Spanish-speaking minority program in the Southwest; July 12, 13, 14, 1943. Typewritten report on file at School of Inter-American Affairs.

———— (5085)
Farm Security Administration and the Spanish minority group. Mimeographed report dated 1943.

CULBERT, JAMES I. (5086)
Distribution of Spanish-American population in New Mexico. *Economic Geography,* 19:171-76, April 1943.

DEHUFF, ELIZABETH WILLIS (5087)
Say the bells of old missions. St. Louis, B. Herder Book Co., 1943.
Folk tales of New Mexicans.

ESPINOSA, AURELIO M. AND J. MANUEL (5088)
The Texans: a New Mexican folk play of the middle 19th century. *New Mexico Quarterly Review,* 13:299-308, Autumn 1943.

GOLDSTEIN, MARCUS S. (5089)
Demographic and bodily changes in descendants of Mexican immigrants. Austin, Institute of Latin American Studies, University of Texas, 1943.

GONZALES, HENRY A. (5090)
New Mexico's Spanish-speaking people contribute to the war effort. Typewritten article dated May 24, 1943, prepared for the Coordinator of Inter-American Affairs to be used in cooperation with the Office of War Information. (Copy on file at School of Inter-American Affairs.)

HARE, ELIZABETH SAGE (5091)
The wood carver of Cordova. *Travel,* 81:20-21, 32, May 1943.

HAWK, ALICE MAE (5092)
An investigation of the parallel development of the picaresque novel and the Hispanic folktale. Unpub. Master's thesis, UNM, 1940.

JOHANSEN, SIGURD (5093)
Family organization in a Spanish-American culture area. *Sociology and Social Research,* 28:123-31, Nov.-Dec. 1943.

LONGMORE, T. WILSON AND HITT, HOMER L. (5094)
A demographic analysis of first and second generation Mexican population of the United States: 1930. *Southwestern Social Science Quarterly,* 24:138-49, Sept. 1943.

LOOMIS, CHARLES P. (5095)
Ethnic cleavages in the Southwest as reflected in two high schools. *Sociometry,* 6:7-26, Feb. 1943.

———— (5096)
Hard work and thrift among the Spanish-Americans. Unpub. ms. on file at Harvard University Library.

LOOMIS, CHARLES P. AND NELLIE H. (5097)
Skilled Spanish-American war-industry workers from New Mexico. *Applied Anthropology,* 2:33-36, Oct.-Nov.-Dec. 1942.
See (3482).

LOOMIS, CHARLES AND GRISHAM, GLEN (5098)
The New Mexican experiment in village rehabilitation. *Applied Anthropology,* 2:13-37, June 1943.

LUDI, PHILLIP M. (5099)
Radio programs to improve Spanish-American minority status. *New Mexico School Review,* 23:12, Oct. 1943.

MCWILLIAMS, CAREY   (5100)
> *Brothers under the skin.* Boston, Little Brown, 1943.

MARTINEZ, REYES N.   (5101)
> *The day of departure.* Unpub. ms. in files of New Mexico Writers'
> Project, Santa Fe.
>> Spanish-American folk custom.

MERA, H. P.   (5102)
> *Spanish-American blanketry; its relationship to aboriginal weaving
> in the Southwest.* Unpub. ms. in possession of the author.

MILLER, MARGARET   (5103)
> Religious folk art of the Southwest. *Bulletin of the Museum of
> Modern Art,* 10:3-11, May-June 1943.
>> Santos.

MORRILL, H. D.   (5104)
> Teaching English to Spanish children. *New Mexico Journal of
> Education,* 14:9-10, Nov. 1917.

MULKY, CARL   (5105)
> Program for tuberculosis control among Spanish-speaking people.
> *New Mexico Health Officer,* 11:13-16, Sept. 1943.

NATIONAL CATHOLIC WELFARE CONFERENCE   (5106)
> *The Spanish-speaking of the Southwest and West.* Washington,
> Social Action Dept., National Catholic Welfare Conference, 1943.
>> Report of conference held in San Antonio, July 20-23, 1943.

OFFICE OF WAR INFORMATION, BUREAU OF INTELLIGENCE,
SPECIAL SERVICES DIVISION   (5107)
> *Spanish-Americans in the Southwest and the war effort.* Report
> no. 24. Washington, Aug. 18, 1942. Processed.

ORTEGA, JOAQUIN   (5108)
> *A statement of the distressing economic situation of the Spanish-
> speaking minorities in our country and on a possible immediate
> action program to ameliorate it.* Submitted to the Office of Pro-
> duction Management, Jan. 1942. (Unpub. ms. on file at School
> of Inter-American Affairs.)

RUSSELL, DANIEL   (5109)
> Problems of Mexican children in the Southwest. *Journal of Edu-
> cational Sociology,* 17:216-22, Dec. 1943.

SAPOSS, DAVID J.   (5110)
> *Report on rapid survey of resident Latin American problems and
> recommended program.* Processed report dated April 3, 1942.
> (Copy on file at School of Inter-American Affairs.)

SCHOOL OF INTER-AMERICAN AFFAIRS   (5111)
> *Recent educational and community experiments and projects in
> New Mexico affecting the Spanish-speaking population.* Mimeo-
> graphed report prepared for use in connection with the Confer-
> ence on Problems of Education Among Spanish-Speaking Popu-
> lations of Our Southwest, Santa Fe, Aug. 19-24, 1943.
>> Contains reports on Nambe Community School, San Jose Training School,
>> New Mexico Highlands Summer Workshop and Institute of the Air, New
>> Mexico Spanish Research Project, vocational and industrial education pro-
>> grams, social studies curriculum development, SCS, NYA, WPA, Barelas
>> Community Center, and the School for the Rio Grande Valley.

UNITED STATES DEPARTMENT OF LABOR, CHILDREN'S BUREAU   (5112)
> The Children's Bureau and problems of the Spanish-speaking minority groups. Washington, April 1943. Processed.

UNIVERSITY OF NEW MEXICO, HIGHLANDS UNIVERSITY, AND
COORDINATOR OF INTER-AMERICAN AFFAIRS   (5113)
> Committee reports of the "Conference on educational problems in the Southwest, with special reference to the educational problems in Spanish-speaking communities," held in Santa Fe, New Mexico, Aug. 19-24, 1943. Processed. (Copy on file at School of Inter-American Affairs.)

WATKINS, FRANCES E.   (5114)
> A bridal chest of Spanish times. Masterkey, 18:13-14, Jan. 1944.

WECKLER, J. E.   (5115)
> Cundiyo, a mountain village in New Mexico. Unpub. ms. in possession of the author, Rosenwald Foundation, Chicago.
>> An analysis of community life in terms of the relations between inherited and acquired status. Will contain chapters descriptive of the general social life of the village and other chapters concerning relations of the people of Cundiyo to other Spanish-American, Indian, and Anglo communities.

WOLFF, KURT H.   (5116)
> San Cristobal, New Mexico. Sociological study of a small, rural, Spanish-Anglo valley community. Unpub. ms. in possession of the author, Southern Methodist University.
>> Includes information on location, history, racial composition, origin and mobility of population, marital status, property and income, occupations, education, language, culture diffusion, housing, health, religion, recreation, social stratification, and culture contacts.

WOODS, BETTY   (5117)
> New Mexico's Methuselah. NM, 20:20, 34, Feb. 1942.
>> 116-year old Herman Perez of Deming.

————   (5118)

> Timeless town. NM, 21:16-17, 38-39, Aug. 1943.
>> Cordova.

ZELENY, CAROLYN   (5119)
> Conflict and accommodation in a dual-ethnic community in New Mexico. Doctor's thesis in preparation, Department of Sociology, Yale University.

Fiction and Drama

BRIGHT, ROBERT   (5120)
> The life and death of Little Jo. New York, Doubleday Doran, 1944.

CRICHTON, KYLE   (5121)
> The proud people. New York, Scribners, 1944.

MARTIN CURTIS   (5122)
> The hills of home. Boston, Houghton Mifflin, 1943.

General

ABOUSLEMAN, MICHEL D., COMP.   (5123)
> Who's who in New Mexico, v. 1. Albuquerque, Abousleman Co., 1937.

ADLER, S. W.   (5124)
    Medical care for dependents of men in military service. *American
    Journal of Public Health,* 33:645-50, June 1943.
        Program of New Mexico State Department of Public Health.
ADVISORY COMMITTEE FOR RURAL NEW MEXICO   (5125)
    Description; purpose; program. 1942. Processed.

——————   (5126)
    Prospectus of the Advisory Committee for Rural New Mexico.
    1942.

——————   (5127)
    Report of the Committee on Education. June 1942.
ALLEN, KENNETH   (5128)
    History's highway to New Mexico. *Travel,* 78:26-28, 35, April
    1942.
ANDERSON, CLINTON P.   (5129)
    The adobe palace. *NMHR,* 19:97-122, April 1944.
        Santa Fe.
ANONYMOUS   (5130)
    Albuquerque, New Mexico. *National Magazine,* 21:574-, 1904.
——————   (5131)
    Archbishop of Santa Fe. *Life,* 15:72-74, Dec. 20, 1943.
——————   (5132)
    The environs of Santa Fe. *Design,* 43:15, April 1942.
——————   (5133)
    Life goes to a sheep ranch in lambing time. *Life,* 15:114-16, 119,
    July 5, 1943.
        Near Grants.
——————   (5134)
    Meeting the teacher shortage in New Mexico. *School and Society,*
    57:683, June 19, 1943.
——————   (5135)
    Oil from Portales. *Rural Electrification News,* 8:11, 17, Oct. 1942.
        Boosting peanut acreage by means of electric power.
——————   (5136)
    School attendance shows a slight decrease. *New Mexico School
    Review,* 22:6, April 1943.
——————   (5137)
    School maintenance budgets for 1933-1934. *New Mexico School
    Review,* 23:22-23, Oct. 1943.
——————   (5138)
    Statehood claims of New Mexico. *Out West,* 18:217-, 1902.
——————   (5139)
    Vice-regal palace at Santa Fe. *American Architect,* 30:151-, 1890.
ARCHAEOLOGICAL INSTITUTE OF AMERICA, SCHOOL OF AMERICAN
RESEARCH   (5140)
    Representative art and artists of New Mexico. Santa Fe, 1940.
BABCOCK, J. W.   (5141)
    Statehood rights of Arizona and New Mexico. *Independent,* 60:
    505-, 1905.

BANDELIER, ADOLPH F. A.   (5142)
The unpublished letters of Adolph F. Bandelier, concerning the writing and publication of The Delight Makers. New York, Chas. P. Everitt, 1942.

BARKER C. M.   (5143)
A report and summary of studies of lands and land administration. *New Mexico School Review*, 23:14-15, Feb. 1944.

BARKER, CHARLES B.   (5144)
Some observations on leasing of state grazing lands. *New Mexico School Review;* 23:30, Sept. 1943.

BARKER, S. OMAR   (5145)
Foothill freight. *NM*, 21:22, 36-38, Aug. 1943.

———   (5146)
Longhorn heritage. *NM*, 20:12-13, 33, Feb. 1942.
    Personal experiences in early 1900's.

BARNES, BERNARD O.   (5147)
Administration of in-service training in the municipal schools of New Mexico. Unpub. Master's thesis, UNM, 1943.

BERT, A. L.   (5148)
Oil town. *NM*, 22:10-11, 31, March 1944.
    Artesia.

BLOOM, LANSING B., ED.   (5149)
Historical Society minutes, 1859-63. *NMHR*, 18:247-311, July 1943.

BOOTH, ALFRED W.   (5150)
The Portales region: a pump irrigation district in the Llano Estacado. *Economic Geography*, 18:97-105, Jan. 1942.
    Water resources of the region and their relation to the economics of crop production.

BOYD, J. V.   (5151)
Reorganization of county school administration in New Mexico. *New Mexico School Review*, 23:10-11, Sept. 1943; 23:7-8, Jan. 1944.

BRANDON, T. L.   (5152)
A parent discusses pupil transportation. *New Mexico School Review*, 22:13, April 1943.

BRUNNELL, HORACE P.   (5153)
The division of responsibility in the financial administration of municipal and independent schools in New Mexico. Unpub. Master's thesis, UNM, 1941.

BURRIS, QUINCY GUY   (5154)
Institute of the air. *New Mexico School Review*, 23:4-5, Sept. 1943.

CAMPA, ARTHUR L.   (5155)
Proposal for a folk music repository for New Mexico. Unpub. ms. dated Sept. 15, 1941, on file at School of Inter-American Affairs.

CARR, LORRAINE   (5156)
My neighbor is an artist. *NM*, 21:14-15, 31, Dec. 1943.
    Taos art colony.

CARTER, JOHN, JR.   (5157)
Dry-farming investigations in northeastern New Mexico, 1936-1943. NMAES, Bulletin 312. State College, March 1944.

CASSIDY, INA SIZER   (5158)
Art and war in New Mexico. *NM,* 22:19, 37, Feb. 1944.

———   (5159)
Painter of old houses. *NM,* 20:22, 26, June 1942.
    Regina Tatum Cooke.

———   (5160)
Sun paintings. *NM,* 21:22, 31, March 1943.
    Art of Pansy Stockton.

———   (5161)
Wood carver of Kingston. *NM,* 21:20, Feb. 1943.
    Bill Johnson

CATON, W. BARNIE   (5162)
A study of the extension division of the University of New Mexico, with emphasis on the period 1928-1938. Unpub. Master's thesis, UNM, 1939.

CHERRINGTON, BEN M.   (5163)
What Americans think about post-war planning in the Rocky Mountain region. *Foreign Policy Reports,* 18:276-78, Jan. 15, 1943.

CHOKLA, L. M., TRANS.   (5164)
One-storied America: Santa Fe. *Southwest Review,* 28:394-401, Summer 1943.

CLARK, N. M.   (5165)
Cowboy beef; Bell ranch in New Mexico. *Country Gentleman,* 112:12-13, April 1942.

CLEVELAND, H. I.   (5166)
Plea of the women for statehood of New Mexico. *National Magazine,* 16:709-, 1902.

COCKERILL, P. W.   (5167)
Labor needs for seasonal operations on New Mexico farms. NMAES, Bulletin 299. State College, Jan. 1943.

COFFEY, LAURENCE C.   (5168)
Legal restrictions governing teachers in their employment and work. Unpub. Master's thesis, UNM, 1937.

CONDON, DAVE   (5169)
The show goes on. *NM,* 20:28, Aug. 1942.
    Las Vegas rodeo.

CONDON, JANE   (5170)
A-carding around Albuquerque. *NM,* 21:12-13, 46, 48, Sept. 1943.

———   (5171)
Grant County passes the ammunition. *NM,* 21:14-15, 33-34, March 1943.
    War activities.

CONSTANT, M. D.   (5172)
Pioneering de luxe. *NM,* 20:18-19, 38, Aug. 1942.
    Near Santa Fe.

COOK, HELEN FETTER   (5173)
Saddle maker of Santa Fe. *NM*, 21:18, 35-36, Aug. 1943.

CROOK, ALICE M.   (5174)
The house by the trail. *NM*, 21:10, 29-30, Feb. 1943.
> Old Baca home at Las Vegas.

DARGAN, MARION   (5175)
New Mexico's fight for statehood, 1895-1912. *NMHR*, 18:148-75, April 1943.
> *See also* (4010).

DAVIES, GERALD L.   (5176)
. Some problems of salary scheduling. *New Mexico School Review*, 23:8-10, Jan. 1944.
> At Santa Fe.

DEFOURI, J. H.   (5177)
Santa Fe in the past. *Catholic World*, 37:549-, 1883.

DEHUFF, ELIZABETH WILLIS   (5178)
The revelation of Cristo Rey. *EP*, 49:200-03, 1942.

DIEFENDORF, J. W.   (5179)
New Mexico schools at war. *New Mexico School Review*, 22:19, Nov. 1942; 23:18, Dec. 1943.

—————   (5180)
Unpublished survey of nearly a thousand New Mexico high school graduates to ascertain what percentage entered college and why the others did not. Ms. on file at School of Inter-American Affairs.

DRING, RUTH   (5181)
Literary backgrounds of the Santa Fe trail. Unpub. Master's thesis, UNM, 1934.

EGERTON, KEARNEY   (5182)
Adobe renaissance. *The Rio Grande Writer*, 1:14-16, Spring 1942.

ENDLICH, F. M.   (5183)
Mining regions of southern New Mexico. *American Naturalist*, 17:149-, 1883.

ESPINOSA, GILBERTO   (5184)
Should the teaching of Spanish in the public schools from the fifth to the eighth grades be made compulsory? Unpub. ms. on file at School of Inter-American Affairs.

ESTERGREEN, MARION   (5185)
Taos dolls. *NM*, 22:18, Feb. 1944.

FALLS, ANNA E.   (5186)
The Ganado mission. *Practical Home Economics*, 20:375, Oct. 1942.

FERGUSSON, ERNA   (5187)
New Mexicans all. *New Mexico School Review*, 23:2-3, Jan. 1944.

FITZPATRICK, GEORGE   (5188)
Fiesta city. *NM*, 21:9-13, Aug. 1943.
> Santa Fe.

FITZPATRICK, GEORGE (continued)   (5189)
    Rural metropolis. *NM*, 21:7-9, 34, Dec. 1943.
        Las Cruces.

FLORES, JOE   (5190)
    *A summary of the sessions on employment, labor, and trade re-
    lations, June 29, 30, and July 1, 1943. Institute on Inter-American
    Problems in the Rocky Mountain Region.* Denver, Rocky Moun-
    tain Council on Inter-American Affairs in cooperation with the
    Inter-American Workshop of the University of Denver, 1943.
        Deals particularly with problems of Spanish-Americans.

FORT, LEWIS D.   (5191)
    The tenderfoot tries ranching. *NM*, 21:19, 35-36, July 1943.

FRENCH, SISTER FLORITA   (5192)
    The history of St. Vincent Academy. Unpub. Master's thesis,
    UNM, 1942.

FRITZEN, IRVING S.   (5193)
    Ganado mission. An oasis in Navajoland. *Santa Fe Magazine,*
    37:9-15, June 1943.

FULLER, CLARISSA   (5194)
    *Frank Hamilton Cushing's relations to Zuni and the Hemenway
    Southwestern Expedition.* Unpub. Master's thesis, UNM, 1943.

GARDNER, ESTHER DALTON   (5195)
    A study of the life and works of Charles Fletcher Lummis. Unpub.
    Master's thesis, UNM, 1941.

GILBERT, HOPE   (5196)
    He found six of the fabled Seven Cities of Cibola. *Desert Maga-
    zine,* 5:5-10, April 1942.
        Life and work of Frederick Webb Hodge.

GREENE, E. L.   (5197)
    Rambles of a botanist in New Mexico. *American Naturalist,* 12:
    172-, 208-, 1878.

HARDY, A. V.; WATT, JAMES; DE CAPITO, T. M.; AND
KOLODNY, MAXWELL H.   (5198)
    Studies of the acute diarrheal diseases. I. Differential culture
    media. *Public Health Reports,* 54:287-300, 1939.
        Includes New Mexico.

HARRINGTON, E. R.   (5199)
    Copper goes to war. *NM*, 21:10-11, 31-33, March 1943.
        Grant county mining.

————   (5200)
    Ghost town manganese. *NM*, 20:10-11, 32, March 1942.
        Lake Valley mining area.

————   (5201)
    Here's your tin. *NM*, 21:7-9, April 1943.
        Catron, Sierra counties.

————   (5202)
    The metals of war. *NM*, 20:7-9, 32-33, April 1942.
        Location and extent of minor metals.

HEFFERNAN, VIOALLE CLARK (5203)
Thomas Benton Catron. Unpub. Master's thesis, UNM, 1940.

HESSELDEN, LOUIS G. (5204)
New Mexico architecture. *New Mexico Quarterly Review,* 13:
326-32, Autumn 1943.

HEWETT, EDGAR L. (5205)
Campfire and trail. Albuquerque, UNM Press, 1943.

———— (5206)
New Mexico needs a hall of records. *EP,* 50:178-82, Aug. 1943.

HILDWEIN, H. L. (5207)
Translating promise into production. *Extension Service Review,*
13:63, April 1942.
New Mexico's food for freedom program.

HOOD, MARGARET PAGE (5208)
Pintos have priority. *NM,* 21:16-17, 34-35, July 1943.

HOUGH, H. W. (5209)
New Mexico's Taos County draws attention. *Adult Education
Bulletin,* 6:37-38, Dec. 1941.
Harwood Foundation.

HOWARD, R. G. (5210)
Terraces quadruple pinto bean yields. *Soil Conservation,* 8:14-
15, 22, July 1942.
At Edgewood, New Mexico.

HULL, J. (5211)
Clovis manager plan ousts politics. *National Municipal Review,*
31:438-39, Sept. 1942.

HUNTER, RUSSELL VERNON (5212)
Latin-American art in U.S.A. *Design,* 44:20-21, March 1943.

INSTITUTE OF INTER-AMERICAN PROBLEMS IN THE
ROCKY MOUNTAIN REGION (5213)
*A summary of the sessions on housing, health, nutrition, public
assistance, and recreation, July 6, 7, 8, and 9, 1943.* Denver, Rocky
Mountain Council on Inter-American Affairs in cooperation with
the Inter-American Workshop of the University of Denver, 1943.
Deals mostly with problems of Spanish-Americans.

JARRETT, AL W. AND SIMMS, HARPER D. (5214)
*Land of the sun, link of the Americas. Sketch for a Southwestern
movie.* Unpub. illustrated ms. dated October 16, 1942, on file at
School of Inter-American Affairs.

JOHANSEN, SIGURD AND ROSOFF, MILTON (5215)
Community planning in Eddy County, New Mexico. NMAES,
Bulletin 297. State College, Dec. 1942.

KELEHER, JULIA (5216)
The land of Shalam. Utopia in New Mexico. *NMHR,* 19:123-
34, April 1944.

———— (5217)
Old days in old Albuquerque. *NM,* 20:22-23, 54-55, Jan. 1942.

KERR, W. E.   (5218)
    The Eddy County teachers' and principals' salary schedules. *New
    Mexico School Review,* 23:2-3, Nov. 1943.

KIDDLE, LAWRENCE B.   (5219)
    Los nombres del pavo en el dialecto nuevomejicano. *Hispania,*
    24:213-16, 1941.

KNOX, NANCY C.   (5220)
    On location. *NM,* 20:18-19, 34-36, Feb. 1942.
        Filming of a movie about Spanish-speaking New Mexicans.

KUBLER, GEORGE C.   (5221)
    Two modes of Franciscan architecture: New Mexico and Califor-
    nia. *Gazette des Beaux Arts,* 23:39-48, Jan. 1943.

KUTNEWSKY, FREMONT   (5222)
    Science at Socorro. *NM,* 20:14-15, 32-33, Feb. 1942.
        Work of School of Mines and State Bureau of Mines.

————   (5223)
    Vocational college. *NM,* 21:12-13, 33-34, June 1943.
        State Teachers College, Silver City.

————   (5224)
    War mines at Grants. *NM,* 21:11-13, 30, Feb. 1943.
        Fluorspar.

LABORATORY OF ANTHROPOLOGY   (5225)
    *Tentative proposal for a program of regional inter-American ac-
    tivities.* Submitted to the Coordinator of Inter-American Affairs,
    1942. (Unpub. ms. on file at School of Inter-American Affairs.)

LANTZ, EDITH M.   (5226)
    Home dehydration of chile. *Journal of Home Economics,* 35:222-
    24, April 1943.

LEWIS, A. H.   (5227)
    Statehood for New Mexico. *Booklover's Magazine,* 7:150, 1906.

LIST, O. W.   (5228)
    Home economics teaching in New Mexico. *Journal of Home
    Economics,* 35:158-59, March 1943.

LUDI, PHILLIP   (5229)
    Shall the teacher contract law be strengthened. *New Mexico
    School Review,* 23:7-8, Dec. 1943.

MABRY, THOMAS J.   (5230)
    New Mexico's constitution in the making—reminiscences of 1910.
    NMHR, 19:168-84, April 1944.

MCALISTER, BRODE BART   (5231)
    *The county and city superintendencies of New Mexico; a com-
    parative study.* Unpub. Master's thesis, UNM, 1940.

MCCONNELL, V. P.   (5232)
    Dutch immigrant farms for freedom in a new land. *Soil Conser-
    vation,* 8:219-21, April 1943.

MCDONALD, SISTER MAURA   (5233)
    *Contributions of the Dominican sisters of Grand Rapids, Michi-
    gan, to education in New Mexico.* Unpub. Master's thesis, UNM,
    1942.

MCIVER, ZADIE RUNKLES (5234)
Linguistic borrowings from the Spanish as reflected in the writings of the Southwest. Unpub. Master's thesis, University of Texas, 1939.

MCLENATHEN, C. H. (5235)
A defense of New Mexico. *Outlook,* 73:226-, 1902.

MCWILLIAMS, CAREY (5236)
Ill fares the land. New York, Little Brown, 1942.

MASTERS, MARY J. (5237)
New Mexico's struggle for statehood, 1903-1907. Unpub. Master's thesis, UNM, 1942.

MILAM, PAUL W. (5238)
Industrialization of the Southwest. *Southwestern Social Science Quarterly,* 22:300-10, March 1942.

MILLER, C. A. (5239)
Santa Fe. *Overland Monthly,* n.s., 4:337-, 1884.

MITCHELL, A. J. (5240)
The effect of bilingualism in the measurement of intelligence. *Elementary School Journal,* 38:29-37, Sept. 1937.

MOODY, C. A. (5241)
New Mexico and Arizona. *Out West,* 24:136-, 1905.

MORANG, ALFRED (5242)
Art exhibition. School children of Madrid have exhibition at State Museum. *New Mexico School Review,* 22:24, April 1943.

NAEGLE, CONRAD K. (5243)
The history of Silver City, New Mexico. Unpub. Master's thesis, UNM, 1943.

NANNINGA, SIMON PETER (5244)
The New Mexico school system; a textbook for use in the course entitled "The problems of education in New Mexico." Albuquerque, UNM Press, 1942.

—————— (5245)
New Mexico's sources of revenue for public schools. *American School Board Journal,* 107:35-37, Oct. 1943.

NATIONAL EDUCATION ASSOCIATION (5246)
Federal aid for education; a review of pertinent facts. National Education Association, Research Bulletin, Sept. 1942.
Statistics on school costs by states.

NATIONAL RESOURCES PLANNING BOARD (5247)
The Pecos River joint investigation. Reports of the participating agencies. Washington, GPO, 1942.

NEW MEXICO AGRICULTURAL EXPERIMENT STATION (5248)
Trends in the production and demand for New Mexico pinto beans. Press Bulletin 978. State College, Sept. 29, 1943.

—————— (5249)
The water-feed-livestock balance in New Mexico in relation to meat production. Press Bulletin 974. State College, Aug. 27, 1943.

NEW MEXICO PUBLIC SERVICE COMMISSION   (5250)
Annual reports, 1942—date.

NEW MEXICO SCHOOL REVIEW   (5251)
The post-war school in New Mexico. A symposium. *New Mexico School Review,* 23:10-11, Feb. 1944.

NEW MEXICO STATE CORPORATION COMMISSION   (5252)
Annual reports, 1912—date.

NEW MEXICO STATE DEPARTMENT OF EDUCATION   (5253)
Biennial reports, 1912—date.

NEW MEXICO STATE DEPARTMENT OF PUBLIC HEALTH   (5254)
Annual and biennial reports, 1919—date.
> 1919-1934 reports issued biennially as separate publications; 1934-1940 published biennially in *New Mexico Health Officer;* annual reports 1941—date continued in *New Mexico Health Officer.*

————   (5255)
Vital statistics in New Mexico. *New Mexico Health Officer,* Dec. 1942, June 1943.

NEW MEXICO STATE DEPARTMENT OF PUBLIC WELFARE   (5256)
Annual reports, 1938—date.

————   (5257)
Report on general assistance. Santa Fe, March 1944. Processed.
Statistical study of relief recipients.

————   (5258)
Survey of medical and health status of recipients of public assistance. Santa Fe, Jan. 1944. Processed.

NEW MEXICO STATE INSPECTOR OF MINES   (5259)
Annual reports, 1912—date.

NEW MEXICO TUBERCULOSIS ASSOCIATION   (5260)
Annual reports, 1922—date.

ORTEGA, JOAQUIN   (5261)
The advisability of establishing a School of Indian Affairs on the campus of the University of New Mexico. Unpub. statement submitted to Office of Indian Affairs on file at School of Inter-American Affairs.

————   (5262)
Inter-American relations in New Mexico. Proposal for an over-all program submitted to the Division of Inter-American Activities in the United States of the Office of the Coordinator of Inter-American Affairs. Unpub. ms. dated May 6, 1943, on file at School of Inter-American Affairs.

————   (5263)
Plan for an American conference on bilingualism. Submitted to the Committee on Modern Languages of the American Council on Education, May 6, 1941. Ms. on file at School of Inter-American Affairs.

ORTEGA, JOAQUIN (continued) (5264)
Plan for a Southwestern conference on bilingualism. Submitted to Governor John Miles of New Mexico, April 16, 1941. Ms. on file at School of Inter-American Affairs.

————— (5265)
Proposal for a regional workshop on inter-American problems in the Southwest. Unpub. ms. dated Sept. 1943, on file at School of Inter-American Affairs.

————— (5266)
Request for co-sponsorship and financial support of an American conference on bilingualism. Unpub. ms. on file at School of Inter-American Affairs.

————— (5267)
Schools of philosophy for agricultural leaders; proposal for a four-day school in Albuquerque. Unpub. ms. on file at School of Inter-American Affairs.

————— (5268)
Suggestions for a Mexican regional project at the University of New Mexico. Part of a general plan for specialized research projects of an international nature submitted to the Rockefeller Foundation by the School of Inter-American Affairs. Ms. on file at School of Inter-American Affairs.

PALLARES, ARTURO MENSES (5269)
Rehabilitacion rural en los Estados Unidos. Washington, Union Panamericana, Oficina de informacion obrera y social, 1943.

PEARCE, THOMAS M. (5270)
New Mexican folk etymologies. *EP,* 50:229-34, Oct. 1943.

————— (5271)
Some anthropological terms used in the Southwest. *EP,* 50:130-41, June 1943.

PIJOAN, MICHEL (5272)
Certain factors involved in the struggle against malnutrition and disease, with special reference to the Southwest of the United States and Latin America. Inter-Americana Short Papers VII. Albuquerque, School of Inter-American Affairs, 1943.

————— (5273)
Food availability and social function. *New Mexico Quarterly Review,* 12:418-23, Nov. 1942.

PILLSBURY, DOROTHY L. (5274)
Ancient adobe soil. *Common Ground,* 3:44-48, Summer 1943.
Santa Fe and the war.

PINGREY, H. B. (5275)
Income and cost of cattle ranching in southeastern New Mexico, 1941. NMAES, Press Bulletin 956. State College, 1942.

POLDERVAART, ARIE (5276)
The New Mexico statutes: observations in connection with their most recent compilation. *NMHR,* 18:52-59, Jan. 1943.

PRINCE, L. B. (5277)
The palace at Santa Fe. *Independent*, 52:2431-, 1900.

REBOLLEDO, ANTONIO (5278)
Report of progress of the New Mexico Spanish Research Project made to Governor John J. Dempsey and the State Board of Education, February 26, 1943. Unpub. ms. in possession of Dr. Rebolledo, New Mexico Highlands University.
> An analysis of Spanish language teaching in the grades and high schools of New Mexico with recommendations for improvement.

REDFIELD, GEORGIA B. (5279)
Prisoners of war. *NM*, 21:19-21, 40, Aug. 1943.

REID, J. T. (5280)
Accomplishments of the Taos County Project for the two-year period, July 1, 1940 to June 30, 1942. Unpub. ms. dated Sept. 23, 1942, on file at School of Inter-American Affairs.

——— (5281)
Adult education and community welfare. *Adult Education Journal*, 2:183-85, Oct. 1943.
> At Peñasco, New Mexico.

——— (5282)
Proposal for a Southwestern Spanish-publication bureau. Submitted by the Taos County Project, June 1941. Ms. on file at School of Inter-American Affairs.

——— (5283)
Status of the Taos County Cooperative Health Association. Unpub. ms. dated Sept. 23, 1942, on file at School of Inter-American Affairs.

——— (5284)
The Taos County Project; second annual report, July 1, 1941-August 31, 1942. UNM Bulletin, Catalog series, v. 55, no. 5, Sept. 1, 1942.

——— (5285)
The Taos County Project, Harwood Foundation, Taos, New Mexico. Suggested program of activities, January 1, 1943 to December 31, 1943. Unpub. ms. dated Dec. 3, 1942, on file at School of Inter-American Affairs.

RHODES, L. H. (5286)
Allocation of maintenance funds to the administrative units within the county. *New Mexico School Review*, 23:8-9, Dec. 1943.

SAN CRISTOBAL VALLEY SCHOOL (5287)
Valley News. Mimeographed periodical bulletin giving news of the school and community, 1938-1943.

SCARRITT, ED (5288)
Fiftieth year. *NM*, 21:16-17, 28-30, April 1943.
> New Mexico Military Institute.

SCHOOL OF INTER-AMERICAN AFFAIRS (5289)
Barelas Community Center. A number of manuscripts dealing with the activities of the Center on file at the School.

SCHOOL OF INTER-AMERICAN AFFAIRS (continued) (5290)
A nutrition-education-land experimental school. Statement presented to the Health Division of the FSA, Dec. 1942. Ms. on file at the School.

—————— (5291)
Nutrition project organized by the School of Inter-American Affairs with the cooperation of the San Cristobal Valley School. Unpub. ms. dated June 1942 on file at the School.

—————— (5292)
An over-all picture of the extra-curricular activities in inter-American affairs of the University of New Mexico. Unpub. ms. dated Oct. 1942 on file at the School.

—————— (5293)
Request to the Rockefeller Foundation for a grant-in-aid for the establishment of a folk music repository at the University of New Mexico. Unpub. ms. on file at the School.

—————— (5294)
Suggestions for a Spanish radio program to be broadcast from Albuquerque. Submitted to the Office of War Information, Dec. 14, 1942. Unpub. ms. on file at the School.

SCHROEDER, ERNA (5295)
From the Southwest. *Progressive Education,* 20:136-38, March 1943.
> Changes in elementary education in Albuquerque resulting from war.

SCHUSTER, ERNEST O. (5296)
Pancho Villa's shadow. Unpub. biography in possession of the author, Springfield, Oregon.
> Includes an account of the raid on Columbus, New Mexico.

SCOTT, DUNCAN (5297)
Saving soil and men. *NM,* 21:18-19, 28, Feb. 1943.
> New Mexico State Prison Farm.

SEDILLO, MELA (5298)
A plan for a pan-American art exhibition and conference. Unpub. ms. on file at School of Inter-American Affairs.

—————— (5299)
A program of New Mexican crafts for the San Cristobal Valley School, 1942-1943. Unpub. ms. on file at School of Inter-American Affairs.

—————— (5300)
A proposed five year plan for the Southwestern and Mexican arts and crafts. Unpub. ms. on file at School of Inter-American Affairs.

—————— (5301)
Proposed program of professional courses in occupational therapy and vocational guidance for the University of New Mexico. Unpub. ms. dated November 1942 on file at School of Inter-American Affairs.

—————— (5302)
Report of a field visit to the San Cristobal Valley School, May 29, 1942. Unpub. ms. on file at School of Inter-American Affairs.

SININGER, HARLAN W.   (5303)
Budgetary procedure in New Mexico. *New Mexico School Review*, 23:10, 14-17, Dec. 1943.

SMITH, GEORGE WINSTON   (5304)
New Mexico's wartime food problems, 1917-1918; a case study in emergency administration. *NMHR*, 18:349-85, Oct. 1943; 19: 1-54, Jan. 1944.

SMITH, HENRY NASH   (5305)
Kit Carson in books. *Southwest Review*, 28:164-89, Winter 1943.

SNOWDEN, GEORGE   (5306)
Political participation of Negroes in border states. Unpub. Doctor's dissertation, Indiana University, 1943.

SPECTOR, BERTHA KAPLAN AND HARDY, A. V.   (5307)
Studies of the acute diarrheal diseases. II. Parasitological observations. *Public Health Reports*, 54:1105-13, 1939.

SPRINGER, EDWARD PAUL   (5308)
A study of student publications in the public high schools of New Mexico. Unpub. Master's thesis, UNM, 1940.

STALLINGS, ROBERT R.   (5309)
Readiness differences of urban and rural children. Unpub. Master's thesis, UNM, 1939.

STEVENS, F. E.   (5310)
History of New Mexico. *Kansas City Review*, 8:690-, 1884.

STODDART, LAURENCE A. AND SMTH, ARTHUR D.   (5311)
Range management. New York, McGraw-Hill, 1943.

STORZ, G. C.   (5312)
Enseñando la historia de Nuevo Mexico. *Hispania*, 25:194-98, May 1942.

TAOS COUNTY PROJECT—HARWOOD FOUNDATION   (5313)
A five year plan. Unpub. ms. dated June 12, 1942, on file at School of Inter-American Affairs.

TIDESTRON, IVAR AND KITTELL, SISTER TERESITA   (5314)
A flora of Arizona and New Mexico. Washington, Catholic University of America, 1942.

TIGHT, W. G.   (5315)
Higher educational institutions of New Mexico. *Science*, n.s., 18: 85-, 1903.

TRUE, CLARA D.   (5316)
A new venture in the Española school. *New Mexico School Review*, 22:4, May 1943.

TRUMBO, THERNON MARCOS   (5317)
Fiesta in Tortugas. *Desert Magazine*, 7:18-20, Dec. 1943.

USDA IN COOPERATION WITH NEW MEXICO STATE COLLEGE AND
THE UNIVERSITY OF ARIZONA   (5318)
Range and livestock production practices in the Southwest. USDA, Misc. Pub. 529. Washington, Nov. 1943.

USDA, BUREAU OF HOME NUTRITION AND HOME ECONOMICS   (5319)
Rural family spending and saving in wartime. USDA, Misc. Pub.
520. Washington, 1943.
> Includes Luna County, New Mexico.

USDA, FOREST SERVICE   (5320)
*Statistics, Southwestern region, Arizona and New Mexico, March
1, 1941.* Washington, [1941].

USDA, SCS   (5321)
*Proposal for a joint action and training program in conservation
for Mexico and the United States.* Albuquerque, SCS Southwest
Region, 1942. Typewritten. (Copy at USDA Library, Albuquerque.)

USDA, WAR BOARD   (5322)
Farm war program community victory council for New Mexico.
Albuquerque, 1942.

USDI   (5323)
*Transcript of title of the Maxwell land grant situated in New
Mexico and Colorado.* Chicago, Rand-McNally & Co., 1881.

VILLANUEVA, RAMON ESPINOSA   (5324)
Lo que vimos en las escuelas del estado de Nuevo Mexico. *Boletin
de la Union Panamericana,* 77:614-18, Nov. 1943.

WALLIS, MARIE POPE   (5325)
Social service special delivery. *American Unity,* 11:7, 13, March
1944.
> Community program of School of Inter-American Affairs.

WALTER, PAUL, JR.   (5326)
Community improvement contest. Unpub. ms. dated Feb. 21,
1942, on file at School of Inter-American Affairs.

WARE, SHIRLEY   (5327)
Styled in Santa Fe. *NM,* 21:16-17, 31, Dec. 1943.

WHITE, EVA BECKER   (5328)
*Evidences of need for speech training for activities outside the
classroom by teachers of New Mexico.* Unpub. Master's thesis,
UNM, 1938.

WILCOX, INEZ H.   (5329)
Country town. *NM,* 20:7-9, 34, Feb. 1942.
> Dexter.

WILSON, D.   (5330)
Domenech's seven years in New Mexico. *Canadian Journal of
Industry,* n.s., 7:47-, 1862.

WOODMAN, F. L.   (5331)
Industrial art at Magdalena High School. *New Mexico School
Review,* 22:4, Nov. 1942.

WOODS, BETTY   (5332)
Mormon town. *NM,* 21:16-17, 34, Oct. 1943.
> Virden.

WPA, WRITERS' PROGRAM, AMERICAN RECREATION SERIES   (5333)
New Mexico. Northport, Long Island, Bacon & Wieck, 1941.

WYNN, DUDLEY   (5334)
A program in corrective speech for the Taos County Project. Unpub. ms. dated June 26, 1942, on file at the School of Inter-American Affairs.

WYNN, DUDLEY, ED.   (5335)
The School for the Rio Grande Valley: a symposium. *New Mexico Quarterly Review,* 12:295-300, 1942.

AUTHOR INDEX

Neumann, David L., 130,1164-1166
Nevins, Allan, 3062
New Mexico Agricultural Experiment Station, 5248,5249
New Mexico Assn. on Indian Affairs, 131, 1167-1170,1847,1851,2309-2312
New Mexico Bureau of Immigration, 4416-4420
New Mexico Highlands University, 4421,5113
New Mexico Highlands University, Department of English, 2313
New Mexico Historical Records Survey, 132, 4422-4446,4845
New Mexico Land Planning Consultant,4447
New Mexico Land Use Advisory Council, 133
New Mexico Normal University, see New Mexico Highlands University
New Mexico Public Service Commission, 5250
New Mexico School Review, 5251
New Mexico Secretary of State, 4448
New Mexico Special Revenue Commission, 4449,4450
New Mexico State Board for Vocational Education, 4451,4452, see also New Mexico State Department of Trade and Industrial Education, New Mexico State Department of Vocational Education
New Mexico State College, 134,4453,5318
New Mexico State College, Extension Service, 135,3566,4454-4456
New Mexico State Commissioner of Public Lands, 4457
New Mexico State Corporation Commission, 5252
New Mexico State Department of Education, 5253
New Mexico State Department of Public Health, 4458,5254,5255
New Mexico State Department of Public Welfare, 136-138,4459,5256-5258
New Mexico State Department of Trade and Industrial Education, 3567; see also New Mexico State Board for Vocational Education
New Mexico State Department of Vocational Education, 139,3568,3569,4460,4461; see also New Mexico State Board for Vocational Education
New Mexico State Employment Security Commission, 4462
New Mexico State Engineer, 4463,4464
New Mexico State Inspector of Mines, 5259
New Mexico State Park Commission, 4465
New Mexico State Planning Board, 140-144, 4465a-4469
New Mexico Territorial Governor, 4470
New Mexico Tuberculosis Assn., 5260
New Mexico University, see University of New Mexico
New Mexico Writers', Music, and Art Projects, WPA, 3570
New Mexico Writers' Project, WPA, 145,3571-3576,4471; see also Federal Writers' Project, Writers' Project
Newcomb, Franc J., 1171-1180,1243,4904
Newcomb, Mrs. Frances L., 2314
Newcomb, Rexford, 3577
Newell, F. H., 4472,4473
Newell, W. W., 1181
Newherne, R. E. L., 2315
Newman, S. S., 1064
Newton, Mrs. E. E., 1182
Newton, Elsie, 1183
Nicholas, Dan, 764
Nicholl, Edith M., 3063
Nicholl, M., 4474
Nicholson, A., 4884
Nirdlinger, Charles F., 1184
Noftzer, Lee J., 4475
Noll, Arthur H., 1852
Norris, Theodore, 2316
Northern Pueblos Agency, see USDI, Office of Indian Affairs, Northern Pueblos Agency
Northrop, Stuart A., 4476,4477
Nusbaum, Aileen, 2317
Nusbaum, Mark E., 3064
Nylander, J. H., 4478
Nymeyer, Robert Bert, 594,4479

O

Oakes, Maud, 4905
Ober, F. A., 4962
Oberg, Kalervo, 146,4150
Obregon, Baltasar de, 2487,2538

Ocaranza, Fernando, 2598
O'Connor, Thomas F., 3064a
Oestreich, W. C., 4480
Office of Education, see USDI, Office of Education
Office of Indian Affairs, see USDI, Office of Indian Affairs
Office of War Information, 5107
Ogle, Ralph H., 3065
Oglesby, Catharine, 2318
O'Gorman, John J., 2599
Olden, Sarah Emilia, 4481
O'Leary, John, 4481a
Olson, Walter O., 2319
O'Neil, James B., 3066
O'Neill, Kate Nevin, 2600
Onion, Charles C., 3759
Opler, Morris Edward, 31,147,148,765-782, 4885,4886
Orchard, William C., 595
O'Rourke, Thomas P., 2601
Ortega, Joaquin, 149,4481b-4484,5108,5261-5268
Orth, George S., 1853
Osanai, Iva, 1373
Osborn, M. M., 150
O'Seasnain, B. P., 4485
Ostermann, Leopold, 1185-1193,4486
Otero, Adelina, 3578
Otero, Miguel, 3066a-3069
Otero-Warren, Nina, 3579-3582
Otis, H. G., 783
Otis, Raymond, 2320,3583,3760
Overholt, M. E., 1194
Overpeck, J. C., 4147,4487
Owens, John G., 1854
Owens, Sister Mary L., 3070
Owens, Sister M. Lilliana, 3071,3072

P

Pacheco, Leonides, 4487a
Pacific Railroad Surveys, 3073
Paddock, William Fred, 3713
Page, Mrs. Dorothy, 3584
Page, Gordon B., 1195,1196
Pallares, Arturo Menses, 5269
Palm, Rufus A., Jr., 2602
Palmer, Edward, 784,1197,2321-2324
Palmer, Frank L., 1198
Palmer, R. S., 4488
Pancoast, C. L., 1855,3074
Pannell, Herman Clay, 151
Parke, J. G., 3075
Parker, K. W., 4806
Parker, Neuman R., 4489
Parker, Samuel, 3076
Parker, William Thornton, 3077
Parks, Charles E., 4490
Parks, Mary Hitchcock, 1856
Parr, V. V., 4491
Parrish, Randall, 2603
Parsons, Edward, 3078
Parsons, Elsie Clews, 152-159,1199-1201, 1857-1905,2325,2326
Parsons, Francis, 4492
Patterson, George L., 1202
Patterson, J. C., 2603a
Patterson, W. L., 3079,3080
Pattie, James O., 3081
Patton, F. H., 4493
Paul, Hattie Belle, 2327
Paulus, Lena, 160
Paxon, F. L., 3082-3084
Paynter, Elizabeth Ann, 4494
Paytiamo, James, 1906
Peabody, Charles, 596
Peabody, O. W. B., 3085
Pearce, T. M., 161,295,2835,4495-4501,5720-5271
Peatfield, J. J., 1203
Peck, Walter E., 4502
Peet, Stephen D., 597-600,1204,1907-1911,2604, 4963-4967
Peixotto, Ernest C., 4503
Pelzer, Louis, 3086
Pennsylvania, University of, 601
Pepper, George H., 602-604,1205-1210
Perea, Fray Estevan de, 2467,2605
Perrine, Fred S., 3087,3088
Perry, R., 1211
Persinger, Clark E., 4504
Peter, W. W., 1212,2328
Peters, DeWitt C., 2802,3089-3091
Peters, J. Henry, 2329
Peters, Leroy S., 4505

SUBJECT INDEX

Bernalillo County
  archives, 4425
  consolidated schools, 4380
  Justice of the Peace courts, 3859
  juvenile delinquency, 3949
  resources, 4416
Beverages
  Apaches, 31
Beveridge, Albert J., 4361
Bibliography, 264-323a,4842-4848
  agricultural economics, 313
  agriculture
    Indians, general, 274,275
    Navajos, 320
  American frontier period, 323a
  anthropology, 306
  archaeology, 303,304,306
  Arizona, 264
  Athapascan languages, 300
  Bandelier, A. F. A., 287
  Catholic church, 276
  conservation, 278
  education, 273a
  erosion, 278
  ethnography, 265,298
  ethnology, 265,298,306
  folk music, 284,4843
  forestry economics, 314
  Fray Alonso de Benavides, 286
  government documents, 311
  historical manuscripts, 277
  immigration, 289a
  Indian
    art, 273,283,318,427
    arts and crafts, 283
    ethnobiology, 288
    industries, 318
    languages, 300
    legends, 317
    linguistics, 321
    music, 319
  Indians
    general, 289,298
    Jemez area, 303
    Mexican immigrants, 268a
    Mexican period, 266,267,269,271,292,296,307-309,
      323a
    Mexicans, 289b
    Mimbres Valley, 304
    minority groups, 273a,4846
    Mogollon culture, 304
    music, 284
    national monuments, 316
    national parks, 316
    Navajo irrigation, 320
    Navajos, 290
    Southwest, 295,307a,310,4847
    Southwestern life, 273b
    Spaniards, 266
    Spanish
      archives, 272,307-309,312
      ballads, 297
      folklore, 270,291,4843
    Spanish-colonial period, 266,267,269,271,272,
      292,296,307-309,312,323,4848
    stone lions, 1818
    travel narratives, 322,1058
Biculturism, 169-172
Bilingualism
  as educational problem, 3979a,4582,4583,4585,
    4587,5240
  conference, 5263,5264,5266
  effect on cultural relations, 4582
  in courts, 4493
  should be developed, 3605
Billy the Kid, 2751,2777,2779,2786,2803,2849-2854,
  2863,2907,2916,2962,2970,3033,3069,3098,3109,
  3118,3149,3158,3162-3164,3195,3196,3204,3239
Biographies
  collective, 4506
Birds
  Pueblo art designs, 1492
  Zuni pottery decorations, 1493
Biscuit ware area, 561
Bishop's Cap find, 382
Bishop's Lodge, 4675

Blankets, see also weaving
  Indians
    general, 2211,2235
    Navajos, 118,822,823,907,955,1014,1017,1020,
      1023,1024,1027,1031,1079,1093,1135,1137,1139-
      1144,1186,1202,1203,1206,1207,1280,1281
Blazer's Mill, 3116
Blood types
  Navajos, 2060
  Pueblos, 1388,2060
Boarding schools, see schools
Body economy
  relation to acculturation, 4514,4515
  Spanish-Americans, 3586,4513a,4515
Bonework
  Hawikuh, 484
Bonilla, Antonio de, 2645
Book circulation, 4136
Border patrol, 4540
Bosque farms
  cost of living, 112
  in-group dissolution, 111
  institutions, 110
  integration, 111
  level of living, 112
  social organization, 3480
  social participation, 4319
  social relationships, 110
  standard of living, 112,4321
Bosque Redondo
  Navajo migration, 2771
  Navajos at, 819,2993
Botany, see also ethnobotany
  economic, 3133
  Zuni, 1393
Boundaries, 3854
  county, 3968
Boundary
  international, 4240
  Texas-New Mexico, 5048
Bourke, John Gregory, 2755,2759
Bows
  Mogollon, 471
Bows and arrows
  Indians
    general, 2292
Branding, 3837
Bread making
  Pueblos, 1845
Breadstuff
  Zuni, 1532
Bridges
  Spanish-colonial, 2455
Brown, W. C., 2823
Buffalo, 3250
Buffalo hunting, see hunting
Bullwhacking, 3251
Bultos, 3689,3690
Burros, 4665
Bursum Bill, 22,261,1395,1398,1406,1423,1513,
  1609,1661,1678,1960
Business conditions
  Albuquerque, 4309

C

Cabeza de Vaca, Alvar Nuñez, 2436,2441,2448,
  2471,2505,2547,2642,2643,2671
Cabezon
  economic conditions, 225
  range survey, 4158
  social conditions, 225
Cacti
  utilization, 29,2316
Cadastral engineer
  archives, 4592
Calendar
  ceremonial
    Picuris, 159
  Indians
    general, 2125
    Isleta, 1869
    Laguna, 44
    Navajos, 1174
    Zuni, 1990
Calhoun, James S., 2790,2862
Camels
  use in Southwest, 2726,2930,3008,3088,5072
Cameron Creek Village, 367,371,372
Camino militar, 2484
Camp Maddox, 2824

Culberson-Stephens Bill, 14
Cults, *see also* religion
　Pueblos, 1429,1886,2030
　San Felipe, 1476,1478,2042
　Taos Pueblo, 1787
　war god
　　Pueblos, 1836
　Zia, 1984
Cultural areas, 2254
Cultural contributions
　Indians
　　general, 2095,2237
Cultural description
　Acoma, 155,1391,1437,1486,1488,1695,1729,1730,
　　1906,2034,2049
　Anglos, 106
　Apaches,　716,717,726,728,729a,730,732,733,758,
　　2131,2150
　Atarque, 103
　Cuba Valley, 146
　Cundiyo, 117
　Indians
　　general, 106,2061,2127,2135,2143,2187,2208,
　　　2289,2326,2337,2350,2360,2362,2411,2416
　　New Mexican, 106,2124,2162
　　Southwestern,　2144,2148,2182,2232,2255,2256,
　　　2368
　Jemez Pueblo, 1762,1919
　Jicarilla Apaches, 148
　Laguna, 155,1700,2028
　Navajos, 831,879,880,922,924,931,947,962,1019,
　　1034,1035,1068,1083,1095,1099,1182,1184,1187,
　　1191,1197,1198,1209-1211,1217,1221,1224,1232,
　　1238-1240,1246,1248,1249,1262,1267, 1286, 1288,
　　1292,1293,1297,1301,1302, 1314, 1326, 1335, 1342,
　　1347-1349,1358,1570,2106,2127,2131,2150,4889,
　　4890,4920
　New Mexico, 161,3843,4013,4077,4209,4246,4332,
　　4369,4535,4606,4788,4822,4840
　New Mexico in 1620's, 2457
　Pueblos, 733,1217,1348,1443,1446,1453,1462,1507,
　　1520,1521,1538,1570,1572, 1578, 1579, 1581, 1590,
　　1595,1597,1598,1600,1606,1607,1607a,1615,1657,
　　1686,1694,1714,1739-1741,1773, 1774,1793, 1802,
　　1820a,1944,1949,1950,1963,2009,2047,2289,
　　2589,4969,4970
　Questa, 186,4536a
　Rio Grande Valley, 4086,4129,4208
　San Geronimo, 136
　San Ildefonso, 1518
　Santa Ana, 1722,2043
　Santa Clara, 1635
　Santa Fe,　3167,3280,3844,3985,4156,4157,4185,
　　4238,4485,4490,4563,4574,4634,
　Southwest,　3833,3836a,3937,4014,4083,4186,4237,
　　4318,4410,4485,4501,4503,4559,4578,4759
　Spanish-Americans, 25,58,106,166,1217,3256,
　　3269,3280,3298,3357,3359,3388,3443,3445,3452a,
　　3464,3512,3558,3578,3581,3637,3643
　Taos Pueblo, 1424,1646,1794,1839
　Tewa Pueblos, 2131
　Villanueva, 138
　Zia, 1925,1984
　Zuni, 1425,1472,1519,1525,1527,1528,1644,1731,
　　1751,1777,1817,1887,1951,1992,2002,2106,2131,
　　4940,4950
Cultural development
　El Cerrito, 108
　Southwest, 80
Cultural history
　Pueblos, 69
　Southwest, 80
Cultural influence
　Spanish-Americans, 3318
Cultural interpretation
　New Mexico, 4303,4343
Cultural isolation
　New Mexico, 40
Cultural relations
　effect of bilingualism on, 4582
　primitive, 547
　Rio Grande Valley, 4062,4149
　role of education in, 4482
Cultural resistance
　Navajos, 1233
Cultural resources, 179
Cultural stability
　Navajos, 1006

Cultural status, *see* status
Cultural values
　Indians
　　general, 2199,2347
　　New Mexican, 3269
　Spanish-Americans, 3269
Culture
　prehistoric, 629,648,668,669
　　Cimarron Valley, 630,631
　Pueblos, 654
　Spanish
　　survival in Southwest, 3672
　Zuni, 13
Culture patterns
　Atarque, 103
　Navajos, 1006,1064,1198
　New Mexico, 106
Culture sequences
　Zuni, 1781
Cundiyo
　acculturation, 3641
　cultural description, 117,5115
　economic life, 117
　food economy, 3641
　nutrition study, 3367,4515
Cundiyo grant, 219
Curanderas, 3288
Curricula
　high schools,　75,3899,3912,4130,4358,4414,4478,
　　4602,4640
Curry County
　agricultural economics, 4164
　agricultural hazards, 97
　agriculture, 97,162
　farm organization, 4768
　folk customs, 4616
　high school consolidation, 4128
　history, 4663
　rehabilitation, 162
　school finances, 4104
Curry County farms
　income, 162
Curtis, Mary Todhunter, 3224
Customs, *see also* folk customs
　Acoma, 190,1930,1995
　baptism
　　Spanish-Americans, 3487
　Cochiti, 1592
　courtship
　　Pueblos, 1674
　Coyotero Apaches, 784
　Indians
　　general, 2323,2350,2355
　　New Mexican, 2079
　　Southwestern, 2168
　Isleta, 152
　Jemez Pueblo, 1662
　Laguna, 190
　mortuary
　　Isleta, 1409
　　Navajos, 980,1264,1274
　　Sandia Pueblo, 1409
　Navajo women, 987
　Navajos,　831,874,904,1288,1299,1301,1302
　Picuris, 159
　Pueblos, 1537,1674,2027
　religious
　　Spanish-Americans, 3528,3545
　　Taos, 3528
　Taos County, 3540
　San Felipe, 157
　Santo Domingo, 157
　social
　　Albuquerque, 50
　　Spanish-Americans, 50,61
　Taos Pueblo, 1838,1914
　wedding
　　Pueblos, 1674
　　Spanish-Americans, 145,3302,3488,3547,3637,
　　　3665
　Zuni, 1990,2003
Cutting, Bronson M., 3999,4629,4793,4795

D

Dairies
　economics
　　Mesilla Valley, 4231

Navajos (continued)
  sudatory, 48,1196
  sun god, 4906
  sun symbols, 1177
  superstitions, 1345
  surgery, 1158
  sweat baths, 1081,1196
  symbolism, 121
  syphilis, 983
  taboos, 1092,1176,1310
  tanning, 1102,1277
  telephone, 1279
  trade, 131,262,814,827,903,953,989,990,1145,1350
  trading posts, 814,827,1145,1350
  transvestites, 1007
  tribal council, 1155
  tuberculosis, 894
  use of jimsonweed, 1001
  use of turquoise, 995
  venereal disease, 1216
  verse rhythms, 1333
  vocational education, 816
  war dance, 1200
  warfare, 1002,1344,2722,4894,4910
  weaving, 118,821-823,838,844,852,883-885,893,
    900,902,907,908,910,911,928,955,959,982,985,
    1010,1014,1017,1020,1023,1024,1027,1031,1055,
    1069,1070,1079,1088,1093,1118,1135-1144,1166,
    1169,1186,1202,1203,1206,1207,1231,1236,1240,
    1276,1280,1281,1356,1366,2252,2329,4902
  wind way ceremonial, 929
  witchcraft, 1048,1049,1061,1156
  wool, 900,959,1056
Navy department
  archives, 4442
Negroes
  education, 4050,4051
  political participation, 5306
  with Spanish explorers, 2684
New Mexico Education Association, 3953
New Mexico Historical Review
  index, 268
New Mexico Normal (Highlands) University
  history, 4526
  Institute of the Air, 5154
New Mexico Public Service Commission, 5250
New Mexico Relief & Security Administration
  relief expenditures
    Rio Grande watershed, 212
New Mexico State Corporation Commission, 5252
New Mexico State Dept. of Education, 5253
New Mexico State Dept. of Public Health, 5124,
  5254
New Mexico State Dept. of Public Welfare, 5256
New Mexico State Inspector of Mines, 5259
New Mexico State Prison Farm, 5297
New Mexico Tuberculosis Assn., 5260
Newspaper circulation, 4136
Night chant
  Navajos, 1050,1116,1120,1201
Niza, Fray Marcos de, 2430,2434,2437,2441,2505,
  2624,2667,5016
Nomadism
  Navajos, 79
Nomads
  prehistoric, 374
Nomenclature
  kinship see kinship terms
Number systems, see also counting systems
  Acoma, 2407a
  Apaches, 2407a
  Indians
    Southwestern, 2407a
  Navajos, 2407a
Numerology
  Zuni, 1863
Nursing, 3803,3804,4055,4649
  American frontier period, 3121
Nutrition
  Cañon de Taos, 3367,4515
  Cundiyo, 3367,4515
  effect on acculturation, 4514
  Spanish-Americans, 3366a,3367,3409,3586,4513a-
    4516,5213,5272,5273,5290,5291
Nutrition education, 4171

O

Oatman girls
  captivity, 3172
Ocate Creek watershed
  water facilities plan, 204

Occupation shifts
  effect on rural life, 4210
Occupational therapy, 5301
Occupations
  Anglos, 151
  Manzano, 88
  Mexicans, 3344,3519a
  Navajos, 1089
  Pueblo girls, 1410
  Pueblos, 151
  relief workers, 4832,4833
  Spanish-Americans, 151
  Tewa basin, 241
  Valencia County, 3963
Office of Indian Affairs
  accomplishments, 2357
  criticism of, 2358
  directed acculturation program, 90
  educational policies, 36
  health activities, 2385,2403
  Navajo education program, 74
  Navajo program, 120
  relief expenditures
    Rio Grande watershed, 212
Oil, 4047,4348,4351,4525a
Oñate, Cristobal de, 5045
Oñate, Juan de, 2459,2513,2527-2531,2548,2572,
  2600,2653,2658,2659
Oratory
  Spanish-Americans, 10
Orchard, Sadie, 3203
Orchards
  Manzano, 4167
Origins
  Navajos, 820,915,916,1042,1053,1192,1257,1290,
    1324,1328
  Pueblos, 1455,1638
  Zuni, 1449,1481
Ornamental designs, see designs
Ornaments
  Spanish-colonial, 3366
Otermin, Antonio de
  reconquest attempt, 2517,2519
Otero, Miguel, 3067,3068
Otero County
  archives, 4433
  school finances, 4809
Otowi, 688,691
  artifacts, 665
Our Lady of Light Academy, 3072
Ouray, 3166
Outlaws
  American frontier period, 2860,2948,2965,3110,
    3127
Overgrazing, 41,4804
  Navajo lands, 78
Overland mail, 2932
Overpopulation
  Navajos, 78

P

Paa Ko ruin, 664
Padilla, Fray Juan, 2506
Pageantry, see ceremonies
Painting, see also art
  Indians
    Southwestern, 2201
  Jemez Pueblo, 1924
  Navajos, 2198
  Pueblos, 1386,1413,1567,1572,1676,1683,1687,
    1691,1712,1848,1851,2198
Pajarita Park
  archaeology, 454
Pajarita plateau
  pottery, 530
Pajaritan culture, 465
Palomas River watershed
  water facilities plan, 198
Paper bread
  Pueblos, 1933
  Santa Ana, 1933
Parent-teacher association, 4644
Parks
  national, 261
    bibliography, 316
Parochialism, 169
Parsons, Edward, 3078
Partido system, 32,126,209
  Tewa basin, 241
Parturition myths
  Navajos, 1109

Passion play
  at Red River, 3644
Pastoral resources, *see* resources
Pathology
  dental
    Zuni, 1795
Patron-peon system, 3637
Patterns
  cultural, *see* cultural patterns
Pattie, James, 2728,3081
Peanuts
  Portales Valley, 4137,5135
Pecans, 3976
Pecos bull, 324
Pecos Pueblo, 341,347,468,506,523-529,532,671,4858
  artifacts, 523,529
  migration, 1943
  musical instruments, 596
  pottery, 534-536
  physical anthropology, 495,584
  revolt against Spanish, 2426
Pecos River, 4153a,5247
Pecos River basin
  resources, 4406
Pecos River watershed
  conservation program, 4707,4713
  flood damage, 3879
Pecos Valley
  antiquities, 384
  history, 4052
  irrigation, 4301,4350
Peña Blanca, 2670,5082
Peñalosa, Diego Dionisio de, 2512,2518
Penitentes, 2,7,1923,3258,3302,3337,3392,3447,3497,
  3502,3509,3527,3531,3544,3548,3559,3583,3651,
  3652,3684,3693,3698,3822,4834
Peralta, Pedro de, 2567
Perchas Creek watershed
  water facilities plan, 198
Perea, Fray Estevan de, 2467,2605
Personal narratives, *see* narratives
Personality
  Hopi, 100
  Indians
    New Mexican, 51
  Isleta, 16,17
  Mexican Indians, 51
  Navajos, 100,101,812,1192
  Pueblos, 114,1545,1550
  San Ildefonso, 1442
  Spanish-Americans, 10,24,114,117,184,3264,3352,
    3389,4482
  Zuni, 1644
Perversion
  sexual
    Indians, 2213
Petroglyphs, 403,644
  Chiricahua Apaches, 803
Peyote, 147,2315
  Apache use, 147,780
Peyote cult, 2260,2331,4996
  Taos Pueblo, 1787
Peyote rite
  Apaches, 147
Peyton, John Rowzee, 2546
Philosophy, *see also* social philosophy
  Pueblos, 2058
  religious
    Indians, 2401
Phonograph
  introduction to Taos, 3040
Physical achievement, *see* achievement
Physical characteristics
  Navajos, 82,847,856
  Spanish-Americans, 3692
Physical description
  Pueblo region, 1716
Physical education
  high schools, 4130,4358
Physical measurements
  Navajo women, 856
Physical status, *see* status
Physiography, 4079
  Rio Grande Valley, 1694
Pictographs, 395,403,427,594,644,2353
  El Rito de los Frijoles, 392,449
Picuris, 1832,4873
  ceremonial calendar, 159
  customs, 159
  dances, 1855
  folk tales, 1671

Picuris (continued)
  government, 159
  grazing resources, 1744
  legends, 1551
  music, 1671,1941
  religion, 159
Pigments
  Indians
    Southwestern, 2177
  pottery, 447
Pike, Zebulon M., 2856, 2929
Pike's expedition, 2842, 3095-3097
Pine
  use by Southwestern Indians, 2370
Piñon industry, 4234,4312
Piñons
  place in Spanish-American life, 3938
Pinos Altos, 2694
Pinto beans, *see* beans
Piro language, 438
Placement
  teachers, 3898
Planning
  agricultural, 134
  land use, 115,1217,4533
    Navajo area, 4722
  post-war, 5163
  regional, 258
Plays
  religious
    Spanish-Americans, 26
    Spanish-colonial, 2425
    Taos Pueblo, 1425
    Zuni, 1506
Pneumonia control program, 4046
Po Shu Onige
  archaeology, 511
Poe, J. W., 3099
Poetry, *see also* folk poetry
  Acoma, 1524
  Indians, 2073,2402
  Navajos, 1330,1333,4909
  Pueblos, 1523,2073
  ritual
    Zuni, 1482
  Santo Domingo, 1564
  Southwestern, 3847
  Zuni, 1766
Pojoaque
  grazing resources, 1744
Pojoaque district
  conservation, 4726
Police
  Apaches, 712
Political conditions
  New Mexico in 1906, 3998
Political education, *see* education
Political life
  Spanish-colonial, 2451
Political organization
  Indians
    general, 2287
  Navajos, 1004,1315
  San Felipe, 2042
Political parties
  labor record, 4044
Political status, *see* status
Politics, 4085
  feudal aspects, 4629
  Rocky Mountain area, 4043
  influence on higher education, 4058
  Pueblos, 1674
Pony Express, 2761,2809,3216
Pope, William Hayes, 4784
Population, 142
  Apaches, 809
  Cochiti, 1981
  foreign born, 4139
  Indians
    general, 2345
    New Mexican, 2258
  Isleta, 1869
  Jemez-Tewa area, 223
  Mexican, 5094
  middle Rio Grande area, 223
  Navajos, 839,840,1009,1097,1357
  New Mexico, 4252-4255
  north-central New Mexico, 127
  Pueblos, 2011,2012,2018
  prehistoric, 650